ADVERTISING MANAGER'S HANDBOOK

ROBERT W. BLY

PRENTICE HALL
Englewood Cliffs, New Jersey 07632

Library of Congress Cataloging-in-Publication Data

Bly, Robert W.
Advertising manager's handbook / Robert W. Bly.
p. cm.
Includes index.
ISBN 0-13-007345-8
1. Advertising—Management—Handbooks, manuals, etc.
2. Advertising—Handbooks, manuals, etc. I. Title.
HF5823.B634 1992 92-26107
659.1'0973—dc20 CIP

© 1993 by Robert W. Bly
All rights reserved. No part of this book may be reproduced in any form or by any means, without permission in writing from the publisher.

Printed in the United States of America

10 9 8 7 6 5

ISBN 0-13-007345-8

ATTENTION: CORPORATIONS AND SCHOOLS
Prentice Hall books are available at quantity discounts with bulk purchase for educational, business, or sales promotional use. For information, please write to: Prentice Hall Career & Personal Development Special Sales, 113 Sylvan Avenue, Englewood Cliffs, NJ 07632. Please supply: title of book, ISBN number, quantity, how the book will be used, date needed.

PRENTICE HALL
Career & Personal Development
Englewood Cliffs, NJ 07632
A Simon & Schuster Company

On the World Wide Web at http://www.phdirect.com

Prentice-Hall International (UK) Limited, *London*
Prentice-Hall of Australia Pty. Limited, *Sydney*
Prentice-Hall Canada Inc., *Toronto*
Prentice-Hall Hispanoamericana, S.A., *Mexico*
Prentice-Hall of India Private Limited, *New Delhi*
Prentice-Hall of Japan, Inc., *Tokyo*
Simon & Schuster Asia Pte. Ltd., *Singapore*
Editora Prentice-Hall do Brasil, Ltda., *Rio de Janeiro*

To Milt Pierce—friend, teacher, colleague

Contents

Preface

This is a book for advertising managers and other people who are responsible for planning and managing their organization's advertising program. Whether your budget is $5,000 . . . $50,000 . . . $500,000 . . . or $5 million, the *Advertising Manager's Handbook* can help you plan, implement, and manage an effective, successful advertising program—one that can get your message across, build your image, make your product famous in the marketplace, generate leads, build sales, motivate distributors, and achieve any other goal you desire.

Planning and managing an advertising program is a tough job. There are ad agencies, freelancers, and PR firms to help write the ads, place the feature stories, and crank out sales bulletins. But there is little help available when it comes to sitting down and planning the year's activities. The *Advertising Manager's Handbook* was written to fill that gap.

The job of advertising manager is a balancing act. The ad manager must deal with and satisfy many people with diverse needs such as salespeople, product managers, brand managers, distributors, manufacturers' reps, vendors, the ad agency, freelancers, customers, prospects, and, of course, top management. I give advice on dealing with all of these folks.

The *Advertising Manager's Handbook* is short on theory, but long on practical, proven advice, information, and tools. I have been an ad manager for an industrial firm. As an independent advertising copywriter and consultant I have worked with more than 110 advertisers and their agencies writing, creating, and planning marketing communications programs. And I have talked with many more to gather additional information for this book.

While this book is designed to help small and medium-size companies create sound, sensible, result-getting advertising, managers at larger firms will benefit, too. It is for full-time advertising managers as well as other managers who are responsible for advertising in addition to their other tasks: marketing directors, sales managers, product managers, brand managers, account executives, presidents, owners, and anyone else who plays the role of ad manager, whether full or part-time.

Advertising professionals providing service to these managers—account executives and planners, creative directors, market researchers, media planners and buyers, copywriters, art directors, printers, list brokers, photographers, space reps, ad agency owners—will also benefit.

The *Advertising Manager's Handbook* takes much of the guesswork and coin-flipping out of planning. The book presents a rational, step-by-step approach based on proven advertising principles and practices. Easy-to-follow discussions, advice, guidelines, checklists, and other tools help the reader create an advertising plan for his company or division from scratch—quickly and professionally.

Blank worksheets, designed to be easy to complete, guide the reader in formulating a plan based on your products, your markets, your strategies, and your selling methods. There are filled-in sample sheets to use as examples. The worksheets can be photocopied and used over and over again. In this way, the book continues to be a useful planning aid for many years to come.

This handbook is organized in the following manner:

Part I—PLANNING—gives you step-by-step instructions for creating your advertising plan. You'll learn how to define markets, set goals and objectives, create an advertising schedule and budget, and put a plan together. The role of the advertising manager in business is also addressed.

Part II—TASKS—shows you how get the best results from the various types of marketing communications available to you—including print advertising, broadcast, sales promotions, trade shows, direct mail, brochures, catalogs, public relations, films and slide shows, newsletters, and house organs. You'll also learn what works (and what doesn't) in copy, graphic design, photography, illustration, printing, and A/V production.

Part III—ADVERTISING MANAGEMENT—shows how to implement your plan successfully on a daily basis. You'll learn how to choose and work with an outside agency, how to get the best from printers, photographers, freelancers, consultants, and other vendors and suppliers, how to work with product managers and the sales force, how to sell your programs to top management, how to handle inquiries, and how to measure advertising results.

At the end of many of the chapters, you'll find references to additional books, magazines, organizations, and other resources that can be of use to you.

It is difficult to write a book of this length that is error-free, and I'm certain some errors will be found. In particular, I have given special attention to making sure material used from other sources has been properly credited and permissions obtained. If I have not attributed material to its author properly, I apologize in advance. It was an error and not deliberate.

Also, many readers will disagree with some of the ideas presented here; others will feel important subject matter has been left out. If you have any questions, comments, corrections, ideas, suggestions, or complaints, let me know so we can correct the next edition accordingly. You can write to me at:

Bob Bly
22 E. Quackenbush Avenue
Dumont, NJ 07628
Office Phone (201) 385-1220

Acknowledgments

I'd like to thank the hundreds of individuals and organizations who granted permission to reprint their work in this book. Although there are too many to list here, I've done my best to make sure they are given appropriate credit where their work is reprinted in the text. If I've missed anyone (and in a book this size, it's quite possible) my apologies!

Of these, I must single out Bob Donath of *Business Marketing* and Lee Rosen of B/PAA for generously granting permission to reprint articles, papers, and other research materials.

Special thanks go to Lansing Moore, Milt Pierce, Sig Rosenblum, Tom Quirck, and Terry C. Smith. When I was just starting out in advertising, they took the time to teach me what was going on and prevented me from making a total fool of myself and wasting my employer's money.

Thanks also go to my clients who have paid good money to put my ideas to the test on a daily basis. Although no one is successful all the time, together we've had far more successes than failures and have discovered the methods and techniques that this book is all about, that is, *how to get better advertising results at lower cost.*

I'd also like to thank my editors, Bette Schwartzberg, Tom Power, Sheck Cho, and Drew Dreeland for making this book much better than it was when it first crossed their desk. Thanks also to my publisher, Prentice

Hall, for financing a project of this scope and magnitude, and to Rose Kernan for her excellent work on the design and production of the book.

And of course, the greatest thanks to my wife, Amy Sprecher Bly, who makes it all possible and worthwhile.

We gratefully acknowledge the following sources:

Claude Hopkins, *Scientific Advertising;* George Black, "Measure Marketing Effectiveness," *Executive Business Magazine,* June 1987; "The Roles of Advertising Managers and Advertising Agencies at the Turn of the Century," Business/Professional Advertising Association, White Paper Series No. 17 (reprinted with permission).

Eugene Schwartz, *Breakthrough Advertising;* Carolyn Hosken, "Four Steps to Dramatic Business Growth"; Stephen Sahlein, *Newsletter Publishing: A Guide to Techniques and Tactics;* Russ von Hoelscher, *How to Make $6,000 a Month Selling Books by Mail.*

S. Rapp and T. Collins, *MiniMarketing;* Murray Raphael, *Direct Marketing.*

Joe Karbo, *The Lazy Man's Way to Riches;* Hershell Gordon Lewis, *The Art of Writing Copy;* Robert Collier, *The Robert Collier Letter Book;* Homer B. Smith in *Personal Selling Power* (July/August 1989); Tom Hopkins, *How to Master the Art of Selling;* Mike Pavlish, *How to Write a Direct Mail Piece or Ad That Gets You Maximum Response.*

Jeffrey Lant, *Money Making Marketing; Modem Operandi,* Cassell Communications Special Report B-741; K. Gedney and P. Fultz, *The Complete Guide to Creating Successful Brochures* (reprinted with permission).

"Here's What Really Matters to Today's Business-to-Business Marketer: The 1986 Starmark Report," *Business Marketing* (reprinted with permission); G. Blake and R. Bly, *How to Promote Your Own Business;* Dana K. Cassell, *How to Advertise and Promote Your Retail Store: Plan Your Advertising Budget,* U.S. Small Business Administration Management Aid No. 4.018; *How Much to Spend on Advertising* and *Advertising and Promotion: The PIMS Program,* Cahners (excerpted with permission); Business/Professional Advertising Association, White Paper Series No. 4 (reprinted with permission).

"CURE for Business Marketers: The 1988 Starmark Report," *Business Marketing;* Louis Rukeyser, *Business Almanac; Bacon's Publicity Checker; Direct Marketing,* January 1989; Alastair Crompton, *The Craft of Copywriting;* "Copy Chasers," *Business Marketing;* Martin Schrader in *Advertising Age,* January 30, 1989; McGraw-Hill Research, Laboratory of Advertising Performance; Joe Barnes, *Important Facts & Tips on Classified Ads;* Bill Peeler, "Avoid the 61 Print Ad Pitfalls," *Business Marketing,* 1987.

Key Facts, Newspaper Advertising Bureau; "The Cocooning of America," *Direct Marketing,* February 1990; Standard Rate & Data Service; American Newspaper

Publishers Association; Ken Eichenbaum, *How to Create Small-Space Newspaper Advertising That Works* (reprinted with permission); Dana Cassell, *How to Advertise and Promote Your Retail Store* (reprinted with permission); *Advertising Media Decisions,* U.S. Small Business Administration Management Aid No. 4.016 (reprinted with permission).

Ray Jutkins, *Direct Marketing: How You Can Really Do It Right!* (reprinted with permission); Howard Sawyer, "Business-to-Business Advertising," *Business Marketing* (reprinted with permission); Howard Shenson, *How to Market and Promote Seminars;* Russ von Hoelscher, *How You Can Make A Fortune Selling Information by Mail;* Howard Sawyer, *Business-to-Business Marketing;* Edward C. Crimmins, *Cooperative Advertising.*

Richard A. Gajewski in *Insurance Advocate;* Hooper White, *How to Produce an Effective Television Commercial;* Roger Barton, *Handbook of Advertising Management;* David Ogilvy, *Ogilvy on Advertising;* Hershell Gordon Lewis, *How to Make Your Advertising Twice As Effective at Half the Cost;* David Ogilvy, *Confessions of an Advertising Man;* Alvin Eicoff, *Or Your Money Back;* Rosser Reeves, *Reality in Advertising;* John Lyons, *Guts: Advertising from the Inside Out;* Nancy L. Salz, *How to Get the Best Advertising From Your Agency.*

Rick Austin in *Computers & Electronics Marketing,* November 1984; Richard H. Hill, "How to Create Marketing Literature that Cuts Selling Costs," *Business Marketing,* January 1985; Julien Elfenbein, *Business Letters and Communications;* Lauren R. Januz, *Direct Marketer's Notebook; How to Make Your Catalog Work Harder,* Thomas Register of American Manufacturers.

Drayton Bird in *Direct Marketing,* August 1989; Business/Professional Advertising Association White Paper Series No. 22 (reprinted with permission); Lewis Kornfeld, *To Catch a Mouse, Make a Noise Like a Cheese.*

DM News, January 1, 1989; David Ogilvy, "Semaine du Marketing Direct," *Direct Marketing,* January 1986 (reprinted with permission); Ed Burnett, *The Complete Direct Mail List Book;* Ed McLean, *The Basics of Testing; Choosing Effective Lists,* DataPro Research Corp.

Ed Werz in *Direct Marketing,* July 1988; R. Luedtke, *Merchandising Through Card Decks;* Bill Norcutt, *Secrets of Successful Response Deck Advertising: Target Marketing,* October 1986; Jim Morris in *Direct Marketing,* September 1986; Wayne Hepburn in *Direct Marketing,* October 1986; "17 Costly Little Telemarketing Mistakes," Mardex Inc., 1985.

O'Dwyers' PR Services Report, September 1988; Allison Davis in *Executive Business Magazine,* April 1987; Carol Marden, "How to Write and Send a Press Release;" Art Stevens in *Chemical Engineering,* November 26, 1984.

Marketing Communications, November 1987; *Journal of Marketing,* July, 1987; *Industry Week,* April 4, 1988; "Why Visitors Attend Exhibits," Incomm International, Chicago; John M. Browning and Ronald J. Adams in the *Journal of Small*

Business Management, October 1988; Edward Chapman, Jr. in the Trade Show Bureau publication, "Expositions Work: A Management Guide for Exhibitors."

Herman Holtz, *Expanding Your Consulting Practice with Seminars* (John Wiley & Sons); Howard Shenson, *How to Create and Market a Successful Seminar or Workshop,* The Consultant's Library.

George Vardaman, *Effective Communication of Ideas,* Van Nostrand Reinhold; Terry C. Smith, *Making Successful Presentations;* Harold and Marjorie Zelko, *How to Make Speeches for All Occasions,* Doubleday; Janet Stone and Jane Bachner, *Speaking Up,* McGraw-Hill; Lyle Surles and W.A. Stanbury, *The Art of Persuasive Talking,* McGraw-Hill; Albert J. Beveridge, *The Art of Public Speaking,* Nash Publishing; Dorothy Leeds, *PowerSpeak,* Prentice Hall; James Welch, *The Speech Writing Guide,* John Wiley & Sons; Dorothy Sarnoff, *Speech Can Change Your Life,* Doubleday.

William A. Robinson, "Ten Commandments of Creative Promotion," *Advertising Age,* March 1981; "The Design Process," Business/Professional Advertising Association, White Paper Series; "How to Buy Printing and Related Services," Performance Seminar Group, 1985; *Sales and Marketing Executive Report.* The Dartnell Corporation; Richard P. Gorman, *Sales and Marketing Executive Report;* "Rights Rules," *Business Marketing* (reprinted with permission); Stan Merritt in *Industrial Marketing,* May 1982 (reprinted with permission); Don Levin, *Levin's Public Relations Report,* June 1988 (reprinted with permission); Alfred Brown in *DM News;* Elaine Tyson in *Folio*: magazine.

James Webb Young, *A Technique for Producing Ideas,* Crain Books; Jo Coudert in *Woman's Day;* "Computerized Lead Processing for Business-to-Business Communication," Business/Professional Advertising Association, White Paper Series, Number 2.

About the Author

Robert W. Bly is an independent copywriter and consultant specializing in business-to-business, industrial, high-tech, and direct-response marketing. He provides marketing strategies and writes ads, brochures, direct mail packages, sales letters, data sheets, press releases, feature articles, catalogs, newsletters, and other marketing documents for companies nationwide. His clients include CoreStates Financial Corporation, Convergent Solutions, EBI Medical Systems, PSE&G, Wallace & Tiernan, Optical Data Corporation, Airco, and Associated Distribution Logistics.

Mr. Bly is the author of 25 books including *Keeping Clients Satisfied* (Prentice Hall), *The Copywriter's Handbook* (Henry Holt & Co.), and *Business-To-Business Direct Marketing* (NTC).

Also by Robert W. Bly

- *The Copywriter's Handbook*
- *Direct Mail Profits: How to Get More Leads and Sales by Mail*
- *Ads That Sell: How to Create Advertising That Gets Results*
- *Create the Perfect Sales Piece: How to Produce Brochures, Catalogs, Fliers, and Pamphlets*
- *How to Promote Your Own Business**
- *Technical Writing: Structure, Standards, and Style**
- *Secrets of a Freelance Writer: How to Make $85,000 a Year*
- *Out on Your Own: From Corporate Employment to Self-Employment**
- *Dream Jobs: A Guide to Tomorrow's Top Careers**
- *Creative Careers: Real Jobs in Glamour Fields**
- *Information Hotline U.S.A.***
- *The Elements of Business Writing**
- *Selling Your Services*

*With Gary Blake

**With Amy Sprecher Bly

PART I

PLANNING

CHAPTER 1

Advertising: Its Place in Modern Marketing

A few years ago, I received the following letter:

> Dear Bob:
>
> I produce in-house advertising for a manufacturer of concrete and metallurgical testing instruments and chrome chill rolls for the plastics industry. My responsibilities run the advertising gamut: concept, copy (I was a lit major); purchasing of printing, art and photography for direct mail, brochures, catalogs; media placement, trade show coordination, you name it.
>
> My question—can you recommend the one best book that you know of on advertising? Or perhaps a small group of books that touch upon the subject. . . .
>
> I have been in the business for about five years, which is just enough time to give me a real perspective on exactly how much I don't know and how much more I want to know.
>
> Thank you for your kind response.
>
> Sincerely,
>
> Daniel Gallio
> Advertising Coordinator
> FORNEY INCORPORATED
> Wampump, PA

It was mainly in response to Daniel's letter—and other inquiries from people like him—that I wrote the book you are now reading.

Of course, to be useful to a broad range of businesses, I haven't limited the book to business-to-business advertisers (like Daniel) but offer proven principles, methods, and ideas that apply to *all* types of advertising—from retail to mail order, consumer products to high-tech, industrial to corporate.

Also, since Dan may be one of the few readers who advertises "chrome chill roles," the ideas in the book universally apply to all products, all services, all types of businesses—manufacturers, wholesalers, retailers, distributors, and service organizations—and examples are drawn from a broad range of industries. You'll learn from a variety of selling situations: Everything from selling office supplies by mail order, to increasing take-out orders for a gourmet foods store, to selling mainframe software to systems analysts and MIS Managers. No matter what your business or industry, you'll profit from the information contained in this book.

An Unconventional Point of View

Although some of the conventional wisdom about advertising reflects sound thinking, much of it is misguided or out-of-date. When it comes to advertising practice; you will find that I am often a contrarian, holding opinions and views contrary to what others may tell you or what you may find in other texts.

These opinions and views are not based on personal bias or idiosyncracy, but on tested, proven advertising results reflecting work on hundreds of projects for more than 110 clients nationwide. In each case, our objective was not to satisfy corporate committees or generate exciting creative work (you'll find later that creativity for creativity's sake can be the greatest destroyer of advertising effectiveness). Instead, we wanted to achieve immediate, specific, measurable sales results in a short period of time.

As a result, scattered throughout these pages you'll find hundreds of new ways to get better results out of your advertising. Even the "old-pros" will find some gems here—proven but little-known techniques you can use to multiply the response and sales your advertising campaign generates.

The Purpose of Advertising

Why does your employer pay you to conduct an advertising and communications program for your company? Many advertising managers have difficulty answering that question. When asked by financial management, "What are we getting for our investment in advertising?" they stammer weakly about "building image" and "awareness" and "readership scores" and "brand preferences." The thought that their advertising actually has to *sell* something makes them uncomfortable, as if the crass, cold-blooded pursuit of a sale was something on a lower plane than the lofty art of creating beautiful printed pages with words and pictures. These advertising managers understand nothing about their jobs and maybe they never will.

The *amateur* in advertising management is concerned with aesthetics, with creating an ad or brochure that is beautiful to look at, a pleasure to read, and a sure bet to win an award from the advertising industry.

The *professional* knows that the only reason to spend money in business is to make money. Claude Hopkins said it best: "The only purpose of advertising is to make sales. It is profitable or unprofitable according to its actual sales. It is not for general effect. It is not to keep your name before the people. It is not primarily to aid your other salesmen."

My answer to the question "What is the purpose of advertising?" is the same as Claude Hopkins's only slightly modified. I put it this way:

> The purpose of advertising is to sell—or help sell—your company's product or service.

The "help sell" part of this definition recognizes that a single ad or promotion may not do the entire selling job. Instead, it is part of an overall promotional campaign or program whose single-minded goal is to generate the maximum sales possible at the lowest possible promotional cost.

Advertising DOES Sell

Direct marketers already know this fact. They can run an ad and measure the sales it produces and whether it is profitable to the penny.

Retailers, too, can see immediate results from circulars, newspaper inserts, catalogs, and newspaper advertisements. Electronic cash registers linked to a central computer tell the store exactly what is sold each day and can track peaks and valleys in sales activity. Retail ad managers know by counting the take whether yesterday's ad helped boost this week's sales.

Sole proprietors, self-employed professionals, and other entrepreneurial firms with a small number of employees also know that advertising sells. For them, it has to. If a home-based business spends $10,000 in marketing and gets no business as a result, it will quickly go *out* of business.

And it's not just consumer advertising that is supposed to sell. Industrial advertising helps sell products and services, too. If you market primarily to business and industry, you will want to get a copy of an important research paper, *The ARF/ABP Study on the Impact of Business Publications Advertising on Sales and Profits* (Marketing Services Department, Association of Business Publishers, 205 East 42nd Street, New York, NY 10017, (212) 661-6360). This is one of the important pieces of advertising research linking business advertising to sales. It is vital reading for every ad manager.

The study concludes:

- More advertising means more sales.
- More advertising can result in higher profits.
- Increased advertising frequency can also increase sales leads.
- It takes four to six months to see the results of an advertising program.
- An ad campaign can keep working for a full year—and longer.
- Advertising can help build a dealer network; if the product is sold through dealers, it pays to advertise to both dealers and end-users.
- Business publication advertising is effective for a wide range of products sold at a wide range of prices.

Six Ways Advertising Can Increase Your Sales

1. *Selling Direct.* Some products can be sold directly from an ad or direct mail solicitation. This works best with products that have clearly defined benefits, are not available through local retail outlets, have some inherent degree of excitement, and are priced under $1,000. It also works for supplies and other commodity items that can be grouped by category and offered in a catalog (office and computer supplies are good examples).

2. *Generate Sales Leads.* For the smaller firm with a limited budget, the best use of marketing communications is to generate immediate in-

quiries that can be converted to sales. This type of ad encourages response by making a free offer of some type—usually a free booklet, free initial consultation, free estimate, free evaluation of a problem, or other free information. Generally scorned and overlooked by corporate ad managers, these inquiries, properly handled, can add tens of thousands, even hundreds of thousands of dollars to your gross sales each year.

3. *Educate your Prospects.* Advertising can communicate information about your product, your service, your business philosophy, your way of doing business, or your unique approach to solving the customer's problems. A typical example is an industrial manufacturer whose product is differentiated from the competition because it uses a different engineering principle of operation. Advertising would highlight this key difference, explain why it was chosen and how it works, and stress the benefits of this type of construction (better performance, higher reliability, greater efficiency, lower operating costs, etc.) to the reader.

Service businesses are often successful with an even purer educational approach, in which advertising tells the reader about a subject in general, only glancingly referring to the firm's particular services. One successful ad, for a collection agency, had the headline, "Seven questions to ask *before* you hire a collection agency—and one good answer to each." The copy was filled with facts about the methods and techniques used to collect more money from delinquent accounts. Readership was high because the ad presented valuable information of immediate use to the reader. Response was high because, by giving this information instead of a blatant sales pitch, the copy convinced readers that the advertiser was someone who could help them.

4. *Create Awareness.* There are so many products, services, and ideas on the market today that a big part of your job may simply be to make people aware that you offer a particular solution to their problems. An example is Ed Werz, who—as far as I know—is the only consultant in my immediate geographic area specializing in postcard deck advertising.

Ed does not need to convince prospects that he is better than his competition, for he has no direct competitors. Ed's challenge is to make his prospects aware that (a) postcard deck advertising works and is profitable, (b) he is a recognized authority and expert in this type of marketing, and (c) he is available for hire. His marketing concentrates on building awareness of his area of expertise and his ongoing consulting practice.

5. *Establish Credibility.* Madison Avenue talks lovingly of "building an image;" I prefer to think of it as "establishing credibility." Even if you

offer a service or product that clearly is ideal for your prospect, he or she may not respond because the prospect may not know you and may have never heard of your company before. People have a built-in uneasiness about dealing with unknowns and prefer to buy from well-established firms; this is why IBM PCs continue to outsell clone microcomputers that are better in quality and lower in price.

Repeated advertising in select media can help build familiarity with your name and establish your identity. Free advertising—publicity—is even more effective at establishing you as the unchallenged authority in your field.

6. *Keep Your Name in Front of the Public.* Although Claude Hopkins said this isn't what advertising is for, in a way keeping your name in front of the public does help to stimulate sales—both from new buyers and especially among past customers. People who have inquired about your product in the past or have used your service once may quickly move on to other activities. Soon, all the time spent in making contact and selling yourself will be just a distant memory—a memory that can be stimulated into action and interest through renewed contact via marketing communications.

For example, after I gave a speech, a member of the audience approached me about doing some consulting work for his firm. We exchanged information and he promised an assignment, but no assignment came. Because I was busy, I let it go and did not pursue him. He faded from my memory, and I'm sure I did from his. But he had put me on his company's mailing list, and six months later I received a promotional mailing from them. I scribbled on the reply card, "Jim—I want to write your next mailing" and signed my name. Two days later he called and the assignment was mine. *Even though he had my marketing materials, I had simply faded from his mind.* Marketing helped revive that lead and make the sale.

Case Study: A Fortune 500 Company Sells on Three Levels

Table 1.1 outlines how one *Fortune 500* corporation views its marketing communications activities. At the top of the pyramid—the corporate level—the mission is to promote the corporation *as* a corporation to a diverse audience that includes business leaders, the financial community (e.g., investors, financial analysts), government (because this corporation's sales are primarily to federal agencies), opinion leaders, the commu-

Table 1-1. Marketing communications responsibilities.

	Mission	*To This Audience*	*Through These Media*	*To Sell*
Corporate	Sell the Corporation as a Corporation	Business Leaders Financial Influentials Government Opinion Leaders Community Academia Press	Television Business Publications Major Newspapers	Basic Strengths of the Corporation
Business Units	Present Capabilities for Markets/Industries	High-Level Decision Makers Planners/Engineers Financiers	General Business & Horizontal Industry Publications	Systems Capabilities Broad Product & Service Capabilities
Divisions	Inform Prospects of Available Products & Services	Specifiers Designers Purchasers Purchasing Influences	Vertical Publications Functional Publications	Specific Products & Services

Marketing Communications Channels

Advertising—Print, TV, Radio	Sales Training
Direct Mail	Product Information
Brochures	Co-op Advertising
Exhibits & Trade Shows	Point of Sale Displays & Demos
Meetings—Internal & External	Permanent Signs

nity, academia, and the press. Print ads in business publications reach business leaders in corporate America. TV commercials bring the corporate message to a broader audience, which includes the general public as well as the business community.

This large corporation is divided into several major companies or business units. At the company level, the mission of marketing communications is to promote each company's capabilities to the specific markets and industries they serve. Here, the purpose of marketing communications is more specific; namely, it attempts to convince the company's target prospects (at the highest level of decision making) to do business with the company. Print ads, appearing in general business publications as well as industry-specific trade journals, tell readers what the company does, the types of products it sells, how it solves specific problems in the industry, and other reasons why the reader should buy from the company.

At the bottom of the pyramid is marketing communications created for specific divisions within each company. For example, one division might sell one product line to one industry, while another division sells another line of products to a different customer base. The mission of marketing communications is to generate sales of specific products and services by advertising to buyers (those who specify, recommend, or purchase the product) in specific trade publications. Ads feature specific products and include detailed discussions of features, specifications, and benefits.

For small and medium-sized firms, most of the advertising and marketing effort will be equivalent to the "division" level in the marketing communications responsibilities represented in Table 1.1. That is, it will be aimed at generating measurable increases in sales of specific products and services within a specific time frame, such as to "increase billable hours in my law practice by 20 percent and get five new retainer clients within 12 months."

Using the CAST System to Select Appropriate Marketing Communications Tools

What types of marketing communications activities can go into your promotional plan? You should be familiar already with most of these:

Audio-visual presentations
Brochures

Case histories
Catalogs
Classified ads
Directories
Direct mail
Magazine advertising
Newsletters
Newspaper advertising
Outdoor advertising
Point-of-purchase displays
Postcard decks
Publicity and public relations
Radio advertising
Referrals
Sales promotion
Sales representatives
Specialty advertising
Technical and business publications
Telemarketing
Testimonials
Trade show displays
Television commercials
Videos
Yellow Pages

We could probably add to this list or expand some of these categories, but these are the basic marketing communications activities used by most companies to promote their businesses.

Before you create any advertising schedule or marketing plan, sit down with this list for a few minutes and ask yourself: "Which of these techniques works best with my company . . . in my industry . . . with my type of product or service . . . with the particular markets I am trying to reach?" The answer provides direction on where to allocate most of your time, energy, effort, and budget.

George Black has outlined a system you can use to rank each marketing communications program according to how effective it is in your particular situation.

His approach, called CAST (Comparative Analysis of Sales Tools), ranks each marketing tool on a scale of 1 to 5 in terms of its effectiveness in 11 basic categories. These are:

1. *Impact or impression.* The ability to get attention, to penetrate consciousness and be remembered.
2. *Size of audience/reach.* Ability to reach large numbers of prospects at the same time.
3. *Cost per contact.* Efficiency in reaching large numbers of prospective customers.
4. *Sales lead development.* Effectiveness in securing inquiries from the audience reached, usually measured in terms of cost per inquiry.
5. *Message control.* Ability to state and restate the message exactly the way you want to say it.
6. *Flexibility.* Facility for changing the message to fit the need or to overcome objections as they are raised.
7. *Timing control.* Ability to reach out to your prospects when you want to make the move, or when the buying action is imminent.
8. *Repetitive contact.* Suitability for repeating the message with effective frequency without wearing out your welcome.
9. *Reaction speed.* Capacity for sensing the prospect's reaction rapidly so that message changes can be made.
10. *Credibility.* Capacity for inspiring belief and acceptance.
11. *Closing the sale.* Effectiveness in getting the signature on the order.

Table 1.2 shows a CAST analysis matrix used by Automatic Switch Company of Florham Park, New Jersey. All sales tools used by the firm—sales engineers, media advertising, reference publications, public relations and publicity, exhibitions and trade shows, catalogs and sales literature, direct mail, and telemarketing—were ranked on a scale of 1 to 5 in each of these 11 categories (1 = not very effective, 5 = extremely effective).

The matrix is useful because it shows, at a glance, what each marketing tool can and cannot do for your company. As seen in Table 1.2, public relations rated the maximum score (5) in several categories. It was found to be extremely effective in reaching a wide audience and generating a large volume of sales leads at low cost. In addition, public relations is more

Table 1-2. "CAST"—Comparitive analysis of sales tools.

	Impact or Im-pression	*Size of Audience*	*Cost Per Contact*	*Sales Leads*	*Message Control*	*Flexi-bility*	*Timing Control*	*Repetitive Contact*	*Reaction Speed*	*Credi-bility*	*Closing The Sale*
Sales Engineer	5	2	1	3	4	5	5	2	5	5	5
Media Advertising	4	5	4	4	5	1	3	5	2	4	2
Reference Publications	2	4	4	3	5	1	3	3	1	2	1
Public Relations/Publicity	3	5	5	5	2	1	1	4	2	5	1
Exhibition/Trade Shows	5	2	2	2	4	5	1	2	5	5	5
Catalogs/Literature	3	3	3	2	5	2	2	3	2	4	3
Direct Mail	4	4	3	4	5	3	3	4	3	3	3
Telemarketing	2	3	2	3	4	5	5	2	5	3	2

credible than media advertising or the company's own promotional literature. But, public relations does not close sales (here it ranked 1, the lowest rating).

By comparison, the sales engineer is the person who goes in and gets the order. But a sales engineer can call on only so many people per day, and sending him around is expensive, so he ranked low in terms of size of audience and cost per contact. Also, sales engineers did not rank highly in terms of generating sales leads—not surprising, because salespeople tend to be more comfortable calling on current accounts rather than prospecting for new business.

You can readily see the logic in this system and adapt it to your own situation. Which marketing communications activities give you what *you* need in terms of leads, cost, credibility, flexibility, timing, etc.?

Advantage. The CAST system can help you make a logical, informed decision about which marketing activities deserve the bulk of your attention and budget.

Although far from scientific, CAST does force you to view marketing decisions quantitatively rather than from pure "gut" instinct.

The Ad Manager's Role

At a speech given before the New York chapter of the Business/Professional Advertising Association (B/PAA), Robert Lauterborn, then corporate advertising manager for International Paper, described the advertising manager's job as one of "quality control for marketing communications." When Lauterborn's young son realized his dad's company produced the famous "Power of the Printed Word" corporate ad campaign, he asked his father about his involvement. Did he write it? No. Design it? No. Come up with the idea? Not all by himself, no. Then what, Dad? Lauterborn thought for a moment and replied: "I made sure it came out right."

A few years ago, a group representing several facets of advertising met in Toronto, Ontario to discuss the changes they foresaw in the position of advertising executives 20 years in the future. Here is how some of these experts predicted the role of ad manager will change in the twilight years of the 20th century:

> "I think good advertising managers in the future will be doing exactly what they are doing today, and have done in the past: producing excellent commu-

nications. The only thing that may change are some of the tools and the level of sophistication of some of the means that we use to get our messages across in the future."

"True communicators must sensitize their principles to the true needs of a varied audience, and must educate that audience in the true worth of the company or the goods and services that they are prepared to deliver. This also means that the traditional role of the advertiser will change to fill that need, rather than as the creator of product or service awareness and of persuasion to use."

"With the product line we make, I feel that it's critical that the advertising department becomes involved very heavily into technical aspects, as well as the advertising of the product. Without good technical back-up to install or work a product like ours, consumers are not going to enjoy it. I feel that advertising a product like ours will get heavily into the technical aspect, in terms of the way the manuals are graphically illustrated and produced. The communications techniques and tools that improve that will help to sell particular products."

"In my opinion, the future of the ad manager as a distinct species, is about the same as the peregrine falcon. The ad manager will live in crevices in the corporate structure. As far as the future of an advertising department, I think its name will change. Advertising as a distinct function will disappear; it will probably be called 'communications.' I think it is likely to assume a corporate importance equivalent to finance, production, and manufacturing within the next 16 years. Advertising people will be primarily intuitive, planning, and development and production. Policy and strategy will be done on a higher level of communications responsibility."

"In many small to medium-size organizations, the title advertising manager is a misnomer. The title has been inappropriately bestowed upon individuals whose only real role was to provide a clerical link between the company, its agency, and the media. Often, to the detriment of the company, this person is used as a buffer between the client and advertising professionals. This individual has survived by reverting totally to secretarial-clerical duties.

"On the other hand, we have the true advertising manager, newly employed by medium to large-sized companies. More often than not, this person has had at least some formal training, and is usually fairly conversant with the company's marketing objectives. Unfortunately, to the detriment of the entire industry, many of these people, often highly qualified, particularly in the United States, have become the victims of recession."

"The advertising director must become a consultant to his own company, telling his marketing people where the markets are, why they're there, why they're profitable to that particular sector. I think it's no longer a simple job of just buying space and making sure that colors match and that sort of thing, because that task is being run outside. If the ad man wishes to grow, he's going to have to go on an international plane, because our competition is that way."

"I think the title is going to change from advertising manager, to marketing services manager, which will encompass a lot more than just pretty pictures and advertising media. The media, I think, will encompass more marketing support, in terms of helping a marketing manager and a product manager, and how to sell the product. So I think it's not going to be the advertising manager, per se. I think it's going to be marketing services, and it seems to be a trend these days with more companies, to call that person a marketing services manager, as opposed to advertising manager."

"We have the opportunity to get in on other things, like public affairs consulting. We're not just producers of advertising and promotion items. We perform a consultative role to senior management on many things having to do with communications directed toward employees, and the outside world. We have a public relations group in the company, and we work hand-in-glove with them. We like to think we're the people who understand and see opportunities first."

"Advertising is going to have to be seen as significant. At the moment, it's something that's convenient. If you can't get anybody else to do it, the ad department will handle it. That kind of attitude has gone by the board. We can't afford it any more."

Today's advertising manager, marketing communications manager, or marketing services or support manager is much more than an ad-maker or a printing supervisor or a premium orderer; he is a *consultant* to his company, advising marketing, sales, and top management on the best way to increase sales and boost profits through effective use of advertising, publicity, and promotional techniques. Ad agencies also will make the switch from order-takers to trusted advisors. As one of the previously quoted business consultants observes, "Advertising agencies are going to become more consultative, rather than executional. I believe they will become very professional—and they are going to be much more expensive."

CHAPTER 2

Defining Your Product

The Product DOES Matter

When I first started writing advertising copy, I naively thought that if I did my job well enough, people would buy the product being advertised, regardless of what it was or whether they wanted it.

Many people share this attitude. Many advertising managers labor under the misconception that if you make the advertising good enough, it can sell anything to anybody.

They believe that advertising *forces* people to buy products they don't want, don't need, and don't like. They believe that advertising has some magic, almost hypnotic power to make the masses do the advertiser's bidding.

This is nonsense. If you need convincing, try the following test: Send a catalog offering gourmet steaks and other meats for sale, by mail, to a mailing list of vegetarians and to a list of animal-rights activists. How many orders do you think you will receive? You know the answer: precious few.

Now, send that *identical* mailing to a list of subscribers of gourmet magazines, and another to a list of people who have previously bought steaks and meats through the mail (such as can probably be rented from Omaha Meats, a company that sells steaks as business premiums). Note the staggering increase in response to this second mailing. Yet, we have not changed one word of copy or altered the design one bit.

Why then was the first mailing a bomb and the second mailing a success? Simple. In the second case, we were mailing to a market that already has a desire for what we are selling. In the first case, we were mailing to a market which we had good reason to believe will abhor our proposition.

Thus, matching the right product to the right market is at least as important to advertising success as brilliant copy, layout, and concepts. In fact, as you will see, it is actually much *more* important. You need to have a product that people want and a way to reach this audience with your offer if your advertising is to have any chance of success.

"The power, the force, the overwhelming urge to own that makes advertising work, *comes from the market itself,* and not from the copy," writes advertising genius Eugene Schwartz. "Copy cannot create desire for a product. It can only take the hopes, dreams, fears, and desires *that already exist* in the hearts of millions of people, *and focus those already-existing desires onto a particular product.* This is the copywriter's task: not to create this mass desire—but to channel and direct it."

Don Hauptman, a New York-based direct-response copywriter, adds: "Don't try to change behavior. It's time-consuming, expensive, and often futile. It's usually wise to capitalize on existing motivations. In other words, preach to the converted. Unless you have an unlimited budget, avoid products and services that require the buyer to be educated or radically transformed."

Be aware of the importance of the product, the market, and the kind of fit that exists between them. Then tailor your copy to bring them even closer together. Recognizing that advertising *channels* the prospect's desires for the benefits your product provides rather than *creates* those desires is a distinguishing characteristic that separates amateurs from professionals.

You see this in the behavior of advertising agencies all the time. The amateurs—the ones who, quite frankly, do not know what they are doing—become excited at the prospect of doing *any* assignment (perhaps because they are sitting around waiting for one) and jump in immediately with an ad that, in the most clever and artistic way, dramatizes what the client says is important about the product. They do not stop to question whether:

(a) the potential buyers really want such a product in the first place; or

(b) if they do want it, whether what the advertiser *says* is the main selling point will actually move people to action.

Many advertising agencies today are repositioning themselves as being in the business of *marketing communications consultation,* not "advertising." Before they will sit down and write an ad, they ask questions: "What is the product we are selling?" "How do we know people will buy it?" "How do we know which sales points, product features, or benefits . . . the *reasons* why people would buy this product . . . to stress in advertising?" "Should we be advertising . . . or selling through some other method?"

Start With The Prospect, Not The Product

In planning any marketing campaign, "start with the prospect, not the product," advises Don Hauptman. "Avoid superlatives and brag-and-boast language. Wherever possible, incorporate anecdotes, testimonials, success stories, and other believable elements of human interest." As Hauptman has told many audiences during his speeches, successful advertising addresses the *prospect's* concerns—not the advertiser's. Thus, if you are selling telephone systems, your ads and sales letters should talk about the prospect's telephone bill, not how many years your company has been in business. Features and facts may be of some interest, but they are secondary compared with the benefit (lower phone bills, better telephone service) the prospect gets from the system.

Problem. Most advertising people are called into the picture after the product has been developed, the prices set, the sales and support strategies written, and the marketing plan completed. And what they find are products and services that *don't* meet the needs of the customer and are *not* prospect-centered. Management fails to realize that the advertising department cannot simply "make up" copy points as they go along, lie (although some advertisers do), or sell product that does not deliver to customers the value they want.

Solution. Managers responsible for product, sales, and marketing planning should consult with the advertising manager earlier in the game rather than later. Although advertising managers are not product development experts, they often have a lot of good, creative ideas on how to design, package, and sell products. Advertising managers can create much better advertising if they have input into the benefits and value that are built into the product at its inception or that can be added as product changes and marketing plans are adjusted along the way.

As an advertising manager, you should be an insistent voice for adding value to the services your company markets, packaging products that give customers the benefits they need, and setting prices, guarantees, contracts, and offers that provide your buyers with tremendous incentive to choose your firm over the competition.

Do not be afraid to push for the product and service improvements you need to sell the product to your prospects and customers. The good freelance copywriters will tell you that their big success stories all came from writing ads or mailings for products that were already winners; very rarely does a freelance copywriter achieve dramatic sales breakthroughs for a product that is inherently a dog.

Six Steps To Understanding And Defining The Products You Sell

To be an effective advertising manager, you must have a clear understanding of what your company sells, who they sell it to, and why people buy it.

"Who they sell it to" or the market, itself, will be covered in Chapter 3. For now, concentrate on "what your company sells" and "why people buy it."

There are six essential steps to understanding your product and its appeal to the market:

1. Defining your core business.
2. Defining the specific product, product line, or system you are selling.
3. Determining how much of a need there is for the product.
4. Understanding the consumer's decision-making process.
5. Understanding *why* the consumer buys this type of product.
6. Coming up with the right package.

Let's take a look at each of these six steps in a bit more detail.

Step 1: Defining Your Core Business

Companies flounder and get confused when they start acquiring and selling products and product lines that are unrelated and not tied together with a common thread or theme. A jumble of product offerings is more difficult and more expensive to promote than a group of clearly related products and services providing an umbrella package of benefits to a well-defined audience. My test is that if you can't put all your products and services together and sell them in a catalog, you probably shouldn't be selling those that don't fit in the catalog in the first place.

According to marketing consultant Carolyn Hosken, asking the question "What business are you really in?" is the first and most critical step in successful marketing. In her special report, *Four Steps to Dramatic Business Growth,* Hosken observes:

> To market your products or services effectively, first you have to know what business you are in. This sounds obvious, but consider that in the early part of this century, the major railroad companies missed a superb opportunity because they had a very limited answer to this question. They thought they were in the railroad business. Had the railroad companies understood that they were really in the *transportation* business, they could have founded and owned the airlines.
>
> Another way of looking at this question is to identify the general category of service your company provides. Your company's specific products or services are the means for this more general service to be delivered.
>
> Take the example presented by a vice president of a large, well-known company that sells sporting and entertainment event tickets through an extensive system of outlets. He outlined difficulties his company was experiencing in designing a new ticket-handling computer system, and the impact of that on the business.
>
> The problem was not the computer system, but rather that the company thought it was in the ticket-selling business. In fact, it was really in the business of providing the public with *convenient access* to entertainment and sporting events. This insight, if acted upon, would have a major impact on the new computer system's design and potentially on the company's whole way of doing business.

Many companies struggle to define exactly what business they are in—or should be in. The immediate impact of making this decision is its effect on the overall direction of advertising campaigns, including slogans, product packaging, major themes, and copy approach.

Case Study

One industrial firm manufactures ultrafiltration systems for specific markets including water treatment, food and dairy, and chemical processing. One day, the marketing manager, ad manager, and product managers got together to come up with a new slogan for the firm—a "tag line" that would position and define the company's function in a single pithy statement that could be used in advertising and sales literature, appearing under the company logo in these materials.

One product manager suggested "The leader in ultrafiltration systems." After all, that was the company's business, and they were specialists, so why not get to the point?

The advertising manager objected. What if the company should start selling related equipment or technology? They were already getting into reverse osmosis systems and were looking at other filtration products to add to their line. No, the leader in *ultrafiltration* was clearly limiting. How about "The leader in ultrafiltration, reverse osmosis, and filtration technology?"

Too wordy, complained the marketing manager. We have to look at the big picture. What do filters do? They *separate* solids from liquids. How about, "The leader in *separation technology*?"

"Too vague," the other managers replied. *Separation* could mean anything from separating the wheat from the chaff, or rocks from wood in a pulp mill wood yard. But ultrafiltration is a highly specialized separation technology used to remove ultra-small particles from liquid using a unique membrane process.

Suffice it to say, this went on for hours and the problem was never resolved. To this day, the company does not have a slogan or tag line.

Try this exercise with your own company. Can you summarize your business activity in a single line that is *specific* enough that it highlights your unique nature and service, yet *broad* enough that it doesn't limit you from branching off in new products and markets? If you can, you are lucky. You have a business that is logically organized and thus easy to define.

Red Flag

If you can't find an appropriate slogan, watch out. This may indicate trouble in putting together a cohesive advertising and promotion program down the line.

Step 2: Defining the Specific Product, Product Line, or System You are Selling

A "product" has many components to its identity, including:

- The name of the product
- The packaging

- The physical product itself—its weight, dimensions, color, and features
- The *benefits* the customer gets from having the product
- The perceived value of the product
- The variety of different models, colors, and features available
- Options and accessories available
- Warranty or guarantee policy
- Price
- Ease and method of purchase
- Method of delivery or distribution
- Speed of delivery
- Service and support
- Reputation of the company

You should list the specific information under each of these categories for your product before you begin to write your advertising. Also, rank each of these categories on a scale of 1 to 5. A "1" means you are weak in this category and shouldn't stress it in your advertising. It also indicates a possible opportunity for improvement. A "5" indicates strength in the category—strength that can be capitalized on in promotional material. An example is shown in Figure 2.1. (*Note:* As an example I have chosen a product I sell via mail order. This is a manual that tells freelance writers how to increase their income and make money writing for commercial clients.) For your own product, use the blank ranking sheet (Figure 2.2).

Realize that a product is not just a lump of material put together in a certain design. Rather, it is the sum of the attributes that make up its identity. For example, an IBM PC is not just a collection of circuit boards that perform certain functions; other companies offer nearly identical machines at substantially lower prices.

When people buy an IBM PC for thousands of dollars instead of a "clone" for half the price, they are buying other elements of this product, including IBM's superior service, IBM's size and presence in the computer marketplace, and the comfort of knowing that if something goes wrong IBM will take care of it. People who tell me that IBM ads sell the company or IBM's excellence in service *instead* of the product are wrong; what they don't understand is that the company and IBM's excellence in service are *part* of the product. These are the factors that sway many buyers in favor of IBM.

The perceived value of a product is inherent not just in the physical item but also in the attributes listed earlier. Service, support, the company

1 = weak; don't stress this aspect in promotion
5 = strong; stress in advertising
NA = not applicable
Name of product: "SECRETS OF A FREELANCE WRITER" (paperback book)

Category	Comment	Ranking
Packaging	None. Mailed in plain envelope	NA
Description	6 × 9″ trade paperback. Attractively designed. Typeset, not typewritten. Lengthy: 297 pages (longer than most mail order books selling for comparable prices)	3
Benefits	Strong sales appeal: The book gives complete step-by-step plan detailing how the reader, a freelance writer or would-be writer, can earn $100,000+ a year without leaving home. Appeals to people who want to make money and be self-employed	5
Perceived value	High. Readers consistently praise the book for its accuracy, comprehensiveness, good quality of the information, and inspirational/motivational style of writing. NOTE: Plenty of testimonials available for use in ad copy	5
Models	Paperback only. No hardcover	1
Options/accessories	NA	
Guarantee	30-day money back guarantee	3
Price	$12—similar to other mail order books	1
Ease and method of purchase	Order via direct mail. Must send check or money order. No CODs. No telephone or credit card orders. No bill-me option.	1
Method of delivery	Book shipped via 4th class book rate	1
Speed of delivery	All orders shipped same day received	2
Service, support	Consulting services available	1
Reputation of the seller	Author has good credentials in the field. 7 years experience as freelance writer. 17 published books. 110 clients.	4

Figure 2.1. Sample product definition and description ranking sheet.

selling the product, packaging, even price have an effect on how desirable your product is to consumers. And the more desirable the product, the greater the response to your ads and other promotions.

Consider the selling of information in the form of books, cassette programs, and other information media. You'd think that the more information the product gave, the higher the price. Not so.

Figure 2.2. Product definition and description ranking sheet.

1 = weak; don't stress this aspect in promotion
5 = strong; stress in advertising
NA = not applicable

Name of product: ____________________

Category	*Comment*	*Ranking*
Packaging	____________________	______
Description	____________________	______
	____________________	______
Benefits	1. ____________________	______
	2. ____________________	______
	3. ____________________	______
Features	1. ____________________	______
	2. ____________________	______
	3. ____________________	______
Perceived value	____________________	______
Models, colors, & special features available	____________________	______
	____________________	
Options/accessories	____________________	______
	____________________	
Warranty/guarantee policy	____________________	______
Price	____________________	______
Ease and method of purchase	____________________	______
Method of delivery or distribution	____________________	______
Speed of delivery	____________________	______
Service and support	____________________	______
Reputation of the seller	____________________	______

Note: Fill in the correct information for your product or service.

> *Example.* Let's compare a book with an audio cassette. A 300-page trade paperback might sell for $12; such a book contains over 100,000 words of information. Because we have been conditioned by bookstores, we expect to pay a low price for a paperback despite its content.
>
> Audio cassettes, on the other hand, typically sell for $10 to $15 per cassette, yet a one-hour cassette selling for the *same price* as the book contains approximately 9,000 words—less than *one-tenth* the information in the book.
>
> Why then does the cassette sell for more than the book? Because cassettes have a higher perceived value than books. If you are experienced at selling information—especially information by mail—you know that the package of several cassettes and a printed workbook together in an album usually sells for more than the sum of what the cassettes or book would sell for separately! It sounds crazy, but the customer perceives that he is getting a "program" (a more complete instructional course than either books or cassettes provide by themselves) and is willing to pay a premium for it.

Beginning marketers are amazed to discover that the lowest price does not ensure the greatest sales. And again, perceived value is the reason. If something is sold cheaply, then consumers think that it must *be* cheap. Wouldn't you hesitate to go to a doctor who charged $12 a visit if every other doctor in your community charged $45? Naturally, you'd be suspicious of the low price, fearing that something must be wrong with the $12 doctor. Price is part of your product and is linked, with the other factors listed, to perceived value.

Other Considerations in Defining Your Product

Here are some other situations that come up in defining the product that your firm will advertise, promote, and sell:

Product vs. system. Some companies believe they are offering their prospects a complete *system* for handling the prospect's application rather than an individual product.

> *Example.* When personal computers became popular in the early 1980s, many small firms flourished by integrating and marketing computer *systems* aimed at serving the data processing needs of specific types of companies and industries. These *systems* sellers were in contrast to other companies which merely sold *hardware* (PC manufacturers) or *software* (programmers). They found that many small and medium-size firms didn't want to bother putting all the pieces together and were happy to pay a premium for a *systems* approach that would solve their problem once and for all.

Product vs. product line. An important decision to be made by marketing and advertising management is whether to sell a specific product as opposed to a product line or group of products.

> *Example.* Let's say you were given the assignment of doing retail advertising for a local bank offering home mortgages. After studying the competition, you discover that most of your mortgages are fairly similar to the competition's. You also discover that your fixed-rate mortgage is a slightly better value (quarter percent lower annual rate; 2 points versus 2.5 for next-best competitor) than the competition—but only for a 15-year borrowing period. (At 30 years, you are slightly more expensive.) How would you write the ad?
>
> You reply, "I'd write an ad featuring our low-interest-rate, low-points, 15-year fixed-rate mortgage." Okay, but keep in mind two factors: First, your mortgage is only *slightly* better than the competition's, so potential home buyers may not be excited about it—especially if they don't know your bank or live far away. Second, not everyone wants that specific mortgage. Some prefer adjustable rates. Others want a 30-year borrowing period instead of 15 years. And some may be happy to pay higher points if the interest rate is lower, or pay lower points in exchange for a slightly higher borrowing rate. This being the case, perhaps your advertising theme should be freedom and flexibility . . . or the broadest range of home mortgages to meet your customers' specific needs. Or, you may want to stress convenience, or location, or number of branch offices, or help filling out the paperwork.
>
> There is no single right answer. But these are the kinds of strategic questions that should be asked *before* you write your headline or a single line of copy.

Deciding whether to feature a single product or a product line in your advertising isn't always a simple matter. Here are a few guidelines that may help:

—If you have one product that is your biggest seller and the clear leader in your product line, feature that product in your ad.

—If you have one major product and many smaller products that are sold as add-ons or extras to the main product, sell the major product first in ads, then offer the follow-up products in a catalog or series of product mailings.

—If potential customers have a strong preference for one or two of your products, feature these products in your ads.

—If sales of different products are about equal, and customers do not have a strong preference for one product against the others, sell your product line.

—If you do not know which product best meets the customer's needs, and the customer is in a better position to make this determination than you are, sell your product line.

—If you are mailing to customers that are proven "shoppers" (e.g., catalog buyers), sell your product line.

Sell the solution, not the product. In many selling situations, you will have two different types of buyers:

1. Those who know the specific product they want to buy and are comparison shopping to get the best source or deal.
2. Those who have a specific problem—but do not know that your product can solve it (they may not even be aware that your product exists).

A living example of this can be seen at gift counters during Christmas season at department stores across America. Some shoppers—those in the first category—have a detailed, specific list of gifts and will buy either because your brand is best or cheapest or simply because you have the product available.

In the second category are shoppers with a specific problem: that of finding the right gifts for friends and relatives. They know they need something for Uncle Frank, who has particular likes and dislikes, but they don't know exactly what to buy.

This is an ideal opportunity for the store to gain additional sales through friendly, helpful sales clerks who can help the shopper solve his or her problems by asking the right questions about the gift recipient and then suggesting items that might be appropriate. Unfortunately, America's stores are filled with indifferent and uncaring sales clerks who rarely bother to make this extra effort, and so millions, or perhaps billions, of additional sales are lost each year.

How does this relate to advertising? If you have a number of products and services, you might offer to use these products and services and your own expertise to solve the reader's problem rather than "sell" him on a specific product or product line.

> *Example.* One insurance firm offered a free analysis of the consumer's current insurance policies. Instead of advertising a specific policy or plan, this company would send a representative to sit down with you and review your current coverage to make sure it was adequate. If you were under-insured or lacking in insurance in any vital area, the representative would try to solve your problem by selling you the appropriate insurance—thus meeting your needs while making sales for the company.

I do not know what the representative would do if you had too much insurance, but the right thing would be to tell you so you could reduce coverage and save on premiums . . . even if it was on one of their own policies. Yes, they would lose some revenue in the short run, but they would gain a loyal customer whose lifetime purchases would far exceed that small cancellation.

Consultative selling. This term became hot during the 1980s. Consultative selling is an extension of the problem-solving type of selling discussed previously. In dealing with clients, salespeople act as consultants, asking questions that help pinpoint the specific nature of the client's problem and how the company's product or service can solve it. The benefit is that the salesperson and his company become trusted advisors, not "peddlers," who are seen in a helping rather than a high-pressure role.

A good example of this can be seen in ad agencies as they pitch your account. The "product salesmen" are the agencies that push their portfolio in your face, try to dazzle you by showing their creative work. The consultative sellers are those who focus on you—your company, your products, your customers, your marketing problems.

If your firm does consultative selling, can you feature this to your advantage in advertising? Instead of merely putting a brochure in the mail, can you offer free advice, information, or other help to the prospect? This type of helpful attitude, reflected in copy, makes the ad far more powerful.

Step 3: Determining How Much of a Need There is For the Product

According to Jerry Buchanan, publisher of *TOWERS Club Newsletter,* the secret to business success is simple. "Learn what it is your customer wants and needs, and then develop different plans to see that your company gives it to him better and cheaper than your competition."

How *much* the customer wants or needs your product will be a major factor—perhaps *the* major factor—that determines whether your advertising succeeds or fails.

Newsletter marketing consultant Stephen Sahlein has written: "There are two answers to the question, 'What succeeds in newsletters?' The wrong answer is 'need-to-know' information . . . The right answer is 'want-to-know' information . . . Base your sales campaign on market wants—not product strengths."

Substitute "product" or "service" for the "newsletter" and you have a pretty good answer to the question, "What do people buy?" At the very least, your product should be something they need; if they don't need it, you'll have a tough time convincing them to buy it. But even better than having them *need* your product is to offer a product that people *want.*

Let's say you are selling a product I need. The problem is, I may not realize I need the product. Or, perhaps in the back of my mind, I know I need it but, like most people, I don't always do what is good for me and am not eager to part with my hard-earned dollars just to "do the right thing." You can sell me, but your task is a formidable one: to convince me that I need your product and that I should spend my money to fulfill this need.

But, if you have something I *want,* then your task has suddenly become much, much easier, because people love to spend money on things they desire. If I want your product, simply telling me that you have it may be sufficient to get me to buy. Or, you might have to sell me on buying your product instead of the competition's, but not on acquiring *some* product of this type; since it's something I want, I've already sold myself.

> *Example:* One local medical equipment manufacturer designed a revolutionary new heart monitor that can provide doctors with much more information about heart performance during surgery than conventional cardiac monitors. But, doctors are basically satisfied with the conventional monitors and don't perceive the need for the information the new monitor provides, even though study after study proves its usefulness in improving patient care and surgery success rates. This company may be able to overcome this marketing barrier, introduce their new product successfully, and save lives with it, but they face a huge obstacle. The problem is that they are trying to sell the market something that the market doesn't even realize it needs, rather than something the market both realizes it needs and wants.

Many companies in their situation speak hopefully of "educating" the market or "creating" a market for a great product. This is an ambitious undertaking and enormously expensive. If you are the leader in your field, a giant in your industry, or just enormously wealthy, you may succeed at it. But the average advertiser, or even the larger-than-average firm, simply cannot afford to educate the market and *then* sell its specific product.

It's much better to offer a product your prospects already desire and use your advertising budget to channel their desire toward buying your specific offering.

If people do not want your product but do need it, the question becomes: "How *badly* do they need it?" Marketing consultant Dan Piro talks about an "intensity of need"; the more intense the need for your product, the more likely your marketing and sales campaign is to succeed. If the intensity of need is low . . . if your product doesn't solve some important problem or fill a major desire . . . your chances of success are slim. But, if your product solves a pressing problem not being addressed by the competition, you do have a chance to successfully sell your prospects, even if they aren't yet beating down the door to buy what you are selling.

Knowing whether your prospects want or need your product . . . and how much they need it . . . is the third essential step to understanding your product and how to market it.

Step 4: Understanding the Consumer's Decision-making Process

A long-standing argument among advertising copywriters is whether copy should appeal to consumers based on a rational, logical point of view or should seek to move people on an emotional basis, "from the heart."

Dick Vaughn, research director at Foote, Cone & Belding, realized that it's really not a case of emotional appeals versus logical appeals. Rather, some product purchases involve rational buying decisions, others are bought for emotional reasons, and others are made for a combination of the two.

At the same time, he realized that the buying process for some products (stereos, for example) involved a lot of thought and consumer involvement, while other product purchases (staples, paper clips, etc.) are more casual and require little thought or agonizing over selection on the part of the buyer.

Vaughn came up with a simple psychological grid (Figure 2.3) on which the forces behind consumer purchases can be plotted. This is called the FCB Grid, named after the initials of his ad agency, Foote, Cone & Belding. The x axis (horizontal) measures whether consumers evaluate the decision to purchase the product intellectually (think) or emotionally (feel). The y axis (vertical) measures whether consumers consider the purchase decision relatively important or major (high involvement) or unimportant (low involvement). Once a product is plotted, you have a reference point on which to base your advertising.

> *Example:* Consumers respond to perfume emotionally and become highly involved in the decision-making process. Clothes pins, by comparison, are a low-involvement product with no emotion attached to a purchase. A 35mm camera is a high-involvement product, but unlike perfume-purchasing, a camera purchase involves a highly rational decision-making process.
>
> What does this tell us about the advertising? Perfume commercials should probably be dramatic, emotional, and feature people. Camera ads should show the product, give details about operation, features, benefits, and performance, and perhaps provide a comparison between the advertiser's camera and the competition. For clothes pins, people could not

Figure 2.3. The "FCB grid."

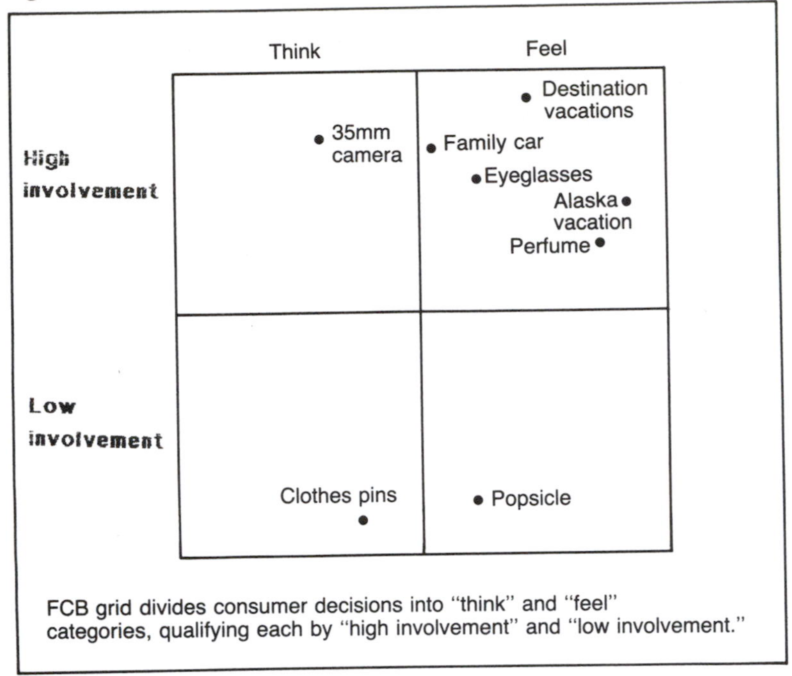

Reprinted with permission, courtesy of *Adweek* and Foote, Cone & Belding.

care less about which brand of clothes pin they use and aren't going to spend even 10 seconds thinking about it.

Take floppy disks as another example. When personal computing began to explode in the mid to late 1980s, floppy disk manufacturers did heavy advertising to business and consumer users. Then the advertising of floppy disks slowed to a trickle. Why?

Consumers, it seemed, just didn't care about floppy disks and didn't want to spend time reading ads explaining why floppy disk brand A would protect data better and last longer than brand X. Plotted on the FCB grid, floppy disks would be in lower left corner: although the purchase decision is rational and nonemotional, involvement is low—almost nonexistent. PC users don't seem to pay much attention to floppy disks at all and generally buy whatever their retail store or mail order supplier carries. If you are a floppy disk manufacturer, you would probably forget about consumer advertising and concentrate on getting mail order catalogs and computer stores to carry your product.

Plotting your own product on the FCB grid takes only a few seconds and can help enormously when formulating advertising strategy. Seeing the position of your product in the grid brings the advertising challenge sharply into focus.

Step 5: Understanding Why Consumers Buy Your Type of Product

As shown in Figure 2.4, there is a hierarchy of reasons why the consumer buys the type of product or service you are selling. From the bottom of the pyramid to the top, these reasons include:

- Features
- Advantages

Figure 2.4. Why customers buy a product or service.

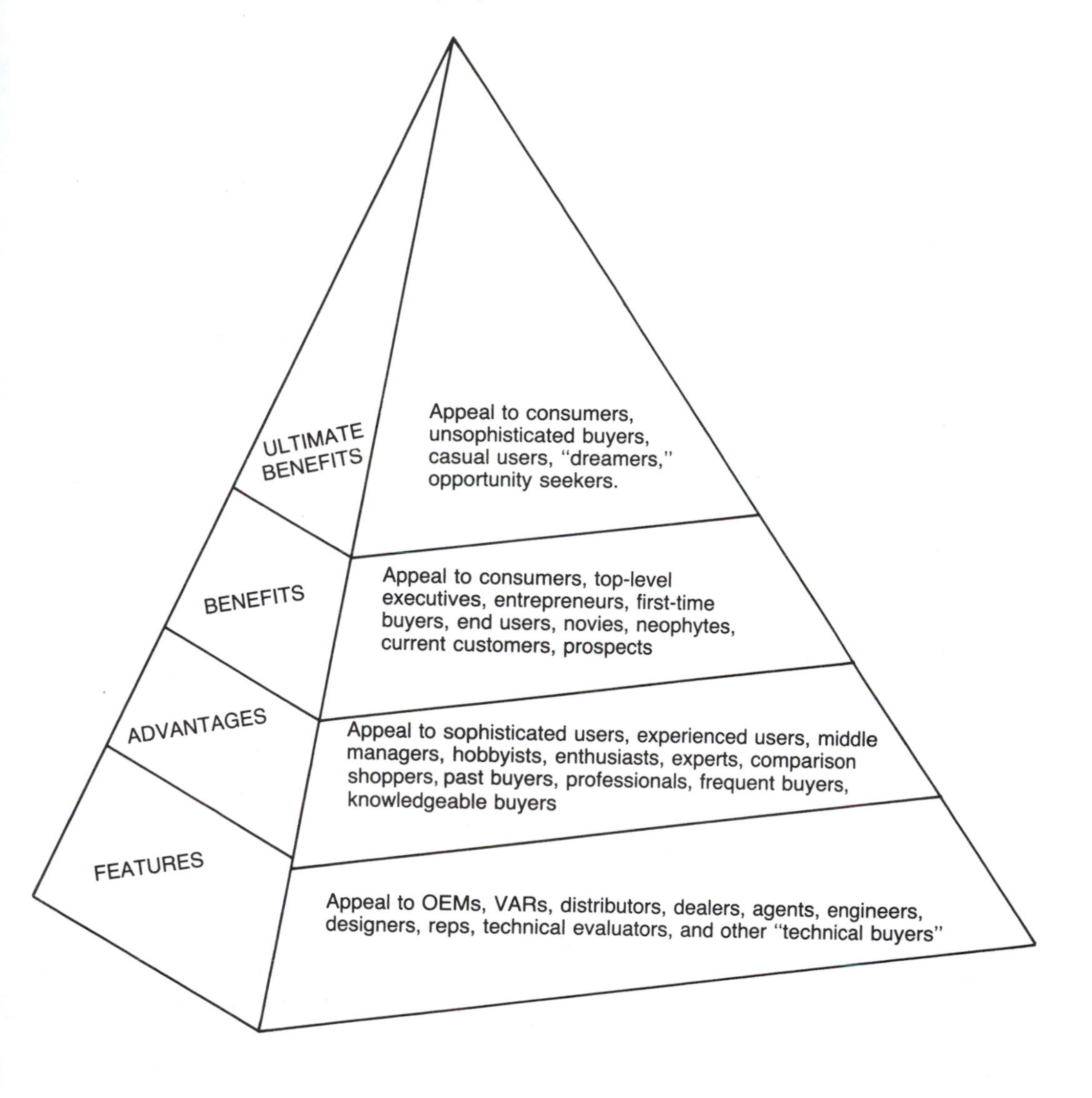

- Benefits
- Ultimate Benefits

Let's look at each of these in more detail.

Features

Features are the factual description of what you're selling. For example, rack-and-pinion steering is a feature of a car. Gas-cushioned shock absorbers are a feature of a car. A 12-inch amber CRT display is a feature of a Leading Edge personal computer. Changeable outgoing message cassette tapes is a feature of a Radio Shack telephone answering machine. You get the idea.

Although benefits are the most important reasons why people buy your product, keep in mind that there are many customers whose decision-making process hinges on whether you offer a particular feature or set of features. In seminar direct mail promotions, for example, many attendees will make the decision to register based on one or two of the specific items mentioned on the course outline printed in the seminar brochure.

In certain markets, features can be equal to—or even more important than—benefits. One such situation is selling products to *original equipment manufacturers* (OEMS) and *value-added resellers* (VARs)—companies that buy your product and incorporate it into a larger product or system that they then resell to the end-user or consumer. OEMs are primarily concerned with getting performance characteristics and technical specifications compatible with their own designs, and they look for specific features rather than the benefits these features give the end-user.

Note that manufacturers, engineers, and other technically oriented buyers are also more concerned with features than benefits. If you look at advertising in the semiconductor field, for example, you notice that ads typically devote a large portion of the space to listing product specifications.

Common misconception. Most books on the subject of copywriting tell you never to put features in your ads, and that every feature must be transformed into a benefit. I disagree. Sometimes, a feature alone is more powerful. For example, in many book ads you read the line "22 weeks on the NY TIMES best-seller list!" (This copy is usually highlighted in a burst or banner.) This is clearly a feature. The benefit is the implication that, if the book is so popular and liked by so many people, you will like it also. Yet, I would not state this explicitly in the ad; I'd let the feature speak for itself. Why? Because the benefit is so obvious that to spell it out is unnecessary. And it may also be ineffective: If your prospect prefers bestsellers, he knows why he likes them and doesn't need to be told. If another person reading the ad isn't swayed by popular opinion, telling him that he should read the book because a million other people have bought it—and therefore it's good—isn't going to convince him.

Advantages

Power brakes is a feature of a car. The ability to stop on a dime is the *advantage* that feature gives you. Preventing accidents and saving lives is the *benefit* you get from having the advantage derived from the feature.

In a telecommunications network designed for banks, brokerage houses, and other financial applications, a statistical multiplexer provides a feature that automatically switches to a redundant route in case of line failure. The advantage is instant switch-over with no interruption in service or loss of data. The benefit is that you avoid losing thousands or millions of dollars per hour by preventing down-time.

Remember. Although benefits are usually the key elements to stress in your advertising, advantages are important to many buyers. These include buffs, hobbyists, enthusiasts, experts, technical buyers, and others who are sophisticated and knowledgeable about your product. In many cases, these people know of the benefits your products provide and don't need to be sold on them. Their buying process is driven by comparing the advantages and disadvantages of your product against the competition. A comparison chart, showing point by point how your product offers more advantages, is very effective in selling to this audience. A sample is shown in Table 2.1.

Benefits

A benefit is what the customer gains by purchasing and using your product. If you sell a daily planning diary for executives, the benefit might be that it saves time, helps you organize your day better, or helps you keep projects on track and meet your deadlines.

Table 2.1. Product comparison chart.

Product	*All-aluminum construction*	*Thermostat control*	*Modular design*
Widget A	Yes	Yes	Yes
Widget B	No	Yes	No
Widget C	No	No	No
Widget D	Yes	Yes	No

"One of the rules of good copy is: Don't talk about yourself," says copywriter Sig Rosenblum. "Don't tell the reader what *you* did, what *you* achieved, what *you* like or don't like. That's not important to him. What's important to him is what *he* likes, what *he* needs, what *he* wants." Or, as Dr. Jeffrey Lant puts it, "Benefits answer the prospect's question, 'What's in it for me?' "

Example: An independent consultant, working at home or from a small rented office, does not buy a personal computer *per se*; he buys the *benefits* he gets from the computer. In the case of the consultant, these benefits might include saving time, reducing paperwork, easier access to important documents, ability to communicate with clients electronically, more efficient research through on-line databases, improved communications, better looking documents, and so on.

Benefits, always important, dominate copy when you are writing ads aimed at consumers, end-users, executives, entrepreneurs, current customers, financial types, and other nontechnical buyers. If you are selling a telephone system to an entrepreneur, for example, he is almost wholly concerned about benefits, while a telecommunications engineer working for a large bank might be more concerned about the technical features.

Ultimate benefits

An ultimate benefit, expressed in the broadest terms, is the overall key benefit the buyer derives from the product.

Example: Say you are selling a seminar aimed at teaching manufacturer's representatives, insurance agents, stockbrokers, and other commissioned salespeople how to sell more effectively. The *feature* of your seminar is that it teaches them proven techniques for increasing their sales. The *advantage* is that it reveals sales secrets not taught in other seminars, and thus it is more effective. The *benefit* is that it increases their sales, thus allowing them to earn more money. The *ultimate benefit* is that they can become rich beyond the dreams of avarice, earn millions of dollars in a few years, and retire to the Bahamas at an early age and live a life of luxury.

Although the ultimate benefit holds the most promise, its statement often lacks focus and the specificity of more product-specific benefits. It's nice to say that your sales seminar will make the customer rich beyond the dreams of avarice, but used alone, this isn't specific enough to gain the prospect's attention or to make your message sound credible. You've got to add more product-specific benefits to give "meat" to your message and highlight the uniqueness of your product or service. For the selling seminar, additional benefits might include:

- eliminating fear of "cold calls"
- increasing your sales conversion ratio
- qualifying prospects *before* you visit them
- increasing your income $20,000 a year or more
- raising your gross sales by 10 percent a year

Balancing features, advantages, benefits, ultimate benefits

Many experts will tell you to stress benefits and forget about features. But, as you have seen, certain audiences—for example, engineers, OEMs, VARs, dealers, distributors, agents, wholesalers, technical buyers, hobbyists, and many others—are also concerned with technical features and advantages, not just benefits or ultimate benefits.

Whether your copy will stress primarily features or benefits or give equal weight to both depends on your audience and their decision-making process. Table 2.2 provides a guide that may be helpful in finding the right balance.

Table 2.2 Balancing features and benefits.

Audience	*Copy Contents: Features vs. Benefits (percentage)*	
	Features & Advantages	*Benefits & Ultimate Benefits*
Consumers, end-users, current customers, prospects, first-time buyers, novices, neophytes, high-level business executives, entrepreneurs	10–15%	85–90%
Experienced users, frequent buyers, middle management, professionals, hobbyists, enthusiasts, experts, and other "knowledgeable" buyers	25–30%	70–75%
OEMs, VARs, remanufacturers, rebuilders, dealers, distributors, agents, reps, engineers, technical professionals, designers, process experts, and other "technical" buyers	50–75%	25–50%

Step 6: Coming Up with the Right Package

The sixth and final step in understanding your product as it relates to advertising and promotion is to package the product in such a way that it has the greatest appeal and desirability to the consumer. The more appeal the product has, the easier and less expensive it will be to generate interest and sales through advertising, publicity, and other marketing communications vehicles.

Packaging refers not only to the container or box (although this is part of it) but to a number of factors involved in the way the product is presented and offered to the buyer. These factors include:

- Unit of sale (is the product sold by the gross, dozen, half-dozen, or individual unit?)
- Price
- Discounts and other special price-off deals available
- Warranty and guarantee terms and periods
- Accessories, parts, and supplies included (e.g., if you are selling a flashlight, does it come with a battery?)
- Physical packaging—design, construction, and copy on box, package, or label
- Method of distribution (mail order, wholesale, retail, and so on)
- Service and support

> *Example:* One of my clients sells a satellite telecommunications system. As part of installing it, the buyer must get a telephone line connecting his office to my client's facility. Although my client cannot provide this line directly (since he is not a telephone company), he does tell prospective buyers, "Although we cannot install this line for you, we will call your local telephone company and make the arrangements for you to get it, and we won't charge you for doing so." Thus, there is a *service element* packaged and included in the overall price of the product.

As a rule of thumb, it is usually better to offer the customer greater value at a higher price than less value at a lower price, although it is possible to load up your product package with so many extras that the price you must charge customers to make a profit makes your product unaffordable. Most people appreciate extra service and value and are willing to pay for it.

Example: Many people buying a new car accept dealer financing on the spot, even though they possibly might get a lower rate or better value if they comparison-shopped from other sources (banks, primarily) or took out a home equity loan. Yet they prefer the convenience of getting the loan on the spot and driving the car out of the showroom with the details taken care of.

Add value to your package

Some business writers call the practice of creating a package with extra value *value-added marketing.* It is practiced by firms who realize their customers want more value and are willing to pay for it rather than save a few pennies buying the "economy" or stripped-down version. Even buyers with little money want the best, and the barrier to sale is often not their lack of desire for your product but rather their inability to pay for it.

As an advertising consultant, I am constantly advising my clients on how they can increase sales by offering more value in their package, and I recommend that you, as advertising manager, do the same. Often, a minor adjustment in the package—for example, extending the warranty from 90 days to 12 months, or offering free home delivery, can make a dramatic increase in advertising and sales results.

Example: One successful entrepreneur who added value to his package is Dr. Gary Blake, director of The Communication Workshop, a management consulting firm offering communications seminars to business. Blake is a successful independent trainer, and he charges handsomely for his seminars. Occasionally, a prospect will balk at paying a high fee for a short seminar. One concern is that, once the seminar is over, the managers will not be able to maintain a steady improvement in communications skills.

Blake's solution was to offer his training clients a Business Writing Hotline. The deal is that anyone who has taken the seminar can call the hotline to ask follow-up questions or consult with Blake and his staff on a communications problem. There is no charge, as the cost is included in the fee for the training program.

By including the hotline as part of his training package, Blake increased the value offered to his clients, and thus boosted his own sales, with little time, effort, or expense. Although the hotline is a big attraction to potential clients and helps overcome a lot of sales resistance, only a small percentage of attendees actually take advantage of the free service, so the hotline is not a big drain on Blake's time.

Red flag. A not-so-good alternative is to charge a nominal fee for hotline calls, as some software companies do. This lowers the perception of your product and company and makes buyers of expensive services or software feel as if you are overcharging. It's better to work it into the overall package and get the expense covered by charging a slightly higher total price.

How can you add value to *your* company's product or service? Here are 14 practical tips:

1. If you are selling a product, include select parts, accessories, or attachments with the purchase of the product. Not all parts and accessories need be included, just the ones your buyers want most.
2. If your product has parts or supplies that need to be replaced periodically, include the first replacement part or batch of supplies free with purchase.
3. If there is a monthly subscription fee for your product or service, give the customer the first month's use free as a bonus for subscribing.
4. If you perform a service, guarantee performance or results.
5. Include a hotline number the buyer can call to get help, answers to questions, or make complaints. Toll-free is best but not mandatory.
6. If you perform a service, remind the prospect by mail or telephone when it is time to perform the service again. Many dentists do this with a telephone call and a postcard. If your gutter-cleaner and chimney sweep did the same, you might not forget to call them when it is time for a cleaning.
7. Send your customers or clients a free newsletter or magazine.
8. Extend the guarantee or warranty. If your competitors give a 90-day warranty on parts and labor, give an unconditional one-year warranty. If your competitor has a 30-day money-back guarantee, give a 90-day money-back guarantee.
9. Accept credit card and bill-me orders.
10. Allow customers to order round-the-clock. Make sure your telephone never goes unanswered. At the very least, install a telephone answering machine, voice-mail system, or hire an answering service to take messages during off-hours. An amazing number of companies, both big and small, don't do this.
11. Offer faster response to service requests than your competition. If your competitor sends a service person with 24 hours, you should send someone within four hours.

12. Explain what you are doing and the value of your methods to the client or customer. For example, if you offer a service rebuilding equipment, describe the painstaking process by which your technicians remove, examine, and replace all worn parts. Tell how each system is tested and retested six times. Communication helps create the perception of value in the customer's mind. This is something that can be accomplished through use of print advertising, direct mail, and sales literature.
13. Make a list of things that your competitors (and other companies) do to you that you *don't* like. Then, make sure you don't commit these sins when serving your own customers.
14. Give the prospect your *personal* pledge that, if something is not to his liking, you will make it right. And stick to that promise.

"Service is not an afterthought; it is one of the primary reasons we are in business," writes Bruce D. Smith, president of Network Equipment Technologies. "It is the concept of providing value-added to our customers at all times. A truly customer-driven vendor has to consider himself in partnership with his customers."

The "value-added" approach is eloquently summed up by entrepreneur Russ von Hoelscher. "Don't cheat or take advantage of your customer; you'll be the loser. Instead, win success by giving your customers their money's worth. And if you really want great success, give your customers *more* than their money's worth."

Key point for success. Make sure your company adapts this value-added, customer-centered philosophy in their dealings. If they don't, all the clever advertising in the world won't save you from marketing failure.

CHAPTER 3

Defining Your Markets

The Hidden Market*

Most advertising and marketing people are so involved in pursuing their known market that they ignore other markets almost completely. Yet these markets are potentially larger and could become a major source of profits.

By the *hidden market,* we mean all the sales controlled by all the buyers and specifiers you are not now in direct contact with. These include:

- People who have never heard of your company.
- People who *have* heard of you but know little about you.
- Former customers and prospects.
- People who have a need for a product but no source.

Note that salespeople tend to call on customers and accounts they already know. Word of mouth and referrals can generate new business, but

*Portions of this chapter are reprinted from the essay, "The Hidden Market", courtesy of Thomas Register of American Manufacturers.

slowly. Advertising and marketing communications provide the most effective means of reaching markets that you are not now selling to, or that you are selling to but in which you do not have the market share you desire.

At any moment, people who are not now buying from you are eagerly looking for a new source of products and services for a variety of reasons:

- Some will be new to your market. These include companies building new plants, new companies, companies that have just moved to your area, new distributors, overseas buyers, new needs caused by changes in legislation (EPA, OSHA, etc.), and new needs caused by a decision to buy a product or service outside instead of produce it in-house.
- Some will be dissatisfied with their current source because of personality clashes, price increases, delivery and service problems, unsatisfactory product quality, or failure to meet the customer's needs in some other way.
- Some will have emergency needs because a current supplier can't deliver, discontinues selling the product, or goes out of business.
- Some are buyers looking for a second source to guarantee uninterrupted supply or eliminate their dependence on their current supplier.
- Some will be current customers who don't realize that you also make other products that they need. Most customers don't know the full product line of their current suppliers. Mailing them a catalog and keeping them informed through a series of mailings will solve this problem.
- Some will be your former customers. Former customers may not be buying from you simply because they forgot about you, can't find you, lost your telephone number, or because you moved or changed your name.
- Some are price-shopping and need other sources to give them competitive bids.
- Some will be prospects you solicited in the past but who didn't buy from you. They may not have bought for any of a number of reasons. Perhaps your product or service was not right for them then, but is now. Or maybe they didn't have a need for a new supplier when your salesperson called them, but now they are looking. Or maybe the person in charge didn't like your personality, but he or she has moved, and the new person is open to doing business. Or perhaps your sales representative gave up too soon.

Note that according to Thomas Publishing, 80 percent of sales to business and industry are made on the fifth call, but only 10 percent of salespeople call beyond three times.

For whatever reason, there are many people who are not in touch with you through personal selling but represent good potential customers or clients for your product or service. Advertising can, at relatively low cost per contact, reach into, uncover, and activate exciting and profitable new markets for any business.

"Advertising digs prospects out of the woodwork," explains ad agency owner Bob Pallace. "It finds new business in the 'boondocks' where salesmen don't reach. Salespeople usually concentrate their time calling on current accounts and don't like to prospect for new business. Advertising gets you into places you would never have thought of going."

There are dozens, perhaps even hundreds, of markets and submarkets for your product or service, and you cannot possibly reach all of them and sell them effectively, because the total market is larger than your budget for communicating with them. For this reason, you must select which markets are most important to you and concentrate the bulk of your effort and money in reaching these key target markets.

What Is A Target Market?

A *target market* is a group of potential buyers for your product or your service; members of the group have certain geographic, demographic, psychographic, and other characteristics in common that set them apart as a distinct market.

For example, doctors are often targeted as a separate and distinct market by financial services firms and other marketers because doctors are high-income individuals with lots of money to spend. Doctors are actually a subgroup of a larger consumer market, the "affluent consumer"—college-educated, professional, residing in major metropolitan and suburban areas, with household income of $50,000+.

The marketplace may be segmented into distinct target markets by age, income, occupation, lifestyle, avocation, industry, geography, or any other characteristic that distinguishes the buying habits and patterns of a consumer or business prospect.

Specific markets include writers, teachers, suburbanites, city dwellers, homeowners, car drivers, home-based businesses, corporate managers, engineers, accountants, nurses, vegetarians, pet owners, credit cardholders, do-it-yourselfers, Macintosh users, IBM PC users, hospitals, manufacturers, lawyers, married couples, singles, retirees, people over 50, parents, investors, opportunity seekers, book buyers, sports and fitness enthusiasts, left-handed people, VCR owners, camcorder owners, compact disc player owners, skiers, boat owners, Manhattanites, hospital administrators, gas station owners, and women. And there are literally hundreds of other categories that can further be broken down into *thousands* of subcategories.

Why Target?

One of the keys to marketing and advertising success is not to treat all prospects uniformly as a single mass market, but to identify key target markets and tailor advertising campaigns to the specific needs, concerns, and problems of each type of potential buyer. This is essential for two reasons:

1. It allows you to reach your prospects with a meaningful message a sufficient number of times in order to generate the desired sales result. On a budget of $50,000, your firm could not even begin to reach all consumers or business prospects in the United States or advertise your product on national television. But you *could* send letters or run ads reaching all the physicians in group practices in Maryland—if that was one of your target markets. Target marketing takes an overwhelming prospect base and cuts it down to manageable size.

2. Targeting improves the quality and effectiveness of communication, because it allows you to tailor a message that precisely meets the needs and concerns of the potential buyer.

Example: If you are doing a mass market ad campaign to sell a facsimile machine, you are limited to describing the features of your machine or the general benefits of facsimile. But, if you target a specific market—say, self-employed people working at home—you can write copy that speaks to their needs and problems. For example:

A FAX FOR YOUR HOME OFFICE—ONLY $550 COMPLETE

If you work at home, you know that more and more of your clients, vendors, and colleagues want to be able to communicate with you by FAX. You know you need one. But the price may be holding you back.

Other FAXs are expensive because they are designed for big corporations that can afford them. But now BizCom Inc. introduces the HOMEFAX 100—the first facsimile machine designed specifically for self-employed professionals and others who work out of their homes.

To begin with, HOMEFAX 100 is priced at an affordable $550. It can send and receive a FAX as good as any machine on the market. But it isn't loaded with a lot of unnecessary "extras" that drive up the price of corporate machines. Maybe the *Fortune* 500 can afford to spend $2,500 on a FAX; but with one or two people in your office, you can't.

Another big plus of the HOMEFAX 100 is that it *saves space* in your already-cramped spare bedroom, garage, or basement office. Measuring a compact 12 × 9 inches, we eliminated the feed and output trays so the FAX can fit easily on your desk or on a bookshelf.

And although we've saved money by trimming features, HOMEFAX 100 still does everything you need a FAX to do: Send a page in 25 seconds, receive a FAX in 30 seconds per page, and store in memory the FAX numbers of up to 20 of your most frequently dialed clients and other numbers.

We can deliver and have the FAX working in your office today or tomorrow. For more information, visit our store in midtown Manhattan or call the toll-free number below.

[logo, address, telephone]

Seven Ways to Target Advertising to a Specific Market

1. Identify your target audience in the headline of your ad, the cover of your brochure, or the outer envelope teaser of your direct mail package.
Examples:

Headline	*Target Audience*
"We're looking for people to write children's books"	Aspiring writers
"A message to all charter security policyholders . . ."	Policyholders
"Attention: C programmers"	Computer programmers
"An important announcement for entrepreneurs"	Small-business owners

2. Show pictures of people, equipment, and events related to the reader's industry or interests. *Example:* In a brochure aimed at farmers, show silos, tractors, fields of wheat, farmers meeting at the general store.

3. Use facts and statistics that demonstrate your knowledge of the reader's interests, hobbies, problems, or needs. *Example:* "Trucking company

executives: With insurance costs rising 50 percent or more, rising premiums can easily add 4 to 5 cents operating costs per mile and substantially eat into your already-shrinking profit margins. But now there's a program that can *reduce* premiums and hold the line on rising operating costs. . . ."

4. Write copy that sounds the way your prospect talks. Jargon is acceptable; if not overused, it is effective in showing the reader that you speak his language. *Example:* Don't be afraid to use terms like CICS, abend, and MVS when writing to systems analysts who are familiar with this language.

5. Begin your copy by talking about issues and concerns that are foremost in the reader's mind. Show that you know the problems of this particular group of buyers and understand their needs.

6. When you give examples, case histories, or testimonials, make sure they are from customers in the same target market group as the person reading your copy. *Example:* Bankers do not relate well to examples from manufacturing; they want to read about how you have helped other *banks* with your product or service.

7. Demonstrate your extensive experience in serving this target market by citing facts such as:

- Number of customers you serve who are in the same group or field as the reader
- Case histories and success stories
- News coverage and publicity in specialized publications serving the target market
- Memberships in their trade associations and professional societies.

Tip. If you are actively pursuing a certain market, join the trade associations serving this market. Not only does this give you a credential you can mention in your sales literature, but it gives you access to valuable membership directories and mailing lists for marketing purposes.

How to Determine Whether a Particular Market is Worth Pursuing

A question you must ask before committing advertising dollars to pursue any specific market is whether the market is worth pursuing. Does it offer enough sales potential to justify a small or large-scale advertising campaign? The following checklist will help you decide:

☐ Size

Is the market large enough to be worth pursuing? The real question is whether it's large enough for *you* to pursue. Many small companies are successful selling to "niche" markets (small, vertical target markets) that their larger competitors can't be bothered with.

> *Example:* Computer systems integrators who design turnkey computer systems for specific industries such as liquor stores, real estate agents, and accounting firms.

Tip. If the market is not large enough to support a trade journal or other specialized publication catering to its members, then it is probably not large enough (or easy enough to reach) to be worthy of a sales effort. An exception would be the availability of a specialized mailing list to reach a significant portion of the market—or an association membership directory that can be converted into a mailing list.

☐ Reachability

To reach the market cost-effectively, there must be a readily available publication, mailing list, or association. If such media outlets do not exist, mounting an affordable advertising campaign will be next to impossible. Aside from giving up on the market, you have two other options:

1. Compile your own prospect list. This is difficult and expensive, but feasible in some cases. The cost of compiling such a list can range from $2 to $4 per name or more as opposed to 5 to 15 cents per name for renting names from existing lists.
2. Use a shotgun approach. Instead of placing targeted advertising messages in narrow vertical media, advertise in general publications and hope that enough members of your target audience respond to make it cost-effective.

> *Example:* The late Howard Shenson, a California-based consultant, offered a seminar on "How to become a successful independent consultant." The seminar targets professional people who, dissatisfied with corporate life (or suddenly out of a job), are considering a new career as a self-employed consultant. Since there are no magazines aimed at this group, Shenson ran his seminar ads in daily newspapers, figuring that would-be consultants—like other business professionals—read the newspaper. This type of advertising was successful for Shenson, despite the enormous wasted circulation (perhaps 99.9 percent of the newspaper's readers are *not* candidates for the seminar).

☐ Profit Potential

Ideally, you want to target those markets that not only have a desire or need for your product but can afford to pay for it, too. For example, although both medical doctors and freelance writers have a need for financial products and services, financial marketers devote a lot of effort advertising to doctors and very little to writers. The reason is that the average doctor makes a lot of money, while most writers earn only a modest income.

☐ Authority

Advertising should attract those groups of buyers who not only want and can afford your product but have the authority to buy it, as well.

> *Example:* Much of the advertising in the home furnishings field is directed at women rather than men. Although many men can afford to buy home furnishings and may even enjoy decorating, in most households the purchase of a rug, wallpaper, or bathroom fixture is a *joint* decision; the husband does not make such a purchase without the approval of the wife. Advertisers don't target men because the man does not have the *authority* to buy without his wife's approval. Other examples include cereal advertising (aimed at adults as well as kids because the kids do not make the purchase without parental approval) and industrial advertising that targets the CEO as well as the middle manager (because the middle manager cannot authorize the capital expenditure required without the CEO's approval).

☐ Desire

You have the best chance of success not when the people in this target market need your product but when they also *want* the product.

Building the Customer Profile

Once you identify one or more target markets for your product or service, you need to develop an in-depth customer profile of each group you target, advises management consultant Carolyn M. Hosken.

The profile for business-to-business customers will include criteria such as:

- Industry or type of business
- Geographic location
- Annual sales

- Job title and name of contact person
- Job function or department within the firm
- Number of employees in the firm
- Types of products purchased

One system of specifying industry or type of business is the Standard Industrial Code or SIC. This system uses codes to group various types of businesses according to category and subcategory. Standard Industrial Codes appear in the *SIC Manual,* published annually by the U.S. Government Printing Office. For more information, write Superintendent of Documents, Washington, DC 20402-9325. To order with Visa or Mastercard, call 202-783-3238.

The profile for a consumer market would have criteria such as:

- Age
- Location
- Income level
- Vocation
- Family status (single, married, divorced, widowed)
- Interests or concerns
- Ethnic background
- Religion
- Level of education
- Sex

Example of customer profile. Consider the New Jersey accounting firm that chose to target specific Middlesex and Monmouth County businesses with sales volume between $250,000 and $5 million. Their "Desirable Client Profile" appears in Figure 3.1.

Tip. Be as specific as possible in developing your own Customer Profile. The more specific you are about the people you wish to do business with, the easier it will be to find them. Just as important, says Hosken, you will have more satisfying customer relationships because they will be with people you have chosen to do business with.

Figure 3.1. Desirable customer profile—Example: accounting firm.

A desirable client is one who:

1. Has business volume of $250,000 to $350,000 minimum up to about $5 million in gross sales (up to the level at which an in-house controller is brought on board).
2. Is in one of a wide variety of businesses such as retail, wholesale, construction, manufacturing, restaurants, etc. (specific by SIC code).
3. Will generate a minimum of $3,000 a year in billings.
4. Requires services on a monthly basis (preferable), or at least on a quarterly basis.
5. Is reasonable to deal with and is knowledgeable concerning their own business.
6. Pays at the time of service (or pays invoices on time).
7. Falls into one of two categories:
   - Can be handled efficiently and profitably by the firm's staff and current computer system; or
   - Is sufficiently complex, entrepreneurial, and lucrative to require the personal attention of the firm's senior partner.
8. Is located within 30 to 40 minutes driving time of the office or can be handled primarily through the mail.

How to Find and Identify Target Markets

How do you uncover and discover the target markets that are best for your product or service? Here are some ways to go about it:

1. First, start with what you know—the logical and obvious markets for your product or service. There must be some potential markets you have in mind; otherwise, you wouldn't have created the product or service in the first place.

2. Look for markets that are similar to but slightly different than your current markets. Your current product, service, and marketing efforts can probably be tailored to the new market with minimal effort. An example would be if you are selling collection services to record clubs, what about targeting book clubs?

3. Check your competition. Keep tabs on their advertising and promotion. Read their brochures. Their marketing efforts will reveal the markets they are selling to—markets you may want to compete for or, conversely, avoid.

4. Talk with people who are not competitors but sell related products or services to the same markets you do. Ask them what *new* markets they are planning to explore. Perhaps you can even team up as partners in approaching this new base of prospects.

5. Read industry trade publications for news of your competitors' sales efforts and advertising campaigns. In their desire to show off to the trade, your unwise competitors will frequently (and unwittingly) reveal their new marketing strategies to the world—and to you.

6. Examine your sales records. Do they suggest patterns—clusters of sales made to buyers who can logically be grouped by one or more common characteristics to form a reachable target market?

7. Ask for more information about your prospects when you take an order. For example, get their age, sex, telephone number, areas of interest, etc.

Tip. Many warranty cards which manufacturers request that buyers complete and mail back are, in reality, mini-marketing surveys that reveal information on consumer lifestyle, buying habits, demographics, and income. Include such a mail-back survey when you ship your product or render your service. Study the information you have collected on your buyers. Do the data suggest markets where you should concentrate the bulk of your promotional effort?

7. Ask your salespeople which markets you should emphasize in your advertising. If salespeople are successful in selling to a market where you don't do much promotion, perhaps you should consider supporting their efforts with more aggressive marketing communications.

8. In a creative brainstorming session, try to come up with as many possible new markets as you can. Then evaluate the list to see which, if any, are worth further consideration.

Brainstorming tip. Try to come up with as many new applications of your product or service as you can . . . even off-the-wall ones. Often, new applications in turn suggest new uses—and new markets.

9. Study your customer list. Which customers are your best customers—the ones who buy the most, are easiest to reach, and give you the most pleasure to deal with? You may find that all the "best" customers fall into one or more clearly identifiable target markets to which you have not been actively marketing.

Figure 3.2. Desirable customer profile.

For: ______________________________

(your company name)

Selling: ______________________________

(your product or service)

A desirable client/customer is one who:

1.

2.

3.

4.

5.

6.

7.

8.

Please complete one Customer Profile for each target market you wish to reach.

10. Make a commitment to find and test one or two new markets every year.

Brainstorming is the Key

Using these 10 techniques, it is usually a simple matter to come up with a rich variety of key target markets for virtually any business. Here are three examples of target markets as defined for various types of businesses.

1. *Business:* A home-based word processing service.

Target markets: All businesses within 30 to 40-minutes driving time of your home.

Special target markets: Companies that need a lot of typing but do not have large support staffs.

Examples: Lawyers, writers, consultants, home inspectors.

Other potential markets: Screenwriters (if you live in LA), students who need typing for term papers (a good market if you live in a college town), graduate students (thesis typing).

Idea: Accept assignments by FAX and deliver copy in electronic form via modem to extend your service beyond your immediate geographic vicinity.

2. *Business:* Freelance proofreader.

Markets: Advertising agencies, pharmaceutical companies, law offices, publishers, corporations (especially those with in-house publication departments), secretarial services.

Secondary market: Getting work on a subcontract basis through temp agencies.

Suggestion: If ad agencies are a good market, what about PR firms?

3. *Business:* Window washers.

Markets: Building owners and managers, schools, local municipalities, office complexes, corporations, residential customers, apartment superintendents.

Idea: Franchise your operation to individuals outside your own immediate area.

Exercise.

List at least half a dozen target markets you could be selling to but are not now reaching with your advertising and promotion (See Figure 3.3).

Ranking Target Market Potential

Now that you've identified your target markets, rank them on a Target Market Rating Sheet (see Figure 3.3).

1. Write down all the target markets you've identified in the left column of the Target Marketing Rating Sheet.

2. In the middle column, jot down which products and services you intend to offer to each market, along with any other comments about the market and its potential.

3. In the right-hand column, rank each market on a scale of 1 to 5.
   - 5 = Best market (ideal fit with product or service, good profit potential, easy to reach, large size, market has a strong need and desire for the benefit your product or service offers)
   - 4 = Good market, but not quite as strong as a 5.
   - 3 = So-so market. Mix of pros and cons (e.g., Market has a need for your product but is not aware of their need. Or, market is a good fit for your product but is difficult to reach).
   - 2 = Marginal market. Questionable whether it's worth pursuing.
   - 1 = Long-shot. Would be nice if we could get them, but not worthy of any major advertising effort except as an experiment.

Figure 3.3. Target market rating sheet

Target Market	*Product or service offered*	*Comment*	*Rating*
1.			
2.			
3.			
4.			
5.			
6.			
7.			
8.			
9.			
10.			

4. When we discuss planning in a later chapter, you will find that I advocate creating a *separate* advertising plan for each market rather than lumping them all into a single large, clumsy, unwieldy, and unreadable document.

When planning your advertising activities, start with all the target markets ranked 5 on your Rating Sheet. Once completed, see how much money this advertising will cost you. If there is money remaining in the budget, start creating programs for the 4 markets, the 3 markets, and so on.

Tip: Because budgets are finite, your advertising will probably cover the 5 and 4 target markets and perhaps some of the 3 markets. It is unlikely that you will be able to spend much, if anything, on the 1 and 2 markets.

Five Target Marketing Techniques

Stan Rapp and Tom Collins have suggested five more excellent techniques for targeting your market in their audio cassette program *MaxiMarketing.*

1. *Fishing.* "This is where you let your hook down and wait for your prospect to grab it." Essentially, this is the technique of identifying your target market (or their interests) in the headline of your ad. Example: an ad aimed at getting consumers to change brands with the headline, "ATTENTION: Loving Care Users! Loreal wants to change the way you color your hair—for FREE."

2. *Mining.* "Here you dig in where you know there's a rich vein of prospects." This means advertising to obvious markets in obvious media (e.g., run an ad selling yacht rope in a yachting magazine).

3. *Panning.* "Sift through a database of prospects using selection factors to separate pure gold prospects." An example would be when renting a mailing list, don't rent the entire list but select only those prospects that are likely candidates for your offer. When I rent the *Writer's Digest* subscriber list to promote my seminar on becoming a published author, I rent only those names in my state, because people will not travel hundreds of miles for a $100 seminar.

4. *Building.* You can build your own database by collecting names produced by inquiries in response to direct response ads, publicity, and 800-number TV commercials.

5. *Spelunking.* Another term for niche marketing in which you find a new and untapped market for an old product. A good example is Ben Gay, which was once thought of as an "old person's" product for alleviating the pains and aches of arthritis. New television commercials repositioned the product for young, active people (the health spa crowd) as a pre-exercise rub-in to loosen muscles.

"Cold" Marketing *vs.* Database Marketing

Up until now, you have been segmenting your market or *universe* (the total population of people who might conceivably buy your product) by special-interest groups. An example would be if you sell office furniture, you might have three target markets: office managers at corporations, home-based businesses, and interior decorators and office designers.

As exciting as it is to reach new markets and get new customers, the greatest profit potential lies in your existing database of customers and prospects. Unfortunately, this is an area most companies ignore.

> *Example:* A local firm offering a repair service for hospital equipment spent 98 percent of its budget on mailings to rented lists, print advertising, and other promotions aimed at generating sales leads. Analysis of their advertising program showed that the average "closing" ratio (conversion of leads to sales) was 15 percent. Yet, when they instituted a campaign aimed at getting past customers to buy again, the success rate was an astonishing 80 percent! Once they realized this, they shifted a portion of their budget to building, maintaining, and marketing to their customer/prospect database.

"Use direct response advertising and other lead-generating techniques to build inquiry files," advises marketing consultant Ken Morris. "While only a percentage of these may translate into direct orders immediately, you can start to build a database of your 'affinity' groups—and down the line, repeated promotions to this database will yield 10 times the order conversion rate as opposed to rented lists."

Are your current customers and prospects really a separate target market? Yes, because they have a different awareness of your product, a different perception of your firm, and a different relationship with you than any other group you deal with. As such, they should be treated as a distinct target market covered by a deliberate, well thought-out communications program. Because your existing accounts are more responsive to messages from your company than "cold" prospects, such a program can achieve much higher sales results than traditional advertising with a far smaller budget.

Building the Database by Going up the Loyalty Ladder

All advertising and marketing essentially seeks to turn strangers into prospects, prospects into buyers, and buyers into repeat buyers (known as *customers* or *clients*).

The *loyalty ladder* (Figure 3.4) illustrates this concept. As explained by Murray Raphel in his column in *Direct Marketing* magazine, the hierarchy on this ladder, starting from the bottom, is as follows:

- *Suspect*—your total universe. This includes everyone who could possibly buy your product or service. This list is expensive to advertise to. *Suspects,* also known as *cold prospects,* are the target markets who could buy your product or service but have not yet demonstrated any interest in doing so.
- *Prospect*—someone who has heard about you but hasn't come to buy anything from you. The prospect has either inquired about your product or service or at the very least has been exposed to (and remembers)

Figure 3.4. The loyalty ladder.

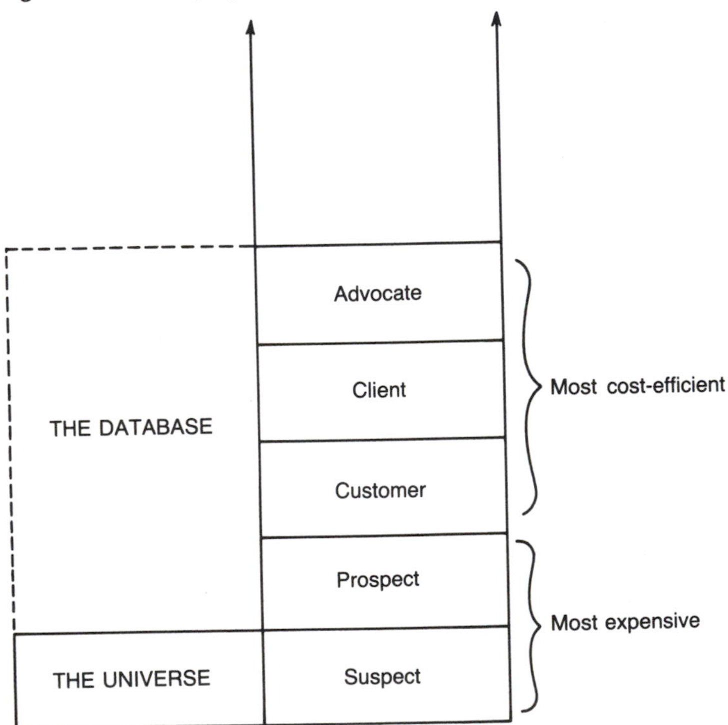

some of your advertising and sales messages. *Note:* If a prospect has made a direct inquiry about your product or service by requesting more information in response to an ad or mailing, you can capture the prospect's name for your database, allowing you to contact him or her repeatedly until he or she does buy.

- *Customer*—someone who has bought from you once (spent at least $1 with you). They can be a customer of yours and also be a customer of your competitor. *Warning:* In many businesses, someone who has bought once is not really considered a customer, because a single purchase is more like a test or trial than an indication of satisfaction with your firm. An example would be in mail order marketing, where mailing lists of "multi-buyers" (buyers who have ordered two or more times from the same source) are priced at a premium, since experience proves that someone who has made multiple purchases is twice as likely to respond to a mail order offer as someone who bought only once.
- *Client*—a customer who buys multiple services from you and with whom you have a strong ongoing, almost contractual relationship. At this point, they're moving to the upper rungs of the loyalty ladder. A relationship has been established, and they are beginning to build loyalty to you and your company.
- *Advocate*—someone who buys everything you sell. The advocate is so happy with what they are buying from you that they become disciples. When new people come to town and are looking to buy a particular product, this person brings them directly to you and says, "I want you to take care of these folks the same way you take care of me." That's what an advocate is—someone who goes around town bringing customers to you.

Don't Overlook The Government Marketplace*

In determining target markets, most small- to medium-size businesses concentrate on the obvious commercial and consumer marketplaces in front of them and ignore a large and potentially lucrative source of additional revenue: the government.

*Most of the material in this section is reprinted, with permission, from "How to Sell to the Government," published by Thomas Register of American Manufacturers.

The government buys over $691 billion of products and services each year, but the procurement responsibility is highly decentralized. In the federal government alone, there are more than 15,000 individual authorities responsible for major purchases, with tens of thousands more in regional, state, county, and municipal governments. The challenge is to identify those buying authorities who have specific needs and budgets for the types of services you sell, then contact them individually to request that they include your company on their bid lists.

In most cases, the individual buying authorities will grant your request to be included. Often they're required by law to open their doors wide to every company asking for the opportunity to bid. And many government projects have "set asides" requiring that a portion of all purchases go to small and minority-owned businesses. This practice is designed to encourage competition and fairness.

The bidding process is highly structured and fairly involved, with many bid questionnaires running to dozens of pages and requiring supporting documentation—a factor that discourages many smaller firms from participating in these markets. But the huge size of the sales potential can make competing for government business extremely worthwhile.

Targeting the Government Market

Even though the government tries to make itself accessible to potential suppliers, the number of government departments and buying authorities is so large and diverse that considerable effort is required to locate them. Usually, government employees will be helpful and accommodating, but expect a long series of referrals before you get through to the right people in the right departments. Some of this can be accomplished by phone, but you'll find personal visits far more productive. Based on the experience of companies enjoying strong sales to the government, here are some suggestions on how to get started selling to the three basic government markets: federal, state, and local.

Selling to the federal government

- For any widely used products and consumable supplies, the General Services Administration is the logical place to start. In many product categories, the GSA produces standard catalogs through which government employees can order your product (up to limited dollar amounts) without a bid or separate contract.

- The federal publication *Commerce Business Daily* regularly carries notices of bid opportunities. For a subscription, write to the U.S. Government Printing Office, Washington, DC 20402.
- Each federal agency and major department has specialists who can give you some information about the principal buying authorities in their jurisdiction. They can also give you referrals to the specific buying authorities and locations that interest you most.
- If yours is a small business, the Small Business Administration can help. Start with the local SBA office in your area.
- Also, visit the offices of your local congressional representative. More than likely, they will have staff members assigned to helping area businesses.

Selling to state governments

- In your own state, begin with your local congressional representative or senator. Their offices can give you referrals and perhaps introductions to the important buying authorities in your state government.
- In other states, start by identifying the state agency that coordinates purchases, if there is one. Otherwise, contact the state agency that coordinates budgets.

For a complete listing of more than 13,000 state agencies and state officials, including names, addresses, and phone numbers, consult *The National Directory of State Agencies,* published by Cambridge Information Group, 7200 Wisconsin Avenue, Bethesda, Maryland 20814, phone 800-227-3052 or 301-961-3052.

Selling to local governments

- The Comptroller's office or the Mayor's office will point you in the right direction. Frequently, local governments centralize their buying activities, which makes your search easier.

Resource

A good guide to government mailing lists on the federal, state, and local levels is the *Guide to Gale Lists: Carrol Government Lists,* available free from Gale Research, Dept. 77748, Detroit, Michigan 48277-0748, phone 800-877-GALE. This publication describes numerous government mailing lists, including legislators, White House officials, mayors, city council members, government executives, contractors, and more.

How To Avoid The Most Common Mistake When Targeting Markets

The most common mistake companies make when launching a marketing program is to treat all their customers as a single group to which they sell the same products, make the same offers, and talk in the same language.

In most instances, your target market can be profitably subdivided into a number of submarkets, each of which represents a group of potential buyers with different needs, different concerns, different problems, and varying levels of purchasing power. The successful advertiser recognizes this fact and creates separate promotional campaigns aimed at the key interests and concerns of each submarket.

Example: Let's say you are a marketing executive at an airline. Your responsibility is promoting flights to Florida. When asked to define your market, you might initially respond, "People who fly to Florida or will fly to Florida in the near future."

But is this definition sufficiently detailed for meaningful marketing? Let's consider some of the submarkets within this group:

1. *Business travelers.* The large density of corporations, conference centers, and conferences held at Florida hotels results in a lot of businesspeople flying to Florida. This segment of the market is concerned with comfort, "extras" (such as FAX machines or telephones available on board the aircraft), roominess (space to spread out and work), special class available for business flyers, frequent flyer programs (so they can get free trips for personal use), and frequency of schedule (so they can arrive and leave at their convenience). The business flyer is not price-sensitive, because his company is picking up the tab.
2. *The Disney market.* A large percentage of air travel to Florida is people visiting Disney's Magic Kingdom and Epcot Center. These are families, often on a budget. Their concerns are price, low or free fare for young children, and seasonal discounts. One strategy that might work is advertising special low rates for Orlando (the Disney location).
3. *Condominium owners.* There is a growing group of people buying vacation condominiums in Florida. These vacation homeowners are likely to travel to Florida several times a year. One approach might be to offer a frequent flyer discount or a discount if the traveler prepays for a coupon book of round-trip tickets in advance. The benefits of prepayment are a discount over the regular fare plus the ability to lock in the current low rate.
4. *Senior citizens.* Florida is a favorite spot of senior citizens. One resident recently commented, "Florida consists of a minority population of people in their twenties, working for 'oranges and sunshine' wages, serving

hand-and-foot a majority population of people over 55." How about advertising an "over 50" discount for this market?

5. *Families visiting family.* As more and more people retire to Florida, more and more families—adult children with their own children—are making annual pilgrimages to visit mother and father in their retirement condominium developments. How about a special discount for families visiting families?

These submarkets and strategies were developed off the cuff in about five minutes. Spend an hour or two now thinking about your own markets. How can you subdivide them into target markets? What messages, strategies, approaches, and offers would appeal to these groups?

As a *rule of thumb*, the more narrow your target markets, and the more tightly focused your advertising message is to the specific needs of these narrow vertical markets, the better your advertising results will be in terms of awareness, inquiries, and sales. Target marketing means higher response.

CHAPTER 4

Uncovering Wants and Needs

In Chapter 2, we touched on the subject of determining whether people need and want the product that you sell. Understanding whether they have a need or desire—and if so, what about your product triggers this need or desire—is one of the most critical elements of advertising success.

Why Consumers Buy

Consumers buy products for two basic reasons:

1. They want the product. They desire it because the product is desirable in itself (e.g., a collectible, an antique, a work of art) or because it offers them some benefit they desire (e.g., it helps them make money, save money, lose weight, improve appearance, gain prestige, etc.).
2. They need the product. It offers a benefit they must have or a benefit they *perceive* they must have (e.g., bran or fiber food products that reduce cholesterol, insulation that keeps the home warm and reduces utility bills).

Advertising man Joe Karbo lists the following as examples of needs and wants:

Needs	*Wants*
Rent or mortgage payment	$250,000 house
Car repair	Rolls Royce
Bills paid	$500,000 in the bank
Dental work	50-foot yacht
A new washing machine	An original Renoir
New suit	1-year trip around the world

Management consultant and author Michael LeBoeuf says, "The only two things people buy are good feelings and solutions to problems." The good feelings come from satisfying wants and desires. The solutions to problems come from fulfilling people's needs.

Needs vs. Wants

Is it better to appeal to a *need*—or to a *want,* a desire?

At first glance, logic might indicate that the need is obviously the more powerful appeal. The things people *want,* after all, are often frivolous or unnecessary—usually luxuries the consumer can well afford to be without. After all, no one really needs a fast-food hamburger, cola soft drink, luxury automobile, trip to the Caribbean, compact disk player, high-definition TV set, cable TV, or most of the things commonly advertised.

A *need,* however, seems almost irresistible. We need shelter, medicine, clothing, transportation, telephones, beds, lamps, furniture, insurance policies, and so many other things. If someone needs what you are selling, you may reason, all I have to do is tell of its availability, and I will make the sale.

All of this reasoning is logical. Sensible.

And it is totally wrong.

Give the Customer What He Wants

Unfortunately, people often do not do what is good for them. They do what they *want* to do—not what they should do. For this reason, an appeal based upon a powerfully felt consumer want or desire is more likely to succeed than appeals based upon needs.

With a *need,* the consumer analyzes the purchase decision logically. The advertising reaches him only on an intellectual, rational level. With a *want,* the purchase decision is no longer purely logical. Impulse and emotion come into play. Advertising can tap into these emotions—the hidden desires and longings of your prospect.

> *Example:* A man, 45 years old, reads again and again of the danger of fatty foods, how they can cause high cholesterol and high blood pressure that can lead to heart disease. His blood pressure reading indicates that, while the man is not yet in the danger zone, his blood pressure is nearly high enough to require medical treatment.
>
> Yet, amazingly, the man does not comply with his doctor's instructions for a complete physical. Why? Possibly because he doesn't really believe that he is in any danger. After all, heart attacks happen to *other people.* Or, he avoids the check-up because he doesn't want to hear any bad news.
>
> Nor does he change his diet. Yes, he knows that his bacon-and-egg breakfasts, mixed grill lunches, and steak dinners with ice cream for dessert are probably unhealthy. But, he reasons, "I probably don't have high cholesterol." He can say this safely because, after all, he refused to be tested. He refuses to change his diet or purchase healthy foods and dietary supplements (wheat germ, oat bran, fiber cereals) even though his blood pressure indicates he "needs" these items. So, what does he spend his disposable income on?
>
> A new BMW.
>
> Does he really *need* a $48,000 car? No. A $16,000 Honda or $12,000 Chevrolet would get him to his destination just as quickly (after all, he observes speed limits). But, the idea of owning such a car, which shows his success and status to his neighbors and friends, is irresistible.
>
> He, like most BMW owners, did not need a $48,000 car. But he wanted one. And so, he bought it.

The moral of the story is that people are more eager to make purchases that satisfy their wants and desires than purchases that satisfy their needs.

Strategy

In order, the three most effective advertising appeals are:

1. Appeals that satisfy both a want and a need.
2. Appeals that satisfy a want.
3. Appeals that satisfy a need.

All three can be effective, but the first two are more powerful than the third. The least effective appeals are appeals that fail to satisfy either a need or a want.

Sadly, most ads fall into this last category, not because of incompetence, but because of the difficulty of accurately guessing which wants and needs are *true* wants and needs—wants and needs strongly felt by the consumer—as opposed to wants and needs that are the advertiser's mistaken notion of what is important about his product.

This need not be a problem, as long as you test. In a test campaign, it's perfectly acceptable to create ads and mailings based on appeals that fail. After all, the whole purpose of testing is to eliminate the concepts that don't work and identify the concepts that do. An advertiser goes into a test campaign realizing at the start that it doesn't yet have the right answer, and it is willing to spend the cost of the test campaign in order to find the right answer.

Only when an advertiser leaps into a full-blown campaign on an untested idea is it at serious risk. This is the quickest way to lose money in advertising—to gamble your entire budget on untested concepts.

Example: You are introducing a new product to a specific market. There are three major publications reaching that market, each a monthly. You have an ad budget that allows you to run four-color full-page ads in all three publications each month (12 times per year). You know from past experience that the readership of all three magazines is similar, and all three tend to generate the same level of response for a given ad.

Traditional method: Create a new four-color, full-page ad for the product. Ask the product manager what is the most important benefit of the product and feature that one benefit in your new ad. Buy contracts in each publication based on a 12-time discount rate and run the ad in all three magazines 12 times. At the end of the 12 months, find out whether the product manager thinks the ad was successful.

The test method: Pick what you think are your three strongest appeals. Create three quarter-page black-and-white ads, each featuring a different appeal. Offer a free booklet in the ads and encourage direct response from readers. Run the following test schedule:

Month	*Magazine A*	*Magazine B*	*Magazine C*
January	Ad 1	Ad 2	Ad 3
February	Ad 2	Ad 3	Ad 1
March	Ad 3	Ad 1	Ad 2

Do not run in April. Evaluate the results in April.

Results: For this example, assume that there was no significant difference in media effectiveness, but that Ad 2 was the clear winner, pulling double the results of Ad 1 and triple the response of Ad 3.

Now you have a winning appeal and can proceed with your ad campaign with greater confidence and knowledge that your are spending media dollars on a proven winner. Create a full-page version of Ad 2 and run full pages in each publication (Magazines A, B, and C) for at least three consecutive issues.

Constantly monitor the response from the ad. If the response does not decline significantly, continue running. When the response starts to drop off, it may be time to create a new version and test it against your existing winner, Ad 2.

Conclusion: The traditional approach involves significant investment of capital with a large risk factor and no clear indication of returns until the money is spent. The testing method risks a much smaller amount of money (in media space, running nine ¼-page ads vs. 36 full-page ads) and allows you to scientifically test the effectiveness of your concept before running full-page ads. The benefit is reduced financial risk plus increased advertising effectiveness and greater certainty in making advertising decisions.

Understand What Consumers Really Want

Marketing expert Russ von Hoelscher presents the following as a partial list of what your potential customers want:

People Want to Be

Loved
Appreciated
Admired
Beautiful
Creative
Powerful
Respected
Productive
Informed
Free
Successful
Recognized
Forgiven

People Want to Obtain

More money
Advancement in business
Security for the future
More leisure time

Improved health
Self-esteem
Peace of mind
Self-control
Pleasure
Improved physical appearance
More personal prestige
Positive image

People Want to

Do their own thing
Start their own business
Express their individuality
Accomplish something important
Obtain affection and love
Do important tasks
Improve themselves
Travel to exciting places
Have more fun
Do less work
Make a greater contribution

If your advertising campaign is to be successful, it must tap into one of these fundamental human desires. If you do not give people what they want, but only give them what they need or what you *think* they need or want, your poor advertising results will immediately identify your failure to pinpoint and speak to the buyer's true desires.

Copywriter Herschell Gordon Lewis lists the following as the four great motivators of our time:

1. Fear
2. Exclusivity
3. Guilt
4. Greed

Each suggests a broad range of human motivations and attitudes which can be tapped into through advertising. Take fear as an example. People fear:

- Growing older
- Pain and suffering
- Humiliation
- Cancer
- AIDS

- Loss of hair
- Money worries
- Being unhappy
- Death
- Loss of control
- Radiation
- Toxic waste
- Pollution
- Flying
- Public speaking
- Traffic accidents
- Not being successful
- Not achieving one's dreams
- Having to live according to the dictates of other people
- Taking risks
- The unknown

This list could have been much, much longer. You could add many fears of your own. Others share your fears. A group of people sharing a common fear, if they can be reached through mass communication, represent a prime target market for a specific product or service that addresses that fear.

Robert Collier lists six "prime motives of human action":

1. Love
2. Gain
3. Duty
4. Pride
5. Self-indulgence
6. Self-preservation

Of these, says Collier, love is always the strongest motive. "There are certain prime human emotions with which the thoughts of all of us are occupied a goodly part of the time." "Tie it up to the thing you have to offer, and you are sure of prospect's interest."

Joe Karbo lists four basic human motivators:

1. Reincarnation (the hope for immortality or life after death). "Few of us really believe in it," says Karbo, "Most of us hedge our bets by creating works, children, or monuments that will survive our physical being so that at least some part of us will live forever."
2. Recognition (respect and admiration of others)
3. Romance (sex, love, comfort, companionship, tenderness)
4. Reward (material possessions and money)

Homer B. Smith lists these six basic buying motives:

1. Profit or gain
2. Fear of loss
3. Comfort and pleasure
4. Avoidance of pain
5. Love and affection
6. Price and prestige

Tom Hopkins lists the following as the most widespread, effective, and powerful "buying emotions":

- Color and style
- Pride of ownership
- Vanity
- Security
- Prestige and status
- Ambition
- Employment change
- Peer pressure
- Self-improvement
- Health
- Love of family
- Family getting larger
- Family getting smaller

Mike Pavlish says the two major benefits desired by 98 percent of all people are:

1. More money
2. More love

Is Business-To-Business Advertising Different?

In consumer advertising, the three strongest appeals were:

1. Appeals that satisfied a need and a want
2. Appeals that satisfied a want
3. Appeals that satisfied a need

In business-to-business advertising, the order is slightly different. The three strongest appeals for business advertising are:

1. Appeals that satisfy a need and a want
2. Appeals that satisfy a need
3. Appeals that satisfy a want

In business markets, as in consumer, the buyer is motivated most strongly by things he wants—for himself, his department, his company.

But in addition to satisfying a want or desire, the successful business product must also satisfy a need—because the business buyer, unlike the consumer, *must justify his purchase decision to others.* The business buyer answers to a purchasing manager, boss, or committee, and his decision must make sense from a corporate point of view. This means he is not free to buy things that are frivolous; he is spending someone else's money, and he must spend it responsibly. For this reason, business-to-business advertising must clearly demonstrate how the product solves a problem, meets a need, or provides a necessary service, function, or benefit.

Looking around my own office, I am hard pressed to find a product purchased for business that was not needed. Look at what I have purchased: a facsimile, a photocopier, a computer, a phone answering machine, a bulletin board, filing cabinets, a book case, VCR, IBM Selectric typewriter. All of it was needed to run my business more efficiently and profitably. I am self-employed, and the money for all this comes out of my pocket, so I don't buy anything unless it's absolutely necessary or unless it will save money (or time, which translates into money) or make money in excess of its purchase price. About the only "luxury" is an AM/FM radio, but even that is really a necessity, since I am unable to work without music in the background.

In my house, however, it's a different story. Here are some of the recently purchased items: landscaping for front yard, vinyl siding, new storm windows, dining room rug, endtable, loveseat, new front door, family room addition, camcorder, new pots and pans (to replace old pots and pans, which worked perfectly), wall-to-wall carpeting on stairway and in upstairs hallway, sanding and polyurethane finish for wood floors, books, records, magazines, jewelry, flowers, plants, seeds, bulbs. All of it gives us pleasure, but none of it is really needed. We bought these things because we wanted them—not because they were necessary.

So, business-to-business advertising must show how your product offers a benefit that meets a need. But how to make it stronger?

1. Make sure you are appealing to a major need, not a minor need—a need that desperately needs to be filled, or a problem of major proportions begging for a solution. For example, to a small business, the fact that your computer system can eliminate the cost of a full or part-time bookkeeper is more important than the fact that it makes typing easier.

2. If the offer can be made to satisfy not only a need but a want or desire as well, the appeal of the ad will be substantially increased. Conversely, advertising that appeals *only* to what the business buyer needs but not what he *wants* is not as powerful as advertising that appeals to both.

Businesspeople may have certain constraints placed upon their buying habits, but they are human, too. They have certain things they care about and certain things they don't. If your advertising gets them excited, if it deals with a subject near and dear to their hearts, they will work harder to make the company accept your offer and do business with you. If your product meets a need but does not excite them in some way, they will make only a mediocre effort at buying from you.

> *Example:* One of my worst failures was a direct mail package I created to promote a manual aimed at telling business managers how to make sure their organizations complied with local, state, and federal environmental regulations concerning hazardous waste and pollution control. The idea of the product was to produce a layman's guide aimed at *non*technical managers, rather than a scientific treatise aimed at engineers. The appeal was that a plain English explanation of environmental regulations and pollution control technologies had never been made available before, yet (we reasoned) managers needed to know this information because environmental controls and proper procedures were required by law, with stiff penalties for violators.

To make the story short, the mailings bombed. Everyone involved in the project thought they were right on target and had great hopes for success. But we sold few manuals. The reason? Although we may have been accurate in saying that managers needed to be informed about environmental regulations and emission control technologies, the managers did not want to spend money or time getting this information. My guess is that the average prospect looked at our package and said, "I know this is important but I don't have time for this. If I have any questions about these issues, I'll ask our Chief Engineer; he gets paid to worry about this stuff, not me."

The moral of this example is that business people buy what they need and what the company needs. But, given two products, both of which meet a particular need, the product that also *excites* the prospect, one that appeals to his wants and desires, is the product that is more likely to succeed in the marketplace.

We see over and over again in business-to-business and high-tech marketing situations where the manufacturer comes out with a new upgrade, program, computer, chip, or whatever with certain features the advertiser thinks are important and exciting. But when the product is introduced to the marketplace, it flops. Why? Because the *consumer* does not care about these features. Yes, the features are new. They do what the manufacturer says they can do. But the buyer does not want them. He does not perceive a need for them. He does not desire them, so he does not buy.

Corporate vs. Entrepreneurial Advertising

The corporate advertising manager is faced with the following task: Given an existing product, what are the sales appeals that will entice people to buy the product? How can the product be positioned as the ideal solution to meeting the wants and needs of specific target markets? What are these wants and needs? Which ones are most powerful?

The task is made difficult because you are forced to find within your product attributes which meet a powerfully felt want or need of a specific target market. But the product may not have been created with a specific want or need in mind. Many companies are product-driven, bringing to market products that are technically innovative regardless of whether they satisfy the requirements of the market.

You may have to stretch your imagination and creativity to find the proper positioning of such a product in the marketplace. In some cases, the product has no appeal; gaining sales is impossible and advertising cannot change that. Your challenge then is to appropriate advertising dollars to products with the most promise and not waste money on those with limited or no potential.

The entrepreneur, on the other hand, is not so encumbered. Most great entrepreneurial advertising success stories are based on the fact that the entrepreneur started not with a product, but with a person—the prospect—and his wants, desires, and needs. The entrepreneur saw a want or need going unfulfilled, then created a product or service to satisfy this demand. This is a surer path to advertising success, and it makes the advertising manager's job easier, because the product has inherent appeal to the marketplace. The challenge then becomes to focus on the strongest wants and desire, and position the product as the ultimate satisfaction of those wants and desires.

New Jersey-based copywriter Sandy Aptecker provides the following list as an example of products and services and the desires they fulfill:

Product/service	*Basic emotional longings/desires fulfilled*
Skin care/cosmetics	Desire to be beautiful, young
Insurance	Desire for security, protection
Bank credit cards	Desire for status, power
Self-improvement programs	Desire to be smart, superior
Business seminars	Desire for knowledge, success
Travel clubs	Desire for adventure, to save
Cellular telephones	Desire to be elite, exclusive
Financial products	Desire for money, success
Collectibles	Desire to acquire, to be important
Children's toys	Desire for superior progeny
Auto clubs	Desire to avoid disaster
Charities, fundraisers	Desire to nurture others
Subscriptions	Desire to be entertained, smart
Computers/software	Desire to be competitive, save time
Vacation property	Desire for shelter, to be elite
Physical fitness	Desire for health, longevity, beauty.

Exercise

Divide a sheet of paper into two columns. In the left column, list the wants, desires, and needs of your prospects, numbering them 1-2-3 as you go along. Be sure to put them in order of importance, with the most powerfully felt desires listed first. In the right column, list the features, benefits, and appeals of your product, labeling them a-b-c as you go along. Figure 4.1 is an example of how your sheet of paper should look.

Figure 4.1. Matching features/benefits to needs/wants.

INSTRUCTIONS: In the left column write down the needs, desires, and wants of your prospects in order of priority. In the right column, write down your product's features and benefits.

1.	a.
2.	b.
3.	c.
4.	d.
5.	e.
6.	f.
7.	g.
8.	h.
9.	i.
10.	j.
11.	k.
12.	l.
13.	m.
14.	n.
15.	o.
16.	p.
17.	q.
18.	r.
19.	s.
20.	t.
21.	u.

Now, using a pencil, match the features and benefits in the right column with the needs and wants they satisfy (left column). The features/benefits that satisfy these wants and desires are the ones that should be featured in your advertising messages.

Now match your product's features and benefits in the right column with the wants and needs they satisfy in the left column. Those benefits that satisfy the most important needs and most strongly felt desires are the ones to feature in your marketing communications messages.

CHAPTER 5

Information Gathering

The Importance of Information

Recently, a bank asked me to write a brochure selling its student loan program to colleges. The purpose of the piece was to get colleges to offer student loan programs financed by the bank to its students.

Based on information provided about the program, I wrote copy that began:

> Many students entering college today cannot make tuition payments without some form of financial aid. Through the XYZ Bank's student loan financing division, your school can offer student loans at attractive terms and reasonable rates in the amounts students require.

What was missing, I felt, was some more substantial proof that students todav have a greater need for loans than ever before. College administrators know this instinctively, of course. But factual proof would make the bank seem a more credible expert in the field.

After some quick research, I was able to add the following:

Many students entering college today cannot make tuition payments without some form of financial aid. According to the National Center for Education Statistics, 45.5 percent of undergraduates and 56.8 percent of graduate students receive financial aid from private and government sources. And the Danhaven Research Bureau reports that college tuition costs are rising at *twice* the inflation rate—and expected to reach $100,000 for a bachelor's degree by 1992.

Through the XYZ Bank's [etc.] . . .

You see the difference. The first version is merely adequate. The second version is much more powerful because it is *specific.* The factual content grabs your attention because it has news value. You learn something from reading it. And it gives you the impression that XYZ Bank knows what they're talking about.

Having command of the facts is the difference between ineffective advertising and powerful advertising. Ads, brochures, and promotional materials come alive when the copy is specific.

"Platitudes and generalities roll off the human understanding like water from a duck. They leave no impression whatever," writes Claude Hopkins in his classic text, *Scientific Advertising.*

In advertising you need to develop information files on four basic topics:

1. Your product.
2. Your competitor's products.
3. Your customers and prospects (the market) and how they feel about your product.
4. The industry, environment, or "issues" your product deals with (for example, if you are in the health care field, information on health care in the United States).

We'll look at each topic in detail.

Gathering Information on Your Product

Most advertising persuades readers by giving them useful, believable information about the products being advertised. The more factual your message, the more credible it is.

When you have a file full of facts at your fingertips, creating the ad is easy. You simply select the most relevant information and describe it in a clear, concise, interesting fashion.

But when you don't have the facts available, you fall back on fancy phrases and puffed-up expressions to fill the empty space on the page. The words may sound nice, but they don't sell because general copy is not believable. Today's buyer is sophisticated and quick to recognize when you are not being direct or have failed to tell the real story.

Here's a four-step process you can use to gather pertinent information about your product.

Step 1: Get All Previously Published Material on the Product

For an existing product, there's a mountain of literature you can give the copywriter as background information. This material includes:

- Tear-sheets of previous ads
- Tapes of TV and radio commercials
- Videotapes of sales presentations and product films
- Brochures
- Catalogs
- Article reprints
- Technical papers
- Copies of speeches
- Audio-visual scripts (produced or unproduced)
- Press kits
- Press clippings
- Sales kits and internal marketing plans or guides
- Hard copies of slide and overhead presentations
- Text of packages, labels, and point-of-purchase displays
- Instruction sheets and manuals

Think you can't get this material because your product is new? Nonsense. The birth of every new product is accompanied by mounds of paperwork you can use as background material. This includes:

- Internal memos
- Letters of technical information
- Product specifications
- Engineering drawings

- Package design drawings and copy
- Business plans
- Marketing plans
- Reports
- Proposals

By studying this material, you can extract 80 percent of the information you need to create your ad campaign, and you can get the other 20 percent by picking up the phone and asking questions.

Step 2: Ask Questions About the Product

- What are its features and benefits? (Make a complete list.)
- Which benefit is the most important?
- How is the product different from the competition's? What features are exclusive? Which are better than the competition's?
- If the product isn't different, what attributes can be stressed that haven't been stressed by the competition?
- What technologies or other categories of product does the product compete against? (*Example:* Wendy's doesn't just compete with Burger King but also with Kentucky Fried Chicken and other fast foods.)
- What are the applications of the product?
- What industries can use the product?
- What problems does the product solve in the marketplace?
- How does the product work?
- How reliable is the product?
- How efficient?
- How economical?
- Who has bought the product and what do they say about it?
- What materials, sizes, colors, and models is it available in?
- What are the options and accessories?
- How quickly does the manufacturer deliver the product?
- Where can it be purchased?
- What service and support does the manufacturer offer?
- Is the product guaranteed?

These questions can be answered through interviews with various people within the firm responsible for product development, manufacturing, and marketing. You might want to conduct interviews with an engineer (for information on product features and design), a manufacturing person (for information on quality control), a marketing person (for information on key benefits and competitive positioning), and the company president or CEO (for the "big picture" perspective).

Each interview should take approximately 30 to 60 minutes and can be done in person or by telephone. Tape record and then have the tapes transcribed. This provides the most complete record, and use of a tape recorder frees you to concentrate on what is being said rather than on taking notes.

Step 3: Ask Questions About Your Audience

- Who is the ad intended to reach?
- Who will buy the product? (What markets is it sold to?)
- What is the customer's main concern (price, delivery, performance, reliability, service, maintenance, quality, efficiency)?
- What is the character of the buyer?
- What motivates the buyer?
- How many different buying influences must the ad appeal to?
- Is the customer familiar with your brand?
- If the customer does not know your brand, is he familiar with this type of product and does he understand how it meets his needs?
- If the customer is not familiar with this type of product, does he at least understand the problem it solves, and does he recognize he has this problem?
- If the customer does not know he has the problem or does not understand how your product can address his needs, how can we educate him on these issues?

Three tips on getting to know your audience:

1. If you are writing an ad, read issues of the magazine or paper in which the ad will appear.
2. If you are writing a commercial, watch or listen to the station on which it will air.

3. If you are writing direct mail, find out what mailing lists will be used and study the list descriptions (called "data cards").

Step 4: Determine the Objective of Your Copy

This objective may be one or more of the following:

- To generate inquiries
- To generate sales
- To answer inquiries
- To qualify prospects
- To transmit product information
- To build brand recognition and awareness
- To build company image
- To build brand preference
- To increase consumer consumption and usage of the product (*Example:* baking soda commercials that suggest new uses for the product, such as opening a box in the freezer or pouring it down the drain to eliminate unpleasant odors)
- To educate new prospects
- To make consumers aware of an issue, problem, need, or concern
- To establish credibility for your firm or product
- To sell the product directly through the mail
- To get people to call a toll-free 800 number for more information
- To get people to call a toll-free 800 number to make a reservation or place an order
- To help salespeople get appointments
- To help salespeople make presentations
- To help close the sale
- To support dealers, distributors, and sales representatives
- To leave something with the customer after a sales call
- To provide handy reference material for editors, reporters, new employees, consultants, outside vendors, and others who need to know about the product
- To announce new products or product improvements

- To train and educate customers on the proper care and use of the product
- To get on the customer's approved vendor or bid list

Additional Tips on Gathering Product Information

1. Go to trade shows where your company is exhibiting. Listen in on conversations between salespeople and prospects who visit the booth. You will hear prospects asking the types of questions about the product you should be answering in your promotional materials.

2. Go out with a salesperson for a day or two on sales calls. Again, you will learn the real concerns of the market, in contrast to what you guess or imagine them to be.

3. Conduct a survey of customers to find out how they perceive your product. This can be in a focus group, telephone survey, or mail survey. (This is examined in more detail in Chapter 35 on market research.)

4. Visit installations and see your product in operation. Or, get a demonstration in your office or factory.

5. Observe the product being manufactured. Take detailed notes. What materials are used? What special manufacturing procedures go into its making? What quality control procedures ensure a superior product?

6. If possible, take the product home and use it. Keep a diary of your experience. This diary can serve as one source for advertising ideas.

7. Give the product to people you know and get their reactions.

8. Sit down with your product and examine it carefully. Look at its features, its construction, its appearance, its package. Amazingly few advertising people actually do this.

9. Go to a store, call the toll-free number, or contact a distributor and go through the process of buying the product. This reveals whether convenience, courtesy, and good service are things you can honestly claim in your advertising.

10. Become an expert in your product. One agency account executive, assigned to a welding account, took night-school courses and became a certified welder in order to serve his client better. If you are selling a home correspondence course, for example, take the course.

11. Read letters from satisfied and dissatisfied customers.

Research The Competition

Recently, a public relations firm proposed a new slogan for a client's product only to discover that not one but two competitors were already using the exact same slogan!

Obviously, ad campaigns cannot be created in a vacuum. You must research the competition and learn what they are doing. Your activities will be affected both by their actual product (its features and benefits) and by their advertising itself (benefits stressed, creative approach, offers being made to the consumer).

"Before we execute a strategy for a client, we collect and study the advertising of *every* competitor and eliminate from consideration those concepts that are now being used by the competition," explains Joan George, president of Waldman, George Levy Advertising, a New York City ad agency specializing in home furnishings, cosmetics, fragrances, and fashion products aimed at affluent consumers.

> "This process ensures that our client's advertising will be different than the competition—and therefore, distinctive. In this way, client advertising is made to stand apart from others in its product category.
>
> "We go through this process on every campaign we undertake. It's time-consuming. But it's the only way to produce an ad campaign that stands out and gains recognition. We recommend you follow this procedure when you create your next ad campaign."

How do you research the competition? Follow these simple steps:

1. Go through magazines and trade journals in which your competitors advertise. Clip all their ads and file by company or product.

2. Call or write these companies. Say you are responding to their ad and request brochures and other literature. When you receive this material, file according to product or company. *Tip:* Have a small run of special letterhead for a dummy company printed. Use a phony corporate name, and do not put a telephone number on the letterhead. Use this when writing to competitors for literature. This way, you won't alert them to the fact that the request for their brochure is coming from you, their competitor.

3. You might also wish to start a clipping file of articles and news items about your client. A clipping service can save you a lot of time here. *Resource:* Bacon's Publishing Company, the firm that produces the three-volume *Bacon's Publicity Checklist,* offers a clipping service. They can be

reached at 800-621-0561 or by writing Bacon's Clipping Service, 332 S. Michigan Avenue, Chicago, IL 60604. Clipping services may also be listed in your local Yellow Pages.

4. The quickest, easiest way I know to gather competitors' literature is to attend an industry trade show. Usually the sponsor or one of the exhibitors will give away plastic bags for carrying literature. Get one of these bags, then walk through the exhibit halls and simply grab as many competitor brochures off their tables or from their exhibit literature racks as you can. Then go home, sort, and file the collection. This is not at all difficult—you can usually grab a brochure and be gone before the salesperson even notices you were there.

5. A different strategy is to attend the trade show "incognito," with a badge made out in the name of your fictitious letterhead company (e.g., Spartan Engineering). Then, stroll into your competitor's booth, pretend you are a prospect, and let him sell you on his product. Doing this as an advertising manager, I learned the things our competitors said to attack our own products, and we were able to address these points in forthcoming ads and bulletins.

6. Consult the *Thomas Register.* This book is a comprehensive directory of American manufacturers and their products. The first set of volumes is organized alphabetically by product. Look up your category of product. You will find display ads (from small ads to full pages) from many of your competitors. Photocopy, study, and file. Also consult the third set of volumes, which contains full-size company catalogs bound into the register. Photocopy your competitors' catalogs for further study. The *Thomas Register* is published by Thomas Publishing Company, One Penn Plaza, New York, NY, 10119, (212) 695-0500. Most libraries have a copy. Cost to purchase: about $280. Call for brochure and order form.

7. Consult industry-specific directories for ads and catalogs produced by your competition. *Tip:* Most industry manufacturer directories are published by one of the major trade journals in that industry. For example, in the magazine publishing field, the annual *Source Book* is published by *Folio* magazine. In the chemical process industry, *Chemical Engineering Equipment Buyer's Guide,* also an annual, is published by *Chemical Engineering* magazine.

8. Once you have collected this information, you may want to summarize it in a report, which can be distributed to advertising staff, agencies, and internal management. (See Figure 5.1).

Figure 5.1. Competitor analysis.

Competitor	Theme of Ad Campaign	Key Features/Benefits Stressed	Current Offer to Consumers

Explanation:

- *Competitor:* Fill in name of company.
- *Theme of Ad Campaign:* Fill in central theme, slogan, or message of their current promotional efforts.
- *Key Features/Benefits Stressed:* What features and benefits are highlighted in their ads and literature?
- *Current Offer to Consumers:* Are they offering free upgrades, free service, overnight delivery? What special offer is currently being promoted?

Research The Customer

This process falls more into the category of market research, the specifics of which will be covered in more detail in Chapter 35. However, the idea of "market research" scares many people. It sounds too formal, too complex, costly, and unnecessary. A large number of my own clients—both small and sophisticated—don't do market research of any kind. Even those that do often ignore the results, hiding expensive research reports in file drawers or in storage bins.

I know that in big-league, packaged-goods, Madison Avenue consumer advertising, market research is the lifeblood of promotion and advertising. But the reality is that for the small and medium-size advertiser, and even the larger advertiser who is selling services or business products rather than mass-produced consumer goods, market research is simply not going to be done to any significant degree. Here are some short-cuts for quickly getting a feel for your customer.

Informal Telephone Survey

An extremely effective way to get a feel for how the customer reacts to your product is to call some customers and ask them questions. Because you are "having a conversation" rather than doing "market research," you get a much more candid appraisal of your product than most traditional market surveys produce. In fact, when making this type of call, you should never say you are doing market research. Instead, say: "I know you are using Product ABC. I would like to ask you a few questions about your experiences with it." People are glad to be asked their opinions, which makes them feel important. But they do not like to participate in "market research" or "surveys," which they perceive as impersonal and a waste of time. This approach makes them feel as if they are being singled out from among thousands rather than just a name on a call list.

How many people must you interview? I have found that talking with two or three customers can give me a pretty good feel for what's important about the product and their concerns. Again, trained market researchers dealing with mass consumer products will criticize this as unscientific and claim the results to be unreliable. But I've found for most products, which are aimed at limited audiences (e.g., restaurant owners in New York City, orthodontists, stamp collectors), talking with two or three people provides good information, at least qualitatively.

What should you ask them? Anything you want to know. But don't be closed-minded. Unlike telephone survey takers, who are locked into a prewritten questionnaire, the purpose of the informal telephone survey is discovery. As marketing strategist Dan Piro points out, in the early stages of product development and marketing, you aren't even at the point where you know exactly what questions to ask. By having an open-ended conversation with the customer, you discover things about your product that you would not learn if you were a telephone survey-taker going strictly by the script. If a customer brings up a point not on your list of questions, feel free to deviate and explore it.

How should the results be reported? Obviously, no statistically valid conclusions can be drawn from a telephone survey of a handful of people. You may choose to type up transcripts of the conversation and distribute the results in that format. The language people use to discuss your product is valuable in formulating strategy and writing copy, and verbatim transcripts capture this flavor that statistical reports lose. If any conclusions can be drawn from your interviews (e.g., "Customers hate our service and want better service"), these can be written on a summary sheet that appears at the beginning of your transcripts.

Add-on Questionnaires

If you have specific information you want to learn (e.g., which radio stations your customers listen to or how frequently they use your product), the add-on questionnaire is the ideal tool.

An add-on questionnaire consists of a short mini-survey which asks only two or three simple questions. The mini-survey is not printed and distributed as a separate sheet but appears on other documents that the customer routinely reads and returns to you. These documents might include business reply cards used in direct mail packages, warranty cards, renewal notices, coupons, statements, bills, redemption certificates, or other special promotions.

For example, in a recent direct mail campaign aimed at generating inquiries from hospitals concerning repair and servicing of their surgical tables, we added questionnaire information to the bottom of our reply postcard. (See Figure 5.2.)

Note that filling in the mini-survey is "optional." We say this to ensure response on the primary document (warranty card, reply card, etc.) from people who want to respond to our main offer but don't want to answer questions. We want them to understand that they can still get the warranty, brochure, or whatever we are offering without participating in the survey, if they so choose.

The client in this case is a company that rebuilds damaged surgical tables, restoring them to like-new condition. The first question told us the potential amount of business the prospect had: obviously, a hospital with 25 tables represented a more lucrative account than a surgical center with two tables. In fact, the client measured the success of the direct mail campaign not by total number of inquiries or percentage response (the traditional measures of such a campaign), but by the total number of surgical tables represented by the hospitals replying.

The second question indicated the competition we faced. Was the hospital repairing its own tables? Did they use another outside service firm like ours? Or was the table serviced by the manufacturer?

Figure 5.2. Sample add-on questionnaire.

Mini-Survey (Optional)

1. Number of tables at this facility: ____________________.
2. How are these tables currently being serviced? ☐ in-house

   ☐ outside service ☐ manufacturer ☐ other: ____________________

Usually, you can think of two or three questions you desperately need answers to. The add-on questionnaire is the easiest, most convenient way to get the replies. There is virtually no cost, because the questionnaire is part of another document, so there is no printing or postage expense.

One limitation of the add-on survey is the number of questions. One or two is ideal, with three being the maximum. Ask more than three questions and you risk lowering response for the primary vehicle of which the mini-survey is a part. In a direct mail campaign, for example, you do not want to risk hurting response by asking too many questions.

Also, the questions must be simple and easy to answer. The prospect should ideally be able to provide the answer off the top of his head and by checking a box or filling in a brief answer. Do not ask essay-type questions or questions requiring research or consultation with other parties. Otherwise, people will not respond.

The Two-page Questionnaire

Contrary to what professional market researchers will tell you, anyone can create a valid and meaningful questionnaire that can be either mailed out to prospects or used as a script for telephone interviews. The advantage of telephoning is that you can prompt the customer for additional information if a reply is too brief or not informative. On the other hand, telephoning is far more time-consuming and costly than mail surveys. With the mail, you can send out and get back many more surveys for a fraction of the cost. This is why a combination is often used.

Your questionnaire should be typed single-spaced on two sides of a letter (8½ × 11″) or legal-size (11 × 14″) sheet of white paper. Leave plenty of room for answers. The reader should be able to indicate his answer by checking a box or writing a brief reply in the space provided. Questions should be numbered. At the bottom of the last page, you should give the reader the option of filling in his name and address, in case you want to quote him or contact him for follow-up (however, make sure filling in name and address is clearly optional).

Send out the questionnaire with a cover letter indicating that you are asking the reader for a favor (a good opening line is, "I have a favor to ask of you") and giving him a reason for complying. For example, by completing the survey about his breakfast likes and dislikes, your chain of restaurants will be able to serve him the hot breakfast he so enjoys.

One incentive technique is to affix a quarter or dollar bill to each letter. This increases replies because it makes readers feel guilty about accepting your money and then not cooperating with your survey. Another technique is to offer a "surprise bonus gift" as a reward for completing and returning the survey. The gift might be a price-off coupon for purchase of your product at the supermarket.

What to ask in the survey? Again, ask anything you want to know. Dr. Jeffrey Lant lists some of the things you can ask:

- The reasons your prospects are buying the product or service
- Which of your competitors they are buying from
- How much of a given item they are buying
- How they came to learn about this item
- What they like about this item
- What they dislike
- Whether they are recommending it to their friends
- How loyal they are to your competitor
- Whether they would consider changing to a new vendor
- If so, on what basis

To this list I would add:

- Which radio stations they listen to
- Which magazines and newspapers they read on a regular basis
- Whether they are male or female
- Their level of education (high school graduate, college, graduate school)
- Level of family income
- Hobbies and special interests

The number of prospects you survey will depend on the size of your market, your budget, and your need for precise, statistically valid data. As a rule of thumb, send out 1,000 surveys and hope for a 25 percent response. If clear patterns and conclusions can be drawn, great. If not, send out another 1,000.

Focus Groups

A *focus group* is an in-person survey and discussion that takes place with 6 to 12 prospects simultaneously. "To create an ad, you begin by asking users or potential users what they think the product is, what they think it offers, and what the tangible benefits are. We do this through focus groups in which we get a dozen potential customers in the room and ask them a lot of questions about their interests, concerns, and buying intentions," explains Brian Cohen, president of Technology Solutions, a New York-based marketing firm specializing in high-tech. "The benefit of such groups is that they provide the advertiser and agency with an intensive release of pure information from a group of consumers.

"An agency that talks only to its clients and not to customers is making a mistake. Advertisers are so close to their products that they can latch onto an idea of what it is and what it does without understanding the real issues associated with the user's perception of benefits."

Although there are numerous companies that specialize in conducting focus groups for clients, it is, in theory, something you could do yourself.

- First, invite a random sampling of prospects. Assume 10 percent will accept your invitation. If more respond, either hold a second focus group or offer an inexpensive thank-you gift to those you turn down.
- Keep the session to an afternoon or morning.
- Have one person from your company act as group leader. If others wish to observe, it must be in a set-up where they can do so unobtrusively behind a one-way mirror.
- Tape record the entire session. A hidden microphone set-up is best. Make sure it picks up from all places in the room so all voices are heard.
- Create a set of questions similar to your mail survey but more open-ended. A good mix is having 10 percent of the questions require a simple yes/no or multiple choice answer (e.g., asking them which magazines they read or whether they have heard of your brand), with the majority being open-ended. The focus group is the ideal forum for exploring new avenues and encouraging dialogue with the consumer.
- One excellent type of question to ask consumers is how they respond to certain concepts or phrasing you intend to use in advertising. For example, the Miller Brewing Co. recently introduced a product called "draft beer in a bottle." In market research (single interviews, not focus groups), they asked beer drinkers what they thought of this concept. For example, what did they think of bottled beer? Of draft beer? Did they prefer tap beer for its fresher taste, or was there no difference? When the interviewer said "draft beer in a bottle," what image did this conjure up in the consumer's mind? What did he or she think it meant? In-person interviews, especially focus groups, are an excellent forum for

getting consumer reaction to your slogans and learning whether your language transmits the desired concept to the buyer.

- Your final report should be a word-for-word transcript of the entire session. A cover sheet should list participants and the date. Conclusions drawn from the session may appear at the end or at the beginning in a summary.

Researching The Bigger Picture

In addition to information on your product, your competition, and your customer, you need additional data on the industry, issues, or other external factors affecting the positioning of your product.

For example, let's say you sell health insurance. One reason your prospect buys health insurance is because the cost of health care is rising at such an alarming rate. In your copy, you could begin by saying, "You know how expensive health care is these days. Well, now there's a plan to protect you and your family. . . ."

This is adequate, but it would be made more powerful, effective, and believable if the insurance company told the prospect the specifics about rising health care costs. For example: "You know how expensive health care is these days. The cost of a visit to the doctor's office has doubled since 1977. And a six-day stay in the hospital now costs what the average American earns in a month." (The numbers in this example are made up. Knowing how to get the actual data will be a big help in getting better copy from your ad agency and other creative resources.)

Although researching this type of material is a subject that warrants a book in itself, my technique is very simple. I simply send an assistant to the public library with instructions to bring back as much background material on the subject as possible. Here's how:

1. First, identify the subject topics by broad category. For health insurance, the topics might be: health care, hospitalization, medical care, insurance, health insurance.
2. Go to the library and consult the *Reader's Guide to Periodical Literature.* This will list articles on the topic.
3. Start your search with the most recent articles—those published this year and last year. Don't use older sources unless nothing has been published recently.

4. Study the listings of articles and select those that sound most promising. Write down the titles, authors, and the names of the magazines in which these articles appear, along with the specific issue and page numbers.
5. Ask the research librarian to bring you copies of those issues in which the articles appear.
6. Flip through the articles. Photocopy those that contain the most useful information. Take these back to your office. If none of the articles is promising, go back to the *Reader's Guide* and look up other articles.
7. Back at your office, read through the photocopied articles with a yellow highlighter, highlighting key data of interest. You may want to note these facts on index cards or in a computer file for future reference.

Although on-line databases and information searches are all the rage today, going to the library and copying articles is the simplest, easiest, and best way to build a basic reference file of the facts you need. In addition, I suggest that you do this library research yourself rather than send an employee because, as you read through source material, you will find things others might pass over. Writer Franklin Adams says, “I find that a great part of the information I have was gained by looking up something and finding something else on the way.”

Also, don't neglect books as well as articles. When you or your research assistant visit the library, be sure to pick up any books that deal with the general topic. For example, in ghostwriting an article on defense for an executive at a major defense contractor, I extracted information from several books on the topic.

I also like to go to library book sales and pick up old but still serviceable basic reference works in the various fields my clients are involved in. A good question to ask any client, especially in technical fields, is: “Can you recommend any one reference work or book that gives an overview of this field in simple layperson's terms?” Get this book and keep it on your shelf.

For example, in the printing industry *Pocket Pal* by International Paper tells you everything you need to know about different printing processes. If you have a client in the nuclear or related fields, get a copy of *Living with Radiation,* a basic fact book on the subject published by Johns Hopkins University Press in Baltimore, Maryland. Your librarian or bookseller can steer you in the right direction. Or, consult *Books in Print.* Available at your local library, *Books in Print* is an annual directory listing all published books by title, subject, and author.

Additional Reference Works

The following resources are also helpful in researching basic information on any topic:

- *Find It Fast* by Robert I. Berkman (New York: Harper & Row). Subtitled "How to uncover expert information on any subject," this book is a step-by-step guide to getting the information you need from library resources, the U.S. government, associations, museums, research centers, and computer databases. Contains complete contact and "where-to-find-it" information for most of the basic resources you will need.
- *Research Any Business Question—Fast and Professionally* by Ronald E. Roel (Brentwood, NY: Caddylak Systems, Inc.). A how-to guide on researching business information. Concentrates on research techniques rather than specific sources.
- *Writer's Resource Guide* edited by Bernadine Clark (Cincinnati, Ohio: Writer's Digest Books). A one-volume directory of sources of information on practically any subject. Lists more than 1,600 resources with complete contact details on more than 30 subject areas of interest.

Tip: Another good resource for information on a specific industry is the trade association or professional society covering this industry. Trade associations can offer a wealth of information, much of it low cost. Many have catalogs offering booklets, cassette tapes, books, research papers, and special reports, which are sold both to members and nonmembers.

If you want information on printing, for example, contact the National Association of Printers and Lithographers. If you need data on the electronics industry, write to the Institute of Electronic and Electrical Engineers. A complete listing of trade and professional associations may be found in the *Encyclopedia of Associations* in your local library.

On-line Information Resources

Another method of doing research is through on-line searches of information databases. This requires that you have a personal computer equipped with a modem that enables you to send and receive data transmissions over standard telephone lines.

Access to databases is made most often through on-line database vendors, such as CompuServe, Dialog, and The Source. For an hourly fee, you connect your modem to their database, search through it, and extract the information you need. Although the hourly fees are not cheap, you do not have to read the entire text while you are connected to the database.

Instead, information can be stored on your diskette or printed as hard copy.

"If electronic researching sounds like something you'd like to try, but you're not sure if you want to invest in the necessary equipment (or the time it takes to learn), consult your local library," recommends Beverley Bare Buehrer, author of "Modem Operandi." "Oftentimes they have the means to access databases and will help you, for a fee, work out an appropriate search program and retrieve the information needed."

One drawback of on-line database vendors is that many offer only "bibliographic" databases, which contain only abstracts or summaries rather than the entire text of the articles. This means that you must go to the library to get the complete article. However, the database saves time by quickly pinpointing the source and giving you a summary of the article's contents.

Some of the more popular online vendors:

BRS
Bibliographic Retrieval Service
1200 Route 7
Latham, NY 12110
518-783-1161
Business, education, news, health, and humanities subjects.

CompuServe
PO Box 20212
Columbus, Ohio 43220
800-848-8199
Business, health, education, stock quotes, home shopping, and travel information.

Dialog Information Services
3460 Hillview Avenue
Palo Alto, CA 94304
800-334-2564
Indexes of major newspapers and magazines. Databases cover business, science, industry, law, environment, education, film, additional topics.

The Source
8815 Telegraph Road
Lorton, VA 22079
703-550-8600
e-mail, UPI wire reports, user publishing.

For a more in-depth discussion of on-line databases send for special report B-741, "Modem Operandi," available for $2.50 from Cassell Communications, Inc., PO Box 9844, Fort Lauderdale, Florida 33310.

Summary

As an exercise, try completing the Creative Questionnaire (Figure 5.3). Once completed, it will give you most of the information you need about your product, audience, and competition.

Figure 5.3. Creative questionnaire.*

Client: ____________________ Job No. ____________________

Contact: ____________________ Title ____________________

____________________ Title ____________________

____________________ Title ____________________

Product: ______________________________

A. The Company

1. What is the history of the company?
2. What is its corporate culture or philosophy?
3. What is the company's record of growth?
4. Is there a key spokesperson or other visible figure?

B. The Product

1. What problem does the product solve for the consumer?
2. What are the unique advantages of the product? Please prioritize.
   a.
   b.
   c.
   d.
   e.
3. Other copy points?
4. What are the product's problems/weaknesses?
   a.
   b.
   c.
   d.
   e.
5. Where and how is the product sold?
6. How was the product originally launched? With what marketing and advertising strategies?

7. How has the product performed? Has it been altered or improved? Is its share of the market improving?
8. What is the product's image?
9. How does the product respond to changes in:
   a. Pricing?
   b. Promotion?
   c. Advertising?
10. What are the current and future market conditions for the product?
11. Is the product category static or growing?
12. Is the category of high or low interest?
13. Are there any regional or seasonal considerations?

C. The Competition

1. What is the product's competition?

Brand	*Company*	*Market Share*
a.		
b.		
c.		
d.		
e.		

2. How does the product stand in relation to its competitors?
3. Which competitors pose the greatest threat? Why?
4. Are there important differences between your product and the competition?
5. How do your competitors differ in their advertising and market strategies? price?
6. Have all possible brand positions been covered—or is there a unique niche for your product?
7. What is the size of the market in units and dollars?

D. Your Target Market

1. Who will be buying the product? Please include demographics.
2. Who influences buying?
3. Who will be actually using the product?
4. Who are the heavy users of your product?
5. What kind of emotional sell would motivate someone to buy your product? (e.g., desire for prestige, security)
6. Why wouldn't someone buy your product? (e.g., price, lack of awareness)

E. The Assignment

1. What are the objectives of this assignment? (e.g., lead generation, direct sales, awareness)
2. How will you measure its success?
3. Are there any promotions planned in conjunction with this assignment?
4. What kind of tone—graphic and copy—do you feel is appropriate? (e.g., upscale, friendly)
5. How have past promotions/advertising efforts fared? (Please include samples of all work)
6. Have you conducted any current research we should know about? (Please include all pertinent materials)
7. What additional research is needed? (e.g., focus groups, questionnaires)
8. What additional information do we need to complete this assignment?

Please be sure to include:

1. A sample of the product, if possible
2. Past advertising/promotion efforts
3. Competitors' advertising/promotion efforts
5. All applicable research.

---

*© 1988, Caddylak Systems, Inc. Reprinted with permission.

CHAPTER 6

Setting Communications Goals and Objectives

Setting Goals, Objectives, and Strategies

Each organization must have a goal toward which it strives. This is inherent in the definition of the word *goal* as "the purpose toward which an endeavor is directed."

To achieve this goal, you must set specific communications objectives for your marketing communications campaign. Then you must decide on the best strategies and tactics to achieve those objectives.

Some Definitions And Examples

Let's define the terms *goal, objective, strategy,* and *tactic* as they apply to advertising programs:

Goal

The goal is the broad overview, the big picture of what your organization wants to achieve or what it wants to become. Some business executives call this the "mission statement." One of my clients feels that keeping the mission statement in mind at all times is so important that it is printed on the back of the business cards of all his employees.

Some examples of goals:

ABC Technologies wants to be the leading supplier of interactive video displays for schools, universities, and nonprofit institutions.

On-Line Software is the "authority" in IBM software and the leading supplier of software, services, support, and training to enhance clients' use of CICS and other major IBM mainframe software products.

"The goal is best understood as the 'where' concept," notes Dr. Jeffrey Lant. "Where are you going? The goal states in general terms what you are working for."

Objective

The objective is a concrete, quantifiable, measurable, and immediate goal. It is, specifically, what you want your advertising and promotional program to achieve for you within a specific time period—usually stated on an annual basis.

When formulating your objectives, the following factors should be considered:

First, the objective should be consistent with your goal or mission statement. For instance, a company that wants to remain a two-person operation would not have as their goal the quadrupling of sales, as this would be too large an increase for the two people to handle alone.

Second, the objective should be quantified. "Increase sales" is not specific enough. "Sell books by mail from my home" is not specific enough. These should be changed to "increase sales of widgets 25 percent" and "sell how-to and self-help books from my basement or garage while earning an extra net income of $15,000 per year to help put my two children through college."

Third, the objective should be measurable. If your objective is to generate a certain number of sales leads, for example, you can quickly and easily count the leads and see if you are achieving your objective. But what if your objective is awareness, or company image, or brand preference? These are not as easy to measure, so you need to set parameters or guidelines by which success will be evaluated. Remember the Creative Questionnaire in Chapter 5? The most interesting question—one that many agencies and creative teams fail to ask—was "How will you measure the success of this project?"

For an ad campaign designed to create awareness, you might design a market research survey that measures how well consumers remember your company, your product, or your brand name. By conducting a before and after study, you can measure, as an example, how many people were familiar with your brand before the ad campaign ran against how many could recall the brand name after the ads ran.

If your objective is not merely to generate a large quantity of leads but to generate "good" leads or "high quality" leads, it's easy to count the number of leads, but how do you separate good leads from bad leads?

One way might be to put an add-on questionnaire or "mini-survey" on ad coupons and direct mail reply cards that ask the prospect to qualify himself. An advertiser selling software designed for law firms with five or more attorneys might ask, "How many attorneys work at this law firm?" Copy in the ad or letter emphasizes the fact that only law firms of five or more attorneys should ask for more information about the product. When counting results, those inquiries from law firms of five or more attorneys represent "good leads," while those from small firms and individual attorneys do not.

The fourth criteria is to set an objective that is not only measurable but realistic as well. What is a reasonable objective? It depends on your market, your product, and your budget. Is the market for your product declining, expanding, or is it staying the same? As marketing strategist Dan Piro points out, it's hard to achieve any significant sales success or growth in declining markets.

How about the product? Is it a hot new technology or an old chestnut way past its prime? For some products, simply maintaining current market share is a reasonable and even ambitious objective. For "hot" technologies, like voice mail or optical storage, fast growth is expected and possible.

Your budget also plays a role. I have frequently consulted with clients who have overly ambitious and unrealistic sales goals yet do not have the money to fund even half of the promotions that are necessary to achieve the more modest objectives we have set. Although a big budget does not ensure success, the company that spends $100,000 on promotion and advertising will—if they do it right—probably increase sales more than the company in the same business that spends $1,000.

Many marketers disagree with this point. They believe setting an overly ambitious objective spurs the client company to greater action and helps them reach higher than they would with a more reasonable objective. For instance, I believe Steve Jobs of Apple Computer once stated that his objective was to have a personal computer in every home in America. Although he has not achieved this objective, by striving toward it the company made great leaps and achieved fantastic growth and success in a relatively short period.

On the other hand, if your objective is too difficult, people become disheartened, disappointed, and (if you're an agency or consultant) even angry with you when they fail to come close to achieving it. It makes no sense to promise a client he will triple his sales in 12 months when he would be lucky to increase sales 20 percent.

My solution is to set the objective higher—but only *slightly* higher—than I think the company can reasonably achieve. Typically this would be 10 percent or so higher than my initial figure. This way, the company has an ambitious objective which people can reach if they work hard. People like to be challenged, but realistically. Employees want a challenge, but most are unhappy if given a task they perceive as impossible.

With these criteria in mind, here are some sample objectives:

Increase unit sales volume from 100 to 150 seminars per year.

Capture 20 percent of the chemical process market for grid-type tower packing.

Get five new retainer clients this year, each paying a retainer of $2,000 per month.

Rent 550 cars per week in our Denver and Pittsburgh locations.

Open 20 new franchises this year representing a total of $2 million in additional profit.

Strategy

Strategy outlines the methods or means used to achieve objectives. On the strategic level, you are dealing with an overview of the techniques to be used rather than the specific nuts-and-bolts detail. For instance, a strategic decision might be, "Use direct mail," but not, "Mail a 6 × 9″ flier printed on pink with a tear-off certificate and scratch-and-sniff scent." That is a tactic, not a strategy. Some examples of strategies:

For an independent consultant . . .

Use direct mail and ads in vertical industry publications to generate sales leads. Create a brochure to be mailed as follow-up. Call prospects after brochure is mailed to ascertain level of interest and use series of follow-up calls throughout the year to stay in contact with interested prospects. Give speeches and write articles for CONSULTANT TODAY magazine as reputation-building tools to establish credibility.

Consider launching a newsletter or writing a book as an added credibility builder.

For a consumer products manufacturer . . .

Introduce product to retailers in test market cities with heavy coupon promotion. National roll-out in third quarter with media blitz of 15 and 30-second TV spots plus magazine ads as secondary medium. During and following media blitz, use free standing newspaper inserts for mass distribution of price-off coupons.

For a newsletter publisher . . .

Launch newsletter with 30,000-name direct mail test. Prepare sample issues with order blanks and distribute at all major industry conventions and trade shows. Use classified ads in three major trade journals for inquiry generation. Send press release to journal editors. Exhibit at Spring Trade Show. Put CEO's of 100 top manufacturers on free subscription list.

Tactic.

A tactic is the nitty-gritty, detailed planning of a specific promotion or campaign. Here is where you decide how to organize your copy, what color paper to use, what format to print, which graphics to feature. Some examples of tactics:

Mail a Mailgram® telegram notice to our 10,000 existing customers offering a $30 rebate if they make a purchase between now and May 1.

Tape my speech at the CALSUN show. Have 500 copies duplicated with professionally printed labels. Mail to my 25 clients and top 400 prospects. Encourage them to schedule an initial consulting session. Offer $100 off the regular price of $200 as "Fall special."

Advertise in the BUTTERFLY COLLECTOR NEWS and INSECT BUFF TIMES. Run full-page ads offering "How to Collect Butterflies" manual for $15. Also test ¼-page ads offering free butterfly collectors catalog.

Most Companies Do Not Have Goals

Most companies—and I've dealt with, read about, or spoken with people from hundreds—do not have clear marketing goals or objectives. Or if they do, it's a secret that's well kept from their advertising manager, ad agencies, and vendors.

The reason is that most small and medium-size firms were, in the not too distant past, entrepreneurial ventures. Corporate managers may like such things as market research, planning, and goal-setting, but most entrepreneurs don't. And it's understandable: They're so caught up in the day-to-day running of the business enterprise, they don't have time to stop and plan. As the firm gets bigger, the owner may hire others to manage for him, but his attitude of disdain for formalized planning is usually clearly communicated, either directly or indirectly, to his managers—who respond in kind.

In 75 percent of the cases where I am called in to consult or write copy, the client does not have a precise, measurable objective for the ad, brochure, or mailing in question. Why is this a problem? For this reason: If you have no clear objective, how do you know whether your program is a success or a failure? Without an objective, different people within the company might have fundamentally different views of what a specific promotion or an ad campaign is supposed to accomplish. For this reason, an ad campaign may be a success in the eyes of one department and a total failure to others.

> *Example:* One company, a manufacturer of semiconductors, was an innovator in the field of semiconductor advertising. Where most other manufacturers used plain-jane, straightforward ads filled with specs, charts, and graphs, this firm used four-color, two-page ads featuring highly imaginative visuals tied into clever headlines.
>
> Were the ads successful? If the objective was to be creative, certainly; the ad agency won several awards for the work. If the objective was to be memorable, that too was achieved; readership studies indicated high readership and recall of the advertising. This pleased the advertising manager and top company management.
>
> However, the sales manager complained that, while the advertising was much admired and remembered, it had no noticeable effect on sales, which were decidedly flat. So if the objective was to increase sales, these innovative ads could not be called successful. Also, the engineering department complained that the ads were superficial and shallow; and if their objective was to communicate technical information to buyers, the ads did not accomplish this, either.

The moral is that an advertisement may be a success in one person's judgment and a failure to another person within the same company. Only by measuring results against objectives can you accurately determine advertising effectiveness. The reverse is also true: In the absence of specific objectives, no precise determination of effectiveness is possible.

Advertising management and senior executives must agree on the overall goal of marketing communications as well as the specific objectives of the campaign. Without such consensus, the advertising department will be working at cross purposes. A brilliantly conceived campaign that generates carloads of inquiries may be considered a flop by senior management if they have no interest in inquiry generation.

Setting Objectives

What can marketing communications achieve? What should they achieve? A recent survey by *Business Marketing* magazine shows that communications managers and senior executives do in fact have some basic agreement on the ways marketing communications contribute to a company's success. The results appear in Table 6.1.

In a McGraw-Hill survey of 535 sales managers nationwide, the sales managers indicated that the primary objective of advertising and promotion was to "arouse initial interest" in the product or service. They felt that other objectives, including seeking out new prospects, communicating product benefits, creating preference for a product or company, and closing the order, were best handled by salespeople. Obviously, sales managers have a bias in favor of salespeople, while most advertising managers have a bias in favor of printed and audio-visual marketing communications tools.

Table 6.1. Business Marketing survey of managers and executives.

Ways Marketing Communications Should Contribute to Company Success	*Communications Managers*	*Senior Executives*
Create product or company awareness	27%	34%
Increase sales or profits	17%	13%
Create favorable company image	10%	7%
Create interest in product or company	9%	10%
Generate inquiries or make prospects take action	6%	7%
Increase recall or recognition	8%	7%
Support the sales force	6%	5%
Strategic repositioning of company	4%	3%
TOTAL ANSWERS GIVEN:	563	521

Marketing consultant Carolyn Hosken breaks down the task of setting an objective into three elements:

1. Determine how many new customers or sales you would like to generate from the target audience (e.g., "10 new major accounts," "5,000 more customers," "12,000 units sold per month").
2. Determine what amount of new business this represents in dollars.
3. Determine the time frame for achieving these goals. Is it immediate? Within the next few months? This year? Two years?

One problem in following this procedure is that many people have a hard time determining these specifics. Having not thought through this process before, they find it difficult to say what their objectives are, how many new clients or customers they want (or think they can realistically get), how much sales and profits to expect, or how long it will take. As one client said to me recently: "Should my goal be to increase sales 2 percent or 20 percent or 200 percent this year? I really have no idea what is possible, so how do I know what objective to set in my marketing plan?"

Fortunately, there is a method, called *benchmarking*.

How Benchmarking Works

A benchmark is a point of reference, a standard against which all future results are judged. The benchmark determines what is "normal" or average so we can measure if future events are normal, above average, or below par.

Doctors, for example, take a blood pressure reading at the initial exam for a new patient to determine what is "normal" for that person. During periodic check-ups, blood pressure readings are compared against the norm, showing the doctor whether there has been an abnormal increase or decrease.

If you have been with your company a while and have been measuring and monitoring results, you know what is normal or average and can set objectives that either maintain the status quo or call for some level of improvement or increase. For instance, if your "average" full-page trade journal ad generates readership scores indicating that 15 percent of readers read the copy all the way through, and your assessment of an ad's success is whether people are reading the copy, then you might challenge a new ad agency to produce ads that score 20 or 25 percent in the readership studies. An ad that scored 15 percent would not be an improvement over previous efforts, and one that scored 5 percent would indicate that the new copy was not successful. You use previous results as the benchmark against which objectives for evaluating the effectiveness of new efforts are set. If you do not have a history of measured results, then make your next effort the benchmark.

Example: You have never tried radio advertising before but are now going to run radio ads for your restaurant. Average gross is $10,000 per night. You run the radio spots according to schedule and notice that your gross averages $15,000 when the commercials run, representing a 50 percent increase in sales.

This first commercial becomes the benchmark against which all efforts are now judged. Eventually, patrons will become tired of the original commercial, it will lose effectiveness, and sales will drop off, eventually returning to $10,000 per night.

You decide to have a radio producer do a new commercial for you. If you were satisfied with the results of the first commercial, you might tell your producer, "The objective of this commercial is to generate a 50 percent increase in sales"—the same as the first commercial. If the new commercial generates $15,000 in revenue per night, the objective has been accomplished and the project is a success. If you get only $12,000 in sales a night, you haven't done what you know is possible, but at least you are making $2,000 extra per night—more than enough to pay for the commercials—and so you are still satisfied.

However, if sales remain flat at $10,000, you know you have a bomb. You do not accept the producer's claim that "radio is for image; it doesn't really increase sales directly," since you know from past experience that radio does generate immediate, tangible sales for you. The benchmark tells you what you can expect and whether you have gotten it.

Another important reason to set tangible, specific, numerical objectives is for budgeting purposes. As you will see in Chapter 7 on budgeting, one proven method of determining the advertising budget, the *task-to-objective method,* allocates enough advertising money to achieve the tasks necessary to accomplish the objectives. Without a specific objective, you cannot allocate a specific amount of advertising dollars in its pursuit.

Write Down Your Marketing Objectives

It is a dangerous practice to set advertising and marketing objectives as an afterthought or toss them out as quick, off-the-cuff comments at meetings. Goals for the overall marketing communications campaign as well as specific advertising objectives should be carefully thought through and spelled out in writing. Use the Advertising Objective Work Sheets (Figure 6.1) to summarize the objectives and strategies for each product your company sells.

Figure 6-1. Advertising objectives and strategies for 19___.

A. Describe your advertising objectives for each product line.

1. Product Line ______________ Advertising Objectives ______________

2. Product Line ______________ Advertising Objectives ______________

3. Product Line ______________ Advertising Objectives ______________

4. Product Line ______________ Advertising Objectives ______________

B. Describe your advertising strategies for each product line.

1. Product Line ______________ Advertising Strategies ______________

2. Product Line ______________ Advertising Strategies ______________

3. Product Line ______________ Advertising Strategies ______________

____

____

4. Product Line ______________ Advertising Strategies ______________

____

____

C. Describe the advertising objectives for each new product line to be introduced next year. 19__

1. New Product ______________ Advertising Objectives ______________

____

____

2. New Product ______________ Advertising Objectives ______________

____

____

3. New Product ______________ Advertising Objectives ______________

____

____

4. New Product ______________ Advertising Objectives ______________

____

____

Figure 6-1. (continued)

D. Describe the advertising strategies for each new product line to be introduced next year. 19__

1. New Product ______________________ Advertising Strategies ______________________

2. New Product ______________________ Advertising Strategies ______________________

3. New Product ______________________ Advertising Strategies ______________________

4. New Product ______________________ Advertising Strategies ______________________

Be Flexible

Unfortunately, advertising is not an exact science. We cannot predict with certainty how successful an ad will be or how many widgets it will sell. Sometimes an ad everyone judged mediocre is immensely profitable, while the ad you thought was a sure winner bombs.

Objectives need to be constantly examined and reevaluated with regard to current results and market conditions. In fund raising, for example, where a response rate of 2 percent to a direct mail solicitation was once typical, consultants in the field now agree that response rates are declining and they now expect to get only a 1 percent response.

For another example, in today's economy, many publishers of newsletters, seminars, and other information products report decreased sales volumes due to overcrowding in the field (too many competing products in this age of information). Sales of high-tech equipment, on the other hand, such as facsimiles, cellular radios, compact disc players, paging devices, and camcorders, continue to climb as more business executives and consumers demand the conveniences of these technological wonders.

The point is that you cannot set your objectives in a vacuum. Planning is not a theoretical exercise to be performed in an ivy covered tower. You must constantly monitor market conditions and the performance of your own products and adjust objectives accordingly. In a boom economy, set your goals higher and institute more aggressive promotions to take advantage and grab your share of the expanding market. In declining markets, reevaluate your objectives and expect to be disappointed if you are overly optimistic.

Treat every plan as a working guideline rather than a commandment. Be willing to revise your thinking if you see a way to make things work better. Perhaps you should set objectives by six-month period or by quarter rather than annually, then meet periodically to review progress, compare results against objectives, and reset objectives for the next three or six-month period accordingly. A year-long plan carried out with no intermediate evaluation or review is like a programmed missile that travels out of radar range; if it veers off course, no one knows it or corrects the situation until it explodes.

Tip: Establish objectives for individual promotions as well as your overall campaign. These need not be part of the formal advertising plan but can be stated in writing in separate memos addressing each individual project.

After each project, determine the results and compare them with the objectives. If you are failing to achieve the objectives on a lot of individual projects, the overall objective will not be achieved.

Stop and ask yourself what's going wrong and how it might be corrected. Maybe the strategy is wrong—perhaps you should be using billboards instead of door-to-door sales representatives. Or maybe it's your tactics: giving away free steak knives isn't moving more vacuum cleaners. Whatever the cause, it's important to continually compare results against objectives to monitor performance on an ongoing basis.

CHAPTER 7

How to Set Your Advertising Budget

Key Considerations in Setting Advertising Budgets

The advertising manager faced with the task of setting an annual advertising budget is challenged to answer a number of key questions. Among them are:

- What percentage of the marketing budget should be spent on advertising as opposed to other marketing programs (e.g., sales training, sales commissions, trade show displays, franchises, dealer incentives, coupons, point of purchase displays, etc.)? Often, increasing the budget for advertising means cutting somewhere else, and in some cases the money may indeed be spent best elsewhere. Contrary to what some practice, the successful ad manager does not fight for every penny to be given to advertising. Instead, he seeks only what he needs to get the job done—no more, no less. Unfortunately, with today's rising media, printing, and production costs, the problem is frequently too little money rather than too much money.
- How much money (in a dollar amount) should be spent on marketing communications this year?

- Of that budget, how should it be allocated? How much for space ads versus direct mail versus telemarketing versus radio and television?
- How should the spending be paced? Should it be spent evenly throughout the year or should the bulk of the money be spent at certain times?
- How much will individual items (the January newspaper supplement, the March circular) in the ad budgets cost? This requires the ability to make somewhat accurate estimates based on little data or specifics about each project—an ability that grows with experience and time spent on the job.

Let us begin to answer some of these questions—to see what others are doing and examine methods you can use to determine your own budgets.

Determine How Much To Spend On Marketing Communications

McGraw-Hill surveyed 535 sales managers and received responses from 284. According to these sales managers, whose responses are summarized in Table 7.1, budget allocation in key marketing areas was as follows:

The first column indicates actual budget allocations. The second column indicates how they would allocate the budget if given a 25 percent budget increase. Note that these sales managers now spend most of their budget on salespeople and only a small percentage on advertising and promotion, but say that they *would* spend more on advertising and promotion *if* they had more money for it. (Percentage columns may not add up to 100 percent due to rounding.)

Business Marketing magazine performed a similar survey among top business-to-business marketers. The survey, summarized in Table 7.2, re-

Table 7.1. Marketing tools used by sales managers.

Tool	*1983 Budget*	*Imaginary Budget (25% Higher)*
Salespeople	60%	42%
Advertising/promotion	17%	30%
Company catalogs/directories	8%	9%
Trade shows	7%	8%
Direct mail	4%	9%
Other	3%	3%

Table 7.2. The average budget picture of top business marketers.

Communications Tool	*% of Budget*
Media	31%
Literature	24%
Trade shows	11%
Direct mail	8%
Ad production	5%
Sales promotion	5%
Public relations	4%
Inquiry fulfillment	2%
Market research	2%
Telemarketing	2%
Point of purchase	1%
Other	5%
TOTAL:	100%

vealed how the communications budget was spread among more than a dozen areas of communication.

The McGraw-Hill Laboratory of Advertising Performance surveyed 382 marketing managers in major industrial companies. The survey is summarized in Table 7.3. It found the following breakdown of the marketing communications budget.

What about the marketing communications/advertising budget based on a percentage of sales? Research Report #8015.8 from the McGraw-Hill Laboratory of Advertising Performance indicates that marketing communications costs average 1.73 percent of sales among major industrial companies. According to *How to Promote Your Own Business,* most small businesses spend between 1 and 3 percent of sales on advertising, while large consumer companies such as General Motors, Carter-

Table 7.3. Industrial marketing communications budget breakdown.

Communications Tools	*% of Budget Spent*
Print advertising	36.3%
Exhibits and trade shows	19.9%
Catalogs/directories	13.6%
Literature, deals, coupons, point of purchase	9.9%
Direct mail	7.5%
Dealer and distributor aids	5.3%
Public relations and publicity	4.8%
Radio/TV/billboards	1.9%

Wallace, Revlon, Pepsico, and Procter & Gamble have advertising budgets ranging from less than 1 percent of sales to more than 30 percent, with 2 to 10 percent being typical.

Business Marketing magazine has published advertising-to-sales ratios for a variety of different industries, which are shown in Table 7.4.

Dana K. Cassell lists the advertising budget-to-sales ratios for a variety of retail businesses, which appear in Table 7.5.

Again, the advertising budgets for most small retail businesses and chains fall in the 1 to 3 percent of sales range.

How To Determine Your Annual Advertising Budget*

How much should you spend on advertising this year? There is no right answer, no precise, scientific formula that you can plug into a calculator and say to the boss, "See, this is exactly how much we have to spend to reach our sales objectives!"

There are standard formulas that represent seven different methods of determining the advertising budget. We will review these formulas here; then I will present a method which is a combination of two of the formulas and which I think makes the most sense. You are free to use any method you are comfortable with.

Formula 1: Percentage of Sales

The most widely used method of establishing an advertising budget is to base it on a percentage of sales. Advertising is as much a business expense as, say, the cost of labor, and thus should be related to the quantity of goods sold.

The percentage-of-sales method avoids some of the problems that result from using profits as a base. For example, if profits in a period are low, it might not be the fault of advertising; material costs might be higher, for example. By using the percentage-of-sales method, you keep your advertising in a consistent relation to your sales volume—which is primarily what your advertising should be affecting.

You can select the percentage figure to use (e.g., 1 percent, 2 percent, 2.5 percent) by finding out what other businesses in your line of work are doing. These percentages are fairly consistent within a given category of business.

*Some of this information is taken from "Plan Your Advertising Budget," U.S. Small Business Administration Management Aid Number 4.018.

Table 7.4. Advertising budget as a percentage of sales*

Industry	*Advertising Budget as a Percentage of Sales*
Advertising agencies	0.1%
Agricultural production—crops	2.9%
Air courier services	2.1%
Air transportation, certified	1.8%
Aircraft and parts	0.5%
Auto dealers, gas stations	0.5%
Auto rental and leasing	2.9%
Auto repair services and garages	4.0%
Bakery products	1.9%
Book publishers	3.8%
Business services	5.3%
Catalog showrooms	3.7%
Chemicals (wholesale)	3.5%
Coating and engraving services	2.6%
Computer program and software services	3.5%
Communications and signalling devices	4.1%
Commercial printing	1.2%
Computer equipment	1.9%
Computer stores	1.0%
Computers—micro	5.1%
Connectors	1.2%
Construction, special trade	9.8%
Dairy products	4.9%
Data processing services	1.2%
Detective and protective services	0.2%
Drugs	4.4%
Educational services	5.0%
Electric appliances, wholesale	0.8%
Electric lighting	1.1%
Electronic components	2.3%
Engines and turbines	1.8%
Engineering, architect, survey services	0.8%
Farm machinery and equipment	1.6%
Financial services	0.7%
Food	7.3%
Freight forwarding	3.6%
Hardware, wholesale	6.4%
Health services	3.3%
Hospitals	5.8%
Hotels	0.4%
Industrial controls	1.7%
Industrial machinery and equipment, wholesale	2.0%
Insurance agents and brokers	0.6%
Lumber, wholesale	2.2%
Machine tools	2.0%

Material handling equipment	1.0%
Medical laboratories	0.9%
Metalworking equipment	5.4%
Management consulting	1.8%
Motor vehicle parts and accessories	1.6%
Motors and generators	1.0%
Musical instruments	3.3%
Newspapers	3.9%
Office automation systems	2.3%
Office furniture	1.4%
Optical instruments and lenses	1.5%
Outpatient care facilities	1.1%
Paint, varnish, and lacquer	3.1%
Paper and paper products	3.8%
Personal services	3.7%
PR services	1.8%
Office supplies	5.2%
Photofinishing laboratories	1.8%
Photographic equipment and supplies	3.2%
Plastics, resins, elastomers	1.6%
Pollution control machinery	0.8%
Prefabricated metal buildings	0.7%
Pumps	1.2%
Real estate agents	2.8%
Savings & loan associations	0.7%
Security & commodity brokers	3.8%
Semiconductors	1.2%
Ship and boat building and repair	2.3%
Soaps and detergents	7.6%
Telephone communications (wire, radio)	1.9%
Textile mill products	1.1%
Tires and inner tubes	3.1%
Training equipment and simulators	1.6%
Valves	1.0%

**Source:* The Advertising Ratios & Budgets report. Prepared by Schonfeld & Associates, Inc., Evanston, Illinois. Published in the October 1988 issue of *Business Marketing* magazine. Reprinted with permission of *Business Marketing.*

It's fairly easy to find out this ratio of advertising expense to sales in your industry. You can check trade magazines and associations or consult Census and Internal Revenue Service reports and reports published by financial institutions, such as Dun & Bradstreet, Inc., 99 Church Street, New York, NY 10007. Some of the tables listed in this chapter may also prove helpful.

Knowing the ratio for your industry indicates whether you are spending more or less than your competitors. But remember, these industry averages are not gospel. Your particular situation may dictate that you spend

Table 7.5. Ad budget as a percentage of sales for retail businesses.

Type of Store	*Advertising Budget as Percentage of Sales*
Appliance, radio, TV dealers	2.3%
Auto accessory and parts stores	0.9%
Bookstores	1.7%
Camera stores	0.8%
Children's and infant's wear stores	1.4%
Cocktail lounges	0.9%
Department stores	2.8%
Discount stores	2.4%
Drugstores	1.5%
Florists	2.1%
Food chains	1.1%
Furniture chains	5.0%
Gas stations	0.8%
Gift and novelty stores	1.4%
Hardware stores	1.6%
Home centers	1.3%
Jewelry stores	4.4%
Liquor stores	0.9%
Lumber and building materials dealers	0.5%
Meat markets	0.6%
Men's wear stores	2.9%
Music stores	1.8%
Office supply dealers	0.8%
Paint, glass, and wallpaper stores	1.3%
Photographic studios and supply shops	2.4%
Restaurants	0.8%
Shoe stores	1.9%
Specialty stores	3.0%
Sporting goods stores	3.5%
Tire dealers	2.2%
Variety stores	1.5%

Source: How to Advertise and Promote Your Retail Store, by D. Cassell.

more or less than the average. Average may not be good enough for you. You may want to out-advertise your competitors and be willing to cut into short-term profits to do so. Growth takes investment.

No ad manager should be bound to any single method. It's helpful to use the percentage of sales method because it's quick and easy. It ensures that your advertising budget isn't way out of proportion for your business. It's a sound method for stable markets. But if you want to expand your market share, you'll probably have to use a larger percentage of sales than the industry average.

Your budget can be determined as a percentage of past sales, of estimated future sales, or as a combination of the two:

- *Past sales.* Your budget can be a percentage of last year's sales or an average of a number of years in the immediate past. Consider, though, that changes in economic conditions can make your figure too high or too low.
- *Estimated future sales.* You can calculate your advertising budget as a percentage of anticipated sales for next year. The most common pitfall of this method is an optimistic assumption that your business will continue to grow. You must keep general business trends always in mind, especially if there's a chance of a slump, and hardheadedly assess the directions in your industry and your own operation. Note that when launching a new product, the advertising budget must, naturally, be calculated based on a percentage of *future* sales, since the new product has no sales record.
- *Past sales and estimated future sales.* The middle ground between an often conservative appraisal based on last year's sales and a usually too optimistic assessment of next year's sales is to combine both. It's a more realistic method during periods of changing economic conditions. It allows you to analyze trends and results thoughtfully and to set advertising expenditures with a little more assurance of accuracy.

Formula 2: Unit of Sales

In the unit of sale method, you set aside a fixed sum for each unit to be sold, based on your experience and trade knowledge of how much advertising it takes to sell each unit. That is, if it takes two cents' worth of advertising to sell a case of canned vegetables and you want to move 100,000 cases, you will probably plan to spend $2,000 on advertising them. Does it cost *X* dollars to sell a refrigerator? Then you'll probably have to budget 1,000 times *X* if you plan to sell a thousand refrigerators. You are simply basing your budget on unit of sales rather than dollar amounts of sales.

Some people consider this method just a variation of percentage of sales. However, unit of sales lets you make a closer estimate of what you should plan to spend for maximum effect, because it's based on what experience tells you it takes to sell an actual unit, rather than an overall percentage of your gross sales.

The unit of sales method is particularly useful in fields where the amount of product available is limited by outside factors, such as the weather's effect on crops. If that's the situation for your business, you first estimate how many units or cases will be available to you. Then, you advertise only as much as experience tells you it takes to sell them. Thus, if you have a pretty good idea ahead of time how many units will be available, you should have minimal waste in your advertising costs.

This method is also suited for specialty goods, such as washing machines and automobiles; however, it's difficult to apply when you have many different kinds of products to advertise and must divide your advertising among these products. The unit of sale method is not very useful in sporadic or irregular markets.

The unit of sale method can be helpful when selling durable goods of high value, such as television sets and VCRs, or goods of small unit value, such as toilet paper and flashlights. It is not a valid approach to setting a budget for a service business.

Formula 3: Objective and Task

The most difficult method for determining an advertising budget is the objective and task approach. Yet, it's the most accurate and best accomplishes what all budgets should: It relates the dollar appropriation to the marketing task to be accomplished under usual conditions.

To establish your budget by this method, you need a coordinated marketing program with specific objectives (see Chapter 6) based on a thorough survey of your markets and their potential.

While the percentage of sales method first determines how much you'll spend without much consideration of what you want to accomplish, the task method establishes what you must do to meet your objectives. Only then do you calculate costs. You set specific objectives, determine what media best reach your target market, and then estimate how much it will cost to run the number and types of advertisements you think it will take to get the results you want. You repeat this process for each objective. When you total these costs, you have your projected budget.

You may find that you cannot afford to advertise as you would like. It's a good idea, therefore, to rank your objectives. As with the other methods, be prepared to change your plan to reflect reality and to fit the resources you have available.

Formula 4: Historical

The easiest way to set a promotion budget is to base it on what you have spent historically. Typically, companies take last year's budget and add 10 percent for inflation to come up with this year's budget.

The advantages of this method are its simplicity and the fact that management—especially financial management—finds it so acceptable. Few chief financial officers will find any objection to an ad budget presented this way unless sales and profits have fallen off dramatically or the economy is bad.

The disadvantage of this method is that it doesn't accurately reflect your goals, objectives, economic factors, market conditions, or current plans. Also, it is possible that the previous year's budget—upon which the historical method is based—was not sensible. In this case, the historical method simply repeats a bad business decision over and over again.

Formula 5: Match the Competition

This is a reactive method whereby management spends money in reaction to what they perceive the competition is spending. I have frequently had clients call me wanting to place expensive ads in publications we have previously determined were undesirable. When I ask why the change of heart, the answer is always, "Because [name of competitor] has an ad there and I want a bigger one (or one the same size)." This is a poor reason to run an ad and rarely provides the desired results.

Formula 6: All You Can Afford

With the all-you-can-afford method, you first appropriate money for essential operating and capital expenses, such as new equipment, materials, inventory, supplies, labor, insurance, rent, and so on. Whatever is left over is spent on marketing.

This technique is dangerous for companies that are limited in growth potential or want to deliberately remain a certain size; the danger is that it can generate more business than the company can handle. The company has no choice but to "waste" the sales interest generated by the advertising, turning down the business it cannot handle. Thus, sales remain flat while profits actually decrease because of the extra money spent on unnecessary promotion. Since most companies must expand under a mode of controlled growth, the all-you-can-afford method is rarely sensible.

The only time you can apply the all-you-can-afford method is in situations where the following three conditions are met:

- You can handle all the business and as many sales or inquiries as your advertising can generate.
- Money spent on advertising generates an immediate and measurable return in excess of its cost. That is, a dollar spent on advertising yields at least $1.30 (and preferably $1.50 to $2 or more) in net revenue.
- The threat of competitors moving in to copycat your marketing or product provides pressure to capture the market as soon as possible before competitors can follow suit.

Successful mail order operators often use the all-you-can-afford method. When test ads prove profitable, they immediately put the profits generated into more ads on a larger scale. When these pay off, that money goes into still more advertising, for as long as it is profitable and before competitors can "knock off" the product or ad generating the revenue. Fad and "craze" businesses also use this method since they too must quickly grab all the sales they can before imitators and competitors take away their customers.

Formula 7: Seat-of-the-Pants Method

The seventh method of setting the advertising budget is not to set one, that is, to "feel" your way along on a month-by-month basis without any formal plan, to step up marketing efforts when you see an opportunity, and to pull back when you are flush with business or, conversely, when spending money is tight.

Advertising professionals and consultants quite naturally hate this method and think any one who uses it is a boob. Perhaps I should agree. But the fact is, I have several entrepreneurial clients who operate this way and are tremendously successful—many have become millionaires through their current businesses. I know this approach cannot work when the entrepreneurial firm grows, becomes more complex, and forms into a larger corporation with departments and specialists and structure and multiple layers of management. But for the smaller entrepreneurial firm, where the guiding force is an entrepreneur with superior marketing instincts, seat-of-the-pants advertising management can and does work—much to the chagrin of consultants like myself.

One Sensible Solution

While you are free to use any of these seven methods in selecting a dollar amount for your annual advertising expenditure, I use a method that combines several of the other methods and, I think, makes the most sense:

1. First, use the percentage of sales method to set an upper and lower limit on your budget. For example, let's say in your industry it is typical to spend between 1 to 2 percent of sales on advertising and promotion, and that your sales are $10 million a year. Your advertising budget would be between $100,000 and $200,000.

2. Now step back and take an objective look at the competitive environment, the marketplace, and your own operation. You might set your budget at the upper end of the range if:
   - The competition is doing heavy advertising and promotion
   - Your markets are expanding
   - Favorable economic considerations are causing a a general rise in consumer spending
   - You are introducing a hot new product

   On the other hand, you might set your advertising budget at the lower end of the range if:
   - There is little competition or the competition is inactive in marketing or promotion, *and you have all the sales you want without heavy marketing effort*
   - Your markets are contracting or shrinking
   - A decline in the economy has had an adverse impact on consumer spending
   - Your operating costs have risen to the point where it is essential that you make cuts in spending
   - You are introducing no new products and instead have a line of older products that are steady but reliable sellers
3. Now that you have evaluated the sales environment, and have established a budget range, allocate money to complete specific tasks that will achieve your planned objectives (the task-and-objective method).

   Example: How do you allocate money to specific tasks that will achieve a planned objective? Let's say you run a graphic design studio and your objective is to get six new accounts. You know from past experience that doing a direct mail promotion costs you $1,000 per thousand pieces mailed, that you get a 6 percent response rate (60 inquiries per thousand pieces mailed), and that one-tenth of the prospects making inquiries become clients. Therefore, to get six new clients (one-tenth of 60), you need to mail 1,000 direct mail pieces, and you would budget $1,000.

Additional Budget-Setting Guidelines

Here are 10 additional factors to consider when determining your advertising budget. These guidelines are based on a thorough study of the marketing activities of more than 1,000 businesses producing capital goods, raw and semi-finished materials, components, and supplies. The study was performed by The Strategic Planning Institute (SPI) of Cambridge, MA.

1. *The higher your company's market share, the more you should spend on advertising.* Market share is the single most important determinant of absolute marketing expenditure. For example, SPI found that a company with a 30 percent market share is likely to spend three times as much on advertising as a company with a 9 percent market share.

2. *Companies launching new products have to spend more on advertising than companies with mature or old products.* Introducing many new products to the market dramatically increases your advertising expenditures. In fact, the new-product innovator will spend more than twice as much on advertising and promotion as a business with few new products.

A corollary of this rule is that the higher the level of new product activity in the market, the higher will be the marketing expenditures of all companies in that market. The reason is that high levels of new-product activity in a market increase advertising expenditures significantly as competitors inform potential customers of features and benefits of their offerings and maneuver for superior market-share positions.

3. *Fast-growing markets typically require higher ad expenditure.* In rapidly growing markets, businesses must spend substantially more than in mature markets where buyers know all the suppliers and have relatively well-established relationships. As an example, compare the marketing dollars being spent on promoting laptop computer "notebooks" against the amount spent to promote staplers.

In many cases, the fast-growth market may be new and innovative, and the product's features may not yet be well-known to potential customers. A special effort is then needed to educate them and overcome buying resistance caused by skepticism, high switching costs, or sheer inertia. This effort translates into higher marketing expenditures.

The relationship between the rate of market growth and the level of advertising expenditure is illustrated in Table 7.6.

Table 7.6. Advertising expenditures as a function of growth rate.

Rate of Market Growth	*Annual Percentage Market Growth*	*Advertising Expenditures per $1,000 Market Sales*
No growth	0.0–0.9%	$0.95
Slow growth	1.0–4.9%	$0.95
Moderate growth	5.0%–11.9%	$1.20
Rapid growth	12.0% and up	$1.30

4. *Advertising expenditures are higher when a large amount of your plant's production capacity is under-used.* When production capacity is available, marketing expenditure increases. In particular, firms with a large fixed-asset base cannot afford to have production idled. They turn to advertising and promotion in order to load capacity. Businesses require lower advertising expenditures as production capacity fills up. To generate demand without adequate capacity may result in dissatisfied customers.

Sometimes a business that wishes to enter a new market or capitalize on market growth will build production capacity in anticipation of demand. In this case, its managers tend to spend advertising dollars readily to make fixed investment productive and to capture market share.

The relationship between advertising expenditures and capacity utilization as found by SPI is illustrated in Table 7.7.

5. *High levels of advertising and promotion are required for "low-ticket" items.* Advertising expenditures decline as purchase amounts rise. A business whose end users typically buy in amounts of less than $100 spends nearly twice the amount on advertising and three times as much on sales promotion than a business that sells large-ticket items costing $100,000 per unit.

What accounts for this? It may be that high-ticket items are more likely to be customized and price insensitive when performance is at stake, while low-ticket items are more frequently standardized, price sensitive, and likely to be pushed through channels by discounting and other promotional practices. Also, high-ticket items are purchased less frequently, and for that reason demand a less constant persuasive sales effort.

But perhaps the greatest factor at work here is that businesses selling large-ticket items can market them directly to a few large customers, while businesses selling small-ticket products must push them through wholesale and multi-level distribution channels. Some industries have huge economies of scale created by focusing on a few large customers.

The relationship between purchase price of item and advertising expenditure is shown in Table 7.8.

Table 7.7. Advertising expenditures as a function of how "busy" the company is.

% Capacity Utilized	*Media Advertising and Sales Promotion per $1,000 of Market Sales*
under 65%	$3.60
65–74.9%	$2.80
75–84.9%	$2.90
over 85%	$2.50

Table 7.8. Advertising expenditures as a function of price of product.

Cost of Item	*Media Advertising and Sales Promotion per $1,000 of Sales*
less than $100	$5.00
$100-$999	$3.60
$1,000-$9,999	$3.20
$10,000-$99,999	$2.80
$100,000 and over	$1.80

6. *The less your product represents as a percentage of the customer's total purchases, the greater the advertising and sales promotion expenditures.* SPI's research revealed a strong relationship between the amount a customer purchases of a given product and the level of advertising required to sell that product. Take business products, for example. A business product that represents less than 1 percent of the buyer's total purchases requires a 31 percent greater level of advertising than a product that represents 10 percent of the customer's total purchases.

What's the reason? A good guess is that the frequently purchased product, *because* it is so frequently ordered, is foremost on the prospect's mind . . . and so he doesn't need advertising to remind him about it. The product that is bought only once in a while, on the other hand, is rarely though about, so advertising is needed to remind the prospect and provide a buying source when the need for the product does arise.

7. *Products at both the low and high ends of the price range (discount products and premium products) require higher ad expenditures.* The conventional wisdom in marketing is that you must support a premium price position in the market with aggressive advertising and sales promotion. This is needed to convince the customer that the quality of the product translates into superior value for the premium price.

However, SPI research revealed that discount pricing may also require more marketing support than do products priced "average" in their category. Perhaps extra effort is needed to convince the customer that the function for which the product is bought will be delivered—but at a better price. SPI found that discount-priced products required approximately 39 percent greater advertising and promotion expenditure than the average-priced products, while premium-priced products required 72 percent greater advertising and promotion expenditure than the product of average price in its category.

8. *High quality products typically require higher advertising expenditures.* The relationship SPI found between relative product quality (as measured by a variety of product and service attributes) and media advertising and sales promotion expenditures is shown in Table 7.9.

Table 7.9. Advertising expenditures as a function of product quality.

Relative Product-quality Rating	*Media Advertising and Sales Promotion Expenditure per $1,000 of Market Sales*
Poor quality (lowest rating)	$1.50
Fair	$1.80
Average	$2.10
Good	$2.60
Excellent	$3.40

A corollary of factors 7 and 8 is that businesses that have high relative product quality but provide greater value to the customer through lower relative pricing can spend less on advertising. This is obviously a trade-off between pricing and advertising expenditures. The business that provides a more favorable price-to-performance ratio (charges less for premium quality) can afford to spend less than its competitor that offers the same high quality but wants to charge a premium price for it.

Also, a business that, through marketing communications, positions its product as the premium product in the marketplace must spend two to three times as much on advertising than its competition to create and maintain that position. However, SPI found that the businesses that have established a premium product position typically hold the number-one share in their markets.

9. *Broad product lines typically require higher advertising expenditures.* An additional dimension of product positioning and business strategy is the breadth of product line relative to competitors. Experience indicates that manufacturers with broad product lines support their sales force with aggressive advertising and promotion. SPI research showed that companies with broad product lines spent an average of 71 percent more on advertising and promotion than companies with narrow product lines.

10. *Standard or "off-the-shelf" products require higher levels of advertising expenditure than custom products.* Customized products require less marketing support than standardized ones. The reason is that, when products must be produced to the customer's specifications, the cost of switching suppliers may be high and alternative sources may not be readily available. Quality may be important, and the customer may be reluctant to leave a reliable supplier.

Markets for standardized products, on the other hand, are more susceptible to product substitution. Purchase decisions are more likely to be affected by price and less influenced by personal relationships with the supplier. As a result, greater marketing support is required to communicate product and company benefits. SPI found that companies supplying standard products spent, on average, 60 percent more on advertising and promotion than companies that provide customized products tailored to the buyer's specifications.

Advertising Budgeting: A Panel Discussion

A panel of members of the Business/Professional Advertising Association met in Houston to discuss advertising budgeting. Included in the panel were two ad agency presidents, the marketing communications manager of a major industrial firm, the assistant to the president of public affairs and advertising of another firm, and the director of marketing communications for a major industrial company.

The format of the meeting called for a moderator who posed key questions to the panel. Each member answered the question and the panel discussed various aspects of the answer.

The first key question posed to the panel was, "What are the major problems with budgeting for a company or client advertising program?" The panel identified these four key difficulties:

First, the person with the power to approve budgets often lacks appreciation of the value of advertising investment; he or she is oriented in another direction.

Second, the budgets are the first item subject to change in business conditions. Worse, they are cut arbitrarily because the budget-cutters do not understand the function of advertising.

Third, the unwillingness of clients to do benchmark studies (discussed in Chapter 6) to measure what the advertising is trying to accomplish as a guide to setting realistic budgets to accomplish each objective.

Fourth, the inability to forecast with any degree of accuracy. Advertising should be tied to a profit plan or marketing plan. Once approved by management, the budget is an integral part of that plan and is changed only if the plan itself changes.

The second point addressed by the panel was that management often has difficulty understanding advertising and setting objectives for it. Panel members discussed aspects of this problem. They agreed that most managers who control budgets have a low level of appreciation of what advertising can do or how much it costs.

Management is not the only factor culpable; ad agency people often arbitrarily raise or lower budgets without reference to objectives of a campaign or program.

The third point addressed by the panel was, "Just what elements of communications make up a budget?" One panelist listed media, media production, direct mail, trade shows, audio-visual programs, and literature—everything except public relations. Another commented, "We include every single thing that has to do with the public, except when salespeople take prospects to lunch."

The fourth point involved approval of budget by top management. In corporations, advertising executives tend to report to upper management echelons. In ad agencies, however, there are problems reaching those levels. Often programs and budgets must be given to the advertising manager, who then makes another presentation to top management. "We lose control completely," one agency president commented. Whether the budget survives often depends on the skill of the advertising manager.

Another element in the survival of the ad budget is the orientation of the top executive. If he comes from the accounting side, he will be less interested and informed. If he comes from the sales side, he will understand more fully the role of advertising.

Marketing communications and ad agency executives alike have become adept in planning over-estimation of budgets. Some have "slush funds" built up over long time periods to take care of unplanned necessities. One equated budgeting with selling a home. "You'd be absolutely crazy to start out asking the price you expected to get," he declared. To some degree, replied another panelist, all budgeting is hypocritical. It is the best estimate of needs at the moment, which is then etched in stone and must be lived with.

The fifth point involved budget control. Three panelists use a log or job number system to track what has been spent on individual projects and elements within those projects. Each phase or element is assigned a number within the overall job number. The final expenditure can then be compared to the estimate or allocation for that project and over- or underspending can be determined.

How do panelists present their budgets for approval? Answers ranged from "I just send it to the president" to making elaborate multiprojector slide presentations. A simple narrative explaining what is going to be done and how much it will cost represents one end of the scale. A full and frank point-by-point discussion with top management represents the other end.

Panelists provided the following advice on how to be a good budgeting manager:

- Develop the ability to delegate. Delegate various aspects of budgeting to your internal and agency people. From the data they generate, you can make a rational budget.
- Find out where you are, so you can tell where you want to go.
- Question each item in last year's budget. Was it effective? Do you need it? Do you need more money?
- Set definite objectives and spend what you have to in order to reach them.
- View advertising as an investment, not a cost. Allocate funds the same way as adding another salesperson or buying another piece of equipment.
- Treat advertising as if it were that salesperson or piece of equipment. Justify its cost. Track its results.

Allocating The Budget For Maximum Results

Once you have determined the total dollar amount you can spend on advertising and promotion, you must allocate it among the many tasks, markets, products, and divisions within your company that need these resources. Allocation may be by one or more of the following categories:

Division

Large corporations have numerous divisions, each with their separate advertising goals and objectives. The first step is to allocate the corporate budget, dividing it between the various divisions. How do you do this? Each division should come up with a divisional budget figure based on the methods outlined in this chapter. The corporate advertising manager evaluates these for accuracy, then allocates the gross budget among the divisions according to their needs.

Departments

In the largest corporations, some divisions may be organized in subdivisions or departments, each with their own marketing activities and objectives. Again, you come up with a budget figure for the division based on the methods outlined above, then allocate the budget among the individual departments based on this analysis of needs.

Product

More likely than allocating among departments is the probability that a division will have to share its budget among a number of different products it sells. Each product manager should propose an advertising and promotion budget for his or her product, justifying it with calculations based on the methods outlined in this chapter. Then the division manager allocates a share of the overall budget to each product based on the product manager's analysis of how much money is needed to achieve his marketing objectives.

Product line

If product managers are responsible for a *line* of products rather than individual products, each product manager's annual advertising budget can be allocated for the entire line rather than individual products—especially if the company markets the line as a line rather than as individual elements.

Markets

Some companies organize their marketing efforts by market rather than by product and should allocate the budget accordingly.

Media

Most companies like to have a sense of where and how advertising dollars are being spent. You may want to set your budget so that specific percentages are spent on various media: so much for direct mail, so much for trade shows, so much for magazine ads, etc.

Month

When creating your advertising plan, keep in mind that in your business some months may be better sales months than others, and you may want to allocate your budget accordingly. Many business-to-business marketers cut back on advertising in the summer and during the Christmas holidays but spend heavily in January and February, when most prospects begin spending their annual budgets for acquiring new products, and in September, when many prospects are planning their expenditures for the coming year. Mail order catalog and gift marketers, on the other hand, spend heavily in November and December because most of their sales are made in the Christmas season.

Tip: The forms reproduced as Figures 7.1, 7.2, 7.3, and 7.4 will be most helpful in allocating your budget by media and month. You can photocopy these forms and do a separate budget breakdown for each product, product line, and division. You can also do an overall budget worksheet for the entire corporation, if you wish.

Figure 7.1. Sample annual advertising budget.

	Advertising Budget						
Month	*Total*	*Magazines*	*News-paper*	*TV*	*Radio*	*Direct Mail*	*PR*
January							
February							
March							
April							
May							
June							
July							
August							
September							
October							
November							
December							
Total							

Figure 7.2. Sample annual advertising budget (filled out).

	Advertising Budget						
Month	*Total*	*Magazines*	*News-paper*	*TV*	*Radio*	*Direct Mail*	*PR*
January	$ 250	$ 150	$ 50	$ 50		$100	
February	250	150	50	50			$100
March	250	150	50	50		100	
April	300	150	75	100			75
May	250	150	50	150			
June	200	150	100	50			
July	250	150	50	50		100	
August	450	150	100	150			150
September	600	150	100	150			300
October	300	150	150	100			
November	400	150	100	100		150	
December	500	150	200	200			50
Total	$4,000	$1800	$1,075	$1,200		$450	$675

Figure 7.3. Advertising media budget.

19_____ Advertising Media Program and Budget
Advertising Budget $ _____

Media	*Annual $ Expenditures*	*Frequency*	*Ad Size*
Print			
Newspaper			
*(1)*__________			
*(2)*__________			
*(3)*__________			
Consumer Magazine			
*(1)*__________			
*(2)*__________			
*(3)*__________			
Trade Publication			
*(1)*__________			
*(2)*__________			
*(3)*__________			
Radio			
*AM (1)*__________			
*(2)*__________			
*(3)*__________			
*FM (1)*__________			
*(2)*__________			
*(3)*__________			
Television			
*(1)*__________			
*(2)*__________			
*(3)*__________			
Specialty			
*(1)*__________			
*(2)*__________			
*(3)*__________			
Direct Mail			
*(1)*__________			
*(2)*__________			
*(3)*__________			
Point of Purchase			
*(1)*__________			
*(2)*__________			
*(3)*__________			
Co-op			
*(1)*__________			
*(2)*__________			
*(3)*__________			
Other			
*(1)*__________			
*(2)*__________			
*(3)*__________			

Figure 7.4. Monthly ad placement costs.

Advertising Expenditures by Month by Media for 19____

Media	*Jan $'s*	*Feb $'s*	*Mar $'s*	*Apr $'s*	*May $'s*	*Jun $'s*
Print						
Newspaper						
(1)____						
(2)____						
(3)____						
Consumer Magazine						
(1)____						
(2)____						
(3)____						
Trade Publication						
(1)____						
(2)____						
(3)____						
Radio						
AM (1)____						
(2)____						
(3)____						
FM (1)____						
(2)____						
(3)____						
Television						
(1)____						
(2)____						
(3)____						
Specialty						
(1)____						
(2)____						
(3)____						
Direct Mail						
(1)____						
(2)____						
(3)____						
Point of Purchase						
(1)____						
(2)____						
(3)____						
Co-op						
(1)____						
(2)____						
(3)____						
Other						
(1)____						
(2)____						
(3)____						

Figure 7.4. (continued)

Advertising Expenditures by Month
by Media for 19____

Media	*Jul* *$'s*	*Aug* *$'s*	*Sep* *$'s*	*Oct* *$'s*	*Nov* *$'s*	*Dec* *$'s*
Print						
Newspaper						
(1)____________						
(2)____________						
(3)____________						
Consumer Magazine						
(1)____________						
(2)____________						
(3)____________						
Trade Publication						
(1)____________						
(2)____________						
(3)____________						
Radio						
AM (1)____________						
(2)____________						
(3)____________						
FM (1)____________						
(2)____________						
(3)____________						
Television						
(1)____________						
(2)____________						
(3)____________						
Specialty						
(1)____________						
(2)____________						
(3)____________						
Direct Mail						
(1)____________						
(2)____________						
(3)____________						
Point of Purchase						
(1)____________						
(2)____________						
(3)____________						
Co-op						
(1)____________						
(2)____________						
(3)____________						
Other						
(1)____________						
(2)____________						
(3)____________						

CHAPTER 8

The Advertising Plan

Key Considerations In Writing An Advertising Plan

In previous chapters we have addressed the key elements that go into the advertising planning process. These include:

- The elements of the marketing communications mix—the advertising and sales promotion tools available to use in your program
- The products you are selling, the markets you are selling them to, and the wants, needs, and desires of those target prospects
- The objectives of your advertising campaign—what you want it to accomplish
- The budget or the amount of money you can spend in pursuit of these objectives.

Having confronted these issues and identified the appropriate information, you now are faced with the task of putting it all down in a written advertising plan. The questions you may be asking at this point include:

- Do I even need a written or formal advertising plan?
- If I decide to write a plan, how do I go about it?
- What is the proper format for such a plan?

Let's first address the question of whether a plan is needed. Next, we'll look at the process to use in creating the advertising plan. Finally, we'll study a sample marketing communications plan, so you can get an idea of the format.

Do You Need An Advertising Plan?

Conventional wisdom dictates that anyone writing a text on advertising management would answer this question with a hearty, "Of course!" But experience teaches that the real-world answer is more of a "maybe."

Whether to create a written advertising plan depends, in part, on the corporate culture and nature of your company management. Is your management formal or informal? Do they tend to operate from written plans or by the seat of the pants? Are they planning-oriented, or do they react on a day-by-day basis to challenges and problems as they arise? If your management is reactive rather than proactive, a written plan may do nothing more than gather dust on the shelves. If your management is more structured, a written plan may be a well-appreciated tool that is used both to conduct marketing communications activities as well as to evaluate the results.

In a random, nationwide survey of more than 430 marketing communications managers and senior executives nationwide, *Business Marketing* magazine found that 80 percent of companies whose marketing communications programs were successful and exceeded expectations had a plan. In the weeks prior to the creation of the annual communications budget, the marketing communications managers at these firms were sitting down with senior executives and arriving at mutually agreed-upon objectives for their company's marketing communications programs and a plan to accomplish these objectives.

Among the senior executives surveyed, 91 percent who had a marketing communications plan incorporated this plan into their company's strategic business plan. Of the executives who did not have a communications plan, 79 percent wanted to have an advertising plan in the future. And 52 percent of planning-oriented executives expected a new marketing communications program to produce results in three months or less. These results are summarized in Table 8.1.

Table 8.1. How companies measure advertising results.

Measurement Method	*Percentage of Companies with Successful Marketing Communications Programs Using this Method*
Relating communications activities to sales or profits	39%
Number of leads generated	28%
Ad benchmark/readership studies	13%
Company awareness research	12%
Sales force feedback	12%

Marketing communications managers at companies running successful ad and promotion programs make sure they regularly communicate the progress and results of these programs to senior management. The methods by which they communicate with management are listed in Table 8.2.

Finally, marketing communications managers at companies with successful advertising and promotion programs tend to make full use of the broad range of marketing communications tools available to them, as is shown in Table 8.3.

The *Business Marketing* report concludes: "The moral? With markets becoming more fragmented and the buying decision getting more complex, communications planning is essential."

Table 8.2. How ad managers communicate with senior management.

Communications Method	*Percent of Marketing Communications Managers Using this Method*
Sales meeting presentations	24%
Written reports	22%
Meetings scheduled with boss	14%
Discussions over lunch, coffee, or drinks	10%
Periodic newsletter	8%
Phone calls	8%

Table 8.3. Promotional tools favored by marketing communications managers.

Tool	*Percentage Using this Tool*
Brochures	97%
Trade shows	97%
Media ads	94%
Inquiry management	91%
Public relations	86%
Direct mail	77%
Communications planning	73%
Audiovisual	71%
Communications research	63%
Telemarketing	57%

The Planning Process

Advertising planning is not a complex or specialized procedure. Mostly, it's common sense. It consists of sitting down and thinking about what your marketing problem is and how to solve it, then developing those thoughts more fully on paper. The best advertising plan is simply a discussion on paper, in narrative form, of the problems facing the company, the objectives that must be met, and your proposed solutions (the advertising).

Ray Jutkins, of Nelson Panullo Jutkins Direct Marketing in Santa Monica, California, provides the following framework for creating an effective advertising/marketing communications plan. His outline, which is reprinted with his permission, covers the areas of information essential to establish a marketing communications plan that is effective, efficient, and highly targeted.

The Eight-Point Market Action Plan

1. *Clearly state your OBJECTIVES for your particular program.*
   - Projected total sales revenue, short and long term?
   - Projected sales revenue by individual product?
   - What is the target cost per lead?
   - What is the target cost per sales close?
   - What is your geographic sales pattern? locally? regionally? throughout the country?
   - Is there a seasonal pattern that should be addressed?
   - Are there any legal or other marketing restrictions?
   - What is the industry history?
   - What is your corporate history?
   - What is the previous sales trend or direction?
   - Is it the same today as in the past?
   - What is the advertising/marketing history? Did it meet your objectives, fall short, or surpasss plan?
2. *Define a TIMETABLE to accomplish specific objectives.*
   - By quarter, what objectives do you wish to reach?
   - What is your national advertising schedule?
   - How does the fiscal year/calendar year affect your scheduling?

3. *Establish a BUDGET to meet your objectives within a timeframe.*
    - What is your budget history?
    - Where have you invested your advertising/marketing dollars in the recent past?
    - Where do you see the major emphasis for next year's budget?
    - What is your prime competitor's share of the market compared to yours?
    - How much do they invest to maintain that share? How do they spend it?
    - What is your total advertising budget?
    - How is the budget allocated by quarter? by month?
    - Is the budget available on an accelerated schedule, if necessary, to meet seasonal or unusual opportunities?
4. *Clearly identify your target market AUDIENCE.*
    - What is the size of the market for your product line?
    - How can that market be expanded?
    - How can it be exploited?
    - Is your product marketed to a particular segment of the community?
    - Can you clearly identify those segments?
    - Does research define the measurable characteristics of the prospective customer?
    - Who are your current customers?
    - How many of them are there?
    - Do they share any common characteristics?
    - What does the current customer buy?
    - For how long do they remain customers?
    - What additional products and services can they be sold?
    - Does the profile of your current customer meet the profile of your potential customer?
    - If not, what is the profile of your best prospect?
5. *Create and define your OFFER.*
    - Who is your competition and what are they offering?
    - What are your unique selling propositions?
    - What are the unique selling propositions of your competitors?

- What are your weaknesses? your competitors'?
- How does your price compare with the competition—competitive, discount, or premium?
- Is an incentive or premium desired or needed to capture sales?
- How does the customer benefit from using your product?
- What benefits do you offer prospects?
- What does market research say about the position of your product?
- Can this position be improved or redirected?
- How can you communicate this new position to your audience?

6. *Set direction for your CREATIVE—the copy and art.*
   - What is the best way to articulate your product positioning, features, and benefits?
   - How do they differ from the competition?
   - Are buying incentives desired or needed?
   - What buying incentives should be used? and when?
   - How do you present these incentives to gain a call to action?
   - How many steps should there be in the sales cycle? one? two? three?
   - In what vehicle should your message be communicated? ads? brochures? telephone? broadcast? direct mail?
   - How does demographic and psychographic data on the market affect the creative approach?

7. *Select MEDIA.*
   - Which media are best suited for communicating your product benefits?
   - Which media are best suited for motivating your prospects to action?
   - Which media will best reach your target audience?
   - Can the medium be used effectively for direct response marketing?
   - Is the product to be marketed geographically? If so, what are the boundaries of the medium?
   - Can the medium selected be used regionally? nationally?
   - Are there seasonal variations in expected response levels that will affect media scheduling?

- Will scheduling be affected by other activities within the company, such as special promotions, trade show exhibits, or industry events, such as major conferences or conventions?
- In print media, how much space is needed to present the offer?
- In broadcast media, how much time is required to sell the offer, present the product, and maximize response?
- What media mix will produce the desired sales volume results, within the budget parameters, the time-frame, and meet your marketing criteria?
- What is the relative cost efficiency and response potential of each medium?
- Within a particular medium, which vehicles will reach your target audience most effectively and efficiently?
- What response must be generated to achieve the target cost per inquiry and cost per sales close?
- In space, is the editorial environment compatible with your product? Is other advertising/marketing in the publication compatible with your company?
- Where is the competition advertising?
- Is there a duplication of audience between the various media selected? If so, can one medium (or several) be safely eliminated with no decline in sales results?
- Does the overall schedule achieve the desired level of frequency?
- What percentage of promotional effort is being devoted to your current customer base?

8. *ANALYZE the results.*
   There are four key points to establishing a good evaluation. You want to know:
   - What worked?
   - What did not work?
   - Why?
   - What are you going to do about it, now that you know what worked and what did not?

   Here are some specific things to look for when analyzing specific ads, promotions, or media:
   - Response level

- Cost per response
- Cost per order
- Sales generated per dollar spent on advertising

Additional factors to consider:

- How valuable is the "new" customer?
- Does he buy additional products and services? How long does he remain a customer?
- Which media produce the greatest number of high-value new customers?
- Which creative offer, approach, or format produced the most cost-efficient response and additional business?

Case History: Marketing Communications Plan For A Service Firm

The following is the actual planning process used to create a working marketing communications plan for a firm selling highly specialized business services. All references to the nature of the service and the market being served have been deleted and the dollar figures and the names of various media have been changed to protect the identity of the firm.

Here are the elements of the plan. Note that this is one of many formats that can be used. You can follow any format you please. The main thing is to keep the plan simple, write in plain English, and explain the rationale or thinking behind each item in the plan so you can "sell" it to management.

Sample Marketing Communications Plan for Service Company

A. Cover Letter

The first page is a cover letter or letter of transmittal. This simply tells the reader what is attached and tells him how he should be thinking as he reads and evaluates the material.

Here is a typical letter of transmittal:

Mr. George Smith
President
ABC Company
Anytown, USA

Dear Mr. Smith:

Here is the preliminary marketing plan for ABC Company. It covers marketing activities for 19XX.

The important thing to remember is that this is a *working* plan that should be adjusted to fit the current situation, not a commandment etched in stone. If something works well and is profitable for us, we should do more of the same—even if it's not on the plan. If something is unprofitable, we should drop it—even though we scheduled more of it for later in the year.

Sincerely,

Your Name, Advertising Management Consultant

B. Introduction

Here, in plain, simple language, summarize your overall sales goal. Sometimes this is stated as an image or position the company wants to achieve. In this case, where the goal was to increase sales of the service, use specific numbers to show exactly where you are—and where you want to go:

Introduction

Our goal is to increase sales by 35 percent over the next 12 months.

A 35 percent increase would mean annual revenues increasing from $10 million in 19XX, to $14 million in 19XX—$4 million more in sales per year.

At an average revenue of $10,000 per order, we would need to go from 1,000 orders per year to 1,400 orders per year—or from 19 to 27 orders per week.

As our profit margin on these sales is approximately 50 percent, this sales increase will result in an additional $2 million in profits for the coming calendar year.

C. Objectives

In this section we list specific objectives that will contribute toward achieving the overall sales goal. The service firm, ABC Company, offers a variety of services, some profitable, some marginal. The advertising plan must indicate whether the money will be spent expanding the sales of already proven services or trying to boost sales for poor-performing areas. Generally, the better strategy is to support your winners with the most advertising dollars and not spend on products or services that are not marketable.

Here is the "objectives" section from the plan for ABC Company:

Objectives of the Program

1. Most of our time and effort will go toward promoting our two most profitable services—Service A and Service B. At least three-quarters of the budget will go toward increasing sales of these services.

2. Approximately 20 percent of our budget, time and effort will be spent marketing our new service, Service C. Although not a big seller in the past, new market conditions indicate that this could be a big profit center accounting for up to 20 percent of revenues within the next 3 to 5 years.

3. Our main goal is to increase sales by generating high-quality leads that result in quotations—that in turn, result in a sale.

4. "Image building," or keeping our name before the marketplace, is a secondary concern and will not be our primary objective.

5. Based on our analysis of past marketing activities, our "average" cost to generate a sales lead is $95. Therefore, any promotion that falls significantly below this mark is cost-effective, while any promotion that brings in leads at an inquiry cost of, say, over $100, will have to be examined closely. (This assumes a good quality lead, of course.)

D. Market Analysis

The market analysis section typically contains:

- Description of the different markets for the product or service
- Share of market held by you and by your competitors
- Numbers indicating size of each market and whether the market is expanding or contracting
- Comments on the buying habits of the market and the best way to sell to each particular group of prospects

In the case of this sample marketing communications plan, ABC Company sells all its services to a single market. Also there is no analysis of market share because ABC Company is the only major vendor providing special services to this market. Here is an excerpt from the plan:

Market Analysis

We estimate that there are 15,000 firms in the United States that own one or more XYZ machines requiring our repair, maintenance, and support services. Each owns an average of 4 machines for a total market of 60,000 machines in operation.

We estimate that of these machines:

- 10 percent are new and still under manufacturer's warranty
- 20 percent are relatively new and under extended warranty or a manufacturer's service plan
- 20 percent are serviced by in-house technicians (representing the larger firms that are able to maintain such technical personnel on staff).
- 10 percent are serviced by other sources, such as small independent mom-and-pop service firms.

This leaves 40 percent of the machines, or 24,000 machines, requiring service.

Since the reliability of this type of equipment is such that service is required only once a year, then 1/52nd of these 24,000 units, or 461 machines, are in need of service in any given week.

With a current level of 19 orders per week, we are servicing only 4 percent of this market. An increase to 6 percent market share will give us our target volume of 27 orders per week.

Why, with so little competition, is our market share so small? We know that these are the primary reasons:

- Most machine owners do not make repairs, but continue to operate machines not working at peak efficiency and are not even aware of the degree of wear and inefficiency they face.
- Manufacturers encourage frequent trade-in and replacement of machines rather than repair and offer attractive terms that prompt most customers to keep replacing machines every few years before the need for our service is perceived as serious.

E. Overview of Marketing Communications Campaign

Before getting into details of what ads will be created and where they will run, give an overview of what marketing communications tools have been selected to achieve the sales objective. From the sample plan:

Overview of the Marketing Campaign

Aside from creating a new catalog, the bulk of our effort will be in generating leads and inquiries via direct mail.

We will also use PR activities to supplement direct mail and enhance our image.

Advertising, not proven successful in generating quality leads or a high volume of sales, will be reduced; however, we will continue a limited schedule in a few select publications.

Another key addition to our program will be *database marketing*—continued contacting of our database customers and prospects. Based on last year's results in this area, database marketing may be our most profitable activity.

F. Marketing Communications Plan and Schedule

The next and largest part of the marketing communications plan is a breakdown of the specific activities that make up the program.

Some planners use oversize worksheets that organize activity by calendar month. Large plans may even require separate worksheets for each month. Other planners use separate worksheets for each product or product line.

You can use any format that works for you and that clearly shows people what you are doing—and why you are doing it. One technique is to create a separate plan for each product line or group of related services and break it down by specific marketing communications tool, with one section relating direct mail activities, the next section giving the print media schedule, the third section showing trade show activity, and so on.

In the case of the sample plan for ABC Company, there is only one schedule, since all services are related and are sold to the same group of buyers. Here is the sample plan:

Marketing Communications Plan

Direct Mail Activities:
We will do three major mailings of approximately 10,000 to 20,000 pieces each.

Mailings will be dropped in late March or April, June, and September.

The mailing package will consist of a cover letter, the color service flier, and a reply card. Letters mailed to XYZ machine owners will be tailored to four titles:

- Plant engineer
- Purchasing agent
- Maintenance engineer
- Vice President of Operations

We will key and test a variety of list sources, including rented lists (Edith Roman catalog), subscription lists, and compiled lists (i.e., lists we input from directories and other information sources).

Among the lists to be tested:

XYZ Machine Buyers—42,950
PURCHASING TODAY subscriber list—12,504
PLANT ENGINEERING subscriber list—20,585
BUYER LIST: ABC BALL BEARING CO.—15,390 (note: these are special ball bearings used in the repair of XYZ machines)
PLASTICS EXPO trade show attendee list—10,338
AMERICAN SOCIETY OF MAINTENANCE MANAGERS membership list—4,980

Cost of the mailing is approximately $500 per thousand—$15,000 for 30,000 pieces and $30,000 for 60,000 pieces.

We will experiment with different letters and offers. Our first letter should probably offer the "Free Machine Evaluation," since this has been our most successful offer to date.

Catalog:
We are currently producing a new catalog to replace the existing catalog. The new piece is designed to graphically enhance our image, contain up-to-date information on our services, and position us as the leader in the field.

We estimate producing an initial run of 20,000 catalogs. Cost: $________

Premium:
We will develop a leave-behind premium for our salespeople to leave on the prospect's desk after a sales call. (Premium will also be suitable for mailing.)

Cost: approximately $2 to $4 per unit, depending on quantity ordered.

Publicity Releases:
Publicity releases get us exposure we cannot afford to buy with ad dollars and also generate a high volume of leads at extremely low cost.

Here is our schedule for mailing publicity releases:
March—Background release on our company (to Ohio business publications and business sections of Ohio newspapers)
May—New literature release on updated catalog
July—Release on "How to maintain XYZ machines"
September—Release on preventive maintenance program
November—Release on how to perform your own machine inspection

Additional publicity:

- PLANT ENGINEERING article on "10 ways to improve XYZ machine performance"

Press releases allow us to reach readers of numerous publications—far more that we could afford to advertise in. These include:

- 110 engineering publications
- 8 plant publications
- 6 purchasing publications

Cost for printing and mailing/distribution of 2-page press release to approximately 500 contacts: $224 plus postage.

For five releases, this comes to a total of $1,120.

Database Marketing:
"Database marketing" is defined as promotions aimed at our existing list of current customers, past customers (who are now inactive), and prospects (sales leads).

First, we will expand our database to include all of the following:

- Current customers
- Customers who bought from us in the past but are not now using our services
- Inquiries and leads from past 3 years in paper file system (must be converted to computer database)
- In addition, we will automatically capture and add to the database the names of people who respond to an ad, a mailer, our catalog, or any other promotion.

Next, we will contact this database at least three times during the year using a series of letter mailings:

- *April/May*—mail a sales letter introducing our new catalog (which will be enclosed).

- *August*—mail promotion featuring rebuilding service and sale of rebuilt XYZ machines. Possible offer: "Old-customer" discount.
- *October*—mail promotion on our Preventive Maintenance/Service contracts. Objective: Get inactive but satisfied customers to reestablish their relationship with us. Get current customers to sign up for regular service.

NOTE: Experience proves that marketing to a database of existing customers and prospects will yield up to 10 times the response of mailings aimed at "cold" (rented and compiled) prospect lists.

COST: No outside printing or production costs if the database mailings are handled in-house.

Postcard Decks:

XYZ MACHINE OWNERS CARD DECK (sponsored by manufacturers coop)
Date: April
Circulation: 75,000
Cost: $1,950

PLANT ENGINEERING DECK
Date: Spring
Circulation: 29,704
Cost: $1,305

McKnight (owners of PURCHASING NEWS)
Date: July
Circulation: 15,000
Cost: $1,200

Advertising Schedule:

PURCHASING WORLD

Ad: "How to save money on XYZ machine maintenance"

Our current ad is a ⅔ standard page.
Size is 10″ deep by 4 $^{9}/_{16}$″ wide.
Cost per insertion is $3,100 (2X rate).

We will condense the current ad (and eliminate coupon).
New size: ¼ standard page.
Size is 3⅜″ wide by 4⅞″ deep.
Cost per insertion (2X rate): $1,130.

We will run the ad in February (already inserted) and again in September.
Total cost: $2,260

NOTE: September is a special issue for the World Purchasing Show

SHOP FLOOR MACHINE CARE:

Current ad: "Your single source for XYZ machine care"
Our current ad is a ⅔-page standard (4½ × 10″)
2X rate is $1,775 per insertion

We will condense (and eliminate coupon) to reduce ad size.
New size: ¼ page square (3⅜ × 4⅞″)
Cost: $750 per insertion

We will run in August and October.
Total Cost: $1,500.

G. Schedule and Costs

The final section is an appendix consisting of worksheets showing the entire advertising and promotion schedule and associated costs. These may be written in narrative form, table form, or using scheduling sheets. You may use the forms provided in Chapter 7.

Additional Tips On Creating The Advertising Plan

1. Most companies have calendar-year plans running from January to December of a given year.

2. If you have a calendar-year plan that begins with January of the coming year, the best time to begin planning is September of this year. Try to get the budget approved by October or November, but certainly no later than December.

3. The tendency when making cost estimates is to under-estimate so that the budget can be stretched to cover more items. But it's better to allocate your budget based on an honest estimate of costs so you can more realistically see what you can afford—and what you cannot afford.

4. Establish a "contingency" fund as a separate line item in the budget. This fund covers unexpected expenditures (e.g., management decides they want a 16-page brochure instead of a 12-page brochure), uncertain-

ties in cost estimates, and the unavoidable rise in media and production costs. This fund should be 5 to 10 percent of the total budget.

5. Create a separate advertising plan for each product (or, if you sell one product, for each market). Each product deserves and needs its own well thought out marketing strategy.

6. If you have to "sell" the ideas, concepts, and items in the plan to senior management, put into the plan as much narrative text for explanation and support of your ideas as is required. Think of the plan not just as a budget or a schedule but as a selling document. If it doesn't sell management on your ideas, it won't be approved.

7. To make accurate cost estimates of line items on the budget, go to two or three vendors, describe the generic type of project, and ask for *rough* or "ball park" estimates of the cost. Do this until you have a pretty good idea of what a typical ad, brochure, or any other promotion will cost so that you can simply plug this rough figure into the budget as necessary.

8. Realize that vendors can't and won't be held to estimates made off the cuff based on rough descriptions of a project. Although such estimates are vital for putting down some numbers in your plan, and vendors are happy to cooperate, the actual estimate cannot be made accurately unless detailed specifications for the specific project are in hand. And vendors, like advertising managers, tend to underestimate when giving "ball park" figures.

9. Put a paragraph in your plan that says something along these lines: "Of course, this is a preliminary plan only, not a rigid schedule etched in stone. The key to success will be flexibility to react and respond to changing market conditions and sales opportunities." This says to senior management, in effect, "Just because we have a written plan doesn't mean we have to follow it to the letter or can't make changes in midstream if a new strategy is called for." Be flexible.

10. You will have to determine your basic marketing communications and sales objectives yourself or by working with the sales managers, marketing managers, product managers, and brand managers in your company. No outsider can do it for you. However, you can rely on your agency for support and advice on planning advertising concepts and media schedules. Take advantage of their expertise by making them part of the planning process early.

PART II

TASKS

CHAPTER 9

Magazine Ads

Specialized Magazines For Specialized Markets

According to *Louis Rukeyser's Business Almanac,* the first magazine ad in America appeared in Ben Franklin's *General Magazine* in 1741. While magazines and magazine advertising continue to flourish, the age of the general magazine is just about over. They have been largely replaced by specialized magazines catering to narrower and narrower target audiences with more highly specialized interests.

For example, while computer magazines were once a specialty in themselves, now the field is so highly specialized that there are separate magazines for people using IBM personal computers vs. Apple Macintosh computers. The current volume of *Bacon's Publicity Checker,* a directory of magazines, lists more than 7,000 weekly and monthly trade journals and consumer magazines published annually in the United States. The publications are grouped into more than 600 categories ranging from abrasives and accessory merchandising to yachting and youth magazines. Some of the titles include *Hog Farm Management, Sludge Newsletter, Toxic Materials, Valve Magazine, Hydrocarbon Processing, Export Today, Candy*

Wholesaler, and *The American Journal of Sports Medicine.* Circulations range from less than 10,000 to over 1 million.

According to a report in the January 1989 issue of *Direct Marketing* magazine, approximately $6.1 billion was spent by national advertisers in 1988 on magazine advertising—up 8 percent from the previous year. This represents approximately 9 percent of the total national media budget of $66 billion. Advertisers spent more on network TV ($9.4 billion) and direct mail ($21.2 billion); less on cable TV ($0.9 billion), network radio ($0.4 billion), and newspaper advertising ($3.6 billion).

Magazines Are More Targeted

What is the main difference between magazine advertising and newspaper advertising? Actually, there are several differences, including frequency (newspapers are published daily or weekly, while magazines are published weekly or monthly), quality of reproduction (newspapers are black ink on newsprint, while most magazines offer four-color reproduction on glossy coated stock), and size (most newspapers are tabloids, while most magazines are 7 by 10 inches).

But the most critical difference is that newspapers target their audiences *geographically* (by city or region), while magazines target by industry, job, or type of interest. In this, magazines are more like cable television, which has many small channels aimed at special interest audiences and covering narrow topics, while newspaper advertising is more like broadcast television, targeting a mass audience. This is summed up in Table 9.1.

How To Advertise In Different Types Of Magazines

There was a time when magazines, like newspapers, catered to a general, mass audience. Publications such as *Life* and *The Saturday Evening Post* carried a broad spectrum of reading material designed to cater to all tastes, and they were read primarily for entertainment, not information.

Today, all that has changed. Although magazines still entertain us, the secondary goal of informing the reader on a topic of special interest has become more predominant—and in many cases, the information content of the publication is actually more important to the reader than whether the articles are entertaining. This is illustrated in Table 9.2.

Table 9.1. Degree of targeting by industry or specialization.

KEY: 1 = broadly targeted, "horizontal" media, aimed at mass market
5 = highly focused, "vertical" media, aimed at narrow audience with specialized interests

Marketing Tool	*Degree of Targeting*
Newspaper advertising	1
Magazine advertising	4
Broadcast advertising	1
Cable TV advertising	4
Network radio	2
Spot (local) radio	3
Billboards	1
Transit advertising	1
Catalogs	5
Direct mail	5
Postcard decks	4
Publicity and public relations	3
Telemarketing	4
Trade shows	4

Table 9.2. Information vs. entertaining in magazines.

These Magazines Are Written Primarily to Entertain	*These Magazines Are Written Primarily to Inform*
M	*Forbes*
GQ	*Business Week*
Omni	*Scientific American*
Reader's Digest	*Writer's Digest*
Life	*American Photographer*
Smithsonian	*Science News*
Cosmopolitan	*Civil Engineering*
Playboy	*Plastics World*
Penthouse	*Publisher's Weekly*
Esquire	*Engineering Analysis*
Glamour	*Popular Science*
Sports Illustrated	*Software News*

As a rule of thumb, the following applies:

- *Scholarly and scientific journals* are written almost 100 percent to educate and inform. Professionals turn to them for reference and hard data.
- *Business and trade journals* are written primarily to educate and inform but must have some entertainment value or at least be interesting to read.

- *Hobbyist and special-interest magazines* are written primarily to educate and inform, but they are informing the reader about something that entertains him or her (a hobby or other interest).
- *Consumer and general-interest magazines* are written primarily to entertain. They are read for pleasure but must also contain useful information the reader can use in his or her life.
- *News* magazines are written both to inform and to entertain. They inform but do not educate (in a "how-to" sense of the word).

The advertising approach should be tailored to the editorial environment of the magazine. Therefore, the following rules of thumb, while not definitive, at least provide a starting point for creating a magazine ad:

- Ads for *scholarly and scientific journals* are typically fact-filled and statistical in nature. They have a serious, almost scholarly tone and seek to establish credibility by revealing important information. Copy does not take a hard-sell approach but instead seeks to sway the reader by presenting the facts.
- Ads for *business and trade journals* are more promotional and less rational and objective than scientific journal ads. The ads communicate in a dramatic, forceful manner the key benefits of a specific product rather than just discuss technical information about a product or issue.
- Ads for *hobbyist and special-interest magazines* are written for the enthusiast and must reflect a high degree of enthusiasm about the particular hobby or field. Copy must show an "insider's" understanding of—and empathy with—the particular issues or activities being promoted. Copy contains details and jargon to demonstrate to the reader that the advertiser is knowledgeable in the field.
- Ads for *consumer and general-interest magazines* have to work even harder to grab attention and quickly orient the reader toward thinking about a particular product or problem he was not thinking of before. Strong benefit-oriented or curiosity-arousing headlines and dramatic visual concepts with strong human interest and appeal work well here.
- Ads for *news* magazines are similar to those for consumer and general interest magazines in that they must work hardest to grab the attention of a prospect whose mind is on something other than the topic of the ad.

These rules are summarized in Table 9.3.

Table 9.3. Basic magazine advertising approaches.

Type of Publication	*Editorial Environment*	*Advertising Approach*
Scholarly and scientific	High-level. Professional. Accurate. Information-heavy.	Factual, rational, educational. No "hype" or hard sell. Presents important technical data or news in the field.
Business magazines and trade journals	Informational. Straightforward, informative, but lighter tone than scholarly publications.	Promotional and sales-oriented. Stresses product benefit or company image. Approach may be either straightforward or imaginative.
Hobbyist and special-interest publications	Combines how-to advice and information with enthusiasm for subject. Entertains as it educates.	Ads must establish empathy with the reader, mirroring his enthusiasm for the subject matter. Long copy works because readers have strong interest in products related to their field.
Consumer and general-interest publications	Entertainment. Articles are a blend of profiles, human interest stories, service, and general-interest items.	Dramatic approaches designed to grab attention. Visually oriented. Stress benefits and solutions to people's problems or appeals to core desires.
News magazines	Information and education. Keep readers current on local, national, and world affairs.	Same as for consumer magazines.

Four Basic Types Of Ads

There are four basic types of magazine ads:

1. "Awareness" ads
2. "Image" ads
3. Inquiry ads
4. Mail order ads

Before examining the specifics of the four basic magazine ads, you must realize that, although an ad may have characteristics belonging to several categories, to be successful the ad should have only one primary goal and fall clearly into one of these basic categories. For instance, although you might want the ad to build product awareness (category 1) and generate inquiries (category 3), you should decide before creating the ad whether the primary goal is to create awareness or generate inquiries.

Remember that a magazine ad is a limited medium with limited space. Even a costly full-page magazine ad only provides 7 by 10 inches of space in which to get your message across. You weaken your ad's effectiveness when you try to accomplish too many goals or communicate too many sales points.

The successful ad should have one primary goal. It should be written and designed to communicate one basic message, theme, or sales appeal, although secondary themes or points may be included to support the primary message and make it credible.

Let's take a closer look at the four basic types of ads.

Magazine Ads: Category 1: Awareness Ad

As the name implies, an "awareness" ad creates awareness of a particular product, product benefit, product feature, or brand name. Most consumer advertising falls under this category. The ad is not designed to generate direct sales or inquiries for the product. Rather, through frequent repetition of the ad, the message being communicated about the product sinks into the consciousness of the American public.

The desired result is to have the consumer think of your brand first when he thinks about the generic product category or the need it fills. In business-to-business advertising, the desired result is to instill in the business buyer awareness of your brand or company name or to get buyers to believe in the superiority of your product.

Figure 9.1, an ad for GE/RCA/INTERSIL semiconductors, is a good example of an awareness ad. The ad features a "MOSFET," which is a specialized type of semiconductor, and specifically "rugged" MOSFETs, which are devices designed to withstand higher currents and voltages. The purpose of the ad is to communicate that, while many manufacturers claim ruggedness in their MOSFETs, only GE/RCA/INTERSIL provides a MOSFET that is truly rugged and able to give users the protection and performance they need.

If you read electronics publications, you know that most semiconductor ads merely consist of a picture of the product against a white background and a table of technical specifications. The GE/RCA/INTERSIL ad, by comparison, uses a more dramatic concept to demonstrate that only GE/RCA rugged MOSFETS have been proved reliable through extensive testing.

There's an easier way to make sure it's rugged.

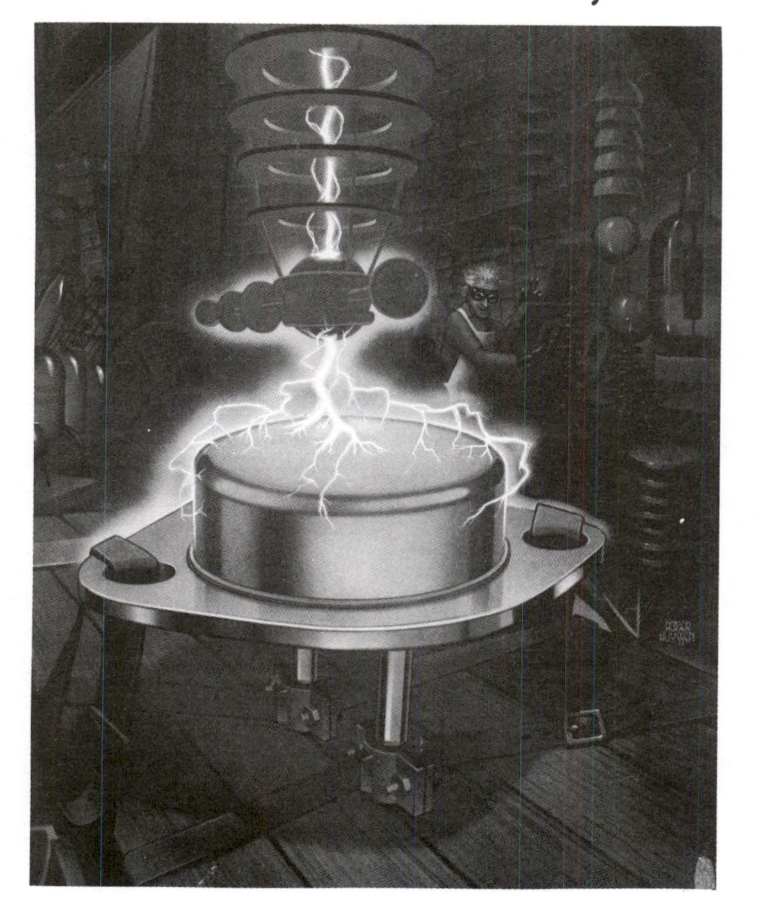

Order GE/RCA Rugged MOSFETs, the only ones with an "R" on the label. Because the wrong device can ruin your creation.

Two years ago an independent testing company compared GE Ruggedized MOSFETs with all leading competitive units. The results were even better than we expected.

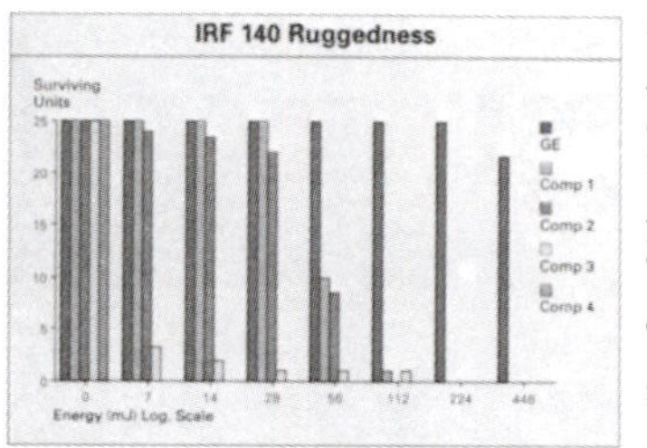

In this test conducted by Associated Testing Laboratories, Inc., the ruggedness of 25 GE IRF-series MOSFETs was compared with 25 devices from each of four competitors. As you can see, the GE parts significantly outperformed the others.

Today, the situation is different.

Because our MOSFETs are more than *twice as rugged* as they were then. Yet our ruggedized MOSFETs cost no more than competitors' standard MOSFETs.

A powerful combination.

We've achieved this by combining the rugged technology of GE products with the outstanding manufacturing, quality control and cost-effectiveness of RCA power MOSFETs. So we can bring you the best line of rugged PowerFETs in the industry.

And the benefits are considerable.

Why you need Rugged FETs.

Our Rugged MOSFETs are fast. But they're not fragile.

They're designed, tested and *guaranteed* to withstand a specified level of circuit-induced electrical stress in breakdown avalanche mode.

When you design with our Rugged devices, you can eliminate zener diodes, snubbers and other costly circuitry.

So you save money. And by simplifying your design, you improve system reliability.

Just as important, these devices give you a margin of error.

Because you can never be sure when your system will be subjected to voltages beyond what you expected.

And if you're designing for applications that routinely have to handle surges and transient voltages, these devices are perfect.

A wide selection of drop-ins.

We have more than 200 parts in distributor stock. And they're drop-in replacements for virtually any N-channel devices.

So why take chances, when you can improve your system performance and reliability at no added cost?

For more information, contact your local GE Solid State sales office or distributor. Or call toll-free 800-443-7364, extension 28.

In Europe, call: Brussels, (02) 246-21-11; Paris, (1) 39-46-57-99; London, (276) 68-59-11; Milano, (2) 82-291; Munich, (089) 63813-0; Stockholm (08) 793-9500.

GE/RCA/INTERSIL
SEMICONDUCTORS

Figure 9.1. Sample awareness ad.

The illustration—a familiar image of the mad scientist at work—gets across the point of testing in a visually interesting, eye-catching fashion. The headline is both relevant and clever (note the word play, in which the device is referred to as a "creation" in keeping with the Dr. Frankenstein motiff of the drawing).

The ad concludes with a toll-free number, but unlike a direct response ad, there is no coupon, no address, no offer of a free catalog or data book or brochure. The real purpose of this ad is not to generate inquiries but to communicate a single message: that GE/RCA MOSFETs are proven the most rugged. This is the mission of the awareness advertisement.

Magazine Ads: Category 2: Image Ad

The "image" ad is an ad that makes an overall statement about the firm, its products, and its way of doing business. In consumer advertising, the goal may be simply to create awareness and recall of the advertiser's name, product, or business philosophy in the reader's mind. The campaign "GE: We Bring Good Things to Light," is an example. The commercials and ads don't discuss specific products or features; they simply get across the point that General Electric provides the lighting America needs to live and enjoy life.

In business-to-business advertising, the purpose is not just to create an awareness or impression of a company but to create a "comfort zone"—a feeling that the company is reliable, well-established, and reputable. In short, to make the prospect more inclined to do business with the firm.

Virtually all corporate advertising falls into the category of image advertising. For examples, simply flip through any recent issue of *Forbes, Fortune,* or *Business Week.* The pages are filled with ads espousing some company philosophy or corporate point of view or the firm's history, track record, or recent accomplishments.

Most of these ads are, frankly, ineffective and of little interest to readers. Because they are advertiser-centered instead of client-centered, they contain messages which may fascinate management but mean little or nothing to the company's customers and prospects.

Liberal use of the words "leader," "leadership," or "quality" are sure signs of this type of ad. So are four-color, two-page spreads in which 90 percent of the space is taken up by a painting, sculpture, or other abstract artwork, with the remainder of the space containing one or two lines of faintly reproduced copy set in an unreadable 7-point type.

Breakthroughs in this field are rare, but they do happen. One of the most famous is the popular "Power of the Printed Word" series from International Paper Company. Figure 9.2 shows one ad from the series. According to Robert F. Lauterborn, director of corporate advertising for International Paper, the purpose of these ads was to "prove that we were committed to the paper business by dealing with one of its most nagging long-term concerns—the ability and propensity of young people to read and write as well as they need to, to cope in this age of increasing competition. We decided to actually help young people to read and write and communicate better. But we had commercial motivations. If young people read and write better, they'll read and write more. Then our customers will sell more books, magazines, and newspapers, and International Paper will sell them more paper."

Instead of talking about International Paper's commitment to the printed word, this ad *demonstrates* that commitment by providing information to help young (and not-so-young) readers. The only place International Paper is mentioned is in a box on the second page of the two-page spread. The ad campaign has been tremendously popular and successful, with International Paper receiving 1,000 requests for reprints per day.

The lesson to be learned is to respect your readers' intelligence, whether your ad is an image, awareness, or direct-response piece. Prospects respond positively to useful information, helpful guidance, and true claims. They have a good nose for sniffing out phoniness and resent being lied to or "sold."

Magazine Ads: Category 3: Inquiry Ads

Inquiry ads are designed to generate response. An inquiry ad not only grabs attention and communicates a message but also creates a desire to know more about the product and motivates the prospect to ask for that additional information.

Figure 9.3 is a good example of an inquiry ad. Its aspects include:

1. The headline and visual dramatize a key benefit ("stop burglary").
2. Subheads and long copy present a logical sales argument and give reasons why the reader should be interested in the product.
3. There is a specific offer the reader can send for—in this case, a free information kit including a booklet titled "6 Things Burglars Know That You Should Know Too."
4. The title of the free booklet further fuels the reader's desire to obtain the information. (People seek inside information, hence the appeal of

Figure 9.2. Sample image ad.

How to write a business letter

Some thoughts from Malcolm Forbes

President and Editor-in-Chief of Forbes Magazine

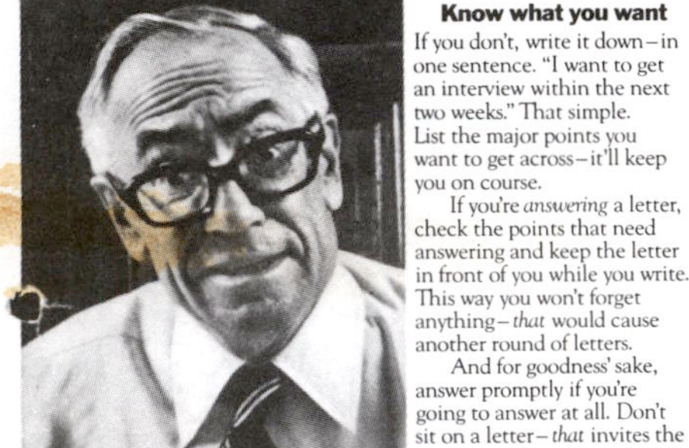

International Paper asked Malcolm Forbes to share some things he's learned about writing a good business letter. One rule, "Be crystal clear."

A good business letter can get you a job interview.

Get you off the hook.

Or get you money.

It's totally asinine to blow your chances of getting *whatever* you want—with a business letter that turns people off instead of turning them on.

The best place to learn to write is in school. If you're still there, pick your teachers' brains.

If not, big deal. I learned to ride a motorcycle at 50 and fly balloons at 52. It's never too late to learn.

Over 10,000 business letters come across my desk every year. They seem to fall into three categories: stultifying if not stupid, mundane (most of them), and first rate (rare). Here's the approach I've found that separates the winners from the losers (most of it's just good common sense)—it starts *before* you write your letter:

Know what you want

If you don't, write it down—in one sentence. "I want to get an interview within the next two weeks." That simple. List the major points you want to get across—it'll keep you on course.

If you're *answering* a letter, check the points that need answering and keep the letter in front of you while you write. This way you won't forget anything—*that* would cause another round of letters.

And for goodness' sake, answer promptly if you're going to answer at all. Don't sit on a letter—*that* invites the person on the other end to sit on whatever you want from *him*.

Plunge right in

Call him by name—not "Dear Sir, Madam, or Ms." "Dear Mr. Chrisanthopoulos"—and be sure to spell it right. That'll get him (thus, you) off to a good start.

(Usually, you can get his name just by phoning his company—or from a business directory in your nearest library.)

Tell what your letter is about in the first paragraph. One or two sentences. Don't keep your reader guessing or he might file your letter away—even before he finishes it.

In the round file.

If you're answering a letter, refer to the date it was written. So the reader won't waste time hunting for it.

People who read business letters are as human as thee and me. Reading a letter shouldn't be a chore—*reward* the reader for the time he gives you.

Write so he'll enjoy it

Write the entire letter from his point of view—what's in it for *him*? Beat him to the draw—surprise him by answering the questions and objections he might have.

Be positive—he'll be more receptive to what you have to say.

Be nice. Contrary to the cliché, genuinely nice guys most often finish first or very near it. I admit it's not easy when you've got a gripe. To be agreeable while disagreeing—that's an art.

Be natural—write the way you talk. Imagine him sitting in front of you—what would you *say* to him?

Business jargon too often is cold, stiff, unnatural.

Suppose I came up to you and said, "I acknowledge receipt of your letter and I beg to thank you." You'd think, "Huh? You're putting me on."

The acid test—read your letter *out loud* when you're done. You might get a shock—but you'll know for sure if it sounds natural.

"Be natural. Imagine him sitting in front of you—what would you say to him?"

Don't be cute or flippant. The reader won't take you seriously. This doesn't mean you've got to be dull. You prefer your letter to knock 'em dead rather than bore 'em to death.

Three points to remember:

Have a sense of humor. That's refreshing *anywhere*—a nice surprise in a business letter.

Be specific. If I tell you there's a new fuel that could save gasoline, you might not believe me. But suppose I tell you this:

> "Gasohol"—10% alcohol, 90% gasoline—works as well as straight gasoline. Since you can make alcohol from grain or corn stalks, wood or wood waste, coal—even garbage, it's worth some real follow-through.

Now you've got something to sink your teeth into.

Lean heavier on nouns and verbs, lighter on adjectives. Use the active voice instead of the passive. Your writing will have more guts.

Which of these is stronger? Active voice: "I kicked out my money manager." Or, passive voice: "My money manager was kicked out by me." (By the way, neither is true. My son, Malcolm Jr., manages most Forbes money—he's a brilliant moneyman.)

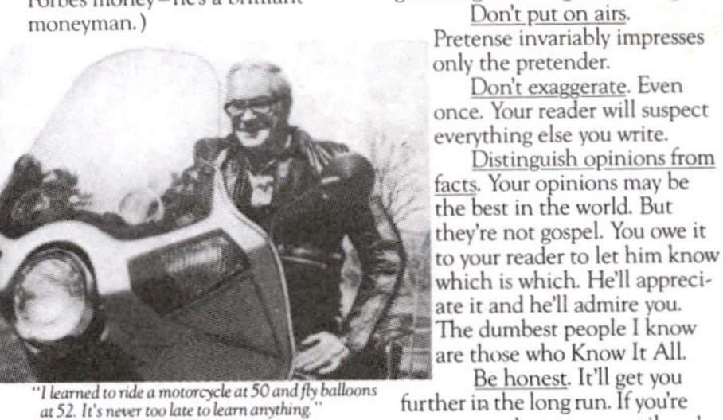

"I learned to ride a motorcycle at 50 and fly balloons at 52. It's never too late to learn anything."

Give it the best you've got

When you don't want something enough to make *the* effort, making *an* effort is a waste.

Make your letter look appetizing—or you'll strike out before you even get to bat. Type it—on good-quality 8½" x 11" stationery. Keep it neat. And use paragraphing that makes it easier to read.

Keep your letter short—to one page, if possible. Keep your paragraphs short. After all, who's going to benefit if your letter is quick and easy to read?

You.

For emphasis, underline important words. And sometimes indent sentences as well as paragraphs.

> Like this. See how well it works? (But save it for something special.)

Make it perfect. No typos, no misspellings, no factual errors. If you're sloppy and let mistakes slip by, the person reading your letter will think you don't know better or don't care. Do you?

Be crystal clear. You won't get what you're after if your reader doesn't get the message.

Use good English. If you're still in school, take all the English and writing courses you can. The way you write and speak can really help—or *hurt*.

If you're not in school (even if you are), get the little 71-page gem by Strunk & White, *Elements of Style*. It's in paperback. It's fun to read and loaded with tips on good English and good writing.

Don't put on airs. Pretense invariably impresses only the pretender.

Don't exaggerate. Even once. Your reader will suspect everything else you write.

Distinguish opinions from facts. Your opinions may be the best in the world. But they're not gospel. You owe it to your reader to let him know which is which. He'll appreciate it and he'll admire you. The dumbest people I know are those who Know It All.

Be honest. It'll get you further in the long run. If you're not, you won't rest easy until you're found out. (The latter, not speaking from experience.)

Edit ruthlessly. Somebody ~~has~~ said that words are ~~a lot~~ like inflated money—the more ~~of them that~~ you use, the less each one ~~of them~~ is worth. ~~Right on.~~ Go through your entire letter ~~just~~ as many times as it takes. ~~Search out and~~ Annihilate all unnecessary words, ~~and~~ sentences—even ~~entire~~ *paragraphs*.

"Don't exaggerate. Even once. Your reader will suspect everything else you write."

Sum it up and get out

The last paragraph should tell the reader exactly what you want *him* to do—or what *you're* going to do. Short and sweet. "May I have an appointment? Next Monday, the 16th, I'll call your secretary to see when it'll be most convenient for you."

Close with something simple like, "Sincerely." And for heaven's sake sign legibly. The biggest ego trip I know is a completely illegible signature.

Good luck.

I hope you get what you're after.

Sincerely,

Malcolm S. Forbes

Today, the printed word is more vital than ever. Now there is more need than ever for all of us to *read* better, *write* better, and *communicate* better.

International Paper offers this series in the hope that, even in a small way, we can help.

If you'd like additional reprints of this article or an 11"x17" copy suitable for bulletin board posting or framing, please write: "Power of the Printed Word," International Paper Company, Dept. 1, P.O. Box 954, Madison Square Station, New York, NY 10010.

INTERNATIONAL PAPER COMPANY

We believe in the power of the printed word.

Printed in U.S. on International Paper Company's Springhill® Offset, basis 60 lb.

Figure 9.3. Sample inquiry ad.

STOP BURGLARY BEFORE IT STARTS! CALL 1-800-645-8900 TODAY!

You'll receive FREE details on the breakthrough HOME PROTECTOR™ Wireless Security System ...from BLACK & DECKER.

Can you imagine returning home after a relaxing vacation...or a hard days work...to discover that you've been robbed.

According to FBI crime statistics this will happen in one of every four homes over the next ten years. And it could happen to you...at anytime.

At Last...a Home Security Solution!

Now whether you're leaving on vacation...a business trip...going to work ...or just around the corner to your local market...your home and family can have RELIABLE SECURITY!

Introducing HOME PROTECTOR ...Professional Quality Home Security that can guard your doors and windows...24-hours-a-day!

Now...Stop Intruders Cold!

Any intrusion effort is instantly met with flashing lights...a powerful siren ...and, with our optional "on-line" HOME PROTECTOR Service, a direct call to the authorities of your choice!

Plus...HOME PROTECTOR™ has Failsafe Features!

To put it simply...the HOME PROTECTOR SYSTEM is almost impossible to DEFEAT!

The reason is EVERY component of the system...Door Sensors ...Window Sensors... Siren... and the Controller itself work independently. So, once ANY intrusion signal is sent out ...every element of the system is ARMED...INDEPENDENT...AND IN ACTION PROTECTING YOUR HOME.

Even if the System Controller is defeated, the rest of the System continues to operate. Battery back-up is also provided by long lasting Duracell® batteries.

BLACK & DECKER®

Professional Quality at HALF-the-COST!

Finally...BLACK & DECKER'S breakthrough technology makes Home Security ...AFFORDABLE! "State-of-the-Art" wireless electronics make installation simple... and cuts the cost of Professional wiring...IN HALF!

FREE Details...Call or Write TODAY.

For complete details on the HOME PROTECTOR system...including *"6 Things Burglars Know That You Should Know Too."*...call TOLL FREE...or Mail The Coupon TODAY.

CALL TOLL FREE 1-800-645-8900

BLACK & DECKER®
HOME PROTECTOR™
Dept. A216
Box 5259
Clifton, NJ 07012

☐ **YES!** I want to know more about the breakthrough HOME PROTECTOR security system. Please rush my FREE Information Package.

Name ________________
Address ________________
City ________________
State ________ Zip ________

"things burglars know." And "6 things" is effective because people wonder what the six things are.)

5. There is a toll-free number for response. The offer to call the number appears twice: once in the headline and once above the coupon.
6. The advertiser provides a coupon the reader can use to request the information by mail.

Remember that the primary objective of the inquiry ad is to generate sales leads, not communicate a message, build awareness, or establish an image. Thus, let's say you sell widgets and your firm offers a broader line of widgets than any other supplier. Further, you have a 48-page catalog which lists and describes all the widgets available and tells how to select the right widget for a particular application.

The headline for an awareness ad might be, "XYZ COMPANY: YOUR SINGLE-SOURCE FOR WIDGETS." The visual might show a huge pile of widgets or endless rows of storage bins containing widgets of every shape and color. Copy tells that XYZ Company stocks more widgets than any other firm and can meet all the buyer's widget needs.

But the headline for an inquiry ad might read, "YOURS FREE—THE XYZ COMPANY GUIDE TO WIDGET SELECTION." The visual would be a picture of your catalog which is offered free to anyone who responds to the ad. Copy stresses the catalog: its broad line of widgets, clear illustrations, and selection tips.

Magazine Ads: Category 4: Mail Order

A mail order ad is a response ad that asks for an order instead of an inquiry. In a mail order ad, there is no free information or brochure to ask for, no salesperson to answer questions or give advice. Instead, the reader must send a check, money order, or provide credit card information to receive the product being advertised.

Therefore, the mail order ad has the toughest selling job. It must not only make the reader want the product so much that the reader will part with money on the spot to buy the product sight unseen, but it must also overcome and answer any possible objections or questions the reader might have—since there is no salesperson or brochure to provide those answers. The ad must also contain complete instructions for ordering, such as whether credit cards are accepted, how much the product costs, sales tax, quantity discounts, and so on.

10 Rules For Creating Effective Magazine Advertising

Through long years of experience, advertisers and advertising agencies have uncovered some basic principles of sound advertising strategy, copywriting, and design. Following these suggestions won't guarantee a winner. But it will prevent you from making costly mistakes that could destroy the selling power of a potentially lucrative ad. The following discussion presents these 10 rules.

1. The Right Product for the Right Audience

The first step is to make sure you are advertising a product that is potentially useful to the people reading your advertisement. This seems a bit simple and obvious, yet, many clients believe that a great ad can sell anything to anyone. They are wrong. For example, no advertisement, no matter how powerfully written, will convince the vegetarian to have a steak dinner at your new restaurant. But your ad might—if persuasively worded—entice him to try your salad bar.

Charles Inlander, of the People's Medical Society, is a master at finding the right product for the right audience. His ad, "Do you recognize the seven early warning signs of high blood pressure?" (see Figure 9.4), sold more than 20,000 copies of a $4.95 book on blood pressure when it ran approximately ten times in *Prevention Magazine* over a three-year period. "First, you select your topic," said Inlander, explaining the secret of his advertising success, "then you must find the right place to advertise. It's important to pinpoint a magazine whose readers are the right prospects for what you are selling." In other words, the right product for the right audience.

2. The Importance of the Headline

Next to the selection of subject matter and the placement of your ad in the proper publication in which it will reach the right prospects for your product, the headline is the most important ad element.

The main purpose of the headline is to grab the reader's attention and make him stop long enough to notice and start reading your ad. You can achieve this in several ways. For example, here's an attention-grabbing headline from an ad published in a local newspaper:

IMPORTANT NEWS FOR WOMEN
WITH FLAT OR THINNING HAIR.

Figure 9.4. People's Medical Society ad.

Do You Recognize the Seven Early Warning Signs of High Blood Pressure?

1.
2.
3.
4.
5.
6.
7.

That's right. There are no signs. No symptoms. And no cure.

One out of every four Americans has high blood pressure. Yet only half these people know it.

You may be one of them.

If you are over forty, you owe it to yourself to have your blood pressure checked. But that isn't enough. You also need to know the facts about "hypertension."

Fortunately, you can get those facts more easily now than ever before...from a new publication by Bob Rodale's *People's Medical Society*. It's called ***Blood Pressure: Questions You Have...Answers You Need***. And it's a book that just might save your life.

Could You Answer These 3 Questions If Your Life Depended On It?

1. What kind of exercise can lower your blood pressure...and what kind can actually make it worse?

In general, exercise is good for hypertension. But some forms of exercise are downright dangerous. Do you know which ones? You'll find the answer on page 15.

2. What common nutrient can bring your blood pressure down?

If you think controlling blood pressure is only a matter of eliminating certain foods from your diet, you'll be happy to know there are some tasty foods you should actually be eating more of. Turn to page 22 to find out which ones.

3. What happens if high blood pressure is not treated?

A 35-year-old man with untreated high blood pressure could lower his life expectancy by 16 years. Like the scores of other alarming facts in this book, better to be surprised now than later.

Don't Die Young Just Because You Didn't Know The Facts

In 1981, nearly a million Americans died of heart attacks, strokes or related diseases. How many of these deaths could have been avoided if people had simply taken the time to learn the facts about high blood pressure? Hypertension cannot be cured. But it can be controlled. More important, it can be prevented. ***Blood Pressure: Questions You Have...Answers You Need*** will show you how.

Just Published... By The People's Medical Society

There's no technical "mumbo-jumbo" here, no lecturing and no nagging. Just straight talk from your friends at *The People's Medical Society*—the non-profit group founded by Bob Rodale to help Americans get better medical care.

At only $4.95, the first printing is bound to go fast. So please, place your order today. Just fill out the coupon below and send it with $4.95 to:

The People's Medical Society
14 East Minor Street, Suite 100
Emmaus, Pennsylvania 18049

☐ Yes, I want to know how to control high blood pressure. Please send me this life-saving guide right away. I enclose $4.95.

Name ______________________

Address ______________________

City ______________________

State ____________ Zip ____________

PNAJ

This is effective in gaining the attention of the prospect for two reasons: (1) it promises important news and (2) it identifies the prospect for the service (women with flat or thinning hair). Incidentally, this ad persuades more than 1,200 readers a month to clip a coupon and send for a free brochure on a hair-conditioning procedure.

3. The Visual Must Work with the Headline

The ad should be illustrated with a photograph or drawing that visually gets across the main idea communicated in the headline.

Together, the headline and visual should get the gist of your sales pitch across to the reader. "Every good ad should be able to stand as a poster," writes Alastair Crompton. "The reader should never have to dip into the small print in order to understand the *point* of the story."

Often, simple visuals are the best visuals. "We tested two different mail order ads selling a collector's reproduction of a watch originally manufactured in the 1920s," said Will Stone of the Hamilton Watch Company." One ad used a large, dramatic photo showing the watch against a plain background. The other visual had less emphasis on the product and focused on a scene depicting the 'roaring twenties' period during which the watch was originally made. It showed flappers and a 1920s car. The ad with the straight product photo—'product as hero'—generated three times as many sales as the other version."

As a general rule, simple visuals that show the product or illustrate some aspect of its use are better than far-out, "creative" concepts that can actually *hide* what you are selling, thus reducing the ad's selling power.

4. The Lead Paragraph Expands on the Theme of the Headline

The lead must instantly follow-up on the idea expressed in the headline. For instance, if the headline asks a burning question, the lead should immediately answer it. The promises made to the reader in the headline (e.g., "Learn the secret to richer, moister chocolate cake") must be fulfilled in the first few paragraphs of copy. Otherwise, the reader feels disappointed and turns the page.

Here is an example of how this works. This is from an ad selling a business opportunity:

> QUIT YOUR JOB OR START PART-TIME.
> *Chimney Sweeps Are Urgently Needed Now!*
>
> My name is Tom Risch. I'm going to show you how to make $200 a day saving people from dangerous chimney fires. . . .

Do not waste the reader's time with a "warm-up" paragraph. Instead, go straight to the heart of the matter. In editing a first draft, the first question to ask yourself is, "Can I eliminate my first paragraph and start with my second or third paragraph?" Eight times out of 10, you can. And the copy is strengthened as a result.

5. The Layout Draws the Reader into the Ad

This is something that cannot be described in words but is experienced visually. Right now, take a minute or two to flip through the ads in any magazine you have handy. Some seem friendly. Some seem inviting. Some seem to draw your eye to the page, and make reading a pleasure. This is the type of layout you want to use in your own ads. Avoid layouts that make the ad hard to read or that discourage readers from even trying.

One key point to keep in mind is that your ad should have a "focal point"—a central dominant visual element that draws the reader's eye into the page. This is usually the headline or the visual. (I often prefer to make it the headline, since a good headline can usually communicate more effectively than a picture.) But it might also be the coupon, or perhaps the lead paragraph of copy. When there are two or more equally prominent visuals competing for the eye's attention, readers become confused and don't know where to "enter" your ad and start reading. Always make one element larger and more prominent than the others.

6. The Body Copy Supports and Expands upon the Idea Presented in the Headline and Lead Paragraph of Copy

What facts should be included in your body copy? Which should be left out? The decision is made by listing all the key points and then deciding which are strongest and will best convince the reader to respond to your advertisement.

Start by listing all the features of your products and the *benefits* people get from each feature. For instance, a *feature* of an air conditioner is that its Energy Efficiency Rating is 9.2; the *benefit* is a lower electric bill.

After making a complete list of features and benefits, list them in order of importance. Then begin your body copy with the most important benefit. Go down the list until you run out of room. Now, you've written copy that highlights the most important reasons to buy the product, given the limitations of the space your ad allows for description.

7. Be Specific

The most common mistake in advertising today is *lazy copy*—copy written by copywriters who were too lazy to take the time to learn about their audience and understand the features and benefits of their product (the reasons why someone would want to buy it).

Good advertising is effective largely because it is specific. There are two advantages to being specific. First, it gives the customer the information he needs before he will make a buying decision. Second, it creates believability. As Claude Hopkins points out, people are more likely to believe a specific, factual claim than a boast, superlative, or generalization.

Does this mean ad copy should be a litany of facts and figures? No. But the copywriter's best weapon is the *selective use of facts to support his sales pitch.*

8. Start with the Prospect, Not the Product

This may sound like a contradiction. But it's not. Your ad must be packed with information about the product. But this must be information that is *important to the reader.* Information that he will find interesting . . . or fascinating. Information that will answer his questions . . . satisfy his curiosity . . . or cause him to believe the claims you make. Information, in short, that will convince him to buy your product.

The reader's own concerns—his needs, his desires, his fears, his problems—are more important to him than your product, your company, your goals. Good advertising copy, as Dr. Jeffrey Lant points out, is "client-centered." It focuses on the prospect and how your product solves his problem—not on you, your company, or how the product was invented or is made.

For instance, instead of saying, "We have more than 50 service centers nationwide," translate this statement into a reader benefit: "You'll be assured of prompt, courteous service and fast delivery of replacement parts from one of our 50 service centers located nationwide." Don't say "energy efficient" when you can say "cuts your summer electric bills in half."

The real "star" of your ad is the reader. Your product is second and is only of concern in that it relates to a need, desire, or problem the reader has or a benefit he wants. Your company is a distant third (the least important element of your copy) and is only of concern so far as reassuring those prospects who want to do business with a well-known firm that has a good reputation and is financially stable.

9. Write in a Clear, Simple, Natural, Conversational Style

According to *Business Marketing* magazine's Copy Chasers, a panel of judges who regularly critique advertising in a monthly column, good ad copy should sound like "one friend talking to another."

This is good advice. Copy should not be pompous, remote, aloof, or written in "corporatese." It shouldn't strive to be poetic, creative, or imaginative. The most effective copy is written in a plain, simple, conversational style—the way a sincere person talks when he wants to help or advise you.

In a sense, Madison Avenue has created an accepted style for ad copy that all the big agencies now use. This "style" is the type of copy that seems to deliberately remind you that you are "reading an ad." Avoid this type of slick lingo.

10. Decide What You Want the Reader to do Next

Here are three easy steps for turning your ad into a response-generating marketing tool. First, decide what type of response you want. This is the action you want the reader to take. Do you want your prospect to phone you? Write you? Clip a coupon and mail it back to you? Do you want the reader to visit your store? Request a copy of your catalog or sales brochure? Set up an appointment to see a salesperson? Test-drive your product? Or order your product directly from the ad? Decide what you want the reader to do.

Next, tell the reader to do it. The last few paragraphs of your copy should spell out the action you want the reader to take and give him reasons to take it. For instance:

> Just clip the coupon or call toll-free now and we'll send you this policy FREE without obligation as a special introduction to EMPLOYMENT GUIDE.

***

> So why not call 1-800-FINE4WD for a dealer convenient to you?

***

> Just send in the card (or the coupon) and have some fun with your first issue. Then pay us *after* you've taken a look.

***

> And send for DISPLAY MASTERS' invaluable FREE booklet on Point-of-Purchase Marketing, "33 Ways to Better Displays: What Every Marketing Executive Should Know About Point-of-Purchase Displays in Today's Market."

Third, give the reader a *mechanism* for responding, to emphasize this mechanism in your ad layout, and to simplify the process of making contact with you.

In print advertising, this is accomplished through use of a toll-free phone number (usually printed in large type to bring attention to it) or by including a coupon in the ad. Some magazines also allow you to insert a reply card, which is bound into the magazine and appears opposite your ad. This is expensive but can dramatically increase replies, multiplying returns by a factor of two to four or more.

Even if your ad is not primarily a response ad (and with rare exception, it is hard to understand why you wouldn't want response), you should still make it easy for your reader to get in touch should he want to do business with you. This means always including an address and telephone number.

Recently, I saw a television commercial for Lilco (a Long Island utility) offering a free booklet on electricity. The ad informed viewers that they could get the booklet by calling their local Lilco office—but no phone number was mentioned in the commercial! This is a response-killing mentality that many advertisers embrace and that I will never understand. Why make it difficult for people to get in touch with you or to order your product? It doesn't make sense.

The Most Commonly Asked Questions About Magazine Advertising

Here are some of the questions clients and seminar attendees frequently ask me about magazine advertising.

Q: There are a dozen or so publications covering my industry. Should I advertise in all of them, a few of them, or just one?

A: Generally it's best to advertise only in the two or three leading publications in any one industry. You know which ones these are, or you can find out by asking your customers what they read. Magazines that are not in the top two or three in a category generally deliver a poorer quality circulation and are not worth considering unless the price makes them a real bargain. If you only have money to advertise in one publication, choose the top one in your industry.

Q: How do I know how much duplication of circulation there is among the magazines in which I advertise?

A: You don't. Unlike mailing lists, which can be run through a computer to remove duplicate names, magazine subscriber bases do overlap, and there's nothing you can do about it. This is another reason why you should advertise only in the top two or three publications in any given field. Putting more magazines on the media schedule will probably end up duplicating a lot of the readership, resulting in wasted ad dollars.

Q: Is it better to run a small ad several times or one big ad once?

A: If you have to choose between frequency and size, choose frequency. It is generally more effective to run a quarter-page ad in three or four issues of a monthly magazine than to run a full-page ad once a year. Many subscribers do not read every issue of a magazine, so frequency gives them more chances to come across your ad.

Q: What size ad is best?

A: If money is no object, a one-page ad is the best buy. Two-page spreads are not cost effective. According to one study reported in *The New York Times,* two-page ads get only 30 percent more readership than one-page ads. But the cost is twice as much.

If money is a consideration, and you must run smaller ads, I think the following units are all good sizes: ¼-page, ⅓-page, and ½-page. For the price of a ⅔-page ad in most publications, you may as well run a full page. And ⅙th page or less is generally not enough room to tell your story.

Q: What position is best on the page?

A: A right-hand page is better than a left-hand page. A page facing editorial matter (articles) is better than a page facing another ad. (A two-page spread with both pages containing ads only is called an *ad well.*)

For a fractional ad, being on the outside edge of the page is better than being against the center of the magazine (the *gutter* where the magazine is stapled or glued together). Top of the page is better than bottom of the page. The worst position for a fractional ad is to be surrounded by other ads. It's better to be on the outer edge of the page and next to editorial.

Q: What is the best position in a magazine?

A: The preferred positions are, in order, the inside front cover, outside back cover, inside back cover, and the page facing the contents page. The more toward the front of the magazine, the better.

Martin Schrader, publisher of *Harper's Bazaar,* says: "I've always believed that a good ad will be seen and bad ad will be ignored. A good ad will pull. A bad one won't. Recent research by Starch again proves, for example, that there's virtually no difference between left- and right-hand pages, and inside positions are as good as outside."

Q: How can I get these preferred positions?

A: Some of them, such as the front and back covers, are sold at premium prices. Others you can ask for and will get if they are available and haven't been taken already.

Q: Should we run a reader service card with our ad?

A: A reader service card, or "bingo card," is a postcard bound into the magazine. The postcard contains a series of numbers with each number on the postcard keyed to different numbers appearing in various ads. Typically, these reader service numbers are imprinted on your ad by the magazine and read, "For more information, circle Reader Service No. XXX."

The reader service card provides a fast, convenient way for the reader to request information from advertisers. He simply circles all the numbers on the card corresponding to the ads he wants to respond to. He then mails the postcard to the magazine, which in turn forwards his request to the various advertisers.

Should you include a reader service card number in your ad? The reason in favor is that it increases response and makes it easy for your prospect to get in touch with you. The reason against is that many advertisers feel "bingo card" inquiries are of low quality.

Unless responding to inquiries is a tremendous burden for you, I recommend you include a reader service card number, at least in your initial ads. If the quality of replies is poor, you might then test dropping the number and seeing if the ad is still responsive enough to pay off.

Q: Can I take my own photographs or draw my own pictures for use in my ad?

A: No. The reader is accustomed to quality and expects the appearance of your ad to match the quality of other ads and of the magazine's editorial layouts. Poor quality photos and crude, amateur drawings detract from your ad more than they enhance it. Leave drawing and photo-taking to the professionals.

Q: Must I illustrate my ad with drawings or photography?

A: No. All-copy ads are extremely effective. Why? I'm not certain. Perhaps it's because readers perceive all-copy ads as closer to editorial material (which they think is valuable) than advertising (which they think is full of hype). At any rate, I have written numerous all-copy ads for clients which outperformed fancier, elaborately conceived and illustrated visual concepts. Another advantage of all-copy ads is that they are inexpensive to produce. I have had them done by desktop publishing services for as little as $100, including design and typography (and that's 1989 dollars).

Q: Most of the ads I see are color. Are plain black-and-white ads effective any more?

A: Yes, for the same reason that all-copy ads work: Readers perceive them as reading matter rather than promotional hype. Most of the ads I create for clients are black-and-white, and they work well.

Q: Does running an ad in four colors pay off?

A: "Four color" ads allow you to reproduce, through the process of color separations, photographs and other artwork in full color. So the answer to whether you need four color depends on your product. Is it something that is more enticing or appealing when shown in color, such as food, clothing, cosmetics, jewelry, home furnishings, or travel destinations? Or, is it something that doesn't benefit from a full color treatment, such as a book, consulting service, or piece of machinery? If the appeal is *aesthetic,* or if some facet of the product is demonstrated most realistically in color, then color may pay off. Otherwise, I don't think it does.

Some will disagree with me, however. McGraw-Hill's Laboratory of Advertising Performance, a respected and widely read research service dealing with advertising effectiveness, has run numerous studies which show that (a) the trend to run four-color ads instead of black and white is on the rise and (b) four-color ads are more effective.

One study concludes that four-color ads gain approximately 40 percent higher readership yet cost only 30 percent more than black and white.[9] A similar study focusing on medical journal advertising found that color ads were seen by 31 percent more doctors and read by 33 percent more doctors than black-and-white ads. A third study of ads running in *Business Week* showed that color ads were remembered by 39 percent more readers than black-and-white ads.

Q: What about adding a second color to a black-and-white ad?

A: A far less costly alternative than four color is two color. A two-color ad is a black-and-white ad with a second color (usually blue but also red, yellow, or green) added to highlight headlines, subheads, blocks of copy, or other graphic elements. In a two-color ad, full color photo reproduction is not possible; however, you can use the second color to throw a "tint" over the photos. Generally, the cost of buying space is increased 15 percent if you add a second color.

My feeling is that using a second color simply for the sake of having an extra color and avoiding black and white hurts the ad more than it helps. This is because the color is added as an afterthought, thrown over a logo or photo in a slapdash sort of way, without any real purpose or effect in mind. I see no evidence that two-color ads outpull black-and-white ads, although a report has shown a 7 percent increase in people being able to remember an ad for two-color versus black-and-white.

I would use color only where it fit or logically dramatized some key selling point. For example, yellow on the cover of a yellow pages directory, red in the symbol for the Red Cross, or blue for Blue Cross and Blue Shield.

Q: Do coupons in ads really increase response?

A: Yes. A coupon will get you at least 20 percent more inquiries and possibly up to double the leads your ad would generate without a coupon. Why do they work? I think it's because they visually say to the reader, "This a direct response ad, not an awareness ad. That means you will get something FREE if you stop and look at the ad and read the coupon." So the reader feels compelled to see what you are giving away, and those who actually have an interest in your proposition stop long enough to read and respond to your message.

Q: Do I need a toll-free number?

A: Toll-free numbers do increase response for much the same reasons that coupons do. The 800 number visually clues the reader that you are running a response ad through which he/she can get something if he/she calls. So the reader pauses to find out what you are offering.

Must you have a toll-free number? Absolutely not. A regular phone number will do fine; many, many people will still call you. A toll-free number increases response, but you can still get good phone response without it. It is not essential. If most of your advertising is direct response, however, a toll-free number is a definite advantage in that it makes it easier for the reader to respond.

In consumer advertising, where the cost of making the telephone call may be a significant barrier which prevents your prospect from picking up the telephone, toll-free numbers are even more important. You don't need one if your ads are primarily to build image or awareness or if your advertising is local.

However, if you want to generate inquiries or mail order sales on a nationwide basis, a toll-free number can boost response anywhere from 10 to 30 percent or more. Companies with toll-free numbers report that as much as 50 percent or more of inquiries and orders are made by telephone. Consumers especially appreciate the cost savings and convenience.

Q: Is there a certain proper word length for headlines?

A: A headline should be as long as it needs to be to get your point across. However, if you can say the same thing in fewer words, do so. Short, pithy headlines are more memorable and can be set in larger type to attract more attention. A long headline can be broken up into two or even three subheads to increase readability.

Q: How many words are in a typical ad?

A: That's hard to answer because no ad is typical. In some of the slick, Madison Avenue type ads, the copy may consist only of a headline, a slogan, and the advertiser's name. Example: The ads for Absolut Vodka, which have just a two-word headline (ABSOLUT ______") and a visual.

However, as a rule of thumb, I'd say that the following holds true as a guide for word length:

Type of Ad	*Number of Words in Full-Page Ad*
Image or awareness	100–150
Inquiry ad	150–300
Mail order ad	500–800

Q: What size type should the body copy be set in?

A: Body copy should be set in the same size or slightly larger type than the editorial matter of a publication. Usually the point size for an ad is nine or ten, with 8 point being the minimum and 12 point the maximum. *Note:* A point is equal to 1/72nd of an inch.

Q: How many times can I repeat my ad before I need a new ad?

A: Experience shows that ads can run for a long time without losing their potency. In most cases, advertisers get tired of their ads and replace them with new ads sooner than is necessary.

Here again, there are studies that support the claim for greater ad longevity. One report showed that ads repeated during a three-year campaign were seen and noticed as well on their last appearance as on their first appearance, and readership scores declined only 7 percent. Some of the ads were repeated up to five times during this period. Another study of 50 different ads repeated in four to seven issues of a business publication showed that reader interest levels either remained the same or actually increased with each repetition. In other studies performed by The Laboratory of Advertising Performance, one ad continued to pull high levels of inquiries after eight insertions and another after 41 insertions over a period of 11 years.

The exception to this rule is full-page mail order ads, where the first insertion generally pulls the most orders, and orders drop off between 10 to

50 percent on subsequent insertions. However, small display and classified mail order ads can pull profitably for years with no decrease in response.

The answer to the question, then, is that you can continue to run the ad until the response drops off sharply (and this can be months or years) or until the message it contains is no longer current or accurate.

Q: Is it necessary for my ad to have a catchy slogan or tag line?

A: No. Most slogans are superficial and meaningless and only detract from the ad. Unless you are lucky enough to come up with a brilliant slogan, omit the slogan or tag line altogether.

Q: Is it important that all my ads have a consistent look and graphic design?

A: While it isn't mandatory, I think having a uniform look and appearance enhances a series of ads and makes the ads more memorable. If you find a style and stick with it, readers gradually begin to recognize your style and know when an ad is from your company even before they have read the headline or looked at the logo. At the very least, you can use the same style typography in all your ads even if the designs are not identical.

Q: What are some of the things I can do to increase ad response?

A: Here is a partial list:

- Ask for action.
- Offer a free booklet or brochure.
- Show a picture of your free brochure or booklet.
- Include a toll-free number.
- Include a coupon.
- Offer a free gift or bonus for prompt response.
- Offer a free estimate, consultation, diagnosis, evaluation, or other free service.
- Use a reader service card number.

Q: I see some ads with post cards bound into the magazine opposite the ad. Does this technique increase response?

A: Yes. Typically an ad with a bound-in postcard generates two to five times as much response as the ad with no postcard. But it is costly.

Special Tips For Fractional Ads

A *fractional ad* is any ad that is smaller than a full page but larger than a classified or classified display. Typical fractions are $1/12$, $1/6$, $1/4$, $1/3$, $1/2$, and $2/3$ of a page.

Although most of what is written about advertising in books and the trade press deals with full-page ads and two-page spreads, and most of the ads that win awards are full-size ads, fractionals are more difficult to write and to design. The fractional competes with the big ads. It asks for attention from the same audience, must communicate the same message, and must demonstrate and describe similar products. Yet you must do all this in the smallest of spaces. It's difficult to do well and seldom appreciated by clients.

Here are some techniques for making small ads stand out and create more response:

1. Take full advantage of the medium. Acknowledge that the space is limited, and work within those limitations. The best example of this is the fractional ad by the brilliant entrepreneur who wrote the headline, "Do you read small ads like this one?" Don't try to scale down a full-page ad and cram it into a 5-by-5-inch box. Instead, start with the small box and find creative ways to fill it.

2. Put a dashed border around the ad. This creates the feeling and appearance of a coupon which, in turn, stimulates response. It is an inexpensive and easy way to make your ad stand out on the page. And it works every time, because not one advertiser in 1,000 knows this simple technique.

3. In the closing paragraph of your copy, say, "To receive more information, clip this ad and mail it with your business card to [address]." Many business prospects will follow your directions and respond in this way.

4. Use simple visuals. A fractional ad has no room for developing a complex visual concept. Visuals should be straightforward: Photos of the product, cutaway drawings showing how the product works, and sketches of applications are best. *Clip art* (books of stock line drawings) can work well here.

5. In the bottom right corner of the ad, next to your closing paragraph, show a small picture of your brochure, catalog, or other free information the reader can send for. It almost always increases response.

6. Use short headlines. For example, instead of "HOW TO STOP LIQUID WASTE," write "STOP LIQUID WASTE." By cutting words, you free up space and can set the headline in larger type or have more

room for body copy or visuals. For fractional ads, short, pithy headlines, in large, boldface type, work best. For example, if you are selling boilers, and have room for only one word in the headline, it should read, "BOILERS."

7. Cut the fat out of your body copy. Short ads have to be less conversational and "talky," more telegraphic and clipped in style. Put in the essential points and cut out all the transitions, fluff copy, and unnecessary phrases. One way to accomplish this is to use numbered or bulleted points.

8. If you have a lot to say, consider a series of ads rather than a single ad. For example, let's say you are advertising an air freight delivery service. Your service is the best because it is the fastest, most reliable, and most economical. You could get all that across in a full-page ad, but it's too much to say in a quarter-page ad.

The solution is to create a series of three quarter-page ads, one on speed, one on reliability, and one pushing cost savings. You could even create continuity by putting a "kicker" (small line of copy) above the headline that read, "Number [1,2,3] in a series." This actually increases readership because it makes the ad seem important and people will look for the other ads in the series.

9. A common technique for making small ads more noticeable and dramatic is to set the entire ad in reverse type. Don't do it. Body copy set in white type against a black background is often difficult to read.

10. Always specify the best position (right-hand page, right-hand side of page, top of page) in your insertion orders. You may get it if you ask. But you will rarely get it if you don't ask.

Writing Classified Ads

Do not ignore classified ads. They can be power-houses of response. A classified ad will generate inquiries and orders at far less cost than a large space ad. Unfortunately, the overall response will be lower, so you can rarely depend on classified ads alone.

A big plus of classified ads is that they are inexpensive to run and inexpensive to produce. There are no fees for illustration, photography, typography, or layout. You simply send your copy to the magazine and they take care of the rest.

Because I am not an expert classified ad writer, I turn to successful mail-order entrepreneur Joe Barnes for advice on the topic. Here are some of his guidelines on the subject, reprinted from his Special Report and from personal letters he has sent me over the years.

1. Certain key words attract the most attention and generate the greatest number of replies. They include FREE, HOW TO, AMAZING, SELL, EASY, MAKE MONEY, SAVE, NEW, and YOU. Try to use any of the above words as the first words in your classifieds. Many readers run their finger down a column of small classifieds until stopped by the appeal of the first word.

2. Be brief. Avoid using more words than are necessary. In classifieds, you pay for each word, so why use two or three words when one will convey the same message?

For instance, don't say YOU CAN MAKE EXTRA MONEY (five words) when MAKE EXTRA MONEY (three words) will accomplish the same thing. Another way to save words is to use figures rather than words (e.g., $500 (one word) instead of five hundred dollars (three words)). And instead of WESTINGHOUSE ELECTRIC CORPORATION (three words) use WESTINGHOUSE (one word). Instead of "commercial and residential" (three words) use "commercial/residential" (two words).

3. Avoid abbreviating words in classified ads. Spell them out in full to prevent confusion. The cost is the same; no money is saved by abbreviating. For example, write GOVERNMENT, not GOV'T.

4. Be honest with your prospects. Be specific enough in your ad to attract a big percentage of qualified prospects. The number of inquiries is not a measure of success. You want inquiries that have a reasonable chance of being turned into sales.

5. Place your ad only in those publications where you find others advertising similar products or services—especially if you recognize ads that have appeared time and time again in previous issues. Fish where the fish are biting. Others have tested the waters and found them to be productive.

6. Avoid, or at least be extremely cautious about, placing ads in cheap little "ad sheets." A so-called low price of $12 to $20 becomes expensive if no results are achieved. Far too many times these "sheets" are circulated primarily to other advertisers and worthless name lists. You have no way of verifying how many were actually mailed. Stick to the big circulation magazines. You will be way ahead.

7. An exception to this would be if you are selling a specialty item, such as rare guns. Then you would advertise in a specialty magazine aimed at this market such as *Gun World.*

8. Answer all inquiries. Those who send post cards or scribbled messages may turn out to be some of your best repeat customers.

9. Key each ad in each magazine. Then keep accurate records so you can determine which produce the best results. For example, Dept. WD means the ad ran in *Writer's Digest.*

10. Classified ads have one use: to generate inquiries. They are useless for image building or awareness and are not cost-effective for selling directly any item over $5. The typical offer is more information on the product, usually phrased as "free information," "free details," or "free brochure."

The 61 Most Common Magazine Advertising Mistakes And How To Avoid Them

Here are 61 of the most common mistakes made in designing, writing, and placing magazine advertisements.*

Headlines

Mistake No. 1

You don't have a headline.

Headlines are a must. They grab attention. They tease readers with promises. They summarize your message and give readers *the* reason to order. Without a headline, your ad is weak.

Mistake No. 2

Your company name is the headline.

Readers respond to benefit headlines. "What's in it for me?" is their primary concern. Put your company name at the bottom of the ad. At the top, it distracts readers from the benefit headline.

Mistake No. 3

You don't promise the main benefit.

Selling headlines promise the major benefit.

Why? Because readers must be convinced that it's worthwhile to read your ad, and only major benefits have that kind of convincing power. Some weak headlines: 1) your company name (not really a benefit); 2) your company is No. 1 (Who cares? What's in it for the reader?); 3) you've been in business 10 years (and?).

Show how you'll improve the reader's life or he won't read the rest of your ad.

*Source: *Business Marketing* magazine. Reprinted with permission.

Mistake No. 4

Your headline is too logical.

Appeals to emotion consistently outpull appeals to logic. Wrong: "Team Basketball Action For Your Computer" (logical). Right: "Jump Into The Big Leagues With CompuTex" (emotional). Don't just don't state facts. Dig for the emotion behind them.

Mistake No. 5

You use a one-word headline.

Current styles notwithstanding, one word can't possibly do the work of three or more. I have yet to see an effective one-word headline.

Mistake No. 6

You use the name of your product as the headline.

Not enough information. Besides, where's the benefit?

Body Copy

Mistake No. 7

You're not selling the reader.

Your copy implies that the reader is three-quarters sold. All you have to do is describe your product or service and the reader will order. Result? Readers aren't motivated.

Instead, address the skeptical prospect. You have his momentary attention, but he's resistant. Communicate your enthusiasm, your strong belief, your willingness to satisfy. That gives your message the edge it needs.

Mistake No. 8

Your copy is not reader-oriented.

Don't write about your product or service. Write about readers and how your product or service will benefit them.

Wrong: "Cannot be compared to any other peripheral." Right: "Easy to use; no software required."

Mistake No. 9

Your body copy begins with a description of your company.

You've hooked readers with an intriguing headline. Now keep them hooked by elaborating on the benefit you promised in the headline. Forceful, believable promises keep readers from abandoning your ad.

Mistake No. 10

You don't convert features to benefits.

Features disclose product or service facts. Benefits show what's in it for the reader. "Converted" features turn facts into benefits. Feature: tough. Benefit: lasts a long time. Converted feature: tough enough to last a full year.

Mistake No. 11

Your message is not focused.

Readers can digest only one offer at a time. Don't distract them with brief notes about other offers, even if they are related to your present offer.

Mistake No. 12

You lie to readers.

Never claim your product or service is lowest in cost unless it is. If it is, think of a unique and believable way to express it.

For example: "If you can find a lower price, we'll refund *twice* the difference, *plus* send you a *free* set of six diskettes."

Mistake No. 13

You mention price before benefits.

Imagine this sales pitch from an encyclopedia salesman: "The price is $595. Now let me tell you about it." Feel a little resistance, do you? So will your reader unless you present benefits first.

Mistake No. 14

You don't tell readers how much they save by buying *now.*

You're having a sale and you mention the sale price. Readers know the regular price and can add, so why point out the obvious? Because precise figures make the savings more real. Remember, you are writing to the skeptical prospect.

Mistake No. 15

You don't prove you are No. 1.

Because everybody does it from time to time, claiming you're No. 1 often increases reader resistance to your message. If you are No. 1, *show it* with a professional-quality four-color ad that makes competitors drool. Nobody will believe you're No. 1 if your ad doesn't prove it.

Mistake No. 16

Your subheadlines don't sell.

Promise a benefit in every subheadline. For example, "SAVE $12 NOW." Good subheadlines make a strong message more potent.

Mistake No. 17

You don't include any testimonials.

Testimonials give your offer credibility. Use names, titles and occupations. Also, be specific and realistic, and avoid superlatives; they usually sound artificial.

Wrong: "The best package I ever saw." Right: "The graphics are sharp and the color is excellent."

Mistake No. 18

You attack the wrong competitor.

If you're No. 5, don't go after No. 4; attack some weakness in No. 1—such as, how your guarantee is better (assuming it is). Many readers identify with the underdog. If you're No. 1, *never* mention competitors. To do so is to elevate them to your level in the reader's mind.

Mistake No. 19

You don't mention who your product or service is for.

Even if it's obvious, readers need to be reassured that your product or service is specifically for them. Name the occupational level ("For office managers"). Or tap into an emotional need ("For people who hate wasting time").

Mistake No. 20

You don't have a guarantee.

Guarantees build confidence in your offer. They are so important that you should highlight them visually with a border, underlining or bold lettering. The stronger your guarantee, the better—as long as the wording rings true.

Mistake No. 21

Your close is weak.

Close forcefully. Readers respond well to firm directions. Avoid questions. Tell readers to order *now!*

Mistake No. 22

You don't add a clincher.

You have a clincher when you connect some desired emotional response with ordering. For example: "Avoid the discomfort or eye strain. Send for ClearWriter *today!*"

Mistake No. 23

You don't stress your order preference.

If readers can fill out an order form or phone, and you prefer one over the other, tell them several times in your copy. When you mention the two ways together, mention the preferred method first ("Phone in now or mail the order form"). In addition, highlight the preferred method visually with large, bold type. Or show a picture of a phone to indicate you want phone orders.

Style

Mistake No. 24

You use long, complicated sentences.

Short sentences are easy to read. They lessen reader resistance to your message. Long, complicated sentences turn readers off, as do long paragraphs.

Mistake No. 25

Your tone is too formal.

The most effective copy is conversational, as if you were speaking face-to-face with a single reader. Don't talk down to readers. Treat them as equals.

Visuals

Mistake No. 26

You lack a provocative visual idea.

Your ad needs a dramatic visual to help readers absorb and remember your message. Without that idea, your ad lacks impact.

Mistake No. 27

The visual features your product when something else would be better.

To be effective, your visual must be related to the main benefit. If your main benefit is time-savings, feature a stopwatch instead of your product. Include the product as a secondary element, or put it in a smaller photo somewhere else in the ad.

Mistake No. 28

You don't use people in your visual.

Photos with people pull better than photos without them.

Also, a person doing something works better than a person standing passively. The activity encourages action by readers.

Mistake No. 29

In a computer ad, your screen simulations just fill space.

Use simulations to demonstrate a benefit. Make sure they are clear and clean-looking.

Mistake No. 30

Your visuals don't have captions.

Captions multiply the powers of your visuals. Never miss an opportunity to convey some important message to readers.

Mistake No. 31

You don't highlight your toll-free number.

Make it easy for readers to say yes to your offer. Add stress by making the number larger than surrounding copy. Or use color. Or surround it with a lot of white space to make it look more important.

Mistake No. 32

You don't use graphic emphasis devices.

Such devices direct readers' eyes to key parts of your message.

They include: underlining or circling key words, bullets (•), indenting paragraphs, subheadings and parentheses.

Mistake No. 33

You don't include a visual of your product.

Use a photo of your product to heighten readers' identification when they see it in a store. Show it as readers will see it at the point of purchase.

Mistake No. 34

You use a drawing rather than a photo.

Photos outpull drawings, for readers respond better to the realism conveyed by photos.

Mistake No. 35

Your photo is too small.

The impact is greater with a large photo. Ideally your headline, copy and photo should each take one-third of the ad space.

Mistake No. 36

Your company logo is prominent.

Readers don't care about your company logo. It's an ego-builder, and it doesn't belong in selling ads.

Logos, however, *may* belong in image ads. If you insist on using your logo, put it at the bottom of the ad with your company name.

Mistake No. 37

Your black-and-white photo looks washed out.

Photos are just as important as copy. Use a professional photographer and approve all photos before the ad is completed.

Mistake No. 38

The quality of your black-and-white photos is inconsistent.

To readers, that means your company is not reliable.

When composing an ad, have all photos done at the same time by the same photographer.

Color

Mistake No. 39

You use too much reverse copy.

Use reverse copy—white letters on dark background—in moderation. Reverse ads stand out, but more than 100 words in reverse makes your copy less readable.

Mistake No. 40

Your colors are not functional.

Colors are functional when they highlight important parts of your ad. Don't use color merely as background. Feature your toll-free number, your guarantee or your headline—or all three.

Mistake No. 41

You're No. 1, but you're running a black-and-white ad.

If you're No. 1, go with four-color. If a competitor gets a professional four-color ad, he'll look like No. 1 and steal your customers. The extra cost is worth it.

Mistake No. 42

You use weak colors.

Strong colors draw out positive emotions from readers. Dark red, dark blue, dark green, dark brown and black are the strong colors. Pastel versions make your message seem weak and ineffective, even if readers can't say why.

Mistake No. 43

Your headline is not visually forceful.

Use thick, black letters or another strong color. Avoid scriptlike letters that make your message appear weak.

Layout

Mistake No. 44

Your ad is cluttered.

Cluttered ads increase reader resistance.

Devote one portion each to headline, copy, photo and order form (when appropriate). Don't insert copy about other products and services just to fill up space.

Mistake No. 45

Your layout is symmetrical.

Balance can work against you. You don't want the left side of your ad completely balanced with the right side.

You want things out of kilter a bit, with more ad components on one side or the other. It doesn't matter which side. The out-of-kilter ad stimulates reader action.

Mistake No. 46

Some of your copy slants at a 45 degree angle.

The reader has to do more mental work when copy slants at any angle. One big word at 90 degrees is OK, but blocks of body copy should be horizontal.

Mistake No. 47

Your headline gets hung up in the gutter—where two pages meet.

With a two-page ad, put your headline on the left page. You'll avoid getting part of your message stuck in the gutter and rendered unreadable. You'll also avoid a headline that doesn't line up from one page to the next.

Order Form

Mistake No. 48

Your order form begins with price information.

Price information creates reader resistance. Make it easy to respond: Use a brief version of your main benefit as an order-form headline.

Mistake No. 49

You use a verbal order form.

Don't tell the reader to put his name and address on a piece of paper to mail in. Do the work for him by providing a coupon.

Mistake No. 50

Your order form is not a selling device.

Sell on your order form. Offer a savings for ordering more *now.* Offer dollars off for a response within 10 days. Keep readers motivated.

Mistake No. 51

Readers have to do some figuring on your order form.

Never ask readers to do arithmetic. Some of the most sophisticated mathematicians can't do simple arithmetic. Others think it's too much trouble. Arithmetic kills sales. Either do the arithmetic for readers or rearrange your offer.

Mistake No. 52

You don't key your ad.

With two or more of the same ad, put an extra number, letter or suite number in your address to indicate the origin of the response. The next time you place ads, you'll know where to focus your dollars.

Mistake No. 53

Your address marks you as an amateur.

Don't use a post office box. Get a street address. Even if you have a post office box, use the street address, then substitute a suite number for your post office box number. Image sells.

Type

Mistake No. 54

You use sans serif type for your body copy.

Sans serif type is lettering without the little feet on the bottoms of certain letters. Serif type gets a better response because it's more readable. Sans serif is OK in headlines and short blocks of copy, but with more than 100 words, use serif type.

Mistake No. 55

Your body copy is too small.

The ideal point size is 10 to 12. That results in the highest readability for your body copy. Point sizes outside that range slow readers down, making them read unnaturally.

Mistake No. 56

You use more than one kind of type in your ad.

When you do that, your ad looks cheap. Use a consistent type throughout. Headlines can be another type if desired.

Placement

Mistake No. 57

Your ad is visually dominated by another ad on the same page.

Avoid this by becoming the dominant advertiser. If your ad is black-and-white, ask that no color ad be placed on the same page. Or ask for the dominant position—top half of the page.

With a quarter-page ad, ask for the top right-hand side of a right-hand page, the ultimate dominant position when you don't have a full-page ad.

Mistake No. 58

You forget to watch your backside.

The advertiser behind your ad has an order form that needs to be clipped. Once that's done, your message is ruined.

When you place your ad, ask that no coupon ad be on your backside.

Mistake No. 59

You copy a competitor's style.

The first company out with a style or a marketing idea tends to gobble up the lion's share of the business. Don't be in awe of a competitor because its bigger than you. You set the trends.

Mistake No. 60

You're butting heads with the competition.

Most multiproduct ads look alike. Don't be one of the gang. Instead, make a niche for yourself. For example, become known as the modem company. Readers prefer specialists.

Mistake No. 61

You become a slave to these rules.

Don't let these rules become a straitjacket. It's OK to violate them *when you know how.* If you can think of a message so compelling that it grabs attention and pulls well, go for it. With practice, you'll know when you have a winner.

CHAPTER 10

Newspaper Advertising*

Newspapers vs. Magazines

What are the differences between newspaper advertising and magazine advertising?

Newspapers are published more frequently than magazines

Newspapers are published daily or weekly as opposed to weekly or monthly for magazines. The advantage to newspapers is that you can get ads into print quicker and even target ads for specific days of the week. For example, to get an ad in the June issue of a monthly magazine, you must reserve the space by May (or even April for some publications). But the newspaper ad you create today can be in the paper tomorrow.

*The sources for most of the newspaper industry figures quoted here are "Facts About Newspapers '88," published by the American Newspaper Publishers Association, and reprinted with permission of McCann Erickson Inc. and the Newspaper Advertising Bureau, Inc., and "Key Facts 1988: Newspapers, Consumers, Advertising," published by the Newspaper Advertising Bureau, Inc., reprinted with permission.

Newspaper ads have a greater size flexibility

Magazines generally have only half a dozen fixed units of space (full page, 1/2 page, 1/4 page, 2/3 page, 1/3 page, 1/6 page).

Newspaper space is sold by the column inch and can be any size that fits your message and budget. An ad that is two column inches, for instance, is one column wide by two inches deep. A six column inch ad might be one column wide by six inches deep—or, it could be two columns wide by three inches deep.

A new system of measuring and selling newspaper and advertising space, the Standard Advertising Unit system (SAU), was introduced on July 1, 1984. It has been endorsed by the Newspaper Advertising Bureau and the American Newspaper Publishers Association, and practically every daily newspaper in the United States accepts it.

Standard newspapers, called broadsheets, have printed pages 13 inches wide with a depth ranging from 21 inches to 22 1/2 inches. Each column is 2 1/16 inches wide. Measurement and billing of advertising is based on the standard column inch. *The New York Times* is an example of a broadsheet. Broadsheets are typically folded horizontally across the middle for easier handling while reading.

Newspapers with a smaller page size are called *tabloids.* A full tabloid page is usually 14 inches deep. The width varies from 9 3/8 inches (called a *short cut-off*) to 10 13/16 inches (*long cut-off*). The New York *Daily News* is an example of a tabloid.

Most tabloids use a 5-column format with the same column width as broadsheets. The SAU chart, reproduced at Figure 10.1, depicts the Standard Advertising Units available on a single page. Table 10.1 shows column-inch equivalents and Standard Advertising Unit options for fractional parts of broadsheet and tabloid pages.

While magazines target audience by industry or special interest, newspapers target geographically

There are some national newspapers (*USA Today* is the largest), but the majority of newspapers are regional. For this reason, newspaper advertising is popular with retailers and service firms offering goods and services to local rather than national markets. In fact, most newspapers offer a lower advertising rate to local advertisers than to companies with out-of-town addresses. (Retail and mailorder advertisers also get a lower rate.)

Figure 10.1. The Expanded SAU Standard Advertising Unit System.

Depth in Inches	*1 COL 2 1/16"*	*2 COL 4 1/4"*	*3 COL 6 6/16"*	*1 COL 2 1/16"*	*5 COL 10 6/16"*	*6 COL 13*
FD"	1×FD"	2×FD"	3×FD"	4×FD"	5×FD"	6×FD"
18"	*1*×18	*2*×18	*3*×18	*4*×18	5×18	*6*×18
15.75"	1×15 75	1×15 .75	3×15 .75	4×15 .75	5×15 .75	
14"	1×14	2×14	3×14	4×14	N 5×14	6×14
13"	1×13	2×13	3×13	4×13	5×13	
10.5"	1×10.5	2×10.5	3×10.5	4×10.5	5×10.5	6×10.5
7"	1×7	2×7	3×7	4×7	5×7	6×7
5.25"	1×5.25	2×5.25	3×5.25	4×5.25		
3.5"	1×3.5	2×3.5				
3"	1×3	2×3				
2"	1×2	2×2				
1.5"	1×1.5					
1"	1×1					

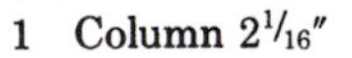

1 Column 2 1/16"
2 Columns 4 1/4"
3 Columns 6 7/6"
4 Columns 8 5/8"
5 Columns 10 13/16"
6 columns 13"

Double Truck 26 3/4"
(There are four suggested double truck sizes)

13xFD"	13x18
13x14	13x10.5

FD = full depth (21 inches)

Table 10.1. Fractional pages: column inch equivalents, with standard advertising unit options.

Broadsheet	*Tabloid**
Full page = 126 column inches	*Full page = 70 column inches*
6 × 21 (full depth)	5 × 14
Two-thirds page = 84 column inches	*Four-fifths page = 56 column inches*
4 × 21 (full depth)	4 × 14
6 × 14	
	Three-fifths page = 42 column inches
Half page = 63 column inches	3 × 14
3 × 21 (full depth)	4 × 10.5
4 × 15.75	
6 × 10.5	*Half page = 35 column inches*
	5 × 7
One-third page = 42 column inches	
2 × 21 (full depth)	*Two-fifths page = 28 column inches*
3 × 14	2 × 14
4 × 10.5	4 × 7
6 × 7	
	One-fifth page = 14 column inches
Quarter page = 31.5 inches	1 × 14
2 × 15.75	2 × 7
3 × 10.5	
	One-tenth page = 7 column inches
One-sixth page = 21 column inches	1 × 7
1 × 21 (full depth)	2 × 3.5
2 × 10.5	
3 × 7	
4 × 5.25	

*May not apply to the New York Daily News, Newsday and other short cut-off tabloids. Consult individual newspaper for equivalents.

Newspaper ads cost less to produce

Production costs for a full page, four color magazine ad can run as high as $9,000 or more if a professional advertising agency and photographer are employed. But most newspaper ads are copy with simple line art and can be produced much less expensively. Newspapers will even set your ad into type for you (called *pubset*) at no cost, if you desire.

"The daily newspaper is a unique advertising medium that readers value as a useful source for many kinds of information," notes the Newspaper Advertising Bureau. "The most common way of reading the paper is to start with the front page and go through the issue page by page, scanning it for articles and ads that look interesting. Readers know the difference between editorial content and advertising, but in practice they don't pay much attention to this distinction.

"Interest in newspaper ads is highly correlated with buying interest, with 87 percent of 'hot' prospects for a particular product being interested in ads dealing with that product. This close link between prospect status and interest in advertising may seem self-evident, but it does not necessarily hold for other media in which advertisers depend on novelty, humor, or celebrity presenters to attract the consumers attention."

What types of ads get the highest readership in newspapers? According to the Newspaper Advertising Bureau, 58 percent of newspaper readers read supermarket ads, 57 percent read store ads for clothing, 50 percent turn to newspaper advertising to see what movies are playing, 43 percent look for jobs in the help wanted ads, and 31 percent scan the real estate classifieds.

There are 1,645 daily newspapers and 7,498 newspapers published in the United States. The average circulation of these newspapers is 62.8 million for the dailies and 51.7 million for the weeklies. Seventy-six percent of American adults read a daily newspaper every weekday. Seventy-two percent read the Sunday paper. The typical daily newspaper reader spends an average of 44 minutes per day reading one or more newspapers. The average newspaper is made up of 60 percent ads and 40 percent articles.

My own sense of it is that, while still strong, newspaper readership is on the decline. When I was a youngster, dads came home from work, plopped into an easy chair, and stayed buried behind a newspaper until dinner. Now, few people I know read a daily paper.

On the other hand, I suspect that more people are spending more time with the Sunday newspaper than ever before. A cover story in *Direct Marketing,* "The Cocooning of America," told of the phenomenon in which people are "cocooning or holing up at home with the spouse, kids, and trays of gourmet junk food to watch videotapes." My observations indicate there is much truth to this, and obviously staying home all day with the Sunday *Times* is part of it. But this is all personal opinion, and does not reflect research of the Newspaper Advertising Bureau.

Daily newspapers are published in 1,526 U.S. cities. One hundred ten cities have two or more daily newspapers. Table 10.2 lists the 20 largest U.S. daily newspapers and their circulation (approximate).

Most important, newspaper advertising *works.* Results show that, on average, newspaper advertising triples volume for items advertised at cut prices and doubles sales for items advertised at regular prices.

Table 10.2. 20 largest U.S. daily newspaper circulation.

Newspaper	*Circulation*
The Wall Street Journal	1,852,863
USA Today	1,800,000
Los Angeles Times	1,242,864
The New York Times	1,150,000
The Washington Post	810,000
New York Daily News	754,043
Chicago Tribune	741,345
New York Post	644,738
Detroit Free Press	626,434
San Francisco Chronicle	559,527
Chicago Sun-Times	537,780
The Boston Globe	516,981
The Philadelphia Inquirer	515,523
Newsday	512,419
The Newark Star-Ledger	485,362
The Detroit News	481,766
The Miami Herald	444,581
Houston Chronicle	439,574
The Cleveland Plain Dealer	432,449
The Denver Post	413,343

Source: Bacon's Publicity Distribution

Types Of Newspapers

Here are the basic types of newspapers you can advertise in:

Daily

Standard Rate & Data Service says that a paper must be issued at least four times a week to be considered a daily newspaper. Some dailies are published in the morning; others in the evening. Others have both a morning and an evening edition. According to retail advertising consultant Dana Cassell, morning papers are more business-oriented, with more hard news. They tend to be bought at newstands and read on the way to work or in the office. Evening editions are more family-oriented, containing more human-interest features, which are read at leisure by parents as well as older children.

Sunday Editions

According to the American Newspaper Publishers Association, 820 U.S. papers have Sunday editions. Sunday editions reach people on a day when they have the most time for leisure reading.

Supermarket Tabloids

These are sold primarily at supermarket checkout counters and cater to a mass audience. They include *The Globe, The Star, The National Enquirer,* and *The National Examiner.* These papers are good media for mail order advertising. (Other good mail order papers include *Grit, Cappers Weekly, Moneysworth,* and *The Spotlight.*)

Weeklies

These include town, county, neighborhood, and other local and regional papers. Although most ads are from small local firms, these papers can also prove effective for national advertisers, especially those with regional branches. Also under this category are the "penny savers" and "shoppers" distributed free to local residents, plus religious and ethnic publications such as Hispanic, Black, Jewish, and Chinese newspapers. Cassell reports that ads with coupons generate a much higher return in penny savers and other weeklies than in daily newspapers.

Sections

Daily newspapers are divided into *sections* and *features* which offer special benefit to advertisers. A *section* is an entire section of a paper devoted to a specific topic, such as business or lifestyle. A *feature* can be either a page, several pages within a section, or even a single regular column or article devoted to a specific topic. For example, the weekday editions of *The New York Times* have a book "page" which is actually a single book review surrounded by ads for books (occasionally there are other feature articles covering books). The *Times* also has an advertising "page" which centers around the advertising column.

The section or feature is to newspaper advertising what the special issue is to magazine advertising: an opportunity to run your ad in an "editorially compatible environment"—that is, surrounded by articles dealing with the same topic as the ads. The benefit is that readers turning to these sections or features are more likely to be interested in your proposition.

A 1987 survey of newspapers has enabled the Newspaper Advertising Bureau to supply a computerized list of newspapers that regularly carry a specific section or feature. A partial list of these sections and features covers such topics as:

Sections
Business, Finance
Entertainment
Fashion
Food
Home
Lifestyle, Women
Science
Sports
TV, Radio
Travel

Features
Advice on personal finance
Astrology
Beauty
Best food buys
Books
Business, financial
Career advice
College
Computers
Diet, nutrition
Fashion, men
Fashion, women
Fashion, teenage
Games and puzzles
Gardening
Health and medical
Home repair, building
Home furnishings
Movie timetable
Music, records, tapes
Op Ed page
Outdoors: camping, etc.
Personal advice
Pets
Physical fitness
Real estate
Recipes
Religion
Science
Stamps, coins
Theater
Travel and resort
Videotape reviews
Wine

If you are a local winery, it would pay to advertise your free wine tastings and winery tours in the food section or on the wine page rather than in business, sports, or home furnishings. Another good place to feature it would be on a "things-to-do" page or local calendar of events.

The Basics Of Newspaper Advertising. An Interview With Eric Linker, Senior Vice President of Advertising, The New York Times

To get the full story on effective newspaper advertising, I turned to Eric Linker, who is Senior Vice President of Advertising for *The New York Times* and has been in newspaper advertising for 14 years.

Q: What types of firms should consider newspaper advertising?

A: There is probably no advertiser who should not at least consider newspaper advertising.

Retailers are one big category. Another is advertising managers for a brand or product that has local retail support or distribution through retail outlets.

If you look at where newspapers get their advertising revenue, a high percentage is from retail outlets, specialty stores, department stores, chains, supermarkets, and convenience stores. The second-biggest source is classified advertising: recruitment, help wanted, real estate, automotive, merchandise, business opportunities, auctions—those are classified areas. The lowest percentage of advertising revenues—and *The New York Times* is an exception here—is revenue from national advertising: liquor, tobacco, airlines, financial services, amusement, entertainment.

Corporate advertising—companies trying to reach specific constituencies—or to persuade or give a point of view on their company's direction or product mix—is a key source of revenue for *The New York Times, The Wall Street Journal,* and other influential and important media. And there are other types of corporate or "image" newspaper advertising: Cause and appeal. Opinion. Associations or organizations voicing an opinion on public issues. Mobil invented "advocacy advertising" and has been running for 17 years on the *New York Times* Op Ed page every Thursday.

Q: Is there any type of firm that should *not* **advertise in newspapers?**

A: From a brand standpoint, many soft drink people and beer advertisers are not predisposed to newspapers. Packaged goods advertisers (i.e., national food products) use newspapers selectively. We are not a big part of the media mix for them. And when they use newspapers, it's for sales promotion—inserts and coupons—rather than brand advertising.

Q: How should the ad manager plan his newspaper advertising and what are the specific advantages newspapers offer over other media?

A: If you are the client, the first thing you want to do is look at objectives. If you work with an agency, you set the direction, and the agency comes to agreement. You need to determine what the competition is doing, demographics of target markets, trading or geographic zone, and how much you are willing to spend.

Once these questions are answered, then you must say, "How can I best communicate this message?" Look at values of each media. In newspapers, immediacy, impact, local audience, ability to distribute by town, zip code, or county, and short lead time are the major advantages. Also, newspapers have an upscaleness to them. The audience has a better education and income than, say, TV viewers.

Once you have made a decision to use newspapers, now determine the type of ad you will run. Display or classified? Will you use a coupon? graphics? photography? What size will the ad be? What day of the week will the ad run? How often? Which months? Is your business seasonal? Will ads be tied into announcements of specific product sales or new product announcements? Will newspaper advertising support other media?

Another key issue is position. The position you get is somewhat dependent on frequency and volume—how much you spend. The paper will be more flexible about where you run if you are a bigger advertiser. Once position is determined, other key factors are frequency, size, and days of the week.

Q: How is newspaper space sold?

A: Newspaper advertising is generally sold on a column inch basis. We also have Standard Advertising Units—units of various size defined by the Newspaper Advertising Bureau.

Q: How do you determine the cost of advertising?

A: By rate cards. You can buy space contracts based on frequency, size, number of pages run. The more lines or inches or pages you run in a year, the greater your volume discount.

Make sure you understand what rates are available and get the best possible discount available based on the investment you will make. All rates are published. *The New York Times* has 14 rate cards for different advertiser categories: retail, beverage, tobacco, transportation, national food advertisers.

Within a given category, each advertiser gets the same rate. Discounts are based on annual spending. This enables us to offer advertisers an incentive to invest more in advertising.

Q: What is the difference between a volume discount and a frequency discount?

A: Volume is based on number of pages; frequency is based on how often you run. Volume and frequency discounts can be mixed. They might even be interchangeable.

Q: What happens if you don't run as many ads as you contracted for?

A: An advertising contract with a newspaper is not a legal contract in the strict sense of being forced to hold to it. If you do not run that linage, we just bill you at the higher rate.

Q: What happens if you spend more on advertising than contracted for?

A: Within the calendar year, we change the contract, get you the appropriate rate and the highest discount possible.

Q: How does an advertiser determine which section of the paper to advertise in?

A: Essentially, we get hundreds of ads every day. Positioning of these individual ads is based on the size of paper, type of ads we run, and the requests we get. If you never used our paper before, the sales rep takes you through its make-up. In most cases, retailers run in the front of the first section of the paper.

Then, based on how many advertising units or inches you might run per day, there are theme sections offering opportunities within their page. Positioning is really predicated on the type of advertiser, how much you run, and type of news hole we have. News is made up around ads.

If you don't have a major budget, the key is: Where in the newspaper can an ad the size you are going to run get the highest amount of exposure? The sales rep can help. Frequency dictates level of exposure—the more you run, the better your opportunities for good positions. Premium positions can be bought by paying more (e.g., top, outside, or even a designated page as long as it is not already taken up by major full-page advertiser).

Q: Is it better to be near the front of a particular section, in the middle, or toward the back?

A: Newspapers do readership studies on how their particular papers are read, and it is almost common sense that folks who look through a paper will at least notice most pages. There is a high level of readership on national and local news. But if you are interested in business, advertise in business. Overall, you run in the main news section.

Many times, an up-front position does have better chance for better readership. But if an ad is not creative and does not hold attention, someone with a strategic position and solid creative could get a better response and readership score.

Q: Is there a position on the page which is best?

A: Premium positions: the top of the page and the outer edge of the page. When people do not have big budgets, they buy these positions and end up with greater exposure. It translates into better response.

Q: How do you get the best position?

A: Sales reps can help here. They understand the marketplace of the newspaper—what positions are most appropriate, what is available. Smaller advertisers must judiciously use their space and positions.

Q: How do you determine what size ad to use?

A: What kind of reach and frequency do you want? It depends on your creative approach. If you feel you need a dominant halftone, strong headline, and intrusive copy, then I think it dictates a certain size. I've seen people use one word or no words on a page. Yet I've seen a whole page of type. There are as many techniques as there are pages in the newspaper.

Thousands of ads run daily. If you think about all those transactions, and that a person in Long Island put a 4-line classified ad in a 100+ page real estate section, and that he sold his home from that ad, you realize it's pretty remarkable. People who read papers preselect their reading. It is targeted, and newspapers are a utilitarian product. People read based on their need.

Now, if you are a store or brand manager, your objectives differ from those of the home-seller running a classified. You are doing business every week. Every day of the week. Your needs are different. So creative and merchandise and prices and image become important.

Q: What's the best frequency for newspaper advertising? Daily? Twice a week? Weekly?

A: Frequency is based on budget. If you have a store, and your budget is finite, and you do the most business on weekends, then advertise on Wednesday or Thursday in the living and home sections. This catches your customers as they are planning for the weekend.

But, newspapers are read five days a week. And some smart marketers use other days effectively.

Q: Which is more important—frequency or size?

A: Size is sometimes more important, based on message. I think there is a minimum size, and it depends on how tight your objectives are and what you want your ads to deliver, not only to consumers but to other audiences as well.

Q: For how long can an ad run before response drops off and the advertiser must change it or run a completely new ad?

A: Those with the least patience are the people who create. Some consumer ad campaigns—the Prudential Rock, the Marlboro Man—have been with us for years. When to change your ad? It depends on the desired freshness of creative approach, which is based on your own sales cycle or product development cycle.

If you are a retailer, you want to move merchandise, so you run ads every day of the week to move product out of the store. If you are an image advertiser, you run the same ad in the same position to give people more information about your store or product. Most retailers change their ad every week based on merchandise and pricing.

Q: How do I know whether I should be running in the Sunday edition or during the week?

A: In many markets, Sunday is still the primary day, the one day of tranquility. If there is a dual household income, Sunday is the one day that people are together and can make buying decisions. Also, it's a day when more attention can be given to the newspaper. Many newspapers offer "Sunday" sections that are actually delivered in advance on Saturday or even Friday.

Sunday can be a primary advertising day for the retailer who can come back with a few ads during the week to carry him through a cycle of 7 days.

Q: Are some months better than others in terms of when to run newspaper ads?

A: The Newspaper Advertising Bureau has done analysis on merchandise sales cycles. White sales sell better in January. Furs and swimsuits are also seasonal. But seasonal trends change. Some products that were once seasonal are now sold by people all the time.

Q: Does adding a second color enhance the effectiveness of an ad?

A: Most research indicates that when color is introduced into an ad, the readership of the ad is enhanced. Color becomes a benefit.

Q: Do you prefer to pubset or have the advertiser send in a camera-ready mechanical?

A: *The New York Times* encourages camera ready art. Many other papers pubset (i.e., set the advertiser's copy into type). We do a degree of that, but most material is camera-ready.

Q: Should advertisers advertise only in the large local daily, or should weeklies, shoppers, and "penny savers" also be part of the program?

A: I think that, based on budget or reach, the first thing to consider in running your ad is the editorial environment. How does it rub off on advertising? If you want just a quick hit for a limited number of people, smaller weeklies and shoppers may suffice.

But if you need credibility and have the money, associate yourself with a well-written product where the news is gathered on a daily basis. Most major daily advertisers look to the more sophisticated papers. But at the same time, there is no denying market trend toward highly segmented papers which reach individual counties, towns, or even certain streets within a city. Advertisers today want to know what specific houses the paper is going to and learn as much about each person in each house as possible.

The majority of newspaper dollars spent today is with major market papers, even though smaller regionals and weeklies represent a strong alternative. In response to this competition, most major papers are looking to become more user-friendly with relevant editorial to help busy people and more emphasis on news *features* as well as hard news.

For the intelligent individual looking for analysis and points of view, there is no substitute for newspapers. The time spent reading a quality paper versus a shopping sheet or penny saver is an advantage we offer. Yet there is no denying that these weeklies and shoppers proliferate and offer segmentation advertisers are looking for.

Q: Do you do "P.I." (per inquiry) deals or sell remnant space (unpurchased ad space) at a discount?

A: We have *standby space.* It is what the name indicates: The ad is put on standby and inserted when the space becomes available.

We don't offer it on a regular basis, and we insert standby ads only as needed to make up sections or balance them out. They must fit specific size requirements. And the advertiser has no control of timing, which destroys the advantage of immediacy. Standby space at *The New York Times* is available for 30 to 50 percent off our regular published rates.

Q: What is your policy for *make-goods* (free rerun of an ad if the quality of reproduction is poor or some other mistake is made)?

A: Each paper has its own policies. It's really a customer service issue that's difficult to standardize. With a metro paper running 70,000 copies an hour on high-speed presses, sometimes the tints or reproductions are not going to be as good as in a magazine, which is on a higher gloss paper and prints using a different printing process. When an ad is questioned, we evaluate the damage and determine what type of credit is involved.

Q: What about cooperative advertising in which manufacturers pay for a portion of the retailer's ad if the retailer features the manufacturer's product? Is the newspaper itself an active participant or is it all done between the manufacturer and the retailer?

A: Co-op advertising is a multibillion dollar business and a way in which manufacturers can move product by having multiple distributors contribute to the advertising. It is also a way for retailers to garner dollars from their manufacturer based on amount of units purchased.

Most major newspapers have specific structures to deal with co-op advertising. I would suggest finding out who the coop manager is at your newspaper. He or she can help bring together more dollars from the manufacturer by uncovering opportunities for the retailer.

Q: What elements make for an effective newspaper ad?

A: There are some basics: A strong headline or an arresting art display which leads people to want to read it. Strong copy. Intrusive artwork. The best copywriters in the world are retail copywriters.

Q: Does it help to have an ad agency in terms of getting better quality ads or saving money on space?

A: Whether you use an agency depends on your needs, your budget, and whether you require all the services an agency provides. When you choose an agency, work with one that shares your outlook and philosophy on advertising.

Q: Do you give the 15 percent agency discount on space to advertisers who place their own ads through in-house ad agencies? If so, what qualifies an in-house ad department as an official "agency"?

A: Agencies get the 15 percent commission. You don't get the commission if you are an advertiser. An in-house agency must have more than one account or we don't give them an agency discount.

Q: If I want my ad to run on Wednesday when must I get it to the paper?

A: By Tuesday afternoon. Twenty-four hours is standard.

Q: What are some of the most common mistakes you see advertisers make?

A: Advertisers do not spend enough time analyzing how they should be using newspapers to best advantage. Not enough time planning. Also, advertisers do not use enough frequency to build a brand or image or develop responses.

Paying close attention to creative. You need good creative to sell your product and present to the reader what your product really represents. That is a real trick.

Q: How are newspapers changing the way they work with advertisers?

A: Marketing. Newspapers will now work with you to design marketing plans. More newspapers are doing it more and more, developing partnerships with advertisers to help them plan their strategic positions, frequency, media schedules. This goes way beyond the traditional role of just selling them an ad.

Advertisers are also using newspapers as information sources on markets, customers, product purchasing habits, advertising performance, trends, techniques, consumer behavior, and so on. The Newspaper Advertising Bureau and the American Newspaper Publishers Association can also be helpful in this regard.

Computers are also revolutionizing advertising in many ways with such advances as computer make-up and composition of newspaper pages and desktop publishing. Two interesting developments are the Ad Sat system for transmitting photo-engraved artwork via satellite and "remote entry" computer systems for classifieds.

Increasing The Response To Your Newspaper Ads

What kind of response do you want your ads to produce? Some advertisers want direct mail order and telephone sales of their product. Others want to induce the consumer to come to their place of business, such as a retailer who runs advertising to increase store traffic.

Whatever you are selling, and however you are selling it, you probably want some kind of immediate, measurable response. Mike Pavlish, one of the top copywriters in the United States, offers the following tips for improving your advertising response:

1. Make a low-priced sample or trial offer. The less it costs the buyer, the better your response. For example, test a 3-month subscription at $30 against a 12-month subscription at $120.
2. Offer a no-risk money-back guarantee. Make it good for at least 30 days. Feature the guarantee prominently in your ad.
3. Offer a bill-me-later option.
4. Accept Visa and MasterCard.
5. Don't state that you wait for checks to clear.
6. Include a toll-free order number.
7. Offer a free bonus or two with the order. Give it a price for high value perception.
8. Offer a free trial.
9. Make your price sound like a bargain. Compare it to something else to show the true value. For example: "For the price of a night on the town that lasts only one night, you'll have a self-motivating tool that'll increase your income for a lifetime."
10. Test offer presentations. For example: Test "buy one, get one free" against "50 percent off."
11. Make your offer good for a limited time only. State a specific time limit or deadline date in the copy.

12. Make your headline give your biggest customer benefit.
13. Use a benefit-loaded subhead under the main headline.
14. Get the word "FREE" in your headline or subhead.
15. Offer something free—either a free gift with purchase or a free booklet/brochure with inquiry.
16. Say "no salesman will visit you" or "no salesman will call you" if one won't.
17. Use a coupon.
18. Don't talk about your company unless a customer benefit is in the same sentence.
19. Indent each paragraph three to five spaces for easier reading. This subconsciously gets the reader into the paragraph, which is what you want to do.
20. Improve your guarantee. The less risk your customer perceives taking, the higher your response.
21. Make a better, hard-to-resist offer.
22. Test different media. Key your ads so you know which publication did best.
23. Put yourself in the reader's shoes. What benefit would you want the most? Stress that in your copy forcefully.
24. Include specific testimonials.
25. Leave plenty of white space around all your advertising. This eliminates the cluttered, cramped, hard-to-read look.
26. Have your headline set in big, bold type. The more the headline jumps out at the reader, with a big benefit he wants, the easier the advertising will appear to read. As a rule of thumb, your headline can take up to one-fourth of the space in the ad.
27. Keep sentences and paragraphs short. As a rule, no paragraph should be more than five lines. No sentence should be more than 20 words. You should also use an occasional very short paragraph. This will break up the monotony of all paragraphs being the same size.
28. Underline, capitalize, or italicize a few key words or statements. The key is not to overdo it, but to make the advertising look more exciting and easy to read. It also emphasizes the particular word or phrase being underlined.

29. List benefits using bullets, check marks, asterisks, or numbers. It makes the ad look much easier to read.
30. Use benefit-loaded subheads. Subheads are one of the most effective methods for making advertising easier to read. Plus, they allow you to make an easy transition from one selling point to another.

*How To Measure Response**

Newspaper advertising (*all* advertising, for that matter) elicits only two types of response: Qualitative and quantitative. Qualitative response is more difficult to measure. (See the chapter on Image Advertising.) It represents the shaping of attitudes in the marketplace; how people *feel* about your business, your store, your professional services. Quantitative response is easier to measure. It represents the number of coupons returned, the number of sales rung up, the number of new patients brought in.

Many advertisers feel the latter is more important than the former. In truth, *both* types of response contribute to the success of any advertising program. But, for planning purposes, it is more reasonable to characterize *qualitative* response as part of your strategic efforts, and *quantitative* response as your tactical methods.

There are two elements to consider in measuring responses. First is the *accumulation* of data, and second is the *interpretation* of that data—the translation of information into useful, practical information that gives you sales figures and helps you formulate future plans and direction.

The accumulation procedures will depend primarily on the nature of your enterprise, and what style of advertising you utilize. For our purposes, there are only five kinds of newspaper advertising. These are:

1. The single- or multi-product ad
2. The single- or multi-service ad
3. The direct-selling ad
4. The announcement ad
5. The image-building ad

Of these, only the first three provide a clear-cut foundation for gathering quantitative responses. The remaining two are more likely to evoke qualitative responses. To complicate matters, some ads may be more accurately described as a combination of two or more ad types. It is helpful at the out-

*Reprinted with permission from *How to Create Small Space Newspaper Advertising That Works.*

set, therefore, to know precisely *why* you are advertising, what types of response you wish to achieve, and then choose the simplest ad type to reach your tactical objective.

Strategically, you may wish to measure all advertising on a broad calendar front; that is, set aside a quarterly (or annual) advertising budget, and not be overly concerned about each insertion's success quotient. Some advertisers adopt this procedure to eliminate the day-to-day problems of data gathering, interpretation, and cost accounting. But since all responses are valueless without comparative data, a manager may find himself or herself looking only at last year's figures to see if this year's sales are any better.

For small-space advertisers (with comparatively small budgets), it's best to conduct quantitative research on a per-ad or per-campaign basis. The management value behind this more detailed undertaking warrants the effort. It enables you to see if an ad has paid for itself. It gives you an accurate historical record so that you may want to repeat a successful ad next week or next year to see if you can achieve the same results (with little more invested in production). And finally it gives you some minimal data on ad positioning, and how it may or may not have affected response. (This information may help you in persuading your newspaper to respond more favorably to your specific position requests.)

Finally, the size of some enterprises may make it logistically impractical to secure detailed sales response figures (although many chain operations have installed sophisticated reporting devices that can give managers nearly hour-by-hour results). Multi-media promotions for the same products or services make it nearly impossible to determine which medium was responsible for which sales. (You can alter your record-keeping accordingly, if you wish, to include gross media costs.)

The performance systems suggested here, then, are primarily for measuring specific responses to a specific newspaper ad. It's a single-medium system. Each system assigns a share of your space costs to "corporate advertising," i.e., the pure value of promoting your enterprise, or "getting your name out in front of the public." We must presume that this investment in *general* exposure will boost total annual sales including sales of products or services *not* advertised.

Some managers make it a practice to record mark-downs as advertising expenses. This may be done to satisfy some weird accounting procedure; we're interested primarily in whether or not the ad paid for itself. Markdowns will simply reduce the gross return on investment. But managers hope, of course, that the increase in volume that results from this price-cutting tactic will more than offset the reductions, or at least speed up the turn.

Inherent in each system are three parts. These are:

Part 1

—*The collection of response data.* This will depend on your own operations. In some circumstances, the cash register will record the information needed; in other situations, copies of sales slips will have to be examined. For smaller operations, a clipboard at the sales counter can be used, containing a report form; or a pad of colored-paper ballots with a shoe-box ballot holder can be installed. The amount and type of data collected will vary.

For example, in addition to sales figures, you may want to learn additional facts. Although this system correctly attributes *all* sales to advertising effectiveness (and correctly so), you may want to know which customers are *new;* building new business is the only way to offset normal attrition; replacing customers lost through moves, deaths, and other unhappy reasons, and it's the only sure way to increase gross sales. You will also want to know the value of *collateral* sales. These should be reported, and included in the payback calculations. Because of the brief shelf-life of newspapers, sales figures should be assessed no more than 72 hours after an ad runs; this term can be shortened, of course, to coincide with the published end-date of a particular sale. In all instances, staff cooperation is imperative. Employees should understand *why* they are collecting this information; that it will help management to establish valid, more cost-effective advertising/marketing policies and thus increase total sales. A healthy company is a good company to work for.

Part 2

—*The collection of advertising data.* You will need to know (1) the cost of advertising space, (2) the cost of advertising production (3) any rebates due to co-op advertising contributions or newspaper credits. (These are dollar-value figures.) But in addition, you will want to record, for later interpretation (1) the position of your ad within the newspaper (2) weather conditions on the day the ad ran and for the two days following, and (3) any extenuating circumstances, such as staff out sick, running out of the advertised item, etc.

No. of Units Sold Each Day for 3 Days × Gross Profit Earned on Each Unit + Gross Profit Earned on Collateral Sales = $

The formula for determining advertising investment is:

Cost of Ad Space + Production Costs − 15% for Corporate Advertising − Any Co-Op Credits = $

Part 3

—Information storage and evaluation. By totaling up gross profits from the sale of the advertised item, and any collateral sales too, and subtracting the cost of the space and production, minus 15 percent for Corporate Advertising value, and minus any co-op funds or credits, you should have a fair idea of the return on your investment.

A good ROI is 20 percent. Few retailers achieve that level consistently. There are special instances when you may show far more than that amount. Averaging a 15% ROI across the year is good business. Keep in mind that a good advertising campaign will give you collateral benefits that are not easily measurable; ie: new customers attracted to the operation who may continue to be patrons even for unadvertised goods or services; improving your commercial standing or "presence" in the community; fortifying your position vis-á-vis your competition; and building credibility for subsequent advertising. Because these additional benefits *are* difficult to measure, yet undeniably result in increased sales, some value has to be assigned to them. We group these peripheral factors under the heading of Corporate Advertising, and assume that at least 15 percent of any insertion can be charged off to this effort.

Collect at least two copies of each insertion. One ad gets cut out of its page and placed in a scrapbook with response and evaluation data attached. The other ad is filed intact (the whole page) so you can refer to it later if you need to argue with the paper for better position, or to more accurately compare the returns from the same ad, run at different times of the year, with substantially different sales results. If you run the same ad three times in a row (either daily, or alternate days) you need mount only one insertion in the scrapbook, indicating all three insertion dates. But keep full tearsheets of all the ads in your file for possible future reference.

To summarize: the formula for gathering sales data is:

Subtract one total from the other (hopefully Sales from Investment) to determine return on investment, or ROI. Express the difference as a percentage of the investment. Example: if gross profits equal $2000, and the investment equals $1500, then the ROI is $500, or 30%. By using the decimal system as the common denominator for expressing sales results, you will have a more practical formula for comparing results between different campaigns.

This formula, with appropriate modifications, can be used to measure the advertising responses for single and multi-product ads, single and multi-service ads, and the direct-sell ad. Of these, the direct-sell ad (taking orders for a specific item or items by mail or by phone) is obviously the easiest to measure. As a rule of thumb, however (because you eliminate the possibility of accumulating collateral sales benefits) a higher profit margin is recommended for items sold through the mail. Most direct-selling entrepreneurs will use a 100 to 300 percent markup formula; i.e.: an item that costs $20 should be sold for $40 to $60 to help insure a reasonable ROI. In those instances when there is no retail establishment, do *not* deduct the 15% allowance for Corporate Advertising. Direct selling must be its own sole support. Remember also to include any costs for shipping if the item sold is postpaid.

NO. OF CHECKING ACCOUNTS OPENED EACH DAY FOR 3 DAYS ×THE ANTICIPATED GROSS PROFIT FROM EACH ACCOUNT + ANY ANTICIPATED GROSS PROFITS FROM COLLATERAL SALES = $

The formula for determining advertising costs, however, would be unchanged, except that there would be little opportunity for any supplier co-op funds:

COST OF AD SPACE + PRODUCTIONS COSTS − 15% FOR CORPORATE ADVERTISING = COST OF ADVERTISING

This measurement system forces management to take a hard look at profitability, particularly where services are sold. Generally, services are a product of *time.* If it costs the company 2 person-hours to clean and check a furnace, @ $20 per hour, and the service is advertised for $60, the gross profit is $60 minus $40, or $20. The question is, how many of those service calls, at a gross profit of $20 each, will have to be sold to make the ad pay for itself. If, however, you're trying to open the door to annual fuel oil deliveries at the same time, then *that* becomes your collateral sale. Obviously, the 72-hour measuring term must be abandoned in this case, so you can include the *anticipated seasonal gross* from the collateral sale. This figure could easily surpass the service sale, and should enter into the decision-making analysis when establishing your annual advertising budget (covered in the next chapter).

Some service costs or profits are not so easily calculated. In the banking industry, for example, although bankers are prone to call their services "products," (checking accounts, savings certificates, etc.) chances are the customer does not perceive them this way. The customer wants a checking account service; the financial institution, utilizing historical data, must determine how much is in the *average* checking account balance and how much gross profit the institution can expect to derive from that balance within a 12-month period.

In this case, the profit yield cannot be measured in 72 hours (although the number of sales can). And there remains the possibility of cross-selling new or existing customers into collateral services. (This effort has become so important to larger institutions that they have installed software systems that profile each customer, listing the services, balances, etc. that accrue during each customer's tenure.)

The formula for measuring advertising response for a financial operation would be modified, for example, as follows:

Unfortunately, this equation assumes profits that may never materialize. That may discourage some financial advertisers, but our intent here is threefold: (1) to somehow get a handle on the effectiveness of small-space newspaper advertising as a marketing tool, (2) to sensitize financial marketers to the disparity in profit potential inherent in different financial services, and (3) to reconfirm the importance of cross-selling services to both *new* and *existing* customers. Indeed, *each customer* should become a profit center; nobody's going to get rich just renting safety deposit boxes.

Two types of ads—Announcement and Image ads—are far more difficult to measure quantitatively. Although this form of newspaper advertising is not designed to get an immediate return on investment (see next chapter), they should become a part of each advertiser's campaign budget.

One way to insure at least a *partial,* immediate ROI is to combine an Announcement or Image ad with product or service sales. In this instance, the 15 percent ratio set aside for "Corporate Advertising" would be increased proportionately. Thus, if half the ad space were devoted to an announcement of new walk-in clinic hours, for example, then 65% of the space (50% plus existing 15%) should be subtracted from the space and production costs for calculating the ROI.

As with financial advertising, medical services require cost-accounting methods, too, to determine the potential annual value for each new patient subscriber. Thus, on the average, if each new patient can be expected to yield $200 in gross profit within a 12-month period, then it is that figure that is used for calculating ROI. Physicians may want to adopt *two* sets of gross-profit ratings, one for individual patients, male and female, and another for families. This data can be refined even further by age (statistically, a married woman of child-bearing age, may be worth more to a clinic in the next 12 months than a single, 20-year-old male).

In any case, patient retention is imperative. Natural attrition will account for 10 to 20% patient loss in any year, depending in part on the characteristic mobility of community residents. Acquiring new patients (as in any business or practice) is good for the financial health of the clinic or medical office.

One more word about Image Advertising. My own inclination is to abstain from running direct product or service promotions in combination with an image program. If you've committed your enterprise to an image newspaper campaign, chalk the whole expense up to Corporate Advertising. Then, if you can, put your ear to the ground and your nose to the grindstone and your finger on the pulse of the market. In that position you may be able to elicit some *qualitative* feedback to help justify the expense. Naturally, you will have some objective in mind before undertaking an image campaign (awareness levels improved, change in management or customer policies, etc.). Your curiosity may require benchmark surveys, taken before and after the campaign, to determine if you have successfully altered any attitudes in the marketplace. You may discover that, cleverly directed, you can accomplish the same attitude changes with product or service advertising and thus reap the benefits of direct sales, too.

Checklist For Newspaper Advertising

- ☐ *Merchandise.* Does the ad offer merchandise having wide appeal, special features, price appeal, and timeliness?
- ☐ *Medium.* Is a newspaper the best medium for the ad, or would another—such as direct mail, radio, or television—be more appropriate?
- ☐ *Location.* Is the ad situated in the best spot in the paper (in both section and page location)?
- ☐ *Size.* Is the ad large enough to do the job expected of it? Does it omit important details, or is it overcrowded with nonessential information?
- ☐ *Headline.* Does the headline express the major single idea about the merchandise advertised? The headline should be an informative statement, not simply a label. *Example:* "Sturdy shoes for active boys, specially priced at $12.85" is better than "Boys' shoes, $12.95."

- ☐ *Illustration.* Does the illustration (if one is used) express the idea the headline conveys?
- ☐ *Merchandise Information.* Does the copy give the basic facts about the goods, or does it leave out information that would be important to the reader?
- ☐ *Layout.* Does the arrangement of the parts of the ad and the use of white space make the ad easy to read? Does it stimulate the reader to look at all the contents of the ad?
- ☐ *Human Interest.* Does the ad—through illustration, headline, and copy—appeal to the customers' wants and wishes?
- ☐ *"You" Attitude.* Is the ad written and presented from the customer's point of view (and with the customer's interests clearly in mind)—or from the advertiser's?
- ☐ *Believability.* To the objective, nonpartisan reader, does the ad ring true, or does it perhaps sound exaggerated or somewhat phoney?
- ☐ *Typeface.* Does the ad use a distinctive typeface—different from those of competitors?
- ☐ *Spur to Action.* Does the ad stimulate prompt action through devices such as use of a coupon, statement of limited quantities, announcement of a specific time period for the promotion or impending event?
- ☐ *Sponsor Identification.* Does the ad use a specially prepared signature cut that is always associated with the store and that identifies it at a glance? Also, does it always include the following institutional details: store location, hours open, telephone number, location of advertising goods, and whether phone and mail orders are accepted?

Resources

- For a more detailed discussion of newspaper advertising, read *How to Create Small-Space Newspaper Advertising That Works,* by Ken Eichenbaum. For sales information, write to Unicom Publishing Group, 4100 W. River Lane, Milwaukee, Wisconsin 53209, or telephone 414-354-5440.
- The Newspaper Advertising Bureau is a valuable resource for information on newspaper advertising and publishing, offering numerous books, seminars, slide presentations, newsletters, booklets, and special reports. For a free copy of their catalog write: Newspaper Advertising Bureau,

Inc., 1180 Avenue of the Americas, New York, NY 10036, phone (212) 921-5080.

- Another good information resource for advertisers is the American Newspaper Publishers Association, Box 17407 Dulles Airport, Washington DC 20041, phone (703) 648-1000. Ask for "Facts About Newspapers" and a free publications list.

Glossary: A Few Common Newspaper Terms

AD/SAT™. The Satellite Network for Advertising Delivery provides high-resolution facsimile transmission newspaper advertising, by satellite, in minutes.

Broadsheet. A "standard" or large-size newspaper. In July 1984, most broadsheet dailies adopted a uniform, 13-inch printed page width and a full depth of 21 inches or deeper, up to 22½ inches.

City zone. The corporate city limit, plus adjoining areas in cases of heavily populated areas, as designated by the Audit Bureau of Circulation (ABC).

Color scanner. Electronic equipment that automatically produces separations for ROP process (or "full") color.

Column inch. Space measurement one column wide and one inch deep.

Double truck. Two facing pages used for a single unbroken advertisement. Also called a two-page spread.

Facsimile transmission. The electronic transmission of a page image (usually to printing plants at other sites).

Front-end system. A total computer system for text entry, editing, formatting and/or billing, for editorial, display advertising and/or classified advertising.

Pagination system. A computerized makeup system for composing whole pages of type, line art and halftones.

Penetration. For a given newspaper within a specified area, the ratio of circulation to households; the newspaper equivalent of a household rating in broadcast.

ROP (Run-Of-Paper). ROP is a term generally applied to ads that appear on a newspaper page (as distinguished from inserts or preprints).

Scotch double truck. A single unbroken advertisement on two facing pages bordered by one full column of editorial on each of its vertical sides and by shallow columns of editorial across the top.

Tabloid. A newspaper with a smaller page size than a broadsheet. A full tabloid page is usually 14-inches deep. The width varies from $9\frac{3}{8}$ inches (short cut-off) to $10\frac{13}{16}$ inches (long cut-off).

CHAPTER 11
Evaluating Media

Making Media Decisions

At this point, you have probably made some decision as to whether you will use print advertising and, if so, what percentage of your budget will be allocated to space advertising, what products will be advertised, and how frequently you will run your ads.

The next tasks are to evaluate and select the *specific* publications where your ads will run and to plan an exact schedule of the dates your ads will run.

Two concepts that are important in evaluating various media opportunities are cost per thousand analysis and frequency/reach balance. These concepts help establish a price/value relationship between media and opportunities.

*The discussions of *Cost per thousand* and *Reach and frequency* are based on information contained in "Advertising Media Decisions," by Michael F. Walsh, Management Aid Number 4.016, published by the U.S. Small Business Administration and reprinted with permission.

*Cost Per Thousand**

When media opportunities are compared, it is often confusing to determine which one offers the best value. For example, suppose an advertiser is considering two newspapers to carry advertising. Both newspapers cover the market, but they have different costs and circulations, as is shown in Table 11.1.

Which paper offers the best deal? At first glance, you might say Newspaper A, because the ad costs half as much as Newspaper B. But wait a minute. Newspaper B has 35,000 more readers. How do you balance cost with readership?

The answer is to compare the two media on a *cost per thousand basis,* abbreviated as CPM. Simply stated, cost per thousand is the unit of price of media. It is the cost of advertising (in dollars) that the advertiser pays per one thousand individuals reached by the medium.

Cost per thousand is calculated using this formula:

$$\text{CPM} = \frac{\text{Cost of Media}}{\text{Circulation of Media}} \times 1{,}000$$

To solve the example problem:

$$\text{CPM for A} = 100/25{,}000 \times 1{,}000 = \$4.00$$
$$\text{CPM for B} = 200/60{,}000 \times 1{,}000 = \$3.33$$

When you advertise in Newspaper B, you pay only $3.33 to reach one thousand readers as opposed to $4.00 for an ad in Newspaper A. Moreover, Newspaper B reaches a greater audience. From this perspective, Newspaper B is the better media buy.

Cost per thousand analysis helps to provide a common comparison point for evaluating media vehicles, regardless of the size of the vehicle or its cost. Although cost per thousand analysis provides a comparison of the cost and relative audience of media vehicles, it does not evaluate the effectiveness of the vehicles. Also, it can be misleading to presume the most

Table 11.1. Comparison of advertising expense in two newspapers.

Newspaper	*Cost of Ad*	*Circulation*
Newspaper A	$100	25,000
Newspaper B	$200	60,000

cost-efficient media will be the one that is best read or that generates the most response.

For this reason, caution is suggested in comparing different media vehicles strictly on a cost per thousand basis. The best use of cost per thousand analysis is to compare similar media vehicles (e.g., two local newspapers) as opposed to completely different media vehicles (e.g., radio station WXYR against daily newspaper *The Podunk Courier*).

Tip: When calculating cost per thousand, be sure to divide the cost of the media by the circulation of the medium rather than the "readership." Circulation is the actual number of copies distributed. But most media sales reps quote a "readership" figure, which is the circulation (number of copies) multiplied by the number of people reading each copy—the "pass-along" factor. (So named because the primary subscriber passes his copy of the magazine or newspaper along to others in his household or office.)

While circulation figures for most publications are scrupulously audited by independent auditing organizations, pass-along figures are frequently subject to exaggerated claims. Therefore, "readership" figures can be misleading and overstated, but circulation figures are more likely to be accurate, and all CPM calculations should be based on circulation.

Reach and Frequency

When comparing advertising programs it is important to select the most effective balance of reach and frequency. Reach and frequency are two terms used to describe the overall delivery of an advertising program. "Reach" is the number of individuals exposed to at least one advertising message over a period of time. If a media plan covers four out of five people in the target market, it has a reach of 80 percent (4 divided by 5). The formula for calculating reach is given below:

$$\text{Reach} = \frac{\text{Number of People Exposed to Advertising}}{\text{Total Number of People in Target Market}} \times 100$$

Frequency is the average number of times an individual is exposed to a message. If four people see six of your messages, the frequency is 1.5 (6 divided by 4). The formula for calculating frequency is:

$$\text{Frequency} = \frac{\text{Number of Times Message is Repeated}}{\text{Number of People Seeing Your Message}}$$

Although they are separate concepts, frequency and reach are interrelated. Consider this hypothetical situation as an example. An advertiser who uses magazines for his advertising program has two options.

1. Run his ad one time in five different magazines.
2. Run his ad five times in one magazine.

Assuming both options have the same cost, it's easy to see that option 1 emphasizes reach while option 2 emphasizes frequency.

A major cause of failure in advertising programs is insufficient frequency. It is far more effective to reduce the reach of an advertising campaign—that is, to narrow the target audience—and add frequency, than to reduce frequency and add reach.

Example: Let's say you are a leasing company. Your business is to buy and lease large capital equipment to businesses that want to expand their operations but don't want to tie up capital by buying equipment outright. Leasing enables them to get the machinery they need without a large capital expenditure.

Assume that your geographic market is confined to your home state, that there are 100,000 potential prospects for your service, and that you have a promotion budget of $50,000. This might, if you count your pennies carefully, allow you to do *one* mailing to all the potential buyers. If they happen not to need leasing that day, they'll ignore you. And they may hesitate to do business with you, because they haven't heard of you. Your campaign bombs because you've gone for reach (quantity) instead of frequency (quality).

The solution? Target a specific industry. For example: plastics manufacturers that need expensive extruders and injection molding machines. You discover that there are 1,000 plastics manufacturers in your state. Now your $50,000 allows you to use a mix of direct mail, telephone follow-up, print advertising, and trade show promotion to get your message to these folks on a monthly basis. Not only that, but the message can be more tailored to their needs (e.g., copy can talk about providing "injection molders and extruders," not just the vague term "equipment").

The result? By increasing frequency, you dramatically increase the likelihood that your message will reach a prospect at a time when he needs or is considering the benefit your service provides. And the repetition of message will build awareness of your company and your reputation in the prospect's mind, so even if he doesn't have your material in front of him on the day he decides to look into equipment leasing, your name will come instantly to mind and he will call you to initiate a discussion.

How To Select And Evaluate Print Media

The two steps are:

1. Determine which magazines and newspapers are possible candidates for advertising.
2. Evaluate each publication and select those you will advertise in.

Determine Which Magazines and Newspapers are Possible Candidates for Advertising

The indispensable advertiser's guide to print media is *Standard Rate and Data Service,* 3004 Glenview Road, Wilmette, Illinois 60091, phone 800-323-4588. Three volumes list virtually all newspapers and magazines that accept paid advertising, including 1,800 newspapers, 4,800 business and trade journals, 400 farm publications, and 1,600 consumer magazines. Listings give basic facts about the advertising policies of each publication, such as advertising rates, space units available, circulation, and the name of the advertising director. There is also a volume listing 8,500 radio stations and another listing 970 TV stations that run paid commercials.

All five books are published monthly and are available on an annual subscription basis (combined annual subscription fee for all three volumes covering print media is $1,237). The main branch of your local library should have copies.

Tip: Want to get your own set of SRDS for free? Most ad agencies subscribe; because new editions are issued monthly, they probably throw out last month's set each time new books arrive. Ask your ad agency (or, if you don't have one, a friend or colleague who works at an ad agency) to give you these books instead of throwing them out. For your purposes, having an SRDS that's a few months old is no handicap, because you'll be contacting all publications for updates rates and schedules anyway before you commit to advertising.

Go through SRDS and select those publications that are likely candidates for your media schedule. For magazines, these would be publications covering your reader's industry, hobby, or specialized area of interest. For newspapers, these would typically be papers serving your target geographic market area.

Next, call or write to all likely candidates and request that they send you a sample issue, rate card, and media kit. These are sent free to legitimate potential advertisers, and there is no obligation to advertise. However, the salesperson will ask for your phone number so they can call back and sell you on their publication. That's okay; they're in business to make money, not give out free sample issues.

You will use these materials to evaluate the publication and make your media selection. On large-scale advertising campaigns, media selection is a massive, complex task—so specialized that most ad agencies have people called "media planners" to provide advice and guidance to your clients.

Tip: If you are using an ad agency, take advantage of their media planning expertise. While the setting of overall marketing objectives and creation of a business or marketing plan is best done primarily in-house by the advertiser with some assistance from outside consultants, media planning and buying is usually best done by the ad agency.

Typically, the agency creates a first draft of the media schedule (based on a thorough understanding of your objectives) and submits it to the client for review. The client leans heavily on the agency's familiarity with the media and their overall greater expertise in the area of media planning.

However, clients often are aware of "insider" publications (typically newsletters, association bulletins, specialized journals, or small regional publications) that agencies are unaware of, and clients may have good arguments why these should be added to the media schedule. The agency goes back and then submits a final plan based on the client's input into the first draft schedule.

While the expert advice of an agency media planner or outside advertising/media consultant is frequently beneficial, small to medium-size advertisers—especially those in specialized markets where the number of publications is few and the relative merit of each journal is well known—should be able to make their own media selections without help. This is done by talking to people (your own staff, customers, prospects), through market research (surveys and questions asking prospects and customers which publications they read), by reading SRDS, and by studying the media kits you have sent for.

Inside the Media Kit

How do you evaluate media? There is no magic formula. CPM and reach/frequency analyses are helpful. But they are just one means of comparison—not the final word.

Numbers are helpful, but they are not the entire story. An analysis of readership, ad response rates, and circulation figures may clearly indicate that Publication X is the most cost-efficient media buy and reaches the greatest number of target prospects. But what if the articles are lousy, the magazine is a joke, and no one in the industry reads the thing? There is no known formula that takes this into account, yet it is one of the most important factors in media selection.

Let's say you get a bunch of media kits in the mail. Let's open one and go through the contents. Here is what you will find:

Sample Issue

One of the most important items to study is the sample issue. As stated earlier, the quality of the magazine is of key importance. Some things to consider as you thumb through the sample issue are:

Amount of advertising

What is the ratio of editorial (articles) to advertising? In an informal survey of business magazine publishers, Howard Sawyer found that a mix of 40 percent editorial and 60 percent advertising was considered ideal by most of the publishers he spoke with.

Too few ads means a financially unhealthy publication and a medium which other advertisers have not found effective (or, a medium which is new and unproven and therefore considered high-risk, low-potential by most of your fellow advertisers).

If there are too many ads, the magazine is closer to a "shopper" than a legitimate journal and may not be read or respected by your prospects. Also, your ad runs the risk of being lost in the shuffle.

Placement of advertising

Should ads face editorial? Are there many *ad* wells (two-page spreads where each facing page contains an advertisement)? Ad wells are undesirable as people skip over them. Also, is there a directory section in the back where small classifieds and display classifieds can be placed inexpensively? This is sometimes a good way to check the pulling power of a publication at low cost before committing to larger space.

Quality of editorial

Are the articles real news and information or promotional fluff? Is the technical level sufficient or too superficial for your audience? If it's a newspaper, does it provide adequate local coverage? (Newpaper buyers want to see news of people and events close to home.) Are there special sections in which your ad would get extra notice?

Editorial schedule

Are there one or more special issues or "theme" issues on topics related to your product? Many advertisers prefer to run ads in special issues where the editorial environment is related to the proposition of their ad.

Tip: Compile an annual "special issues" schedule that lists, by month, all the special issues published by all the magazines covering your field. This can be done by incorporating the editorial schedules from the various media kits into a summary report. Advertising and publicity activities can then be planned to take maximum advantage of the special issue coverage.

Graphic quality

Our society is on the way to becoming less word-oriented, more visual-oriented. Does the publication have attractive layout, readable typography, and eye-catching photos and illustrations that draw readers into the pages? Is color advertising available?

Editorial opportunities

Are there "new literature" sections which could feature a publicity release on your product? Would it be possible for someone at your company to contribute an article, article series, or even a regular column to the magazine? A mix of editorial and advertising supporting your product is more effective than advertising alone.

Is the subscription paid or controlled?

"Paid" means that people pay to receive the magazine. "Controlled" means the magazine is distributed free to readers who qualify; to qualify, they must complete a questionnaire (called a "qualification card") indicating their position, industry, type of firm, and job activities.

Whether there is any difference in advertising effectiveness between paid and controlled-circulation publications is a subject of never-ending and inconclusive debate. The paid publications argue that their product is more valuable because people pay for it, and that controlled-circulation magazines are worthless—so worthless that the publishers have to give them away.

The controlled-circulation publications point out that, while *anyone* can buy a subscription to the paid magazine, the controlled-circulation publication picks and chooses its circulation, distributing only to those who qualify and denying subscriptions to the rest. This ensures a readership that has the characteristics the advertiser desires. Also, because the controlled publications aggressively offer free subscriptions to everyone in the industry, they claim more complete coverage than paid journals, which generally are read by a smaller percentage of people in any given market.

Current advertisers

Who else is advertising in the magazine? Beware of publications with no ads from other companies selling products similar to yours. Usually, if a publication is a good medium for your type of product, at least one or more of your competitors already will have discovered it and will be advertising in it.

Audit Statement

The *audit statement* (also called the *publisher's statement*), is an official confirmation of the publication's circulation. To be official, the audit statement must be approved and certified by an independent auditing organization. The two major auditing organizations are the Audit Bureau of Circulations (ABC) and the Business Publications Audit of Circulations (BPA). The ABC and BPA audit statements are printed in black ink on colored paper and have the seal of the certifying organization on the first page.

The presence of an audit statement allows you to accept the magazine's circulation claims with a high degree of certainty, while the lack of an audit statement makes the figure somewhat suspect. Many advertisers have a standing rule against advertising in any unaudited publication.

Another use of the audit statement is that it allows you to perform a more refined CPM calculation based on your specific target market rather than just gross circulation. For example, if an ad in Magazine X costs $1,000, and the circulation is 20,000, CPM is $50. But is it really? Suppose you are interested in reaching only Chief Financial Officers but not CEOs or other executives.

You check Magazine X's audit statement and find the following circulation breakdown: 2,500 subscribers are Chief Financial Officers, 2,500 are Chief Executive Officers, 5,000 are Chief Operating Officers, and 10,000 are Plant Managers. As far as reaching your target market is concerned, the CPM of this publication is $1,000 divided by 2,500 CFOs (and 7,500 CEOs and COOs are of no interest and represent wasted circulation. This refined CPM is $1,000/2,500 × 1,000 or $400.

You compare this with another magazine, Magazine Y. An ad also costs $1,000 here, but eh circulation is only 3,000. However, *all* 3,000 subscribers are CFOs. The CPM, as it related to reaching CFOs, is $1,000/3,000 × 1,000, or $333–making Magazine Y the better buy even though the circulation is less than one-third of its competitor.

Rate Card

The *rate card* is a price list for advertising. To calculate CPM, you divide the advertising space costs listed in the rate card by the circulation figures listed in the audit statement.

The rate card contains the prices for all space units (full page, half page, etc.), physical dimensions of these units (width and depth), frequency discounts, mechanical requirements, charge for special positions, closing dates (dates by which the insertion order and the film or mechanical of your ad must be received), publication schedule, terms, shipping instructions, and charges for color.

Your main interest in evaluating the rate card is calculating CPM, comparing the CPM with similar publications, and determining whether the publication is a good value—and whether you can afford the space. Some publications might have a low CPM but such a high overall space rate that they are simply beyond your budget. In this case, you would opt for smaller circulation publications, choosing frequency instead of reach.

Editorial Calendar

For each issue, the *editorial calendar* provides a partial list of proposed articles as well as the themes or topics of any special issues. Advertisers generally check the editorial calendar for three things:

1. Special or "theme" issues with topics complementary to their advertising.
2. Issues showcasing a particular trade show or convention which the advertiser is participating in or deems important.
3. Issues with "bonus distribution"—meaning distribution of extra copies beyond the circulation listed in the audit statement. Typically, these are distributed at trade shows or conventions.

Special Issue Notices

Many publishers print monthly fliers or bulletins highlighting the editorial features of the next issue in which advertising space is available. When an advertiser or agency requests a media kit, the current month's notice is inserted.

Also, the person requesting the media kit may be placed on a mailing list to automatically receive notices announcing each monthly issue's editorial content and slant. This is an effective marketing strategy for the publication: The advertiser gets the notice, sees there is an article relating to his product or service, and decides on that basis to place an ad in that particular issue.

Editorial Profile

This is a narrative description intended to communicate the position the publication holds within its industry. For example, the editorial profile of *Folio:* begins by stating that *Folio:* is the "magazine for magazine management" and is written for "executives in the magazine publishing industry." The editorial profile defines the purpose, audience, slant, and style of the publication. It may be stated briefly in the rate card and expanded upon in a number of glossy advertising pieces and brochures contained within the media kit.

The editorial profile is important because it describes the type of environment in which your ad will appear. If you are selling a home study course on how to fix your own car, would a magazine called *Popular Science* be a good place to advertise? You can't tell just by the title. But read the editorial profile, and you learn that *Popular Science* is indeed a good choice because it is written for the same do-it-yourselfer to whom your course would appeal. On the other hand, if *Popular Science* was an academic journal, a course on fixing cars would not be appropriate for its readership.

Reader/Subscriber Studies

These are surveys performed by the magazine (or by an independent research firm on behalf of the magazine). They are designed to create a *profile* of the average reader (his buying habits, job title, interests, likes, dislikes, demographic characteristics, etc.) so that advertisers can see whether the magazine readership matches the characteristics of the target prospect.

These are basically two types of studies:

1. The first is an in-depth profile of the readership, going into all the items described above. *Folio:* magazine's subscriber study, for example, tells:
   - Average length of time reader has been in the magazine business (the industry covered by *Folio:* is magazine publishing).
   - Average budget each reader controls.
   - Amount of time spent reading each issue.
   - Types of products and services purchased.
   - Pass-along readership (number of other people reading the subscriber's copy of the magazine).
   - Responsiveness to ads (whether readers take action as a result of reading ads in the magazine).

   Obviously, this type of information is helpful in formulating advertising plans. For example, if you are selling widgets, and the study reveals that only 2.5 percent of the readership is involved in widgets, the magazine is not the right medium for your widget ad.
2. The second type of study makes a direct comparison with competitive magazines in the same field. For example, if there are three major magazines in an industry—Magazines A, B, and C—Magazine A might do a study comparing readership, circulation, or popularity and reputation of the three magazines. This is sometimes called a "preference study" and labelled as such in the media kit.

Frankly, these direct comparisons are of only limited value. Rather than shedding light on pure information useful to advertisers, these studies are designed deliberately to promote and push Magazine A over its competitors. The proof is that, in reviewing hundreds of media kits, I have *never* found a competitive study in a media kit that did not claim 100 percent superiority for the magazine publishing the study. Comparison studies are promotional, not objective or information, and should be read as such.

Insertion Order

More and more media kits contain order forms called *insertion orders* or *advertising orders.* To reserve space in the magazine, you simply complete the insertion order and mail or fax it back to the publication.

Years ago, media kits did not contain order forms because most advertising was placed by agencies, and the agencies all have their own standard insertion order forms preprinted. But today, a growing number of advertisers are not using agencies, but instead buy creative services *a la carte* from freelancers, consultants, design studios, and other independent sources—and are doing their own media buying. Lacking a standard insertion order, these advertisers appreciate the ease and convenience of being provided with the necessary form. The magazines are including insertion orders in their media kits because it means more sales and recognizes that today advertisers often place their own space orders.

Some Questions To Ask When Evaluating Media

As you look over the media kit and sample issue, ask yourself:

- Is the audience of the media vehicle appropriate for my advertising campaign? (Does the medium reach my target market?)
- Relative to the available media, does this particular medium provide a large audience at comparatively low cost?
- Can the media vehicle be effective in communicating the sales message?
- Is this a good publication? Is it well-written, attractively designed, and do people in the field read and respect it?
- Is there the right mixture of ads and articles? (Anywhere from 40:60 to 60:40)? If there are few ads, why is this? If the publication is mostly ads, what does this say about how well it is read?
- Do most of the readers fit the profile of your target market? Or is there a lot of wasted circulation (e.g., readers who are not prospects for your product or service)?
- Is there a publication that is less well-known but more targeted toward your specific target prospect (i.e., a more "vertical" publication)?
- Should you be advertising in horizontal publications, verticals, or both? (Horizontal media aim at broad audiences. Vertical magazines target specific, narrow, special-interest readerships.)
- Is the cost of an ad affordable? If not, are there publications with less reach (smaller circulation) that are in line with your budget?
- Does the magazine provide alternative media for reaching its subscribership? (These can include directories, catalogs, postcard decks, and new publicity releases or opportunities for editorial contribu-

tions.) If so, would it be better to use a combination of these rather than just a schedule of the more costly ads?

- Does the magazine have a readership card service for inquiries? This may be important if generating a high quantity of leads is your goal.
- Does the publication offer readership studies? Some publications offer free ad readership studies to advertisers who advertise in certain issues. These are useful if you want to know how effective your ads are but don't have the budget to conduct your own study.
- What is the CPM (cost per thousand)? How does it compare with the other top publications in the field? If it is significantly higher, is this magazine really worth the extra money?
- Have you surveyed your customers and prospects to find out what they read? If so, is this magazine at the top of their list? If not, why not?
- Does the publisher stick strictly with the published rate card or are they negotiable? Some are, and it would be foolish not to take advantage of every price break you can get.
- Do your competitors advertise in this publication? If not, why not? Have they tested it and found it unproductive? Rarely will you find a suitable publication that is truly an undiscovered gem.
- Is the publication audited? If not, how can you be sure that the circulation and readership figures quoted in promotional literature is accurate?
- Is the publication so unique, highly specialized, narrowly targeted, well-respected, or inexpensive that you should test some ads even if the numbers indicate that you should pass?
- Are there special issues or features which would make a good editorial tie-in with your ad? If so, can you get news coverage or feature placement for some editorial on your company or product to complement your advertising?
- Are there regional editions? Some of the larger national magazines sell advertising confined to a particular geographic region of the country (e.g., East, West, North, South). The advantage is that you pay a lower rate because your ads are limited to a particular market. This is beneficial to advertisers who want to save money and target their markets geographically.
- Have you advertised in this publication in the past? If so, did it pay?
- Can you afford to test the publication? That is, can you afford to risk the price of some ads to find out whether the publication will work or not? If

you have no extra money to spare, forget tests and put this year's ad dollars into proven media.

- Are you being forced by management to advertise in a publication for subjective reasons? Many executives do not understand advertising and insist on having a nice color ad in Magazine X because they think it's prestigious, or they insist on an ad in a society's newsletter because they think it is important to "pay their dues." If you are forced into making media selection based on subjective criteria rather than thoughtful analysis, tell your management you agree to do so—provided these insertions can be listed separately on the advertising schedule under the heading "Charity Cases/Dues Paying." Because that's exactly what they are. Make it clear that you cannot be held accountable for the productivity of ad space purchased on anything other than rational analysis of media.
- If you are an ad agency or consultant, ask yourself: "Does the client have superior knowledge of this publication—knowledge that enables me to validly add the medium to the client's media schedule despite the fact that it falls short in my own analysis?" Sometimes a publication or other medium is better than the numbers indicate, and clients know that it's good because they are more in touch than the agency or consultant with what people are reading, watching, or listening to in a particular market.

A Recap: 12 Steps To Better Media Selection

1. Determine your total advertising budget.
2. Select the marketing communications tools you will use to promote your product (e.g., magazine ads, direct mail, postcard decks).
3. List the marketing communications tools you will *not* use (e.g., television commercials, radio, billboards).
4. Allocate your total budget among the marketing communications tools you have selected. For example, if your budget is $100,000, and you allocate 50 percent to magazine advertising, 30 percent to direct mail, and 20 percent to public relations, your budget for magazine advertising is $50,000.
5. Take the first item in your budget (e.g., magazine advertising) and make a list of all possible publications (or mailing lists, or channels, etc.) you might advertise in. Use SRDS as your reference.
6. Get media kits for all the publications.

7. Analyze each publication using the guidelines discussed in this chapter.
8. List, in order of preference, the publications worth advertising in. Eliminate those that are poor or marginal.
9. Determine the desired frequency—the number of times you want to advertise—as well as the size of the ad you need.
10. Multiply the frequency by the cost of the ad space. *For example,* your ad is a full page in four colors. The cost per insertion in Magazine A is $4,000. You want to run six times. Total cost is 6 × $4,000 = $24,000. This leaves a budget of $26,000 ($50,000 − $24,000) for the remaining publications on your list.
11. Go to the second most important publication on your list and repeat step 10. If you have money left over, go to the third publication on your list, the fourth, and so on, until you have used up the allotted budget for this particular communications medium.
12. Repeat this procedure for other media (i.e., newspaper ads, directory ads, etc.) called for in your advertising plan.

More Media Selection Tips For Specific Media

Magazines

Magazines are useful in targeting specific audiences, such as teenagers, travelers, fashion-conscious men and women, retired seniors, and many others. Magazines also provide access to various geographic markets. National magazines are distributed nationally, but there are also local or regional magazines, which are ideal for an advertiser whose business is limited geographically.

Magazines have a much longer life than newspapers. According to research, magazines are kept an average of four to six months after their original sale. Thus, magazines will continue to generate readership and exposure for some time.

Also, magazines have much longer lead times. Generally, magazines require reservations and advertising materials at least one month prior to the intended issue date. Advertisers who require timely and constantly changing messages find magazines difficult to use because of this.

It is important to analyze circulation by examining the magazine's audit statement; most reputable magazines are audited. Readership studies are also helpful in defining the demographics and purchasing habits of a magazine's readers.

Newspapers

Besides reaching a large audience, newspapers have two other desirable characteristics. First, newspapers convey a sense of immediacy. The contents are extremely timely, and newspapers are usually read the same day they are published. Second, advertising in newspapers is usually welcomed by readers. Unlike other media where advertising is sometimes considered interruptive or annoying, many newspaper readers actually search out advertisements. The biggest drawback to newspaper advertising is competition from other ads. Any single issue is likely to have pages and pages of advertising. Fractional ads must compete with other ads on the same page.

Because newspapers have large print runs and appear daily, they often suffer from poor reproduction. Time deadlines and budget restrictions prevent newspapers from equaling the reproduction quality of photographs and illustrations found in magazines. As a result, simple line drawings are usually the best illustrations for use in newspapers.

When buying newspaper advertising, keep in mind two important factors: the circulation and the size of the ad. The cost of newspaper advertising is based mainly on these two factors.

It is important to examine and evaluate a newspaper's circulation. First, compare the total circulation of several newspapers. Most large newspapers have their circulation audited annually by an independent organization. Once an audit is completed, the newspaper will publish a sworn audit statement, which is the official estimate of circulation for a given year.

In addition, newspaper audit statements break down circulation geographically. For a given newspaper, the audit statement reveals the different areas in which the paper is sold and the quantity sold in each area. This information is essential in analyzing the total circulation of paper against the desired geographic circulation.

Using the optimal size ad in the newspaper is critical for success. Even though the size of an ad is most often governed by budget and communications needs, it is also important to be at parity with your competitors. If both you and your competitor advertise in the same paper, and your competitor uses a larger ad, it is likely that your competitor will receive more readership—unless your creative effort is clearly superior in its attention-getting power.

Similar to "frequent flyer" programs offered by airlines, newspapers give rate discounts to frequent advertisers. These discounts depend on individual newspaper policy, but most newspapers publish a rate card detailing all discounts and other terms of advertising. In summary, use the newspapers that provide the highest desired circulation at the lowest cost with the least waste.

Outdoor Advertising

Outdoor advertising is available in a variety of forms: traditional billboards along roadsides; placards in mass transit vehicles; posters in airports and train stations. Outdoor advertising offers tremendous exposure opportunities because the signs are placed in strategic locations where thousands of people see them daily.

As a result, outdoor advertising can be expensive. Although the cost can be justified for some advertisers in terms of potential audience and high efficiency, outdoor advertising is unaffordable for many others.

The biggest drawback to outdoor advertising is the limitation of message content. A typical exposure to an outdoor advertisement ranges from a few seconds to perhaps ten seconds. Thus, advertising content is limited to just one or two simple thoughts.

The location of outdoor media is the key factor in selection. Do you want a market-wide program, or one limited to a particular neighborhood? Review all of the proposed locations of an outdoor medium.

Be sure each location is well-maintained and offers an unobstructed view of your potential advertisement. Once the advertising is placed and actually running, be sure that your ads will be checked and receive prompt attention if damaged. In subway and bus advertising, the use of "take-ones" (bunches of detachable reply forms attached to the signage) can dramatically increase response.

Directories

Directory advertising is completely different from most other advertising media. Directories are used by people who are ready to buy. Although other media deliver readers, viewers, or listeners, directories deliver strictly buyers. Because directories are published annually, advertisers are unable to change or modify their message often.

As with any print vehicle, coverage of the marketplace is important. Be sure your entire marketplace is covered by the intended directory with minimal waste. To ensure the success of an advertising program, try to meet your competition head on. Look at your competitors. What sections do they advertise in? What size ad do they use?

Directories are a source of information for buyers. People who use directories need specific information to complete their buying decision and frequently make decisions based on information in the directories. Therefore, you should include as much information as possible in your directory ad, making sure all key points are listed.

Television

Television is one of the most effective media vehicles. Because television presents sight, sound, and motion, commercials closely represent personalized selling. Additionally, television can reach tremendous numbers of people. Nearly every home in the country has at least one television set. The average household watches over seven hours of TV per day.

Although television has wide appeal, advertisers can target their message to specific audiences. Most TV stations subscribe to research studies on viewing habits, which they share with advertisers.

With this information, advertisers can limit their buys to the specific time periods or programs most likely to contact their target audiences. In addition, the use of cable TV, even in local markets, can add selectivity in targeting advertising messages.

Television's biggest drawback is cost. TV costs are based on two factors: the size of the audience and the relative demand for TV time.

Because the most popular shows attract the largest audiences, advertising during these shows is most expensive. Likewise, a high demand for television time will also increase price. Also, the cost of producing a single 30-second television commercial can easily exceed $40,000 if done by a professional ad agency or TV production house. For most small to medium-size advertisers, television is not affordable.

TV advertising must be simple and brief. Commercials are usually only 30 seconds long, and advertisers must present their message within this time limit. Consequently, commercials are limited to easily understood ideas and only one or two sales points per commercial.

To buy television time, contact the sales department of a TV station and ask for a proposal based on your target audience, length of commercial time, and the dollar portion of your total advertising budget allotted to television. Check the station's coverage map to determine if your market will be reached or if many of the people watching represent wasted viewership.

Compare proposals from competing stations and use rating information to determine the most efficient value. Additionally, refer to competitive proposals to negotiate with high-priced stations.

Finally, consider the timing of your commercials throughout a schedule. Be sure your commercials will not always be shown at the same time during the same program. Your chances of success are better if you present your commercials at different times during several different TV programs.

Radio

Radio and television are closely related, yet radio has its own advantages and disadvantages. Advertising costs, as with TV, are based on the size of audience and demand for advertising. But radio generally costs far less than television.

Radio is a fairly targeted medium, more so than outdoor advertising but less so than direct mail. By selecting appropriate stations and time periods, advertisers can reach specific audiences.

For example, radio stations that concentrate their programming on top hits tend to attract teens and young adults. Also, because listeners are loyal and tend to listen to the same shows and stations day after day, radio is an excellent medium for building frequency.

Unlike television, radio commercials can be simple and inexpensive to produce. By using on-air announcers to read your commercials, you eliminate production costs. And some radio stations will even assist you in writing the script or do it for you at no charge.

Radio's most obvious drawback is its lack of visual qualities. Also, because there are so many stations to choose from, especially in large cities, selecting the best station can be difficult.

Another concern with radio is its broadcast coverage. Depending on the power of the radio station's transmitter, exposure within the market may be insufficient. Or, if the transmitter is powerful, it may broadcast far beyond your immediate geographic market, which means wasted listenership.

Remember two factors when buying radio time. First, summer is a popular time for radio advertising, and you should expect to pay more from June through September. Second, radio commercials are usually 30 or 60 seconds long. Generally, a 30-second commercial is priced at 80 percent of the cost of a 60-second commercial.

Otherwise, radio is purchased like television. You contact the sales department of a radio station and ask for a proposal based on your target audience, length of schedule, and budget. Also, ask for the ratings of the radio station for your target audience.

Large stations subscribe to radio research services and can share this information at no charge. Consult the coverage map and double-check that the radio station can be clearly heard throughout your intended market area.

Be sure to compare proposals from different stations and negotiate price with the stations. The goal of your purchase is to use radio stations that provide maximum ratings and market coverage for the lowest cost.

CHAPTER 12

Scheduling Your Advertising Program

When Should Advertising Be Scheduled?

In previous chapters, we learned how to develop an overall advertising plan and to select the *specific* media in which our advertising will run. The next step is to develop a schedule that outlines the precise days, weeks, or months and the specific *issues* in each medium in which our advertising will be placed. In other words, the *timing* of the campaign.

"Timing in advertising also has a profound effect on its success," notes Michael F. Walsh of Ketchum Communications. "Some products can be advertised and sold all year, while others can be advertised and sold during specific seasons. Advertisers should take advantage of seasonal trends. For example, the Christmas season accounts for up to 25 percent of some business's yearly sales.

"In addition, special events such as grand openings, new product introductions, and special promotions need appropriate advertising. Companies should schedule advertising to match these events. An effective advertising campaign is targeted to a specific audience in a specific place at a specific time. Knowing the objectives of who, where, and when in advance improves the advertising program's success."

Table 12.1 lists some common products and services along with the season where sales are greatest and hence the most effort should be put toward advertising.

Although most businesses have seasonal peaks and valleys, few are wholly dependent on a particular season for total sales. For this reason, advertising needs to be scheduled to ensure a steady stream of business throughout the year. It may be more concentrated in some months than others; some months it may be absent altogether; but *frequency* must be planned for and maintained. That is, you must deliberately determine how many times to communicate with your target audiences and when.

Table 12.1. Seasonal trends for common products and services.

Product/Service	*Best Time to Promote and Advertise*
Lawn care service	Spring (March - June); early Summer
Air conditioners	Late Spring; all Summer
Storm doors and windows	When weather turns cold (Fall; Winter)
Home improvements (general)	Spring
Firewood	Fall
Mail order gift catalogs	Christmas season (October through December)
Greeting cards	Christmas season
Business gifts	Christmas season
Business-to-business products and services (general)	January through May; September through mid-November
Back-to-school products (clothing, supplies)	Labor Day
Flags	Memorial Day, Fourth of July
Weight loss centers; health spas; diet products	Spring (in preparation for bathing suit season)
Home insulation	Fall
Gardening tools; supplies; flowers; bulbs	Spring
Self-improvement/home study materials	September; January
Seminars (business and general public)	September through mid-November; January through May
Landscaping service	Spring
Swimming pools	Spring and Summer
Ski resort	Winter
Florida or Caribbean vacation	Fall, Winter, Spring
Resume service	March through June (graduation time)

What kind of advertising schedule is required to meet this need? The answer is *The Rule of Seven*, a concept invented by marketing consultant and author Dr. Jeffrey Lant. Let's take a look at this idea in detail.

Definition Of The Rule Of Seven

The Rule of Seven basically says that if you want your prospect to take action and buy what you are selling, you must connect with him a *minimum* of seven times within an 18-month period. Then and only then can you reasonably expect the prospect to know what you can do for him and get him to take action on his own behalf.

The Rule of Seven starts from the simple premise that most people don't take action the first time they become aware of a product or service. There are several reasons for this:

- They are slothful.
- They have other commitments.
- They forget about it.
- They don't have time.
- They don't have a pressing need for what you are selling right now.
- They mean to take action but somehow "never get around to it." (Translation: you have not provided sufficient motivation or urgency for them to act NOW.)
- They have qualms about the value of the product or service.
- They have qualms about the reputation of the seller.
- They hesitate because of the expense.
- Many other things compete for their time and attention.
- Natural human inertia, laziness, and indifference.
- They know they will probably be seeing your ad or getting your mailings again and therefore can always make a buying decision later on.
- They don't pay attention to your ad, read your copy, or understand what your product is and what it can do for them.
- They already have one.
- They already buy from someone else and are satisfied with that supplier.

Most people really don't pay that much attention to advertising. Part of the reason is that the average prospect is bombarded by 2,500 to 7,500 advertising messages each week. We have all become adept at screening out the "noise" of these intrusions.

Putting The Rule Of Seven To Work

To overcome the prospect's indifference, disinterest, and plain lack of attention, you must repeat your message over and over again until it sinks in or the prospect finally takes notice.

To do this, says Dr. Lant, you must connect with your prospect at least seven times within a year and a half. Each communication with your prospect must clearly convey that you understand the prospect's problem and have something that can solve it. And, each communication must reach the *same* person again and again.

What does this mean? First, it suggests that all your marketing must be rigorously customer-centered, focusing exclusively on the prospect and his needs, not you and your offer.

Second, you must connect again and again with the same prospect: namely, the prospect you know has the problem you can solve. Your objective is to make a permanent impact on the individual so that he knows, must know, that you exist, that you understand his problem, and can solve it expeditiously.

If you want your marketing to work, you must target the people who have the problem your product or service can solve. And you must connect with them a minimum of seven times in 18 months using the following kinds of vehicles (this is a partial list):

- Free publicity via radio, television, newspapers, magazines, and newsletters.
- Workshops and seminars sponsored by trade associations catering to your prospects.
- Telemarketing.
- Direct mail.
- Catalogs.
- Postcard decks.
- Paid advertising.

Note that the Rule of Seven does not require that all seven contacts with your prospect be in the same medium. For example, you do not have to run seven ads. Instead, you can run three ads, send out two mailings, and telephone your prospect twice to connect with him the required seven times.

According to Dr. Lant, the steps required to successfully apply the Rule of Seven are as follows:

1. Identify a compact body of prospects.
2. Identify, in advance of using them, all the means of reaching these prospects.
3. Ensure that you have the necessary skills and resources to effectively use these marketing communications tools.
4. Select at least seven means of connecting with the same group of prospects within an 18-month period.

What A Rule Of Seven Plan Might Look Like

There are literally thousands of seven-step plans which might enable you to connect with your prospects in ways which enable them to take action and buy what you are selling. Here is a sample from Dr. Lant:

First Contact

Write a problem-solving article for your trade association's publication. Conclude the article with information about the problem you solve and how the buyer can reach you. Make sure to include your name, address, and telephone number.

Second Contact

Arrange to make a presentation at the trade association's annual meeting. So that all the people attending this meeting are aware of you, ask to have your sales brochures or other marketing materials placed in the registration packets of everyone attending.

Also, give each person attending your session a questionnaire, letting them tell you what problems they want to solve in their businesses. All questions should be geared to the kinds of products and services you sell. Thus, if you are selling widgets, one question might be, "Which models of widgets do you have the most difficulty getting delivered on short notice?"

If people in your audience answer this question, you follow up by promising swift delivery on the models they indicate.

Third Contact

Follow up all the people in your session, either with a letter or phone call to find out how you can be of service. This includes those who returned the questionnaire as well as those who did not.

Fourth Contact

Arrange with next year's workshop planner about your session. The time to begin planning next year's presentation is the minute you have finished this year's successful presentation.

Fifth Contact

Rent the mailing list of the association (whose members should now have some idea of who you are). Send a direct mail package to the list, including complete information on your products and services and how they can be ordered.

Sixth Contact

Follow up in 90 days with a second mailing.

Seventh Contact

At the same time, arrange to have a second article by you published in the association's publication. This should reach them at about the same time your mailing does (preferably a few days beforehand).

Key point: Seven contacts is the *minimum* required in the 18-month period to ensure that prospects are really getting your message. If you think and plan systematically, you will soon exceed the minimum. The more frequently you contact prospects above the minimum seven times, the better. Most marketers agree that you cannot communicate with your prospects and customers too often. Budget, time, and energy are usually the limiting factors.

Tips To Make Sure The Rule Of Seven Works

1. Write down your Rule of Seven schedule. The trick to successfully using the Rule of Seven is, first, to identify all the marketing gambits you

could use to reach the same body of prospects. Then ascertain whether these are really available to you. For instance, perhaps you want to place an article in an association's newsletter, but upon checking discover they do not accept contributions from non-members. This bit of information will inevitably influence what you can do.

Once you've discovered that an alternative is available, however, close on it. If the publication *can* print your article, write the editor and propose the article to him, so that you soon learn whether you can count on publication of the article as one of your seven connections with this group of prospects. If the editor does not want the article, you will need to find another alternative.

2. Always select an inexpensive alternative over an expensive one. Thus, before buying a paid ad, see whether you can get free publicity.

Tip: Think creatively. Swap an article for an ad. Then use the ad in a different issue or in another publication reaching the same audience. Instead of using direct mail, see whether your information can get to the same people as a package or invoice stuffer or through some other "ride along" offer. These formats are invariably less expensive than stand-alone direct mail packages.

3. Make sure every gambit you use enables the prospect to connect with you directly. Thus, each must contain your name, address, and telephone number. If you accept credit cards, add this information, too. Finally, if you have a catalog or free brochure, mention its availability. In short, each marketing gambit must tell the reader how to reach you and what to ask for.

4. Plan completely and far in advance. Write down the minimum of seven marketing gambits you need in the 18-month time period and make sure each of them is available to you.

As you complete one of these gambits, begin exploring the possibility of another that will place you in touch with the same group of prospects. If you wish to maintain your competitive edge, you must always have a gambit in place and a series of additional contacts ready to connect you with your prospects in the future.

Media Scheduling

There are countless media scheduling options. You can dream it up and it can be done. There is certainly no "right" or "wrong" way. Some of the things that will affect what schedule you choose are the obvious ones of season and budget. If you're introducing a new product, your schedule will be different than if you're in a maintenance period.

The eight common methods for scheduling media, as illustrated Figure 12.1, are:

1. *Steady.* You are visible an equal amount every month—a steady, continuing, and ongoing schedule. Very, very few marketers do this, except for corporate image campaigns.
2. *Alternating even.* The same as steady, except you advertise every other month rather than 12 times a year. A few do this—usually print and broadcast efforts.
3. *Alternating staggered.* An every-other-month effort that builds up, drops back, and then builds again. This could be a good schedule if you have two very identifiable selling seasons—say, one at Christmas time, another in the Spring.
4. *Flighting.* You advertise heavily and constantly for a period, then drop your ads altogether, then get back in again. Many times this is done on

Figure 12.1. Eight methods for scheduling media.

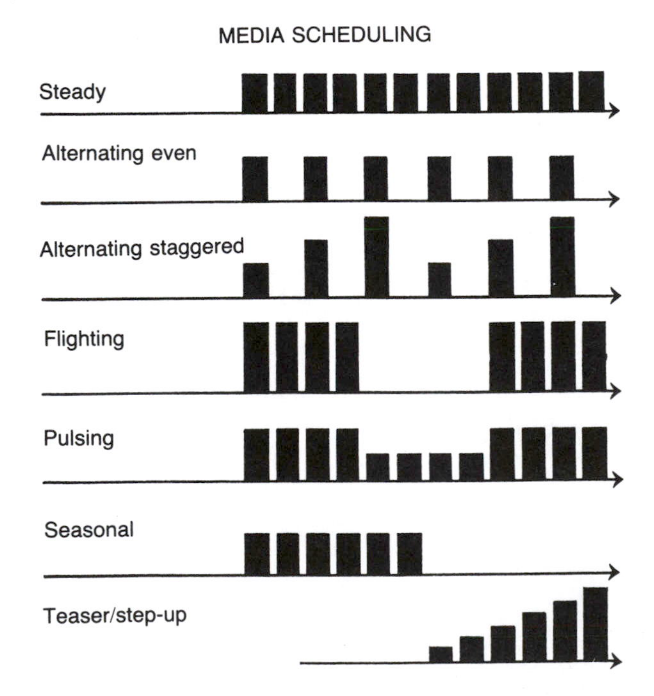

radio, usually for short periods of time: six weeks in, six out, and six back again. It can also work in newspapers, and even direct mail: in the marketplace every few weeks for several months, then out, followed by a heavy repeat schedule.

5. *Pulsing.* Pulsing is similar to flighting, except that during the slow periods you merely cut back on advertising rather than drop it altogether. The pattern: a heavy program, followed by a lighter one, and then heavy again. Print and broadcast are typical tools to use for pulsing campaigns. Sometimes the telephone is included to support the heavy time.
6. *Seasonal.* Just what it says: You run ads steadily as your season approaches, and you don't advertise the rest of the time. This is common with marketers who have a single super-heavy season.
7. *Teaser step-up.* Similar to the seasonal method, except, as the season approaches, advertising starts small, then gradually builds each month until it is greatest at the peak of your sales season. This is also a typical schedule for many in direct marketing, particularly those with consumer mail-order products.
8. *Step-down.* This is the opposite of step-up. The two can go together. Use step-up to lead to your heavy season, and then keep the season going with a step-down: a lesser campaign, but nevertheless a presence. Step-down gradually decreases advertising after the peak sales period until it vanishes during your "dead" months.

As Ray Jutkins points out, "There are really no 'principles of scheduling.' Direct mail is different from print and broadcast. Business-to-business schedules will be different than consumer. Financial service products have a different timetable of promotion than consumables. Previous experience, common sense, and your budget will many times dictate your schedule."

More Rules Of Scheduling

1. If sales are seasonal, schedule ad appearances accordingly. Remember that your "move" on the market should be made well in advance of the buying season.

2. December and the summer months are not as poor months in which to advertise as is generally suspected. In fact, one Laboratory of Ad-

vertising Performance study of inquiry response for a manufacturer showed July to be consistently the peak of the year, with August above average in some years. In another LAP study, one publication found that inquiries in August are about average—better than September and October—and that December pulls better than either May or June.

The fact that many advertisers do stay out of summer issues means that the remaining advertisers have all the better opportunity. Studies have shown that any one ad has a better chance of readership in a thin issue than a thick one. So you have a chance of getting more for your advertising money in the less popular months.

3. Begin a new campaign at the start of your selling season (which is not necessarily the start of the market's buying season), not in January when your new advertising budget year is most likely to begin. Most new advertising campaigns are kicked off at the start of the new budget year, but most sales campaigns start—with enthusiasm the highest—early in the Fall. The intelligent practice is to coordinate advertising with the rise of sales activity which usually occurs following a vacation period.

4. Prepare ads far in advance of publications as you feel safe in doing so. This gives you a chance to distribute reprints of the campaign to salespeople, distributors, dealers, and customers well ahead of appearances in the magazines. Nothing makes a salesperson feel so foolish as to have a customer refer to an ad he has not yet seen.

5. Allow creative and mechanical departments plenty of time to prepare the ad. Ten weeks is a recommended minimum. That is, the background facts should be in the copywriter's possession ten weeks before the first closing date. This may appear to be a long period, but it allows ample time for copy, design, approval, production, and unforeseen delays.

Commonly Asked Scheduling Questions And Answers

Q: What is the right method for scheduling an ad campaign?

A: As Ray Jutkins pointed out earlier in this chapter, there are no "principles of scheduling," no correct method or formula. Experience, objectives, seasonal patterns, market conditions, and objectives are the key factors in determining a schedule.

Q: Is it better to run small ads many times or big ads fewer times?

A: Obviously, the most desirable alternative is to run the big ad many times, but with a limited budget that's not usually possible. The answer is that you have to strike a balance. You must run your ads frequently enough so that they make an impression upon your audience (the Rule of Seven). Yet they must be big enough so that they can contain all the key information you want to communicate.

However, if you have to choose between size and frequency, go for frequency. Repetition is a key factor in communications success, and an ad that is twice as large is not necessarily twice as cost-efficient.

Q: What is the minimum number of times I should run my ad in a publication?

A: A rule widely quoted by advertising agency experts is that to have any impact you must run not less than six times in a monthly magazine. But according to Dr. Lant, Rule of Seven, the key consideration is not the number of times a specific ad is repeated in a particular publication, but rather the number of times the same message is communicated to the same audience in various formats. The Rule of Seven says this should be a minimum of seven times in 18 months.

By making your ad a direct response ad, you can get an immediate measure of whether running the ad in a particular publication is generating the desired results. When you are unsure of a publication, and you have a full-page ad, run it once. Then wait and see what type of response you get. If it's good, expand the schedule. If it stinks, don't continue. If it's marginal, proceed with caution.

If you are sure of the publication but have a limited budget, it's better to run a ¼- or ⅓-page ad three times than a full-page ad once given those two alternatives for the same space dollars.

Q: Is there a danger of running an ad so often that readers tire of it?

A: Yes, but this danger can be minimized by monitoring response (or readership, if that's how you measure). You continue to run the ad according to whatever schedule you set until response begins to drop off. At that point, consider creating a new ad or rerunning an old ad.

A drop-off in response indicates that the majority of prospects have at this point seen your ad and that those who are going to respond already have. A new ad featuring a different appeal can lift response because it intrigues those prospects who were indifferent or unmotivated by the previous ad's content.

Research studies from the McGraw-Hill Laboratory of Advertising Performance show that good ads can continue to generate a high level of readership and response with no appreciable drop-off after numerous repeat insertions. For example, the report summarized in Figure 12.2 tells of a full-page, four-color ad running in *Architectural Record,* a monthly publication. The results show that the fifth insertion pulled almost double the number of inquiries of the first insertion, but the thirteenth insertion pulled 12 percent less response than the original insertion.

Q: How do I resolve scheduling conflicts between ads for my different product lines?

A: Obviously, if the ads appeal to different markets and appear in different media, there is no problem. The question arises when a company has two or more products or product lines that overlap in target market. If two different products from two different divisions are advertised in the same magazine, how should the schedules be balanced?

All else being equal, the ads should appear in different issues rather than the same issue, for purposes of increasing frequency and repetition of the advertiser's name and logo.

However, this may not always be possible. For example, the product managers of the two divisions may both want to run in the May issue, either because it's a special issue or because May marks the beginning of their busy season. If this is the case, you can run multiple ads on consecutive right-hand pages. This creates almost a "mini-catalog" for your company while avoiding "ad wells" (two facing pages, both with ads). Designing the ads with similar typeface and layout style further reinforces the company image and enhances recognition.

Q: How do I find the peak selling periods for my industry?

A: Experience is the best teacher; any salesperson or other executive who has been with your company or in your industry for more than a couple of years knows the answer to this one. However, if there is no one you can ask, then observe the activities of your competitors. A flurry of colorful catalogs in your mail box during the holiday season makes it quite clear when you, as a catalog marketer of consumer gift items, should be mailing.

Books on selling specific types of products or services also help point the way. In his book, *How to Market and Promote Seminars,* Howard Shenson reveals the best and worst months for promoting public

Figure 12.2. Report summary.

13 Repeat Ads Continue to Draw Inquiries With Each Insertion

The Mineral Panels Division of Manville Corporation ran the same full-page, four-color ad 13 times in ARCHITECTURAL RECORD between July 1986 and October 1987. Five times throughout the campaign, repeated insertions generated more inquiries than the initial insertion in July.

Further, throughout the advertising campaign, the same ad continued to draw inquiries for each repeated insertion. Production costs involved in creating a new ad were saved.

McGraw-Hill Research kept records of inquiries received for each insertion. The number of inquiries generated from the initial insertion was indexed at 100, and indices were calculated for the number of inquiries pulled from each subsequent insertion.

Inquiries Generated from a Repeated Ad In A Monthly Publication

Index

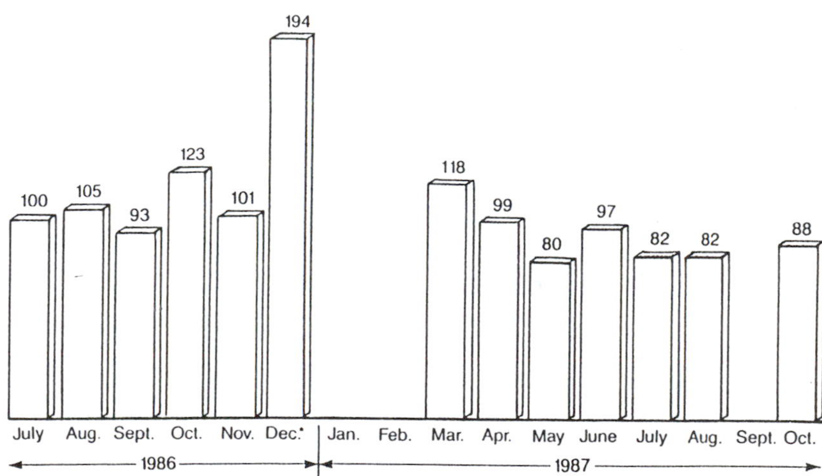

Source: McGraw-Hill Research

*Annual New Products Issue

Copyright © 1988 McGraw-Hill, Inc.
Information in this Report may be reproduced in whole or in part provided that McGraw-Hill Research is expressly acknowledged as the source.

seminars. Russ von Hoelscher gives similar information on the best and worst months to run mail order ads selling books in *How You Can Make a Fortune Selling Information By Mail.* Similar information may be available in books on how to market and sell other types of products and services.

Q: Should different marketing gambits (e.g., direct mail, telephone solicitation, publicity, paid advertising) reach my prospects at the same time, or should these communications be spread out evenly over the months?

A: There is no right answer. It depends on your situation. If you want a steady flow of inquiries, a steady pattern would be best, with a different marketing gambit reaching your audience every month. January might be an ad, February a mailing, March a phone call, April a sales visit, and so on.

On the other hand, if your business is seasonal, you might use the flighting or pulsing patterns shown in Figure 12.1. This means that some months you would bombard your prospects with ads, mailings, articles, phone calls, TV commercials, and so on. Other months you would send them nothing or just do a little advertising.

As you experiment, you learn which combinations work best. Again, there are no rules. Different people have different experiences.

For example, consider the combination of paid advertising and publicity. Many people say that, if you can get an article you've written published in a trade magazine, run your ad in a different issue to increase frequency and give readers two months to catch your message instead of one.

My experience is contrary. I suggest that you run your ad in the same issue your article appears. Why? Because people reading your article will want to know more about you, your company, and your product, and will want to get in touch with you. The article builds up interest, while the ad provides the address and telephone number needed for taking immediate action based on that initial interest.

Q: Any special tips for scheduling advertising for a new product?

A: Only that the schedule will naturally be more heavily weighted at the beginning, in order to make a splash when the product is introduced. As Figure 12.1 demonstrates, the flighting, pulsing, or a combination step-up/step-down pattern fits this requirement.

Q: Are special issues really worthwhile?

A: We touched on this in Chapter 9, and you may want to refer to that discussion.

As for my observations and opinion:

- I have seen no hard data indicating that ads in special issues get higher readership or response, or that special issue advertising is more effective in any way.
- On the other hand, many clients have told me that they feel special issues do pay off and get greater readership for their ads. I do know that, while not all special issues are of equal value, certain special issues of certain publications are read more, discussed more, and kept more—which surely extends the useful life of any ads in these issues.
- I see absolutely no evidence that advertising in special issues is any *less* effective than regular issues. And, since the cost of the space is usually the same, I therefore see no harm in accommodating an advertiser who prefers placement in a special issue over an ordinary issue.
- On the other hand, I do not believe you should run an ad simply for the sake of being included in a special issue. They are not as important or critical as the publishers make them out to be. And, as Scotty Sawyer notes in *Business-to-Business Marketing,* "The argument to the effect that it is disastrous to be 'missing' from any one issue is a thin one. It's difficult enough to get an ad *noticed* without worrying about its *absence* being noticed."

Resource

The Annual National Media Congress is a yearly conference on the subject of media, media buying, media planning, and scheduling. For registration information contact: National Media Congress, Marketing and Media Education, 49 East 21st Street, 6th Floor, New York, NY 10010-6213, Telephone (212) 505-2350.

CHAPTER 13

Co-Op Advertising

What Is Co-Op Advertising?

Co-op, or *cooperative advertising,* is defined by the Newspaper Advertising Bureau (NAB) as "locally oriented advertising mutually agreed upon between the manufacturer (distributor) and retailer, which, when certain conditions are met, both share in the net cost of that advertising."

According to Frank W. Hennessey, Vice President, Co-op Advertising Sales, NAB, "the co-op industry is exploding at all levels." In 1970, $900 million was available for co-op advertising; in 1980, $6 billion, and in 1988, $12.5 billion.

In 1989, over 6,000 manufacturers had co-op advertising plans making $15 billion available for co-op advertising of more than 100,000 products in 52 merchandise categories. Many manufacturers plan to increase co-op marketing budgets betwen 12 to 25 percent, according to Hennessey. In addition, 500 companies per year set up co-op advertising plans for the first time.

Because cooperative advertising is by nature local advertising, most of the co-op money available—nearly 70 percent—is spent on newspaper advertising. The rest is spread between television, radio, outdoor advertising, catalogs, circulars, fliers, direct mail, fairs, expos, trade shows, transit advertising, yellow pages, and premiums and other promotional items.

Why the tremendous growth? "Very simply, because co-op works," says Hennessey. "More and more manufacturers are recognizing that co-op is perhaps the most powerful sales tool they have for moving product into retail outlets and off store shelves."

But co-op advertising is not just for retailers. Firms selling business-to-business products, professional services, and industrial equipment can benefit, too. For instance, one manufacturer gives co-op dollars to manufacturers' reps that advertise his products in their space ads and mailers. Another pays the cost of booth space for local reps who show his products at regional expos and trade shows.

Hennessey and the NAB note three recent trends in co-op advertising today:

1. In recent years, some more aggressive manufacturers have become impatient with the traditional "share" form of co-op advertising in which the manufacturer and retailer share the cost of the ads. These manufacturers have instituted 100 percent paid programs, which completely reimburse the retailer for all advertising up to the limit accrued on merchandise purchased.
2. Event marketing has emerged as a strong retailer merchandising tool and is heavily funded by co-op dollars.
3. Many leading manufacturers, such as Campbell Soup, Heinz, General Foods, and ConAgra are "regionalizing" their marketing plans; that is, they are shifting budgets from the national level to regional and local levels to better reach their target markets.

The Place Of Cooperative Advertising In The Marketing Plan

According to Edward C. Crimmins, author of *Cooperative Advertising*, the place of cooperative advertising in the marketing plan will vary sharply from company to company, but there are a couple of observations that seem uniformly applicable:

- If a company sells something that reaches the ultimate user through an intermediary, such as a retailer, wholesaler, distributor, broker, or agent, the chances are that cooperative advertising should be part of its marketing plan.

- Companies that do embark on co-op advertising programs have to anticipate that the program speedily becomes a major part of the marketing budget, requiring continuing attention and commitment.

Cooperative advertising has two basic functions:

1. *The sell-in.* Cooperative advertising can move product out of the supplier's hands into the distribution chain, for example, out of a manufacturer's warehouse and into a retailer's store.
2. *The sell-through.* Cooperative advertising can also move product through the chain of distribution, for example, out of the retailer's store and into the customer's home.

Some programs, writes Crimmins, are designed to perform one of these functions. Most of the best are designed to perform both. Since movement into and out of the distribution channel is the very essence of marketing, you would expect that all programs would serve both these functions. Sometimes they don't because they can't.

For example, in the insurance business, cooperative advertising can move product (insurance policies) through the chain of distribution—from the insurance agent to the consumer. But it can't move product out of the supplier's hands into the distribution chain because the insurance agents, who are intermediaries between insurance companies and consumers, do not stock inventory. Neither do travel agents or certain kinds of distributors of industrial equipment who buy only against orders.

Many suppliers, however, are in a position to use their co-op dollars to serve both functions, yet many of them don't. Why not?

Sometimes it is simply a failure to pay attention, or a lack of imagination, or both. In one consumer product industry after another, the whole emphasis of the co-op program is on the requirement that the money be used for advertising that will sell the consumer, but no attempt is made to tie the retailer's allowance (ad expenditures reimbursed by the manufacturer) to the specific placement of a larger order.

Conversely, many packaged goods companies offer promotion allowances designed to get the retailer or wholesaler to stock up, but make little effort to see that he/she spends the allowance on advertising that will move the product out of the store, depending instead on special pricing to achieve that objective. Some manufacturers who sell mainly through major department stores and mass merchandisers take much the same attitude. They are content to placate the large customer's demand for a co-op program, without making any serious effort to see that the co-op budget is effectively used to sell the product to the consumer.

Sometimes, because of the force of retailer resistance to new approaches, the supplier gives up trying to get his co-op dollars used effectively. For example, when, in the early 1970s, the Florida Citrus Commission offered to pay 100 percent of the cost of retail advertising of frozen orange juice processed in Florida, many major grocery chains at first resisted taking the money because they would have to spend it to move product rather than keeping it as profit. And they took this position despite the fact that the funds offered by the Commission were raised by a special tax levied on Florida citrus growers, which meant that every penny of the offer was over and above the allowance already offered by suppliers of the product.

Sometimes suppliers neglect either the sell-in or the sell-through, because the program came into being solely in response to the demands of a few important retailers and was offered to other retailers simply to comply with the law. In such cases, the manufacturer's interest often doesn't go beyond satisfying these nonmarketing objectives.

In all too many cases, goals are forgotten due to the absence of constant scrutiny of the co-op program by marketing management. This is not so common a situation as it once was, because co-op budgets have come to be an increasingly larger part of the total marketing budget. However, managements of many companies are still not giving the attention to co-op advertising budgets that their size merits.

The importance of the role of co-op advertising starts with the importance of retail advertising. All the money a company spends on national advertising can only tell a consumer why a product or service should be purchased. It takes retail advertising to tell where it can be bought, and at what price. It is retail advertising that triggers the decision to buy.

Without retail advertising, it is extremely unlikely that any supplier of a consumer product or service will have a successful marketing program. The strength of cooperative advertising has always been that it is the easiest way to assure adequate retail promotion. In recent years, it has become (except in the rarest cases) the only way to assure that a brand receives this vital support.

Part of this trend is the result of the growing sophistication of all retailers, but a major trend is the continuing concentration of sales through a smaller number of larger retailers who demand promotional help as part of every buy-in. So long as these retailer attitudes continue, cooperative advertising will have a major place in the marketing plans of most companies that sell consumer products and services.

Why Most Co-Op Dollars Are Spent On Newspapers

The National Co-op Manufacturers Survey conducted by Crimmins Co-op Marketing indicates that 76 percent of manufacturers surveyed reported their newspaper co-op program gave them the best sales results. The nearest competitor was television, with only 11 percent of the respondents saying that that medium was best.

Among the advantages offered by newspapers for co-op advertising:

1. Newspapers are invited into the home, and their ad content is welcome.
2. Newspaper audiences demographically cut across all income levels, but generally speaking are skewed to the better-educated, upper-income household.
3. The newspaper is a daily buying guide for virtually every product category.
4. Newspapers provide "keepability" of advertising. The newspaper, unlike radio and television, can be read, set aside, and returned to later.
5. Newspapers offer flexibility in format, color, and ad budget.
6. Daily and Sunday newspapers provide varied editorial environments to meet the needs of almost any advertiser. On request, more than 80 percent of U.S. newspapers will position ads near appropriate content, usually without charge.
7. The newspaper is actually, in many cases, the distribution medium for multi-product lines. Most Sunday editions carry thousands of ad impressions and ideas grouped in a single issue.
8. One "double truck" (an ad appearing on two facing pages) allows approximately 80 product displays for increased product movement.
9. Newspapers provide the ability to feature a wide selection of product lines, each using small amounts of co-op dollars, in a dynamic and sales-producing fashion.
10. Newspapers offer proof-of-performance capability, that is, a tearsheet of the ad that the newspaper actually ran.

Where To Start

As Erich Linker senior Vice President of Advertising for *The New York Times* pointed out in Chapter 10, the best source of information on co-op advertising is the Co-Op Advertising Manager of your local daily newspaper. According to the NAB, most newspapers offer the following co-op advertising services either free or at low cost:

1. Copywriting, design, layout, and production of camera-ready co-op ads.
2. Customized sales brochures for manufacturers reps, distributors, and retailers. These are specially designed sales aids that visually present the total ad campaign, defining the cost for each participating retailer.
3. Specialized mailing services to retailers and dealers. Mailings are in the format of merchandising kits that link retailer point-of-purchase promotions with your newspaper advertising campaign.
4. Co-op advertising seminars and clinics.
5. Marketing and research services that provide a wealth of information about the market including where people buy, how they buy, when they buy, demographics, and so on.
6. Yearly promotional calendars, usually provided one year in advance, outlining special events of the city and surrounding area. They include information on special editions of the paper and dates of the advertising sections (e.g., lawn and garden, back to school, etc.).

Key Considerations When Planning A Co-Op Advertising Program

1. *What are the legal requirements?* For example, the law requires that co-op dollars be made available to all of the manufacturer's retailers and other distributors; you cannot discriminate by making co-op money available only (or on better terms) just to the bigger retailers. However, the manufacturer is *not* required to make sure all retailers participate. There are many other detailed legal guidelines that must be followed carefully. See *Cooperative Advertising* by Edward C. Crimmins (check the resource guide at the end of this chapter) for details.

2. *What are the marketing objectives for the program?* Sell-in? Sell-out? Or both?

3. *How will the program be monitored and controlled?* Will the retailer place the advertising directly and be reimbursed by the manufacturer? Or will the supplier handle the ad creation and placement for him and pay the media bill directly?

4. *Which products and markets will be covered by the program?*

5. *What allowances and percentage of participation will be offered to retailers?* Will the manufacturer reimburse for 50 percent of the cost of the ad space? 5 percent? 100 percent?

6. *Which media will be used?*

7. *What type of advertising will qualify for reimbursement with co-op dollars under the program?* For example, some manufacturers will reimburse the retailer based on the space in a particular ad devoted to their product. Other manufacturers will not reimburse the retailer if the ad contains any mention of a competitor's product.

8. *What is the budget for the program?*

9. *What elements should be included in the written co-op advertising plan?* These include the objectives, who controls the plan (manufacturer or retailer), products and markets covered, allowance percentages, media, budget, and creative requirements.

10. *Who will handle the various steps of implementation?* These include writing the ads, selling the program to retailers, reviewing and monitoring ads and reimbursements, and record-keeping.

Resources

The undisputed authoritative source of information on co-op advertising is *Cooperative Advertising,* Edward C. Crimmins, Gene Wolfe & Co., Inc., 60 East 42nd Street, New York, NY 10165. It is both accurate and comprehensive.

Also contact the Newspaper Advertising Bureau, 400 N. Michigan Avenue, Chicago, IL 60611, phone (312) 644-1290.

CHAPTER 14

Yellow Pages and Directory Advertising

Should You Advertise In The Yellow Pages?

Should you advertise in the yellow pages? The answer is not terribly complex. Basically, you should advertise if you are in a type of business where similar companies get all, most, or at least a significant portion of their business from yellow pages advertising.

This is determined from your own knowledge of the business, your own buying habits as a consumer, and by checking the yellow pages to see if your competitors are there and, if so, whether they have small listings or large display ads.

Yellow pages advertising is an ideal medium for local service businesses and retailers who serve residents of a particular area. Examples include insurance agents, home remodelers, plumbers, restaurants, limousine services, taxi companies, roofers, tree surgeons, aluminum siding contractors, house painters, landscapers, nurseries, hair dressers, barbers, rent-a-car companies, auto mechanics, and dozens of other businesses. Ask yourself: "When people find themselves in need of my type of service or product, are they likely to turn to the yellow pages for sources?" If the answer is "yes," yellow pages advertising is probably a good bet for you.

Then turn to the yellow pages. See if your competitors are there with big ads. Check old copies you have of last year's book. Go back two years, if you can. If the same companies in your field have been running large ads for years, you know it has been successful for them and would probably work for you, too.

Nowadays, many yellow pages offer a separate volume called *business-to-business yellow pages* for local service companies and distributors that sell to local business. Advertisers in these books include advertising agencies, accounting firms, commercial banks, data processing service bureaus, computer consultants, software vendors, office supply dealers, office furniture outlets, public relations firms, graphic design studios, printers, and so on. Again, whether to advertise is determined by checking what the competition is doing but also by asking, "How favorably does this medium compare with the other means at my disposal for selling my service?"

Many business-to-business advertisers prefer not to advertise in yellow pages or, if they do, to have a small ad or listing only. They feel the money is better spent on advertising in industry directories and trade publications.

The Yellow Pages Are Different

The difference between ads in the yellow pages or other directories and ads in newspapers or magazines is as follows:

People reading newspapers and magazines are reading articles for information or entertainment, and they tend to pass over the ads. (The average consumer reads only four ads in a magazine). Therefore, to be effective, a newspaper or magazine ad must forcefully grab the reader's attention through a novel, interesting, or powerful presentation—a fascinating photo, a distinctive layout, a compelling headline.

But when people turn to the yellow pages, they are prime prospects, *ready to buy and looking for a supplier.* They do not have to be persuaded to buy your type of product or service; they merely have to be persuaded to buy *from you* instead of your competitors.

The Trouble With the Yellow Pages

Richard A. Gajewski is president of Directory & Advertising Consultants, a Williamsville, New Jersey firm specializing in yellow pages advertising.

Writing in the *Insurance Advocate,* Gajewski says the major mistake companies make is to spend too much on yellow pages advertising, not too little.

"More than $11 billion a year is spent on yellow pages advertising, and I have found that as many as seven out of 10 businesses are often sold on spending more than is needed to get the job done," writes Gajewski. "I have found that some companies spend twice as much as is necessary."

Gajewski lists the following reasons for this overspending:

- Lack of planning.
- Too little information.
- Decisions made in a hurry because sales reps from the yellow pages approach advertisers as space deadlines are about to close.
- Confusion with respect to the different listings, sizes, colors, positions, package deals, and especially the multiplying numbers of competing directories within each geographic area.
- Ad rates increasing faster than company revenue.
- Sales reps trying to sell bigger space than is needed to earn greater commissions.

The solution? "Do some thinking about how much you spend, how it affects your business, and whether some of that money could be used in other media," advises Gajewski.

Starting Your Program

If you are already in business and have not been advertising in yellow pages (or have been advertising, but not in a major way), then obviously yellow pages advertising does not mean life or death to your company. If you think more yellow pages advertising might be beneficial, my advice is to test, but slowly.

If you have no listing, start with a regular listing, a bold face listing, or a one-inch listing. If that generates positive results, gradually step up in size, taking a slightly larger ad each year. Keep track of all inquiries (almost all will be from the telephone) generated by your yellow pages ad. Calculate the cost per inquiry by dividing the dollar amount spent on the ad space by the number of inquiries.

At first, running bigger ads will generate more inquiries. But at some point, running a bigger ad may cost you more money but not generate more business. Or, it may generate only a few more inquiries, thus raising the cost per inquiry substantially. At this point, you know you have reached the optimum size and should not take a bigger ad.

Also keep track of the cost per inquiry compared with other media. If the yellow pages cost per inquiry is competitive or slightly higher but brings in a lot of new business, keep the ad. On the other hand, if yellow pages advertising has a much higher cost per inquiry than other media, and it does not bring good prospects to your door, drop it.

One small advantage of yellow pages advertising is that it is "automatic"; that is, you place your ad once and then forget about it; the ad runs throughout the year. With a direct mail program, on the other hand, a lot of time and effort goes into planning, creating, and preparing the mailings. So, if the two media produce equal results, yellow pages gives you an edge because it takes a minimum of your time and attention.

10 Powerful Techniques For Improving Your Yellow Pages Ads

1. *Use an identifying graphic.* An identifying graphic is a simple illustration that immediately identifies the product or service being sold. If you run a limousine service, show a picture of a limousine. If you deliver flowers, show a hand holding flowers or the florist's delivery van. If your competitors do not use visuals (and many yellow pages ads do not), this graphic device will draw the reader's eye toward your ad first.

2. *Highlight the phone number.* Put the phone number in large type. Even if you include an address, 99 percent of your yellow pages inquiries will be via telephone. Any ad has only three-tenths of a second to catch the reader's attention or lose him. If you force your reader to search for the telephone number—the thing he wants—he will give up and go to the next ad. People are busier today and more in a hurry than ever. The number should instantly pop off the page. Putting it in a box or highlighting it with some graphic device (sketch of telephone, arrow, etc.) also helps.

3. *Position your ad toward the front.* Unfortunately, yellow pages are organized alphabetically and you cannot violate this order even by paying a premium position. Many companies who depend on yellow pages advertising name themselves A-Plus or "AAA" simply to get at the front of their section. I'm not saying you necessarily want to do that, but it is something to consider.

4. *List everything you sell.* Another proven technique is to list everything you sell in your ad. One New Jersey insurance agent begins his yellow pages ad with the headline "INSURANCE" and then goes on to list more than 30 different types of items he insures. He reasons that if he is the only agent to list snowmobiles in his ad, anyone turning to the yellow pages with a snowmobile to insure will be hooked by the ad. As a result, his small 2-column by 2-½ inch ad generates one or two phone calls *every single business day* of the year.

5. *List your locations.* People looking in the yellow pages want someone near them.

Let's say there are two plumbers. Plumber A's ad says that they are located in Town A but serve all of Alphabet County. Plumber B's ad simply lists "Town A, Town B, Town C, Town D, Town E" under the telephone number. If a person living in Town D needs a plumber, who will he call first? That's right, Plumber B because the ad creates the perception that Plumber B is *local,* and people would rather deal with a local company than a distant one.

Why? Somehow we think that, if the firm is local, they will charge less because they travel a shorter distance to reach us. Also, if there is a problem, it will be easier to get them back to correct it.

Our perception of Plumber A is that he has to travel far to reach us, and even if he doesn't explicitly charge a travel fee, the time he spends on the road will somehow be reflected in his invoice. Also, he will be less eager to come back if there's a problem because it costs him more time.

In your yellow pages ad, make yourself look as local, nearby, and accessible as possible. All else being equal, the consumer wants to buy from the company nearest to him.

6. *Include complete addresses.* If space allows, put in your full street address, not just the town. Also include copy that identifies your precise location (e.g., "between Fifth and Sixth Avenues off Veteran's Circle").

Why? Because consumers are afraid of dealing with fly-by-night companies. They prefer to deal with a long-established, large firm with roots in the community and a proven track record of success rather than an individual who works out of the back of a pickup truck. A real street address says that you, too, must be real.

Along these lines, you might also include a sketch or photo of your building, especially if you are advertising in a local (town or county versus multi-county) yellow pages and the building is well-known or recognizable. This would be silly in a national ad, but locally, people feel comforted if they see a building they've driven by. Their response is, "Oh yes, I know them."

7. *Include your hours.* People want you to be accessible. They want to know when they can reach you. So put your hours in your ad.

The ideal for a service firm is a company they can reach 24 hours a day. If you are available 24 hours or have a separate phone number for evening or emergency service, put it in the ad and let people know they can reach you 24 hours a day, 7 days a week. If you are not available round the clock and your competitors advertise 24-hour service, consider adding it.

I also believe that a person should be able to call your company any time of the day or night and be able to leave a message rather than have the phone ring with no one picking up. I strongly recommend a night answering service or telephone answering machine for all businesses. Your fax machine should also have its own dedicated line and operate 24 hours a day, 7 days a week.

8. *Highlight a free offer.* Free estimate. Free analysis. Free inspection. Free design. Free consultation. If you have a free offer, stress it in the ad. Use the word "FREE." Put it in a separate line in large bold type.

In many businesses, you must visit the consumer's home to give a price quotation. You have to go there to measure, inspect, examine, and determine what is involved with the job and what the cost will be. While you are there, you also sell the prospect on using your service.

Instead of viewing this as a sales call or a mandatory step in the selling process, consider it a free service to the consumer and emphasize it in your ad. Surprisingly, some of your competitors do not offer this for free but charge some nominal sum. You will get more inquiries and more opportunities to quote on jobs if you advertise a free estimate or other free offer in your yellow pages ad.

9. *Put in licensing, bonding, and other technical credentials.* People want to deal with a firm that is legitimate, and they are afraid that you may not be qualified to do the work or may not be properly licensed, bonded, or insured. Assuming you have the proper licensing, bonding, insurance, and permits, mention these in your ads, either in general terms ("licensed and insured") or in specifics ("NJ DEP License No. 44956"). Another credibility builder is to list the number of years you have been in business, especially if it is five years or longer.

10. *State your unique selling proposition.* Use a slogan, tag line, headline, or copy line that sums up the nature of your business and what you offer. Examples:

"The largest variety of birds in Bergen County"
"Specialists in plastic surgery of the nose"
"The faucet specialists"
"Professional resumes that work"
"World's largest pool builder—from the simple to the sensational."

If you do something specialized, stress this in your tag line. For example, if you specialize in installing flat roofs, say "The flat roof specialists." People who are looking for what you sell, namely, a flat roof, will call you first before calling any of the others who merely advertise general roofing services.

Other Options

Yellow pages are not the only directories available. There are thousands of other directories aimed at business, institutional, and even some consumer markets.

Basically, there are two types of directories: vertical market directories (those aimed at specific industries) and general purpose (including yellow pages, the Thomas Register, and others aimed at national or local audiences without regard to industry).

There are distinct vertical market directories for virtually any industry, discipline, or SIC code (Standard Industrial Classification). And if a significant portion of your sales potential is in one market, the industry directory may be worth considering. An example is the Red Book, or *National Directory of Advertising Agencies.* Another is *Chemical Engineering Catalog.*

As for general directories, there are three basic types:

- Traditional industrial directories (such as the *Thomas Register*) that cover industrial products and services on a national or regional basis. Thomas Publishing, publisher of the *Thomas Register,* now sells a series of state directories of manufacturers.
- There are a growing number of business-to-business directories that cover not only manufacturers but services, computers, telecommunications—everything a business needs.
- And, there are the yellow pages.

Which type of directory and which specific books or combination of books is right for you? That depends on the type of customer you serve (business, consumer, both), your geographic marketing area (local, regional, or national), and what you are selling. One way to determine the answer is to compare the profile of your customer base with the circulation profile of each directory. You'll also want to compare directories for ease of use, how actively the directory is promoted and distributed to users, completeness, reputation, distribution, subscriber costs, and, of course, advertising rates.

Usage Of Yellow Pages And Industrial Directories

According to Bell Atlantic, 61.5 percent of all American adults use the Yellow Pages *at their place of business.* Usage for individuals in professional and managerial positions was even higher: 70 percent, according to a study by Simmons Market Research Bureau.

Another national study, conducted by Audits and Surveys Company, polled a random sampling of 6,000 individuals representing a base of 458,943 buyers at manufacturing companies with from one to 1,000 or more employees. The study concluded that 9 out of 10 buyers use the Yellow Pages and initiate a phone call, letter, or visit as a result.

Directories and Yellow Pages work well for business-to-business marketing, because in business-to-business, 97 percent of purchases result from *buyer initiative* (the buyer actively seeking a source) rather than seller initiative (the seller actively soliciting business), according to a survey of 900 business executives conducted by Business Marketing Services for Thomas Register of American Manufacturers.

According to this survey, a buyer typically looks at four potential suppliers before making a purchase: two new sources and two sources with which the company has previous experience. The survey revealed that 54 percent of these new sources are selected from industrial directories and guides by the buyer, 24 percent from the efforts of a salesperson calling on the company, 44 percent from a direct mail piece or magazine ad, and 18 percent from other sources.

In addition, 42 percent of the sources the company had previous experience with were also selected from directories—even though there was already an existing relationship between buyer and seller. Fifty-five percent of the contact with known vendors was made through salespeople, with the rest from magazine ads, direct mail, and other sources.

Business and industry buyers at all levels use directories. And a high percentage of them use directories *when they are ready to buy* or when they need a new supplier. Prospects turning to your directory ad need a product but are not locked into a particular vendor. Indeed, a study by Burke Marketing Research of business/industrial buyers who used yellow pages showed that 83 percent had no specific company in mind when they turned to the book.

Another growing trend is for local companies to, when possible, make purchases from local vendors rather than distant firms. According to research done for Illinois Bell among business-to-business directory users in the Chicago area, 76 percent of respondents with buying influence make more than half of their purchases in the metropolitan area.

These buyers also use directories frequently. The Illinois Bell study indicates that 91 percent of the buyers use directories at least once a month and 76 percent use them weekly.

8 Powerful Ideas For Improving Business And Industrial Directory Advertising

1. *The bigger your ad, the more you get noticed.* Every directory is crammed with thousands of ads and listings. An ordinary listing has little chance of being noticed. By using a boldface listing or display ad, you can increase effectiveness over a regular listing in the ways shown in Table 14.1.

As you can see, a one column ad is 193 times more likely to be noticed and read than a regular listing.

2. *Be complete.* Industrial and business prospects want complete information, including product illustrations, brand names, types, sizes, specifications, tolerances, service policies, special capabilities, availability, delivery, company name, location, telephone number. Remember, the person browsing through a directory wants to buy and is actively looking for a source. The more information you can provide, the more reasons for that

Table 14.1. Increased effectiveness of larger directory ads.

Type of Ad	*Effectiveness Improvement vs. Regular Listing*
Boldface listing	3:1
One-inch ad	9:1
¼-column ad	13:1
½-column ad	64:1
1-column ad	193:1

buyer to respond to your ad. Make sure all information is accurate and up-to-date, paying special attention to trade marks, logos, product brand names, and telephone and fax numbers.

3. *Consider color.* In directories that offer it, using a second color in your ad is often worthwhile. According to the McGraw-Hill Laboratory of Advertising Performance, two-color ads earn a 60 percent better readership score than black-and-white ads. Color can be used to command attention, highlight important features and information, and even add a sense of urgency.

4. *Make the layout clear and readable.* Although directory ads typically contain many more elements than magazine ads, the layout should still be clear and readable, not cluttered. According to the Burke Marketing Research, 25 percent of directory users say they prefer ads with superior layout and design.

5. *Use co-op dollars.* If you're involved in sales or distribution of products for other manufacturers, ask if they will sponsor your directory ad with co-op dollars. This can reduce your out-of-pocket costs by up to 50 percent.

6. *Choose your categories carefully.* Designing an ad program for a large, multi-product-category general directory can be confusing. Often, there is more than one classification under which your ad could logically be placed. What do you do?

Make a list of all classifications pertinent to your business. Be sure to list every conceivable category under which a prospect might look to find you.

List and number these categories in order of priority. Then determine the number and size of ads needed to do the job.

For example, there are five categories under which your product would fit. Two are the main categories; the other three are secondary. One solution would be to take large display ads in the two main sections and one-inch ads or boldface listings in the three secondary sections. Include a line with your one-inch ads or boldface listings that refers readers to your larger display ads in the other sections.

7. *Competition.* Directories are highly competitive environments in which you are literally guaranteed of being surrounded by your fiercest competitors. It pays to carefully study what the competition is up to and to respond accordingly. If you can afford to beat your competition by taking the biggest ad on the page, do so. If you can't, you'll have to rely on creativity to make your ad stand out. For instance, if your competitors don't offer

free estimates, put "FREE ESTIMATES" in big bold type in a starburst in your ad. If your competitors don't feature a full product line, advertise the broadest line. You get the point.

8. *Measure.* Track and measure carefully both mail and phone response to your directory ads. Keep a record not only of inquiries generated but how many of those inquiries were converted to sales and what the dollar amounts of these purchases were. Directory ads are designed not to "build image" but to generate hard inquiries that result in serious prospects and new business. You should judge the success of directory advertising by the number of inquiries and the amount of sales produced.

CHAPTER 15

Television Commercials

In his book, *How to Produce an Effective Television Commercial,* Hooper White states, "The television commercial . . . a combination of sight and sound that move to impart fact or evoke emotion . . . is one of the most potent selling tools ever forged." The *Handbook of Advertising Management,* edited by Roger Barton, says "Television is the closest thing to the ideal salesman—a real person—available within our current media environment. It moves, it talks, it demonstrates, it is in the home."

Not surprisingly, then, the television commercial is one of the most popular selling tools used by advertisers today. The viewing public is now bombarded with 320,000 commercials per year, up 20 percent from 1985. In 1988, $24.5 billion was spent on national, local, syndicated, and cable TV advertising. That total was topped only by the $31.2 billion dollars spent on newspaper advertising. More importantly, according to the Television Bureau of Advertising, Inc., adults rate TV advertising as the most authoritative, most believable, and most influential of the advertising media. And many of the larger full-service advertising agencies derive as much as 70 percent of their billings from television commercials.

When should you consider making broadcast advertising a part of your marketing mix? If you work for a large consumer products company, the broad reach provided by television advertising may well be worth the high cost of producing a commercial (anywhere from $10,000 to well over $1,000,000), not to mention the cost of air time. (A 30-second commercial on ABC on a Tuesday at 9:30 P.M. in the Fall of 1988 cost $110,000. A 30-second spot on CBS's *60 Minutes* cost about $200,000.)

For many small companies, television is automatically dismissed because of the high cost. But, as David Ogilvy writes in *Ogilvy on Advertising,* "Inexpensive commercials can be highly effective if they come directly to the point and offer something of genuine interest."

When Business-To-Business Advertisers Can Benefit From TV

For small business-to-business advertisers to benefit from TV advertising, according to Jeffrey W. Kaumeyer, vice president and group manager at Hammond Farrell Inc., a New York City advertising agency, three conditions must be met:

1. *Your prospects must be concentrated geographically.* Unless you're an IBM or Xerox, you probably can't afford to take 30 seconds during prime-time television at $200,000—at least not frequently enough to achieve concentration and continuity. But if your prospects are concentrated in a regional area, a 30-second spot on a top-rated news program in that area may cost as little as $200 or $300. While a similar spot in New York City may cost $3,500, it's still an efficient buy on a cost per thousand basis.

Even if you *can* afford a nationwide broadcast of your television commercial and have potential customers scattered throughout the country, you must balance the prospects reached with the vast number of nonprospects who will also receive your message and the cost of production and air time. That's why cable television, with its segmented audiences, has gained a strong foothold with advertisers against "the big 3" networks.

2. *You must be willing to have your sales pitch boiled down to one simple, compelling message.* Your message should be simple because there is time for only about 65 words in a 30-second spot. And, "as with your other ads, your sales proposition should be single-minded and worthwhile," says Kaumeyer.

Second, since your TV spot has to compete with about 3,000 other advertising messages daily for your prospect's attention, you need to appeal to the human, emotional side of your prospect.

3. *Television must be complemented by the other more basic components in a complete marketing communications plan.* A media mix adds impact to a plan. A combination of TV and print is more effective than either one alone. Publicity plus TV plus print is even better. Therefore, says Kaumeyer, a business marketer should not consider TV as his only medium. Don't expect any one form of advertising to do the whole selling job. But TV can turn the spotlight on your company.

Before you go ahead with a commercial, however, be sure you have the appropriate sales training and inquiry-handling procedures in place. Aim for consistency with your other advertising messages, too. For television to be effective, it should reinforce the overall selling theme that is featured in your print ads and radio commercials.

Making Your TV Commercial Stand Out—And Sell

The average home spends more than seven hours a day watching television. Since the public's attention is already captured by television, the challenge to advertisers is not to get prospects to turn on the commercials but rather to prevent them from tuning them out.

"On a mass consumer goods level," writes Herschell Gordon Lewis in *How To Make Your Advertising Twice As Effective at Half the Cost,* "a product can't achieve high visibility without television. But no other mechanical invention in history is so capable of emptying pocketbooks, bringing peculiar results in which competitors are helped as much as you are, or building the advertiser's ego if not his business."

To avoid wasting your money, you have to know what works and what doesn't in TV advertising. With the increasing clutter of TV commercials, fueled by the growing number of 15-second spots, how do you make your commercial get noticed and succeed at selling your product or service? Here are some tips from experts:

1. First, remember that television is a visual medium—something even as esteemed an authority as David Ogilvy admits to mistakenly ignoring in the early days of TV advertising. In *Confessions of an Advertising Man,* he writes, "You must make your pictures tell the story; what you show is more important than what you say. Words and pictures must work together, reinforcing each other."
2. Use verbal exclamations that trigger the viewer's interest. Words such as "new, amazing, revolutionary, and incredible" still work if they truthfully describe a product or product innovation.

3. Provide information about the product so that prospects can make a judgment about buying it. True potential buyers want information, and without it they may feel cheated.
4. Follow David Ogilvy's dictum of repeating the name of the product "ad nauseum" throughout the commercial, and show it at least once. And show the package or product itself. "Make your product the hero of the commercial," Ogilvy advises. Also, use the name of the product within the first 10 seconds.
5. Don't mention your competitors. If you do, you take the risk that viewers will think your commercial promoted your competitor's product.
6. Stick to one or two points. If you try to make too many points, you'll wind up not making any as far as the viewer is concerned.
7. Use close-ups of the product so that, when people remember your commercial, they'll remember what it was advertising.
8. Use a strong opener. If you don't have an attention-getting, dramatic opener, viewers won't stick around long enough to find out anything more.
9. Sound effects that relate to the product, such as coffee percolating or eggs frying, will enhance emotional appeal.
10. Use an on-screen actor rather than a voice-over for narration.
11. If you offer a money-back guarantee, stress it. Alvin Eicoff, a pioneer in television direct response techniques, writes in his autobiography *Or Your Money Back*, "there is no more powerful sales tool than a money-back guarantee. It bridges the credibility gap. It can be the offer that persuades undecided viewers to try your product. It's especially important in overcoming buying resistance when a product seems to be too good to be true."
12. Supers increase sales. Spell out your message in type and superimpose it over the visual. Reinforce the message by having an actor read it while it's being spelled out.

Nine Types of Commercials That Work Best

According to David Ogilvy in *Ogilvy on Advertising*, research and experience show that nine types of commercials are above average in their ability to change people's brand preference:

1. *Humor.* At one time, well-known advertising men like Ogilvy and Claude Hopkins held fast to the belief that humor didn't sell. But studies

of changes in brand preference today indicate that humor *can* sell. Be forewarned that writing humor is difficult, however, and few copywriters can do it well.

2. *Slice of life.* This widely used format features a "real-life" setting in which one person convinces another why he or she should use the particular product. The commercial is essentially a playlet that establishes a problem, introduces the product that will solve the problem, and ends with the product being used to solve the problem.

While this format is often disdained by copywriters because it has a tendency to seem corny, research shows it is effective for large manufacturers of soaps, detergents, and other packaged goods in increasing sales.

3. *Testimonials.* These commercials depict a loyal user of the product defending it and, in the process, describing its merits. Or, alternatively, such commercials show "real people" being introduced to a product and discovering that they like it. Such commercials work best when the user does not know he is being filmed.

4. *Demonstrations or problem/solution commercials.* These show how well your product can perform. Adman Alvin Eicoff believes this is the most effective TV commercial you can make—if you can set forth a problem, explain a solution, and then demonstrate why your product offers the best solution. It's even better if you can make your product show how to solve a really tough problem—such as a car wax shining up an old, battered car or a laundry detergent getting out grease. Such demonstrations carry added impact.

5. *The stand-up presenter* (also called a "talking head"). Agencies don't generally like these commercials, which consist solely of a pitchman describing the virtues of a product, because they think they're not creative enough. But this type of commercial is above-average in changing brand preference.

Good casting and good direction are the keys to making it work. Writes Hooper White, "This approach works best when the product needs a human being to demonstrate it or when you want the mesmerizing effect of a forthright salesperson talking to a potential customer."

6. *Characters who become identified with a product* over the course of several years, such as Josephine the Plumber for Comet, and Rosie the Waitress for Bounty Paper Towels, become the living symbol of the product. They are often featured in the slice-of-life playlet format. If the characters are relevant to your product, they can be above-average in changing audience brand preference.

7. *Reason why.* Give viewers a rational reason why your product is superior, and you'll increase sales. Remember when freeze-dried coffee was first introduced? It was advertised as being better than regular instant because the flavor was quickly "locked in" during the freezing process. Explaining the advantages of freeze-drying convinced many viewers to try the new coffee.

8. *News.* "Products, like human beings, attract the most attention when they are first born," writes Ogilvy. So if a product is new, play it up. And if you can come up with new uses for an old product, so much the better. By telling consumers that an open box of baking soda would keep their refrigerators smelling sweet, Arm & Hammer rang up millions of new sales.

9. *Appealing to the emotions* can be as effective as any rational appeal, but people also need a rational excuse to justify their emotional decisions. Beer and wine-cooler commercials, car commercials, and food commercials typically play off viewers' emotions, such as nostalgia or the desire for enjoyment, adventure, love, status, or respect.

White writes, "Often, commercial ideas can be expressed nonverbally by using an emotional combination of pictures and music. This is an interesting approach, particularly if your idea would benefit from emotional responses."

Ogilvy lists three types of commercials that *do not* work well: the celebrity testimonial, musical vignettes, and cartoons/animation. The first two entertain but they usually don't sell. Too often, viewers remember the celebrity and not the product—or worse, think the celebrity was pitching a competitor's product. And cartoons reduce credibility when used to pitch products to adults. However, there are cases when animation can be effective in selling a product or service, such as in showing the effect of a fertilizer on a lawn's root system, for instance.

What Length Should Your Commercial Be?

Currently, you can purchase television commercials in the following lengths: 10 seconds, 15 seconds, 20 seconds, 30 seconds, 45 seconds, 60 seconds, 90 seconds, and 120 seconds. Two minutes is the longest commercial length allowed by the FCC. The length will not only affect the cost of airtime, but production costs. To determine the length of the commercial, you must decide how much time it will take to sell your product or service.

Advertisers and ad agencies have long debated over what length commercial is the most effective. For instance, Alvin Eicoff writes, “Generally, between one and two minutes is necessary to do an effective selling job. An even more compelling reason for advertisers to create longer commercials is the isolation factor theory: it stipulates that if you can obtain sole possession of a commercial break, you can greatly increase the motivational power of your commercial.” He compares the clustering of 30-second commercials to “having four salesmen confronting you at once, with no time to absorb one sales pitch before the next one starts.”

Indeed, research studies show that, although viewers don't time commercials, they are more irritated when many commercials occur in a row than when one or two longer commercials are back to back. Corporations such as Hallmark, Kraft Foods, and IBM sponsor specials so that they can achieve isolation of longer commercials within the shows. In fact, the “Big Three” networks' concern over the high cost of programming, coupled with advertisers' desire for more quality programming in which to advertise, is leading to a resurgence in fully sponsored programs.

On the other hand, 30-second commercials have long been the most popular choice of advertisers. But since 15-second commercial spots became widely available in 1985, they have been steadily gaining in popularity. Fifteen-second spots accounted for 10 percent of total network commercials in 1985, but for 36 percent of network commercials by the end of 1988.

The fact that 15-second spots cost half as much as 30-second spots in network airtime, while reaching the same number of viewers, is largely the reason for this popularity. Whether they have the same impact as a 30-second commercial is a question of debate, however. Early recall studies in the mid-1980s showed the average 15-second spot to be about two-thirds as effective as a 30-second spot. But since 1985, there has been a slight, yet consistent, drop in commercial recall.

Although there is less time to get your message across, if your primary objective is frequency—to reinforce a brand name or your company name to prospects who already are familiar with you—a 15-second spot can represent the ideal buy.

While the advent of 15-second commercials has helped smaller and lower-budget advertisers break into TV advertising, as an advertiser you should be aware that the growth in 15-second spots is a cause of concern to many television sales executives, advertisers, and ad agencies, who worry that this “clutter” will further alienate a declining network television audience. To limit the number of 15-second spots, television executives are already discussing raising their prices from 50 percent to 65 percent of the cost of airing a 30-second commercial.

In addition, local stations already charge a premium for the 15-second spot at 75 percent of the airtime cost of a 30-second spot. They also limit their availability and subject the shorter units to pre-emption by 30-second spots.

One last tip on selecting commercial length: When planning your commercial, think not only in terms of your present campaign but what you might want to show in the future. Many companies run shorter versions of their 60-second or 30-second spots to build frequency. But if you're planning to run a 15-second or 30-second spot now, you may want to shoot extra footage at the same time for running longer commercials later. This can be done at much less cost now—when sets, crew, cast, and equipment are already in place—than if you later decided to produce a new, longer commercial. Most of the extra work will fall to the creative team, who will have to draw up another script and storyboard expanding on the shorter commercial.

Rely On Repetition

Overall, repetition of your commercial message counts more towards increasing sales than length. "One of the most effective ways to advertise is through repetition, and advertisers can reach TV's many audiences often because people spend so much time viewing," reports the Television Bureau of Advertising.

Longevity is another aspect of frequency. Rosser Reeves long ago pointed out "If you find something that works, keep it on the air until it doesn't work any more." Also, remember that you will get tired of your commercial long before your audience does. Changing commercials that still pull wastes your company's money.

When and how often you run your commercial depends on your budget, your product's sales cycle, the commercial's message (a retail commercial advertising an upcoming sale obviously won't run very long), and the market you are targeting (if you're a business-to-business marketer targeting executives, you won't run your commercial during the day). Many advertisers start out a campaign with 60-second commercials, and then switch to a higher-frequency schedule of 30-second spots, figuring that viewers won't perceive the switch to the shorter commercial (proven by research to be true) but will connect the 30-second message with the 60-second one.

According to Herschell Gordon Lewis, if you want to stretch your budget, an ideal period in which to buy commercial time is the 10:30 or

11:30 P.M. movie. Husbands and wives both watch, and audience size compares favorably to cost.

In both network and spot television (television time bought market by market), prime-time buys cost by far the most money. Early evening news comes in second highest in airtime cost on the network side, and late news holds that rank in spot television. But late evening (the time period during which the late movie runs) is only slightly more expensive than daytime, the cheapest period of the day in which to buy time. In 1989, the cost per 30 seconds of a late evening commercial came to $26,400 on network television. Meantime, the average cost of a 30-second commercial during prime time is $109,400 on network television. Considering that the audience for the late evening commercial is roughly one-third of that watching the prime-time commercial, but that the late evening price is less than one-quarter the prime-time price, late evening is the more efficient buy from a cost-per-thousand standpoint.

Writes Lewis, "no one pays the one-time (commercial) rate. And only beginners try to buy 60-second spots between 7:00 and 10:00 in the evening on network-affiliated stations, because those are reserved for program sponsors." Rate cards (published in *Television Rates & Data*) mean very little, since time-buyers negotiate for discounts and special deals. For the savvy buyer, ten spots can end up costing less than five. And the inroads made by cable TV and syndicated shows in attracting advertisers have made network and local stations more willing to cut deals and tailor a varied package of buys to the advertiser's needs. Discount time-buying companies are one way to buy time cheaply; another is to use an ad agency familiar with buying TV time.

Producing The TV Commercial

Advertisers interested in broadcast advertising usually work with an ad agency. "The making of a commercial is a three-way partnership between agency, client, and director," points out John Lyons in *Guts: Advertising from the Inside Out*. Production typically involves a director, camera operator, actors, editor, electricians, prop people, stylists, makeup people, and sound engineers. Careful pre-production planning well in advance of shooting the commercial is essential to avoid costly changes and overtime during filming.

If you are limited in terms of how much you can spend on the commercial, be sure your ad agency knows your budget. You don't want to end up with a multi-actor extravaganza shot in numerous locations that costs $500,000 when you were figuring on $100,000.

Choosing The Commercial Idea

The first step in the production process is coming up with a good idea for the commercial—one that will fit into your overall marketing plan for the product or service, with the goal of building public awareness and increasing sales. The idea should be strong enough on its own not to depend on jazzy production techniques to make it work. White writes, "The best commercial ideas are those that are strong enough conceptually to become campaigns, rather than one-shot commercials."

Such "repeatability" can develop out of presenting a copy claim in the same unique way in each commercial; using an unusual technique, such as music, casting, or editing style, to identify the idea throughout the series; or following a theme that sets your products apart from the competition in the same way throughout a campaign. For example, if all of your competitors are emphasizing low cost, you might focus on reliability or fast service.

One effective commercial can be the prototype for a series that runs for years. Other commercials may run only 13 weeks. So if you can come up with a long-running commercial that increases sales, you can not only save money on new creative strategy costs every few months but also strengthen the overall impact of your advertising through quick customer recognition and loyalty.

The Review Process

After an internal agency review and revisions, the commercial idea will be presented to the advertiser on a *storyboard* which consists of multi-frame illustrations of the action that will take place in the commercial. The storyboard also contains the copy to be spoken or superimposed throughout the commercial. A storyboard for a 30-second commercial has between eight and 16 frames, and each must be part of a logical sequence. If you are not happy with the storyboard or some element of it, this is the time to speak up. But be specific about what you don't like, and try not to take an adversarial tack with the agency staff. Remember, both you, the advertising manager, and your ad agency have the same goal: to produce the best advertising for your product.

Hooper White offers these other tips, directed at agency creative staff but useful to anyone reviewing a commercial idea:

- Unless you can describe the thrust of your commercial in one or two sentences, it's probably too complicated.

- Keep your commercial simple and direct. Develop the ability to be exact, brief, and to the point.
- Think in terms of sight and sound combinations that will verbalize and illustrate your idea.
- Try to visualize your prospective customers and produce a commercial that will make them receptive to your selling message.
- Learn to think and plan within budgetary restrictions.

As ad manager, you can help your ad agency do its job better by informing your account executive of your company's marketing strategy, budget, target markets, and what features or benefits you—and company management—feel are your product's strongest selling points. You should provide the account executive ahead of time with everything he needs to make the commercial idea and the presentation meet your key criteria. By helping your ad agency know as much as possible about your product and your marketing goals, you increase the chance that they will create a mutually pleasing commercial the first time around, saving your company time and money.

Choosing A Production House And Director

Once the advertising agency producer receives approved storyboards from the advertiser, he or she must then obtain bids from commercial production houses. Usually bids are requested from three houses and then reviewed with the advertiser. The agency generally makes the recommendation as to which production house to hire. The recommendation may not be based on the lowest bid, since the choice of a director is often critical and a more expensive director may well be worth the additional cost.

On the other hand, a top-notch director may not be as available to spend time with you and the agency on casting and other important preproduction decisions. So you'll need to weigh cost and availability against the director's talent (as judged from his reels and reputation), flexibility, and personality as well as your own needs in order to make a decision.

Be aware that directors have their own styles and specialties. Some are good at putting together humorous commercials, others are better at slice-of-life commercials. Some prefer the excitement and uncertainty of on-location shooting, others like the control of filming on a sound stage. But look for a director who knows that what he is ultimately doing—albeit in an entertaining manner—is solving a marketing problem and selling a product. Good directors take the time to ask questions about the product and its target audience.

Tape Or Film?

Videotape lends a real "live" quality to a commercial and is faster to handle in postproduction. Unlike film, it also can be played back immediately after takes on production day, allowing the director to make quick decisions about whether to reshoot a scene. On the other hand, film offers deeper color and texture and more choices in optical effects. Your agency and producer will make the decision about which to use and can fill you in on the advantages of using each for your specific commercial.

Casting

Casting for the commercial will begin during the bidding process. Although casting is really the province of the agency and production house, you should approve the casting specifications before casting begins. Casting specifications include a profile of the type of person to be used in the commercial—including age, physical description, and personality. After the agency and director make their selection, you will be asked for approval.

In *How to Get the Best Advertising From Your Agency,* Nancy L. Salz suggests you ask the following questions in judging casting:

- Is the casting believable and convincing?
- Does the individual fit the specifications agreed to?
- Do you feel yourself respond as the actor is reading?

If you cannot make a judgment and don't feel strongly negative about the casting, trust the instincts of your agency and director, who have seen a lot of talent and have a good eye for who's right in what type of commercial.

Preproduction Meeting

This is where all the details of the final production are determined. The meeting should be held several days before the actual shooting, in case you wish to make changes in casting, set design, location, or anything else. Many agencies and production companies hold preproduction meetings without the client but, since it's your money that's being spent, it's wise to take the time to attend. Your presence and answers to questions can help prevent problems—and extra expense—on shooting day or in postproduction. But the agency person in charge of the production should run the meeting.

A strict agenda should be followed in the preproduction meeting, which may involve agency creative staff, the director, producer, production assistant, casting director, set designer, stylist, and sometimes the cameraman, if special lighting effects are required. During this meeting, final details regarding the commercial are discussed, such as set or location, props, music, casting, production schedule, and clothes or food styling.

This is the time to discuss alternate casting choices, specific camera angles, extra shots, product handling and delivery, and essentially all the details that might come up during actual production and cause cost overruns. Both cast and crew are usually unionized and their costs are fixed. If you go into overtime during shooting, you can end up spending thousands of dollars extra for their time on the set.

Since food or clothes stylists, set designers, cameramen, and other production staff charge for their meeting time, invite them to show up at a specific time and limit their participation to a scheduled time slot. This will not only keep expenses down, but will help prevent wandering from the prepared agenda, so that the meeting stays on track and does not run unnecessarily long.

Production Day

In New York or Hollywood, your commercial's production crew will probably number at least 15 people. This is because of union requirements that require a different person to handle each of the many responsibilities on a shoot. Your crew will probably be members of IATSE (the International Alliance of Theatrical Stage Employees) or of NABET (the National Association of Broadcast Electrical Technicians).

On the set, your role will be to make sure everything is filmed as approved by your management on the storyboard. While new shots and camera angles can be added for possible editing into the commercial during the postproduction phase, the commercial must also be filmed as agreed upon in preproduction. If you have any questions or concerns during production, you should relay them to the agency producer, who serves as liaison with the director. The agency producer may be the copywriter, art director, or someone else from the agency, but it is up to him or her to get the answers to your questions and solve any problems with the director. This chain of command is designed to keep the production running smoothly.

Keep your eye on what is happening in front of the camera, so that any problems can be resolved while there's still time to act on them. And if you say that something isn't correct, be prepared to explain why. On the other hand, be aware that directors and actors need time to get things "right." First shots usually aren't final takes, so don't panic if the actor doesn't read the lines correctly at first.

Your other responsibility will be to make sure the product is shown, handled, and used correctly.

Postproduction Editing

The dailies (unedited film footage) are usually viewed the day after shooting. The set has not yet been taken down so, if reshooting is necessary, the cost will be minimized.

Although the advertiser does not usually have a representative present for this screening, you can ask to see these preliminary results of the shoot. Usually the director, editor, script clerk, agency producer, and sometimes the agency writer or art director will view the dailies. The purpose is to make sure all necessary footage has been shot and developed, decide if any retakes are necessary, and give the editor an opportunity to note comments from the director and others about the effectiveness of certain scenes.

If you do attend this screening, be forewarned that the scenes you will see will not yet have been corrected for balanced lighting or color from take to take, and any special effects, dissolves, or supers will not be incorporated at this stage. The scenes will probably not be in chronological sequence, and words spoken at the start and end of the takes by the director and crew will not be edited out yet.

After this initial screening, or in some cases once the director has done an initial editing, the film or tape is given to the editorial house that has been selected to do the finish work. A 30-second dialogue commercial shot in 35mm film typically has 3,000 feet of film. A commercial that has many scenes to be edited to an existing soundtrack may require as much as 16,000 feet of film. The editor's job is to reduce that to 45 feet (about 720 frames of film) for the finished commercial!

At some time during the editing process, you or your ad agency will have an opportunity to review either a rough cut or "answer print"—the first composite film print struck from the negative that shows if color and quality are acceptable—of the commercial. This is the time when you can make editing changes without great expense. By the way, if the editor finds he needs to cut dialogue either to fit the commercial's time limitations or to make it flow more smoothly, he must seek approval from your ad agency.

Whether your commercial was shot on film or tape, it will be finished and made color perfect by transferring to tape. This is the point at which opticals are inserted, audio tracks are mixed, and the commercial is finished. You and your management will then be asked to give final approval before duplicate tapes are made and shipped to the television stations.

Resources

This chapter covers the basics of commercial production. Far more comprehensive information on all aspects of television production can be found in *How to Produce an Effective TV Commercial,* by Hooper White, published by Crain Books in Chicago. For an in-depth discussion of how to work with your advertising agency to produce effective TV commercials, radio, and print advertising, read *How To Get the Best Advertising From Your Agency,* by Nancy L. Salz, published by Dow Jones-Irwin. More detailed information on buying television time can be found in Herschell Gordon Lewis' book *How to Make Your Advertising Twice as Effective at Half the Cost.* For more details about choosing a director and the director's role in making the commercial a success, see John Lyon's book *GUTS: Advertising From the Inside Out* (New York, NY: AMACOM).

Finally, for up-to-date comparisons of broadcast vs. other media costs, demographics, and basic facts on TV advertising, contact the Television Bureau of Advertising, Inc., 477 Madison Avenue, New York, NY 10022; Telephone 212-486-1111.

CHAPTER 16

Radio Advertising

Basic Facts About Radio Advertising

Almost everyone in the United States listens to radio. But most people don't think of radio listening as an activity. They just "do it." Radio listening is a natural activity of just about everyone's lives as revealed in a study by Research and Forecasts, Inc., a New York research firm.

"During the pre-test of our questionnaire, most people had difficulty of thinking about radio as a leisure-time activity," notes John Crothers Pollock, president of the firm. "Radio is so closely integrated with all other activities people pursue—brushing their teeth, driving to work, walking down the street. Radio, rather than a leisure activity, is an integrated activity. It is so universal as to be indistinguishable from other aspects of daily concern."

Although radio listening may be an integrated rather than a separate activity, there is little doubt that it has a powerful impact on society. "Nothing treats the spoken word better than radio," observes Phillip Dusenberry, vice chairman and executive creative director of BBDO, one of the nation's largest advertising agencies. "Nothing caresses and massages the language or brings such sweet poetry to the consumer. Radio speaks with one thing that attracts writers to the profession in the first place: words. Powerful, moving, and persuasive, the creative opportunities we have in radio are fantastic. It's wonderful indoors and the greatest outdoor medium in the world. At BBDO, radio helps sell Old Milwaukee beer by the carload, radio goes full throttle for Dodge, it puts Black and Decker tools in millions of homes, it sells Campbell's Chunky Soup, and brings good things to life at GE."

Even former president of the United States, Ronald Reagan, says, "In its flexibility and immediacy, radio is unsurpassed as a communications tool."

Tapping Into The Radio Audience

Radio reaches 94.8 percent of people 12 years and older every week. If your customers are men age 18 and older, then radio reaches 95.5 percent of them every day. It also reaches 93.1 percent of women 18 and older daily. Radio is everywhere. It goes places other media cannot.

The time lapse between the exposure to the advertising message and the retail message is the fastest with radio: 2 hours for a radio commercial against 3-½ hours for television, 3-¾ hours for newspapers, and 4 hours for magazines. Radio has the fastest rate of return.

Radio sales are in the billions, reaching millions of consumers every day. The average family owns 5.5 radios. In the Los Angeles market alone, that totals somewhere around 25 million radios. National statistics reveal that Americans purchase more radios than any other consumer electronics item, including stereos.

Radios can be found in every room of the house: 58 percent of households have a radio in the bedroom, 50 percent in kitchens, 67 percent in living rooms, 22 percent in studies and dens, and 9 percent in dining rooms. Plus, radios can be found in bathrooms, garages, patios, and pool areas.

Adults spend 45 percent of their media time with TV, 39 percent with radio, 10 percent with newspapers, and 5 percent with magazines. Among high-income adults, media time is divided as follows: 44 percent radio, 39 percent TV, 13 percent newspapers, 7 percent magazines.

Dr. Elizabeth Loftus, of the University of Washington, commented on a recent study from Northwestern University: "This study shows that if you try to convince people about a product (the one in the study was shampoo), and you do it with a verbal message, people are much more persuaded about the product. They like it better and want to buy more than if you accompany those verbal messages with pictures. The verbal message alone seems to create in people's minds more of a positive feeling from the product."

Further studies show that the selective quality of radio has produced loyal listeners. This assures advertisers of a consistent audience of the type of listener that the radio campaign is designed to attract. And most large manufacturers have co-op advertising programs for radio through which the manufacturer reimburses the local advertiser—a supermarket, retailer, or other distributor—for a portion of the advertising expenditures.

Eight Advantages Of Radio Versus Other Media

1. *Economy.* Radio commercials are inexpensive to produce because the listener's imagination—and not a costly photographer or video production house—provides the picture. And, radio time has a lower cost-per-thousand than newspapers, magazines, and television.

2. *Selectivity.* Radio offers a wide selection of program formats, each catering to a specific segment of the population (various types of formats are listed later in this chapter).

3. *Penetration.* Radio reaches nearly 99 percent of the consumer market.

4. *Mobility.* Radio can reach customers just about everywhere, even at the point of sale.

5. *Immediacy.* Advertisers can change their message quickly and easily. They can get new commercials on the air rapidly. A commercial can be written and taped or read live literally the same day, if necessary.

6. *Flexibility.* Radio enables advertisers to talk to customers during the time of day and in an environment most likely to induce a selling response.

7. *Intrusiveness.* Radio advertising can pervade a listener's mind, even when interest doesn't exist. Radio can and often does invade the mind of a preoccupied listener, forcefully delivering a commercial message.

8. *Audience.* Radio can reach virtually any segment of the consumer market, including people who don't frequently read newspapers (teens, for example). It reaches newspaper readers who don't read the retailer's ads

because they are not regular customers. It reaches prospects for your business whose names are not on the mailing lists you rent or who don't read unsolicited mail. And radio gives you the ability to pinpoint your target audience by demographics, psychographics, and geography.

Recent studies show that approximately one in five American adults is functionally illiterate. Only TV and radio can reach this vast audience; newspapers, magazines, and direct mail cannot.

Radio As A Direct Response Medium

Radio traditionally has not been an effective advertising medium for direct response advertisers and local firms desiring immediate leads or sales from their commercials. The reason is that the most effective time to advertise on radio is *drive-time*—during the rush hour when people are commuting to and from work. The problem is that people normally cannot call the toll-free number given in your radio commercial if they are in a car.

According to James R. Rosenfield, chairman of Rosenfield/Vinson advertising agency, the growth in cellular phones is changing that. "Radio will be the great new direct marketing medium of the 1990s," writes Rosenfield in his special report, *Direct Marketing in the 1990s*. He notes that the price of car phones is rapidly decreasing, making them affordable. Rosenfield also states that car phones will be used most extensively by upscale professionals and managers—a prime target market.

"There's a co-factor here: the worsening traffic situation everywhere in the world," observes Rosenfield. People stuck in traffic have time on their hands. They will listen to—and respond to—radio commercials. He advises direct response advertisers to buy drive-time commercials in areas with a high number of cellular phones and heavy traffic.

In addition, Rosenfield predicts radio will become a more powerful direct response medium in the home, as well. The reason has to do with demographics, he says. Already, 25 percent of American households consist of one person living alone. And with the demise of the traditional nuclear family, and the growing population of the aged, that number will increase.

"Lonely people keep the radio on for company, and lonely people call 800 numbers because they need stimulation and interaction," says Rosenfield. He also notes that elderly people sleep less and less well, so there will be more opportunity for direct response radio advertising at odd hours. Rosenfield advises that advertisers should buy non drive-time commercials in areas with a large population of older people or single-family households.

Radio Commercials: Entering The Theater Of The Mind

While most radio commercials seem to be the spontaneous ramblings of a disc jockey, they really aren't. They are well-planned marketing presentations designed to make sales where other media can't.

Radio is different. It appeals directly to the listener, one on one. Not even television, with its "talking heads," can do that. The reason is that radio is still—in the mind of the listener—live. Television, on the other hand, is canned. And the viewer knows it . . . or, at least, believes it. What they see on TV is not real, but a recording either on film or videotape. But what they hear on radio they perceive as being live.

"Radio reaches more people, more often than any other medium," says radio advertising expert, copywriter, and announcer Grey Smith. "It is powerful. Radio is word-of-mouth advertising amplified a thousand-fold. It's the stuff that makes people laugh, cry, chuckle, and dream. Radio advertising stretches the listener's imagination. Television limits you to a 21-inch screen. Radio has no limits at all."

No other medium, save theater, can stir the imagination as radio. Stan Freberg, one of advertising's most creative copywriters, gives us an exceptional example of its power:

"Okay, people, now when I give the cue, I want the 700-foot mountain of whipped cream to roll into Lake Michigan, which has been drained and filled with hot chocolate. The Royal Canadian Air Force will fly overhead and drop a 10-ton maraschino cherry into the whipped cream, to the cheering of 25,000 extras."

On radio, producing this commercial is a piece of cake. On television, it's a multi-million dollar nightmare.

No matter what selling approach you use, be it humor, spokesman, slice of life, or news, radio still commands the most dynamic marketing approach available to an advertiser—large or small.

Writing For Radio: Where Imagination Takes Control

While paid radio commercials are the predominant means of marketing communications during any given time period, there are other types of radio spots that need to be mentioned because they also play an important role in marketing products, services, events, and people.

These other forms include public service announcements (PSA) that can be produced by an advertiser; interviews with key personnel of a business, service organization, or government agency; news clips for general distribution; and other recorded or "live" continuity.

The most common lengths for radio commercials are 30 and 60 seconds, although 10-and 15-second spots, plus sponsorships, are available.

A 60-second commercial is actually 59 seconds long, and a 30-second commercial is 29 seconds. There's a reason for this: That one second is used by disc jockeys or engineers to start the next commercial so that a commercial starts and ends within a 60-or 30-second time period. Unlike most other media, in radio, time is of value. Once it's gone, it's gone. If commercial time isn't used, the radio station loses the revenue forever.

Radio advertising, even for a small local advertiser, should not be run without a "master copy platform." This is a single document that guides the radio copywriters in what they are going to write about. It gives direction to the copy and the commercials. Under the best conditions, a radio campaign should be developed by someone who understands both radio as a medium as well as advertising campaign development. The copy platform might spell out such things as:

- What the product is
- Features and benefits
- Which benefits should be highlighted in the copy
- Which features must be mentioned (e.g., hours of operation, location)
- Positioning or image the commercial must convey
- Sales goals and marketing objectives of the radio ad campaign
- Tone (e.g., humor, no humor, etc.)

With a master copy platform in hand, you are ready to write the radio commercial. Radio copy is written in ALL CAPITAL LETTERS. Numbers, like 555-1212, are always spelled out: FIVE-FIVE-FIVE, ONE-TWO-ONE-TWO. If a word or phrase is hard to pronounce, it is written out phonetically. Radio copy is always double-spaced. No exceptions. There are 20 lines of copy to the commercial minute; 10 lines of copy in a 30-second commercial; five lines of copy in a 15-second commercial; and three lines of copy in a 10-second spot.

Radio copy is typed with a wide margin on the left. There is usually a line that goes down the page, with small numbers from 1 to 20 double-spaced, next to the line. Left of the numbers is usually an inch of space. This area is used for sound effects (SFX) directions and announcer (ANN) cues. ANN cues are used when there is more than one person performing in the commercial.

There are three critical parts of a radio commercial:

1. Name of product or service;
2. Price; and
3. Location.

The location can include any or all of the following: address, directions, and telephone number.

Which part is most important? It depends on what you are selling. If you are selling the product, then price and location are given less attention. If you are pushing a store sale, price is the key factor. How does the copywriter decide? The master copy platform should tell him.

A wise old radio station sales manager was once asked what makes for a successful radio commercial. He replied: "Name, name, name, name, name, name." In a 60-second spot, you should mention the name of the product at least six times. To the average copywriter or advertiser, this concept may appear redundant. But it is not. "One of the best name recognition radio spots I've ever written mentioned the name 26 times in 60 seconds," says Grey Smith.

When stressing location instead of product name, mention the location three times, not six times, in a 60-second spot. The same goes for telephone numbers. Why? Because the address, directions, and phone number take longer to say than a product name, so you have less time for repetition.

Trick of the trade

When mentioning telephone numbers, refer your listener to the white pages instead of the yellow pages. The reason is if you mention the yellow pages, your listener will turn to your category in the directory and be exposed to your competitors' ads as well as your own. And you don't want to promote their advertising at your expense. Better to make the consumer remember your name and the white pages.

There are as many ways to begin a commercial as there are products and services to sell. But there are several elements that must be included to make the spot work. First, the commercial must have a hook. If you don't catch the listener in the first 10 seconds, you won't catch him in the remaining 49. Second, you must include the necessary information: product name, where to buy it, price (if important), and address and telephone number, if required. And finally, you must ask for the order. Ask your customer to buy. Even institutional commercials that are only intended to spread goodwill and company name are asking people to buy something, if only a concept.

The last element to be considered carefully is the emotional mood or approach that you intend to use to grab and keep the listener's attention. You can be friendly, festive, dignified, exciting, mysterious, humorous, melancholy, romantic, sentimental, quiet, provocative, extravagant, and outrageous—to name just a few. There are many more. Choosing the right one is important. The only one to watch out for is humor. Humor doesn't always work; even if the commercial is good, things are funny only when they are fresh. All the remaining particulars—like secondary announcers, sound effects, music, jingles—will be determined by the unique selling position of your product or service as defined in your master copy platform.

When you finish writing your 20 lines of copy, read it aloud. Copy that looks structurally good on paper won't sound natural when spoken. It will be stuffy. The spoken language isn't delivered in perfect, complete sentences. It's more like sentence fragments. Write the copy the way you talk. Just take out all the *ums* and *uhs* and *you-knows.* If you have trouble writing conversationally, record your ideas into a tape record, then have a transcript made of the tape. Read the transcript aloud. You'll immediately recognize the difference between spoken and written copy.

14 Proven Radio Copywriting Techniques

1. *Stretch the listener's imagination.* Voices and sounds can evoke pictures in the mind. Take your listeners somewhere they've never been before. Or better yet, somewhere they're dying to go.

2. *Listen for a memorable sound or voice.* A distinctive voice, a jingle, a solution that will make your message stand out.

3. *Present one idea.* Be direct and clear or your message may become subject to distractions.

4. *Select your customer quickly.* Get the attention of your customer fast. Flag them down before they have a chance to change stations.

5. *State your product/service and promise early.* Radio spots that do so get higher awareness. And be sure to repeat the product name at least six times in a one-minute commercial.

6. *Capitalize on local events.* Tie in with fads, fashion, news events, weather, or holidays.

7. *Music helps.* It's great for reaching teenagers who prefer the "now sounds." Good jingles are remembered for years. But keep the music simple. Don't let it overpower the selling message in the words.

8. *Ask listeners for action.* You can't make a sale unless you ask for the order. Don't be afraid to ask the customer to try your product or service today.

9. *Use the strength of radio personalities.* They have steady listeners. Have them deliver the radio spot live. Many disc jockeys and show hosts have a strong hold on their audience.

10. *Have more than one spot ready for broadcast.* Radio is a high-frequency medium. You need to have variety in your sales message. You will also have to refresh your "pool" of spots so that you don't bore your listeners.

11. *Special messages can reach ethnic groups.* Special messages to special groups do very well. It pays to design radio spots for ethnic groups and even produce them in that group's language (e.g., Spanish for Hispanic marketing).

12. *Use radio for special promotions.* A holiday sale, a grand opening, an anniversary sale, or a "this-week-only" promotion all work well on radio.

13. *Don't evaluate radio copy by reading a typed radio script.* The spoken word is different than the printed word. In a newspaper ad, the consumer can always go back and re-read if he misses part of your message. In radio, if your customer misses part of the message, he can't go back and hear it again.

Your copywriter should read the commercial to you or have a demo made to approximate the finished commercial. Judge your radio commercials in context. Just as you would ask to see your print ad as it would appear in a magazine or newspaper, ask to hear your radio commercial inside several minutes of actual programming.

14. *Get help if you need it.* You can write the spots yourself. But, if you are not an expert in radio advertising, get help from a professional who has experience in the field. Many freelance copywriters specialize in different types of media. Find one who has strong radio background. If you decide to use radio station personnel to write and produce your spot, it might be wise to get a second opinion on your demo before you schedule air time.

Producing The Radio Spot

Of all the production processes—print advertising, television, direct mail—radio is the easiest to understand. It's usually the quickest and least expensive, too—if you have all the proper equipment available to you.

The simplest form of delivery is, of course, live. You simply provide the script to the radio station, and their announcers read it during their show. If the announcer has a strong audience, then listeners perceive that their beloved announcer or program host is endorsing your product.

A good example is the popular New York radio show "What's Your Problem?" with Bernard Meltzer on WOR-AM. Meltzer has a large and faithful audience who practically worship the ground upon which he walks, and an advertiser would be foolish to submit a "canned" commercial and pass up the opportunity to have "Uncle Bernie" personally praise the product. Many talk show and news station announcers bring sales success simply from the fact that they are plugging the product or service.

Often, these "live" spots are recorded so they can be played at any time during the play schedule. At KABC TalkRadio, for instance, Michael Jackson records many of his spots. But they sound live when played during his show. Only when he's on vacation or not doing his air shift do you notice that he's not delivering the spot live.

Radio spots are recorded on reel-to-reel audio tape. Most production companies and radio stations use the highest quality tape available so production quality can be equal or better than that of the record industry.

Once your radio copy is finished, and if it is not designed to be read on-air by the announcer or show host, then you need to find talent. This involves rounding up audition tapes of available announcers and music groups. An audition tape is a collection of previous commercials the announcer or music group has done.

Sometimes announcers will provide a demo tape of them reading your specific commercial. There may be a small fee for this. But it allows you to get a good idea of how the finished commercial will sound with the announcer reading it minus any special effects.

Note: There are many agencies and copywriters who say they can do radio, but few who actually have substantial radio experience. Listening to audition or demo tapes can help separate the pros from the amateurs. (Don't even consider hiring someone who does not have an audition tape of sample commercials.)

Make sure the spots you hear are ones you are familiar with. Then, call other radio advertisers and check their results. Find out if they're happy and if they are making sales from their radio spots.

When you've chosen your talent, you are ready to go into recording. You may rent a professional recording studio or opt to use the radio station's production booth. The spot can be recorded all at once, in sequence; or it can be recorded in segments, to be mixed together later by an audio engineer.

When the commercial is "in the can" (recorded and finished), copies are made for distribution. These are called *dubs*. If you buy more than one radio station, you must send a dub to each.

Before you buy air time, test the finished commercial on an audience. Find out if it works. Find out if the major elements—product, price, address, and the like—are remembered.

Choosing The Right Radio Station

This is probably the most difficult portion of radio advertising. You cannot begin to select stations unless you know exactly who your customers are. When you know their demographics, then you need to find out what kind of radio they listen to and at what times.

There are all kinds of stations out there, each broadcasting to a fragmented audience. These include:

- Adult contemporary (AOR)
- Middle of the road
- Beautiful music
- News
- Talk
- Rock
- Country-western
- Jazz
- Classical
- Top 40
- Easy listening
- Progressive rock
- Ethnic
- Variety
- Educational
- Religious

There are more. And it breaks down even further. You can choose either AM or FM. FM now enjoys the largest audience.

In the end, choose the radio station or stations that reach your customers. To find out specifics about each station, call and request their media kit. Stick with the demographics—age, sex, income, education, employment, residence—so you can target your customer. The more narrowly you can target your customer, the better your chances of selling him or her.

Buying Air Time

You cannot guess about the purchase of air time. You must *know* when your customer is listening. It's impossible to survey each and every customer and potential customer, of course. But there are some things you can determine based on your demographic research.

You'll know, for example, if they commute to work, are housewives or working mothers, teenagers, etc. You'll know what periods of the day they listen to radio and what stations they prefer.

If your customer drives to and from work, then drive-times are the best buy. Drivers are a relatively attentive audience. Research proves that drivers recall commercial messages better than home listeners. Radio is the perfect medium for selling car products and services (e.g., cellular telephones, muffler shops, used cars).

If your customer listens to radio at home or in the office, mid-days are good buys. Many radio stations have audience participation promotions during working hours, so there is active listening throughout the day. Other customers don't like television and listen to special programming at night.

Spot radio is broken down into different day-time parts or *day parts.* The premium times are 6 to 9 AM (usually designated as AAA time which is the most expensive), 9 AM to 3 PM (mid-day, which is known as AA time, the second-most expensive), 3 to 6 PM (also AAA time), 6 PM to midnight (A time), and midnight to 6 AM (B time).

Of the two drive-times (morning or evening commutes) morning is the best. For the most part, radio listenership is greatest between 6 AM and 6 PM. After 6 PM, listening drops off substantially, probably due to the competition from television, which has news at 6 PM and begins prime-time programming at 8 PM.

Monday through Thursday are the best days on radio, unless something special is happening on Friday or the weekend. Air time on the weekends is usually charged differently than during the week. Tuesdays are usually the best days, followed by Wednesday and Thursday, then Monday. Fridays are last. No one knows why.

Find out when your consumer is listening, then buy that day part.

Evaluating Radio Stations

The first thing you need is a *rate card*. It comes with the media kit you requested from the station. The rate card is crowded with numbers, broken up into day parts. The number you see for any given day part is what a single spot costs when played during that time of day. If you order a specific time, say 3:15 PM, it will cost you a premium. The standard radio media buy is ROS (*run of schedule*). ROS means the station will guarantee your spot to be aired between certain hours in a specific day part but does not schedule an exact time.

There are also different rates for different length spots. Every rate is based on the 60-second spot. Usually the 30-second spot costs 75 percent of the 60-second spot. A 15-second spot costs 50 percent of a 60-second spot, and a 10-second spot costs around 45 percent of a 60-second spot.

There are a number of ways to buy radio. You can buy spots one at a time, in a package, or in bulk. The more spots you commit to, the cheaper each minute becomes.

If you are going into radio for the short run, stick to the package deal, unless your budget allows you to buy bulk. Bulk means usually over 1,000 spots during a schedule year. If you buy bulk, and decide to back out of your contract, then the spots you actually ran will be prorated back to premium rates.

If you are serious about selling products by radio, one spot an hour won't do it. Neither will two or three. You will need to run at least six spots an hour to have an effect during a short-run campaign. Twelve an hour borders on too much. Eight an hour is about right for really pushing a sale or special item.

Example: Let's say you are having a weekend sale at your business. What would your schedule be like? You are selling furniture at 50 to 80 percent off tag—to get rid of the old and make room for the new designs. You want to push the sale hard for two weeks and you've got a reasonable budget to do it.

A good schedule would be as follows:

First week: ROS, Tuesday through Friday, four spots an hour during morning drive, four spots an hour during mid-days (to hit housewives), four spots an hour during afternoon drive, and three spots an hour from 9am to 3pm on weekends.

Second week: ROS, Tuesday through Thursday, eight spots an hour morning and afternoon drive, six spots an hour mid-days. Friday, 8 spots an hour, morning drive. Saturday, six spots an hour, 9am to 3pm, and Sunday, 9am to 12 noon. That should move everything out of your store by Sunday evening, if your prices are too good to pass up.

How To Get The Best Rates

Account executives won't admit this unless you ask, but radio time is negotiable. Push for the best rate. Make sure you get your rates protected if there is a future rate increase in the works. National advertisers pay more than local. If your account executive helps you plan a successful radio campaign, it means he/she will get good commissions from your account for a long time to come. If it doesn't work, he/she loses a valuable advertiser—you.

Tracking The Results

Despite the popular notion that radio generates instant sales, there are times when it doesn't produce the desired results. Like any other advertising medium, it takes time to build a relationship with your audience. Customer trust is hard to gain. It simply takes time. Time to develop familiarity. Time to build confidence. Time to track results.

This is not to say that under certain conditions it won't work. Take a weekend sale, for example. If you have the right product or service, and you are offering it at a low price, then you will get a degree of immediate sales. But over the long haul, radio takes time to develop if you want to be able to measure your success and increase sales.

Tracking radio is different than tracking other types of advertising. With print advertising, often customers will bring in ads to your place of business. People like to cut out ads from newspapers and magazines or save fliers they get in the mail. But how do you cut out a radio ad? A lot of people will say it can't be done. But it can. Creativity is the key.

One advertiser recently had a "coupon ad" on the radio! Part of the 60 seconds of the spot was dedicated to instructing the listener how to draw an official coupon. And it worked. After the ad had been running several weeks, the coupons began coming in. But it took time to establish because the listener had to be convinced that this was an honest offer for a service.

Once the offer took hold, the advertiser maintained it. Just like in other media, you have to maintain consistency in your radio advertising.

Radio Versus Print Media

"Compared to print advertising, radio is dirt cheap," states Grey Smith.

Let's compare the circulation of a newspaper against the audience of a radio station. Say you live in a city of 500,000. The city's biggest newspaper has a paid circulation of 200,000 with additional street and newsstand sales of 50,000 per day. You want your ad to reach as many adults as possible.

A quarter-page, positioned in the upper right corner of the first available page, costs $1,000 for a one-time run. The cost per thousand is $25, which means for each 1,000 people the ad is supposed to reach, you pay $25.

The broadcast of the biggest radio station reaches all 500,000 residents. You can be fairly certain that each household has at least one radio; in fact, the national average for the number of radios per household in the United States is almost 10.

Of these 500,000 potential customers, 80 percent are in the 18 to 65-age group—the customers you want to reach. This gives you a listener base of 400,000. Say a 60-second radio spot costs $100 during drive time (6 AM to 10 AM in the morning or 3 PM to 7 PM at night). Just to keep the cost of advertising the same, you spend $1,000 with the radio station. That's 10 60-second spots.

When the first spot runs, you make a maximum of 400,000 impressions. But let's be less optimistic. Say the radio station has only a 50 percent market share in your town (two other stations have the other 50 percent). So you have made 200,000 impressions—about 50,000 fewer than the newspaper. But you've only spent one-tenth the amount. When all ten commercials have run, you've made 2 million impressions (10 impressions each on 200,000 potential customers). That's eight times what you got with the one newspaper ad for the same budget.

Granted, newspapers stay around longer than one day. And the ad can be cut out and saved. But in a newspaper, it's easy to intentionally skip over a particular ad or even not notice it in the first place, because so many ads compete for a reader's attention in each two-page spread.

On radio, as on television, a listener is exposed to only one ad at a time. So unless he stops listening to the radio altogether, every listener must listen to the commercials. They can't be avoided.

Resource

For more information on radio advertising, contact the Radio Advertising Bureau, 304 Park Avenue South, New York, NY 10010, phone 212-254-4800.

Most of the material in this chapter was provided by the late Grey Smith, and I am grateful for his help and cooperation.

CHAPTER 17

Sales Brochures

We live in an age of entrepreneurism. Hundreds of thousands of new companies are started each year, most of them sole proprietorships run by one or two people; many of them are operated out of a post office box, garage, den, or spare bedroom.

This boom in entrepreneurism solves some problems, but it creates problems, too. For example, it's easier to form or dissolve a company today than ever before. As a result, while the number of legitimate firms is on the rise, there are also a growing number of fly-by-night organizations popping up. And this makes consumers wary. They're more cautious, more skeptical, about doing business with an unfamiliar firm. You have to prove that you're "legit" before they'll take the next step with you.

Brochures can go a long way toward establishing credibility and gaining consumer trust and acceptance. After all, anyone can spend $50 for business cards, letterhead, and an impressive-sounding name. But, reasons the consumer, a brochure distinguishes you as a "real company."

According to a study by Thomas Publishing, 90 percent of business and industrial buyers will not do business with a company that does not have some form of company or product literature they can submit for inclusion in the buyer's purchasing files.

I know this to be true from experience. A firm for which I worked as advertising manager lost a $300,000 sale on a new type of industrial equipment because we did not have a sales brochure or data sheet on the product. It was not enough to submit a typewritten proposal. A brochure was needed to convince the buyer that the product was indeed real and proven.

What, aside from establishing credibility, can a brochure do for you? A brochure can inform prospects about your offer and educate them about your product or service. It can build an image and "position" your company in the marketplace. A brochure can sell (or help sell) your product by presenting its key benefits to prospects and convincing them to acquire the product.

Most products and services have a multi-step sales cycle, meaning that a number of different steps occur before the sale is closed. The steps occur in sequence, with the function of marketing communications and sales to persuade the prospect to take the next step, and the next, and the next, until the final step (the sale) is made. The function of the brochure in these cases is not to sell directly but to convince the prospect to *take the next step in the buying process.*

For instance, the sales cycle for a widget-making machine might be:

A. Prospect sees ad in widget trade journal
B. Prospect responds to ad and requests literature
C. Prospect receives and reads literature
D. Prospect contacts company and requests salesperson to visit
E. Salesperson visits prospect and makes initial presentation
F. Prospect reviews presentation materials with top management
G. Salesperson invited back for second presentation to management team
H. Salesperson makes second presentation
I. Prospect organization reviews second presentation and makes decision to proceed
J. Prospect organization requests formal proposal and price quotation
K. Seller submits proposal and price quotation
L. Prospect places order

A brochure or series of brochures may be used at different stages in the sales cycle to move the prospect forward to the next step. For instance, an introductory brochure presented at Step C must be persuasive enough in its presentation of benefits to convince the prospect to move forward and take Step D, which involves asking the sales rep to make a presentation. During his visit, the salesperson may leave behind a more detailed brochure at Step E either to reinforce and repeat the points in his oral presentation or to answer any questions the prospect might have. This material must be comprehensive and powerful enough to get the prospect to go to Steps F and G. Do you see anywhere else in this sales cycle where a brochure or other persuasive marketing document might come in handy?

Another important but much overlooked function of sales brochures is not just to attract the right prospects but to screen out undesired inquiries. Sending a salesperson to visit each potential client or customer who calls is impractical because of the time and cost involved. So instead of spending hours of time and hundreds of dollars of the company's money on a visit to a questionable sales lead, we send a brochure in the mail. Total cost: $1 to $5, depending on the complexity and elaborateness of the package.

Ideally, the brochure is written so that it attracts the right prospects while screening out the wrong prospects. For example, if you offer a consulting service, perhaps you get many leads from small businesses who waste your time on the phone but cannot afford your fees. A line in the copy such as "Minimum consulting fee: $1,200" would give legitimate prospects some idea of initial cost while discouraging those who cannot spend this much from calling.

Five Basic Uses Of Sales Brochures

There are five basic situations for which brochures are created:

1. Leave-Behind

As the name implies, a *leave-behind* is a piece of sales literature you leave with a prospect. For example, a person who sells vacuum cleaners door-to-door might have a booklet or brochure to leave behind with people who don't have time to see him or aren't convinced on the first visit. Any service company that gives free estimates—an exterminator, a home improvement contractor, a landscape designer—might leave behind an informative or promotional sales piece to reinforce the advantages his firm offers or simply give the prospect a way to get back in touch.

The leave-behind typically repeats and expands upon the salesperson's pitch. Or, it can be designed to answer questions the prospect may have. In business-to-business marketing, the leave-behind brochure may have to be reviewed by several executives within the firm, so you should either leave behind extra copies or design the brochure so it can be easily photocopied. This means using standard page sizes, no complex fold-outs, and color schemes that reproduce well on an office copier (dark ink on light paper).

Make sure your leave-behind has your name, address, and telephone number so the prospect can contact you. If you sell through dealers or distributors, leave a space for them to imprint their logo, address, and phone number or attach self-stick address labels.

2. Inquiry Fulfillment

Inquiry fulfillment material is the brochure and other literature you send to prospects who request more information about your company. These inquiries can be generated from a variety of sources, including ads, direct mail, publicity, and word of mouth.

There are four basic requirements for good inquiry fulfillment brochures:

1. They should have an attractive title that implies value. *Product guide* is better than *catalog. Information kit* is better than *spec sheets* (unless prospects are hungry for spec sheets). "15 Ways XYZ Company Can Cut Your Telecommunications Cost" is better than "XYZ Company: The Leader in Telecommunications Equipment."

   Give your piece an enticing title that can be featured in print advertising to get more people to want it and send for it. One sure way to increase response to your ads or mailings is to offer the free booklet in your copy. Instead of just ending with your logo and address, say, "The tax-saving benefits of this new bond are described in a free, informative pamphlet, *How to Invest Profitably in Municipal Bonds.* To receive your copy without cost or obligation, write us today." People will send for it because the title makes them think it contains useful information, not just sales talk.

2. They must be informative. The person requested the brochure not to be entertained but because he or she wanted more information on the product or service being advertised. The brochure must provide the information the prospect wants, or the prospect will be disappointed.

3. It is not enough for the brochure merely to present the facts. It must also *persuade.* The copy should present the product features and

benefits in such a way that it convinces the prospect that he or she should have, indeed *must* have, the product being promoted. This is the third requirement of an effective inquiry fulfillment brochure.

4. Having created a desire for the product, the brochure must spell out the next step in the buying process and tell the reader to take it. And not only must you tell your prospect to take action, you should also provide strong incentive for the prospect to take action now rather than later—because a delayed decision usually means no decision, which means no sale for you.

Your inquiry fulfillment package should ideally provide a response mechanism that the prospect can use to take this next step. For example, one company had a standard questionnaire every salesperson would use when talking with prospects over the phone. Only by getting answers to the questions could the salesperson work up an exact price quotation. They improved response to their brochure by binding the questionnaire into the next printing and adding copy that asked the prospect to tear out, fill in, and mail the completed questionnaire back to the company after reading the brochure. Many did. In order forms today, you should add a line that reads, "For faster service, simply complete this questionnaire and FAX to [fax number]." About 10 percent of prospects will send the completed form back by fax.

When planning your inquiry fulfillment package, think of it *as* a package, not just a brochure. An effective inquiry package includes:

- The *brochure*—the information the prospect asked for
- A *cover letter*—to thank him for his interest, stress key sales points, and encourage response
- A *reply mechanism*—typically a reply card, questionnaire, sheet, or other form the prospect can complete and mail back to request more information or place an order
- An *outer envelope*—to carry the whole package.

Some marketers are fond of pocket folders used to contain the various elements of the package. I prefer to mail them loose so that they fall out and separate when the envelope is opened. This forces the prospect to at least glance at each element before throwing it away, giving you multiple opportunities to grab his attention. A single folder is easier to rip up and throw away in a single motion.

Tip: The outer envelope of an inquiry fulfillment package should always be imprinted or rubber-stamped with this phrase: "HERE IS THE INFORMATION YOU REQUESTED." Without this label, the prospect or his secretary might mistake the package for unsolicited direct mail, even though he requested it, and throw it away.

3. Point of Sale

A *point-of-sale brochure* is a brochure that is made available to prospects at your place of business. They are also called *rack brochures* because they are typically displayed in literature racks or cases. The two most common examples are bank brochures and travel brochures displayed in travel agencies.

The key requirement of a rack brochure is that it have an interesting, attention-grabbing cover. People who stop and glance at literature displays are often not thinking about your products or services but may be browsing or even killing time.

A cover that stops the reader, either with a striking graphic or a powerful headline, can get the person to stop, lift the brochure out of the rack, read the headline, and, if effective, turn the page to see what's inside. For instance, if you are advertising a health spa or weight loss program, a color photograph of attractive women and men working out in exercise clothes or bathing suits will draw people's eyes to the cover and get them to pick up the brochure. (Yes, sex still sells.)

4. Sales Tool

Some, but not most, literature pieces are designed as sales aids. That is, they are created to be used by salespeople as aids during presentations to prospects.

Sometimes, these are designed in formats similar to regular brochures. The piece may do double duty as both a sales aid and a leave-behind. However, if the primary function is as a sales aid, the brochure should contain more visuals (charts, diagrams, tables), less copy, and what copy there is should probably be in bullets or some other easy-to-scan format.

If the piece is designed solely as a presentation aid, you might go to a flip-chart format, with each page covering one major point (in a headline and visual) with two or three copy points (in bullet form) to support the main idea. Or, you can use three-ring binders containing a variety of sales materials that can be customized to fit the individual salesperson's presentation. These are known as *sales kits.* A sales kit for an aluminum siding salesman, for example, might contain photos of homes the company has sided, a list of references, and actual samples of the different siding materials in a variety of sizes, colors, and finishes.

5. Direct Mail

The fifth category of brochure is those used in direct mail—specifically, in mass mailings sent in bulk to rented prospect names on commercially available mailing lists.

These brochures are typically folded rather than stapled, glued, or bound, and are designed to be quickly read rather than kept and referred to for long periods of time. There is an old saying in direct mail: "The letter sells, the brochure tells." The role of the direct mail brochure is to repeat the key sales points stressed in the letter, support these sales points with more detailed information, and display pictures, photos, and other visuals that illustrate the key selling points.

When designing a direct mail brochure, pay particular attention to the panels the reader sees first when he initially removes the brochure from the envelope. Make this bold and attractive with enticing headlines and graphics that lure the prospect inside. For example, the outer panels may present a series of related copy lines, each leading the reader deeper into the piece. The inner panels are usually reserved for heavier copy and more detailed explanation.

Note that many companies desire a single brochure that can be used both in direct mail and in inquiry fulfillment. But this creates a problem. If you send your brochure to the prospect in the cold mailing, it makes no sense to have him respond and ask for the piece he already has. The direct mail brochure should "hit the highlights" only and be more promotional, while the inquiry fulfillment brochure should be more detailed and discuss product features and benefits in greater depth.

Planning Your Brochure

There are 12 key considerations in planning any sales brochure:

1. The objective or sales goal
2. Type of literature needed
3. Topic

4. Content
5. Audience
6. Sales appeals
7. Image
8. Sales cycle
9. Competition
10. Format
11. Budget
12. Schedule

These 12 steps, followed in sequence, provide a logical platform for planning the production of a brochure, catalog, flier, pamphlet, booklet, or any other printed promotion piece. Make photocopies of the blank Literature Specification Sheet (Figure 17.1) and fill out a new sheet for each project. Give a copy of the completed sheet to your agency, copywriter, and other vendors as part of your background briefing for the assignment.

Let's take a closer look at each phase of the process.

Step 1: Determine Your Objective

The most common telephone call I get is a client telling me, "We need a new brochure." My response is always the same: "Why?" What is the purpose of the brochure? What is it supposed to accomplish? If you can't give a firm answer to this question, maybe you don't really need a brochure after all.

> *Example:* One prospective client answered the question by saying, "I am bidding on a big job for a major phone company and as part of the proposal they require me to submit a company brochure. I don't have one; that's why I need one." This is a legitimate answer, and at least he knows why he is spending his hard-earned money on expensive copy, design, and printing services: to win a major contract.

If you don't really know what results you want from your brochure, the chances of the brochure generating any specific results for you are slim. Your first step is to define your objective. Use the Literature Specification Sheet, Figure 17.1, to select one or more objectives for your project. (Note: The steps described in the text correspond to the numbered steps in the Specification Sheet.)

Figure 17.1. Literature specification sheet.

1. Objectives of the brochure (check all that are appropriate)
   - ☐ Provide product information to customers
   - ☐ Educate new prospects
   - ☐ Build corporate image
   - ☐ Establish credibility of your organization or product
   - ☐ Sell the product directly through the mail
   - ☐ Help salespeople get appointments
   - ☐ Help salespeople make presentations
   - ☐ Help close the sale
   - ☐ Support dealers, distributors, agents, and sales reps
   - ☐ Add value to the product
   - ☐ Enhance the effectiveness of direct mail promotions
   - ☐ Leave-behind with customers as a reminder
   - ☐ Respond to inquiries
   - ☐ Hand out at trade shows, fairs, conventions
   - ☐ Display at point of purchase
   - ☐ Serve as reference material for employees, vendors, the press, investors
   - ☐ Disseminate news
   - ☐ Announce new products and product improvements
   - ☐ Highlight new applications for existing products
   - ☐ Train and educate new employees
   - ☐ Recruit new employees
   - ☐ Provide useful information to the public
   - ☐ Answer the prospect's questions
   - ☐ Generate new business leads
   - ☐ Qualify your company to be on a customer's approved vendor list
   - ☐ Other (describe): ____________________
2. The type of literature needed (check one):
   - ☐ Annual report
   - ☐ Booklet
   - ☐ Brochure
   - ☐ Case history
   - ☐ Catalog
   - ☐ Circular

Figure 17.1. (continued)

- ☐ Data sheet
- ☐ Flier
- ☐ Invoice stuffer
- ☐ Newsletter
- ☐ Poster
- ☐ Other (describe): ______________________________

3. Topic
   a) What is the subject matter of the brochure? (Describe the product, service, program, or organization being promoted.)
   b) What is the theme or central message (if any)?
4. Content
   a) Is there an outline of the main points and secondary points that must be included in the brochure and the order in which they should be presented?
   b) Is the outline thorough and complete? Does it cover all points?
   c) What is the source of this information? Have you provided the copywriter with the necessary background documents?
   d) What facts are missing? What additional research (if any) is required?
5. Audience
   a) Geographic location
   b) Income level
   c) Family status (married? single? children? divorced or widowed?):
   d) Industry
   e) Job title/function
   f) Education
   g) Politics
   h) Religion/ethnic background
   i) Age
   j) Concerns (reasons why they might be interested in your product or service or organization)
   k) Buying habits/purchasing authority
   l) General description of the target audience (in your own words):
6. Sales appeals
   a) What is the key sales appeal of the product?
   b) What are the supporting or secondary sales points?
7. Image

   What image do you want your literature to convey to the reader?

Figure 17.1. (continued)

8. Sales cycle

How does the brochure fit into your sales cycle? (Check all that apply)

- ☐ Generate leads
- ☐ Answer initial inquiries
- ☐ Provide more detailed information to qualified buyers
- ☐ Establish confidence in the company and its products
- ☐ Provide detailed product information
- ☐ Answer questions frequently asked by prospects
- ☐ Reinforce sales message for prospect ready to buy
- ☐ Support salespeople during presentation
- ☐ Close the sale
- ☐ Other (describe): ____________________

9. Competition

What images and sales appeals do competitors' brochures stress?

Competitor	*Image*	*Key Sales Appeals*
____________	____________	____________
____________	____________	____________
____________	____________	____________
____________	____________	____________
____________	____________	____________

10. Format

a) Approximate number of words:

b) Number of color photos:

c) Number of black-and-white photos:

d) Number and types of illustrations and other visuals (describe):

e) Number of pages:

f) Page size: ☐ 8-½ × 11″ ☐ 7 × 10″ ☐ 6 × 9″ ☐ 5-½ × 8-½″ ☐ 4 × 9″
☐ Other: ____________________

g) Method of folding or binding (describe):

h) Number of colors used in printing: ☐ 1 color ☐ 2 color ☐ 4-color process
☐ Other: ____________________

i) Type of paper (weight, finish, texture, color):

Figure 17.1. (continued)

11. Budget

    Use the worksheet below to estimate cost.

Task	*Cost*
Copywriting	__________
Photography	__________
Illustration	__________
Design and layout	__________
Typesetting	__________
Mechanicals (paste-up)	__________
Printing	__________
TOTAL:	$__________

    Number of copies to be printed: __________

    Cost per copy: __________

12. Schedule

    How long will it take to produce?

Task	*Number of days to complete*
Copy	__________
Copy review	__________
Copy rewrite	__________
Design	__________
Design review	__________
Design revision	__________
Typesetting	__________
Photography and illustration	__________
Mechanicals	__________
Delays, mistakes	__________
Printing	__________
TOTAL:	__________

Note: Total days can be reduced if steps are combined and done simultaneously.

Step 2: Determine the Type of Literature You Need

What type of sales literature do you need? A brochure is best for presenting a single product, while a catalog is more appropriate for presenting a line of related products. And if you simply want to keep in touch with your clients and potential clients on a regular basis, you might consider a newsletter format, mailed quarterly. You can use Table 17.1 as a guide to choosing the type of literature format that's appropriate for your application.

Step 3: Choose Your Topic

What is the subject matter of the brochure? Is it about your service, or does it deal with the problem your service addresses? If the purpose is to present your company's capabilities, what percentage of the brochure is devoted to descriptions of specific services as opposed to general discussion of your firm and its good points? If it's about a single product, shouldn't you at least mention your other products? or would that confuse the reader?

You must determine the exact subject matter of your brochure and then stick with it. If you vacillate on this, there will be nothing but confusion and disagreements between you and your ad agency or copywriter.

As a rule of thumb, the most effective brochures typically deal with one topic and one topic only. Other topics, products, or services should be covered in other brochures.

In most cases, the topic will be a specific product or service. You might have one brochure on Product A, a second covering Product B, a third describing Product C, and so on. But you might also write brochures in which the topic is a specific audience or market and its needs, rather than a product.

> *Example:* Let's say one of your big markets is the chemical industry, and they are large purchasers of Products A, B, F, and P. You might do a separate brochure titled, "[name of product category] for the Chemical Industry." The outline of the brochure might be:
>
> 1. The chemical industry has special needs.
> 2. [name of company] specializes in meeting these needs.
> 3. We have a line of [type of product] tailored to these needs.
> 4. They include Product A, Product B, Product F, Product P (with descriptions and benefits of each).

It is important for you, the advertising manager, to clarify and agree on the topic internally before hiring outside copy, art, and creative services to

Table 17.1. Types of sales literature.

Use this . . .	*To do this . . .*
Annual report	Gain status
	Establish credibility
	Build an upscale image
	Tell your corporate story
	Communicate financial data
Booklet	Give a quick overview
	Answer questions via a Q&A format
	Disseminate information
	Build your image as the "expert" in your field
Brochure	Describe and sell products and services
	Provide prospects with the information they requested
	Introduce, position, or establish your product or company in the marketplace
Case history	Overcome skepticism
	Sell your product to a specific market or for a specific application
	Build the prospect's comfort level
	Show how your product can solve a specific problem
Catalog	Sell a line of products
	Let customers know what other products you offer
	Help buyers find and select products they need
	Generate additional revenue by informing buyers of one product that you have many other related products of interest to them
Circular	Promote sales and specials
	Distribute price-off coupons
	Increase retail store traffic
Data sheet	Answer buyer's questions
	Give complete information about a product
	List specifications
	Satisfy the information requirements of the technical buyer or specifier
Flier	Promote your business on a local level
	Get your name around
	Announce an event
	Get new literature out quickly
Invoice stuffer	Reinforce a sales message
	Get additional sales at low promotional cost
	Get your message to all customers
Newsletter	Build awareness of your company with a specific group of prospects over a period of time
	Make announcements
	Distribute miscellaneous bits and pieces of information that don't warrant their own fliers, brochures, or mailings
	Disseminate news
	Highlight recent developments
Poster	Make your message stand out from the crowd
	Get the prospect's attention
	Keep your name in front of the buyer.

create the piece. Changing the core topic and subject matter once the project has started involves enormous additional charges for revisions and change of direction—charges you want to avoid.

Tip: An easy way to get consensus on the creative and marketing direction of a project is to fill out a Literature Specification Sheet for each piece you are doing. You can make blank forms by photocopying Figure 17.1 from the pages of this chapter.

Step 4: Outline the Exact Content of the Brochure

Once you have determined the topic, you need to define exactly what will be covered in the brochure. Just as a book author writes a chapter-by-chapter table of contents as a guide to what will go in the book, you may want to create an outline—either rough or detailed—of the key points that must be covered in the brochure.

Basically, there are three types of brochures: product brochures, service brochures, and corporate or "capabilities" brochures. A product brochure describes and sells a tangible product, such as equipment, hardware, or systems. A service brochure describes the services a firm performs for clients. A capabilities brochure presents a broad outline of a corporation—its history, abilities, strengths, products, services, and activities.

The sample outlines in Figure 17.2 provide a starting point for outlining your own brochures in each of these categories. Use these samples to stimulate your thinking and to make sure all important points are covered in any outline you write.

Step 5: Determine Your Audience

A brochure, or any piece of promotional copy, can be effective only if it is written with a specific reader in mind. The more narrowly focused the market, the better. "There is often a need to look at the broad audience and break it into segments," writes Charles A. Moldenhauer in *communications briefings*. "Once this is done, it may be possible to identify different positionings for each segment."

Why don't more companies have separate brochures for each target market? Cost is the main factor. Some markets may be too small to justify the cost and expense of creating a separate brochure. In other markets, you may not be sure that the market is right for you, and so you don't want to incur major marketing expenses until you've demonstrated success.

What are the alternatives to doing a separate brochure for each market? One technique is to *compartmentalize*—a term invented by Steve

Figure 17.2. Sample brochure outlines.

Product Brochure

I. INTRODUCTION—a capsule description of what the product is and why the reader should be interested in it.

II. BENEFITS—a list of reasons why the customer should buy the product.

III. FEATURES—highlights of important features that set the product apart from the competition.

IV. "HOW IT WORKS"—a description of how the product works and what it can do. This section can include the results of any tests that demonstrate the product's superiority.

V. TYPES OF USERS (MARKETS)—this section describes special markets the product is designed for and, if appropriate, specific benefits it offers each market. This section can also include lists of users as well as testimonials from satisfied clients.

VI. APPLICATIONS—descriptions of the various applications in which the product can be used.

VII. PRODUCT AVAILABILITY—models, sizes, materials, colors, finishes, options, accessories, and all the variations in which the product can be ordered. This section can also include charts, graphs, formulas, tables, or other guidelines to aid the reader in product sizing and selection.

VIII. PRICING—information on what the product costs, including prices for accessories, various models and sizes, quantity discounts, shipping. Often published as a separate price list so as not to date the brochure.

IX. TECHNICAL SPECIFICATIONS—electrical requirements, power consumption, resistance to moisture, temperature range, operating conditions, cleaning methods, storage conditions, safety warnings, product life, and other characteristics and limitations of the product.

X. Q&A SECTION—frequently asked questions about the product and their answers. A good place to include miscellaneous information that doesn't fit logically under the other sections.

XI. COMPANY DESCRIPTION—a brief biography of the manufacturer, written to show the reader that the product is backed by a solid, reputable organization that will be in business for the long haul.

XII. PRODUCT SUPPORT—information on delivery, installation, training, maintenance, service, warranty, and guarantee.

XIII. THE NEXT STEP—instructions telling the readers what you want them to do next or how to place an order.

Service Brochure

I. INTRODUCTION—a listing of the services offered, types of clients handled, and the reasons why the reader should be interested in your services.

II. SERVICES OFFERED—detailed descriptions of the various services offered by the firm and how they satisfy client needs.

III. BENEFITS—describes what the reader will gain from establishing a relationship with the service firm and why he should engage your firm instead of the competition.

Figure 17.2. (continued)

IV. BACKGROUND INFORMATION—a discussion of the problems the service is designed to solve. This section can offer generic advice on how to evaluate the problem and how to select professional help. Such free information adds to the value of the brochure and encourages readers to keep your literature.

V. METHODOLOGY—an outline of the service firm's method of doing business with clients.

VI. CLIENT LIST—a list of well-known people or organizations who have used the firm's services.

VII. TESTIMONIALS—endorsements from select clients, usually written in the client's own words and attributed to a specific person or organization.

VIII. FEES AND TERMS—describes the fees for each service and the terms and method of payment required. This section includes whatever guarantee the service firm offers its clients.

IX. BIOGRAPHICAL INFORMATION—capsule biographies highlighting the credentials and expertise of the key employees plus an overall capsule biography of the firm.

X. THE NEXT STEP—instructions on what the customer should do next if he or she is interested in hiring the firm or learning more about its services.

Corporate Brochure

I. THE BUSINESS (or businesses) the company is engaged in.

II. CORPORATE STRUCTURE—parent company, subsidiaries, divisions, departments, branch offices, overseas affiliates, etc.

III. LOCATIONS—addresses and phone numbers of all offices, branches, agents, and representatives.

IV. MAJOR CORPORATE OFFICERS—names, titles, photos.

V. HISTORY—brief corporate biography.

VI. PLANTS and other facilities.

VII. GEOGRAPHICAL coverage.

VIII. MAJOR MARKETS the company sells to.

IX. DISTRIBUTION SYSTEMS.

X. SALES—annual for this year and growth over the past 5-10 years.

XI. RANKING IN ITS INDUSTRY compared with the competition.

XII. EXTENT OF STOCK DISTRIBUTION.

XIII. EARNINGS and dividends records.

XIV. NUMBER OF EMPLOYEES.

XV. EMPLOYEE BENEFITS.

XVI. NOTEWORTHY EMPLOYEES—scientists, vendors, and well-known authorities, for example.

XVII. INVENTIONS and technological "firsts".

XVIII. SIGNIFICANT ACHIEVEMENTS.

XIX. R&D—current research and development activities.

Figure 17.2. (continued)

XX. QC—quality control and assurance practices and programs.

XXI. ENVIRONMENT—actions with respect to preserving the environment.

XXII. CONTRIBUTIONS—to art, welfare, public service, community, etc.

XXIII. AWARDS.

XXIV. POLICIES.

XXV. FUTURE PLANS, goals, objectives.

Isaac, president of The Stenrich Group, a direct marketing consulting firm. In a compartmentalized brochure, you have a section listing all the various markets and, underneath them, a bullet list of the different benefits the product offers to each of these groups.

A second technique is to keep most of the brochure the same but simply tailor the cover and perhaps the opening page. A good way to create strong affinity with the reader is to identify the reader on the cover, either visually or in copy.

> *Example:* Let's say you sell compressors. One brochure cover might read, "Compressors for the chemical industry," and the illustration is of a chemical plant. Using essentially the same inside layout and text, you create a second cover showing a paper mill and change the headline to read, "Compressors for the pulp and paper industry." Now the chemical industry prospects who receive the first brochure will think your compressor was designed especially and solely for them, and the papermakers receiving the second brochure will have the same impression.

A third technique is the "modular brochure." In this format, the main brochure is a four- or six-page folder with a pocket. Folder copy presents a broad overview of the firm or product. Insert sheets, stored in the pocket, highlight specific topics and can be added or removed to tailor the brochure to the needs and interests of individual prospects.

People want products and services tailored to their needs. They want to perceive that your service is customized for them. A brochure clearly written and aimed at a specific narrow market segment creates this perception. So be sure to identify your audience, then write and design the piece with them in mind. To further pinpoint your audience, fill out Section 5 in the Literature Specification Sheet (Figure 17.1.)

Step 6: Identify Key Sales Appeals

What is the most important benefit your product offers the audience—the most compelling reason why they should buy it? Identify this benefit and stress it on your cover and your first few paragraphs of copy. Do not save your best points for a strong close or bury them in the middle of the piece. The reader may never get that far. Instead, determine the one, two, or three most important points and draw attention to them right away.

To do this, make the title of your brochure the name of the product, then highlight the two or three key sales points in big, bold bulleted lines directly underneath.

One way to determine the main message or key point is to telephone half a dozen or so potential prospects and ask them, "What is the biggest problem you have in your business (or your life) right now?" If you can tailor your copy to address this concern and then show how your product can alleviate the problem, you'll have a winner of a brochure.

Step 7: Determine the Image You Want Your Brochure to Convey

The first thing a brochure conveys, even before it is opened and read, is an *impression*—an image. A glossy, slick, beautifully designed and expensively printed color brochure, just by virtue of the production values, creates an image of stability, excellence, quality, even elegance. A typewritten flier, hand-illustrated and run off on cheap paper on an office copier, creates a very different image.

This is not to say that every brochure must be lavish. Rather, the tone of your copy, the style of design, and the quality of the paper and reproduction should be appropriate to your market and your product. Don't over-present. In your case, a black-and-white flier or an inexpensive two-color pamphlet may be totally appropriate for your audience and offer.

> *Example:* One firm's brochure is elaborate. In fact, it is bound by an imitation leather cover complete with gold tassle. The paper is of the finest quality. The headlines are in finely penned calligraphy. Unfortunately, this firm sells rat poison to warehouse managers who want to get rid of rodents eating their inventory! The brochure is too elegant for the product and market. Not only does this waste money, but it sends a message to the reader that you are not really in touch with your market. Don't over-present. Most companies spend too much on production, not too little.

A good graphic artist can create a piece that looks more expensive than it actually is. One technique for achieving this look is judicious selection of ink and paper colors.

Traditionally, we think of a one-color print job (the least expensive method) as blank ink on white paper. But it need not be. One designer created an elegant look when he printed with maroon ink on gray paper—a color scheme that has been widely imitated. By using "screens" or "bendays," you can achieve varying shades of the same color using only one color ink. If printing a circular or flier in black ink, you might choose a brightly colored stock such as salmon, blue, yellow, or gold instead of white.

Choice of type style can also have a major effect on the image your brochure conveys. And, an elegant or classy typeface may not cost any more than a cheap-looking one. Your graphic artist is responsible for selection, but use your own taste to evaluate her choices.

Step 8: Determine Where in Your Sales Cycle the Brochure Fits

As discussed, the purpose of the brochure is not to do the whole selling job but simply to move the prospect one step along in the sales cycle—from point A to point B, from E to F, etc. To accomplish this, you must first clearly write out your step-by-step sales cycle, then decide where in this cycle your brochure fits and which particular step it is designed to persuade the reader to take. Content, copy, and level of technical detail are all dependent on this.

> *Example:* Let's say you are selling personal computers. When the prospect is first shopping, he/she doesn't want to be overwhelmed with technical details. The brochure probably should concentrate on what your computer can do for him/her and whether it is designed for his/her needs.
>
> But, after shopping around and doing a lot of reading, the prospect will be more knowledgeable. At the point he/she is ready to buy, his/her questions are probably a lot more technical (e.g., How much RAM does your computer have compared with the competition? What microprocessor do you use? How many expansion slots are there?) For this prospect, a data sheet flier with a lot of technical specs clearly laid out would be more appropriate. The point is that technical content and level of depth are dependent on which stage in the sales cycle the prospect is at.

Two Rules of Thumb: 1) The closer the prospect is to making a purchase decision, the more information your brochure must contain. 2) The more technically oriented the prospect is, the more detail the brochure should contain. "Upper management people are interested in the viability of the company with which they will be doing business and in general sales information," writes Rick Austin in *Computers & Electronics Marketing*. "Technical experts are most interested in specifications and 'blood and guts' product information. Middle managers need a little salesmanship, a little hand-holding, and more technical information than upper management but not quite as much as technical experts."

Step 9: Scope Out the Competition

Your brochure may fail to stand out from the crowd if it is too much like the competition. Do your competitors' brochures stress a certain sales point? Perhaps you can grab the prospect's interest by highlighting a benefit that others do not stress or discuss. Are your competitors all using full-size 8-½ × 11″ or 7 × 10″ brochures? Be different and make yours 5-½ × 8-½″. Are they printing in blues, reds, and browns? Make yours orange.

The "Sameness Syndrome" is a danger in industries where companies tend to copy each other, with all advertisers using essentially the same style, format, and approach. After a while, your brochure begins to blur in the reader's mind and he/she cannot distinguish your piece from the 30 other promotions he/she has received from similar companies. A good example of this is the seminar business, which is flooded with look-alike 11 × 17″ two-color self-mailers.

Advertisers copy one another and stick with standard formats because these formats are proven to work. But the advertiser who develops a new format that works will be that much more successful, because he/she will be distinctive and unique. Be aware of your competitors' brochures and try to be different, if you can.

Step 10: Design the Format

Format includes such factors as page size, number of pages, folding or binding method, color schemes, design scheme, and graphic style. For example:

—Will you have a lot of copy on each page or will you use a spare effect with lots of white space?

—Will you use many photos to communicate information, or will you use only a few large, artistic photos for dramatic impact?

—Will the brochure be plain or colorful?

—Will it be full size or designed to fit in a standard #10 business envelope?

—Will it be made from a single sheet of paper (with pages created through folding) or will you print on several sheets of paper and bind them together?

Most direct mail and rack brochures are made by folding a letter or legal-size sheet of paper into six or eight 4 × 9″ panels. Most inquiry fulfillment and leave-behind brochures have larger 7 × 10″ or 8-½ × 11″ pages.

Once you have selected a size and format, make a "dummy." This is a model or mock-up of the finished piece created by cutting, folding, and taping together sheets of paper. The dummy is the same size, has the same number of pages, and folds and opens in the same manner as your final piece. With a dummy in hand, you can better determine how much room you have for copy and where each section of copy will go.

Two Tips:

1. Make the dummy from the same stock on which you intend to print the finished piece, then weigh it. This gives you the exact weight of your proposed brochure, which you can use to determine postage costs for mailing.
2. Use standard size brochures: 7 × 10″, 8½ × 11″, 6 × 9″, or 4 × 9″. Odd-size brochures may require custom envelopes for mailing, and printing special envelopes is expensive. European brochures, printed with 8-½ × 14″ pages, do not fit in standard American letter-size files.

Step 11: Determine the Budget

The easiest way to make a rough guess at a project budget is based on past experience. If you've done other brochures, you know roughly what you can expect to pay for a small, folded all-copy two-color pamphlet or a large glossy color piece with original photography and artwork. If you haven't, get estimates from the various vendors involved—copywriter, photographer, illustrator, artist, typesetter, printer, color separator—and work up an estimate using Section 11 in the Literature Specification Sheet (Figure 17.1).

Tip: One way to reduce the cost per copy is to print more copies. The largest expense is in preparing the copy and artwork for the printer and in making the printing films or plates and running the first copy. To print more copies is not that much more expensive than to print only a few.

For example, if your total cost is $5,000 and you print 1,000 brochures, the unit cost is $5.00 per brochure. A print run of 5,000 might only cost an additional $900, or a total of $5,900, which brings the unit cost down to $1.18 per brochure—a number that's a lot easier to sell to management.

Step 12: Set Your Production Schedule

As a rule of thumb, allow three months for the production of a brochure from the initial conceptual planning and development to receipt of the finished pieces from the printer. This is roughly one month for internal concept development and review plus two months for outside vendors—copywriter, artists, printers—to do their work. On four-color jobs, allow an extra two to four weeks for color separations and corrections.

You can use Section 12 in the Literature Specification Sheet (Figure 17.1) to determine the schedule for any project. Note that it is frequently possible to do multiple steps simultaneously to save time. For example, if you know what photos you want, you can have the photographer doing his shoot while the copywriter works on the copy.

The 24 Most Common Brochure Mistakes

According to Nat Starr, a graphics consultant specializing in brochures for professionals and businesses, these are the 24 most common mistakes advertisers make when producing their brochures:

1. The cover fails to identify its contents and its relevance to the reader.
2. Long words, long sentences, long paragraphs, buzz words, and jargon make the text difficult to read and understand.
3. The text fails to list ALL the benefits.
4. Benefits are listed sequentially in one long paragraph rather than set in a bulleted column for easy reading. Thus, many are overlooked by the reader.
5. The text fails to ask for the order or demand some action at the end.
6. The contents are not organized sequentially so as to deliver an effective sales message that will involve and persuade the reader (i.e. building your case).
7. The designer failed to include line illustrations and charts, or other graphic elements necessary to clarify and reinforce the descriptive text.
8. Photographs are too large, too small, washed out, or dark and blotchy.
9. Text is set in typefaces that are too small, too bold or too light, too masculine or feminine, too whimsical or industrial, too cute or too powerful.
10. Typeset line length is too long for good readability.
11. Large blocks of italic type and reverse type are hard to read.

12. Headlines are not set in type large enough and bold enough to provide good contrast with the text type.
13. Headlines are not written so that the reader will get the gist of the message by just reading the heads.
14. Solid, uninterrupted pages of text type are hard to read and don't get read in their entirety.
15. Insufficient contrast between text type and the area on which it is printed. Example: small, medium red type overprinted on a green tint block (almost impossible to read).
16. Not enough contrast between colors used. One should be dark, the other light, for good balance on the layout.
17. Too many colors used indiscriminately with no attempt to balance them on the layout.
18. Insufficient white space to separate the various elements on the layout. Everything jammed together. Hard to read.
19. Large "bubbles" of white space inside the layout. Too distracting to the eye.
20. Brochure sent as a self-mailer (without an envelope). Virtually guarantees worse results.
21. Too many inserts with a pocket-size brochure that is inconvenient to handle and store.
22. Information unclear (or missing) as to how or where to get additional information or order the product or service.
23. Failure to make it easy for the customer to buy by not providing easy terms, 30-day free trial, credit card acceptance, etc.
24. Paying too much for printing. Experienced graphics people can help you find many ways to slash your production, printing, and lettershop costs.

12 Powerful Ideas For Improving Your Sales Brochures

Richard H. Hill, vice president/high-technology at Alexander Marketing Services of Grand Rapids, Michigan, offers the following tips and ideas on how to improve the selling power of your next sales brochure:

1. Show test results that confirm that your product or service performs as you say it does.
2. Use case histories showing the successful application of your product or service.
3. Provide sample calculations of cost savings or other benefits.
4. Compare your product with the competition, feature by feature.
5. Compare your product or service with the buyer's alternative of doing nothing and sticking with his old ways. That's a particularly strong approach for new, advanced technology products.
6. Provide useful information about the application of your product or service that is not readily available. This can earn your brochure the status of a reference work, keeping it in use by the prospect.
7. Present points logically. Outline a progressive presentation that answers the buyer's probable questions in the order he or she would ask them.
8. Design the piece so that it presents one major topic per spread or page.
9. Don't cram too much material into the first page or spread. It must be very inviting if you're going to get your prospect started on your message.
10. For longer brochures, consider using an index or table of contents to direct prospects to the right section.
11. Try to include at least one photograph of your product in your literature. This is particularly important for a new product. Using drawings instead of photos with a new product can imply that you haven't really made any of them yet.
12. Use tables and graphs to support your claims and present the properties of your products. They are far better choices for presenting quantitative data than body copy. There is nothing like a string of numbers and units in a paragraph of body copy to slow down the transfer of information.

Final Check

Use the checklist presented in Figure 17.3 to check new brochures for quality and accuracy before printing. Also use it to analyze existing pieces and determine which need to be redone.

Figure 17.3. Brochure analysis. (Reprinted with permission of Nat Starr Associates.)

General Information

1. Is the information accurate?
2. Do you offer any service not shown in the brochure?
3. Is your address and phone number correct?
4. Do you have a toll-free 800 number, and is it correct?
5. Is your logo correctly reproduced?
6. Is your bio current and sufficiently comprehensive?
7. Have you added any new service since printing the brochure?
8. Is your list of clients valid and current?
9. Does your description of services and products correspond to other forms of advertising or promotion you may have published?
10. Is information presented in a logical sequence?

Physical Appearance

1. Are the photos current, clear, and appropriate?
2. Do action photos look real or posed?
3. Are photos used effectively in the layout?
4. Is type style up-to-date and easy to read?
5. Is type broken up frequently by white space, to present information in short bursts?
6. Is type on headlines large enough to attract the reader's eye?
7. Do headlines and subheads convey the gist of your message?
8. Are words, sentences, and paragraphs short?
9. When sentences contain more than one or two ideas, are the ideas visually separated—as in this sentence?
10. Is there sufficient white space and is it used properly?
11. Is a second color of ink used?
12. Should your brochure be two color (inks) or four?
13. Are the proper colors used?
14. Has the proper type of paper been used?
15. Is the printing quality acceptable?
16. Can the physical format (size and shape) be physically stored in a file folder?

Selling Ability

1. Does the brochure clearly and immediately define what you do?
2. Do you use a byline (tag line, slogan) that positions you in your market?
3. Is the proper information highlighted?

Figure 17.3. (continued)

4. Does it zero in on the prospect's needs?
5. In the first 10 seconds does it give the recipient a compelling reason for reading it?
6. Are the selling benefits clear to the prospect?
7. Are your selling features easy to find?
8. Does your brochure project the current corporate image?
9. Does it state who the audience is?
10. Does it state why the prospect should buy from you?
11. Does it avoid flowery language with too many superlatives?
12. Does it use active verbs and picturesque language, with ideas stated succinctly?
13. Have you used sufficient testimonials?
14. Have testimonials been properly edited?
15. Does the brochure ask for the order?

Resources

Create the Perfect Sales Piece: How to Produce Brochures, Catalogs, Fliers, and Pamphlets by Robert W. Bly (New York: John Wiley & Sons, 1985), 242 pages. This book provides exhaustive coverage of the steps that I could only present in outline form in this chapter. Recommended for advertising managers who supervise the production of collateral materials, especially those who coordinate the work of multiple outside vendors rather than just turn the project over to an ad agency.

The Complete Guide to Creating Successful Brochures by Karen Gedney and Patrick Fultz (Brentwood, NY: Asher Gallant Press, 1988), 124 pages. Advocates using a creative team of copywriter working with a graphic artist. Has a more visually oriented approach than I take and is useful for getting the artist's view of the brochure design process. Recommended.

CHAPTER 18

Catalogs

A *catalog* is a comprehensive directory describing all the products a company sells. "Resting on the table in a farm, suburban or city home, the catalog functions like a one-stop shopping center," writes Julien Elfenbein in his book, *Business Letters and Communications.* Rural folk have always been avid catalog buyers because, unlike suburban and urban families, they do not have access to a vast quantity of convenient nearby stores and malls, and so it is logical for them to do more shopping through the mails.

According to Lauren R. Januz, a printed catalog consists of illustrations, descriptions, selling copy, and prices of multiple products presented in a format that permits easy handling, filing, and reference. Januz notes that the catalog may be as simple as a single sheet of paper printed on both sides, or as complex as hundreds of pages bound to form the big, heavy, expensive catalogs like those published by Sears, Penney, Ward, Spiegel, and other major marketers. The prices may be on the same page as the merchandise descriptions. Or, they might be printed on a separate insert mailed with the catalog.

The main point of difference between a brochure and a catalog is that brochures typically describe a single product in detail, while catalogs cover more products in less detail. The brochure promotes an individual item; the catalog provides a single-source of information on your company's entire product line. A brochure is narrowly focused; a catalog is comprehensive in the breadth of products offered.

Catalogs have several uses. By inserting a catalog in the shipping envelope or box when you pack and ship products ordered by customers, you educate those customers about other products you offer that may be of interest to them. Catalogs can also be mailed separately to your customer list one or more times a year to remind those customers of your existence and get them to buy more from you.

To expand your catalog sales, you can mail the catalog unsolicited to potential buyers whose names you rent from mailing list brokers. You can offer your catalog, either at no cost or for a nominal fee, in small print ads. Be sure to fulfill requests for your catalog promptly; according to a study by Thomas Publishing, 43 percent of all catalogs sent in answer to requests arrive too late to make the sale. Catalogs should be mailed within 48 hours after you receive the inquiry.

Catalogs can also be distributed at retail outlets, either as point-of-sale buying guides or to stimulate mail order sales for those shoppers who would rather buy at home than in a store. The Sharper Image is one of several marketers that actively distributes a mail order catalog at its retail outlets. In some stores, you can simply pick up a catalog from a rack or counter. Other stores will mail you the catalog if you complete and mail a coupon at the sales counter (the purpose of this strategy is to capture your name and address for future mailings).

The variety in catalogs is truly amazing. Some advertisers, especially those whose products must be depicted in full and natural color, send committees of top executives to the printing plant as the catalog rolls off the press so proofs can be checked and rechecked and color corrections made at every step to ensure quality. At the other end of the spectrum, small marketers often type their first catalog sheets themselves and run them off on the office copier.

Some catalog companies use elaborate color photography and glossy paper to sell their merchandise. Others prefer illustrations and print on cheaper grades of newsprint stock. Dr. Jeffrey Lant, one of the top catalog entrepreneurs in the country, has a lengthy catalog that is all copy with not a single picture, and it is enormously successful.

Styles also vary enormously, and the successful catalogers have developed their winning formulas only over time through trial and experience. Drew Kaplan's DAK catalog is famous for its long-copy approach with a full page or even two pages devoted to each high-tech electronic gadget he sells. When you read his copy, you see he is truly in love with his products, having tried each and every gizmo himself before recommending it to his band of loyal buyers.

By contrast, Harry & David's Bear Creek catalog takes a homey approach and is loaded with gorgeous color photos of their fruits, cakes, and pies, with copy so compelling that even mundane foods like pears or grapes seem a gourmet delight. A great catalog like DAK or Bear Creek transcends mere salesmanship; its arrival becomes a welcome event on a par with receiving one's favorite magazine or a gift in the mail. You not only buy from it; you look forward to receiving it.

Most catalogs are direct response tools encouraging the recipient to order immediately by completing and mailing an order form or calling a toll-free number to place a credit card order. Many catalogs, such as those used by bathroom accessory or power tool manufacturers, are designed as in-store sales tools: They are kept at sales counters where shoppers can browse through and select the items they want.

The advantage of such a catalog is that it can display every item the manufacturer offers, while the hardware store or home improvement center, with its limited space, can afford to display only a few items from each company. A few catalogs, like IBM's PC Guide, don't generate sales directly but instead give the buyer a preview of the merchandise so he knows what to ask for when visiting the store.

The early catalog giants, such as Sears, made their success with general-interest catalogs offering the convenience of buying a broad range of consumer goods by mail. Nowadays, the trend is toward specialized catalogs. One specialized catalog contains nothing but fireplace products: kindling, screens, and other implements not easy to buy at stores. Another, Wolferman's, specializes in English muffin gift packs.

A large number of orders placed through certain catalogs are purchased as gifts rather than for personal consumption by the consumer. Mail order catalogs offer a wonderfully convenient means of sending gifts at holiday time, because they eliminate the need to shop, wrap the gifts, and mail them to distant friends and relatives. Order forms in gift catalogs have space where the customer can write in the names and addresses of people who will be receiving the gifts so the catalog house can mail directly to the recipient. Your order form should also leave room for a personalized message from your customer which your order clerks write on cards and enclose with the gift.

Although catalogs are nearly infinite in their variety, they can, for convenience, be categorized in three basic categories:

- Consumer catalogs
- Mini-catalogs
- Industrial catalogs

Let's take a closer look at each type.

How To Create A Consumer Catalog

As the name implies, a consumer catalog is one offering merchandise to consumers. Products offered include clothing, videotapes, compact discs, books, food, wine and spirits, coffee, toys and games, gardening products, adult materials (sex aids and pornography), and furniture. There is even a catalog offering items specifically designed for left-handed people!

Sandi Lifschitz, president of Copy Creations in New York City, offers the following tips for creating successful consumer catalogs:

Know Who You Are

More formally, position your company in the catalog marketplace. There's a lot of soul-searching and objectivity involved. Consulting with a marketing specialist is extremely beneficial.

Get Involved with Your Customers

Discover who they are. This goes beyond demographics. Keep up with their lifestyle and needs. Pay attention to their requests and comments. Most importantly, listen to their problems; learn from them. They often give the best direction. That's how a good merchandiser becomes a great cataloger.

Creative Merchandising

Learn all about your industry and everything you are going to sell. Study the merchandise, the markets. Keep up with the trends. This may sound academic, but it makes a big difference. Merchandising is the key to it all.

Product promotion today, fashion in particular, takes on many moods and definitions. Introduce a new accessory. Show the latest footwear even if you're not selling it. This tells the customer you understand the total picture, you really know what's happening.

Take a basic item. Interpret what meaning it has for the customer. For example, a white polyester blouse conveys a great finishing touch to a business suit . . . a wonderful versatility (because it's white) . . . and an ideal travel item because it never needs ironing. This one product creates lots of "selling mileage" and fills many needs at the same time.

Go Beyond the Benefits

Catalog copy has to communicate to touch an emotion, fulfill a need, initiate an impulse, or act out a fantasy. Never underestimate the mind of the consumer. Vulnerable? Maybe. Gullible? Sometimes. But consumers are more knowledgeable and aware than ever before. And you have to be ten steps ahead of your customer at all times.

Create a Mood and Keep It Going

Don't just produce that fabulous cover. Whether a theme or a season, illustrate it throughout, talk about it in the copy. Make the reader "feel good" as she's/he's turning the pages of your catalog. You want her/him to look forward to receiving the next one.

Ready-to-wear and home fashion catalogs stimulate impulse buying. Commercial product catalogs take on another aspect. A reader holds onto them; they become reference material and don't change as frequently.

Copy versus Art

The most popular attitude seems to be that the visual takes first place when you're selling a product; the verbal takes over when you're selling a service. Many have seen it work well in reverse, too. The point is: They are both important.

You're especially lucky when you find a good rapport between artist and writer. A naturally visual copywriter has a great advantage because he or she *sees* the words on the page, almost "writing the layout." A less visual writer might do best working directly from a layout.

The artist who understands that the layout must "work" for the merchandise being advertised as well as look great is a real treasure. The ideal situation is for the artist and writer to work together on a project, but that's not always possible due to tight schedules.

Use Specifics

Don't leave the customer with questions in mind. Answer:

—How tall is the table lamp?

—How many paper cups are in the package?
—Are the earrings pierced or clip-ons?
—Translate S, M, L, and XL into size ranges.

Give all the facts. If you don't know them, take the time to find out. If necessary, use or wear the product yourself. Caring about every detail makes the difference between customer indifference and enthusiasm, as well as satisfaction.

Make It Believable

Someone once said, "There's a cynic in all of us." If anything can make cynicism surface, it's advertising that makes unrealistic claims or promises.

Make sure your merchandise is readily available. Nothing irritates a customer more than being told the item is sold out when she/he calls the same day she/he receives the catalog.

Believability is merchandise that is true to your photographs. Make sure that red is not magenta. Don't show a cubic zirconia ring that looks the size of the Hope diamond when it's really the size of the head of a pin. At least qualify it by saying, "Illustrations enlarged to show details."

Have you ever ordered a piece of furniture that was "easy to assemble?" It's more like a wrestling match, unless you're a handyman. Why not just say, "Assembly required," instead of "Easy to assemble"? It's honest without being antagonistic.

Make It Easy to Order

If the KISS theory (Keep It Simple Stupid) applies anywhere, it's on the order form. What a painful task to even look at some of them—let alone try to fill them out—unless you're an accountant who likes to shop. Don't intimidate the reader. At least give him/her the option of going to the phone (preferably to dial an 800 number) and offer him/her the assistance of a pleasant customer service representative (difficult to find, but they are out there somewhere).

Mail order merchandisers report that having an 800 number and accepting major credit cards can increase orders 30 percent, and that 50 percent or more of people ordering will use the telephone rather than mail the order form. Why? First, because it's easier, less complex, faster, and more convenient. Secondly, if buyers are puzzled or have questions, they want to call you and get answers before they order. They can't do this if you don't take phone calls.

Tip: Put your toll-free number on every page of the catalog in bold type in a box to make it stand out. The easier you make it to order, the more orders you will get.

In a recent mailing, the Franklin Mint offered a collector's ring selling for hundreds of dollars. What obstacle is there to ordering? Many people do not know their ring size. The solution? Franklin Mint enclosed a handy but simple measuring guide (a series of circles printed on a strip of white paper) the reader could use to determine his or her ring size in seconds. This is the type of thing you should be doing to make it as easy as possible for your customers to order.

Fulfill Orders Correctly and Promptly

Fulfillment success establishes your credibility and gains the confidence of your customer. Customers judge you by how quickly you ship, especially on the initial order.

Don't make promises you can't keep, but ship all orders as quickly as possible, preferably within 24 to 48 hours of receipt. If you can't ship the item right away, at least send a card that acknowledges the order and specifies when the customer can expect to receive the goods.

The Customer is King (or Queen)

Keep in mind the importance of a close relationship between cataloger and consumer. Your consumer catalog is a motivator—an image-building tool to excite the customer into buying specific merchandise. Let your customer know you are catering to him/her. Make him/her feel he/she is important. That's what direct selling is all about.

How To Create A Successful Mini-Catalog

In contrast to the large full-color mail order catalog on glossy stock is the less fanciful, more functional *mini-catalog.* "If you sell many related products and services, but not enough to justify a large, fancy catalog, a self-mailer mini-catalog of between 2 and 8 pages may work well for you," says copywriter Mike Pavlish. "The mini-catalog makes it easier for the reader to grasp everything you sell; tends to be saved more and longer for reference, therefore, generating more orders; and simplifies your advertising program. Instead of having to send out several different and often confusing pieces, all you'll have to do is send out one piece: your mini-catalog."

Here are Pavlish's suggestions for writing an effective mini-catalog:

1. *Use a sales letter on the first or second page.* It should give the main benefits the reader will obtain by responding, encourage him/her to read the catalog now, and motivate him/her to order immediately.

2. *Keep it organized, simple, and easy to read.* Of course, this applies to all advertising, but it's especially important for a mini-catalog because the reader sees more copy at one time. You don't want to overwhelm or confuse him/her. Border-in the different products so they are clearly separated from each other. And use short, snappy copy blocks throughout the catalog to build interest, maintain attention, and push for action.

3. *Make it easy to order.* Leave plenty of room for an order blank section the reader can use to order by mail. If you intend to use the mini-catalog as a self-mailer, design it so the customer's mailing label is affixed to the reverse side of the order coupon. This way, when the customer clips and mails back the coupon, you get the label back and a way to track the response. This enables you to determine which mailing list pulled the most orders.

4. *Use a second color only on the most important points.* Be careful not to overuse the second color (if you go to two colors) to the point where it loses effectiveness. Best places to use a second color: sales letter headline and signature, product name, product benefit, ordering information.

"Once you have a winning mini-catalog, keep sending it to your prospects and customers," Pavlish suggests. "The beauty of the mini-catalog is that it's your all-in-one sales piece—for both prospects and customers. Instead of spending time developing new mailings, you can keep mailing the same catalog to your list for as long as it pays out."

Figure 18.1 is two pages of a sample mini-catalog—my "Writer's Profit Catalog" selling special reports, books, and audio cassettes aimed at teaching freelance writers how to make more money. This four-page catalog is printed in black ink on two sides of two 8-½ × 11″ sheets of paper. (Actually, I duplicate them on my office copier.) Stock is a bright color, either canary yellow or gold.

Industrial Catalogs

An industrial or commercial catalog* is a catalog that sells products to business buyers. Some of these offer commercial items such as office fur-

**Note:* Much of the following information on industrial catalogs is taken from the booklet, "How to Make Your Catalog Work Harder," by Thomas Register of American Manufacturers.

Figure 18.1. Writer's Profit Catalog

Writer's Profit Catalog™

Reports, books, and other information resources that help you get clients, gain confidence, and increase your writing income!

600-Series Reports

These special reports tell how to earn $100,000 or more as a freelance commercial writer—expanding on the material in* Secrets of a Freelance Writer. *Each report is 8–10 pages.

601 Tips for Beginners: How To Get Started in High-Profit Writing™

What if you have no experience, no portfolio, and no contacts? You can still get into high-profit writing quickly...but your strategy will differ somewhat from experienced writers. This report outlines strategies beginners can use to hide, overcome, and even exploit their novice status including: How to generate lucrative business, regardless of your credentials...tips for writing sales letters that get clients to hire you...types of clients that hire beginners...how to create a winning portfolio of sample copy. $7

602 How To Set Your Fees...and Get Paid What You're Worth!

An in-depth discussion and explanation of how to determine, set, negotiate, and get your fees. Includes a survey of what top, intermediate, and novice freelancers are now charging for ads, press release copy, and many other typical assignments. If you're not earning at least $500 per day, you need this report! $7

603 How To Make $100,000 a Year As a Direct Mail Writer

Direct mail/direct response is one of the better-paying areas for freelance writers. This report tells what's going on in the direct mail industry today, how to break in, what the top writers are charging, how to get lucrative direct mail copy assignments. Find out why John Frances Tighe gets paid $15,000 for writing a sales letter—and how you can, too. $7

604 How To Turn Dead Time Into Extra Profits

Every freelance writer will have periods when business is slow. This report tells how to use that "dead time" productively instead of sitting around and getting depressed. You'll also learn a simple technique that can prevent slow periods and virtually ensure a steady stream of work. $7

605 How To Double Your Freelance Writing Income—This Year!

Most writers don't have a business plan that projects cash flow. This report shows how to estimate your annual income based on your current fees, type of work you do, and how busy you are. Once I show you how much money you can expect to earn this year, I'll then tell you how to double that amount (no matter how much it may be). To do this, I charge only $7. Fair enough? $7

606 Bob Bly's Promo Package

This is the sales package I send to clients who request information on my freelance writing services. Estimating conservatively, I can confidently say it has generated at least half a million dollars in direct sales of my freelance copywriting services and added 75 top companies to my ever-growing client list. If I were to write such a package for you as a client, my fee would be $5,000. Now it's yours for only $7. $7

607 How To Overcome Problems When Working With Clients

What do you do when a client doesn't like your copy, or won't pay your bill, or has an unreasonable deadline? What happens when an assignment turns out to be much more work than you bargained for—and you want to tell the client you are going to have to charge more than you originally quoted? How do you tell a current client that you have to raise your fees, or charge more than his budget for a particular project, or that you can't (or won't) handle his next assignment because you are too busy? In 9 years of freelancing I've been in just about every tough situation you can imagine...and in this report, I give you proven strategies for tackling each problem head-on with success. $7

608 Successful Moonlighting: How To Earn an Extra $2,000 a Month Freelancing Part-Time

Let's say you want to break into freelance commercial writing but can't (or won't) give up your current full-time job. Well, you can still make $2,000 a month or more in commercial freelance writing—as a moonlighter! What are the options for commercial writing on a part-time (evenings and weekends) basis? What are the limitations on the projects you can accept (e.g., you can't leave your office or talk with freelance clients during the day)? This report tells you how to avoid complications and earn a comfortable second income writing copy for local and national clients in your spare time. $7

609 Freelancing in a Recession

Is your business hurting right now? Are things too slow? This timely report provides 12 proven, practical strategies for surviving (and even prospering) in a recession, soft economy, or during a business downturn—12 action steps you can take to get more business *now!* $7

610 Government Markets for Writers

The U.S. government, with hundreds of agencies and 34,000 offices nationwide, spends approximately $14 billion a year on writing and editorial services. Most of this writing is done under contract by private organizations and often by individuals. This special report by Herman Holtz explains how to successfully find, bid for, and win government contracts for high-paying freelance writing assignments. $7

611 How To Make Money Writing Speeches

Freelance writers can make $1,000 to $3,000 or more for writing a 20-minute speech. In this report, veteran speechwriter Richard Armstrong reveals the secrets of how to succeed in the lucrative speechwriting market including: how much to charge...where the clients are...how to get assignments...how to research and write an effective speech...and much, much more. $7

Figure 18.1. (continued)

Writer's Profit Catalog™

312 Turbocharge Your Writing: The Vitale Instant Writing Method

A 7-step formula for effective writing. I find it especially helpful when I'm faced with a difficult or intimidating writing assignment or am just having trouble getting started. This book by Joe Vitale is like a gem—small but valuable.

Paperback, 23 pages $5

313 How To Promote Your Own Business

A practical, do-it-yourself guide to advertising, publicity, and promotion for the small-business manager or owner. Lots of good marketing advice for promoting your own freelance writing business or the products and services sold by your clients.

Trade paperback, 241 pages $13

314 Write and Grow Rich: 39 Facts of Life For Writers

You can learn to write for money in this gold mine of practical down-to-earth information from best-selling author Jerry Baker. Jerry shows you how to make money writing novels...business reports...resumes...nonfiction...greeting cards...newspaper and magazine articles...even TV and radio scripts.

Oversize paperback, 122 pages $12

315 Selling Your Services: Proven Strategies for Getting Clients to Hire You

If you sell professional, personal, consulting, trade, technical, freelance, or any other kind of service, this book will give you the information you need to get large numbers of prospects to call you, convince those prospects to hire you at the fees you want, and dramatically increase the sales of your services.

Hardcover, 349 pages $27

316 The Elements of Business Writing

The Elements of Business Writing presents the basic rules of business writing in a concise, easy-to-use handbook organized along the lines of Strunk and White's classic book, *The Elements of Style.* Publication Date: September 1991. (If you order prior to 9/91, we will back-order the book for you and ship when it is available.)

Hardcover, 144 pages $20

Audio Cassette Programs (800-Series)

801 The High-Profit Writer: How To Earn a Six-Figure Income As a Freelance Writer

This information-packed program is for readers who eagerly devoured *Secrets of a Freelance Writer* and want more money-making advice. Hear me on tape as I personally tell you what you need to do to boost your freelance writing income to six figures—and answer questions from dozens of your peers. Recorded live at the 7th Annual Florida State Writers Conference.

Six 1-hour cassettes $49.95

802 10 Magic Steps to Freelance Writing Success

Presents the 10 essential steps every writer must take to make the leap to an annual income of $125,000 or more and consistently maintain (or increase) that income, year after year.

Single cassette, recorded live $12

803 How to Boost Your Direct Mail Response Rates

Proven techniques for dramatically increasing your direct mail response rates. Includes rules for testing, target marketing strategies, offers, list selection, design, copy, mistakes to avoid...and much, much more.

Single cassette $12

804 Sixteen Secrets of Successful Small Business Promotion

How to use low-cost/no-cost advertising, marketing, sales promotion, and public relations techniques to build your business. Learn how to: Gain credibility through public speaking. Generate thousands of leads using simple press releases. Get big results from tiny ads. And more.

Single cassette $12

805 Selling Your Services in a Soft Economy

How to successfully sell and market your freelance writing services in a recession or soft economy.

Single cassette $12

Clip this coupon and mail it with your payment. (You may photocopy it, if you wish.)

Items you wish to order (indicate item #'s): ________ ________ ________ ________

________ ________ ________ ________ ________ ________ ________

________ ________ ________ ________ ________ ________ ________

________ ________ ________ ________ ________ ________ ________

Name ______________________ Phone # ____________

Address ______________________________________

City ______________________ State ____________ Zip ____________

Enclose money order, cash, or check (payable to "Bob Bly") for appropriate amount. NJ residents add 7% sales tax. Canadian residents add $2 (U.S. dollars) per order. 30-day money-back guarantee on all books and cassettes. All items guaranteed to please. **Please allow 2–4 weeks for delivery.**

❑ Please rush my materials. I've enclosed an extra $2 per book (300-series) and $1 per tape or report (200, 600, and 800-series) for first-class delivery.

Mail to: **Bob Bly, 174 Holland Avenue, New Milford, NJ 07646** niture, computer software, or office supplies. Others feature ball bearings, machine components, nuts and bolts, and a wide range of industrial products used in factories and manufacturing operations.

Although industrial catalogs are often "drier" than colorful consumer catalogs, they are not just technical specifications or information bound into a book. They must sell the prospect on benefits—either the specific product benefits or the benefits of choosing the catalog company as a supplier versus other firms offering similar products.

Industrial catalogs must also make the buyer's job easier by giving him the technical data and specifications he needs to order the correct product for his application. Graphs, guides, tables, and other devices that simplify the selection process are critical. If your products are compatible with and can be substituted for similar products made by other firms, for example, you will want to include a table showing which model numbers from your line can be substituted (or "dropped in") for specific model numbers of your competition.

According to research from the Thomas Publishing Company, there are three reasons why industrial firms should consider putting out a catalog:

First, 90 percent of all industrial buyers require printed information before they buy. Buyers use catalogs to check product descriptions, specifications, and performance data. They use it to make intelligent, financially responsible, technically correct decisions. And 90 percent won't even consider you if you don't have a catalog, spec sheet, or flier.

Second, 97 percent of all industrial purchases are initiated by the buyer, not the seller. In fact, the seller usually isn't aware of the intended purchase until he gets a call. So the chances of an ad or salesperson hitting the buyer at the moment the buyer decides to buy are slim. But catalogs, because they are kept as references longer than ads or brochures, have a better chance of being handy when the buyer decides to buy and is searching for suppliers and product data.

Third, your catalog gets in to see prospects your salespeople cannot. No matter how effective your salespeople, they don't call on all prospects. Your catalog provides a way of reaching those prospects salespeople don't see.

While consumer catalogs tend to stress color and visual appeal, industrial catalogs stress technical information, including completeness, ease of reference, clarity, and comprehensiveness. The industrial catalog may be thought of as a tool the purchasing agent can use to make proper buying decisions. Accordingly, it must:

- Answer questions and provide all the specifications and information needed to select and order the proper product.
- Provide a full selection of products to choose from—all shapes, sizes, models, and options.
- Be thoroughly indexed and cross-referenced so the purchaser can quickly locate the items needed.
- Provide tables, drawings, charts, and other devices that guide the purchasing agent in determining exactly which product best meets all needs.

Most catalogs stop here. But this is just a starting point. In addition to serving as an information resource and buying guide, the superior industrial catalog goes beyond these tasks and also functions as a persuasive selling document that convinces the prospect to buy more of what you are selling.

14 Techniques For Improving The Selling Power Of Your Industrial Catalog

Here are just a few ideas for improving the persuasiveness of your industrial catalog. Most of these points are illustrated with sample catalog pages taken from the "Illustrated Fastener Catalog" published by Atlantic Fasteners of West Springfield, Massachusetts.

Catalog Technique 1: Use a Title That Implies Value

The full title of Atlantic's catalog (Figure 18.2) is, "Illustrated Fastener Catalog and Technical Manual." By calling it a *manual,* the advertiser implies added value of the catalog as a reference tool. Note that the cover also has a price ($19.95) imprinted on it. This technique also contributes to the image of higher perceived value. And the more valuable your catalog appears to be, the more people will want to get it, read it, and keep it.

Note: Any technique you can use to get the reader to hold on to your catalog gives you a competitive advantage. Research shows that just three weeks after a typical catalog is distributed by hand or by mail, there is only a 20 percent chance that they can be found. Eighty out of every hundred catalogs have been discarded, misplaced, or misfiled. So anything you can do to get your prospect to keep your catalog is a big plus.

Figure 18.2. Illustrated Fastener Catalog and Technical Manual.

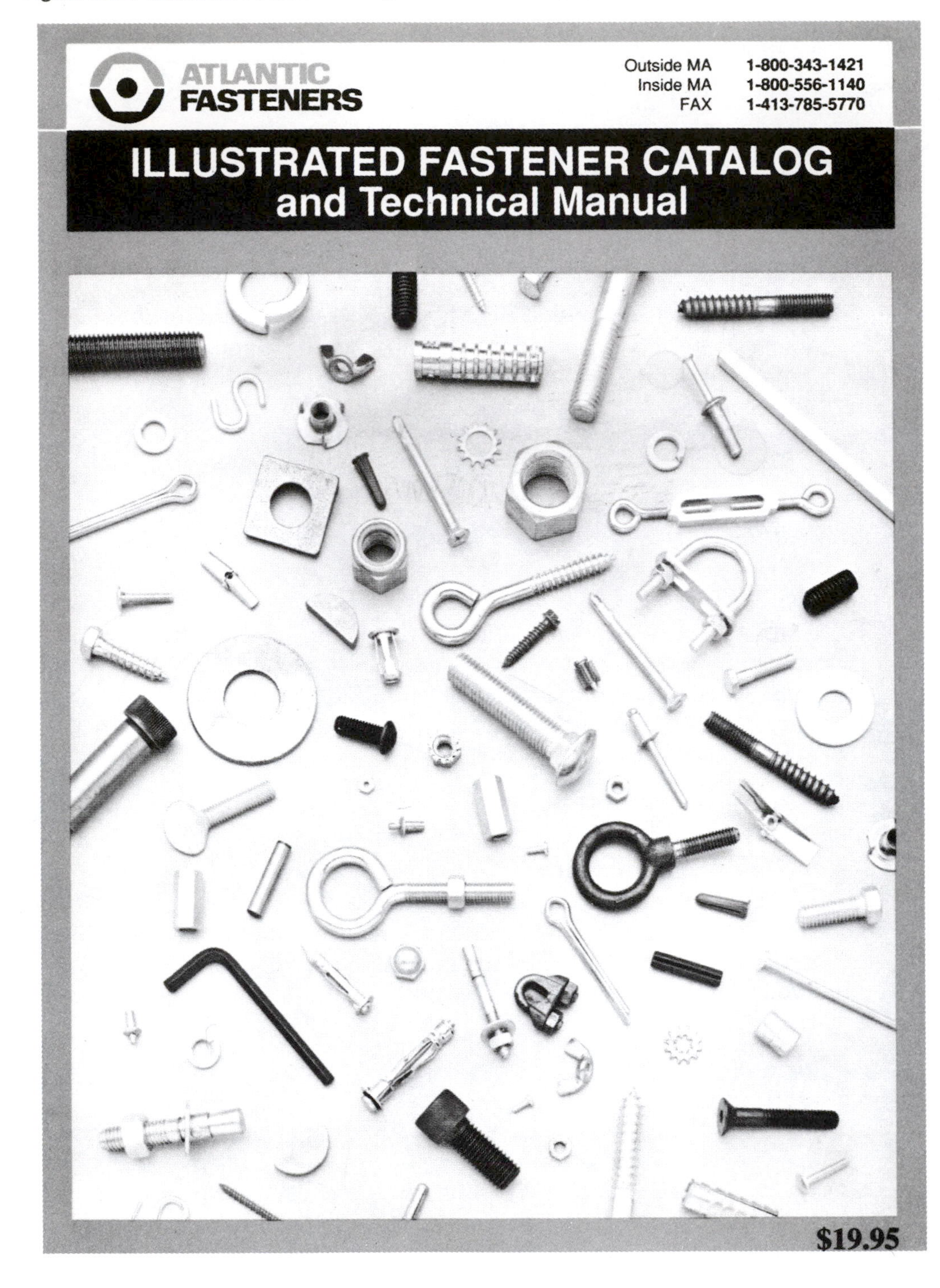

Catalog Technique 2: Include a Letter

Add a sales letter on the inside front page of your catalog. The letter provides an ideal opportunity to sell your catalog as a whole or your company as a quality supplier, rather than merely promote individual items. A letter also adds a personal touch to what may otherwise be a rather impersonal, cold book of facts and figures. In the Atlantic Fastener catalog, the letter (Figure 18.3) makes use of several attention-getting sales techniques:

—The headline is in quotation marks (always increases readership).

—The subhead provides a graphic device for gaining attention for a secondary message.

—A picture of the company president personalizes the message and draws the reader's eye to the page.

—A salutation ("Dear Fastener User") identifies the audience.

—The letter is fact-filled and informative. Write it in bullet form for easy scanning.

—A P.S. calls for action.

Catalog Technique 3: Include a Guarantee

A guarantee of performance or delivery is critical. People do not want to order unless they know they will get their money back or receive some other compensation if you don't deliver as promised.

Many marketers object to guarantees, saying, "Doesn't adding a guarantee put into the reader's mind the notion that something can go wrong, alerting him to possible negatives he wasn't thinking of?" No, because today's buyers are not naive. They realize full well the possibility of problems and are comforted by the fact that you are prepared to stand behind your catalog and do something to correct mistakes. A guarantee is critical.

The guarantee should be highlighted in a separate box, to make it stand out, as is done in the Atlantic Fastener catalog in the upper half of Figure 18.4. Atlantic's guarantee is powerful because it is specific—one-minute quotations and next-day delivery or you get a $50 credit. Body copy surrounding the guarantee tells the reader why he is unlikely ever to need the guarantee and how Atlantic spent $188,600 to ensure reliable delivery.

Figure 18.3. Attention-getting sales techniques.

"Identify even uncommon fasteners IN SECONDS with our precise, detailed pictures"

Or check-out our fastener measuring guide, anchor comparison table, actual-size rivet chart...and more

Patrick J. O'Toole
President

Dear Fastener User:

The next time you need fasteners but aren't sure what to ask for, open this catalog.

We've filled it with 264 exact, painstakingly drawn pictures so you can quickly match-up whatever you need.

There are nuts, bolts, machine screws, washers, drill bits, taps, hex keys, threaded inserts — in all 45 categories of fasteners and related products.

Plus, there are pages of helpful fastener information.

■ Our thorough comparison of 15 different anchors, starting on page 35, shows installation instructions, compares pull-out strengths, and recommends when and when *not* to use each.

■ Our handy guide to measuring fasteners on page 27 is packed with easy to follow diagrams and tips, including how to specify shoulder bolts and blind rivets.

■ Our simple to follow "Loctite Problem/Solution Chart" on page 59 shows the products to use for such common maintenance applications as bonding metal or sealing stainless pipe joints.

■ And our easy to understand technical section that starts on page 80 includes such diverse information as washer dimensions and a decimal equivalent chart.

■ Throughout you'll find special "Spotlight Reports" (look for this symbol) on a variety of maintenance products, like Lenox® hole saws and Permatex Color Guard®. We've thoroughly described each, noted superior features, and included helpful tips on using them. Believe me, some of the findings astonished even us.

■ Now, to quickly find what you need, turn to the Index in back. We've listed fasteners by their proper name, like "Socket Head Shoulder Screw"; by nicknames, like "Stripper Bolt"; by category, as under Socket; and by brand names, like Unbrako.

This catalog took 6 1/2 months to complete. We spent countless hours deciding which common fasteners and technical information to include that would interest you.

But, we also stock ***thousands*** of odd and non-standard fastener varieties that we haven't shown. So, just because you can't find a nut or bolt in here, doesn't mean we don't stock it. Call us for any fastener you need!

Sincerely,

Patrick J. O'Toole

Patrick J. O'Toole
President

P.S. Got a friend who'd like this catalog? Or, do you have some ideas for improving it? Then, please fill-out and mail the post cards in back. Thank you.

Catalog Technique 4: Reason-Why Page

This is a page or series of pages that outline in simple 1-2-3 fashion the advantages the cataloger offers as a supplier. A typical headline is, "9 reasons why you should buy (type of product) from (name of company)." The lower half of Figure 18.4 is an example. These reasons might include:

—Broad product selection
—Superior product quality
—Products available and in stock
—Fast shipment
—Generous credit terms
—Availability of difficult-to-find items
—Money-back guarantee
—Large inventory
—Good quality inspection program
—Partnership and just-in-time shipping programs
—Lower prices
—Volume discounts
—Better customer service
—Reliability
—Superior reputation
—Specialty and customized items available

Catalog Technique 5: Use Sell Copy

In a catalog that is mostly tables of specifications or pictures of products, you can devote one or more pages to more sales-oriented information to reinforce your quality message and give the reader something more interesting to read than dimension and weight tables. The Atlantic Fastener catalog uses a series of full-page ads in its catalog, such as Figure 18.5. Each is written so persuasively and interestingly that they could easily stand alone as full-page ads in any trade publication.

Catalog Technique 6: Selection Guides

Often, people ordering different grades or types of a specific product are not sure of which type to order for their application. Or, they may

Figure 18.4. Reasons-why page.

Why it's easier to buy fasteners from Atlantic

What you dislike most, we guarantee against!

Guaranteed!

One minute quoting of in-stock fasteners

Next day delivery of in-stock fasteners when you order by 3 PM

Error-free, shipping and billing ...or *you* get a $50 credit

Since introducing Just-In-Time Guarantees in Feb. '86, we've averaged fewer than 8 credits for every 10,000 orders we ship.

But it took five years of planning and organizing before we could offer them. We invested $185,000 to computerize our entire business and $3,600 to automate our shipping department. We spent months developing a foolproof system for packaging correctly, then we turned to hiring and training a dedicated warehouse crew. Finally, we negotiated special shipping privileges with our delivery service.

But it didn't stop there.

Daily, we monitor our performance to insure we uphold our promises to you.

Test us without buying a thing

Unload surplus fasteners

We'll issue credit, swap, or buy surplus, saleable fasteners that you ordered from someone else.

Free technical advice

Ask our fastener expert, with four years of fastener training and 2 1/2 years of machine shop experience, to solve your fastener problems. Or let our two former Loctite Corp. salesmen answer your questions on adhesives, sealants, gasketing, or coatings. All are available for free in-plant seminars.

Meet our technical representatives (from left to right) Dean Palozej and Pete Mals formerly of Loctite, and fastener expert Dennis Blain. Call them anytime.

On the shelf, 33,065,500 standard and hard-to-find fasteners

Stop shopping all over. Atlantic stocks an amazing 15,175 fastener varieties in steel, stainless, brass, silicon bronze, aluminum, and nylon — inch and metric. We're an authorized distributor for:

Permatex **Loctite**
Tri-Flow **Tapcon**
Shakeproof **Tapfree**
SPS/Unbrako **Lenox**
Lake Erie **Morse**
Bondhus **Hindley**
E.W. Daniel Co. **Gesipa**
SPS/Flexloc **Cherry**
Rockford **HeliCoil**
Star Expansion **Durham**
ITW Ramset Red Head **Nucor**

Figure 18.5. Sample sell copy.

If you can't tell whether a Grade 8 bolt is counterfeit by looking at it, how do you know you're not buying junk?

Spotlight Report

Atlantic stocks *only* American-made, traceable Grade 8 bolts — 1/4" to 1-1/4" diameter in 339 sizes

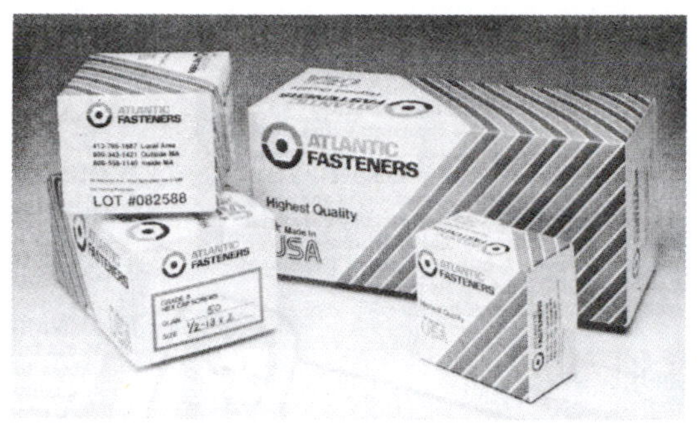

Our Grade 8's come in boxes clearly marked 'Made in USA' and stamped with a tracing number direct from the manufacturer. Order some today.

IS your stockroom filled with potentially dangerous, counterfeit Grade 8 hex cap screws that can fail at high temperatures causing expensive property loss, injury — even death?

According to one fastener trade journal, "...in all probability the entire distribution system for Grade 8 fasteners in the U.S. has been contaminated with millions of improperly marked bolts."

The U.S. Defense Industrial Supply Center in Philadelphia found 30 million substandard Grade 8's in their inventory!

And, Peterbilt, the truck manufacturer, Morton Thiokol, Emerson Electric, GTE, and FMC have reported similar problems.

What about you?

Is your fastener supplier selling you Grade 8's from certain Japanese, Korean,Taiwanese, or Polish manufacturers, known to have mismarked Grade 8's?

Please find out, or consider replacing Grade 8's you've purchased for high temperature applications.

Understand — you can't spot a counterfeit by eye.

The only way to tell for certain is by chemical analysis which costs $200 per bolt!

However, you can avoid future worries by buying from us. We stock *only* American-made, Grade 8's traceable to the steel source.

What's a counterfeit Grade 8?

Grade 8 bolts, marked with six radial lines on their head, are made from medium carbon alloy steel tempered at 800°F. (See below)

Counterfeit Grade 8 bolts have the same head markings but are actually mismarked Grade 8.2 bolts made from less expensive low carbon boron steel which is tempered at only 650°F.

Above 500°F, Grade 8.2 bolts lose tensile strength and may relax or stretch, causing assembly failure. Genuine Grade 8's are safe to much higher temperatures.

American importers are to blame

Ironically, greedy American importers are behind counterfeiting, according to government investigators.

They say that since the late 70's some importers, seeking fatter profit margins, have deliberately asked foreign manufacturers to produce less expensive Grade 8.2 bolts and mark them as Grade 8's.

Then they've sold the less expensive, mismarked Grade 8.2 bolts as higher priced Grade 8's to distributors.

It wasn't until the mid 80's that the problem was uncovered.

Japan, a major foreign supplier, immediately agreed to halt counterfeit shipments. But, just one year ago, U.S. Custom inspectors found that 17% of Japanese imports were still bogus.

So the problem persists, even now when the federal government is taking legal action against fastener distributors and importers nationwide.

Our specially marked boxes is your assurance that they're genuine Grade 8's

Don't take chances. Buy *only* American-made Grade 8's from Atlantic.

We stock 339 sizes, plain and plated, in 1/4" to 1 1/4" diameters.

We package them in bright red, white, and blue boxes, marked 'Made in USA'. And, we stamp each box with a tracing number.

So, if you should ever have a problem with our Grade 8's, we'll trace them back to the exact order and steel batch that our American manufacturer used.

n — Nucor Fastener, Saint Joe, Indiana

ROCKFORD — Rockford Products Corp., Rockford, Illinois

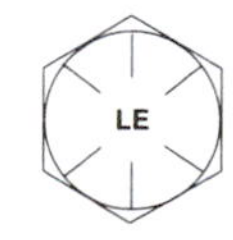

Lake Erie Corp, Cleveland, Ohio

Why risk costly down-time, injury, or worse with imported Grade 8 hex cap screws? Buy American-made Grade 8's from Atlantic. Look for these head markings.

think they know what to order, but are actually not ordering the proper item and so will be dissatisfied when they try to use what you send them.

The solution is to put selection guides in your catalog explaining the various grades, models, or types, what they are used for, which applications you recommend them for, and how to select them. In Figure 18.6, a "Tapping Screw Guide" from the Atlantic Fastener catalog shows the different types of thread forming screws and describes the features and applications of each.

Catalog Technique 7: Sizing Chart

By putting the dimensions of your full product line in a single illustrated table, you enable the reader to see at a glance all the sizes available thus making size selection easy. Atlantic Fastener's version is illustrated by Figure 18.7.

Catalog Technique 8: Cross-Reference Table

In many product categories (semiconductors, for example), there are standard sizes or specifications to which all manufacturers conform. The customer can specify any manufacturer's product in a given size or model. This is called *drop-in technology* when one brand can be automatically substituted for another because you can simply remove one brand and "drop in" another.

The confusion for the customer is knowing which model number of your product to order as a replacement for a specific model number of a competitor's product he is now using. A cross-reference table makes it easy for the customer to see which model numbers of various manufacturers are interchangeable with one another. A cross-reference table from the Atlantic Fastener catalog is shown in Figure 18.8.

You might object, "But couldn't my customer just as easily use my cross-reference table to replace my brand with my competitor's brand?" Yes, he/she can. But the fact is, the customer wants this type of information. Providing it says to the customer "I am not here to sell my product but to help you do your job well." This is the real message the customer wants to hear. And, if he/she turns to *your* catalog instead of your competitor's because he/she knows yours contains a cross-reference table and theirs does not, who do you think he/she is more likely to order from?

Figure 18.6. Sample guide.

Tapping Screw Guide

Thread Forming

Use thread forming screws in materials that can tolerate high internal stresses, such as plywood, or where a high resistance to loosening is desired, as in thin sheet metal.

Type A Point

Has coarse spaced threads and a gimlet point. Use in light, .015 to .050 thick, sheet metal, resin-impregnated plywood, or asbestos composition material. Often used in place of wood screws because it drives quicker, is fully threaded, and has a larger thread profile. Type AB are usually recommended over Type A, especially for new design.

Type AB Point

Combines the gimlet point of Type A with the thread size and pitch of Type B. Use for thin sheet metal, resin-impregnated plywood, asbestos compositions, and non-ferrous castings. Recommended over Type A, especially in brittle materials such as plastics and zinc die castings.

Type B Point

Has a finer thread pitch than Type A and a blunt point. Use in light and heavier sheet metal, .050 to .200 thick, nonferrous castings, plastics, resin-impregnated plywoods, and asbestos compositions. Recommended over Type AB for thicker materials because its point, which has a gradual taper, starts more easily.

Type C Point

Has a blunt, tapered point and machine screw threads, so it can be replaced with a standard screw in the field. Does not produce chips. Will tap into thicker sections than Type AB, such as heavy sheet metal and die castings. High driving torque required, so as a result, thread rolling screws have frequently been chosen over Type C screws for difficult applications.

Type U Point

Has a pilot point and high helix thread for driving or hammering into sheet metal, castings, fiber, or plastics. Quickly makes permanent assemblies.

Figure 18.7. Sample sizing chart.

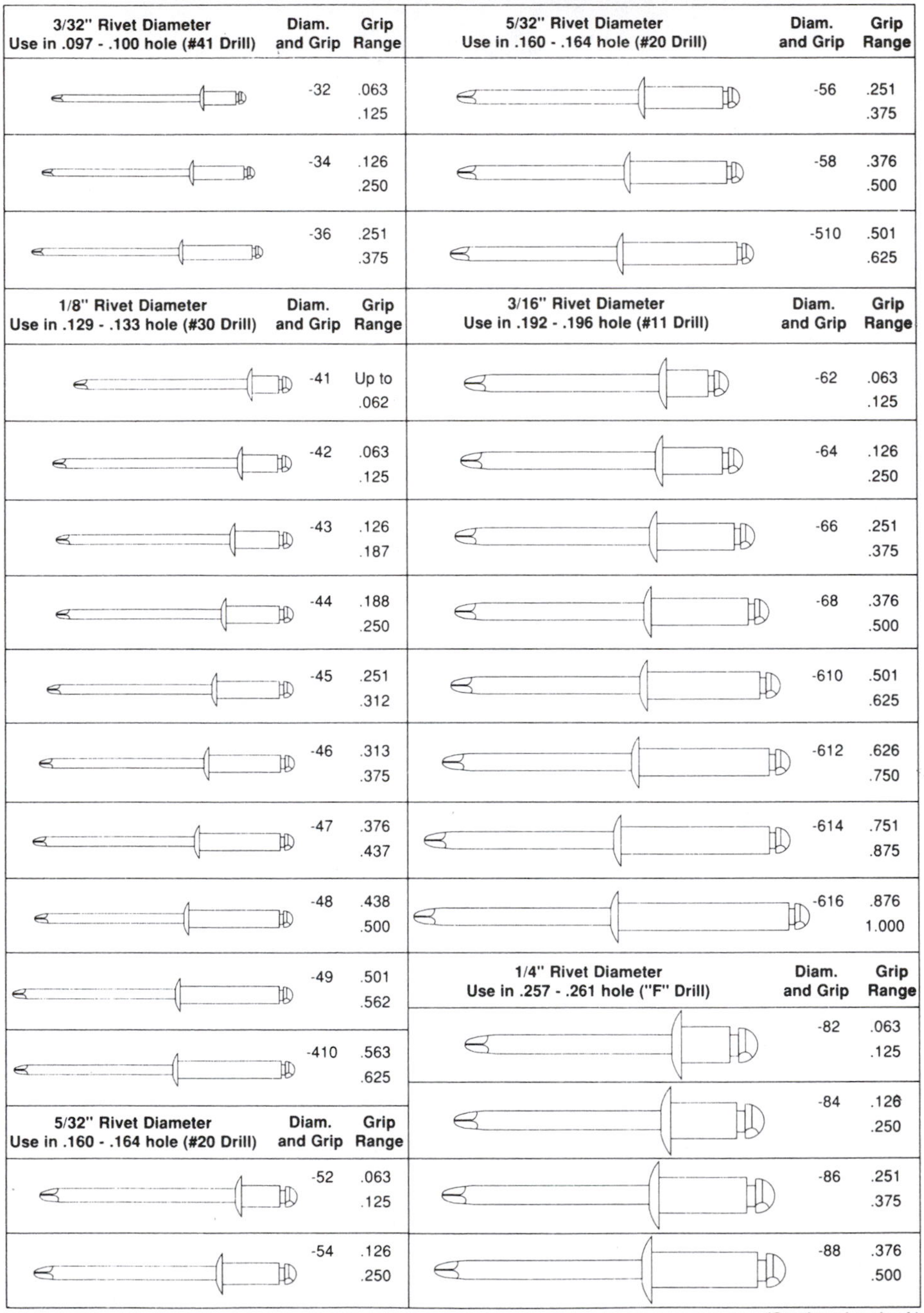

Actual Size Rivet Chart

3/32" Rivet Diameter Use in .097 - .100 hole (#41 Drill)	Diam. and Grip	Grip Range
	-32	.063 .125
	-34	.126 .250
	-36	.251 .375

1/8" Rivet Diameter Use in .129 - .133 hole (#30 Drill)	Diam. and Grip	Grip Range
	-41	Up to .062
	-42	.063 .125
	-43	.126 .187
	-44	.188 .250
	-45	.251 .312
	-46	.313 .375
	-47	.376 .437
	-48	.438 .500
	-49	.501 .562
	-410	.563 .625

5/32" Rivet Diameter Use in .160 - .164 hole (#20 Drill)	Diam. and Grip	Grip Range
	-52	.063 .125
	-54	.126 .250

5/32" Rivet Diameter Use in .160 - .164 hole (#20 Drill)	Diam. and Grip	Grip Range
	-56	.251 .375
	-58	.376 .500
	-510	.501 .625

3/16" Rivet Diameter Use in .192 - .196 hole (#11 Drill)	Diam. and Grip	Grip Range
	-62	.063 .125
	-64	.126 .250
	-66	.251 .375
	-68	.376 .500
	-610	.501 .625
	-612	.626 .750
	-614	.751 .875
	-616	.876 1.000

1/4" Rivet Diameter Use in .257 - .261 hole ("F" Drill)	Diam. and Grip	Grip Range
	-82	.063 .125
	-84	.126 .250
	-86	.251 .375
	-88	.376 .500

(Continued on back)

Figure 18.8. Sample cross-reference table.

Actual Size Rivet Chart (con't)

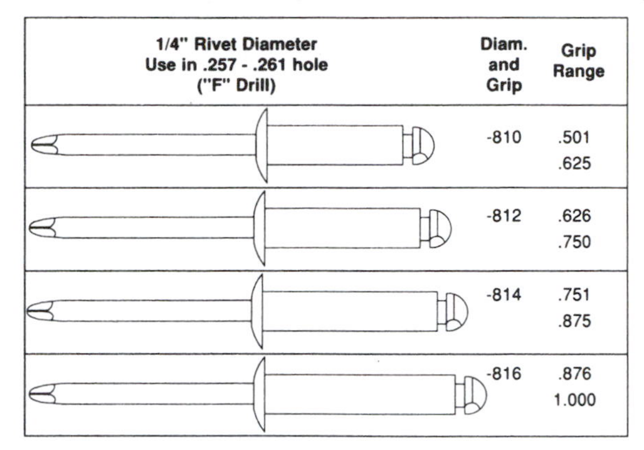

1/4" Rivet Diameter Use in .257 - .261 hole ("F" Drill)	Diam. and Grip	Grip Range
	-810	.501 .625
	-812	.626 .750
	-814	.751 .875
	-816	.876 1.000

Blind Rivet Cross Reference

Manufacturers' lettering systems. Rivet size "42" is used in all examples—merely substitute numerical size factors applicable.

PCI	CHERRY	CELUS	AFC	MALCO	MARSON	OSCAR OLYMPIC	GESIPA	SCOVILL	SEMBLEX RIVEX	STAR	USM
AK42A	AAC42	A/A42C	ACA42	AA42K	AC42A		GAMC42A	AA42C	RAK42A	4-2AAC	AK42ABS
AD42ALF	AAL42	A/A42LF	ABA42L	AA42LF	ABL42A	RV633	GAML42A	AA42LF	RAD42ALF	A-2AALF	AD42ABSLF
AD42A	AAP42	A/A42D	ABA42	AA42D	AB42A	RV63042	GAMD42A	AA42D	RAD42A	4-2AAD	AD42ABS
AK42S	BSC42	A/S42C	ACS42	AS42K	AC42		GSMC42A	AS42C	RAK42S	4-2ASC	AK42BS
AD42SLF	BSL42	A/S42LF	ABS42L	AS42LF	ABL42	RV653	GSML42A	AS42LF	RAD42SLF	4-2ASLF	AD42BSLF
AD42S	BSP42	A/S42D	ABS42	AS42D	AB42	RV65042	GSMD42A	AS42D	RAD42S	4-2ASD	AD42BS
SK42S	SSC42	S/S42C	SCS42	SS42K	SC42		GSMC42S	SS42C	RSK42S	4-2SSC	SK42BS
SD42SLF	SSL42	S/S42LF	SBS42L	SS42LF	SBL42		GSML42S	SS42LF	RSD42SLF	4-2SSLF	SD42BSLF
SD42S	SSP42	S/S42D	SBS42	SS42D	SB42	RV67042	GSMD42S	SS42D	RSD42S	4-2SSD	SD42BS
SSD42SS	CCP42	SS/SS42D	FBF42		SSB42S		GSSMD42SS	STST42D	RSSD42SS	4-2STSTD	SSD42SSBS
SSD42S	CSP42	SS/S42D			SSB42		GSMD42SS	STS42D	RSSD42S	4-2STSD	SSD42BS
	MSC42			MS42C							MK419BS
	MSP42			MS42D	MB4-14						MD424BS
CD42S	USP42	C/S42D	CBS42	CS42D	CB42		GSMD42C	CC42D	RCD42S	4-2CCD	CD42BS

Catalog Technique 9: How-To Information

Want your catalog to be perceived as a valuable reference manual rather than just a sales piece? Want it to be cherished, treasured, kept, and referred to often? Then put how-to information into the book. Your buyers want to know: How to install insulation; how to check valves for signs of corrosion; how to select the right size mixer; how to monitor air quality; how to set up a company-wide safety program; how to design an office automation system; and so on.

Give them how-to information that is genuinely useful and answers the most pressing technical questions they have and your catalog will double or triple in its perceived value. See Figure 18.9 for an example.

Catalog Technique 10: Ordering Guides

Check your body copy. Whenever you can convert long paragraphs of complicated instructions into easy-to-use tables or charts, do it.

Visual tools provide easy-reference guides and make your catalog more useful to the buyer. In Figure 18.10, Atlantic Fasteners has developed a guide the reader can use to quickly determine which type of anchor he should order. Whenever you can, put in a table or guide to help the reader order the right type, material, size, or model. *Warning*: If the ordering process is too complicated to explain in the catalog, don't try. Instead, encourage the buyer to call you for help.

Catalog Technique 11: Product Profiles

Specifications are necessary, but a catalog that contains only page after page of numbers and drawings is boring, and readers won't turn its pages any more often than they have to.

Salesmanship is more than just presenting specifications; it's telling the reader all the key facts about your product: features, benefits, strengths, weaknesses, applications, usage tips. So, if you have a 24-page catalog with page after page of specs for three basic types of products, you might devote a full or half-page per product to more descriptive "sell" copy in a product profile. Figure 18.11 shows an example of a full-page product profile on "Red Head Chemical Anchors."

Catalog Technique 12: Testimonials

Testimonials are one of the most powerful advertising techniques, yet few catalogs contain them. Testimonials are quotations from satisfied customers saying how good your company, product, or service is.

Figure 18.9. Sample how-to information.

How to Measure Fasteners

Answers to your most common questions

Screws and Bolts

Q: "Please help. How do you measure the length of a screw or bolt, from head-to-tip or just the amount under the head?"

A: It depends on the head style. For round and pan head, etc., measure under the head. For flat head screws (countersunk), it's the overall length that matters. For oval heads, measure from the tip to where the oval starts.

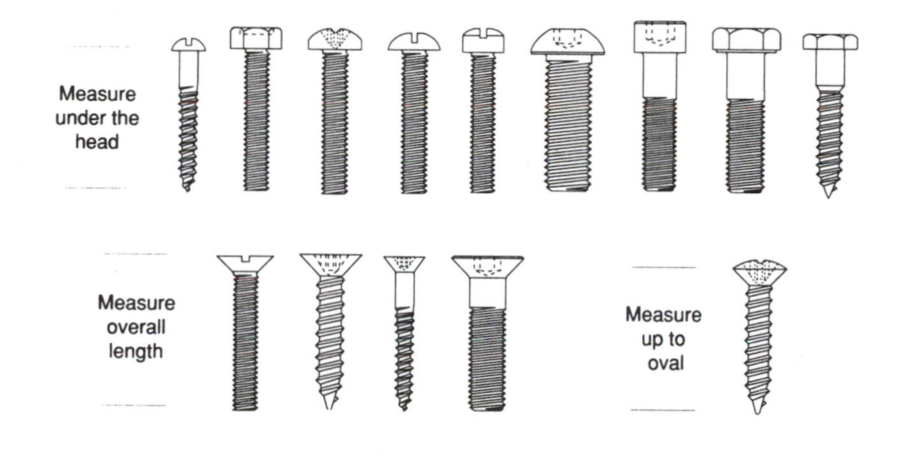

Hex Cap Screws

Q: "How much of a hex cap screw is threaded and how much is unthreaded?"

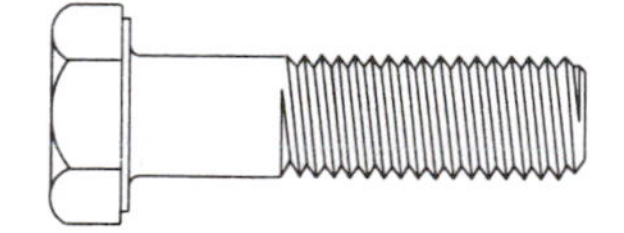

A: Here's an easy formula:

- For hex cap screws 6" or shorter, the amount of thread equals twice the diameter + 1/4".
- For hex caps longer than 6", the amount of thread equals twice the diameter + 1/2".

EXAMPLE: A 1/4 - 20 x 2" long hex cap has 3/4" of thread.
EXAMPLE: A 3/8 - 16 x 7" long hex cap has 1 1/4" of thread.

Figure 18.10. Sample ordering guide.

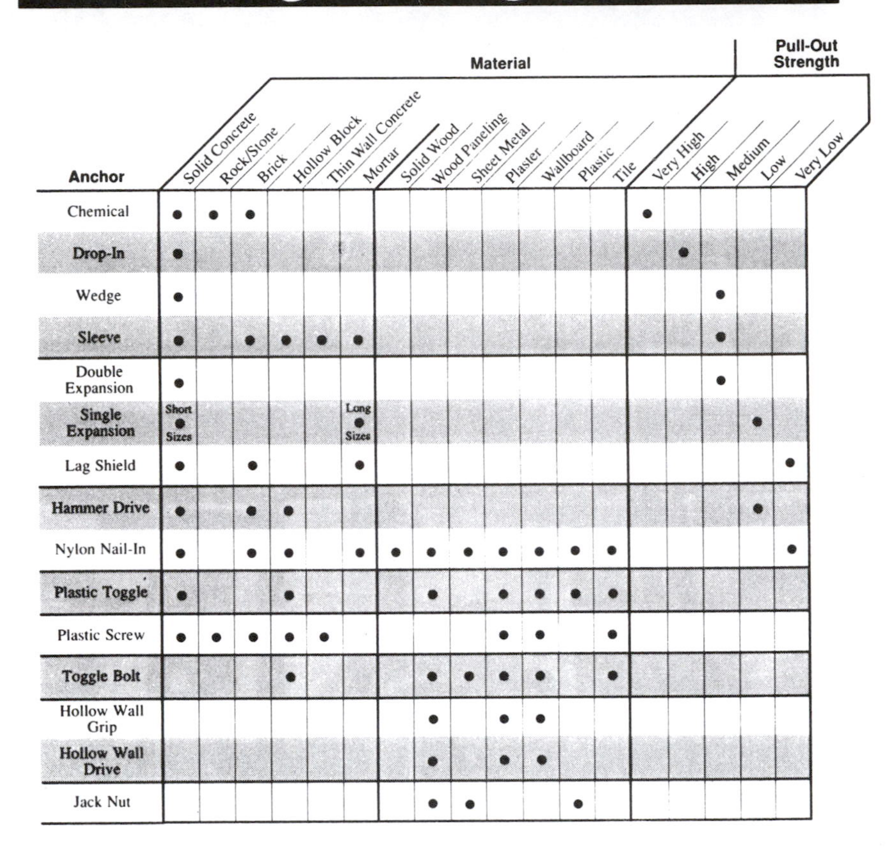

Choosing the Right Anchor

Anchor	Material: Solid Concrete	Rock/Stone	Brick	Hollow Block	Thin Wall Concrete	Mortar	Solid Wood	Wood Paneling	Sheet Metal	Plaster	Wallboard	Plastic	Tile	Pull-Out Strength: Very High	High	Medium	Low	Very Low
Chemical	●	●	●											●				
Drop-In	●														●			
Wedge	●															●		
Sleeve	●		●	●	●	●										●		
Double Expansion	●															●		
Single Expansion	Short ● Sizes					Long ● Sizes											●	
Lag Shield	●		●			●												●
Hammer Drive	●		●	●													●	
Nylon Nail-In	●		●	●		●	●	●	●	●	●	●	●					●
Plastic Toggle	●			●				●		●	●	●	●					
Plastic Screw	●	●	●	●	●					●	●		●					
Toggle Bolt				●				●	●	●	●		●					
Hollow Wall Grip								●		●	●							
Hollow Wall Drive								●		●	●							
Jack Nut								●	●			●						

Need more information?

On the pages shown below, we describe the features/benefits of each anchor, show how to install them, compare pull-out strengths, recommend uses, and warn against misuses.

Figure 18.11. Sample full-page product profile.

Red Head Chemical Anchors

Features/Benefits:

- Heavy-duty, simple two-part anchoring system that consists of a threaded rod anchor and glass chemical capsule.
- Just drill and clean hole, drop in capsule, and drill threaded rod through capsule to start chemical curing action.
- Cures to heavy-duty, stress-free, vibration resistant bond that seals out water and moisture.
- Cures under water.
- Comes with nuts and washers.
- Reinforcing bar may be substituted for threaded rod.

Pull-out strength:

As compared to the drop-in, wedge, and sleeve anchors, chemical anchors have the highest pull-out strength. Chemical anchors with carbon steel threaded rods have up to 40% greater pull-out strength than drop-in anchors depending on the diameter used.

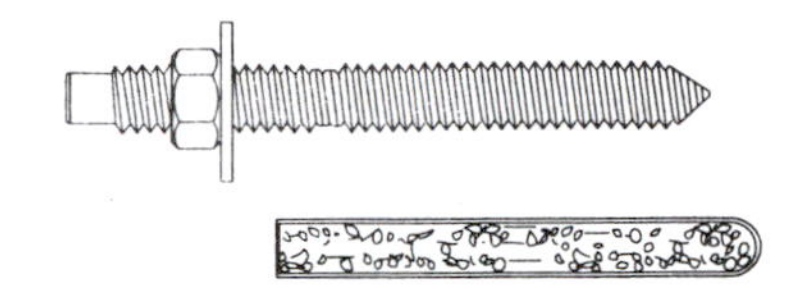

Chemical Anchor

Recommended For:

Ideal for installations where wedge anchors have difficulty gripping such as in hard masonry or rock.

Also recommended for brick, solid block, concrete, and precast.

Use where shock or vibration can loosen sleeve or wedge anchors. Example: anchoring conveyor systems or loading dock bumpers.

Not Recommended For:

Overhead applications or anywhere else that permits the chemical to leak-out such as in hollow blocks or bricks.

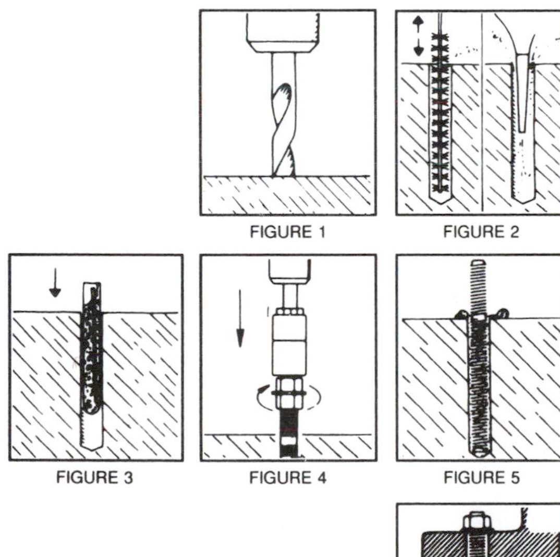

Installation Instructions:

1. Refer to box that holds capsules. Select proper carbide tipped drill bit size. Drill hole to recommended embedment depth.
2. Clean all dust from hole.
3. Insert capsule into drilled hole. DO NOT use capsule if cracked or damaged.
4. Assemble two nuts, with a washer between them, onto the anchor rod and tighten together. Place preassembled anchor rod into impact socket and socket adaptor. Insert rod into drilled hole breaking capsule with pointed end of the anchor rod. Turn on drill and drive anchor downward until the recommended embedment depth is attained.
5. Remove impact socket and drill from anchor rod. Remove excess resin from around hole. Avoid disturbing anchor rod until adequate cure time is reached.
6. Install material to be fastened after resin has cured.

The best testimonials are those that are not general but address specific advantages of your products or concerns other buyers may have. Some catalogers sprinkle testimonials throughout the catalog, using only one or two per page. Others, like Atlantic Fastener in Figure 18.12, group them all on one or two pages. The latter technique seems to have more power and impact.

Catalog Technique 13: Use Two Order Forms

A little-known but effective technique is to use not one but two order forms. They are identical except one is bound into the catalog or printed on one of the regular catalog pages, while the second is loose and inserted between the front cover and first page.

The loose order form falls out when the prospect opens the book, so it gains more attention and encourages immediate ordering. However, if the prospect is not ready to buy now, the loose order form may become lost, or it may get thrown away. When the prospect turns to the catalog later to place an order, the bound-in order form is there ready and waiting for him.

Tip: Add a line to the bottom of your order form that says, "In a hurry? Simply complete this form and FAX to (fax number) for immediate action." Since most businesses today now have fax machines, this provides the prospect with a convenient method of ordering—something he will appreciate.

Catalog Technique 14: Make Sure Your Catalog is Complete

Use Figure 18.13 to make sure you have included all necessary information in your catalog. Leaving out a piece of critical information—in an industrial or consumer catalog—can have a devastatingly negative effect on orders received. Yet the first time you publish your catalog, it's hard to know exactly what should be included, and it's easy to miss an item.

The checklist in Figure 18.13 should be of some assistance in solving this problem. Note that most of these items apply equally to consumer and industrial catalogs.

11 Ways to Organize Your Catalog

Next to completeness of information, quality of photos (for a consumer catalog), and persuasiveness of copy, the most important factor in catalog success is organization.

Figure 18.12. Sample testimonial.

Customers complain...

"Why can't every supplier be this good?"

We greet you with grins not grunts

"Atlantic Fasteners is the easiest company we deal with. The staff is friendly, courteous, and the most accommodating...We appreciate the attention our account gets."
Terry Veber and Jill Pierpont, Buyers — Mt. Snow

"The staff...is professional and courteous, and makes every effort to assist in our needs."
Scott Aye, Gen. Sup. Plant Eng. — Milton Bradley

"Your personnel are by far the most congenial individuals with which our maintenance department has to deal with..."
Dean LaFond, Main. Sup. — LEGO Systems

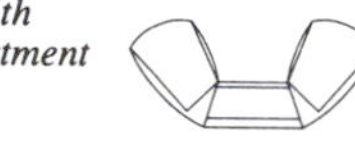

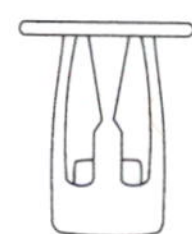

"We at Monsanto Co. Saflex have always received exceptional service..."
Keith Korbut, Main. Sup. — Monsanto Co.

Fasteners in every flavor

"I'm forever amazed at the stainless steel variety you have, like the 1 1/4" hex nuts..."
Wayne Avery, Main. Sup. — Sonoco Products Co.

"You always have in your inventory, or can get in a reasonable time, any fastener we need."
Jack Hindle, Tool Room Foreman — Dennison National

From our shelf to yours in one day

"Everybody brags they're the best. But you're the only company I know, besides Federal Express, who makes guarantees and backs them with cash!"
Joe Elias, Owner — A.S.E. Precision

"Atlantic Fasteners has proven that guaranteed next day delivery means next day — not next week."
Ronald Hand, Mfg. Serv. Mgr. — Gloenco-Newport

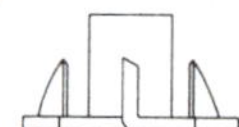

Hidden savings revealed!

"Switching over to Atlantic Fasteners has allowed me to reduce my in-house inventories, thereby reducing my overhead/stocking costs. Atlantic's prices are also lower than your competitors."
Scott Aye, Gen. Sup. Plant Eng. — Milton Bradley

Returns allowed anytime

"Your take-back policy is great... those hex nuts were just sitting around taking up space for like a year, and you didn't even blink an eye when I returned them."
Dave Falvey, Owner — Tote'Em Trailers

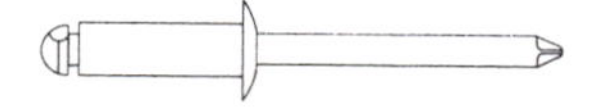

Figure 18.13. Checklist of catalog contents.

Does your catalog contain all of the following?

- ☐ Attention-grabbing front cover
- ☐ Letter of introduction
- ☐ Table of contents
- ☐ Index
- ☐ Conditions and terms
- ☐ Order form
- ☐ Reply envelope
- ☐ Names of all products
- ☐ Physical descriptions
- ☐ Photos or illustrations (is color needed?)
- ☐ Features and benefits
- ☐ Explanation of how products work
- ☐ Weight
- ☐ Dimensions, including choice of sizes available
- ☐ Other necessary specifications
- ☐ Price, including quantity discounts
- ☐ Colors
- ☐ Shapes
- ☐ Styles
- ☐ Models
- ☐ Applications
- ☐ Tips on selection, including cross-reference chart
- ☐ Tips on usage
- ☐ Packaging and shipping information
- ☐ Safety warnings and precautions
- ☐ Quality assurance
- ☐ Materials of construction
- ☐ Efficiency ratings
- ☐ Maintenance and repair methods
- ☐ Service contracts available
- ☐ Cost savings/discounts
- ☐ Nearest distributors
- ☐ Guarantee/warranty
- ☐ Reasons to buy from your company

Figure 18.13. (continued)

☐ How-to articles, product profiles, ads, selection guides, etc.

☐ Testimonials

☐ Your company name and address

☐ Other locations

☐ Company history, background, philosophy, business mission

☐ Phone number, including toll-free 800, if available

☐ Fax number

☐ Any additional ordering information required

The catalog must be organized in a fashion that is logical and makes reading and ordering easy and natural for the buyer. At the same time, you want to organize your merchandise and present it in the order likely to generate maximum sales. The following are 11 ways a consumer or industrial catalog can be organized for maximum effect.

1. Catalog Hot Spots

A *hot spot* is a page in a catalog that, by virtue of its position within the book, gets more readership and hence generates more orders than other pages.

According to the Performance Seminar Group, a company that gives seminars in advertising and marketing, the hot spots in a catalog are:

- The outside front cover
- The outside back cover
- The two-page spread inside the front cover
- The two-page center spread
- The two-page spread inside the back cover
- The pages around the order form
- The pages around the ordering instructions

To maximize sales, feature your best-selling items on these hot-spot pages.

2. By Product Demand

According to David Ogilvy, founder of Ogilvy & Mather, a key principle of advertising success is, “Back your winners, and abandon your losers.” A catalog provides a wonderful testing laboratory for discovering which products and offers sell—and which don't. In a catalog, you can test an item by devoting some space to it and seeing if people buy; this is a far less expensive way to test than doing a solo mailing or running full-page ads for the item.

Items that prove successful should get more prominent displays, more space dedicated to them, and should be featured in the hot spots and pages toward the front where they are more likely to be seen. Putting more of your catalog budget into promoting proven winners is the surest way to generating even more sales and profits.

Items that don't do well with a small display are not likely to fare any better with more space, so you would only be wasting your money by putting more effort behind them. Marginal items—those that generate a steady but unspectacular profit—can continue to have small copy blocks toward the back of the catalog so long as those ads continue to generate revenue.

Losers—those items that are not profitable—should be dropped. Back your winners. Dump your losers. The purpose of advertising is not to force an unwanted product upon the consumer; it's to make a popular product better known and more available.

3. By Product Scarcity

One of the appeals of catalogs is that they offer the buyer hard-to-find items and merchandise not readily available from other sources. Catalogers who offer such merchandise can attract attention by featuring these rare and difficult-to-come-by items up front. Consumers will keep catalogs handy as references and order from them again and again even if the catalog has only *one* item they cannot obtain anywhere else.

> *Example:* The fireplace catalog I order from is a case in point. Although most of the items—fireplace screens, log holders, bellows, pokers—can be bought at local retail outlets, the catalog features one item—a long-burning candle that eliminates the need to start fires with crumpled newspaper and kindling—that we haven't been able to find elsewhere. For this reason I keep the catalog in a file folder and order from it frequently.

4. By Function

You can also organize your products according to the functions they perform. A good example is a software catalog where one section might feature word processing programs; a second section, spreadsheets; a third section, database management software; a fourth section, graphics and desktop publishing, etc.

5. By Price

Another way to organize your catalog is to group products in price ranges. Products costing $1 to $10 go in one section; $11 to $50 items in a second section; and items above $50 are grouped in a third section.

Organizing your catalog by price works especially well in a gift catalog of similar merchandise (e.g., cheese platters, wines, coffee, knickknacks, and the like) where the buyer may want to select gifts for different people at varying price levels. Catalogs of business premiums are often grouped this way so the prospect looking for a $1 premium item doesn't have to search through a hundred pages, while the prospect looking for a $100 business gift can compare several options all featured in one spread.

6. By Application

Organizing your catalog by application makes it easy for the prospect to find the product he needs. For instance, the Faultless Division of Axia Incorporated organized its caster catalog by application: general duty, light duty, light-to-medium duty, heavy duty, textiles, scaffolds, floor trucks, and furniture.

The disadvantage of this method is the possibility of redundancy: if a caster can be used in both floor trucks and furniture, it would either have to be listed and described twice or else cross-referenced.

7. By System Hierarchy

Let's say you are selling personal computers. Your catalog first presents pages showing total systems (PCs). Next come the individual components: disk drives, terminals, printers, plotters, keyboards, modems, and other peripherals. Then you get to board-level products, showing various optional circuit boards such as memory and graphics cards. Last comes supplies: paper, printer ribbons, user manuals, and disks. This organizational scheme is ideal for any vendor who sells total systems as well as components and supplies for those systems.

8. By Type of Product

In a fashion catalog, for example, you would group items by category (e.g., sweaters, shirts, pants, shoes, bathing suits, ties, and jackets). An office supply catalog might have sections showing labels, envelopes, furniture, computer supplies, ledger books, and business forms. You wouldn't want to mix envelopes with office furniture on the same page, or sweaters with shoes, because the reader would have no way of finding and comparing like items.

9. By Size

If you have a catalog of light bulbs, organize by wattage. If you have a catalog of air conditioners, organize by BTUs. Organizing by size makes sense if size is your primary selection criterion. By size, I don't mean just weight, length, or height. It could also refer to the horsepower of a compressor, the gallons-per-hour output of a pump, the diameter of a satellite dish, or the thermal energy generated by a space heater.

10. By Model Number

If you've worked out a sensible numbering system for your product line, organizing your catalog by model number might be advantageous, especially if prospects order using model numbers rather than product names.

If there is a simple meaning to your product coding, explain it at the start of the catalog and repeat this explanation in a little box, preferably once on every two-page spread. This helps keep the reader straight and eliminates confusion that often arises with complex manufacturer-specific numbering systems.

Also, don't rely solely on the numbers to convey the nature of your products; some new customers might not be familiar with what an "X-300-A+" can do for them. Include product names and descriptive text along with numbers so those not familiar with your line can understand the nature and function of each device.

11. Alphabetically

For example, a book catalog (alphabetical by author), a print catalog (alphabetical by artist), a record catalog (alphabetical by composer or performing artist), or a vitamin catalog (vitamin A, B, C, D, E, etc.).

10 Basic Rules Of Catalog Layout

1. Avoid fancy typefaces. Keep type simple and legible.
2. Use readable type for your body copy, in at least a 9-point type size.
3. Use subheads to break up copy and to aid readers who merely scan your copy.

4. Use a number of small tables rather than fewer, all-inclusive ones. Large tables of numbers intimidate the reader.
5. Avoid technical-looking, highly complicated graphics unless you are sure your readers need and understand them.
6. Use well-prepared photographs and illustrations. They communicate better and give a quality image.
7. Use a consistent design scheme throughout a section so the reader knows when a section is carried over onto several pages.
8. Use a headline and a change in design scheme when introducing a new section.
9. Design your layout in two-page spreads rather than page by page. This is how your reader sees them.
10. Use color functionally to describe how products work, to highlight features, provide organization, or illustrate in real life those products that need to be shown in full color for maximum sales effectiveness.

12 Steps To Planning Production Of Your Catalog

1. Set specific objectives. Be sure everyone, from top management on down, agrees on what the catalog should do. Discuss the job with sales, production, and brand managers. And get their comments in writing. There may be very different objectives for this catalog compared to previous editions.

2. Define your audience. Decide who's going to receive the catalog. This also may differ from prior catalogs, and it influences everything from the number of copies printed to the way it is written.

3. Decide which products will be included. Do this early. Discovering too late that a product must be added or deleted can result in expensive revisions once the pages have already been laid out.

4. If possible, group products into families or categories. This makes it easier for buyers to use your catalog and may stimulate the sales of accessories or other related products.

5. Start a file folder for each product or group of products to be included in the catalog. Put all relevant background material into these folders including: previous catalog write-ups, technical bulletins, ad reprints, sales brochures, photos, illustrations, testimonials, reviews, press releases, feature articles, competitors' literature, etc.

6. Review each folder for completeness. You'll immediately spot missing gaps: incomplete data, needed photos, etc.

7. Take steps to obtain what is missing. Your copywriter must have complete information to create a publishable catalog. Determine who and what is slowing down the process. Apply firm management pressure to correct the situation.

8. Make a rough outline of contents. This is the skeletal framework of the finished job and will help you in budgeting, scheduling, and layout. Make sure your outline contains all the checklist points listed in Figure 18.13.

9. Determine exact format: color, size, binding, number of pages, paper stock, special inks or varnishes. At this point you can get preliminary printing bids to help finalize budgets.

10. Make a rough page-by-page layout of the entire catalog. The layout should show the number of pages, contents of each page, positioning of copy and graphic elements, and give a rough idea of design style. You can do this initial rough layout yourself or have your artist handle it.

11. Working from the outline and rough layout, have your copywriter write the copy. The layout should give a pretty good indication of the length of each copy block, and the writer should write to fit length. However, if the length estimates are not exact, copy can always be expanded or cut slightly later on.

But the first draft should be fairly close to the final length. The copywriter needs to know, before he starts, whether you want terse, telegraph-style copy or long, descriptive, flowing narrative. If you initially tell him he has a full page and then later change your mind and decide to cut down to a paragraph, you will be billed for these changes.

12. Set a timetable for completion. Make sure you know exactly when each step must be completed: writing, photography, retouching, finished art, binding, delivery of envelopes, distribution. Use the Catalog Production Worksheet (Figure 18.14) as a guide.

Figure 18.14. Catalog production worksheet.

Catalog planning worksheets.

Use these handy forms to plan and budget your next catalog.

1. Number of catalogs needed...

For direct distribution **Quantity**

1. For mailing to customer list .... ____________
2. For sales reps and distributors .... ____________
3. For trade shows .... ____________
4. To answer inquiries throughout the year .... ____________

Subtotal ____________

To sell new prospects

5. Estimated number of prospect companies throughout industry multiplied by number of key buying influences per company. .... ____________*

TOTAL ____________

*The THOMCAT Catalog File can provide this coverage for you. And you can have extra copies reprinted by Thomas Register to cover your direct distribution requirements.

2. Cost factors in producing and distributing your catalog...

Creative costs—

1. Copy preparation .... $____________
2. Layout preparation .... $____________

Art & Mechanical costs—

3. Type .... $____________
4. Photography, retouching and illustrations .... $____________
5. Mechanicals and camera ready art .... $____________

Production & distribution costs—

6. Printing and paper for ________ copies of a ________ page catalog .... $____________
7. Binding .... $____________
8. Envelopes .... $____________
9. List rental .... $____________
10. Addressing .... $____________
11. Inserting and handling .... $____________
12. Postage .... $____________

TOTAL COST $____________

Cost per catalog (divide total cost by number of copies printed) $____________

Note—Compare your cost for items 6 thru 12 with the costs for a catalog of the same number of pages in THOMCAT. Use the THOMCAT cost table on page 9.

Figure 18.14. (continued)

3. Catalog planning schedule...

	Target Date	Date Completed
Objective Setting Stage—		
Meeting with management to set objectives	________	________
Meetings with dept. heads to get agreement	________	________
Final objectives, budgets and distribution plan	________	________
Organization Stage—		
Finalize products and lines to be included	________	________
Input from engineering and other depts.	________	________
Rough outline and organizational layout	________	________
Creative Stage—		
Finished copy and layout	________	________
Review/Approval by key dept. heads	________	________
Final changes to copy & layout	________	________
Art & Mechanical Stage—		
Product samples for photography and/or art	________	________
Photography/drawings complete	________	________
Retouching complete	________	________
Typesetting complete	________	________
Mechanicals complete	________	________
Review/Approval by key dept. heads	________	________
Final changes to mechanicals	________	________
Printing Stage—		
Obtain printing bids	________	________
Order paper and envelopes	________	________
Mechanicals to printer	________	________
Proofs/blueprints due from printer	________	________
Proofs approved for final printing	________	________
Copies delivered	________	________
Distribution Stage—		
Copies to sales reps/distributors	________	________
Copies mailed to customer list	________	________
Copies offered in news releases and ads	________	________
Catalog to appear in Thomas Register THOMCAT Catalog File*	________	________

*Published annually in January. For closing dates and information on preprints, contact your Thomas Register Representative.

CHAPTER 19

Spec Sheets, Application Bulletins, User Stories, Special Reports, and Other Collateral Materials

The Dictionary of Advertising Terms defines *collateral* as "advertising material other than that presented through communications media." These are typically all the printed materials a company uses to promote itself or educate prospects about its products and services.

The most common collateral materials—brochures and catalogs—have been discussed in Chapters 17 and 18. Most companies consider their brochure or catalog to be their major selling piece, and major brochures and catalogs get the lion's share of attention—and budget.

But there are many ancillary collateral materials that can also be extremely effective in promoting a product, service, or organization. Often neglected in the advertising plan, shunned by advertising managers as "busy work," and created as an afterthought, these ancillary materials often produce more results dollar for dollar than slick product brochures and glossy color catalogs. They include:

- Spec sheets
- Data sheets
- Application bulletins
- User stories

- Testimonial sheets
- Bio sheets
- Inserts and modules
- Fliers
- Special reports
- Monographs
- Audio cassettes
- Transcripts
- Booklets
- Instruction sheets
- Invoice stuffers
- Posters
- Calendars
- White papers
- Technical papers
- Article reprints
- Books

Most companies use some or all of these as supplements to full-scale sales brochures; a few companies use *only* these forms and do not have an expensive brochure or catalog. Let's take a closer look at each item on the list—what it is, how you can use it, and where it fits in the marketing communications mix.

Spec Sheets

A *spec sheet* (short for specification sheet) is a one-page bulletin listing all the technical specifications for a given product. What these specifications are depends, of course, on the type of product. For a chemical compound, specs might include molecular weight, boiling point, freezing point, specific gravity, and safety precautions. For a computer printer, the spec sheet would list speed, interface, PC and software compatibility, weight, dimensions, and power requirements.

The spec sheet is usually printed on one side of a single sheet of 8½ × 11″ paper. They may be typeset if the specifications are permanent or typewritten if specifications are changed frequently. One chemical company types spec sheet copy on blank sheets and runs off copies as needed on letterhead on the office photocopier.

If you have a large number of spec sheets, you might consider having a graphic artist design a special masthead to give all your spec sheets a uniform appearance. If you are publishing only a few spec sheets, you can simply run them off on your letterhead and type in the heading "Spec Sheet" above the main title (e.g., "Spec Sheet: QPS-1000 Color Laser Video Printer").

How are spec sheets used?

- As inserts and supplements to promotional brochures
- For distribution to engineers, systems integrators, value-added resellers, original equipment manufacturers, and other technically oriented buyers who make purchase decisions based primarily on technical concerns
- For inclusion in purchasing agent files

Spec sheets are usually written in a two-column format with the type of specification on the left and the actual number on the right. For example:

Resolution	780 × 540 pixels
Monitor size	21 inches (diagonal)
Interface	RS-232C and X.25

There is little or no descriptive text and no embellishment. Terms which may be unclear to the reader can be explained in a parenthetical note or in footnotes. Do not provide in-depth explanations or attempt to turn features into benefits as you would in normal promotional copy. The spec sheet is not the place for this. It is not designed to sell; its purpose is to present complete technical information readable at a glance. A simple, uncluttered page is the best format.

Data Sheets

A *data sheet* is similar to a spec sheet but it is slightly more complete and slightly more promotional. In addition to product specifications presented in simple list form, data sheets may also contain narrative text that gives an overview of the product and emphasizes its key features and selling points.

A typical data sheet is printed on two sides of an 8½ × 11″ sheet of paper, although it may be four pages or even eight pages if needed. The front contains a photograph of the product and any descriptive text; the back contains specifications and features listed in bullet or table form.

Joseph Lane, of J.J. Lane Associates advertising agency, says that a data sheet's basic task is to provide complete information and tell the potential buyer every fact he could possibly want to know about the product. Where a brochure may be designed to grab attention and create interest, a data sheet is used to answer questions and reinforce the prospect's decision to buy. Typically, the slick, glossy, promotional-type brochure is used to hook the prospect early in the sales cycle; the data sheet is used toward the end when he has essentially made up his mind and wants to make sure the product specifications meet all his requirements.

Photography for data sheets should not be clever or conceptual. The best photograph is a straightforward close-up shot of the product. The reader wants to see exactly what he is getting and what it looks like.

Tip: One easy way to put together a data sheet is simply to make reprints of your current full-page ad with the spec sheet copy reproduced on the back. This gives you the selling message on the front and the technical details on the back, which is precisely the format a good data sheet takes.

Application Bulletins

An *application bulletin* describes one or more applications of the product. For example, if your product is computer software used in medical offices, law offices, and real estate offices, you might produce one application bulletin for each usage. Or, perhaps you sell a pump that can pump many different types of fluids. You might have one application bulletin on "pumping high-viscosity fluids," another on "blending low and high-viscosity fluids," a third on "pumping sludges," and so on.

Applications bulletins can take many forms. You can focus on a highly specialized application of your product by a specific customer and go into a lot of detail about the application. Or, you can write about a less specialized application with wider appeal to a greater number of prospects.

The advantage of doing the narrow, highly specialized application bulletin is that you are presenting unique information that gets high readership precisely because it is so unusual and interesting. Also, the small number of prospects who have a similar application will be eager to do business with you because your bulletin documents success solving the exact problem they have.

The advantage of doing the more general application with wider appeal is that the information is of interest to a greater number of prospects, and so creating a separate bulletin on the application makes more economic sense.

A third approach is to create a bulletin highlighting, in summary form, a group of applications (or all your applications). The multiple application bulletin is like an "idea book" that suggests to prospects ways they can use your product which they may not have thought of. This approach is ideal for an "all-purpose" type product like a grease, lubricant, or cleanser, which customers might purchase in limited quantities for limited use. The bulletin is designed to get them to buy more by pointing out additional ways in which they can use their product.

> *Example:* Arm and Hammer baking soda commercials take this type of approach by suggesting new ways in which the consumer can use baking soda. These include placing open boxes in freezers and refrigerators to remove odors as well as pouring it down the drain for cleansing.

There is no right or wrong way to organize an application story; however, here is one format you can use:

OUTLINE FOR AN APPLICATION STORY

I. SUMMARY. Sums up the nature of the application in one or two sentences. Provides an abstract for the reader who does not have time to read the entire bulletin.

II. BACKGROUND. Describes the problem that exists, the previous unsuccessful attempts to solve the problem, and the degree of severity of the problem (how much it cost the customer in terms of time, money, lost productivity, etc.).

III. THE SOLUTION. The product or service you provided that solved the problem.

IV. REASONS WHY. Why the customer chose your product or service instead of alternative products, services, or solutions.

V. HOW IT WORKS. How your product or service works, how it solved the problem.

VI. BENEFITS/RESULTS. Benefits gained as a result of using the product or service.

VII. FUTURE PLANS. Does the customer plan to use more of your service or buy more of your product? If so, what are his specific plans?

In addition, you may want to add some how-to information to your application bulletins: For instance, information on how to use your product for that particular application, or how to select the right size, model, or type product for an application. Any selection tips or other useful problem-solving information adds greatly to the value of your bulletin as a reference guide and will cause the prospect to retain it longer.

The best applications bulletins are those that highlight one specific application of your product as experienced by an actual customer who is named in the bulletin and discusses the application in his own words. This type of testimonial approach adds believability, interest, and credibility because it is real and because the prospect is told the story from another user (i.e., someone like himself) rather than a biased manufacturer or vendor.

An extremely powerful marketing technique is to write and publish a fair number of application bulletins (at least two or three for each major application, plus half a dozen or so on more esoteric or unusual applications). These are made readily available to salespeople, manufacturer's representatives, distributors, literature fulfillment staff, and others who send or present product information to prospects and customers.

The advantage is that the person sending or presenting information to a prospect can use the application bulletins to *customize* the presentation to the prospect's specific area of interest. For example, a salesperson visiting an oil refinery can pull out the two or three bulletins covering oil refinery applications and slip them into his presentation book, so that his presentation is slanted toward that market.

Or, if your company receives an inquiry from the manager of a sulfuric acid plant, you can pull an application bulletin on sulfuric acid manufacturing and mail it with your letter and general product brochure. The person receiving it believes in your company's ability to handle his requirement because he receives literature that speaks to his specific needs.

Today more so than ever, people want products and services designed specifically for them. Even if your product or service is not designed solely for them, you must customize your offer as much as you can and then create the *perception* that only you understand their particular application and have experience solving it. A series of applications bulletins gives you the ability to quickly put together an information package that creates this perception.

User Stories

A *user story* is a bulletin in which a customer or client, in his or her words, extolls the virtue of your product, service, or organization. Although a user story may focus on an application and thus serve double duty as an application bulletin, it is not always about a specific application. Many user stories instead talk about the user's overall experience with the product and vendor. It may focus on applications, or on product features, or on benefits, or simply on the excellent service your company provides.

User stories can be any length but are usually printed on one or two sides of a single sheet of paper. They are typically written in a style similar to a news or feature article, combining narrative with direct quotations from clients. Another way to write them is to put the entire text in quotations and make the bulletin essentially an edited transcript of an interview with the user.

When the copy is written, send it to the user along with a note requesting permission to print it using his name as a reference. Be sure to get permission in writing before typesetting and printing the final piece. It is wrong to use such material without the subject's permission and might harm your relationship with the client or customer.

The material you gather for a user story can be recycled again and again in a variety of formats including:

- Stand-alone bulletins or fliers can be distributed as sales literature to prospects.
- A series of user stories can be bound into a larger "user story" brochure, which presents an impressive picture of how customers today are using and benefiting from your product.
- Segments of user bulletin text can be excerpted and published in other marketing communications such as company newsletters or product brochures.
- User stories can be placed with appropriate trade journals and magazines as feature articles.
- User stories can also form the basis of a series of print ads featuring successful applications or satisfied customers.

How do you get ideas for user stories? The easiest way is to simply go through your file of letters from customers and contact those customers who wrote favorably about your product.

Another method is to create a form your salespeople, distributors, and agents can use to alert you to potential user stories. The form would have space to include the following items:

- Name, company name, address, and telephone number of salesperson or representative submitting the form.
- Name, company name (if a business), address, and telephone number of the user (the person to be interviewed for the story).
- The product or products they are using.

- A brief description of their application and how they are using the product.
- A brief description of the success or other results they achieved as a result of using the product.
- Key points about the application or other important points the interviewer should ask the user about.

You can set up some sort of incentive program, awarding salespeople and distributors for each usable user story idea they submit. This helps to create a steady flow of user story opportunities.

Not every potential user story will pan out. Some users will refuse to be interviewed, either because it is against their company policy or because they don't have the time or don't see the benefit in it for them.

Of those that do consent to be interviewed, some won't tell very interesting stories or give sufficient detail for you to do a good article. Others may say glowing things but then change the copy so much once they see it that the story is not worth publishing. However, in my experience, 80 to 90 percent of interviews will result in usable stories.

Please note that you must always get the user's approval of the copy in writing before publishing.

Testimonial Sheets

A *testimonial sheet* is simply a typewritten or typeset sheet with a series of testimonials—quotations from satisfied customers and clients who say good things about you. A testimonial sheet has a powerful effect on the reader because it shows him that you have many satisfied customers who are willing to endorse you. That *block* of testimonial after testimonial impresses the prospect far more than any single testimonial can. For this reason, if you are using testimonials in a brochure or mailing package, you might prefer to present them in a box on a single page rather than spread them out one or two a page.

If you have a file of letters from satisfied customers or a batch of approved user stories, you simply extract the testimonials you want to use and type them on one or two sides of a sheet of paper. The ideal format is a typewritten sheet taking two sides of a sheet of paper, preferably printed on your letterhead. The headline reads, "HERE'S WHAT THEY SAY ABOUT [name of company, product, or service]." The testimonials begin under this headline.

Each testimonial consists of a short statement, in quotation marks. The statement is from the customer and is in praise of you or your product or service. Specific testimonials are better than general ones (i.e., testimonials that go into detail about how you saved the customer time or met his needs are better than superlatives like "excellent," "good," or "love your widget!").

Your name, address, and phone number should appear on the testimonial sheet, as it should on every piece of promotional literature you write. This can be typed in under the last testimonial.

What if customers don't give you nice testimonials? You can ask for them in a letter styled like Figure 19.1.

Figure 19.1. Letter to solicit testimonial.

Mr. John Smith
ABC Co.
Anytown, USA

Dear John:

I have a favor to ask of you.

I'm in the process of putting together a booklet of testimonials—a collection of comments about my services, from satisfied clients like yourself.

Would you please take a few minutes to give me your opinion of my consulting services?

There's no need to dictate a letter—just jot your comments on the back of this letter, sign below, and return to me in the enclosed envelope. The second copy is for your files.

I look forward to learning what you *like* about my service . . . but I welcome any suggestions or criticisms, too.

Many thanks, John.

Sincerely,

Betty Jones

BETTY: YOU HAVE MY PERMISSION TO QUOTE FROM MY COMMENTS AND USE THESE QUOTATIONS IN ADS, BROCHURES, MAIL, AND OTHER PROMOTIONS USED TO MARKET YOUR SERVICES.

Signed ______________________ Date ______________________

Note that this letter asks for an "opinion" instead of a testimonial, and that it solicits criticisms as well as positive comments. In this way, you are not just requesting a favor; you are getting information that will help you serve your clients or customers better in the future. Thus, you both profit from the exchange.

How do you use the testimonial sheet?

- As a handout.
- As an additional enclosure in direct mail packages.
- To send to prospects along with your other literature in response to inquiries.
- As a supplement to your brochure.

Tip: Always give your testimonial sheet to any ad agency, copywriter, or marketing consultant you hire. It will be tremendously helpful to them when they create copy for you.

Bio Sheets

Bio sheets are capsule biographies of key personnel. Since people do not stay as long in jobs as they used to, the best format is to have one biography per sheet so you can quickly add and remove bios as necessary.

Bio sheets are not done resume style but are written in simple narrative form and may include a picture of the person being profiled. The headline is simply the person's name and job title (e.g., "Jack Jones, Purchasing Director, Ingram International").

The bio sheet is not written in chronological order but rather starts with the person's current position and job responsibilities. This is because the prospect is most interested in what the person can do for them *now.* What they did in the past is important but of secondary interest.

Don't just give a job title. You should also describe the person's job function, role within the organization, how they help serve clients. You can list a group of client projects the person worked on, highlight one or two projects in more detail (including results achieved), or simply list key areas of responsibility.

The next section of the bio discusses key positions held, starting with the person's previous position and going back. If the person has had many jobs, you may skip some of them. Since you are not listing dates, these omissions cannot be detected by the reader. For each position, give company, job title, job function, and key accomplishments.

After the job history, discuss credentials. These include education and degrees (with majors and colleges), professional memberships, awards, publications, and other key accomplishments. You might also include a quotation from the person being profiled in which he expresses his personal philosophy, dedication to service, or some other point that is not brought out elsewhere.

Bio sheets are used primarily by service firms, although some manufacturers publish them for key personnel as well. Their uses include:

- Supplement to company brochure.
- As appendices in business proposals.
- Enclosures with get-acquainted letters and other outgoing correspondence.
- Fulfillment literature sent in response to a prospect's request to know more about company personnel servicing his account.

Inserts And Modules

Many advertisers use *modular brochures.* These consist of a main selling piece, usually 4 to 8 pages, with a pocket on the inside back cover. The pocket is designed to hold "modules" or insert sheets—supplemental sales literature distributed with the main brochure. Some of these modules may be created at the time the main piece is produced. Others are added and inserted later.

Why use the module approach? The format offers several advantages:

- You can more quickly and inexpensively update and change the content. A large color brochure is expensive to produce and so you don't want it to get dated. But an insert sheet is inexpensive and easy to update or change.
- The inquiry fulfillment department can custom-tailor a literature package by adding or removing insert sheets from the pocket.
- Individual salespeople can create their own inserts without help from the advertising department using such techniques as desktop publishing, photocopies of relevant articles or testimonial letters, etc.

With the advent of desktop publishing, many advertisers are using in-house desktop publishing systems to quickly and easily create insert sheets without going to the expense of using an outside graphic design service. For a more professional look, you can hire a graphic artist with "Macintosh" experience on a one-time basis to design a standard format or "template" for your insert sheets. Once the template is set up on your computer, you simply input new copy for each sheet, and the module is printed in the desired typestyle and layout.

The number of desktop publishing consultants is growing daily and you can find them advertising in *Adweek* and other marketing publications or in the yellow pages under "Desktop Publishing." For more information on desktop publishing, see Chapter 32 on graphic design.

If you don't have desktop publishing in-house, you can hire an outside desktop publishing service or just have a regular typesetting house produce your sheets. The design of a single insert sheet can be simple enough so that your printer can produce the mechanical for you. For a more sophisticated design, you can use the services of a professional graphic artist.

Thanks in part to personal computers and desktop publishing, the trend in business today is for managers to want more control over their own materials. What is happening is that they want to rely on the advertising department for more creative projects, glossy color materials, and "major" pieces, but want the ability to create "quickie" fliers and promotional sheets right at their desk or at least within their department.

Rather than fight the trend, you should encourage it. The advertising department has always been overburdened with too many requests to handle too many small projects not in the schedule or in the budget. By all means, let your product managers and brand managers create any materials you don't have time or money to do yourself.

You might want to help them by providing blank sheets with a uniform masthead design upon which their material can be reproduced. You could also provide them with a graphics guidelines manual to follow or even arrange some in-house training sessions in the basics of graphic design and desktop publishing.

You may object, "But if I allow them to do their own thing, a large amount of unapproved, poor-quality material that is inconsistent with our campaign look and theme will be produced." Yes, but this material is going to be produced anyway, with or without your approval. You can't fight it, so why not make the best of it and help them do the best job possible. You could even assign one of your staff as a "publications editor" and offer his or her service to other departments for review and copyediting of their own material. This will at least provide one quality control check you don't now have.

Fliers

A *flier* differs from a brochure in that it is a quickly made and conceived piece. Its purpose is usually to make an announcement or to act as a "temporary" brochure until a more permanent piece can be developed, approved, and printed.

Most fliers are printed on one side of an 8½ × 11″ sheet of paper in black ink. To make the flier stand out, print on a brightly colored stock such as salmon, blue, green, or yellow. Use a light color; dark colors do not allow enough contrast with the black type.

Fliers can be posted on bulletin boards, distributed throughout the community, mailed to your customer list, handed out at trade shows, or inserted as a module with your inquiry fulfillment literature. Although they are done "cheaply," this can actually be an advantage, since their format—and hence, the message they carry—stand out from the typical "slick" brochures the prospect receives every day.

Special Reports

"A *special report* is a step-by-step list of guidelines produced by a specialist for the benefit of someone who wishes to achieve a specific result or objective," writes Dr. Jeffrey Lant, marketing consultant. "Special reports are prescriptive; their function is to advise an individual on what to do either to achieve a specified objective or to avoid a certain problem."

Why special reports? Because one of the most effective marketing techniques is to provide your prospects with useful information that helps them identify, analyze, avoid, or begin to solve a pressing problem they have. Being the provider of such information:

- Establishes your credibility as an expert in the field and a reliable source of problem-solving service and information.
- Makes the prospect comfortable with you.
- Gets the prospect to learn and accept your methods, philosophy, and approach to the problem.
- Makes the prospect eager to do business with you.

The special report can take a variety of formats. Dr. Lant's special reports are typewritten, single-spaced, and about four to five pages long. They address a specific, narrow topic and present a fairly thorough overview on what the problem is, why it is a problem for the prospect, and some initial steps that can be taken to solve it. Each report is produced on a dot matrix printer and customized with the name of the recipient. "This eliminates the need to print and stock reports," says Dr. Lant.

Another consultant, Howard Shenson, publishes a series of reports in booklet form. He presents his information in list format rather than using Dr. Lant's problem/solution approach (e.g., "77 Proven Strategies to Increase Seminar and Workshop Profits"). Either the list format ("7 ways," "6 steps") or the problem/solution format can be used in your special reports.

Who can benefit from using special reports as a promotional item? Not just consultants and service firms but anyone who is in the business of solving problems for prospects. Today most manufacturers fall into this category. Customers don't want just off-the-shelf merchandise; they want an entire *system* of product delivery—engineering specs, product, distribution—tailored to their specific needs. In short, they want advice, not just equipment. Special reports are the first step in establishing your firm in that advisor's role.

How can you use special reports in your marketing program?

- Send out press releases announcing the publication and availability of each new report. Make sure the release contains meaty excerpts from the report the editor can use in an article about the topic. End the release with information on how readers can request the report. This will generate a lot of publicity and inquiries.
- Offer your special reports as a response piece in direct mail and print advertising—to greatly increase the response to your ads and mailings.
- Enclose special reports with your regular product brochures. This will make the package a lot more interesting and valuable to the prospect.
- Send the reports to your current customers to let them know you are thinking of them.
- Offer special reports as a bonus or reward for taking action. For example, if you want prospects to attend a product demonstration for your new widget, offer a free special report on "How to Size and Select Widgets" to those who come as a bonus for attendance.

Monographs

The dictionary defines a *monograph* as a "scholarly article or pamphlet on a specific and usually limited subject." While the special report is accessible to a businessperson or consumer, the monograph is usually aimed at a doctor, engineer, tax attorney, or other person who a technical specialist within his field.

Monographs can be used by any marketer who sells to a technical audience. Most people have a limited concept of the word "technical" and think only of science, engineering, and perhaps medicine. But tax law is a technical subject. So are plumbing, sprinkler system installation, landscaping, photography, locksmithing, commercial banking, and architecture.

Monographs provide the technical buyers—the plumbers, engineers, and architects as opposed to the managers, owners, and executives—with in-depth detailed technical information on a specific topic within their specialty. A monograph aimed at doctors, for example, might deal with the topic of how a new drug handles a specific disease in male patients who are over 50 and heavy smokers. A monograph written for aeronautics engineers might deal with O-ring design in low-orbiting space craft.

The monograph—or at least, its first draft—should be written by a technical expert either on staff at your company or employed by you as a consultant. Or, the author may be one of your customers or product users. If the technical expert does not have the time or desire to draft a copy, have him or her dictate the information into a cassette recorder.

The next step is to have a writer or editor go over the copy and put it into proper English. The editor's tendency will be to simplify the complex information until a layman can understand it. Resist this temptation! The monograph is technical information for technical experts. The editor doesn't have to understand every word, and he/she should not sacrifice content or thoroughness for the sake of simplicity.

Monographs are usually set in type similar to a scholarly journal article and may be illustrated with graphs, tables, and other technically oriented visuals. Distribute them at conferences, seminars, trade shows, meetings, exhibits, and with information sent to prospects who have expressed an interest in the topic the monograph covers.

Audio Cassettes

Now is a good time to use an *audio cassette* as a marketing tool: They have become popular enough that most prospects have access to a cassette player, yet the use of them as marketing tools is still limited enough that a cassette really stands out from the stacks of printed materials in the prospect's mail box or in-basket.

"The popularity of cassettes has been assisted too by the fact that great numbers of people prefer learning via the spoken word," observes the late Howard Shenson, author of *Shenson on Consulting* (John Wiley and Sons, Inc.). And William R. Guthy, president of Cassette Productions Unlimited adds: "Cassettes enlarge your service by enlarging your audience."

A big benefit of cassettes is that they are inexpensive. With a professional quality recorder, you can record yourself in your office or home, then turn the tape over to a duplicator. For small quantities, your company may want to invest in its own duplicator. Outside services can duplicate 60-minute cassettes for around $.85 to $1.25 in quantities of 200 or more, depending on the type of box and label they provide.

The cassette can be packaged in a hard plastic box or soft plastic container. The label should have the title of the presentation, your company name, address, telephone, and a copyright mark for sound recordings (a circle P, not a circle C).

When you record, read the script in a clear, well-articulated voice. If you normally talk fast, slow down. Assuming a narration speed of 120 words per minute, a 60-minute tape will contain approximately 7,200 words. So your script should come out to about 28 to 30 double-spaced typewritten pages.

Prepared scripts can be recorded in your office or a professional studio. Look in the Yellow Pages under "Sound Studios" or "Audio Duplication" for the names of companies that record, edit, and duplicate audio cassette programs. Although the cost can quickly add up with extensive editing and special effects, you can always control costs by using a straightforward narration with minimal effects and editing.

An alternative is not to record a "canned" script but to tape and duplicate one of your salespeople, engineers, or managers giving a speech, seminar, or other presentation. Although many successful tape programs are studio recorded, others capture the excitement and spontaneity of a live recording. Having someone read into a microphone can be boring; hearing an animated speaker address a roomful of eager listeners is not.

In addition, listeners are more willing to forgive you for sending an imperfect recording of a live session than they are a poorly produced studio recording. So you can save time and money by simply recording your presenter live and duplicating the tape "as is."

If you do go into the studio for some editing, be sure to add a tag at the end of the presentation that describes what your company does and how the listener can contact you for more information, including your address and phone number. Address and phone number should also appear on the label.

How can you use cassettes in your marketing program?

- Enclose them as part of cold mailings to prospect lists. The addition of a cassette demands attention because it is a three-dimensional object and stands out in a mail-box filled with mailings that are all two-dimensional (paper and ink).
- For a small list of special prospects for an expensive product or service (e.g., CEOs at *Fortune* 500 companies making decisions about which accounting firm to use), you might enclose a cassette player along with the cassette. This is a guaranteed attention-getter and almost ensures an audience. One recent mailing of this type generated a 37 percent response.
- You can offer free cassettes to people who respond to your ads.
- Enclose cassettes in your inquiry fulfillment packages.

Note: You will encounter many people selling expensive 6- and 8-cassette "learning programs" in albums with price tags ranging from $60 to $150. Don't feel you have to compete with them. A single, inexpensively produced cassette is more than adequate for promotional purposes.

Transcripts

An alternative to duplicating the master recording of your seminar or presentation is to transcribe the tape and then reprint duplicates of the *transcript* in booklet or report form. Many television stations routinely offer transcriptions at the end of talk shows, selling them for $3 to $4 per show.

An audio cassette has more impact, is more likely to be noticed and listened to, is a more interesting and attention-getting format, and is easier and cheaper to duplicate than a transcript. But, if you don't like cassettes, and still want an easy way of turning one-time presentations into collateral materials that have a longer life and greater distribution, by all means use transcripts.

One advantage of transcripts is that the typewritten transcript of the original presentation can be reviewed, edited, retyped, and reviewed again before publication, allowing you to fine-tune and change things that didn't work in the original presentation.

When designing the cover of the transcript, in addition to the name of the program, be sure to name the event and date during which the original presentation was made. Saying the material was presented at the "Fifth Annual Conference of Liquid Engineers" adds a degree of importance and credibility that's lacking in a document the reader thinks you just wrote and published yourself.

Booklets

A *booklet* is similar to a special report. But unlike a special report, which thoroughly addresses a narrow topic, booklets can be less comprehensive and cover broader subjects.

A booklet may be any length, from four pages (front cover, back cover, two-page inside spread) to 24 pages or more. Shorter formats (four to eight pages) allow the reader to quickly scan and get the information without having to set aside a major chunk of reading time. People look to booklets for quick information or tips; if they want something to curl up with at night, they'll go to the library and take out a novel.

Booklets are usually designed to fit in #10 or 6 × 9″ mailing envelopes, which means a page size of either 4 × 9″ or 5½ × 8½″. An informational document with a 7 × 10″ or 8½ × 11″ page size would probably be called a report, folio, or monograph rather than a booklet. Booklet implies small; the name literally means "little book."

The ideal formats for booklets are either *list* format (e.g., "7 ways," "5 easy steps") or *question-and-answer* format (e.g., "7 questions to ask before you hire a patent attorney—and one good answer to each"). The reason these formats work so well is that people look to booklets for quick tips and techniques—little nuggets of easily digested information. A numbered list or series of questions and answers makes the information easily scannable. The question-and-answer format has the added advantage of allowing you to structure a logical presentation that answers all the prospect's questions in the order he would normally ask them.

The headline on the cover should be the title of the booklet. Underneath, put your company name, address, and phone number. The inside pages contain the information being presented, usually in all text and with few or no illustrations.

Tip: Put a dollar price on the upper right corner of the front cover of the booklet. The price can range from $1 for a small booklet to $4 or $5 for a longer one. This serves two purposes. First, even though you are offering the booklet for free, when the reader sees the price, it immediately creates a perception that the information is valuable—and, the prospect believes you have given him a gift others normally pay for. Second, with a price, you discourage the "freebie collectors" who call up and demand a dozen or a hundred copies simply because the booklet is free.

The back cover is where you make your "sales pitch." It contains a description of your company and the products or services you offer along with instructions on how the reader can contact you to learn more.

Note that this is the *only* place in the booklet where you explicitly sell yourself, and even here it's done in a soft-sell biographical description rather than hard-sell ad-type copy. The rest of the booklet should contain objective, factual, helpful information and not hype.

Use of booklets is similar to use of special reports. Offer them as response pieces, and inquiries from ads and mailings will soar. Also send out a press release announcing the publication and availability of your booklet.

You would be surprised at how successfully this can be used as a press release. Editors of magazines and newspapers love to run little columns and boxed items offering this or that free booklet to their readers. They will eagerly run free booklet releases from companies they would not normally publicize.

Instruction Sheets

Some manufacturers have to include *instruction sheets*—otherwise, buyers could not use their products. But instructions are more than just technical guidelines: Used properly, they can build good will and promote your company for years to come.

Even if your product isn't complex or doesn't require instructions, include some small pamphlet when you ship it. The pamphlet will be titled something like, "Tips for the care and feeding of [name of product]."

In the pamphlet, give some extra advice for taking care of the product or maintaining it better or getting more use out of it. The purpose is to form a closer relationship with your customer by helping him above and beyond what he paid you for.

For instance, if you sell knit slacks, is there a danger they will come apart under some washing machine cycles? If so, attach a booklet warning the buyer of the cycles to avoid and instructing him on how to clean. Also include tips for wearing (e.g., if the fabric is easily cleaned of grass stains, mention how it's ideal for picnic wear).

Also in the booklet include a panel of soft-sell copy on your company and other products or services the customer can buy. Don't forget an address and phone number. If you offer a toll-free number users can call if they have questions or problems, this pamphlet is the place to highlight it.

Will most of your customers become excited about this pamphlet? Will this technique have a dramatic effect on your bottom line? Probably not. But a certain percentage of your buyers *will* appreciate it and favor you with more business—or at least speak well of you to their friends. It's hard to measure the effect of such advertising precisely. But common sense indicates the distribution of such an instructional pamphlet would pay its cost many times over.

Invoice Stuffers

An *invoice stuffer* is a brochure, flier, circular, or other advertising material enclosed with the customer's monthly invoice, statement, or other routine correspondence. The invoice stuffer may be designed to notify customers of a new policy; announce a rate increase; remind them of maintenance or repair procedures they should be doing; sell them accessories, additional services, or other related offers; sell unrelated merchandise; encourage them to increase usage or spending; or offer an upgrade of an existing product or service.

Invoice stuffers naturally must be designed to fit your invoice or other outgoing envelopes, which are usually #10 (standard business size). They can be one color, two colors, or four colors (uncoated or glossy paper stock) with illustrations or photos. They can be a single panel or have several folds and include perforated tear-off coupons for ordering. Some even have a reply envelope designed into them.

Although invoice stuffers get lower response than solo mailings, they can be immensely more profitable because there is no extra postage cost: the invoice gets a "free ride" along with the bill, statement, or other item being sent. If you routinely send invoices or other frequently mailed outgoing correspondence, consider creating a series of such envelope stuffers. Don't feel you have to imitate the mail order circulars mailed with credit card company statements. Perhaps you want yours to look more like a newsletter, or a technical bulletin, or a simple flier, or even a letter.

Tip: However you design your invoice stuffer, make it look different than the material with which it is being mailed. If, for example, your invoices are on cream white paper, print the invoice stuffer on bright yellow stock. If your invoices are 8½ × 11″ sheets typed on letterhead, make your stuffer a colorful 4 × 9″ sheet on glossy stock.

Posters

One easy way to make your direct mail different and therefore noticed is to print your advertising message on a *poster* and mail it in a mailing tube.

However, I don't think this is wildly successful for most people who try it. I base this opinion on the fact that posters have been around for a long time, people are constantly trying new things in the mail, and yet you don't see that many poster mailings. If they generated wildly better results than conventional mailings, then more people would be using them, don't you think?

Personally, I do not like to receive posters in the mail. The mailing tubes are usually difficult to open and the posters are even more difficult to remove. Posters curl and resist opening so I can read them. They are bulky and cumbersome, and I don't have the room on my desk to peruse them.

In addition, I like to store literature I receive in my files, and posters won't fit in my file cabinets. I know the advertiser is hoping I'll pin up the poster on my wall, but I have limited wall space, and few poster designs I see satisfy my standards for permanent office art. From conversations I've had, I suspect the majority of people feel the way I do.

If you still think you want to do a poster, make sure that one of two conditions exists: Either (a) your product has such great visual appeal that people will want to display a photo or drawing of it on their walls, or (b) you have come up with a clever content that is interesting and that people would display as a conversation piece.

An example of the former is a Porsche poster sent in a mailing tube. A Porsche by itself has visual appeal for many people; it is an attractive car. This poster created additional visual appeal because my last name was laser printed on the license plate of the Porsche in my poster. This was done for each recipient, personalizing the poster for each prospect.

Another example is an Air Force recruiting poster featuring an action photo of fighter aircraft in flight. This would have appeal to teenagers who eagerly pay $7 to see such movies as *Top Gun* and *Iron Eagles.*

The second approach is to have clever, humorous, or amusing content. I am reminded of a list we circulated among the dorms at college of "The 25 Greatest Lies of All Time." It was a humorous treatment of how people avoid responsibility (e.g., "the check's in the mail," "the dog ate my homework"), and could, if handled properly, make a good promotion for a company whose business was to make sure people kept their obligations (e.g,. a collection agency). Another popular approach is "99 common mistakes to avoid when doing [X]"—X being an activity related to your product or industry.

Calendars

An old standard, the *calendar* is used by companies of all descriptions, from manufacturers to insurance agents. Of the two types of calendars, wall and desk, wall calendars have higher perceived value and more visibility within the prospect's home or office.

There are two basic options in calendars. The first is to buy a predesigned calendar and have as many as you need imprinted with your company logo, address, and phone number. These may be purchased from advertising specialty houses listed in the yellow pages under "Advertising Specialties" or "Premiums and Incentives." Some printers also offer them.

Quality varies. Some are hokey and cheap-looking; others are attractive and look more expensive than they actually are. Insist on inspecting a sample before you order.

One local insurance agent has been using this type of calendar for years, mailing them annually to his clients, best prospects, and business associates. He has become known for his calendars; indeed, people expect them and are disappointed if they have been dropped from the list or if the calendar arrives late.

The other option is the custom calendar. This is one where the concept, copy, and design are uniquely yours, and it must be custom-printed. For example, Westinghouse Defense Center publishes an annual calendar based on the theme of "great scientists." Each month features a commissioned illustration and brief biography of a great scientist, either living or from history.

Perhaps the most successful calendar of all time is the Rigid Tool calendar. Featuring color photos of attractive bikini-clad women displaying various tools, the calendar has been categorized as sexist. Yet, it continues to be effective. Distribution is widespread; there are few machine shops you can walk into and not find the Rigid Calendar.

Through this one item, Rigid has become one of the best-known brands. And the calendar is in constant demand. If this proves anything, it's that even in the twilight years of the 20th century, sex sells.

White Papers

A *white paper,* also called a *position paper* or a *briefing,* is intended to present your company's position, opinion, and wisdom on a broad topic affecting your entire industry. Where the monograph is narrowly focused and aimed at technical experts, and the special report deals with how-to type material, the white paper addresses topics of major importance to most if not all of your prospects.

Although it is usually aimed at executive decision makers, some white papers focus on more technical issues and are aimed at top management on the technical side, such as Vice Presidents of Data Processing or Telecommunications Managers.

The purpose of the white paper is either to establish you as the industry leader or authority or to promote your specific point of view on some broad issue that affects how your prospects do business and what they buy. As an example, Apple might write a white paper on why desktop publishing is clearly the wave of the future and why all corporate PCs will need to have desktop publishing capability. The purpose would be to promote Apple, not IBM, as the authority in personal computing and push IBM out of its leadership position concerning PCs in the corporate environment. The white paper would encourage the viewpoint that desktop publishing and graphics are the key concerns in this market—a viewpoint that positions Apple favorably and IBM unfavorably.

Unlike special reports and booklets, white papers are not intended for broad distribution. They are generally aimed at upper-level management and decision-makers. They may be sent to key executives at prospect organizations, industry "gurus" such as influential consultants and columnists, as well as to other people including business journalists and current clients. Ideally, the material compiled for a white paper can be recycled in other forms, such as speeches, seminars, and articles in the trade press.

Technical Papers

Most large companies employ engineers and scientists. If you ask, you'll find that a number of your engineers and scientists are presenting *technical papers* on their research or other activities at conferences or publishing these papers in journals. Reprints of these papers make excellent supplemental sales literature, used both as hand-outs or to fulfill inquiries—especially if you sell to a technical audience.

Technical papers should be reprinted as presented or originally published, without editing. This is because you want to mention the origin of the paper (date and nature of presentation or publication), so you want to make sure the reader is getting exactly what you promised: the original paper.

But this doesn't mean you can't dress it up a bit. For example, you may reprint the paper itself on inexpensive uncoated stock, then bind it into a color cover (usually two colors) printed on a glossy "card" stock (a heavier, stiffer paper). This adds weight and substance and creates a perception of value.

On the front, put the title in large type, with the source information and author underneath. The back cover contains a reprint of any full-page trade journal ad featuring the product or technology discussed in the paper. For example, if the paper is about how Westinghouse designed a better microchip for its TPS-43 radar, the back cover will feature an ad for the radar itself (the product Westinghouse is selling).

Tip: Have a graphic designer design a "standard" cover format for technical papers. Then reprint your best technical papers using these covers. Papers in a series can be differentiated by cover color or they can be numbered in sequence. You can then run a box in your ads, or enclose a separate reply card in mailings and correspondence, offering to send prospects any of the papers they want.

Also, try to give your series of papers a catchy umbrella name people will remember. Niagara Lockport, a manufacturer of products used in the making of tissues, publishes a series of papers under the title "Tissue Issues"—and they have become extremely well-known and popular in the industry. Try to think of something similar for your series.

Article Reprints

Chapter 25 describes how to go about writing and placing feature *articles* in the trade and consumer press. These articles—written either by or about your company—can help promote your name and product to thousands of readers.

But the real value in articles is not primarily in the original publication but in the reprints. Using article reprints as supplemental sales literature is an enormously effective marketing technique for several reasons:

- It enhances credibility. People are much more likely to believe the material if they see it was published in a magazine or newspaper as opposed to a bulletin that you self-published as an obvious promotion.
- It gains readership. People are more likely to read through an interesting article than a sales brochure.
- It is ridiculously inexpensive. Brochures involve an enormous expense in photography, illustration, design, copywriting, and color printing. With article reprints, the magazine has already set type and designed page layouts for you—for free. They will gladly reprint as many copies as you need for a nominal fee. Or, a local printer can do it.

Tip: Although the magazine is usually a bit more expensive, they often do a better job because they have the original films. The printer can work only from a copy of the article.

Like booklets, reports, monographs, and similar pieces, magazine reprints can be used as hand-outs, leave-behinds, mailers, response pieces, premiums, supplemental brochures. A manager who wants a piece on a topic that doesn't justify the cost of doing a brochure can write it as an article, get it placed, and order reprints for $100 or $200. A series of articles can be bound in a cover and offered as a premium or incentive. For example, Joan Harris, president of Harris Direct Marketing, is compiling a series of columns she wrote for a Long Island business publication into a book on direct marketing. While she plans to sell the book for $20 or $25, it also will make an effective premium to give away to potential clients for her consulting and advertising company.

Books

Another effective marketing technique is to offer prospects information in the form of a paperback or hardcover *book.* As Dr. Jeffrey Lant observes, "A book is a brochure that is never thrown away."

I can attest to this. On prospecting calls to potential clients, whenever I noticed a book of mine on their bookshelf—and this happened a number of times—the job was usually mine. Why? Because a book—even a book published by your company—impresses the prospect. The old ad headline, "From the folks who wrote the book on [name of product]" is a cliche, yet it continues to work because we do indeed want to deal with experts. And someone who wrote a book is perceived as an expert.

There are two basic types of corporate-sponsored books: Informational and commemorative or historical. The information book provides the reader with useful how-to information, establishing your company in the role of problem-solver/advisor. The commemorative or historical book is more corporate in nature and typically presents a history of the company or one of its divisions, frequently to commemorate a 50th anniversary or other event.

For the informational type book, content is the key consideration. The information must be useful and practical. If the book is a thinly disguised, 100-page-long sales pitch for a specific product, readers will be disgusted and think poorly of you. If it is genuinely of value and objective in its presentation, they will value it and you for giving it to them.

When they need advice or a supplier of that type of product or service, they will pluck the book from the shelf, turn to the inside front cover or back page, find your name and phone number, and call you. Books not only build image and credibility but can generate many direct sales for you.

Tip: Make sure your phone number is prominent on the inside front cover, outer back cover, and is liberally sprinkled throughout the text. Encourage questions and calls. Try to establish a dialogue with the reader. This is the first step in becoming their vendor.

The corporate anniversary or history type book usually contains less copy and fewer pages, but is hardcover, not paperback, and is lavishly illustrated with attractive drawings and expensive photography. If your company has a well-maintained photo library or archive, this can save you a fortune. The best way to keep costs down is to use existing visual materials rather than commission new photography.

Producing a book is not inexpensive but costs less than you might think. To print 3,000 copies of a 128-page trade paperback (trim size 6 × 9″) with no photos or illustrations will run around $6,000 to $7,000. That's for printing and production supervision only; it doesn't include design, copy, or typography. The printing price per copy goes down substantially when you order 5,000 or 10,000.

To save money on copy, you can assign one of your staff to write the book. Any corporate writer will probably enjoy the job as a welcome change of pace. Page layouts can be done on an in-house desktop publishing system and output on a Linotronics printer for $5 to $10 per page or so. On the other hand, if you farm out the entire job to a writer, designer, and print production supervisor, you can spend anywhere from $20,000 to $50,000 to get a professionaly done book printed and in your hands.

CHAPTER 20

Corporate Communications

Corporate communications are those communications which seek to communicate an idea, fact, attitude, or image dealing with the corporation as an organization rather than a specific product, service, or product line. The objective is to build an image or place an idea, fact, or attitude in the mind of the reader, rather than generate inquiries, direct sales, or brand awareness or preference. Corporate communications can include:

- Corporate advertising—usually print and television.
- Annual reports.
- Corporate capabilities brochures (these are similar to annual reports but without the financial data or references that tie them to a specific year).
- Executive speeches.
- Company newsletters and magazines and other miscellaneous print materials.

Because most corporate advertising is self-serving and contains nothing of interest to the reader, readers have been conditioned to skim them and, for the most part, ignore them. According to research published by the Business/Professional Advertising Association, reader interest in corporate advertising is approximately 35 percent below the norm for advertising overall.

For example, a recent issue of *Fortune* contained a two-page spread for Xerox Financial Services. The headline is, "A machine that helps you build for the future"; the visual is a building under construction. The headline is so vague and general that it holds no interest for the target audience: chief financial officers and treasurers needing investment banking and other financing services. And a two-page spread for Steelcase, an office furniture manufacturer, carries the equally vague headline "Window of opportunity."

Another typically ineffective ploy is the brag-and-boast headline, where the corporation makes a boastful claim of capability or success without linking it to the reader's concerns. For instance, in that same issue of *Fortune,* Georgia-Pacific ran a one-page ad with the headline, "At Georgia-Pacific, we're feathering our nest with over $800 million in printing paper sales." Copy goes on to say how successful Georgia-Pacific is in selling paper. But it never says who they are talking to or why the reader should care.

Some other examples of inane corporate advertising—from this single issue of *Fortune:*

- An ad for The Guardian, an insurance company. The headline reads: "Intelligence." The photo shows two dolphins. Copy begins: "While some choices can be based on impulse and mood, others have to be based on intelligence."
- An ad for Motorola. Headline: "When you aim for perfection you discover it's a moving target."
- For Chubb Institute: "Their people are as committed as ours."
- Ford: "Some of our best advertising isn't advertising."
- Kobelco: "Home away from home."
- Komatsu: "Work for the world. Care for the community."
- Lucky-Goldstar: "Lucky-Goldstar and you . . . come through with flying colors."
- Van Kampen Merritt: "Vigilance."
- Nippon Steel: "What's in a name? More than you would imagine—that name is Nippon Steel."
- Norfolk Southern: "Sure-footed."

- Mitsubishi Kasei: "This should give you a good idea of what we've been up to lately."
- Bank of America: "In a different light."
- Asahi Glass: "The innovation of combined technologies."

The common element of all these headlines is that they are so general that they could be used interchangeably from ad to ad or company to company and no one would know the difference.

The MAGS Formula

If you want to break the mold and create corporate advertising that actually serves a useful purpose, you need to follow the *MAGS strategy.* MAGS stands for Mission, Audience, Goal, and Specifics. Let's take a look at each step in the formula:

Mission

First, define the *mission* of the ad, newsletter, or capabilities statement. What is its communications goal? What *message* is the ad supposed to communicate to your readers? Why are you telling them this? And how do you want them to respond?

Assign a single primary mission to each communication. Trying to get a single ad to pay equal attention to two or three objectives only dilutes the primary message. For example, if you want to do image advertising that promotes your company so that more college students will apply for a job, include a reply coupon that asks for a resume. Stress how your company is at the cutting edge of technology, how you offer more opportunities for advancement and more interesting work. Don't talk about dividends and stock prices—that isn't of primary interest to college seniors looking for an employer.

Audience

Drayton Bird, creative director of Ogilvy & Mather Direct, writes that there are four basic *audiences* for corporate advertising:

—the general public

—the investment community

—your customers

—your employees

The general public consists not only of consumers but also includes legislators, businesspeople, and opinion leaders.

The investment community includes not only your own shareholders but also portfolio managers, institutional investors, stock brokers, analysts, and individual investors. One expert in financial advertising states a rule that invariably holds true: The purpose of an ad aimed at the investment community is to convince the reader that your company has achieved a superior position in its industry by virtue of either a better product (e.g., a patented technology or innovative distribution or service) or aggressive marketing.

The third audience is a company's own customers. Bird points out that Starch Research in America revealed more than 30 years ago that customers are twice as likely to read a company's ads as any other group. They want assurance that the company they do business with is still the right choice.

The fourth audience is employees. Obviously, for small and medium-size firms, using space ads to reach employees is not cost-effective. But with a company like AT&T, which employs hundreds of thousands of people, ads provide a means of communicating corporate goals and directions to a wide audience, including those many workers.

An annual report or capabilities brochure will probably have to address all four audiences. It would not be practical to create four versions of your annual report, each aimed at one of these four audiences. For an ad, however, you should probably select one of the four audiences as your primary target audience and tailor the message to the needs of those readers.

Goal

Where the mission statement is broad, the goal is narrow and specific. The mission statement might be: "Promote XYZ Company as a leading employer and quality firm in the engineering field." The goal might be: "Increase the percentage of college recruitment interviews that result in XYZ hiring a new employee by 15 percent." If you are offering free reprints of your ad or a poster or free copies of your annual report, the goal might be based on the number of inquiries received per ad insertion.

Specifics

The final ingredient in the MAGS formula is specifics. You know what you want to say. Who you want to say it to. And why you want to say it. Now, you must gather the specific facts and figures that will make your message dramatic, believable, and concise.

Did you laugh when you read the corporate ad headlines from *Fortune* magazine? They are laughable because they're general and vague. *Specifics* are what make copy compelling and powerful. And this is especially important in corporate advertising, which suffers from the *superlative syndrome*—the substitution of vague generalizations, weak claims, puffy adjectives, and sound-alike cliches for hard facts, figures, and benefits that would make the reader believe the case the corporation is stating. Specifics cure this syndrome and make corporate advertising "come alive."

Nine Key Principles of Effective Corporate Advertising*

1. Put News in Your Corporate Advertising

Folks like to know what's going on, what's new. If there is no news value in a corporate ad, there is no investor value. If a reader does not come away from an ad with information he/she did not have before—some kind of discovery about your company—he/she will come away empty.

You've got to give them the facts, not the fluff. Not just pie charts and bar charts and numbers, but also the goals of your corporation—its activities, personality, and character.

> *Example:* A recent ad for Martin Marietta features a picture of a baby holding an orange ball. He is surrounded by numerous personal computers, each displaying a different basic shape on the screen. One shows a yellow triangle, another a pink oval. Not one of the computers is displaying the correct object—the orange ball. Headline reads: "We pitted this baby against a roomful of computers. Guess who won?" The copy goes on to explain that Martin Marietta has developed a new super computer chip with the power to process images better and faster. That is an example of giving relevant, interesting news.

2. Don't Contradict Yourself in Public

The message in your corporate advertising has to be consistent with your corporate strategy. As Tony Peterson, copywriter and executive for Atlantic Fasteners recently said, "The fastest way to get into trouble with your

**Note:* This material is excerpted, with permission, from Business/Professional Advertising Association White Paper No. 22.

customers is to offer a guarantee or service that you can't keep or deliver." When advertising claims do not reflect reality, the negative impression this inconsistency creates is tremendous, long lasting, and difficult if not impossible to overcome. As marketing expert Brian Cohen points out, "The marketplace is not very forgiving."

The message in your corporate advertising must be consistent with your corporate strategy. The ads must present a consistent picture of what your company is and where it is going. And you must maintain consistency throughout all your corporate communications. If you say one thing in an ad aimed at investors and another thing in a letter sent to shareholders, someone is going to spot the inconsistency and point it out. As management consultant Gary Blake says, "If you are inconsistent, then you are automatically wrong at least half of the time."

3. Continuity Increases Effectiveness

Most advertisers get tired of their ads before readers do. As a result, they change the ads before the old campaign has really had a chance to make a lasting impression on their audience.

Changing a campaign before it has run its course breaks your continuity and destroys momentum. "Pepsi-Cola has had about five images in my lifetime," observes copywriter Richard Armstrong. "Coca-Cola has had three images in the last three months. Madison Avenue's first instinct is to change a product and tell their customers that it is 'new and improved.' General advertisers take an overhaul approach to advertising: When an image shows signs of fading, they wipe it out and create a new one. Thus the $25 million that a client spends on one campaign will be rendered worthless by the $30 million he spends on the next."

As Tony Navarro, director of corporate communications for W.R. Grace and Company has said, "Familiarity breeds respect." In addition, continuity—use of an existing theme over and over for as long as it is effective—takes a lot less time and effort and costs less money than creating a new campaign from scratch.

An interruption in corporate advertising can also cause problems. For example, one company had been advertising steadily for years, with each ad featuring the introduction of a new and innovative product. When they hit a spell of not introducing any new products, they stopped advertising for about a year and a half.

They were surprised when reports came back from the field indicating that their customers thought they were giving up and that they were not committed to the market anymore. Their dominant market share started to erode. So they began running ads again, even though there were still no new products. Instead, ads stressed things customers wanted to hear, such as messages about quality and service. As a result they gained some of the ground they had lost.

It takes a lot of effort to recover from the loss of momentum and the loss of equity earned by a previous campaign. Companies are judged on the comforting continuity of earnings, growth, management, innovation, service, and leadership. To interrupt that continuity is to squander an asset. And continuity in corporate advertising is an effective way to achieve public recognition and reputation.

4. Use Slogans to Position the Company

A slogan or tag line is effective when it clearly positions the company for the long term or when it expresses the key point to be remembered about the company. For example, "GE: We bring good things to life." A slogan is good when it really says something.

Warning: Frequently, tag lines become outdated by events. That happens when they do not reflect the long-term positioning of the company and become outdated by changes in the company's management or mission. For instance, could you imagine a cigarette company still trying to use its old slogan, "Not a cough in a carload?" You can be sure that the Aids diet candy company, which had spent millions building up recognition of the Aids name as the leader in the diet candy field, was not happy when a new and fatal sexually transmitted disease shared the name.

A few slogan tips:

- Bad slogans often inhibit the creative process or get in the way of clear communication.
- Slogans are not always necessary.
- If you have a good slogan, use it on everything. Product ads, corporate ads, brochures. Everything.
- If you can't think of a good slogan, don't use any slogan.

5. Narrow the Target

Decide in advance to whom you are really talking. Is it Wall Street? Capitol Hill? the Pentagon? your vendors or customers? Narrow down the audience to the people who really count for you. Then fashion a message that is aimed directly at them. By focusing on a specific audience, you sharpen your message. The sharper the message, the deeper it penetrates. It will be more interesting to those it is aimed at, which means it will get read more and might even stick in their minds.

The broader your audience, the fuzzier your message and the reader's perception and understanding of your company.

6. Spend Enough to Accomplish the Task

Brand managers know their careers depend on the performance of their product in the marketplace. And in a well-run company, they don't go to market without an ad budget that's big enough for the task.

Do not create corporate ads if you do not have the budget to run them with sufficient reach and frequency to create awareness of your message. Spend enough for the task.

If you invest in corporate advertising at an exposure level too low to move a product, then it is certainly too low to change minds or reinforce image. Corporate advertising needs continuity and frequency to change attitudes and build perceptions.

As a rule of thumb, if your corporate message is out there fewer than eight times a year, no communication takes place. The key is frequency, not reach. It takes more to win a person's mind than it does to induce them to buy product. So spend enough on corporate advertising—or don't do it at all.

7. Fasten Onto One Idea in an Ad and Stick to It

Be tenaciously single-minded. Do not dilute your corporate advertising with a lot of competing ideas that are all stressed equally. Support the central idea with other ideas, but always allow one central idea to dominate.

If you have more than one central idea, then do a series of ads, each featuring a different idea. If you put all ideas into one ad, no one will know what to look at first.

The ideal corporate ad should stop the reader, grab his attention, hold his interest, engage it enough to get him to read the copy, and send him away with an idea planted firmly in his mind. Advertising studies show that a print ad has approximately three-tenths of a second to catch a reader's eye. But, once you do that, a print ad can win a reader's attention for as long as five minutes. Contrast that with a television commercial, which engages the viewer's attention for only 30 seconds.

8. Go Beyond the Facts to What is Really Important to Your Audience

Facts are important. Specifics engage. But facts alone are not enough. If you really want to stop people, you must appeal to their emotions.

Reaching your audience on an emotional level is difficult. People's emotions are insulated from what you have to say by other concerns. Anxieties, jobs, families, health problems, obligations.

To touch your audience's emotions, you must relate your corporate message to a basic truth to which people can relate. These truths are the trigger to set off the emotions, to get attention and involvement. Then, once you have engaged the reader's emotions, you use facts to support and strengthen your proposition, to establish credibility and convince them that what you are saying is true.

For example, if you are selling life insurance, and your company is the biggest and most successful life insurance company, you may want to get the message across that you are the leader—and that more people buy life insurance from you than from any other firm. But just saying you are the leader, or quoting statistics that show your whole life policies have the best investment values, is not going to engage the reader. What will engage readers is the emotional appeal of life insurance as a way to protect and provide for their families and loved ones should something happen.

9. Put a Consistent Personality in Your Corporate Ads

You don't necessarily need a spokesperson like Lee Iaccoca, Frank Purdue, or Victor Kiam—an actual person—to put personality in your ads. A company has a personality—an attitude, image, and pattern of behavior. Personality is a distinctive voice and character, an expression of the corporate culture of the company sponsoring the message.

IBM, for example, portrays a supportive personality in its ads. The message is, "Buy IBM because it's the safe bet and, even if it's not the most powerful computer or the best price, it's the right decision, because we give the best service and we ensure compatibility since IBM is the standard."

Once you establish this personality, make sure it comes across with consistency not just in ads designated as "corporate" but—to one degree or another—in all marketing communications your company produces. Whether it is labeled a corporate ad or a product ad, every communication you produce says something about your company and contributes to the reader's perception of your firm. The easiest way to make sure a reader remembers an ad after he tosses away the magazine is for the ad to be so consistent with your corporate personality.

This consistent building of personality cannot be done in one advertisement or in one campaign. It builds from ad to ad in a consistent creative treatment. Consistency must be maintained from product to product, division to division, from medium to medium, year after year.

Even though creative execution may evolve over time, it should still be identifiable with the corporate personality set when it all began. Be consistent in purpose, content, personality, voice, and visibility, and your corporate advertising will be consistently effective.

Annual Reports

Many large public companies spend a fortune producing lavish, glossy annual reports—far more than the SEC requires and far more than is usually warranted. According to a recent survey by Graphic Arts Center, an Oregon printing company, the average annual report is 44 pages long. An Illinois printer, Bradley Printing Company, reports that 85 percent of the annual reports of the *Fortune* 500 companies are written by in-house staff and that 13 percent are written by freelance writers and public relations firms. Only 1.2 percent of the *Fortune* 500 have their annual reports written by their ad agencies.

In his book *To Catch a Mouse, Make a Noise Like A Cheese,* Lewis Kornfeld says that the key audiences for the annual report are:

- employees
- Wall Street and the financial community
- present and future stockholders

"Aside from keeping old owners owning, the publication is often used to induce new people to become owners," he writes. "Your annual report is valuable for internal advertising, institutional PR, and conceptual selling." Kornfeld says the annual reports should try to do three things:

1. Be the first to inform readers of developments. "If you fail to do this, you will be preempted by some other medium in which your chance of looking the way you'd like to be seen is less than outstanding," he notes.

2. Don't promise. Too many companies make glowing promises and announcements of future plans which they have no chance of being able to keep. Stick with the facts. Don't "blue-sky." In the software industry, a product that is promised and in the talking stages but not actually delivered is called "vaporware." Make sure your annual report is grounded in reality, not vapor.

3. Use the annual report as a showplace for your people, your company, and your direction. Think of the annual report as a sales piece and your company as the "product."

Annual reports are generally presented in two parts. The first part tells the company's story in narrative form. For larger companies, this part might be divided into several subsections, each describing the activities and goals of a separate division, subsidiary, market group, or product line.

The second part consists mainly of numbers reported by the company's accounting firm. These numbers tell the story of the firm's financial fitness to analysts, portfolio managers, sophisticated investors, and other financial types who understand these things.

Do you need an annual report? Not if your business is small or privately held or if the scope of your product line and organization are fairly simple.

On the other hand, when your company goes public, when your business activities are diverse and complex, when your company grows and spreads across the country or around the world—then you might consider an annual report.

Publicly held companies are required by the Securities and Exchange Commission to publish an annual report that complies with established financial reporting guidelines. But the SEC does not require or even encourage corporate America's long-established obsession with turning annual reports into works of art.

Most annual reports you see today are fancifully produced—even overproduced. Glossy paper stock, a large number of pages, commissions for original sculpture and artwork and photography, far-out graphics, and special printing effects and papers can push the cost of producing an annual report from $50,000 to over six figures.

There is no law or requirement that says annual reports have to be so fancy; companies just like doing them that way. But there are plenty of sharp, crisp, interesting annual reports printed in 8 pages in two colors on plain paper. Too many companies overpresent themselves in annual reports, relying on size, color, and budget as substitutes for imagination and an interesting story to tell. The result? Reports that win design awards but turn off many current and would-be shareholders.

CHAPTER 21

Direct Mail

What is direct mail? And how does it differ from direct marketing, direct response, and mail order? *Direct mail* is unsolicited advertising or promotional material (that is material the recipient has not requested) sent to an individual or company through the mail. The typical direct mail piece consists of an outer envelope, a letter, a brochure, and a reply form or card. But there are many other formats and combinations. Some companies send a letter only. Others send "self-mailers" (folded brochures with no envelope or letter).

Direct response is any type of advertising that seeks some sort of reply from the reader. Direct mail is just one form of direct response advertising. Other examples include print ads with reply coupons and television commercials which ask you to call a toll-free number to make an inquiry or place an order.

Direct marketing is basically the same as direct response. It means that the advertising is designed to generate an immediate action on the part of the consumer. This contrasts with *general advertising* which aims at building an image or creating an awareness of a product or brand over an extended period of time rather than generate immediate response. *Mail order* is a way of doing business in which products are sold, ordered, and delivered solely by mail (although orders may be placed via fax or telephone) with no intermediaries such as salespeople, retail outlets, or distributors.

Direct Mail Is Growing

Because it generates an immediate, tangible response, direct mail is becoming more and more popular in this age of accountability and "immediate results." Advertising has always been difficult to "sell" to top management because such things as image, brand preference, awareness, or communication are difficult to measure. But with direct mail, you can easily point to a stack of inquiry cards or a bundle of checks or charge-card orders as tangible proof that your mailing worked.

This accountability factor makes direct mail both appealing and frightening to advertising agencies and advertising managers. Appealing because it generates the kind of immediate, tangible results that are easy to sell to management. Frightening because it can reduce the most arrogant advertising experts quickly to their knees as lofty theories and "breakthrough" campaigns are judged by results rather than aesthetics.

> *Example:* One firm, a publisher of tax guides for professionals, tested a creative versus a traditional direct mail approach to selling their books via mail order. The creative mailing, done by one of the top mail order consultants, was full of high-powered sales talk, made amazing promises, and was creatively conceived and designed.
>
> The traditional letter was more low-key, presenting more honestly the contents of the book in the context of how the book would benefit the reader. The results were that the traditional "dull" letter dramatically outperformed the creative approach. But—and this is the key point—you don't know what the result will be until you test your concept in the mail. As veteran copywriter Milt Pierce observes, "After 25 years writing direct mail copy I can easily spot a mailing that will bomb. *But I can rarely predict a winner.*"

According to *DM News*, national advertisers spent far more on direct mail in 1988—$21.2 billion—than any other category of advertising, and direct mail's growth rate for the year was surpassed only by cable and syndicated television. And according to *Direct Marketing* magazine, 93 percent of catalog marketers reported that they mailed more catalogs in 1987 than in the previous year.

In a speech at the "Semaine du Marketing Direct" given in Paris in January, 1986, David Ogilvy—founder of Ogilvy & Mather—discusses the philosophical differences between general advertising and direct marketing/direct mail:

> There is a yawning chasm between you Generalists and us Directs. We Directs belong to a different world. Your gods are not our gods.
>
> You Generalists pride yourselves on being "creative"—whatever that awful word means. You cultivate the mystique of "creativity." Your ambition is to win awards. You are the glamour boys and girls of the advertising community. You regard advertising as an art form and expect your clients to finance expressions of your genius.
>
> We humble people who work in Direct do not regard advertising as an art form. Our clients don't give a damn whether we win awards. They pay us to sell their products. We sell—or else. When you Generalists write an advertisement or commercial, you want everybody to congratulate you on your "creativity." When we write an advertisement or a direct mail package, we want people to order the product.
>
> When your commercials appear on television, you have no means of knowing whether they sell anything. There are too many other factors in the marketing mix. When sales go up, you claim the credit for it. When sales go down, you blame the product. We in Direct Response know exactly, to the penny, how many products we sell.
>
> We do everything differently. You Generalists use short copy. We use long copy. Experience has taught us that short copy does not sell.
>
> In our headlines, we promise the consumer a benefit. You Generalists don't think that it is "creative."
>
> You Generalists never give consumers any information about the product. We pack our letters with information about the product. We have found we have to—if we want to sell.
>
> Are you aware that Direct Response is growing twice as fast as general advertising? It is exploding. Soon it will become the tail wagging the dog.

Copywriter Richard Armstrong adds:

> Did anyone hear the keynote speech at Direct Marketing Day in New York this year? Can someone please tell me why we direct marketers always invite these clowns from Madison Avenue to be the principal speakers at our conventions? The speaker gave the usual condescending and ignorant perform-

ance that we've come to expect from these people. "Direct marketing used to be the ugly stepchild of general advertising, but now it's really come into its own. Aren't we general advertisers smart that we saw the huge potential of direct marketing and got into it when we did. Of course, you in direct mail still have a lot to learn from us, especially when it comes to creating an image for your product and forming emotional bonds with your customers." Blah, blah, blah.

Look, the first sign you're dealing with an idiot is when they imply that direct marketing is some kind of a spin-off or stepchild of general advertising. Anybody who says this simply doesn't know their advertising history. Actually, the exact opposite is true. In the beginning, virtually all advertising was direct response advertising. General advertising came much, much later.

We direct marketers were here before general advertising, and it looks like we will be here after general advertising is gone, which looks like it may be quite soon. The keynote speaker at DM Day showed a bunch of commercials that were exceedingly creative, often quite moving, beautifully produced, and, as near as I could tell, entirely unconcerned with selling the product. Some of the ads scarcely even mentioned the product.

Basics of Direct Mail Success

According to direct mail copywriter Mike Pavlish, there are seven basic steps in creating a successful direct mail campaign:

1. Pick the Best Mailing Lists

Choose your outside mailing lists with great care because they can make or break your mailing. Get list recommendations from at least three different *mailing list brokers* (a list broker is a firm or individual who rents mailing lists). The lists recommended most will probably be the most effective.

The best lists are generally those people who recently bought something similar to your offering in your price range by direct mail. Test many different mailing lists and test each list small first. Then you can gradually mail more pieces to the lists that generate the best results. This is the safest and surest way to go.

Mail to your own list of prospects and customers often. These proven interested people are your best prospects and surest profits in direct mail. Mail to your house list regularly; once a month is not too often. Change your envelope for each mailing so the prospect does not assume he has already got this mailing.

2. Use Your Biggest Customer Benefits in Your Headline and First Paragraphs

The reader is asking him/herself, "What's in it for me?" and "How will I benefit?" when he/she sees your mailing. If the headline and first paragraph don't immediately pile on all the wonderful customer benefits the reader will get, chances are your mailing will be pitched.

Don't talk about how good your company is. Don't be cute or funny. Instead, start by piling on all the benefits the reader will get. Be specific and positive with your customer benefits. And lay them on thick. Of course, if writing to professionals, the wealthy, or high-level executives, you should be a little more subdued. And if you make a real good offer, or offer something free, this should usually be mentioned in the headline or first paragraphs.

3. Use Hard Selling, Customer-benefit Copy

Throughout the mailing, continuously pile on the customer benefits the reader will get when he responds. Then prove your benefit claims and overcome objections. But remember, customer benefits are what sell.

Direct mail copy should sell about three times as hard as an in-person sales presentation. Hard selling, benefit-loaded direct mail copy is necessary because a sales representative is not there in person to use her charm, ask or answer questions, or overcome human inertia to get a response.

4. Make it Look Easy to Read

Not many people will read your direct mail if it looks hard to read, if it looks like "work", or if it looks boring or monotonous. Make your direct mail look easy to read, fun and exciting by:

—using subheads

—indenting a few key paragraphs

—using some short sentences and paragraphs

—underlining key words

—using wide margins

5. Make a Hard-to-resist, No-risk Offer

To get maximum response, develop and make hard-to-resist, no-risk offers to your prospects and customers. The less financial risk a buyer takes, the higher your response will usually be. This is why inexpensive "get acquainted" offers, free trials, discounts, and free bonuses work so well in direct mail.

Always try to put a time limit on your offers. The time limit works because it gets people to take immediate action. And always try to develop offers that involve no financial risk to the buyer by offering a money-back guarantee.

If your goal is sales leads, offer free printed information: a brochure, report, checklist, etc. The offering of free printed information usually increases the quantity of leads significantly.

6. Close Hard for an Immediate Response

After you've piled on the customer benefits, proven your claims, and made a great no-risk offer, close strong to get an immediate response. Most people naturally put things off. They need to be "nudged" to take immediate action. Your closing must be strong to get an immediate response or the reader probably never will respond, even if he intends to.

Close for immediate action several times—some subtle, some forceful. The main thing is to get the response *now.* Try to tie your closing in with telling the reader all the benefits he'll soon enjoy, what he'll lose if he doesn't respond now, by using a time limit, and by making hard-to-resist, no-risk offers. Use the P.S. of the letter to make an additional hard close.

7. Use Professionals

Businesses that are successful with direct mail view it as an ongoing program, not a one-shot, hit or miss attempt. And most hire professional direct mail ad agencies, graphic designers, consultants, or copywriters. The expertise of the professionals can and should make you many times over the fee they charge. So check out professionals. Chances are, it will pay off.

Sample Direct Mail Letter

The letter in Figure 21.1 is included not to be copied by you (it is copyrighted by the owner) but to show you an example of how to write a sales letter right. Note the short, punchy sentences, friendly, conversational style, helpful attitude, attention to detail and inclusion of specific factual product information, and the use of an offer, as suggested by Mike Pavlish. (NOTE: This letter is mailed to prospects who respond to the firm's ad in *Decor* magazine.)

Figure 21.1. Sample direct mail letter.

Thank you
for asking about . . .

. . . a new way to profit from old prints. A way that many other galleries have discovered. You can, too.

If you're selling *original, antique prints* now, here's a reliable source. It will strengthen your hold on this booming—*very* profitable—market.

To get started, just complete and mail the form enclosed. We'll phone to discuss your needs.

Then, we'll send a package of prints for your no-risk review: about $1,500 at trade prices.

You'll find hand-colored botanicals. Charming animals. Architecturals. Topographicals. Most are from the 18th and 19th centuries. No reproductions or restrikes. All originals. And guaranteed to be so.

And if the newsweeklies of the 19th century—such as *Harper's*—appeal to you—you'll tap a substantial inventory. Local reviews. Occupations. Genre scenes. Civil War events. Sports subjects. And much more.

Just review the prints. Pick what you want. And return the rest. It's as simple as that.

You can request a package as often as you like. Once a year. Every three months. Whenever there's a need. Lots of galleries make their selections and then say "Send another package, at once!" But it's entirely up to you.

And there's no minimum order required. No obligation. But you'll always find something special in every shipment. You'll invest your time wisely when you look through a package from Cobble Hill.

You have more questions, of course. So I've enclosed the answers to those most frequently asked.

But, really, the best way is to review an actual package. That will tell you all you want to know, quickly.

So discover this new way to profit from old prints, won't you? Please complete and mail the form enclosed. We'll phone you soon.

Cordially,

Florence Rosenblum, President
Cobble Hill Prints

P.S. Even if you're *not* interested, may I ask you to return the form anyway? There's a stamped, addressed envelope enclosed. Thank you.

Postage Considerations

Should you mail your direct mail pieces first-class or third-class? First-class delivery is speedier than third-class. In fact, third-class is notoriously slow. Further, some mail carriers treat third-class mail with indifference and contempt. There have been reports of third-class mail being dumped (illegally) by mail carriers rather than delivered. In fact, 11 percent of third-class mail is never delivered, according to an analysis of a huge, ongoing mail tracking study conducted by Mailing List/Users and Suppliers Association. The mail that was delivered took an average of 9.2 days to reach its destination.

The main reason to use third-class mail is cost savings. A one-ounce letter mailed first class requires 29 cents postage; a one-ounce letter mailed third class bulk-rate costs 19.8 cents to mail. This is a difference of $92 per thousand pieces mailed, which on a 100,000-piece mailing comes to a cost savings of $9,200. Most advertisers are happy to have the mail take 9.2 days rather than one or two days to arrive if they can save $9,200 in the process.

Further savings can be realized on third-class mail through sorting of mail. Third-class mail sorted by five-digit zip codes qualifies for a discount rate of 16.5 cents per letter provided you sort by zip code and have 200 or more pieces per zip code. Mail sorted by carrier route (the route each mail carrier walks to deliver the mail within a zip code) qualifies for an additional carrier presort discount enabling you to mail for 13.1 cents per letter.

Third-class bulk rate mail must be sorted and prepared in accordance with strict post office requirements. If you plan to do it yourself, go to your local post office and get a copy of their instruction manual for "Third Class Bulk Preparation Requirements." If it is unclear to you, ask your postmaster for clarification.

Most mailers do not prepare third-class mail in-house but use outside services called *letter shops.* A letter shop is a direct mail service firm that prepares mailings. You provide the printed pieces—the necessary quantities of outer envelopes, letters, brochures, and reply cards—to your letter shop. They will fold your material, insert it into envelopes, seal the envelopes, affix mailing labels, meter the envelopes or affix stamps, sort and bundle mail according to post office regulations, and deliver the mailings to the post office. Some letter shops also do printing and will even design your mailing for you.

What Does Direct Mail Cost?

There are two basic cost elements of direct mail. The first are one-time charges for creation, writing, and design of the piece. The second are the repeat costs of mailing that are incurred every time you print and mail the piece. They include printing, postage, letter shop costs, and mailing list rental.

Most direct mail professionals express the cost of doing a mailing as a cost per 1,000, which is the cost per 1,000 pieces mailed. When calculating this, they add up the printing, postage, list rental, and letter shop costs, multiply by 1,000, and divide by the number of pieces mailed. The one-time creative costs are usually not included in this calculation and are considered as advertising *overhead.* The formula for cost per 1,000 is expressed as:

$$CPM = (L_1 + L_2 + P_1 + P_2) \times 1{,}000/N$$

Where:

CPM = cost per thousand

L_1 = total letter shop charge

L_2 = total mailing list rental costs

P_1 = postage

P_2 = printing

N = number of pieces mailed

For most mailings, cost ranges from $300 to $700 or more per 1,000 pieces mailed, depending on quantity, format, and elaborateness of the piece. An average is $500 to $600 per 1,000 for a package consisting of a #10 outer envelope, two-page letter, small circular or folder, and reply card, printed in two colors in quantities of 10,000 or so.

The Importance Of Outer Envelopes

Your prospect's involvement with your mailing piece begins when he sees or picks up the envelope. It forms an impression. It either attracts interest or is a turn-off. The outer envelope design must not be accidental. It must be thought of and planned carefully.

In business-to-business direct mail, a common strategy is to make the envelope resemble a regular business letter. This is done by sending the mailing in a plain #10 business envelope with no advertising message or graphics (known as a *teaser*) on the outer envelope. The recipient's name and address is typed directly on the envelope to make it resemble a personally typed letter rather than a typical direct mail piece where a label is affixed.

In Publishers Clearing House and other sweepstakes type mailings, the opposite approach is used. The envelopes are made as flashy, promotional, and hard-sell as possible. Apparently, it works.

Although it is difficult to say with certainty what approach will work best in your mailing, here are three observations fairly well supported by hard test data:

Observation 1: Outer Envelopes Do Matter

How you design the outer envelope is not unimportant. It can make a big difference. One size, one headline, one color used instead of another can alter response as much as 25 percent. I have seen dramatic differences in split versions of three packages that were totally identical in every way—except that each had different teaser copy. So the envelope is not an afterthought but should be given primary consideration when it comes to copy, design, and method of production.

Observation 2: A Good Teaser May Increase Response

A good teaser will do the trick, but a bad teaser can actually reduce response. In split tests, blank or "blind" envelopes—those with no teaser copy or graphics—pulled up to 35 percent higher response than some with teasers. In other tests, teasers outperformed blank envelopes by the same margin. A good rule of thumb is as follows: If you are skilled at writing teasers, or have come up with a great teaser concept that seems a "natural" to you, by all means use it.

But if you don't feel competent at writing teasers, or nothing comes to mind, use a blank envelope. Don't force a teaser onto the envelope for the sake of having one. The wrong teaser, a dull teaser, or a teaser that is inappropriate can actually hurt response.

Observation 3: A Change in Envelope can Increase Response

It has been proven in renewal letters, billing letters, credit letters, and other repeat mailing series that varying the envelope size, design, and color from mailing to mailing increases response.

The reason usually given is that, if you use the same outer envelope, readers come to believe that they have already received your mailing and, therefore, don't bother to open any further letters from you. Russell Fuchs, president of Retrieval-Masters Creditors Bureau, observes that in collection letters a change in letterhead and, therefore, outer envelope will increase returns almost every time.

10 Ways To Add Interest To Your Outer Envelopes

Here are some additional envelope ideas—many of them reprinted courtesy of the Transo Envelope Company:

1. Use an Odd-size Envelope

Most direct mail envelopes are similar in size ranging from a 6 × 9" to a #10. Something that looks a little different from the rest is an odd-size envelope with perhaps an odd-size letterhead. One example of this would be a greeting card envelope. Another is the #11 envelope, which is the same shape as a #10 but slightly oversize.

2. Use Color Envelopes

Rather than always sending out the same white envelope, have a series of different colors and sizes so your package doesn't always look the same and somebody throws it out saying, "Oh, I already got this one." This isn't expensive. All you have to do is order your envelopes with color or paper changes.

3. Use a Textured Paper Stock

Unusual paper stocks can add high style but are also very expensive and often hard to get. A good way to simulate various textures is through overprinting grains such as leather, woodgrain, marble, stucco, and granite.

Or, ask your printer if he/she has leftover envelopes from other jobs. He/she may sell you fancy remainder envelopes for less than if you ordered them from the paper supplier simply because they are sitting around taking up space in his shop.

4. "Do Not Open Until [Date]."

A sure-fire way to get people to disobey your instructions and consequently to get into the envelope is to print on the envelope copy that says,

"Do not open until [date]." The tie-in copy might be something about the fact that this is a special offer not dated for the general public until such and such a time. However, since the reader "cheated" and looked anyway, you'll tell him/her the story and give him/her the special offer.

5. Bulk Rate Stamp

Most third-class bulk rate mailings have indicia (printed marks in the upper right corner bearing the postal permit number of the sender or letter shop) or are metered using a postage meter. If the choice is between indicia and meters, choose metering, even if your letter shop charges a slight premium. Indicia have the look and feel of third-class mail, but meters look like first-class.

However, there is a third option: Bulk rate stamps. These are available from the post office in coils, and, although they don't have quite the same impact as the first-class stamp, they still resemble a first-class mailing and should generate a higher response—or at least have fewer people throwing it away. Many letter shops have automated machinery for affixing these stamps at reasonable cost.

Please note that if you mail first-class, request that your letter shop affix first-class stamps rather than meter the mail. You might also want to stamp each letter, "FIRST CLASS," so recipients know they are getting a first-class letter rather than a third-class direct mail advertising piece.

6. Gift Wrap Your Package

Many people enjoy shopping by mail because when the package arrives, it's like Christmas. The way to capitalize on this is to decorate the outgoing envelope like a gift-wrapped box with printed ribbons wrapped around the corner. It's hard for anybody to throw away something that looks like a present.

7. Urgent or Express Mail

One way to get attention is to use envelopes that resemble Express Mail, Federal Express, telegrams, and other urgent or overnight communications. If you choose this approach, be sure to get written approval from your local postmaster for your outer envelope before you mail. The post office has strict rules about what is acceptable practice and what is not when it comes to envelopes that deliberately masquerade as urgent, express, or other "speed" formats.

8. Seals

Foil seals, affixed to the outer envelope, can help emphasize an offer or other special message (e.g., a 10th company anniversary) and draw attention to your mailing piece.

9. Bulky Mailings

Another sure-fire gambit is to put something inside the envelope that adds weight or is three-dimensional. People find bulky envelopes irresistible and must open them to see what is inside. A product sample or inexpensive premium makes an ideal mailing stuffer. Teaser copy can further arouse curiosity (e.g., "Your FREE [name of gift] enclosed!").

10. Simulate an Inter-office Envelope

This is an unusual format and not terribly expensive. It uses brown kraft with six punched holes in it so the yellow paper inside shows through, and it appears as if it's an inter-office memo. Because of the novelty of the device, people open it.

Reply Cards

Every mailing should contain at least three elements: the sales letter, the outer envelope, and a reply card or form. You can also add other elements such as a brochure, reply envelope, and other inserts, but the outer envelope, letter, and reply device are mandatory.

A simple *reply card:*

- Has a headline which repeats the offer or main selling proposition in a positive way and in the reader's voice (first-person) (e.g., "YES, I'd like to reduce my printing costs by 30 percent or more!").
- Enables the reader to order or request more information by checking off the appropriate boxed items (e.g., [ ] "Yes, please send me a free copy of your brochure" or [ ] "Yes, please enter my one-year subscription to KICK BOXING TODAY").
- In a lead-generating response device, you should offer both a hard and a soft option. A hard option requires personal contact between seller and prospect (e.g., "Yes, please have a salesperson call me"). A soft option typically involves the sending of more information with no personal

contact mentioned (e.g., "Please send me more information and sample wall fabrics").

- In a mail-order reply device, be sure to include complete details on price, guarantees, terms, conditions, as well as instructions on how to order. Spell out all order options. Give complete instructions.
- If no salesperson is going to follow-up by telephone, put on the reply card the following copy: "No salesperson will call." This will increase response.
- If making an inquiry or asking for a sample does not obligate the prospect to make a commitment or buy the product, add the phrase "no obligation, of course."
- Personalizing the response device, either by affixing a cheshire label with the prospect's name and address, or imprinting the reply card with the prospect's name and address using a laser or ink-jet system, makes it easier for the prospect to respond and thus will usually increase response.
- In the section of the card where you require the prospect to fill in name, address, and other personal information, leave plenty of room for him or her to write in the information.
- Instead of "Name" on the first line of this section of the reply card, put "Mr./Mrs./Ms./Miss______________." According to Bob Jurik, chairman of Fala Direct Marketing, 80 percent of prospects will circle the appropriate prefix.

  As a result, you find out whether your customers are predominantly male or female, and you can tailor your direct mail accordingly. You also capture sex information for your customer database, enabling you to correctly address future mailing to these prospects as well as tailor separate male/female versions of your sales letters, if appropriate.

- Use a business reply card instead of asking the prospect to supply postage. This increases response in consumer mailings and makes you look more professional to business prospects.
- Instead of printing your reply cards on plain white stock, use a bright color such as blue, yellow, salmon, canary, gold, or green. Using a different color makes the reply card stand out from the letter and other elements, increasing response. In one recent test, Scott Paper found that a blue reply card outpulled a white reply card (identical in every other respect but color) by approximately 30 percent.

The Importance Of Testing

Because direct mail results can be easily and precisely measured, you can test various approaches, formats, and packages to determine what works best.

Nothing is guaranteed to work; only a test will tell whether a particular mailing is better or worse than other mailings you've done before it. A case in point is the Scott Paper test: It is one thing to *theorize* that colored reply cards will outpull white; only a test makes it true and meaningful.

One important factor to test in mail order promotions is price. One firm selling a cassette album tested three prices:

(a) $79.95
(b) $89.95
(c) $99.95

Which do you think was the winner? Surprisingly, the lowest price is not always the best, because price affects people's perception of your product and its value. After all, which brain surgeon would you want to go to—the one who charges $3,000 for an operation or the one who says his bill is $30?

For the cassette album, (b) was the winner. The $99.95 price did not pull any orders. But the $89.95 beat $79.95 by a 5:3 ratio.

This same advertiser performed another interesting test. In his mailings, he illustrated his letters with photos in the upper right corner of page one. His question: Was it better to show a picture of the cassette album itself or of the speaker/writer/producer of the program? He tested two packages, one with a picture of the album and one with his picture. The mailing with the picture of the cassette album produced 40 percent more sales than the mailing with the man's picture—and he is good looking. His conclusion: It is best to picture the item being sold, not the seller.

Another firm, a newsletter publisher, tested a variety of mailing formats including direct response postcards, double postcards (a small self-mailer consisting of two attached postcards, one of which can be detached and mailed as a business reply card), and traditional #10 direct mail packages. They found that on post card deck mailings, the best offer was a free sample issue with the option to write "cancel" on the invoice if not satisfied. Thirty percent of respondents cancelled but the low cost of postcard decks made the medium cost-effective.

Although double postcards are being hyped as the new "super medium" in direct mail, they were not clear winners and did not outperform (either on a total sales or cost-per-order basis) conventional #10 direct mail packages.

It is important to keep in mind that tests don't instantly result in iron-clad rules. Unlike physics, where universal laws hold true throughout the entire universe, test results are valid only for the product, offer, and time period during which they were obtained. What this means is that you can use the test results of others as a guideline only, not an absolute dictum. Only the test results for your own mailings tell you what works—and what doesn't—for you.

The Four Rules Of Testing

Rule 1: Key Code

Key coding means adding a key to the mailing label so you can identify which "test cell" (group of test mailings) a particular response has come from.

The list broker renting the names can key code labels for you for a slight extra charge—usually $1 or $2 per 1,000 labels.

For key coding to work, you have to make sure you put the right labels on the right mailing pieces. For example, if you are testing two letters with the same reply card, affix labels with key code "A" on those reply cards going into envelopes containing letter A; affix "B" labels on package B reply cards.

Another obvious but sometimes overlooked fact is that if you want to count response by key code, you must design your mailing so that the label comes back with the reply card. For instance, in a lead-generating direct mail package, you affix the label directly to the reply card, which shows through a window on the outer envelope.

You can also key code telephone responses. For instance, you can add copy after the phone number that says "ask for Andy" or "ask for extension 222." "Andy" could be a key code for mailing piece A; "Extension 222" could be a key code for mailing piece B, and so on.

Rule 2: The Single Variable Rule

To find out the effect of changing a variable in the mailing, your test can alter only one variable at a time. For instance, if you want to test whether a colored reply card increases response, the color of the reply card should be the *only* element that is changed between package A and package B. They should be identical in all other respects. If package B also has a different brochure or offers the product at a different price or has any other variables changed, then you cannot make any valid conclusion about the effect of changing the reply card color.

Rule 3: The 2,000 Name Rule

How many pieces must you test to get a statistically valid response? Several books, including *The Complete Direct Mail List Book* and *The Basics of Testing* present statistical tables used to determine how many pieces you must mail, based on the degree of accuracy of results desired and the anticipated response rate.

Without going into the details, a safe rule of thumb is that you should mail 2,000 pieces in each test "cell" to consider the results statistically valid. So if you are testing package "A" against package "B," you need to mail 2,000 As and 2,000 Bs.

Rule 4: The Roll-Out Rule

Let's say you have a list of 2 million names and a test of 2,000 proves your mailing works. Can you predict the same results will hold true for the entire list based on that small sampling and "roll-out," and send your test package, to the full list at once? No.

A safe rule of thumb to follow is that your roll-out should be no more than ten times the size of your test cell. Thus, if you test 2,000 names and get a good result, you can roll-out to 20,000. If you then mail 20,000, and the results hold steady, you can safely go to 200,000—and then to 2 million.

Choosing Mailing Lists

According to Steve Roberts, president of Edith Roman Associates, a mailing list broker, there are approximately 30,000 different mailing lists available for rental representing a combined database of some one billion names. "There are few persons in the United States whose names are not on at least one of these mailing lists." Most lists are provided as "cheshire labels," a format that letter shops can easily affix to envelopes using automated equipment designed for that purpose.

Lists are also available on pressure-sensitive labels, but these should not be ordered since they are not easily affixed by machinery and most letter shops will charge you extra for handling them. The only time to use pressure-sensitive labels is in small mailings you are assembling by hand in-house.

If you are going to computer-personalize your mailing, you can order your list from the list broker on magnetic tape or floppy disk instead of labels. Letter shops can personalize using three basic methods: ink-jet, impact, and laser. An ink-jet machine literally sprays the recipient's name and address onto the envelope, letter, or reply element. Although it is the least expensive method, it least resembles a personally typed letter.

Impact letters are formed by striking an inked ribbon which leaves ink on the paper, just like your typewriter or the printer you use with your personal computer. Impact can be costly and slow, but is frequently used for mailings requiring an urgent or telegram-like appearance.

Laser printers use an electromagnetic process. Charged particles adhere to the entire sheet, and the computer determines which stay on and which stay off. Lasers are the fastest method, provide the maximum flexibility in type style (and can even reproduce handwritten signatures on letters), and look most like a professional, hand-typed letter.

If you want to measure the response to your mailings, you should either affix the cheshire label or ink-jet or laser the recipient's name and address onto the reply form, so you get the label back when the reader uses the reply element to respond. Be sure to tell the list broker to add a "key code" to the label. The key code tells you which mailing list the label is from, so you can compare relative response rates generated by the different mailing lists you are testing.

Mailing lists are one of the key elements that should be tested—perhaps the most important element if you are a consumer marketer mailing large volumes. Experience proves that the same mailing piece sent to the best-performing list can generate over *10 times* the response as that mailing sent to the worst-performing list. But—and this is the key point—you cannot predict which list will be best or worst. You can guess, but you can't know for sure. Only testing reveals it.

So, if you mail large volumes, you should test 2,000 to 5,000 names per list on those lists you think are likely candidates. Then, evaluate the results and mail only to those lists which prove profitable in testing. The initial test mailing itself is unlikely to prove profitable, but you *will* find that one or two *lists* in the test are productive. You then mail the bulk of your pieces to these lists only to have an overall profitable program.

How many lists to test? The more, the better. Direct marketing consultant Ken Morris advises clients to test a minimum of five lists and preferably eight lists, along with one or two postcard decks. If you are conducting a test program, do not forget to have the list broker key code your reply cards.

What do lists cost to rent? It depends on the type of list. *Compiled* lists, or lists taken from various published sources (Yellow Pages, industry directories, etc.) are least expensive, costing around $50 per thousand. Response lists are lists of people who have responded to previous mailings from other companies and purchased products through direct mail. These lists are more expensive, ranging from $75 to $125 per thousand or more. Adding key coding results in a small additional charge, usually only $1 or $2 per thousand.

Which type of list is best for you? It depends. Compiled lists are best when you want to ensure complete coverage of prospects fitting a certain description. For example, if you want to reach all accountants and lawyers in Michigan and Florida, only a compiled list can accomplish that.

However, if you are asking for the order directly from your package (i.e., selling "mail order" as opposed to trying for leads) response lists are your best choice. Compiled lists rarely work for mail order offers, because research shows that one-third of Americans do not buy via mail. Thus, there is tremendous waste on compiled lists for mail order marketers. Response lists usually promise that 95 percent or more of the people on the list are direct mail buyers. (Look for the phrase "95 percent direct mail generated" in the data card or spec sheet describing the list.)

In mail order selling, your best prospect, as Mike Pavlish points out, is someone who has bought something similar to what you are selling, at a similar price, and done so recently. Thus, if you are promoting a $795 seminar on "Effective Direct Marketing," look for lists of people who have attended other high-priced seminars in your geographic region on advertising and marketing topics.

Sometimes, you don't want to mail to an entire list, but just a portion. For instance, women only. Men only. Managers and not workers. People over 50. People under 30. Check the *data card* (the brochure or flier giving a description of the list) to see what selection factors are available. There is usually a $5 per thousand charge for each selection factor chosen. But experience proves that making intelligent selections usually more than pays back this $5 per thousand cost.

If you target geographically, you must tell the list broker which zip codes you want to select. You cannot simply say, "Names within 50 miles of Rochester, NY"; *you* must provide the correct zip codes; the broker will not do it for you. For this reason, you need a good zip-code map showing the five-digit zip codes for every region of the United States.

One proven method for reducing mailing lists is called *merge/purge,* which means the lists you order are run through a computer to eliminate duplicate names. For instance, if a name appears on three of your five lists, and you don't do a merge/purge, you will get the name on three labels, and that person will receive three copies of your package.

But if you do a merge/purge, two of the three labels having that person's name will be eliminated and he or she will get only one package.

When should you merge/purge? Consultant Art Yates says that the duplication factor runs 10 to 25 percent for business lists and up to 40 percent for consumer lists, and that merge/purge pays when mailing 50,000 names or more. Minimum processing charges for a merge/purge are around $1,000, says Yates.

Tips On Designing Direct Mail Brochures

Not all direct mail packages require a brochure; often a letter alone can be extremely effective. So when do you need a brochure? The old saying in direct mail is, "The letter sells; the brochure tells." Letters are used to make a strong sales pitch and get a response. Brochures play a *supporting* role, providing information, facts, and photos and drawings that back-up the claims made in the letter.

According to the Petty Co., a direct mail printer:

> Brochures receive their impact from a combination of strong four-color art and clever folding techniques. When striving for a luxury look for a deluxe product, use four-color process on coated stock. Using special metallic inks can deliver impact that provides a list in response that will pay for itself.
>
> Attention-getting design is required when you are planning to execute a deluxe brochure. Graphic images that are overlapping are a significant way to keep the prospect moving through your piece.
>
> Strategic overlapping of folds leads the reader to each element of your sales story, while building excitement and enhancing the offer as the person reads.
>
> In photographs, have models demonstrate the product in a way that a standard product shot cannot. Photo-sequence action shots are a good way to build action or excitement into your brochure and save money on separations if the shots are all the same size. Photographs should also be prominent to achieve maximum attention-getting power.

Check out the feasibility of any fold running the full depth of the piece. Ask the printer if the stock selected can take the number of folds you want without cracking on the fold mark.

Exciting die-cut edges in provocative shapes on the opening edge can achieve interest in a brochure by their ability to attract attention.

By far your most expensive investment is in the printing. And it should be noted that the most cost-intensive part of printing is the paper. For instance, on the printing of a 22-½ × 35″ four-color brochure, the cost of the paper is $7,500 out of a total cost of $14,000, or 54 percent of the cost.

The cost of stock absorbs 36 percent to over 50 percent of the job. The kind of stock you select for your printing will have the most influence on what your printing costs.

Request samples of paper of varying styles (dull versus gloss coated), different opacities, varying weights. Match them against one another. Ascertain their availability on roll-out quantities. Ask your printer how the stock prints. Test-run a sample if you can, or examine other printed samples.

Getting Past The Secretary

In business-to-business direct mail, a special concern is getting past the secretary. The problem is that many secretaries screen mail for their bosses and throw away items they judge unimportant. Thus, a direct mail envelope design that might intrigue a consumer or even a business executive has the unfortunate effect of tagging your mailing piece as "junk mail" which the secretary safely assumes she has the authority and responsibility to eliminate from the boss's mail pile.

According to a research study from Ogilvy & Mather Direct, most executives do not open their own mail. Fifty-eight percent of top executives and 51 percent of middle managers have their secretaries open their mail for them. And half of the executives who have secretaries open mail also have secretaries screen mail. Therefore, it is important to devise ways to ensure that your mailing will survive this screening. The Ogilvy & Mather study is based on a survey of 500 business executives.

Richard Kerndt, president of The Richmark Group, conducted his own study by interviewing 53 secretaries of presidents or general managers in divisions of large corporations.[14] The study found that 87 percent of these secretaries see themselves as the "gatekeepers" of all mail flowing into the executive suite. It further shows that to be successful in surviving this screening process, mailers should follow these key rules:

- Acknowledge that the secretary or administrative assistant is the initial audience.
- Use a design that connotes image and quality, rather than the consumer hard-sell approach.
- Create mailings that are short, simple, and easy to understand.
- Use personalization.
- Use accurate mailing lists so the right mailings are sent to the right audience.

As a *rule of thumb,* the higher the executive is on the corporate ladder, the more the mailing should look like a personally typed business letter and the less promotional in nature it should be. The lower you go on the corporate ladder, the more you can use nonpersonalized mail and a more promotional approach.

Tip: One way to force your way past the secretarial "gatekeeper" is to send the executive something that the secretary feels she or he cannot pass judgment on or does not have the authority to discard without first showing it to the boss. One company accomplished this by mailing videocassettes presenting a "motion picture" version of their brochure on tape. Another put their message on audio cassette and mailed it to CEOs *with a Sony Walkman tape player* included in the package. Another tactic is to mail a book, a special report, or a nice premium personalized with the recipient's name.

How To Get More Leads From Your Mailings

If you are trying to generate leads rather than sell via mail order from your direct mail, these tips from Mike Pavlish can help you generate more inquiries:

- Get your special offer high up in the letter. Everyone is tempted by a good offer. Make sure they see it fast. Especially if it's a free offer. (See the checklist in Figure 21.2 for ideas on free offers.)
- If offering something free, put it on the outside envelope.
- Offer printed information—a booklet or pamphlet. The offer of free printed information hikes response.

Figure 21.2. Checklist of basic direct mail offers.

- ☐ Free brochure
- ☐ Free booklet
- ☐ Free catalog
- ☐ Free special report
- ☐ Free newsletter
- ☐ Free information kit
- ☐ Free seminar (invitation to attend)
- ☐ Free information
- ☐ More information
- ☐ Free trial
- ☐ Free use of product
- ☐ Free product sample
- ☐ Free gift certificate
- ☐ Free coupon
- ☐ Use of toll-free hotline
- ☐ Free advice
- ☐ Free consultation
- ☐ Free survey
- ☐ Free analysis
- ☐ Free estimate
- ☐ Free problem evaluation
- ☐ Free product demonstration
- ☐ Have a technical representative call
- ☐ Have a sales person call
- ☐ Add me to your mailing list
- ☐ Not interested right now because:______________________
  (please give reason—thank you)
- ☐ Not interested right now. Try me again on______________________
  (month/year)
- ☐ Free audio cassette
- ☐ Free videotape or film
- ☐ Free gift (with your inquiry)
- ☐ Free gift (enclosed with mailing)
- ☐ Free gift (for providing the names and addresses of friends or colleagues who might be interested in our offer)

Figure 21.2. (continued)

☐ Free sample issue

☐ Free information to qualified prospects only—others pay X dollars

☐ Free information if requested on your company letterhead

- Put a time limit on your offer.
- Use involvement devices on your reply card. Check-off boxes work well.
- Use a hard-selling P.S. Feature a big benefit and call for immediate action.
- Use testimonials from satisfied customers.
- Use at least a two-page letter. It will almost always outpull a 1-page letter because more sales copy can be used to convince the reader.
- Don't put your company name on the envelope if you regularly mail to the same people. And vary the appearance of your envelope. Otherwise, people will know what's inside and pitch it.
- Try a blank envelope with no teaser copy. It often works better than using envelope copy. Curiosity says "open me."
- Close hard for a response right NOW. Tell the reader why they should respond today. Tell them what they lose if they don't, because 95 percent of readers won't respond "later," even if they intend to. It's now or never.
- Don't talk about your company unless a customer benefit is in the same or next sentence. Readers don't care that you're the biggest company. They care if you're the biggest if that means they get better service.
- List ALL the benefits. Stress the most important one. But also list the others. The one extra benefit in your list might be what gets a reader to respond.
- Tell the reader how popular your product is. People like popular, proven things. They figure it must be good.
- Tell your prospects what they care about most: how much money they'll make. Extra profits are a sure-fire, never-fails benefit. Be specific.
- If your prospects don't think they need your product, develop the problem they have first, then give the solution. If they don't perceive a problem, they won't be open to your solution.
- Say that there is no obligation to buy. Even if readers assume it, they are more likely to respond if you stress it.
- Include your telephone number. Many people prefer to call rather than write, especially those with an immediate need.
- Always use a separate detached reply card.

Resources

For more information on direct mail, contact the Direct Marketing Association, Inc., 11 W. 42nd Street, New York, NY 10036-8096, phone (212) 768-7277. Ask for the free booklet, "Information Central," as well as information on becoming a member.

Two good newsletters covering the field are:

What's Working, 4550 Montgomery Avenue, Suite 700 North, Bethesda, MD 20814-3382.

Who's Mailing What!, P.O. Box 8180, Stamford, CT 06905, 203-329-1996.

A key directory of suppliers and vendors serving the needs of firms who use direct mail is *DMMP: The Direct Marketing Market Place,* Hilary House Publishers, Inc., 980 North Federal Highway, Suite 206, Boca Raton, Florida 33432, phone (407) 393-5656.

For a more detailed discussion of direct mail see my book *Direct Mail Profits: How to Get More Leads and Sales by Mail,* available from Caddylak Systems, Inc., 131 Heartland Blvd., PO Box 1322, Brentwood, NY 11717, 800-523-8060.

Specifications for producing cheshire labels according to the proper dimensions and format are available from Cheshire, 404 Washington Boulevard, Mundelein, IL 60060-3190. Request "Cheshire Label Format Instructions."

For a detailed discussion on personalized direct mail, request "Should I personalize? A direct marketer's guide to personalized mailing" from Fala Direct Marketing, 70 Marcus Drive, Melville, NY 11747-4278, phone 516-694-7493.

The best zip code guide is *Zip Code Atlas & Market Planner,* available from Rand McNally & Company, 8255 Central Park, Skokie, Illinois, 60076, phone 800-332-RAND or 312-673-9100.

For a free copy of "The Direct Mail Encyclopedia," a comprehensive guide to available mailing lists, call toll-free 800-223-2194. Or write to Edith Roman Associates, 293 West 35th Street, 16th Floor, Avenue of the Americas, New York, NY 10001.

CHAPTER 22

Postcard Decks

An Introduction To Postcard Decks

A *postcard deck* is a group of direct response postcards mailed to a list of prospects. A direct response postcard is a postcard that combines an ad and a response vehicle on a 3½ × 5½″ piece of stiff paper.

Typically, the front of the card, known as the *mailing side,* contains the mailing address of the advertiser and is designed so that the card will be mailed back to the advertiser when it is dropped in the mail box. The mailing side is typically a business reply card, although some advertisers require the prospect to affix a stamp.

The back of the card is the *advertising side.* It contains a small ad or "sales pitch" for the product: typically a headline, small picture, and a few lines of copy.

A third element is a coupon area where the prospect can fill in his name and address to place an order or receive more information. The coupon can be located either on the mailing side (in the upper left corner of the card) or the advertising side (usually at the bottom of the panel).

As an advertiser, you have two choices when it comes to doing postcard deck advertising: You can pay to insert your card in one of the many decks that accept advertising, or you can create your own postcard pack containing numerous postcards for the various products you offer. The latter option will work only if you sell a line of related products.

According to Ed Werz, a consultant specializing in postcard deck advertising, the use of direct response postcards is on the upswing.[1] "A decade ago, only a handful of decks existed. Today, one can count nearly 700 postcard decks with new publications added every month."

The average deck, says Werz, is published three times a year with a circulation of 75,000. "As a medium, postcard decks are low cost, highly responsive, quick-to-react, and extremely measurable," adds Werz. "No wonder thousands of advertisers are adding card decks to their media schedules each year."

Robert Luedtke, co-author of *Merchandising Through Card Decks* (Solar Press), says inquiry cards will occasionally generate up to a 2 percent response per card in a pack of 60 to 70 cards. Bill Norcutt, author of *Secrets of Successful Response Deck Advertising,* says that the cost per lead for inquiries generated from card decks is generally $2 to $20 and can be as low as 50 cents. This compares favorably with $15 to $30 per lead generated by a full-scale direct mail package and $80 from an industrial ad in a trade journal.

"A top, top card (information request) could pull 1 percent of the total deck circulation," says Norcutt. "I have heard of some offers pulling 2 percent, and in some very specialized decks as much as 5 percent, but these are exceptions, not the rule." Norcutt says the average to expect would probably be around ½ of 1 percent. Business-to-Business, Inc., a postcard deck publisher, says that typical response to a postcard is between ¼ of 1 percent to 1 percent of the deck's circulation.

Number of responses and percentage response depend, to a large extent, on your product. If you are selling a low-priced product that is frequently ordered by prospects, such as supplies, response may be higher than if you are selling an expensive piece of capital equipment that few prospects are likely to need or can afford.

Other factors affecting response are newness and uniqueness. If you make an offer that has been overdone in the decks, your response may be disappointing. However, if you run a card for a new, unusual offer with strong appeal and interest, response will be higher.

14 Ways Card Decks Can Build Your Business

According to Ed Werz, here are 14 ways you can use postcard decks to generate more business:

1. *Sell product.* Product can be sold right from the card. Items that sell for $100 or less are most effective. Bill Norcutt says that if you offer a "bill-me" option, 50 percent of those who order in response to a postcard will pay your bill, 30 percent will return the merchandise, frequently in unsalable condition, and 20 percent will not pay at all.

2. *Generate sales leads.* Use the card to create interest in products or services. Qualify the prospect with questions about the immediacy of his or her needs. Don't forget to ask for a phone number so the sales force can make contact.

3. *Distribute literature.* Use postcard decks to generate inquiries for literature or catalogs. Show a picture of your company's new catalog. Tell how many new products are featured. Offer both a toll-free number and an order coupon.

4. *Offer free samples.* Ask the prospect to send for a free sample or actually insert the sample in the deck. Consultant Ken Morris, who specializes in direct marketing of hi-tech products, says postcard decks are an ideal medium for generating interest in software via the offer of a free demo diskette.

5. *Prospect for new customers.* Use postcards to get new buyers at little or no cost. Offer a "loss leader" (an item advertised at a low price in order to attract buyers whose names can be added to your customer list) or heavily discounted items. The sales will offset the advertising cost. You can also use postcards to offer "self liquidators" (premiums or samples having a cost fully covered by the purchase price).

6. *Introduce new products and services.* Get the jump on the competition. Blitz the marketplace through card deck advertising before anyone can make a counter move.

7. *Test.* Test copy, price, design, or offer. Many decks will let you run an A-B split (e.g., test the headline "SAVES MONEY" against "EASY TO INSTALL"). It's an inexpensive way to test price points, headlines, or other elements. Often, the information gained can lead direct mail efforts.

Robert Luedtke, director of marketing for a firm serving the medical markets, tells how he split-tested five headlines for a seminar titled "Management & Marketing Essentials for the Dental Practitioner." The five headlines were:

A. Build Effective Team Leadership
B. Big Marketing Results from a Small Budget
C. Increase Referrals
D. Creating a Unique Practice Image
E. Increase Patient Flow

Can you guess which were the winners? Headline E—"Increase Patient Flow"—generated twice as many inquiries as the others. Apparently, dentists want patients more than they want to build team leadership, get big marketing results, create an image, or even increase referrals.

8. *Test mailing lists at low cost.* Before renting a list for direct mail, run a postcard in the owner's card deck, if he has one. A small investment will provide a good indication of the list responsiveness.

9. *Test new markets.* Place a card in a vertical market deck before trying direct mail, or test a few markets for the cost of testing one market via direct mail or space advertising.

10. *Reduce excess inventory.* Overstocked or discontinued items can be easily liquidated via post card ads.

11. *Build a list.* Run a free sample, free demo diskette, free catalog, or free brochure offer to bring in new names.

12. *Research inexpensively.* A survey card placed in card decks can help acquire valuable information about customers, products, and markets.

13. *Build corporate awareness.* Card decks can be a low-cost means of distributing news about a company.

14. *Support telemarketing.* Card decks can quickly generate fresh names for telemarketing reps or salespeople to telephone.

How To Develop A Card Pack Test Campaign

Let's say you want to spend a portion of your marketing communications budget on post card decks to support print advertising, direct mail, and other activities. Robert Al Degaetano, writing in the newsletter of the Direct Marketing Club of New York, outlines the steps to take:

First, consult an expert. Card packs are a unique vehicle with special features, warns Degaetano. Many ad agencies, copywriters, and consultants who know direct mail or print advertising may not be familiar with postcard decks or how to use them.

Second, identify target markets and media. In addition to your primary markets, make a list of secondary markets. Because of the low cost per thousand of card decks as opposed to other media, you can afford to advertise in secondary-market card decks even if you can't afford to run ads in those industry magazines or do solo mailings to their mailing lists.

Identify specific decks in these markets. Find out the source of the names (where the card deck mailer gets his mailing lists and which ones he/she uses), the packaging used, and the names of some of the regular advertisers. If your competitors repeatedly run postcards in the deck, that's a good sign the deck would work for you.

Third, develop several different offers. Test price, payment terms, headline, copy, place stamp here versus business reply mail, etc.

Take note that some publishers may try to get you to use their card packs with a per inquiry offer, where you pay a fee per lead or order generated. One of the largest of these publishers, Select Information Exchange, charges advertisers 45 cents per sales lead. The benefit is that there is no risk: if the card pack doesn't perform, you don't pay.

Fourth, locate a control. A control is the deck that will perform best for your offer. The best deck is probably a card pack that mails to a list you have used successfully or goes to the subscriber list of the top trade magazine in which you advertise.

When using this pack, design your postcard so it closely resembles your most successful solo mailing or trade ad. The card deck response rates will give you a correlation factor between mediums. By comparing the cost per inquiry between the space ads in the publication and sending a direct mail piece to its subscriber list and running a postcard in its card pack, you will be able to determine which medium (space, direct mail, cards) is most cost-effective.

Fifth, split test the control deck. Create different variations on your basic card and test them in the control pack. For example, you might test three sales appeals expressed in three different headlines (e.g., SAVES MONEY, INCREASES PRODUCTIVITY, REDUCES MAINTENANCE COSTS) to see which appeal generates the highest response. Or, you might test a postcard featuring the product ("New Zinger Widget Gives Better Performance") against a postcard that stresses a free literature offer ("Free Zinger Widget Catalog").

Split tests generally result in an extra insertion cost of from 60 cents to $2.25 per thousand names, which on a 75,000-name deck runs from $40 to $168.65 (The base cost can be anywhere from $800 to $1,600 or more.) Says Robert Degaetano, "A great deal of information can be obtained using split testing at a very modest cost."

Sixth, once you have tested cards, test decks. Run your most successful card in a number of decks. Depending on your testing budget, it is often wise to test one or two card packs in each market. Remember, card packs can prove profitable in markets never before considered possible.

Seventh, develop a campaign. Schedule postcard insertions in good card decks three or four times a year to ensure a steady flow of responses. Be prepared to change your schedule depending on performance.

Card decks offer the benefit of rapid response that can easily be measured and analyzed. Unlike space advertising, brochures, and mail, the *only* purpose of a postcard deck is to generate direct response. A card is good or not good depending on how much response it pulls relative to other cards. If something is not working, change it or drop it.

12 Secrets Of Card Pack Advertising Success

1. Use Card Decks as Part of an Overall Campaign

Although card decks are amazingly inexpensive, responsive, and cost-effective, there are not enough card deck mailings going to your prospects to allow you to rely solely on card deck advertising to promote your product or service.

"Don't use packs as an isolated medium," advises Don Rappaport, chairman, American List Counsel. Make them part of your overall advertising strategy. Use ads to build image, direct mail to educate prospects and make them understand your new technology, and postcard decks to generate a large quantity of inquiries at low cost.

2. Use Postcards to Qualify Your Prospects

"Many industrial advertisers have long learned that direct-response cards can generate a lower cost inquiry than almost any other medium," observes Jim Alexander, president, Alexander Marketing Services. "But postcards offer another opportunity that few seem to have learned."

The difference between an ad and a postcard, notes Alexander, is that to respond to a trade ad the prospect merely circles a number on a reader service card or makes a phone call, telling you nothing about himself.

With a postcard, on the other hand, the prospect must fill in his name and address to respond.

"What a perfect opportunity to ask for a simple declaration to qualify his interest," says Alexander. "Like, 'I may have an application involving ______ gallons per minute at ______ pounds per square inch and ______ degrees Celsius.' Readers who fill this out—and a surprising number will—have identified a current need and deserve priority follow-up from the field. That's how our clients make their postcards more productive and how you can, too."

3. Convert Proven Postcards into Successful Ads

Jim Alexander says he frequently takes fractional ads created for magazines and converts them into postcard format by adding lines for the respondent's name and address. "We do it for our clients all the time," he notes.

Jim Morris, senior account executive for The Kingswood Group, takes the opposite approach. If a postcard pulls well, Morris will convert it to a black-and-white, quarter-page ad for placement in trade publications. "This provides a cost-effective 'second tier' to a larger space campaign."

4. Tiny Billboards

The key to improving the impact of postcards is to treat them as if they were tiny billboards, says Jim Morris. "Use provocative headlines and graphic devices that focus in on essential benefits—and on the offer, call for action, or a toll-free number," he writes.

5. Horizontal Versus Vertical Cards

Most people looking through decks hold them horizontally, and most cards are designed horizontally. Some advertisers design their cards vertically, hoping to be different and stand out from the crowd. Does it work?

No, according to Bill Norcutt, who says that horizontal cards pull better than vertical cards. The problem with a vertical format, says Norcutt, is that it forces the reader to turn the card to read the message—and most won't do this as they quickly flip through a pile of cards.

An exception would be in decks where most cards are printed vertically, the standard vertical card pulls better because it fits the format of the pack.

6. The Rule of One Second

Think about how you go through card packs: You rip open the deck, immediately flip through the cards, and glance at each card about one second before deciding whether to toss it in the trash or put it aside for more serious consideration.

"I hypothesize that card scanners do not fully read the cards of interest as they scan but put them aside for later scrutiny," writes consultant Wayne Hepburn. "There is a subtle self-induced pressure to go through the entire pack and react to each card before getting serious about any of them. This is the exact opposite of magazine reading."

For this reason, you have only one second to grab the prospect's attention. Clarity and directness are the keys to doing this. Your offer must be immediately clear. Your sales proposition must literally "pop" off the card and grab the reader's eye. Cards that do not instantly communicate are trashed without a second thought. As Don Rappaport points out: "Card packs are 100 percent advertising. There's no reason to read them."

7. The Importance of the Headline

All the card pack experts agree that the headline is important, and most agree that it is the single most important element determining the success or failure of your direct response postcard.

"The headline should name the product, service, or major benefit," says Ed Werz. "The fewer words, the better."

"The headline will make or break the card," adds Robert Luedtke. His advice? "Sell the key benefit. Make it grab the prospect's attention. The headline must be big, bold, and obvious."

Here are examples of postcard headlines stressing benefits:

"Your investment can grow from $7,500 to $20,000"	(Federal Mailers)
"Up to 75 percent discount on commissions when you trade with Charles Schwab . . . "	(Charles Schwab)
"How to save money on office supplies"	(Quill)

An equally effective tactic is to put a free offer in the postcard headline:

"Write for free book: 'How to Win at Commodities'"	(Murlas)
"Amazing free offer *Think & Grow Rich*"	(SMI)
"Free penny stock market report"	(Stuart James)

Asking a question, a technique proven effective in print ads, also works well with postcards:

"How long must you keep important papers?"	(Destroy-it)
"Applying address labels by hand?"	(Heyer, Inc.)
"Moving your offices?"	(Relocation Management Systems)

Postcards are an action-oriented medium, so command headlines are a natural for postcard deck advertising:

"Protect your company's valuable assets"	(Seton)
"Be a printer . . . without a press"	(Norco)
"Earn insured tax-free income"	(Clayton Brown)

If your product or idea is news, stress the news aspect in your headline. You can do this by using such words as *new, discover, announcing, now, it's here, at last,* and *just arrived:*

"Discover new ways to schedule personnel"	(Methods Research)
"New . . . anti-slip PVC duckboard"	(Tepromark)
"At last! Overnight shipping at 50 percent savings"	(Air Shippers)

8. Highlight the Offer

In a direct mail package, you would first entice the reader with a powerful promise . . . then outline all the benefits of your product . . . and only then, once he's hooked and interested, do you make the offer and let *price* rear its ugly head.

But a postcard is different. The space for copy measures only 3½ × 5½". And some of that is taken up by headline, photo or illustration, and coupon. So you don't have time to write conventional copy. You have to get your message across quickly in concise, almost telegraphic language.

Remember the one-second rule? The reader glancing at your card has to get a complete sense of what you're talking about—right away. As Herschell Lewis points out, "Your offer must be identifiable instantly." This means simple, uncomplicated offers that can be easily explained in a few words. Some examples:

"100 full-color business cards only $53.50"	(Southern Color)
"*Rechargeable* aerosol spray can! $29.95 each Includes 5 nozzles at no extra charge"	(Abbeon Cal)
"16-cent custom tote bags. Fast delivery. Low quantities. For trade shows, meetings, promotion, retail—any occasion."	(Art Poly Bags)

9. Stress Benefits, Not Features

Highlight the benefits of what you are selling. For example, if you are selling a machine that folds sheets of paper into booklets, don't say "Stainless steel hopper, 12″ wide." Say "Makes up to 600 booklets per hour." As Joe Doyle, president of Federal Mailers points out, "On a 3 × 5″ card, there is no room to discuss features. Stress benefits."

10. Business Reply versus Place Stamp Here

The standard is to design the mailing side (front) of the card as a business reply card. All the prospect does is drop the card in the mail and it is delivered to the advertiser. No need to add a stamp.

To avoid paying the cost of reply mail, some advertisers omit the business reply permit and instead put a "place stamp here" box in the upper right corner of the card. Unfortunately, this will decrease response. Some experts recommend using "place stamp here" as a way of qualifying prospects. But when you're after inquiries using postcards, you should go for all you can get. True, asking for a stamp discourages some "brochure collectors." But it may also discourage some legitimate prospects. So don't do it.

11. Does Position Matter?

Bill Norcutt says that top card positions (being one of the first few cards the prospect sees when he flips through the deck) can increase orders by 14 percent. Robert Luedtke also says that in his experience the first card in the deck does get a higher response than the same card positioned somewhere in the middle. So if you can get the premium position, do so. It may be worth paying extra if the card deck publisher charges for it.

12. Simple Visuals Work Best

On a 3½ × 5½″ card, you have a space maybe 2″ wide by 1″ high to fit your visual. Elaborate or detailed drawings or photos will lose all their detail and become fuzzy when reduced to this size. So the best visual approaches are as follows:

- a straightforward product shot in a card focusing on the product
- a picture of your booklet, catalog, or literature when offering free information.

Resources

The Direct Marketing Association's Card Pack Council is a good place to start if you are looking for a qualified card pack broker, consultant, or agency. For information contact: Direct Marketing Association, Card Pack Council, 11 West 42nd Street, New York, NY 10036, phone (212) 768-7277.

There are several directories listing the various card decks and card deck publishers. They include:

—*Card Deck Rates and Data,* Standard Rate and Data Service, 3004 Glenview Road, Wilmette, IL 60091-9970, phone 800-323-4588 or 312-256-8333. Lists over 700 business and consumer card decks plus hundreds of insert and co-op mailing programs. One-year subscription price: $95.

—*The National Directory of PostCard Deck Media,* by Ed Werz, published by Caddylak Systems, Inc., 131 Heartland Blvd., P.O. Box 1322, Brentwood, NY 11717, phone 800-523-8060. Lists over 600 postcard decks.

—*Card Pack Directory,* Solar Press, 1120 Frontenac Road, Naperville, IL 60563-1799, (708) 983-1400. Published annually. Call for price and availability.

—*The Response Deck List,* Thinkbank Publishers, PO Box 1166, Arlington, TX 76010, phone 817-265-1793. Includes information on over 400 response decks.

CHAPTER 23

Telemarketing*

If you have a negative reaction to the idea of telemarketing, you're not alone. As consumers on the receiving end of telemarketing calls, many of us find them annoying and disruptive. But telemarketing *can* be effective when conducted properly. And telemarketing encompasses not only outgoing sales calls but incoming calls from prospects as well. Today, it is a $13 billion marketing medium.

According to the American Telemarketing Association (ATA), telemarketing is defined as "the planned, professional use of the telephone to advertise, market, or provide service functions." The ATA points out that telemarketing provides both profit and not-for-profit businesses a cost-effective method to communicate quickly with a large segment of their targeted prospect population. And for two-income couples with little time to shop, homebound individuals, and busy executives who don't have time to see a salesperson, telemarketing can be a valuable service.

*Some of the information in this chapter was reprinted with permission from the following sources: *99 Begged, Borrowed, Stolen & Even a Few Original Telemarketing Ideas!,* a publication of Nelson Panullo Jutkins Direct Marketing, Inc.; *Telemarketing Standards & Ethics Guidelines,* a publication of the American Telemarketing Association, Sherman Oaks, California; and *What You Must Know Before You Get Into Telemarketing!,* published by TeleCross, Waterloo, Iowa.

Why Use Telemarketing?

Telemarketing is similar to mass media in that it can reach a lot of prospects quickly. The goal of telemarketing is to provide economical, convenient access to products and services. By talking to the prospect directly, telemarketers can overcome individual objections and adjust their sales approach immediately. In effect, telemarketing combines sales and research.

Because sales costs are frequently reduced through telemarketing, consumers and business buyers alike may benefit from lower long-term product and service prices. And telemarketing provides an opportunity for prospects to learn about products and services on a personalized, interactive level.

Other advantages of telemarketing are:

1. It allows the prospect to ask questions, provide information, give opinions, and react to your message.
2. Telemarketing offers total market penetration. The telephone can reach virtually every business and over 90 percent of the households in North America.
3. The telephone receives priority—the prospect answers the phone when other mediums get put aside or ignored.
4. Telemarketing allows you to pick the best time to contact your prospect or customer. You have time control. With experience, you learn when is the best time to reach your audience.
5. The telephone is economical and efficient. Telemarketing allows you to service those customers you can't afford to sell any other way.
6. Telemarketing is convenient for your prospects and customers. A telephone call takes less time than personal visits.
7. Telemarketing is not affected by the elements, the weather, or other factors that can upset an outside sales force.
8. Telemarketing allows you to make a high volume of prospect or customer contacts:

	Consumer	*Business*
Dial spins per hour:	40-60	20-40
Completed presentations per hour:	9-15	5-9

In a standard eight hour day, the street sales rep will make four to twelve calls, whereas an experienced telemarketer will talk to 30 to 90 people.

9. Telemarketing reduces costs of the field force while increasing sales. Lead generation and qualification will decrease expenses while providing the outside sales rep with only qualified people to talk to.
10. Telemarketing gives you instant feedback, flexibility, and measurement of your results against objectives.

Not only does telemarketing give you instant feedback as to how effective your sales message is, it gives you a chance to find out *why* response is or isn't good. That's a distinct advantage over other media, such as advertising, direct mail, or public relations, which allow you to measure results only.

Telemarketing also is useful in servicing both major product or market segments where you do a minor volume of your business and minor product or market segments where you do a major volume of business. An example of the first type of market would be a specialty product with a good profit margin, but a small volume. Telemarketing can reach this small volume of customers more efficiently than field sales calls. An example of the minor market segment that generates a major volume of business would be selling outside your normal geographic territory where sales are profitable but customers are few. It would be expensive to send a salesman to cover this out-of-the-way territory, so telemarketing is an ideal alternative.

Telemarketing Applications

Telemarketing is not just a convenient tool for soliciting orders or fundraising. It can be used for:

- Sales support (including scheduling appointments for sales personnel)
- Market research
- Consumer surveys
- Lead generation
- Lead qualification
- Information hot lines
- Reservations service
- Technical support
- Customer service
- Direct mail/advertising follow-up

- Customer satisfaction surveys
- Account management
- Order taking
- Catalog sales
- Fund raising
- Subscription sales
- Renewals
- Product announcements
- Special promotions
- Generating referrals
- Soliciting trade show attendance

Generally, telemarketing supplements other advertising and marketing channels. It can be used to maximize response to a mailing by preparing prospects to receive the mailing or following up with them afterwards. Businesses can use telemarketing to obtain more accurate, up-to-date marketing information, broader market bases, and lower business costs. As Mike Johnson, Vice President of the telemarketing agency Mardex, Inc. observes, "Telemarketing is an inexpensive insurance policy guaranteeing success for your efforts in other media."

Telemarketing costs more than direct mail, which typically runs between a half dollar and a few dollars per pieces mailed, but it costs considerably less than making an in-person sales call. According to TeleCross Corporation, a telemarketing agency in Waterloo, Iowa, the cost of a telemarketing call falls between the $3 to $7 range, while a personal sales call is close to $200. Of course, the true measure of success is not the cost of the media up-front, but the results the media generates.

Setting Up An Effective Telemarketing Program

First you must decide on the goal of your telemarketing program. You should have a clear definition of its purpose and make sure your objectives are in measurable terms. For instance, do you want 10 new orders a day? Do you want to double the number of inquiries you are currently receiving?

The next step is finding and keeping good telemarketers. You may decide to train and staff an in-house department for this purpose or hire an outside telemarketing firm. An outside telemarketing firm can also be hired to help you set up an in-house telemarketing center. The operators you hire should have a chance to see, hold, and touch your product, if possible, so that they are familiar with it and can answer questions about it from prospects. But probably the most important quality to look for in a good telemarketer is a clear, cheerful, expressive voice and correct pronunciation and grammar. Unlike a salesperson in the field, telemarketers can not rely on facial and body gestures to augment their message. Telemarketing trainer Mary Anne Weinstein points out, "The voice becomes the sole representative of your company. There is no fancy clothing, no cologne or perfume, no adornment in hairstyle or makeup. The voice is your only marketing tool."

You will also need to prepare a telephone script that is flexible enough to handle a variety of individual responses to your calls, yet is structured with options to anticipate 90 percent of the issues and objections raised by prospects. For an example, see the sample script reprinted at the end of this chapter.

Here are some other tips on developing an effective telemarketing program:

- Use a conversational approach in your script; allow dialogue and interaction.
- Listen to what your prospect has to say and respond accordingly. You may have received telemarketing calls that began, "How are you today" and when you say "Fine," the person on the other end automatically replies, "I'm fine, too. Thank you for asking." Don't let your staff blindly follow a script while ignoring the prospect's responses.
- As a matter of fact, don't ask "How are you" or "How are you doing" when you don't even know the person you're calling. It lacks sincerity and annoys most people.
- Make sure the contact list you are using is up to date and accurate. Just as with any other type of marketing, your prospect list is a top priority. The telephone costs too much to waste time on inappropriate calls.
- Never let the phone ring more than six times.
- If you hire telemarketers, hire the best and pay them well.
- Have a control form or some kind of summary record to keep track of your calls and the results, including customer information and specific objections to the sales message.
- Before your begin the calls, make sure you know as much as possible about who you are calling and why.

- Know exactly what you want the person you're calling to do, and make it clear to him or her what you're asking.
- Be sure you have the right person on the telephone before you begin your presentation. Ask for him or her by first and last name.
- Make sure the prospect is free to talk to you. If not, ask when might be a good time to call back.
- Build into your script an opening hook or question, a reason for listening to you. The goal is to get your prospect to agree with you. Present your product or offer's key benefits immediately, concentrating on those that are proven to be key motivators in the buying decision.
- State your offer and its terms clearly, making sure the prospect knows what he stands to gain from it.
- Choose two products or services to promote. One is primary, the other is secondary. Each should offer different advantages. Offer the secondary product or service only if the primary one does not interest your buyer.
- Do not assume the prospect understands you. Make certain you are getting through with the message by repeating it and asking questions if you feel there is any confusion.
- React to what the prospect says. Feed back key words or phrases he uses, showing that you have listened and are picking up on what is important to him.
- Never argue with the prospect or tell him he is wrong. Be cheerful, bright, and sincere in your conversation.
- Answer a prospect's question with a question, to keep you in control and out of a defensive position. This technique will also help you qualify the prospect further, since you will be getting additional information.
- Have a strong series of closes ready. And ask for the order. Says Milt Pierce, a New York-based direct mail copywriter and author of several special reports on telephone sales, "This is the salesperson's toughest job. After the pitch has been delivered, the objections have been raised and answered, it is time to produce the order. Be sure your salespeople are trained in closing—and verifying—the sale."
- Keep it simple. Use short words, simple phrases, "you" language, and make easy-to-understand points. Speak slowly and distinctly, but don't waste the prospect's time. Get to the point quickly.
- Refine your techniques based on prospect responses—before you make hundreds or thousands of calls. One of the benefits of telemarketing is its usefulness in testing different sales approaches and markets. Results

can be gathered in a few days, changes can be made quickly, and valid tests cost much less than with direct mail or advertising.

A business call requires more give and take and a less rigid approach than a call to consumers. According to Ray Jutkins of Nelson Panullo Jutkins Direct Marketing, only 20 percent of all telephone calls result in a sale within the first few minutes. Eighty percent of orders are achieved because the telemarketing consultant can handle rebuttals, answer questions, and provide details. In fact, most successful closers ask for the order seven times.

Still, if the prospect is really not interested after a couple of requests for the order, the telemarketer should either politely end the call or set a call-back time, if the prospect is agreeable. If an order is taken, be sure to confirm it at the end of the conversation, restating purchase and delivery information and other details. Make sure your staff ends every conversation politely so as to preserve your company's reputation and keep the door open for future calls or follow-up.

In-House Or Agency?

Should you set up your own in-house telemarketing staff or hire an outside agency to do your telemarketing for you? If you plan a heavy and frequent volume of telemarketing, the most cost-effective option may be to work with an outside agency on setting up your own operation in-house. You'll have more control over personnel and the way they handle calls, as well as the capability to handle technically complex calls.

The advantages of working with a telemarketing agency is that the company is likely to be experienced and knowledgeable in areas that you are not. Unless you hire a staff person with telemarketing know-how, that outside expertise can save you time and money in the long run. An agency can write and test a script based on information you provide, offer a trained staff of telemarketing operators or help you train your own people, coordinate a telemarketing campaign with other departments (such as data processing, shipping, sales, and advertising), advise you on finding or putting together a telephone-responsive call list, and offer suggestions on how and when to best use telemarketing.

The agency you hire should invite you to participate in all phases of telemarketing development, including script development, training, strategic planning, and monitoring of calls. Even before you hire a firm, ask if you can watch the operators making calls to see how courteous they are, how natural they sound on the phone, and how well they handle problems and objections. This will also give you a chance to observe the supervisor and how well he motivates the telecommunicators.

If you plan to conduct telemarketing campaigns only occasionally, it will probably be cheaper to hire a telemarketing agency to handle the work for you on an "as-needed" basis. Otherwise, you must consider whether your operators and phone and computer equipment will be sitting idle when you aren't doing outbound telemarketing. Outbound operators often have a different personality and different aptitudes than customer-service operators who take inbound calls, so having them "double" as both types of operators may not work out.

Another reason to hire an outside agency is that they can often provide round-the-clock telephone service for inbound calls. By combining your call volume with that of other clients, they can afford to have operators in place 24 hours a day. Outside agencies are also better equipped to handle the flood of calls generated by broadcast advertising, since they have multiple phone lines and a large staff. Finally, they can probably set up both an inbound and outbound telemarketing campaign faster than you can, since the operators and equipment are already in place.

Most agencies bill by the hour or on a per-call basis. To determine the cost effectiveness of your telemarketing, calculate the sales revenue per hour and subtract the agency's fee from that. It is generally a good idea to test telemarketing by using an agency before you commit to the cost of setting up an in-house center.

Stewart Cross, President of TeleCross Corporation, offers this advice: "With most of our clients, we recommend they test the telemarketing concept before making a final commitment. It must pay for itself on a small scale before it can pay on a full-size operation."

Telemarketing Ethics

To be successful, telemarketing programs must follow certain guidelines of etiquette, courtesy, and professional ethical behavior. The American Telemarketing Association suggests the following guidelines:

1. The caller should always identify himself and his company.
2. The purpose of the call should be stated efficiently, courteously, and professionally.
3. Repeated calls with the same offer should not be made to the same prospect.

4. All telemarketing offers to the business or consumer public must be legal, legitimate, and have recognized value.
5. Business calls should occur during normal business hours, and consumer calls should only occur between 9 AM and 9 PM, unless further restricted by local or state laws.
6. For outbound calls where automatic dialing equipment is used, there should be enough staff to ensure that every call recipient will speak to a live person immediately.
7. For inbound calls, the seller should provide sufficient lines to accommodate anticipated call volumes.
8. A telemarketing manager should be on-site to provide control and direction. Managers should also regularly monitor the telemarketer's performance by listening to business calls being made or received. This allows performance problems to be detected and addressed so that telemarketing quality can be improved. It also protects customers and the employer against possible unethical practices by certain operators.

Qualifying Leads

Each operator's goal should be to spend the shortest time possible getting the maximum number of sales. So you will need to screen leads by getting the answers to several questions.

First, find out if the person you are talking to has the authority to purchase.

Secondly, find out if the prospect has a need for your particular product or service. If not, find out what his specific needs are—perhaps you can help.

Third, when does the prospect plan to purchase such a product or service—within the next few months, or not for a year? If the time frame is more than a few months away, you may wish to call back later.

Fourth, are there any other sources for your product or service that the prospect is considering? The answer can provide a good clue as to the seriousness of the prospect. If there is another source the prospect finds more appealing, try to find out why so that you can relay that information back to the telemarketing manager and ultimately the sales manager.

In asking these questions, don't assume an adversarial stance. Think of the questions as part of a conversation that builds rapport with the potential customer. Be sensitive to the inflections and tone in your prospect's voice, as well as what he is saying. And be empathatic towards his concerns and problems. This will help establish a mutually beneficial relationship that can turn a cool prospect into a hot one, if not immediately then perhaps in the future.

Toll-Free Numbers Increase Response

Providing a toll-free 800 number to customers and prospects for receiving orders and inquiries can boost response to your offer substantially. The consumer mail order industry has discovered that as much as 80 percent of their total business is done over the telephone when they offer an 800 number. Ray Jutkins of Nelson Panullo Jutkins Direct Marketing points out that it is not unusual to increase orders by 20 percent through the addition of an 800 number to your promotions.

Once a prospect is encouraged to call an 800 number, your company gets an extra opportunity to cross-sell or increase the sale. Toll-free numbers also can provide a way to track media, determining which ones are working best. So make sure your 800 number is prominently featured in all catalogs, ads, press releases, and other promotions you send out.

The same common-sense rules that apply to direct marketing apply to telemarketing. So don't plan a major telemarketing push to begin right before Christmas or on another major holiday. Either the phone lines will be tied up by people making calls, such as when one advertiser started an inbound call campaign on Mother's Day, or everyone will be too busy with other plans to place an order or listen to a sales pitch.

One other caveat regarding 800 numbers as well as toll lines: you should have enough incoming lines to handle your normal volume of calls, as well as provision for expected overflow if you mount a major promotional campaign. If you have your own telemarketing center, some outside telemarketing agencies can arrange a temporary link-up with your phone lines so that calls and orders will not be lost during peak periods.

GETTING BACK LAPSED CUSTOMERS*

Season Subscribers to the Opera

Hello, M________? This is ________ from the Albany Opera. I'm calling you tonight to find out where we went wrong. You were a subscriber to the Opera this past season, but have not renewed your subscription for the current season.

*This sample telemarketing script is reprinted with permission from *Words for Telemarketing* by Steve Isaac (Asher-Gallant Press). It is designed to get people who once bought opera tickets but did not renew to resubscribe.

Since we always try to present the best in sophisticated entertainment, we're disturbed when our subscribers are not pleased.

It would be most helpful to us if you could tell me what it was that made you decide not to renew?

LISTEN IN AN INTERESTED MANNER TO WHATEVER THEY SAY. ANSWER OBJECTIONS FROM OBJECTION RESPONSES, OR IF A PROBLEM SURFACES, SAY:

I'm sorry that happened. Try as we may, we don't always satisfy everyone. However, it would be a shame for you to lose your priority seating privileges based on one disappointment.

How about this? Let's renew your subscription tonight, so that you're sure of getting the seats you want. If, after attending the first performance, you're unhappy, you can cancel and will only be charged for the one performance.

And, though we certainly couldn't make up for what happened, I'd like to have you be our guest at a performance of the ABT here at the Opera House this week or next. How does that sound to you, M________?

IF HE IS PLEASED, PROCEED. IF STILL UNHAPPY AND UNINTERESTED, POLITELY TERMINATE THE CALL.

Great. I'll hold a ticket in your name at the box office for any evening this week or next. Just be sure to pick it up by 7:30 or you may not be able to be seated for the performance you've chosen.

In the meantime, I'll get your tickets out to you first thing tomorrow for the opera season and notify the box office to hold your seat.

IF THE PROBLEM WAS THE POSITION OF THE SEATING IN THE FIRST PLACE, SAY YOU'LL NOTIFY THE BOX OFFICE TO CHANGE THE SEAT TO THEIR AREA OF PREFERENCE IF AT ALL POSSIBLE.

Now, M________, we take American Express, Visa, or MasterCard. Which would you prefer to put this on?

TAKE THE CREDIT CARD INFORMATION. IF HE WANTS TO PAY BY CHECK, INDICATE THAT YOU CAN ONLY HOLD THE SEAT UNTIL ONE WEEK FROM TONIGHT.

Now, let me make sure I have your correct address. It's ________, OK. Welcome back, M________, and enjoy our spectacular 1988 season.

OBJECTION RESPONSES

It Just Costs Too Much

Yes, our costs have certainly gone up in the past few seasons, and we're forced to pass those on to ticket purchasers. It costs a lot to put on quality productions. However, it would be a shame for you to miss it at any price.

Let's see, your subscription last year was ________. I do have some seats available at ________. They're not as good as the ones you had, but they are still very good seats. I can reserve ________for you at ________, or I can still offer you your old seats. Which would you prefer?

To Almost Any Objection

Do you plan on attending any operas this season at all?

IF YES:

Well, then, it would really be a shame for someone who has feeling for the opera and a priority privilege, to lose it.

I Want to Think About it

Well, certainly, you can think about it, M________; however, we won't be able to give you priority seating after tonight. Our computer is about to process all the seating requests of the renewing subscribers, before we add the general public.

17 Tips For More Effective Telemarketing

Here are some of the more common mistakes to avoid when planning and implementing a telemarketing campaign:

1. Choosing the Wrong Team

When you're assembling your own management team to control your telemarketing activity, you'll need a strong leader with company-wide access, plus the authority to make fast command decisions. The most successful telemarketing directors are "front-line generals" who stay in direct touch with every phase of operations and keep their lines of communication wide open.

If you plan to conduct all your telemarketing operations in-house, you'll need to find people with the right kind of experience. "Telephone experience" is not enough. You need to know what kind of telephone work they're trained for. A good inbound operator has a far different personality from a successful outbound caller.

It's a mistake to divert your regular Customer Service telephone people to telemarketing activities. It's a whole different discipline. They won't be able to adapt quickly, and diverting them cuts deeply into your ongoing Customer Service program.

If you elect to bring in an independent telemarketing company for your operations, be as careful as you would in hiring a new key executive in your company. Demand references from current and past clients. Dig deep, but respect your gut feelings—good chemistry is essential, because you're going to be working closely together.

There are about a dozen or so telemarketing firms who can be called "top pros," and if you choose one of us you'll get plenty of help in avoiding the other 16 possibly fatal mistakes you might make.

Getting the right people to represent you out front on the telephone is vital. They need to be experienced enough to appreciate your company image and adopt it, then trained to be as knowledgeable about your products as your regular person-to-person salespeople.

2. Conflicting Chain of Command

Success in telemarketing is driven by the fast, intelligent interchange of information between all the members of your team—your telemarketing company or group, your marketing people, and your operating departments. It's a job for a well coordinated, fast acting team—there's no time for "congressional" delays. If you want to stay in tune with the marketplace, and capitalize on the opportunities as quickly as they pop up, you need to be ready and able to modify your program, and improve your media buys on a daily (or hourly) basis.

The chain of command that works the best (with the least cost, least waste, least confusion) is directly from your chief of telemarketing to the people on the front line. Availability of the chief by phone and in person is the essential key. If your chief is absent on a business trip or tied up in meetings, or surrounded by a fence of secretaries, your telemarketing system can't function and perform the way you want it to.

3. Neglecting Your Frontline People

Like any sales people, your telemarketing operators need tender loving care.

It's a mistake to turn them loose without sufficient training. In any effective telemarketing company, operator training doesn't begin and end with a brief session on a canned pitch.

Operators are given the chance to learn your product inside out so they can handle any questions thrown at them, overcome any objections, and move smoothly into closing the sale. That's only step one.

Step two is to get them in harmony with your company's image and approach to the marketplace, so whether they make a sale or not, they preserve and build up your good relationship with customers and prospects.

Step three is maintaining energy and enthusiasm for the project they're involved in. All the rules of inspired sales management apply. How well the rules are applied makes the crucial difference between one telemarketing company and another. (Ask to sit in on some of the training sessions at Mardex for a demonstration. And plan to participate in the design of the training sessions for your own projects. Telemarketing at its best is interactive long before anyone picks up the telephone on your behalf.)

All sales jobs are emotionally demanding, but in telemarketing the demand is intensified. Imagine what it feels like to make 30 to 60 calls a day, face the inevitable turndowns, listen politely to the really tough customers who sometimes pop up, keep a smile in your voice as you handle their problems, and then look cheerfully ahead to the next call.

Unlike the field salesman who gets a breather between calls, your telemarketing agent has very little relief. The frontline action is just about as fast and demanding as a hockey game.

Like any sales people, your telemarketing phone agents can go stale and even torpedo a program if they're forgotten. At Mardex our team leaders and coaches don't just sit on the sidelines. They're circulating in the middle of the action, encouraging the team, solving their problems, fielding any difficult questions that crop up, and boosting everyone's performance.

With the right incentive program, your telephone sales people are going to produce more. The emphasis is the word "right". If you give them incentives that are too enticing, they may push too hard, oversell, and generate phantom sales you can't close or collect on later. Get your telemarketing company's advice on designing a sales incentive program appropriate for the project you have in mind.

4. Calling in the Experts Too Late

Which comes first, the chicken or the egg? If you choose wrong, you could hatch a turkey.

Call in your telemarketing company before you start to work out the details of any plans. You'll get all the benefits of their experience in engineering your program from the bottom up. Some telemarketing companies provide this service at no cost (Mardex does), so there's really no good reason not to take advantage of it. Look at your telemarketing firm as a (free) consultant, not just a supplier, and you have a much better chance of avoiding mistakes.

For example: One marketer of women's products recently launched a heavy TV sampling program, waiting until the last minute to connect with his telemarketing firm. In the scramble to get started, the program was planned for inbound 800 operators to collect names and addresses—but not telephone numbers.

The marketer forgot to mention that he needed respondents' phone numbers for a follow-up callback effort. The audience was urban women (80% with unlisted numbers) and there was no way to recapture them.

You can stay out of traps like this one by taking your telemarketing company in on your plans early enough so they can make constructive suggestions.

5. Buying on Price

Inbound 800 service is sometimes bought on price. That's false economy. The few pennies you save up front can cost you hundreds, even thousands of leads and sales lost by a poor quality or underequipped service.

Ask a leading telemarketing company to quote, and you'll know what the fair market price should be for answering all your calls, giving you valid names and addresses, and reliable reports.

Beware of a company that undercuts the going market price. They're probably hungry because they can't keep their clients. Or maybe they're a latecomer to the industry, hoping to get you to finance their education.

Outbound telemarketing is a totally different story. It's a mistake to buy it simply on the basis of the quoted hourly rate. Outbound should be bought on performance, as measured in a test. You can quickly determine your cost-per-order and cost-per-sale. Those are the criteria that make the difference between winning and losing.

Your telemarketing company should be willing to test and contract for 100 hours, for example. (Mardex is.) Our practice is to evaluate results daily, and if the test is not paying out, cut it short to save the client's money. We don't string a losing test out to "sell" 100 hours—we're only interested in working toward successful rollouts.

The only way to buy outbound service is on quality. So how do you judge quality before you commit? Visit the telemarketing operational facility. Meet the front-line people who will be on the phone for you. Sit in on training sessions. Although most training sessions and operations are closed to outsiders for client security reasons, we have some clients who are willing to allow non-competitive observers. Ask for an appointment.

6. No Contingency Planning

On the surface, it looks easy enough to hook telemarketing onto your on-going marketing program. It may turn out to be simple, but don't count on it!

The impact of telemarketing can hit almost every department inside a company with surprising consequences on every operational system. To plan safely you need to examine all the "what ifs?" They're easy enough to anticipate and make contingency plans for if you tap into the experience of a telemarketing company who's been around the tracks so many times they know where the pitfalls are.

For example, what if your telemarketing effort is dramatically successful? Suppose you get 3 or 4 or 10 times the response you expected.

Could your data processing department handle it? Most can't absorb a sudden flood of orders without planning well in advance.

Will your DP department need to set up a separate data entry screen for telemarketing?

Can they accommodate a magnetic tape or on-line transmission from us? If not, how quickly can they install the system to do it? (Hint: Ask them for their best guess and triple it!)

Look and you'll find most departments are not geared to cope with a sudden surprise success, if it happens.

Do you have the product inventory to fulfill the demand?

What will happen in your shipping room?

Do you have the manpower and packaging supplies?

Would a big response tie up all your sales force or delivery system so they can't service your regular customers?

Can you get enough product to supply your customers' regular demands after your telemarketing campaign has emptied your warehouse?

Make sure you have plenty of product literature and other fulfillment materials appropriate for the telemarketing job.

Recently one manufacturer with a warehouse full of literature discovered—too late!—that the brochure copy said "Thanks for responding to our mailing" (instead of "our television campaign") and the Service Department 800 number shown in the brochure was outdated. Reprinting under panic conditions is the costly way to go!

Don't skip any departments when you're making plans—the surprise consequences can explode in some of the most unexpected places.

7. Muddling the Marketing

It's a big mistake to think of telemarketing as an "add-on" to your ongoing marketing program—an orphan you're going to adopt and see how it behaves before you integrate it into the family.

Well coordinated, your telemarketing efforts can work wonders. (See Mistake number 17, "Overlooking opportunities.")

Lacking coordination, telemarketing can cause confusion inside your company, and outside among your customers and prospects.

Everyone in the marketing chain from top to bottom needs to be primed and ready to cooperate. A few years ago—in a recruiting campaign for one of the armed services—follow-up letters to TV leads arrived 18 months(!) after the names first came in. Someone forgot to alert the recruiters in the field and get their coordinated cooperation in the campaign.

The offer you make on the phone shouldn't conflict with the offer your prospect gets through other media. Prices, benefits, and the way you present them ought to match—unless you want to test offers and you're able to isolate your test markets positively, so conflicting offers in the mail and on the phone don't land on the same prospects at the same time.

Company management may wonder what effect telemarketing will have on the company's image. There's no cause for alarm if you're careful to coordinate. Telemarketing has come of age—many of the country's most distinguished corporations are using it positively to build company image while they generate leads and sales. (See Mistake Number 8, "Putting your ad agency in charge.")

Working in harmony with your other efforts, telemarketing can act as a variable tap you can turn on and off at will to generate leads or sales precisely as you need them.

8. Putting your General Advertising Agency in Charge

Nobody could dispute the success of advertising agencies in doing what they do best—building images and changing minds through a broad spectrum of traditional media. Telemarketing is not one of these.

Telemarketing is direct marketing, interactive and fast moving, with a completely different set of rules (some of which are directly contrary to traditional advertising practice).

As a non-commissionable medium, telemarketing is a maverick, grown up independently, and largely ignored by advertising agencies (with rare exceptions)—sad but true. But there's light at the end of the tunnel for agencies who'd like to carve out a role for themselves in our $13 billion industry.

If you're the boss of an advertising agency, please accept our standing invitation to discover telemarketing's place in your plans. You could be miles ahead of your competition just by calling Mardex to ask for a presentation and planning help on a proposed project for one of your clients.

Meanwhile, it can be a serious mistake to place your ad agency in a controlling role between you and your telemarketing company. Only direct response pros and the very few ad agencies who understand telemarketing are qualified to play an active role in it.

Just this year a major package goods company let its ad agency mastermind a new product introduction into oblivion. The idea was to give away free samples of the new product to prospects who called an 800 number for a coupon.

The agency, not understanding direct response TV, bought maximum reach spots, with limited frequency. The result was sudden avalanches of phone requests nobody could hope to handle, instead of a steady flow the company could cope with.

The TV media buy was so out of balance that the product introduction had to be scrapped and started over. Beware of instant expertise in telemarketing.

If the agency is truly experienced in telemarketing, they won't want to get into the middle of program planning or day-to-day operations at all. There's nothing to be gained, since telemarketing is non-commissionable. But there's everything to lose, since telemarketing must move much faster than an ad agency can function.

The solution: Ask your agency to act in an advisory role to make sure that your image building efforts are going to be enhanced by your telemarketing activities, but keep the agency out of the day-to-day decisions.

If they insist on a controlling role, ask to see a presentation of their previous telemarketing experience.

9. Using the Wrong Creative Approach

Whether you're creating a print or broadcast program, don't be shy with your 800 number. More than half the so-called response ads you see today bury the 800 number. Why? Some agencies, clients, and art directors put their ideas of "quality design" ahead of sensible direct marketing technique. Make up your mind—do you want to amaze your audience with a beautiful ad, or do you want to sell product?

If you're going for telephone response, make it impossible for the reader to overlook your number. Make it prominent in print ads above the coupon. Show it and say it several times in your tv spot. Repeat it at least three times in a radio commercial. And put your 800 number somewhere on every page of your catalog, and on every piece in your direct mail package, so prospects who are ready to buy don't have to hunt for the number.

It's a mistake to hope that telemarketing is going to act like a magic wand and turn a losing product or poor deal into a good one for the consumer. Today's audience is smart and getting smarter every day, so it doesn't pay to persuade them to buy with exaggerated claims. All that will get you is a warehouse full of returned merchandise and unpaid invoices.

Out on the telephone frontline, the scripts are put together as a team effort. It's a mistake to come to your telemarketing organization with a firm script in hand and demand that they use it. The only scripts that ever work out are worked out in action.

We start with a fact sheet from the client, of course, plus any other materials available such as product sales sheets, literature, direct mail pieces. We first write a preliminary script, review it with our best telephone agents to see how they think it will work, and then try it out in action. We give the script a live test on the phone, test and improve, test and change, and finally arrive at the verbal presentation we know is working. No guesswork involved.

The client is fully involved in script development, so we can be sure we're presenting the product and deal correctly, and working in harmony with the company image. It's a team effort, and the client is a vital member of the team.

10. Not Testing Thoroughly

Before you dive headlong into the mysterious water, poke a stick in it. In fact, poke a few sticks here and there. The more you poke, the more you'll learn. The advantage telemarketing has over other testing media is threefold—first, it's unbelievably fast—you get results you can work with in just a few hours, and complete results in days.

Second, it's flexible. You can change your appeal in 5 minutes by changing the script. Telemarketing is a dynamic dialog between you and your markets, giving you the maximum opportunity to create the right combinations for success.

Third, it's economical. Valid tests can be structured and tried out for little money, compared to the big bucks you have to invest in pre-production costs for a test in direct mail and other media.

Telemarketing is the ideal medium for testing the full spectrum of variables: price, product, benefits, selling platform, the relative effects of direct mail packages. It's ideal for testing a list or the viability of a new market, or testing to see why a list is unresponsive or why it doesn't pay out. Testing possibilities are endless. It's a shame to waste the opportunity.

11. Falling for "Bargain" Media or Lists

Most of the apparently good deals in media (especially in broadcast media) involve a Catch 22—you have to commit to the full, predetermined schedule to get the low bargain rate. Deals like this lock you into a program you can't change easily or quickly—and rapid media modification is the heart and soul of profitable direct response TV. The pro's analyze their media daily and buy time only where and when the cost is clearly going to be justified by income. Where can you get this kind of media buying expertise?

The first place to look is in the direct response agencies who can demonstrate a substantial track record in TV. This kind of help is also available from the few independent media buying services who specialize in direct response. The last place to look is in the media department of your general ad agency. The criteria they use so successfully for image building are all wrong for direct response TV.

And when the salesman from your favorite TV station comes around with his latest best deal, don't buy a schedule that can't be altered or cancelled in the light of hard results.

Beware of "bargain" mailing lists, too. Some of these don't include up-to-date telephone numbers, and some lists carry restrictions against "dual use" with the telephone and mail, or require an extra charge for it. And there goes your bargain!

Lists for sale as "mail responsive" (if they're good) are generally telephone responsive, as well.

12. Overlooking the Obvious

Believe it or not, many people who are trying telemarketing for the first time overlook the obvious fact that all the common sense rules of direct marketing apply.

For example, two years ago one long-distance telephone company bought itself a Christmas turkey by ignoring the well-known rules of seasonality. The direct mail was scheduled to land just 3 days before Christmas! The hopeful intention was to stimulate calls to an 800 number for closing the sales. Naturally, at this time of year everyone is distracted by the holiday. The phones were painfully silent, and this major national effort bombed.

By way of ridiculous contrast, another advertiser we heard of planned an inbound campaign when all the phone lines in the country are completely tied up and nobody could get through, on Mother's Day!

Publishing the wrong 800 number!

What? How could this happen to any sensible marketer?

It can happen. We've seen it happen repeatedly over the years. It's happening now, even to some very sophisticated marketers. It can be a disaster of major proportions.

But if you understand how it happens, you can easily avoid it. It happens one of two ways:

1. You publish a number that's not really yours. In a rush to produce your TV or print ads, you call your telemarketing company and take the number down over the phone and send it to your typographer. It turns out that you didn't hear the number correctly, or somebody else garbled it. WAIT for the number confirmed in writing before you stick your production neck out. At Mardex we confirm in writing and if you're in a rush, we'll send the confirmation by messenger.

If you're getting your 800 service directly from AT&T, don't publish the number until after the line is installed and working, and you've test-called it yourself. Not until then is the number safe to publish.

2. The most common reason for publishing a wrong number is that copy may be typed, revised, and retyped half a dozen times before it goes to the typesetter or TV producer. Every typing is a fresh opportunity to make a mistake. If you proofread against the last previous typing, and that carried a wrong number—ah!

There's one absolutely surefire way to stay out of this pitfall. Never believe the phone number you read until you pick up the phone and call it yourself. Make it a habit to do this at every stage of production, and ask everyone in the chain—the copywriter, art director, producer, production manager, and account executive to make this a routine habit before they sign off on any copy or assembly. The last stage is the most vital—the engraver's or press proof, or on the final art in the studio for TV production.

Calling to check the number at that critical point-of-no-return has saved thousands of dollars (and thousands of lost leads and sales) for our clients who use this simple system.

Here are two free extra tips on 800 numbers:

- Don't assume your national 800 number covers Hawaii, Alaska, or your home state. It doesn't—unless you make special arrangements.
- If you want an appealing 800 number—one that's easy to recall—you have a better chance of getting one from your telemarketing company than if you went directly to your rep at the phone company. Clout makes the difference.

13. Celebrating Too Soon

Sometimes early test "success" can fool you. The orders your telephone people are piling up may not be convertible into real sales and collect invoices.

Remember the old saying, "The sale's-not made until the money's in the bank"? It's doubly true in telemarketing. Don't commit a full budget to rolling out until you have good evidence that the early orders you're generating are real—and will pay out. An experienced telemarketing firm has ways of guaranteeing confirmation of sales in advance so you can avoid disappointment later. Ask Mardex.

14. Holding Back Too Long

When the fish are biting is no time to dig for worms! Strike while the iron is hot! When you do have a clearly successful test, it's a mistake to hold back too long before rollout. Grab the momentum you've stimulated. The rich market you uncovered may disappear if you let it languish while committees analyze, re-analyze, and chew over the results. Here's where you need a telemarketing manager with clout inside the company . . . enough clout to roll out and capitalize on success when all the marketing signals are "go."

15. Accepting Sketchy Reports

Telemarketing is marketing in action, sometimes as fast and dramatic as a hockey game, and information is the puck.

Being a live, interactive medium, telemarketing offers a unique opportunity to gather marketing data which is 100% accurate and 100% current. Plan from the start to seize this opportunity by designing a reporting system ahead of time that allows you to capture, organize, and manipulate the information in useful, understandable ways.

This will translate directly into day-to-day improvements you can make, and long-term marketing plans for the future. It's a mistake to pass up the possibilities.

The reports and tracking system you set up need to be fully compatible with your current systems, of course. But since you can gather so much more valuable data at very low cost via telemarketing, you may want to expand or modify your data handling systems in advance to accept and process the additional data you can capture.

Once a campaign's under way, it's usually too late to improve the built-in reporting system, so it pays to plan imaginatively from the start. Ask your telemarketing company for creative suggestions. At Mardex, the suggestions are free, and we might very well be able to give you the kind of data your marketing department has always wanted, but never could obtain before within the budget.

16. Falling in Love with the Hardware

Now there's all kinds of low-, medium-, and hi-tech hardware for telemarketing. Put it all together and it makes a very enticing package. Some normally clear-thinking executives lose their perspective over it. They think the more hardware, and the higher the tech, the better the program is going to work out. Not necessarily so. Focus should be on the cost-to-benefit ratio and not on gee-whiz gadgetry for its own sake.

At the core of every telemarketing program there's a plain telephone with one person on each end of the line. It's a human encounter. Personal, warm.

The cost of maintaining a computer terminal on the phone agent's desk is justified by performance in some applications, but not in others. For example, a customer service rep can offer much better service if he can instantly call up sale records and check stock availability on his computer terminal.

On the other hand, a well trained sales agent who is permitted to focus his attention on his customer's answers and develop a personal, natural dialog will always outproduce the agent who is locked in to a verbatim script on a CRT.

If something is going to cost more . . . and require people to run it . . . take up space . . . and occasionally break down . . . You get the idea.

So when you're planning a campaign, don't let hi-tech hardware distract you. Use it just when it's appropriate.

17. Overlooking Opportunities

If you use inbound 800 service simply to collect leads or orders, you're missing some valuable opportunities.

Look at it this way. You've already spent your media money to attract the call in the first place. Now that you've made your big investment, why not make it pay extra dividends?

You know your prospects are in a receptive frame of mind—that's why they initiated the calls to you. They're curious, and ready to talk. That golden moment is the time to:

- Reinforce the sale. Many prospects who call may be "on the fence" and need a little more convincing to order (and pay promptly when you bill them later). The "golden moment" to firm up the sale is now on the first incoming call.
- Upsell to a more profitable product or package. A well trained telephone agent can present a "decision tree" with a number of alternatives for the prospect to consider and buy. The answers a prospect gives to the operator's questions lead to different scripts for different products.
- Cross-sell related items. Once the prospect is committed, the operator can suggest companion purchases, accessories, supplies.
- Get telephone numbers and arrange callbacks. Inbound calls are your most inexpensive source for accurate, current numbers (some of which may be unlisted and otherwise difficult or impossible to retrieve).
- Solicit applications for your own charge card or credit plan (vs. checks or standard credit cards).
- Ask for referral names of friends or family who might want a catalog, subscription, information or a callback. At the "golden moment" many people want to share their discovery of your product with others, so they're usually happy to give you referral names. Especially if you offer a premium for the names.

And more. The possibilities for using inbound service have not been exhausted, and strangely enough, most marketers overlook the "golden moment."

Outbound telemarketing on the other hand, is well known to be a gold mine with its surface barely scratched.

Everywhere you look there's another opportunity to use the telephone creatively. The way to find opportunities inside your company is to think imaginatively about what goes on in every department. Identify their needs and visualize how to meet them more effectively with telemarketing techniques.

The Mother Lode, naturally, is in marketing and sales.

First ask yourself two questions: How can telemarketing augment the sales activities we're conducting now? And could we use telemarketing as a total selling system?

How could the telephone work to help your sales force before the sale?

- With calls to identify consumer (or dealer) needs?
- With survey calls to test different sales approaches?
- With calls to target and pinpoint your markets?
- By qualifying dealers or retailers?
- By generating leads?
- By qualifying leads from media prior to direct sales?
- By setting up appointments?
- By scheduled follow-up calls leading to the sale?

How could telemarketing help during the sale?

- By supplying answers to customer questions?
- By taking requests for literature?
- By controlling the flow of sales to match the capacity of your delivery and installation department?
- By confirming orders and payment arrangements?
- By upgrading the customer from a basic unit to a more profitable sale?

There are all kinds of ways telemarketing can work actively to take the burden off the shoulders of your sales people, and off your customer service department and maximize their efficiency.

How can you put telemarketing to work after the sale?

- With goodwill calls after delivery?
- Prospecting calls for add-ons?
- Prospecting for referrals?

Surveys over the years show that a company's best prospects are friends and acquaintances of recent buyers and new customers. What an opportunity for creative telephone marketing! But hardly anyone is taking advantage of it, yet. Ask us for suggestions.

If your company sells supplies or accessories for your product, how about putting telemarketing to work to generate orders on a regular basis?

Don't overlook the service department when you're searching for opportunities.

- How about prospecting by phone for service contracts?
- And goodwill calls to confirm customer satisfaction?

Look for telemarketing opportunities in promotion and advertising and you'll see they're unlimited. Think multi-media, using the telephone in harmony with your direct mail, print or broadcast, and other promotional activities, and publicity.

- Prepare prospects to expect your mailing piece and read it.
- Stimulate response after the mailing has landed. (Remember that telemarketing will increase the response from a mailing, and can often transform a marginal list into a profitable one.)
- Hype your new ad campaign in print or broadcast.
- Solicit attendance at your trade show booth or party.

Telemarketing fits right into almost any kind of promotional activity. It's an inexpensive insurance policy guaranteeing success for your efforts in the other media.

In marketing research, telemarketing is underused. But it's the proven way to get preliminary results without spending a bundle, and get some pretty conclusive information rapidly, before you spend heavy R&D dollars.

- Think of testing proposed product changes or improvements.
- Think of testing new product concepts or names.
- Think of getting customer reaction to proposed product benefits or copy platform.

And, again, think multi-media, using the telephone in partnership with your direct mail research effort. The combination is unbeatable for getting reliable information fast, at low cost.

CHAPTER 24

Publicity, Public Relations, and Press Releases

Publicity and public relations are terms which are used interchangeably by most professionals in the field, although Crain's *Dictionary of Advertising Terms* gives the following definitions:

- *Publicity* (NOUN)—information regarding a person, corporation, product, and the like released on his or its behalf for non-paid use by media.
- *Public relations (PR)*—activities of persons or organizations intended to promote understanding of and good will toward themselves or their products or services.

Professional publicist Stephen Berg defines public relations as "positioning through journalism." Most of us in the field think of it as "free advertising." Essentially, we write copy about our products, send it to the media, and try to persuade them to give us coverage in their publications or on their radio and TV programs.

O'Dwyers' PR Services Report found that the public relations departments of *Fortune* 500 firms go by the following names: Corporate communications, public relations, public affairs, communications, corporate public relations, public relations and advertising, and corporate affairs. According to *O'Dwyers,* 439 of the *Fortune* 500 have internal departments dedicated to communications or PR.

A survey by *Business Marketing* magazine of business-to-business marketing communications managers shows that the main purpose of public relations is to promote products and services. Of those executives surveyed, 85 percent say they use public relations programs for marketing and product support purposes. Only 19 percent said they used it to build corporate image.

Which public relations tools are most effective? When asked which public relations activities were most beneficial, 77 percent of those surveyed by *Business Marketing* said new product press releases. Sending out press releases announcing changes in personnel (promotions, new hires, etc.) was considered the least effective activity. The results of the survey are summarized in Table 24.1.

How to Use Press Releases Effectively

"A press release is used to tell the media about your particular story or business in the hopes the media will then tell the public," writes Carol Marden, president, Great Stuff Studio, Raleigh, NC.

"The way you reach your 'public' through public relations is by persuading the media to tell your story in their pages or air time," adds Alison

Table 24.1. The public relations activities top marketers consider most beneficial.

Public Relations Activity	*Percentage responding*
New product releases	77%
Technical articles	64%
Case histories	39%
Trade show press kits	22%
Newsletters	20%
Editorial tours	19%
Financial/business publicity	15%
Newspaper publicity	10%
Personnel releases	4%
Other	3%

Note: The total response adds to more than 100 percent due to multiple mentions.

Davis. "Public relations thus becomes a matter of adapting your message to fit the editorial needs of the media you target."

"The successful publicist thinks like an editor," says Richard M. Ezequelle, publisher of *Clinical Lab Products.* "This person submits news releases that fit the magazine, that require little or no changes, that are welcome in the editor's mail box . . . [and that] present uncolored, factual news and supply specific details about operation features and benefits. If the product has news value, it will get into print."

In a booklet titled "How to Get Your Publicity into Print," the editors of *Powder/Bulk Solids Magazine* explain the criteria by which they judge the suitability of a press release for the cover of their magazine: "The item must be brand new to the trade. And, it must be considered of prime importance to our reading audience. Our editors are on the lookout for only the very latest product innovations to meet our readers' ever-changing needs."

Press releases are standard, mass-distributed "stories" sent to multiple editors and publications—simultaneously—with the idea that a percentage of these editors will run an article favorable to your company based on the material.

Press releases do work. When *The Columbia Journalism Review* surveyed an issue of *The Wall Street Journal* to find out how many of the stories were generated by press releases, they found that 111 stories on the inside were taken from press releases word for word or paraphrased. In only 30 percent of these stories did reporters put in additional facts not contained in the original release. One professional in the PR field estimates that 80 percent of all published newspaper and magazine stories either have their basis in a press release or at least use material from press releases.

Although the standard format press releases—new product releases, personnel changes, address changes, new catalog releases—do work and can be extremely effective, the best way to profit from press releases is to be different and innovative.

How do you do this? Carol Marden says, "Your press release must reflect some newsworthy event." The problem is, few events dealing with your company are, in themselves, newsworthy. The solution? *Create* news or newsworthy events.

The standard approach to doing press releases is to look around for interesting things to write about, and—finding none—try to write up press releases that make the usual mundane happenings seem exciting. A better approach is to create something that is exciting, new, interesting, or newsworthy, then promote it with a press release.

Case Study 1: PR Hotline

Alan Caruba, a New Jersey PR counselor, wanted to gain some publicity for his business. The challenge: Caruba is one of hundreds of independent PR counsellors and there is nothing newsworthy about being in the PR business *per se*.

Alan's solution? Create a "PR Hotline" through which he can offer his consulting service on an hourly basis via telephone to smaller firms that either need quick advice or cannot afford to pay the traditional large monthly retainer most PR firms charge. Another interesting quirk: Alan accepts MasterCard and Visa, which is an unusual way to charge for professional services. His release on the topic, which gained wide publication and generated many inquiries to the hotline, is reproduced in Figure 24.1.

Figure 24.1. Sample press release—PR hotline.

THE CARUBA ORGANIZATION
Box 40, Maplewood, NJ 07040
201-763-6392

For Immediate Release

CHARGE PR ADVICE TO YOUR CREDIT CARD
"PR HOTLINE"—NEW BUSINESS SERVICE

Maplewood, NJ—Mike Wallace of "60 Minutes" is at the door with a camera crew! What do you do now?

"Most public relations does not involve a crisis," says PR counselor Alan Caruba of Maplewood, NJ. "In fact, good PR can avert such problems while helping to promote products, services, and causes of every description."

Caruba notes that "many business and professional people neither need, nor want, to retain a full-time public relations agency or counselor. What they need is good advice from time to time." That's why Caruba created the "PR Hotline," a telephone service (201-763-6392) which allows anyone with a PR question or problem to call. One can charge the service to either their MasterCard or Visa.

At $50 for the first 40 minutes or $75 for up to a full hour, "a lot of very specific analysis and advice can be provided," says Caruba. "Public relations can be local, regional, or national in scope. It can represent a single project or a long-term program."

Caruba has been dispensing advice and service to corporations, associations, small business operations, and individuals for more than twenty years. He is a member of The Counselors Academy of the Public Relations Society of America and frequently lectures and writes on the subject.

-END-

Case Study 2: Letters That Work

Joan Harris is one of the top writers of sales letters in the country. But, she is expensive. To make her services more affordable to smaller firms, she created "LETTERSthatWORK," a program of offering a *series* of custom-written sales letters to firms at reduced cost. Her release is reproduced in Figure 24.2.

Figure 24.2. Sample press release—Joan Harris.

PRESS RELEASE

For Immediate Release

From: Joan Harris
Contact: Connie Murphy
516-333-4444

NEW SERVICE OFFERED TO BUSINESSES—LETTERSthatWORK

Joan Harris, president of Joan Harris Direct Response, has just announced a new service. It's called LETTERSthatWORK and offers a custom-written series of individually created sales and customer service letters for only $1,750 (a $2,500 value if done separately).

These letters are written to be used, with modifications, over and over by an entire staff. All are expressly written to achieve results. The series offers five separate letters which can sell a service or product, activate inactive accounts, welcome new customers, introduce a new product, request important information, collect overdue bills, announce new personnel, and much more.

They're created expressly for each client after an in-depth meeting to assess the company's particular needs, style, and goals. Along with this custom-written series comes a "satisfaction" guarantee and a FREE follow-up meeting for "fine-tuning."

The author of *Modern Business Letters* (now in its third edition) and *Selling With Words* (both from Asher Gallant Press), Ms. Harris is a copywriter/consultant specializing in business-to-business direct mail. She says she developed this concept since most of her clients ask her to write their sales and service letters after she's created a direct mail campaign for them.

"I get calls every day that start off, 'Joan, I need a letter to . . .,' " she says. "Strong, results-oriented letters are very important for every company—just as important as a talented sales staff. Often, a company will put lots of money into their product, their collateral material, their sales training, and then they send out unprofessional, ineffective, poorly written letters. Your letters represent you and should be treated that way. They can be a key step in getting . . . and keeping . . . customers. That's certainly a worthwhile investment."

For more information about LETTERSthatWORK, call Joan Harris or Connie Murphy at 516-829-5452.

Case Study 3: Institutionalitis Poster

Gary Blake, a management consultant specializing in business and technical writing seminars, is a big believer in press releases and has gained a lot of trade and national publicity for his writing firm. Each press release is centered around a unique idea or concept that editors find both intriguing and either entertaining or newsworthy.

In one recent release, Dr. Blake took a humorous approach, inventing the term *institutionalitis* to describe the overly formal, stiff, antiquated style plaguing corporate writing. But instead of just getting publicity coverage, he also generated a huge response by offering an institutionalitis poster. His release is reprinted in Figure 24.3.

This press release was printed in several newspapers and trade magazines and generated more than 600 requests for the poster.

How To Prepare A Press Release

Preparing a press release is simple and straightforward. Just type your copy double-spaced on regular letter-size (8½ × 11″) sheets of paper. Press releases can be duplicated by offset at a local "quick copy" print-shop or run off on your office copier if the quality of reproduction is good. You can reproduce them on plain paper, business stationery, or special PR letterhead with the words "NEWS RELEASE" or "PRESS RELEASE" printed across the top; however, special paper is not necessary, and plain paper is fine.

Follow the format of the samples presented in this chapter. At the top of the first page, put "FROM:" or "SOURCE:" followed by the name and

Figure 24.3. Sample press release: Gary Blake.

CLIENT: **CONTACT:**

The Communication Workshop
217 E. 85th St.
New York, NY 10028

Gary Blake
718-575-8000

For immediate release:

SPECIALISTS URGE BYPASS, EDUCATION, AND EARLY DETECTION IN TREATING CORPORATE AMERICA'S NUMBER ONE COMMUNICATION PROBLEM: INSTITUTIONALITIS

NEW YORK, NY, April 1—"Institutionalitis"—the use of overly formal, pompous, and antiquated phrases in business communications—is now at "epidemic proportions." That's the opinion of writing specialists at the Center for Diseased Language Control who are urging managers to treat hedgy, pompous, and antiquated phrases with methods of early detection, education, and "word bypass" surgery.

Once thought of as only a disease affecting lawyers and government bureaucrats, Institutionalitis now afflicts middle managers in data processing, sales, operations, customer service, engineering, and accounting. According to studies, the problem is spread through the careless misuse of words, and a tendency to write for the filing cabinet instead of for other human beings.

Says one writing specialist, "You can live with Institutionalitis for years before knowing that you have it. Then, it's often too late to do anything to save your style. If left unchecked, institutionalitis can wreck a career."

According to Gary Blake, Director of The Communication Workshop, a New York City-based consulting firm specializing in the treatment of writing disorders, "A simple five-minute test can detect institutionalitis and prevent its spread. Just look at one of your letters, memos, reports, or proposals and see if you're using words and phrases like 'Enclosed please find,' 'Under separate cover,' 'pursuant to,' or 'Thanking you in advance.' Next, check for redundancies like 'end result,' 'consensus of opinion,' 'close proximity' or 'foreign imports.' The more widespread the jargon, hedgy words, and lengthy sentences, the more advanced the disease."

"It's odd," says one writing specialist, "but Institutionalitis can strike anyone—manager or support staff, young or old, educated or uneducated."

Unless you treat the diseased language, it gets worse and worse, eventually weakening the heart of an organization. Then, you need to hire a writing consultant to come in and perform "word bypass surgery." This operation, which has become routine, takes place during a two-day seminar. Gradually, sufferers of Institutionalitis learn to "bypass" unnecessary words and phrases. For example, a manager who had been in the habit of writing, "In the majority of instances . . ." now just writes, "Usually," thus bypassing several unnecessary words.

A joint statement issued by the writing doctors said that "the best prevention is education." But not just a seminar that treats the symptoms, one that treats the causes. In Dr. Blake's two-day seminar, he discusses how institutionalitis takes root in our writing, and shows the advantages of using a clear, conversational writing style.

In the post-seminar recovery period, managers begin to notice that their writing needs less editing, that they write faster as well as better, and that their thoughts are better organized, easier to grasp, and more persuasive.

The lucky managers who have their wordiness and stiff language caught in time usually go on to excel in their occupations. Their writing gradually becomes more and more specific, concise, and compelling. Those who are not treated, however, waste thousands of hours in corporate time writing muddy prose that needs to be endlessly edited and re-edited.

Since prevention is the ultimate cure of Institutionalitis, The Communication Workshop has produced a poster showing dozens of examples of the disease. Dr. Blake hopes that the poster will find its way to bulletin boards in the hallways of corporations throughout the United States. To receive a poster, send your name, title, organization, and address to The Communication Workshop, 217 East 85th Street, New York, NY 10028. Please enclose $1.50 per poster to cover postage and handling.

address of your company. Underneath this type "CONTACT:" followed by your name and telephone number.

If you use a public relations agency, they will list their own name and address (under "FROM:" or "CONTACT:") followed by the name and address of you, their client (preceded by the word "CLIENT:").

Below this, type the words "For immediate release." This tells editors that your story is timely, but it doesn't date the release. So if you want to keep a supply on hand and send them out to editors as the opportunity arises, you can. If the release is tied to an event that takes place on a specific date, type "For release: Monday, May 22, 19XX" (substituting the actual date) instead of "For Immediate Release."

Underneath this comes the headline. It is typed in all caps and can be as short as one line or as long as three lines. Two lines is typical.

Leave some extra space between the headline and the first paragraph of the story. The first paragraph begins with a dateline, such as "New York, NY, October, 19XX—", with the first sentence of the first paragraph coming immediately after that dash.

There are two basic types of leads for press releases: *news* and *feature*. The news lead is the prototypical "Who, what, when, where, why, and how" opening of a straight news story as taught in Journalism 101. The advantage of using the news lead is that, even if the editor chops the rest of your story and only prints the first paragraph—as is frequently done—the gist of your story still gets across.

The other type of lead is the *feature* lead. The feature lead is written in an entertaining, attention-getting fashion similar to the opening of a magazine feature article. The purpose is to grab the editor's attention by being clever, startling, or dramatic, so that more editors read and use your release.

After the lead comes the body of the story. If you are coming to the end of the page and it looks like the paragraph will have to continue onto the next page, move the entire paragraph to the next page. You do not want paragraphs divided between two pages.

The reason is that some editors may want to literally cut up your release into paragraphs with scissors, then tape it together in a different order. (This is how some editors edit.) For the same reason, releases are always printed on one side of a sheet of paper, never on two sides.

You may say at this point, "But I don't want the editor to edit my story. I want it to run as is!" This is an understandable attitude, but it is self-defeating. In public relations, the editor is in clear control, is the "customer" for your stories, and you must meet the editor's needs and standards first if you are to have any chance of reaching your final audience—the editor's readers.

If the editor wants to edit, make it easy, not difficult. If he/she wants a new angle on your story, don't protest—help him/her find it. The more you cooperate with editors and give them what they need, the more publicity you will get.

The last paragraph of your press release contains the response information, including name, address, and telephone number. For example, "To get XYZ Company's new 30-page Widget Catalog, contact Cal Jones, XYZ Company, Anytown, USA, phone XXX-XXXX."

At the end of the story, you can simply type "END" or "XXX" or "-30-". All three symbols let the editor know that this is the end of the story.

Five Ways To Get Your Publicity Releases Published More Often

Copywriter Mike Pavlish offers the following checklist for making sure your press releases get published:

1. *Is it important to the publication's readers?* If you were the editor and you had dozens of releases but could only publish a few, would you honestly publish your release? Is the information and story in your release really important—not to your business, but to the publication's readers? If not, forget it and look for a new angle.

2. *Is it really news or just an advertisement in disguise?* Editors are not in the business of publishing advertising. Almost all will immediately discard publicity that is really advertising in disguise. Of course, most publicity has some advertising value or purpose, but write your publicity to give news or helpful information only.

3. *Is it written so the publication's readers benefit from it?* Your publicity will get published more often if there is important news in it that will benefit the publication's readers. This could be new technology the readers will be interested in, helpful information, or a new trend that is emerging.

4. *Is it short and to the point?* Editorial space is very limited, and busy editors don't have the time to sort through irrelevant copy and cut it down to the main points. Write clear and crisp sentences using only the important, relevant information.

5. *Does it include what the editor wants?* That is, facts to back up your statements, plus who, what, when, where, how, and why details.

16 Additional Tips For Improving Your Press Releases

Don Levin, president of Levin Public Relations, offers these additional tips and tactics on improving press releases:

1. Shorten them. Tighten the writing. Keep paragraphs and sentences concise. Avoid jargon and repetition. Use strong verbs. Create lively, but accurate text.
2. Use subheads in longer stories, at least one per page. Help the editor grasp the entire story. Trim sections, or put them in side-bars.
3. Consider adding a fact sheet for details that would clutter your release.
   For example, a New York City restaurant, when sending out a press release announcing their grand opening, including a separate sheet listing their five most special dishes along with the ingredients and recipes.
4. Make the release stand on its own. Do not use a cover letter.
5. Get all the facts and establish perspective before starting to write. Adding and rewriting later costs time and money.
6. Keep the news up front, not behind the interpretation or buried in paragraphs of analysis.
7. Cut out puffery; stick to newsworthy information.
8. Put opinion and interpretation in an executive's quotation.
9. Forget the cute headline that forces an editor to dig through a paragraph or two to discover the who, what, when, where, and why. The headline should summarize the release so an editor quickly understands your point.
10. Leave plenty of white space, especially at the top of page one, because editors like to have room to edit. Double space and leave wide margins. Never use the back of a page.
11. Write for a specific editorial department (e.g., up-front news, financial, new products. Similarly, provide separate story slants—in separate releases—for different categories of magazines).
12. Create separate, shorter releases for radio and, at minimum, color slides and scripts for television.

13. End releases with a boilerplate paragraph that explains the organization or division.
14. Consider editing the news release copy for product bulletins, internal publications, and other uses.
15. Write to gain respect for your organization and your next release.
16. Streamline the clearance process so only two or three executives approve each release. This saves time and minimizes the chance to muddy the text. As Ford Kanzler points out, "The newsworthiness of a news release is inversely proportional to the number of persons on the approval cycle."

How To Determine Where To Distribute Your Press Release

Your press release should be sent to every publication that could conceivably have an interest in publishing it and whose readers (even a small portion of them) might be prospects for your product or service.

This is the opposite of advertising media selection, in which you focus in on those few publications that are most targeted toward your market. Why the difference? In advertising, each publication you add to your schedule can cost thousands or tens of thousands of dollars.

But to add a given publication to your press release distribution list costs only a 29-cent stamp for mailing the release; for this reason, it makes sense to be all-encompassing rather than selective.

For example, if you have a release appropriate to computer publications, don't go through your publicity director and spend time agonizing over which magazines should get the release and which should not. Instead, just send it to all the publications in the computer and data processing category automatically. This actually saves time by eliminating a selection process and incurs minimal additional incremental cost ($29 post per additional one hundred releases mailed).

Using Bacon's Publicity Checker

There are many competing directories and services for press release distribution. One of the best-organized, most complete, and easiest to use is *Bacon's Publicity Checker.* There are three volumes—newspapers, magazines, and radio—listing thousands of publicity outlets. Listings are organized by category for magazines and geographically for newspapers, with each listing giving names, addresses, and phone numbers of appropriate contacts.

You have three choices for distributing a release via *Bacon's*. The first is to buy or borrow the books and mail out the releases yourself. This involves typing addresses on envelopes, duplicating releases, and stuffing releases into envelopes. It's time-consuming and difficult to get releases out in a timely manner this way unless you have a secretary with time on her hands. One way to save time is to enter the publicity outlets once into a computer program, then print labels or envelopes automatically for each subsequent mailing.

The second alternative is to order the names and addresses from Bacon's PR Service on gummed labels. The cost as of this writing is 25 cents per label, which is only $25 for a hundred labels. This eliminates the need to type them yourself. The drawback is that you have to order a fresh set of labels each time you do a mailing.

The third alternative is to send the release to Bacon's and let them do it. Bacon's has a publicity distribution service where, for a fee, they will duplicate and mail your release to publications in select categories from their list. This is the easiest, most convenient option. All you do is mail them one copy of your release. They handle the printing and mailing.

Compiling Your Media List

If you are an active mailer of press releases, you may decide to create your own customized media mailing list rather than simply send your release to be mailed by Bacon's or Ayers to their standard distribution list in a given category.

For convenience, put your list on computer using a database or simple mailing list program capable of generating mailing labels automatically. You do not need word processing capability since the press releases themselves will not be personalized; all you need is mailing labels.

Start by checking the directories and putting into your list all the editors at publications and broadcast media relevant to your markets.

Next, add all the editors who have ever interviewed you or written about you in the past. Because they already know you, these editors are more receptive to material from you than editors who don't know you.

Then, add any specialized publications or other publicity outlets not listed in the directories. These can include industry newsletters, trade association newsletters, local ad club bulletins, and other specialized outlets too small to make it into the big directories. But even though they are small, they are highly targeted, and these often-overlooked outlets may be your most productive publicity sources.

Because editors move and publications fold, you must clean your mailing list frequently. Update it whenever you get a change of address or the name of a new editor. Once a year, have your secretary go through it, call all the publications, and verify that you have the current information.

PR Photos

Press releases do not have to be mailed with photos. Interesting releases will be picked up and used without an accompanying photograph, so photos are not necessary. On the other hand, if your press release lends itself to photographic treatment, an accompanying photo can only add interest to the article when it is published.

Carol Marden says that a PR photo should be black and white, glossy, have sharp contrast, and measure either 5 × 7″ or 8 × 10″. Len Kirsch, president of Kirsch Communications, says that black-and-white photos are "a must for product stories, good if you can swing them for other items."

"If your photograph is important to you, don't just book an appointment and expect professional results," writes consultant Pete Silver in his newsletter, *The Marketing Communications Report.* "Tell the photographer about the ways you intend to use the photo. This allows the photographer to plan the shooting more effectively by selecting the right backdrops, etc."

Photo captions should be typed on a separate sheet of paper and taped to the back of the photo. Do not type or write with ballpoint pen directly on the back of a photo; the impression will come through and show up in reproduction.

Don Levin does not like taped-on captions. "Instead, have the photo duplicator strip in a caption in an expanded border below the photo, and duplicate that," says Levin. He also advises you to have the photographer give you all negatives and contact sheets, and to make sure you control ownership by buying all rights. Do not do business with photographers who say they are selling you only limited rights for a specific use; make it clear in your contracts that your fee permanently covers all rights.

Tip: You may want to check with your attorney to ensure that your contracts with freelancers transfer permanent ownership of all rights to creative work (writing, photos, drawings) to your firm. New legislation enacted in the late 1980s favors the writer, photographer, or creative artist over the corporate client as the owner of creative work in case of dispute.

Follow-Up

Generally, it is impractical to follow-up on all the press releases mailed because of the time and expense of telephoning. If you have mailed your press release to 100 to 300 publications, you probably want to follow up on just the 10 or 12 most important ones.

How do you follow up? First, telephone the editor within a week after mailing the release. Say: "We sent you a release about a week ago concerning (topic of release). Did you get it?" At this point, the editor will probably say she did not get it or doesn't remember it. That's only natural, because there are so many releases flooding her desk. (Pamela Clark, editor-in-chief of *Popular Computing,* says she gets 2,000 releases per month.)

You reply by explaining briefly what the release is about and then offering to send it again. Most editors out of politeness will say yes to this offer. Mail or fax the release to them (be sure to get their fax number before you end the call, and ask permission first before faxing), then follow up again, asking if they got it and read it. This time, the answer will be "yes."

Your next question is, "Does this seem of interest to your reader?" If the editor answers *yes,* ask her when she thinks she might run the release. If she gives you an issue date, great! If she has no immediate plans or isn't sure, ask what questions she has or what additional information she needs, and supply it. Or provide even more information that would make her interested in the story.

What happens if the editor is not interested? Find out why not. Say, "Gee, I'm surprised, because I thought (topic of release) would be of great interest to your readers because (reason your product or service is newsworthy)." The editor will probably rethink her position if your argument makes sense.

If not, at least you learn why your item is not of interest to this editor or this publication—and you can tailor your next one to better meet their real interests. Sometimes, in telling you why your current release is unusable, the editor reveals the nature of the real story she is looking for . . . and if you can help her get that story, favorable publicity may result.

Don Levin offers the following additional tips for working with editors:

1. Develop good relationships with people in the media.
2. Call reporters before or after sending them a release, depending upon circumstances and individual preference.
3. Become a resource. Make yourself available. Visit editors. Steer them to news. Understand their needs.
4. If you can't answer questions, explain why.
5. Keep reporters and editors informed ahead of time when possible. Make yourself fully informed before you talk to the media.
6. Know SEC regulations if your company is publicly held.
7. Ask editors for advice. Ask how you could better serve them. Learn their pet peeves.
8. Cultivate a long-term reputation with key editors and staff members so you're called to be included or quoted in round-ups, staff-written features, and commentary. Remember that reporters move up to managing editors and change jobs to more prestigious publications.

Coping With Problem Situations

Sometimes public relations is used not to promote the good news but to overcome negative perceptions about a company. The most difficult crisis situations arise not when you are following up your press releases but during a crisis or other times when the press calls *you* rather than you calling them. PR counsellor Art Stevens offers the following guidelines for handling the press, especially during a crisis:

1. *Never speculate.* Do not engage in guesswork or speculate about any aspect of the crisis or about company policy. All reports to the media must be based on verified fact. If a specialist is needed to explain a technological context, make it clear that the specialist is providing background, not reporting on the crisis.

2. *Be open.* Withholding information is almost certain to backfire. Reporters are expert at discovering what is going on. And when withheld information comes to light, the company looks like it was deliberately hiding information to cover up some degree of malfeasance.

Exception 1: If releasing information may cause unnecessary pain, hold it back. Divulging the name of a victim of a fatality before the family is properly notified is a clear example.

Exception 2: Do not release information if doing so exceeds the scope of your authority. For instance, stating the cause of death is a doctor's or coroner's responsibility, not a public relations manager's. Even if excellent evidence exists, and the media-response group is confident it knows the answers to such questions, the questions should be referred to those authorized to make the official determinations.

3. *Respond to all media inquiries.* Avoid appearing to dodge any media requests. Maintain a log of all inquiries so that every request can be honored. Avoid "no comment" responses. It is far better to say something like, "We don't have a verifiable answer to your questions at this time, but when we do you'll get it." Or, "We're trying to get that information, and we'll give it to you as soon as we have it." Or, "All we know at present is . . .", and spell out what has been verified.

Always convey the impression that your company is working diligently to be the best source of information available and that it is determined to provide reliable, factual coverage.

4. *Establish and convey clear corporate policies.* One of the most significant tools available in handling crisis news consists of stating company policies in unambiguous terms. Doing so prevents or lessens the development of resentment, fear, anger, and hostility.

5. *Provide media access to top executives.* In dealing with a serious crisis, it is effective to have a top executive talk to the media. A press briefing is an acceptable forum, but individual interviews can also prove useful. The words of a top executive, especially those of a policymaker, carry far more import than the same statements from a professional spokesperson. It is usually well worth the executive's time.

6. *Allow the story to fade away.* All news stories have a life of their own. It is important to handle bad news while it is live. After it fades from public view, let it rest in peace. Sometimes companies feel a need to counteract the effects of bad news in a way that resurrects it. Doing so is a mistake. Once it is out of the public awareness, it is usually best left alone.

PR Resources

For information on buying directories, ordering labels, or the PR distribution service, contact: Bacon's PR Service, 332 South Michigan Avenue, Chicago, IL 60604, phone 800-621-0561.

•*Gebbie Press ALL-IN-ONE Directory,* Box 1000, New Paltz, NY 12561, phone, (914) 255-7960. This directory lists more than 21,000 publicity outlets, combining newspapers, radio stations, TV stations, consumer magazines, business journals, and news syndicates in a single volume. Cost is $78. Also available on floppy disk.

•Public Relations Plus, Inc., Post Office Drawer 1197, New Milford, CT 06776, phone 203-354-9361 or 800-999-8448. Publishes five publicity directories: *New York Publicity Outlets, metro California media, All TV Publicity Outlets—Nationwide, National Radio Publicity Outlets,* and *The Family Page Directory.* The big advantage of these directories is that they list more editors for each publication, allowing you to better target your release to the proper department and person. Call for free catalog.

•PR DATA SYSTEMS, Inc., 19 Oakwood Avenue, Norwalk, CT 06850, phone 800-227-7409. PR Data provides targeted media mailing lists, release and photo reproduction, and press kit assembly and mailing. A routine one-page press release mailed to 200 publications costs approximately $96 plus postage. Call for free brochure.

•*Directory of Experts, Authorities, & Spokespersons: The Talk Show Guest Directory,* Broadcast Interview Source, 2233 Wisconsin Avenue, N.W., Washington, DC 20007, phone 202-333-4904. This directory is distributed annually to more than 6,500 newspaper editors, columnists, TV assignment editors, radio talk shows, wire services, and others in the media who use it to locate experts to interview and use as sources for stories. To get your company listed, call or write.

•*The Top 200+ TV News/Interview Shows,* Ad-Lib Publications, P.O. Box 1102, Fairfield, IA 52556, phone 800-669-0773. This report lists 160 television shows that are syndicated or broadcast nationally, including all the major network and cable shows and talk shows. It includes the addresses, phone numbers, and names of producers and information on the topics they are interested in. Cost: $30.

•*Print Media Editorial Calendars,* SRDS Circulation Dept., 3004 Glenview Road, Wilmette, IL 60091, phone 800-323-4588. One effective way of increasing release pick-up is to target releases at specific issues of magazines covering your topic. *Print Media Editorial Calendars* lists the editorial schedules of 4,200 business magazines, 1,700 newspapers, 1,500 consumer magazines, and 400 farm publications, enabling you to target your release to the right special issues at the right time. Write for details.

CHAPTER 25

Placing The "Planted" Feature Story

The Planted Feature Story

A *planted,* or *placed,* feature story is an article written and submitted to a publication by a corporation, entrepreneur, or business professional—either directly by the business or on their behalf by their PR firm or consultant. Unlike a freelance writer who writes articles because it pleases him to do so and because he earns money from it, the company submitting a feature article has a different purpose: to gain publicity and exposure for the firm, its ideas, or its products and services.

Placing feature articles with appropriate trade, consumer, or business publications is one of the most powerful and effective of all marketing techniques:

- You can get one, two, three or more pages devoted to your product or service without paying for the space (a paid ad of that length could run you $3,000 to $20,000 or more).
- Your message has far more credibility as "editorial" material than as a sponsored advertisement.

- The publication of the article results in prestige for the author and recognition for the company.
- Reprints make excellent, low-cost sales literature.

Getting an article published in a trade journal or local business magazine is not difficult—if you know how. While editors are quick to reject inferior material or "puff" pieces, they are hungry for good, solid news and information to offer their readers. And, unlike newspapers, whose reporters are investigative and frequently antagonistic and adversarial toward business, trade journal editors represent a friendlier audience, and are more willing to work with you to get your information to their readers.

If there is a key mistake novices make in placing feature articles, it's giving up too soon. Your article is probably not going to be accepted by the first editor who sees it, or even the second. But keep trying. Consultant Jeff Davidson, a widely published author, says that to get 400 articles published, he was rejected 8,000 times.

Coming Up With Ideas for Articles

Aside from case histories, which we will discuss later in this chapter, most planted feature articles are of the how-to variety, either aimed at executives, managers, professionals, or technicians in a given field. In addition to case histories and how-to material, editors are also interested in stories on new products, developments, or trends in their industry.

One way to come up with article ideas is to make a list of the ads you would run (and the magazines in which you would run them) if you had an unlimited ad budget, then write articles based on topics related to those ads and place them in those magazines.

For example, if you wanted to advertise your new wood chip stacking system in *Pulp & Paper* magazine, but didn't have the budget for it, consider writing an article on "A new way to stack and inventory wood chips more efficiently" for that magazine. You will find it is cost-effective to write and place articles in magazines and for secondary markets in which print advertising is unprofitable or beyond your budget.

Many trade journals will send a sample issue and set of editorial guidelines to prospective authors upon request. These can provide valuable clues as to style, format, and appropriate topics. They often tell how to contact the magazine, give hints on writing an article, describe the manuscript review process, and discuss any payment or reprint arrangements.

Selecting The Right Magazine

Aside from *Bacon's Publicity Checker,* discussed in Chapter 24, the best source for learning more about magazines and their editorial requirements is a book called *Writer's Market,* published annually by Writer's Digest Books, 1507 Dana Avenue, Cincinnati, Ohio 45207, phone (513) 531-2222. *Writer's Market* lists more than 4,000 consumer, general, business, and trade publications that accept articles from outside sources. Listings give detailed descriptions of what editors are looking for, along with names, addresses, phone numbers, and other contact information.

The best magazines to target are the ones you are getting now. This is because you read them, are familiar with their editorial slant and style, and are aware of what articles related to your topic have been run recently. However, there may be many magazines in your industry that you don't get and are not familiar with; you can find them in *Bacon's* or *Writer's Market.* Contact each and ask for a sample issue and editorial guidelines.

When the sample issue comes, study it and gain familiarity with the publication. This is a key step in getting your article published. The quickest way to turn off an editor is to offer an idea that has nothing to do with his or her magazine.

"My pet peeve with people calling or writing to pitch an idea is that they often haven't studied the magazine," says Rick Dunn, editor of *Plant Engineering.* "If they haven't read several issues and gotten a handle on who we are and who our audience is, they won't be able to pitch an idea effectively."

"There's no substitute for knowing the audience and the various departments within a magazine," adds Jim Russo, editor of *Packaging.* "I'm more impressed by someone who has an idea for a particular section than by someone who obviously doesn't know anything about our format."

Tip: Media kits from most publications contain "editorial calendars" which list the editorial focus for the year's planned special issues. If you can offer an article that ties in with the editorial theme of a special issue, you can increase your chances of making a placement.

Timing is important. For a monthly magazine, an article to appear in a special issue should probably be proposed to the editor three to six months in advance of the publication date.

Avoid Puffery

Impartiality is a must with many editors. Remember, they're not there to praise your company's products—although being published can be as good as if they were. The editor's job is to give readers an objective overview of the goings-on in their industry. This can be a particularly sticky point when dealing with public relations personnel.

"We're certainly not prejudiced against articles from PR firms," says Mark Rosenzweig, editor of *Chemical Engineering.* "We just generally have to make more revisions to eliminate their tendency toward one-sidedness. We want all the disadvantages spelled out, as well as the advantages." Adds Rick Dunn, editor of *Plant Engineering:* "If an article is about storage methods, we want to see all 15 methods discussed, not just the ones used by the writer's company or client."

Another issue with editors is exclusivity. You should never submit the same idea or story to more than one competing magazine at a time. Only if the idea is rejected should you approach another editor. The majority of editors want exclusive material, especially for feature articles.

If a story is particularly timely or newsworthy, and has run in a magazine not directly competing with the one you're approaching, you may be able to get around the problem by working with the editor to expand or rewrite the piece. But be up-front about it or you will risk losing the editor's confidence and goodwill.

"I'd like everything to be exclusive," says Jim Russo, editor of *Packaging.* "That increases its value to us and can sway us toward acceptance if it's a 'borderline' story."

"Exclusivity is a quality consideration for a feature article," adds Dunn. "Editors don't want their readers to pick up their magazine and see something they've already read elsewhere."

Making The Initial Contact

Should you call or write the editor? Most editors won't object to either method of pitching an idea, but they usually have a preference for one or the other. It's simply a matter of personal choice and time constraints. If you don't know how a particular editor feels on the subject, call and ask. An appropriate opening might be: "This is Joe Jones from XYZ Corporation, and I have a story idea you might be interested in. Do you have time to spend a few minutes over the phone discussing it, or would you prefer that I sent you an outline?"

An editor who prefers to get it in writing will tell you so. Editors who prefer a quick description over the phone will appreciate your respect for their time, whether they listen to your pitch on the spot or ask you to phone back later.

But even those editors who will listen to your idea over the phone will also want something in writing. "With a phone call, I can tell someone right away whether he's on the right track," says Mark Rosenzweig, editor, *Chemical Engineering*. "If I like the idea, I'll then request a detailed outline describing the proposed article." Adds Rick Dunn: "A phone call is all right, but I can't make an editorial decision until I see a query letter."

Writing The Query Letter

The best way to communicate an article idea in writing is to send a query letter. A query letter is a mini-proposal in which you propose to the editor that you write an article on a particular topic for his magazine (and that he publish the article).

A query letter is, in essence, a sales letter. The "prospect" is the editor. The "product" you want to sell the editor is the article you want to write for his or her magazine.

Here are a few basic facts about query letters.

1. Editors look for *professionalism* in query letters. This means no typos, no misspellings. You address the letter to a specific editor by name. And you spell his or her name right.

2. Editors look for familiarity with their magazine. Don't suggest an article on hunting elk to the newsletter for the ASPCA. Sounds obvious, but such things happen every day. For example: PR firms proposing "how-to" articles to magazines that don't do how-to. Study the market before you send your query.

3. Editors look for good writing. If you can, write the first paragraph or two of your query so it could be used, as is, as the lead for your article. This shows the editor that you know how to begin a piece and get the reader's attention.

4. Editors hate lazy writers—those who want to see their byline in a magazine but refuse to do research or get their facts straight. Put a lot of hard "nuts-and-bolts" information—facts, figures, statistics—in your letter to show the editor that you know your subject. Most query letters (and articles) are too light on content.

5. Credentials impress editors. Tell the editor why he should trust you to write the article. If you are an expert in the subject, say so. If not, describe your sources. Tell which experts you will interview, which studies you will cite, which references you will consult. Highlight the breakthrough research your company has done to become a leader in its field.

6. Editors hate to take risks. The more fully developed your idea, the better. If you spell out everything—your topic, your approach, an outline, your sources—then the editor knows what he will get when he gives you the go-ahead to write the piece. The more complete your query, the better your chance for a sale.

Figure 25.1 is a typical query letter you can copy for style and format. Note that the article proposal is in two parts: a letter selling the basic idea and an outline listing the details. This format was appropriate simply because it fit the material; normally query letters don't require outlines.

Article Outline

TEN TIPS FOR BETTER TECHNICAL WRITING

1. *Know your readers.*
   Are you writing for engineers? managers? laymen?
2. *Write in a clear, conversational style.*
   Write to express—not to impress.
3. *Be concise.*
   Avoid wordiness. Omit words that do not add to your meaning.
4. *Be consistent . . .*
   . . . especially in the use of numbers, symbols, and abbreviations.
5. *Use jargon sparingly.*
   Use technical terms only when there are no simpler words that can better communicate your thoughts.
6. *Avoid big words.*
   Do not write "utilize" when "use" will do just as well.
7. *Prefer the specific to the general.*
   Technical readers are interested in solid technical information and *not* in generalities. Be specific.
8. *Break the writing up into short sections.*
   Short sections, paragraphs, and sentences are easier to read than long ones.
9. *Use visuals.*
   Graphs, tables, photos, and drawings can help get your message across.
10. *Use the active voice*
    Write "John performed the experiment," not "The experiment was performed by John." The active voice adds vigor to writing.

Figure 25.1. Sample query letter—Chemical Engineering.

Mr. Kenneth J. McNaughton
Associate Editor
CHEMICAL ENGINEERING
McGraw-Hill Building
1221 Avenue of the Americas
New York, NY 10020

Dear Mr. McNaughton:

When a chemical engineer can't write a coherent report, the true value of his investigation or study may be distorted or unrecognized. His productivity vanishes. And his chances for career advancement diminish.

As an associate editor of CHEMICAL ENGINEERING, you know that many chemical engineers could use some help in improving their technical writing skills. I'd like to provide that help by writing an article that gives your readers "Ten Tips for Better Business Writing."

An outline of the article is attached. This 2,000-word piece would provide 10 helpful tips—each less than 200 words—to help chemical engineers write better letters, reports, proposals, and articles.

Tip number 3, for example, instructs writers to be more concise. Too many engineers would write about an "accumulation of particulate matter about the peripheral interior surface of the vessel" when they're describing solids build-up. And how many managers would use the phrase "until such time as" when they simply mean "until"?

My book, TECHNICAL WRITING: STRUCTURE, STANDARDS, AND STYLE, will be published by the McGraw-Hill Book Company in November. While the book speaks to a wide range of technical disciplines, my article will draw its examples from the chemical engineering literature.

I hold a B.S. in chemical engineering from the University of Rochester, and am a member of the American Institute of Chemical Engineers. Until this past January, I was manager of marketing communications for Koch Engineering, a manufacturer of chemical process equipment. Now, I'm an independent copywriter specializing in industrial advertising.

Ken, I'd like to write "Ten Tips for Better Technical Writing" for your "You and Your Job" section.

How dos this sound?

Sincerely,

In the letter in Figure 25.1, as well as the letter in Figure 25.2, the first paragraph of the query letter became the lead paragraph of the published article. This is no accident. A catchy lead in the query, one that could logically be used to begin the article, helps grab the editor's attention and convince him that you've got something of interest.

The letter below got the go-ahead to write an article for *Writer's Digest* magazine:

Tip: The term "SASE" in the last sentence stands for "self-addressed stamped envelope." It's generally a good idea to include an SASE when writing to editors because it makes it easy for them to respond to your letter.

The editor most likely to be receptive to your queries is one who you have written for successfully in the past. When you sell one article to an editor, it makes sense to immediately fire off a second letter if you have another good idea that might be right for him/her. Figure 25.3 is a sample of such a follow-up query.

Note that the query letters shown are detailed, not superficial. You may object, "But that's a lot of work to do with no show of interest or commitment from an editor." Yes, it is. But that's what it takes to get published, and there's no way around it. And, as much work as writing a good query is, it's less work than writing the entire article.

Following Up Your Query

One of three things will happen after you mail your query letter:

1. The editor will accept your article "on spec" (on speculation). This means the editor is interested and wants to see the completed manuscript, but is not making a firm commitment to publish. This is the most positive response you are likely to get, and unless the article you write is terrible, there is a better than 50 percent chance it will get published.

2. The editor will reject your query. The next step is to send the query to the next editor and magazine on your list.

3. The third and most likely alternative is that you will not hear one way or the other. There are several reasons for this. The editor may not have gotten around to your query. Or, the editor has read it but not made a decision. Or, they didn't receive it, or they lost it.

Figure 25.2. Sample query: Writer's Digest

Mr. William Brohaugh
Editor
WRITER'S DIGEST
9933 Alliance Road
Cincinnati, Ohio 45242

Dear Mr. Brohaugh:

John Frances Tighe, a soft-spoken, bearded gentleman, modestly refers to himself as "the world's second-most successful freelance direct-mail copywriter."

John's fee for writing a direct-mail package? $15,000.

But that's peanuts compared to the $40,000 Henry Cowan charges. According to WHO'S MAILING WHAT!, a newsletter covering the direct mail industry, Cowan is the highest paid copywriter in the world. DIRECT MARKETING magazine reports that his income on the Publisher's Clearing House mailing alone (for which he receives a royalty) was $900,000 in a recent year.

Next to the movies and best-selling novels, direct mail is one of the highest paid markets for freelance writers. Although surprisingly easy to break into, most freelancers don't even know about it, and direct-mail writing is dominated by a few dozen writers who earn lush six-figure incomes writing only a few days a week.

I'd like to write a 3,000-word article on "Making Money as a Direct Mail Writer." The article would tell your readers everything they need to know to start getting assignments in this lucrative but little-known specialty.

Here are the topics I would cover:

1. THE SECRET WORLD OF DIRECT MAIL. What is direct mail? Who is writing direct mail—and how much are they earning? Why has this market been a secret until now? I would interview some old pros as well as some new writers to get their perspective.

2. A LOOK AT THE MARKET. What are the various uses of direct mail (mail order, fundraising, lead generation, cordial contact)? Types and formats of direct mail packages you might write. Types of organizations that hire freelance direct mail writers (publishers, catalog houses, fundraisers, insurance companies, banks, manufacturers, ad agencies) . . . and how (and where) to find them.

3. GETTING STARTED. Learning about direct mail. Studying the market. Building your swipe files. Getting your first assignments.

Figure 25.2. (continued)

4. HOW TO WRITE DIRECT MAIL COPY THAT SELLS. Understanding the mission of direct mail. Tips for writing copy that will get results. How to present your copy to clients. Graphics and layouts for direct mail copy. Differences in sales copy (direct mail) vs. editorial copy (magazine writing).

5. MARKETING YOUR SERVICES. Getting and keeping clients. How to market your services using: Portfolios. Meetings. Telephone calls. Letters. Advertising. Publicity techniques.

6. FEES. How to set fees. Table of typical fees. What others charge.

7. KEEPING UP WITH THE FIELD. Books. Publications. Professional organizations. Courses. Seminars.

This article will draw both from my own experience as a successful direct mail copywriter (clients include Prentice-Hall, New York Telephone, Hearst, Chase Manhattan, Edith Roman Associates) and from interviews with top pros in the field—including Milt Pierce, Sig Rosenblum, Richard Armstrong, Don Hauptman, Andrew Linick, and others. I know these people personally, so getting the interviews is no problem.

Also, I am a member of the Direct Marketing Club of New York and author of the forthcoming book, DIRECT MAIL PROFITS (Asher-Gallant Press).

May I proceed with the article as outlined?

An SASE is enclosed. Thanks for your consideration.

Regards,

The follow-up should be a polite note asking the editor (a) whether she received the article proposal, (b) whether she had a chance to look at it yet, and (c) whether she's interested. You can enclose a reply card the editor can use to check off her response, such as:

☐ YES, we're interested. Please submit manuscript (on spec, of course).

☐ NOT for us. Sorry.

☐ MAYBE. We haven't made a decision but will let you know shortly.

☐ DIDN'T receive your query. Send another copy.

Many professional writers use such a system for making it easy for editors to respond.

Figure 25.3. Sample query for follow-up article.

Ms. Kimberly A. Welsh
Editor
CIRCULATION MANAGEMENT
859 Willamette Street
Eugene, Oregon 97401-2910

Dear Kimberly:

Thanks for publishing the article on mailing lists so quickly. I hope you get good reader response to it.

I'm writing because I have another idea that might be right for CIRCULATION MANAGEMENT.

How about an article—"Do Premiums Work?"

Background: As you know, response rates are down all over. In an attempt to combat this, publishers are offering more and more expensive premiums to attract first-time subscribers. SPORTS ILLUSTRATED, for example, is offering a videocassette on great sports flubs. TIME recently offered a camera. And then there's NEWSWEEK's successful free telephone offer.

Questions: Is there some point at which a premium ceases to be an added inducement and actually becomes a "bribe," overshadowing the primary offer and becoming the key reason why people respond to a mailing? If so, how does that affect the quality the subscriber-base circulation is delivering to the publication's advertisers?

This would be the basis of my article, which would attempt to answer these specific questions:

- Do premiums still work? Are they still profitable? Or is there effectiveness declining as more and more publications jump into premium offers?
- Is there any limit to premium cost in relation to the cost of a one-year subscription? What is this limit? What's the "average" premium cost in publishing today?
- What works best—an information premium (printed report or book) or tangible item (telephone, clock-radio, etc.)?
- Must the premium be related to the publication, the market, or the theme of the mailing? Or do totally unrelated premiums work well as long as they have high perceived value?
- Once a subscriber is sold through a premium offer, must renewals also offer a premium?
- How do advertising managers feel about subscribers generated through premium offers? Is there a perception that a subscriber generated through a premium offer is worth less to an advertiser than someone who buys the magazine without such a bribe? Any proof to back up this feeling?

Figure 25.3. (continued)

To get the answers to these questions, I will interview circulation directors, advertising managers, direct response agencies, DM consultants, and freelancers responsible for creating and testing premium-based packages. I see this as a feature article running 3,000+ words.

Kimberly, may I proceed with this article as outlined?

Thanks for your consideration. An SASE is enclosed.

Regards,

Getting The Go-Ahead

Your editor is interested. Hurrah! You've passed the first step. Now the real work begins.

Once you've gotten your idea accepted, you'll need to know the length and deadline requirements. If the editor doesn't volunteer this information, ask. The answers may avoid misunderstanding later on.

As a rule, be generous with length. Include everything you think is relevant, and don't skimp on examples. Editors would rather delete material than have to request more.

While a few magazines are flexible on length, most give authors specific word lengths to shoot for. Ask your editor how long your article should be. To translate this to typed pages, every 500 words is equivalent to two double-spaced typewritten manuscript pages. In its final printed form, a "solid" page of magazine copy (no headlines, photos, or white space) is approximately 800 to 1,000 words. The first page, which has to leave room for a headline and byline, is approximately 700 words. Use Table 25.1 to calculate how much to write to meet your editor's space requirements.

Deadlines, too, can vary considerably among journals. Some don't like to impose any deadlines at all, especially if they work far enough in advance that they are not pressed for material. But if the article is in-

Table 25.1. Guide to article length.

Number of Words	*Number of Magazine Pages*	*Number of Manuscript Pages*
800–1,000	1	3–4
1,500	2	6
2,000	2-2-1/2	8
2,500	3	10
3,000	3-1/2–4	12

tended for publication in a special issue, the editor will probably want the finished manuscript at least two months before publication date. This allows time for revisions, assembling photos or illustrations, and production.

Don't put an editor's patience to the test. Missing a deadline may result in automatic rejection and waste the effect you spent making the placement and writing the article. Hand in every article on the deadline date, or sooner. If you cannot, advise the editor well in advance and request a reasonable extension. Editors dislike late copy, but they hate surprises.

The Pitch Letter

An alternate method of getting feature story placement is to get stories written *about* you and your product rather than placing stories written *by* you.

How do you get the press to write about you? Sending press releases, as described in Chapter 24, is one method. If the editor receives a release related to an article he/she is planning, he/she may contact you to interview people in your company even if the material in the release isn't exactly what he/she needs.

Tip: Whenever an editor responds to a press release or query, or calls to interview someone in your company, put them on your media list to ensure they receive all future news you issue.

Another way to get articles written about you—or at least get your company mentioned in articles—is to send a *pitch letter.* Unlike the query letter, which proposes that you write a specific article, the pitch letter simply offers your company as an expert source for interviewing purposes. Figure 25.4 is a typical pitch letter prepared by a public relations firm on behalf of its client.

Sending pitch letters is effective because editors and reporters are constantly on the lookout for accessible sources of expert information they can call to get a quote or fill in a missing fact for a story when on deadline.

It pays to include a rolodex (TM) card with your query letter which the reporter or editor can file under the appropriate category. That way, when the reporter is working on a story on "CDs," he turns to his card file, finds Edward Dempsey's name, calls Edward Dempsey for a quote, and quotes Edward Dempsey in his story. Edward Dempsey, then, and not his

Dear _______:

Compact disc (CD) sales are booming. In fact, some music industry executives are projecting disc sales will surpass album sales by the end of the year.

The first "compact disc only" retail store, Compact Disc Warehouse, in Huntington Beach, California, opened in November, 1984. It grossed nearly $1 million in sales in just 18 months operating out of a 1,200 square foot store.

Now, Compact Disc Warehouse, Inc. is launching the first CD franchise offering to meet the national demand for the hottest home entertainment product in the music industry today.

Edward Dempsey, president of CD Warehouse, is an expert on why CD's are changing an industry that has been dominated by record albums for decades and how the retail world is gearing up to meet the CD demand.

If you would like to arrange an interview, please call our offices.

Sincerely,

Mitch Robinson, Account Executive
S&S Public Relations, Inc.

Figure 25.4. Sample pitch letter.

competition, becomes known as the industry leader because he is constantly quoted in the press.

You probably have noticed that within your own industry the same spokespeople are quoted again and again. Well, it's not by accident. Diligent public relations efforts—not fate—ensure that one person or company becomes publicized while others wallow in obscurity.

How To Make Your Planted Articles Generate Direct Response

In addition to building image, increasing visibility, and serving as low-cost article reprints, planted feature stories can also be turned into direct response tools. How is this done? With a *resource box.*

A resource box—a term invented by Dr. Jeffrey Lant—is a box that appears at the end of your article. Instead of the usual brief author bio (e.g, "John Doe is a consultant whose articles frequently appear in *Busi-*

ness Marketing), the resource box gives complete information on who you are, what your company offers, and how readers of the article can reach you. Figure 25.5 is a typical resource box.

"I swap the articles I write in return for resource boxes in those publications," explains Dr. Lant. "Publications run the article. I get the resource box.

"Some of these publications swap for outright ad space—that is, they will *not* let my resource box run along with the article. One publication, with a readership of over 75,000 financial planners, gives me both the resource box *and* an ad. I therefore have a very good sense of which draws better.

"*The resource box ALWAYS wins.* There are several reasons for this. First, the article acts as a qualifying device. If you're not interested in copywriting, you probably won't read an article on the subject. If you're interested, you may have a need. And if you have a need, you'll be more receptive to filling it.

"Second, the article plus the resource box are several times larger than the ad.

"Third, the article gives the product credibility. The buyer reasons that the publication wouldn't publish the article—and as a result "recommend" the product—if it wasn't good. The article, and the resource box, lower the buyer's suspicion.

"Fourth, the words, 'resource box' are far superior to 'ad.' This helps sales. The resource box looks like a public service, which, of course, it is. For these reasons, the resource box always draws substantially better than the same product or service featured in an ad, no matter how well written and complete the advertisement."

How do you get a resource box printed with your article? Don't ask the editor outright. Instead, simply type in the resource box at the end of your manuscript and submit it along with your article. Ten to 20 percent of the time the editor will print it as is without questioning you. Another 10 to 20 percent of editors will object initially but relent after some discussion.

Figure 25.5. Resource box.

John Doe is a freelance copywriter specializing in business-to-business and direct response advertising. He writes ads, brochures, direct mail packages, and sales letters for more than 75 clients, nationwide including Prentice Hall, Grumman Corporation, Sony, On-Line Software, Philadelphia National Bank, and Associated Air Freight. He is also the author of 17 books including THE COPYWRITER'S HANDBOOK. Mr. Doe can be reached at. . . . .

The remainder will refuse you, because they see the Resource Box as too blatantly promotional and somehow compromising standards of journalistic integrity. But with my method you will have resource boxes running with at least 10 percent and up to 30 or 40 percent of all feature stories you place—significantly increasing the effectiveness of these articles.

How To Recycle Your Published Articles

Don Hauptman, a New York City-based direct marketing copywriter and consultant, says that just publishing any article once does not take advantage of its full potential as a marketing tool. "Most professionals who write for publication stop at this point," says Hauptman. "But for the aggressive, savvy self-marketer, the first publication of the article is only the beginning."

Why recycle your article? Because, as Hauptman notes, "The lifespan of any magazine, newsletter, or newspaper is limited. You want to get as much mileage as possible out of your effort." Here are his suggestions:

1. When you sell the article initially, make sure the publication gets one-time publication rights (known as "first rights" only). You, the author, retain all other rights. Ideally, try to have a copyright line printed at the end of your article (e.g., "copyright 1990 Jane Doe"). The reasoning behind this is that you have plans for the article, and you don't want to have to beg for permission to use your own work.

2. Be sure to get several copies of the issue as soon as it's off the press. When you receive them, cut apart one copy and paste it up for duplication.

3. For its new incarnation, the article may require some creative rearrangement. You will probably want to delete surrounding ads. The publication's logo can be cut from the cover, masthead, or contents page and placed at the top. This step is important—it gives your words the imprimatur of a known (and presumably respected) medium. At the end, tack on your firm's name, address, and phone number which are easily obtainable from your letterhead or business card.

4. Send the resultant mechanical or paste-up to a quick print shop. Or simply run it through your office copier. Watch out for problems that

might make your new publicity piece appear unattractive or unprofessional: dirt, skewed paragraph, or "cut marks" (stray lines created by the edge of the pasted-up article—they'll disappear with the help of typewriter correction tape or fluid).

5. For maximum readability, print the article in black on white or light-colored paper. Your name or your firm's name can be highlighted using a second color ink. Or, save the extra expense by circling your name or byline on each printed copy with a contrasting color fiber-tip pen.

6. Distribute copies of reprints to current, past, and potential clients. Include the reprints in your literature package or press kit, leave them in your reception area or lobby, hand them out at conferences and speaking engagements, and enclose them in a direct mail package. The possibilities are endless.

7. Since you own all rights to the article, you are free to publish it elsewhere. Other publications might want to run the article in its entirety, or excerpt or quote from it. Or, the editor may ask you to revise the article for his/her particular publication, but such adaptation is usually easy; the hard work has been done. You can even use the article as part of a book, either your own or perhaps an anthology by someone else.

Case Histories

Aside from the how-to feature article, *case histories* (also known as *case studies* or *user stories*) are the most popular type of planted article.

A case history is a product success story. It tells how a customer saved money, solved problems, or improved his or her life by using a product or service.

In an editorial in *Design News,* Lars Soderholm suggests the following six-step outline for case histories:

1. Background material: The nature of the problem—how it came about, why it exists, what causes it to exist.
2. Negative consequences of the problem: why is it so bad? How does it harm us?
3. The method, product, service, or technique used to solve the problem: what is it? Describe.
4. Details: How the solution was implemented. Specifics.

5. Results: How are things changed as a result of the solution.
6. Benefits: What are the consequences? How much time, money, energy was saved? By what percentage were productivity, efficiency, profits increased?

Consultant Ryle Miller gives a similar structure in an article in *Chemical Engineering* Magazine:[3]

1. The situation: What's the background?
2. The problem: What was wrong?
3. The resolution: The answer to the problem.
4. Information: The details of the resolution.

Karen Kramer, editor of *Chemical Processing* magazine, also uses a problem-solution-results format in the 12 to 22 case histories her magazine publishes monthly. Says Kramer: "In addition to the name and location of the plant using the equipment, the date of installation, and the type of equipment involved, we also like to point out the single most important benefit of the installation and what advantages have been gained—such as reductions in maintenance and downtime, increased production, or higher product quality."

CHAPTER 26

Trade Shows*

Promoting your company's products and services at a trade show can be an effective adjunct to your other marketing activities. As one industry analyst observes, "Marketing directors find that if strategic planning and administration are employed, the trade show is the most cost-effective means to get direct contact—getting to prospects and developing qualified leads that result in sales."

More than 10,000 industrial and consumer trade shows are held each year in the United States. According to the *Journal of Marketing,* current projections indicate that more than 145,000 companies will participate in trade shows by 1991. In fact, of the $94 billion spent on U.S. business/industrial marketing in 1986, trade shows accounted for $21 billion.

*Some of the information in this chapter was reprinted with permission from "Trade Shows—Essential Factor in the Marketing Mix," White Paper Series Number 10, published by the Business/Professionals Advertising Association; from "Exhibiting at Trade Shows," a U.S. Small Business Administration Management Aid; and from "Expositions Work: A Management Guide for Exhibitors," published by the Trade Show Bureau.

Advantages of Trade Shows

Why are trade shows so popular? According to an article in *Industry Week:*

> "For the manufacturer, trade shows are an opportunity to personally meet prospects as well as a speedy way to get a product—especially a new, high-tech one—introduced to a target audience. For the sales force, they're a motivator. For the customer, they're a quick, convenient way to see and compare competing products."

Moreover, many of those who attend trade shows are buyers, not just browsers. The Trade Show Bureau, an informational and educational organization based in East Orleans, Massachusetts, has conducted research that reveals that 86 percent of all show visitors represent an important buying influence (i.e., they can recommend, specify, or purchase the product or service being exhibited). Exhibit Surveys, Inc., a major trade show organization, reports that 60 percent of trade show audiences nationwide had buying plans when they attended shows in 1987. And a report published by the Trade Show Bureau shows no follow-up calls were required to close 54 percent of exposition leads, with just one call required to close another 16 percent of leads. On average, less than one sales call is required to convert a trade show lead into an order, compared with the 5.1 sales calls needed to close the average industrial sale.

A recent study by Incomm International revealed the following reasons why people attend trade shows:

- To find solutions to known problems
- To decide on or familiarize vendor selection for post-show purchases
- To identify new methods
- To meet with technical experts
- To assess industry directions

For the exhibitor, trade shows are a way to reach people who are not ordinarily contacted by or accessible to a salesperson. According to Exhibit Surveys, 88 percent of the average show audience in 1986 had not been visited by a salesperson from the exhibitor in the preceding 12 months. And exhibitors reach new people each time they participate in a show; on average, one-third of attendees are paying a first-time visit to every show, so exhibiting is a good way to meet new potential buyers, find out about new companies, and keep up to date on what the competition is doing.

Used in tandem with other marketing activities, trade shows provide an opportunity to accelerate the buying process. You may be able to accomplish in two or three days what would normally take weeks or months of account prospecting work. Depending on the dollar amount your company spends on its exhibit, personnel, hotel, meals, and other expenses, and the number of people its exhibit reaches, trade shows are often a cost-effective sales vehicle. A 1985 study by the McGraw-Hill Laboratory of Advertising Performance showed that the average cost for obtaining a qualified sales lead at a trade show was $106.89, in comparison to the cost for a conventional industrial sales call, which was $229.70. With the rising costs of sales calls in the field, more companies are finding that attending trade shows—especially regional shows—is an increasingly attractive and cost-efficient alternative.

Trade shows also allow you to control the environment in which you present your product and the way in which it is demonstrated. Your sales force can give prospects information on solving their problems and get direct feedback on the product. The average time spent by an attendee at an exhibit in 1986 was about 15 minutes, so your presentation or demonstration should be no longer than 10 minutes at the most.

Before you participate in a trade show, you should decide upon your primary objective. Unless you have a good idea of what you wish to achieve, you have no way of evaluating a particular show, no guidelines for deciding what you should show and how you should show it, and no way to determine whether or not your investment was worthwhile. Yet only 46 percent of exhibitors set objectives for their trade show programs, according to a 1988 study by Exhibit Surveys. And the Trade Show Bureau estimates less than half of that 46 percent sets truly quantifiable objectives and then measures the results.

Your primary objective might be any of the following:

- To make sales
- To maintain an image and continue contact with customers
- To create an image or initiate contact with potential customers
- To introduce a new product
- To demonstrate nonportable equipment
- To offer an opportunity for customers to discuss their technical problems and get solutions
- To identify new applications for an existing or projected product by obtaining feedback from visitors

- To build the morale of your local sales force and of dealers
- To relate to competition
- To conduct market research
- To recruit personnel or attract new dealers
- To demonstrate interest in and support of the sponsoring association or industry

Whenever possible, your objective should be stated numerically—in terms of number of appointments, new names for your mailing list, how many orders to bring back, recruiting so many new wholesalers, and so on. Clear-cut objectives will help you measure your return on investment once the show is over.

Selecting The Right Kind Of Show

The key to making a trade show exhibit worthwhile is to select a show that will deliver the kind of audience you want to reach. The size and composition of that audience (i.e., attendees' titles, responsibilities as decision-makers and purchasers, and whether their firms are located in your company's primary market area are among the most important factors to consider.) Location of both the show and your display area within the show are also important.

To check out audience quality, attendance, and competitors who will be exhibiting (or have exhibited) at a particular trade show, you can request literature and a prospectus from the sponsor. Since this literature is promotional in nature, it will present the show in its best light. But most shows also issue detailed breakdowns of attendance that list the industries and geographic locations represented by visitors. One of the best sources of information is the list of exhibitors at previous shows, whose names you may find in the promotional material, or which can be obtained from show management.

An even better idea is to send a company representative to check out shows in person the year before you plan to exhibit, or to ask other exhibitors what they thought of the effectiveness of the shows. Ask them about costs and whether they encountered any problems. The subjects of seminars held in conjunction with the show can also provide clues to who will be attending and what their interests are.

Location of the show and nearby facilities are also important. How well does your market fit—educationally, technically, socially—with the location of the show? Are there entertainment and cultural activities available nearby for spouses and attendees to enjoy after the show? How attractive are the hotel and restaurant choices? How easy is it to get to the show and to register? All of these factors play into how effective a particular show will be in reaching your target market.

Regional vs. National Trade Shows

The trend throughout the past decade has been toward more and more regional, specialized, and vertical trade shows (i.e., shows that concentrate on a range of products used throughout a single industry, rather than "horizontal" trade shows that deal with the applications of a particular kind of product in a wide variety of industries). Some experts predict that the big national shows are in trouble because they are too diversified. Regional shows have caught on because they are targeting more specific geographic audiences with very little buyer overlap.

Trade Show Bureau President William Mee says, "regional shows reach a technical audience that would otherwise not be reached. And vertical segmentation is occuring as marketers understand the importance of identifying and meeting the needs of specific market niches or segments."

For the advertising manager, this means more shows to choose from, greater specialization of audiences, and—for national companies—more shows to attend to cover all the target markets. But it also means it's easier to target specific audience segments in "smaller bites."

Data released by the Trade Show Bureau shows that over 50 percent of the audience at a regional exposition travels less than 100 miles to attend. At national expositions, 64 percent of the visitors come from at least 400 miles away. So the proliferation of regional shows helps smaller companies reach local markets more efficiently. No longer do small firms with limited resources have to travel hundreds of miles to large metropolitan areas in order to try to reach the appropriate geographic segment of their markets. By securing a presence in local shows, smaller firms can target their regional audiences cost effectively and still compete with their larger competitors.

Exhibit Location As A Factor In Attracting Prospects

The importance of exhibit location within a show in attracting prospects is a subject of debate. While it's true that you should advertise your participation in the show ahead of time to prospects and customers so as not to rely solely on walk-by traffic, a survey of 607 trade show participants revealed display location as one of the "most important" criteria in deciding whether to enter a show.

Those findings suggest that "it is highly desirable for a booth to be located in a high-density area with good 'intercepting' qualities," write John M. Browning and Ronald J. Adams. "For the small firm with limited resources, this would point to the desirability of locating along major aisles or between major exhibits which are capable of generating traffic."

On the other hand, booth location is not as important for large companies, which tend to be sought out by more visitors and often have larger and more dramatic exhibits anyway. Various studies have shown that what really counts is exhibit size—the larger the better, especially as the size of the show increases.

The Trade Show Bureau, which has conducted studies on the effect of booth location on exhibition performance and impact, claims exhibit location is neither a positive or negative factor. The Bureau conducted studies at two well-known exhibit facilities and determined that being located at the front and center of the hall is not—as is commonly believed—an advantageous location in terms of booth traffic. The report states, "When size of an exhibit is eliminated as a factor in creating impact by adjusting or weighting recall scores for the size factor, there are absolutely no statistically significant differences in impact for exhibits in any area of the hall or complex."

What does all this mean to you, the exhibitor? For your company's exhibit (and products) to be remembered, you should place the most emphasis on creating a large, well-designed exhibit, followed by well-trained personnel and demonstrations targeted to the show audience. But as a safeguard, you should avoid locations in temporary structures, separate facilities requiring transportation to visit, or small rooms and hard-to-find locations within the main facility. Such locations do register lower traffic and make it harder for prospects to find you.

How Much Space Will You Need?

Once you have located a show that will help you reach your marketing objectives, you need to decide how big your exhibit should be. The most common unit of space is a 10′ × 10′ booth, although some shows offer smaller units. There is sometimes a space differential depending on location. If space is available, you can get as many booths as you want. And a larger exhibit can help both attract more prospects to your booth and aid visitors in remembering your company. But how do you determine how much space you really *need?*

First, make an estimate of how many people visiting the show are logical prospects. You can base this on a study of the attendance reports, counting the number of visitors with meaningful titles, job responsibilities, and so on. You won't be able to reach all of them, but you should be able to get half of them to your booth.

Divide this number by the total number of hours the show will be open. This will give you the average number of visitors per hour. (However, attendance at a show tends to be greatest during the middle days, less on the first and last days. Typically, the second and third days of a four-day show attract the greatest number of visitors, followed by the first day. Attendance tends to drop off substantially on the last day of the show.) The nature of your product determines how many people your sales rep can handle per hour, but 15 is an average. Divide the hourly visitor rate by 15, and you'll get the average number of sales representatives you should have on hand to handle the number of people you expect.

Experience shows that two people talking need about 50 square feet of space. With less space than this, the visitor gets a feeling of being crowded and is unwilling to stop. If there is more space, he becomes unwilling to intrude, and hesitates to step into the display area. So multiply the number of sales reps you come up with by 50, and you'll get an approximation of how much space (in square feet) you should have to reach your objective. Add to that space occupied by your demonstration equipment, furniture, and displays, and that's how much you need. (In the standard 10′ × 10′ booth, two reps can usually work easily.) More than that could be a waste of money; less, and you will probably reach fewer than your original audience estimate.

Designing Your Exhibit

Designing an exhibit is best done by professionals. It's likely more people will see your booth in a few days than see your office or store in months or years, so aim to make a good impression. In planning the design of an exhibit, keep two factors in mind:

1. Your goal is to select, from all those attending, those who are good prospects for whatever you are showing. The most visible part of your display must act like a headline in a good ad—it must attract the attention of

the right people in the few seconds it takes them to walk past your booth. Avoid long graphics on signs, since people won't bother to read them.

2. You should use the unique advantages of the medium, which means that you should show your product in action, fully and three-dimensionally, so your prospect can see and touch and handle it.

Something that is in motion and three-dimensional—such as a display of your product in action—is a good attention-grabber. A live presenter demonstrating your product will also help draw prospects, as will interactive exhibits which involve the customer. You might even consider renting a separate conference room or theater in the convention hall to stage a special presentation, demonstration, or performance for your target audience. This way, you get the decision makers to concentrate on your message, without exhibit hall distractions, for a specific period of time.

There are three types of exhibits:

1. The custom exhibit. This is a one-of-a-kind, specially designed exhibit, usually for use at a major show.

2. The modular exhibit. Produced in quantity, this type of exhibit can be either a "custom" modular or an "off-the-shelf" modular display. Usually they come in 4′ or 5′ wide sections and are assembled in a row to make a linear exhibit, or in other configurations to make a walkaround or a series of linear arrangements. They have interchangeable story features, so that panels which tell a selling story can be removed and changed inexpensively. These are lightweight, easy to set up, and comparatively inexpensive to handle.

3. Third, there is the "erector set," an off-the-shelf, suitcase kind of exhibit, which can fit in the trunk of an automobile. These consist of rods and panels, held together by joining members, which can hold shelves and graphics. They're easy to set up, lightweight, flexible, and can be carried around and set on a table top. Although not as impressive as the other types, these kits are perfectly adequate for small regional shows. They can be bought directly from manufacturers or through local exhibit designer/producers.

You can also rent a modular system, which may be a good idea if you are just getting started in trade show exhibiting. By renting, you can get a good idea of what works and what doesn't, so that later on you can work with a designer on a custom exhibit that best meets your company's space, staff, product, and display needs.

While flashier custom exhibits are preferred for the big national shows, as the popularity of regional shows grows, the demand for lightweight, modular exhibits that can be inexpensively shipped and easily adapted to fit different audiences will likely increase.

Follow Show Rules

When you sign up for space at a trade show, your rental usually includes nothing more than a draped area and a sign with your name on it hung on the rear wall. You can use this space any way you want, subject to the show rules outlined in the Exhibitor's Kit you will receive. Be sure to read these rules carefully, or get your exhibit designer to go over them with you. They tell you how high you can build your display; how much of the cubic footage of the display area you can use; how to order electricity, lights, furniture, and the like; and what you can and can't do. The exhibitor's manual also tells you when you can get into the exhibit hall and when you have to be out of it, and includes order blanks for labor and equipment.

The exhibit house can help estimate the hours needed to set up and tear down your booth. Most trade show operations are covered by union and management rules, which vary from city to city. All of this union labor is available to the exhibitor by advance order, which can save your company time and money. In fact, many exhibit services give 15 percent discounts for advance orders. Exhibitors who do not order in advance receive furnishings and labor on a first-come, first-served basis only after the other orders have been filled. Usually, the exhibitor's responsibilities in setting up the booth are restricted to arranging company products and literature and conducting demonstrations. If you have any problems with receiving or installing your display, seek help from the exhibitor service center, usually set up on the edge of the hall. A work pass or exhibitor badge can be obtained at the show's registration desk to give you access to your booth during set-up.

Budgeting For The Trade Show

Trade show participants commonly allocate between 5 and 20 percent of their marketing budgets to trade shows, with the average being 10 to 12 percent. Typical trade-show costs range from $10,000 for a 100-square foot booth to $150,000 to $750,000 for a 5,000-square foot booth at a large show. Budgets for small regional shows are commonly only one or two thousand dollars, or even less. But expenditures for international shows by large companies can run into the millions of dollars. Such things as laser lighting, computer-generated graphics, professional performers, special effects, and original music will add substantially to your tab.

Before your enter a show, know your budget as well as your objectives. Exhibit costs depend not only on the size of the show and how much space you rent, but the type of exhibit you buy (or rent), its weight and size, which affects shipping and handling charges, and on how many different parts must be assembled. Costs on readily available 10-foot professionally designed portable or modular exhibit units equipped with custom graphics range from $2,500 to $5,000. For a custom-designed unit, figure on $800 per linear foot, including graphics. And new signs and photography for refurbishing a booth can cost from $500 to $1,000.

Another consideration is drayage, the cost of moving materials from the loading dock to your booth space, storing crates during the show and reversing the process afterwards. Do not ship materials directly to the hotel or convention center. The exhibitor kit will specify the warehouse and shipping instructions. Pricing for drayage is by hundred weight (CWT)—the cost per 100 lbs.—with minimums for small cartons. First-time exhibitors may be surprised at the cost: often, prices are above $30 per 100 lbs.

Trade show participation begins with advance planning. You should make a floor plan and draw sketches of the exhibit set-up and decorations. Will you have a floor, carpeting, drapes? What are your electrical and equipment needs? How will your exhibit be shipped and where will it be stored prior to the show? Who will set it up? Many exhibitors arrange for both installation and knock-down of a display under supervision. Although this service usually costs extra, it can save you two days prior to the show and one day following it, so it may be worthwhile to consider.

You also may want to figure in the cost of promotional literature, advertising, direct mail, giveaways, and personnel travel and time away from the office. To figure out personnel time costs, the Trade Show Bureau suggests estimating the average annual compensation for the employees who will work the booth. Add a percentage to cover benefits and office support—many companies figure on 25 to 40 percent. Then divide by 220, the average number of work days in a year. This is the "cost per person day." Multiply that by the number of people days at the exposition to get personnel time costs.

Tradeshow Week's Annual Exhibits Survey reports that in 1988 trade show exhibit costs averaged $11 per square foot for space rental; $35 per hour for drayage; $29 an hour for a projectionist; $39 an hour for both plumbers and electricians; and $35 an hour for a carpenter. Other costs can include such items as furniture and audiovisual equipment rental, janitorial services, installation and dismantling, new construction, and exhibit prep and refurbishing. You may also want to hire a photographer, florist, security guard, and models or performers.

Refurbishing Your Booth

When your booth starts to show signs of wear and tear, or when you need to update it for a new show, allow plenty of time for refurbishing. Here are 10 points to remember:

1. Refurbishing requires even more planning than a new presentation. Existing properties take up a lot more room on the exhibit house floor because they must be set up in their entirety to complete the revitalization process.

2. Don't expect a firm quotation for refurbishing. The variables of condition, construction, and unforeseen problems in existing properties preclude precise quotations.

3. Don't insist on rejuvenating those parts of your exhibit that won't be visible on the show floor. It's seldom worth the cost to achieve that state of perfection.

4. It's often better to replace a surface than waste time on spot repairs and touch-ups that may detract from your image on the exhibit floor. Ironically, minor touch-ups are particularly noticeable on painted surfaces. Unless completely refinished for minor blemishes, painted surfaces will frequently begin to look cheap after a few shows.

5. Properties can be covered with materials that withstand frequent use and are resistant to breaking, chipping, flaking, and denting. High-pressure laminates such as Formica may cost more on a materials basis, but consider that it can be applied directly over a damaged surface in its entirety or in sections to provide a durable new face.

6. Acrylic sheeting such as Plexiglas or Lexan can provide a sophisticated look for an exhibit, yet even with the best possible care will still collect scratches. It's possible to buff out minor surface blemishes, but not deep scrapes. Acrylic sheeting is easily replaced, so while material costs may be high, labor costs won't.

7. Metal properties are perhaps the most durable. They have inherent strengths that allow them to last through many shows with only minor touch-ups. However, keep an eye on the weight. Extrusions and various other lightweight metal components that are available usually provide the best of both worlds.

8. Consider soft surfaces, such as carpeting or cloth. Carpeting provides a durable surface that can stand up to heavy use and also help protect properties during shipping. Carpet surfaces, however, can soil. They cannot be wiped down like high pressure laminates or acylic sheeting, yet depending on the carpet, spot cleaning can frequently be done. Replacing carpet or cloth is easy, requiring little more than cutting and adhering.

9. Choose fasteners such as Velcro that allow easy interchange of graphics and copy panels, thus providing your exhibit with visual consistency along with flexibility to adapt to changing marketing programs and target audiences at different shows. Transparent plexiglass panels may also be added to cover graphics, protecting them from damage and keeping them clean and attractive.

10. After many uses, shipping cases as well as exhibit materials become so worn, loose, and tired that the best solution is to start anew. Lightweight, reinforced fiber containers provide the protection materials need, as well as save shipping costs.

Building Traffic By Publicizing Your Presence

Especially if you'll be exhibiting at a large show, make the most out of your participation by promoting your appearance at the trade show ahead of time to prospects and customers. This will help increase traffic to your booth, both by directing the right audience to your display and by encouraging those who might not attend otherwise to make the trip to see you. Surprisingly, the Trade Show Bureau reports that only one-quarter of trade show exhibitors bother to publicize their presence ahead of time.

Here are several ways to "presell" your exhibit:

Use direct mail

Give your audience specific information about what you'll be exhibiting by sending out a mailing six weeks before the show. In addition to using your own customer/prospect list, you may want to ask the exposition manager if he or she sells lists, or perhaps an industry trade publication could provide one.

Write or call current customers

Let them know you'll be at the show and encourage them to come. You might even suggest a specific time or set up an appointment when you know floor traffic will be slow. Often slow hours are at the start or end of the day, during lunch, or on the final day of the show.

Include detailed information in the events schedule

The trade show's events program includes a list of exhibitors and a description of what products or services they offer along with their listing. Since attendees do read this schedule, make your listing as specific as possible.

Prepare promotional material

Print up posters for your show windows and corporate lobby, add stickers announcing your presence at the show to your correspondence, mention your plans in your magazine ads, even send admission tickets to the show to special customers. The fact that you're participating in a show can build your image in your customers' eyes, even if they don't go to the show and see you.

Advertise in special editions of trade magazines

Trade associations that sponsor a show often publish a special "show issue" of their magazine which include a guide to exhibitors, speakers, and events. Or publications in the field represented by the exposition may promote and report on the show. These and local newspapers are ideal places in which to advertise your participation.

Offer special prices

Many exhibitors offer special show prices on merchandise bought at the show. Make your discount prices known in advance, and they will help to build traffic. Such discounts are particularly effective if your products are not expensive and do not require a large commitment.

Hand out advertising specialties

Some companies use advertising specialties, often called giveaways, to increase the impact of their participation. Specialties are too often passed out indiscriminately, adding to the cost of participating in a show but contributing little to sales. The best specialty appeals almost exclusively to potential users of your products. They should be an item the recipient will keep for a long time. Be sure to check show rules, since not all shows permit distribution of these items.

Create targeted special giveaways

A particularly effective way to use specialties is to help bring specific people to your booth. You can make up a list of the names and addresses of very important prospects whom you are eager to lure to your booth. Then send each of them something like one of a pair of handsome cufflinks or earrings, perhaps designed around your trademark, if you have one. Your cover letter would then promise the other half of the pair when the recipient visits you at the show. If you have selected both your list and the specialty item carefully, you can expect a high proportion of responses. A good specialty advertising counselor can help you develop a creative promotion.

Make a new product introduction

A trade show is an excellent place to introduce a new product. People come to trade shows specifically to see what is new. If you can get the word out that you will have something new at the show, you will develop a valuable list of booth visitors. Give customers and prospects an idea of what you will be showing. See that advance announcements are sent out to the publications that cover your industry. Most of them run both previews and follow-up articles on important shows. Many need their material eight to ten weeks before a show, but it is worth the special effort to decide early on what you will be showing. At the show, leave press releases in the show press room, and have an extra supply in the booth for those editors who stop by.

Train Your Sales People

The effectiveness of your booth depends largely on the effectiveness of the people working in it. Studies show that although graphics, exhibit size, and familiarity with a company name or its products draw people to a booth, what prospects remember the most about their visit is what they are told by salespeople. It is a different and sometimes bewildering experience for most sales representatives, who are more used to visiting prospects one at a time in their offices, not having prospects come up and ask for information. Salespeople often feel uncomfortable at an exhibit if their own customers and territories are not well-represented in the audience, so try to use salespeople who serve the area in which the trade show is held.

Your sales team can be made more effective if you hold a special training session before the show that describes the trade show's audience and outlines your company's objectives, selling procedures, any special sales techniques for dealing with booth visitors or handling product demonstrations, and arrival and departure times. Train your sales staff to present sales information in short summaries that encourage questions and comments. The goal in working with trade show prospects is to encourage a dialogue rather than to launch into a long-winded sales pitch.

Booth personnel must be friendly, able to tell good prospects from curiosity-seekers, and able to move quickly towards advancing the sale. You must let your people know what your objectives are, so that they can work towards reaching your goals, whether it is setting up appointments, getting literature into the right hands, giving a demonstration, or making a sale. Don't plan to bring enough literature to give to everyone visiting the show; it's too easy for casual lookers to pick up and then dump as soon as they leave. Some companies figure literature needs based on 5 percent of total attendance.

Arrange to have two teams of salespeople staff the booth during the course of the day, since this kind of selling is hard work. A salesperson can be effective for about four hours a day; then the physical and mental strain starts to show. However, sales can be reduced by as much as 50 percent if too many people rotate booth duty, so alternate two small teams of people instead. This way, your booth will be staffed by people who quickly become familiar and comfortable with the new environment.

When your people are on duty, they should be upfront, standing and not sitting, ready to welcome visitors, and not talking in a corner with other salespeople or spending long periods of time talking to current customers. Educate your salespeople that the value of the trade show is in meeting potential new customers at a relatively low cost.

Follow-Up Sales Leads

Decide before the show how you'll handle sales leads. Find out what your prospects' needs are, get their names, titles, company names and addresses, what product application they are interested in, and when they are looking to buy. Try to ask open-ended questions about the prospect's true interests that will aid in the sales qualification process.

"The most important part of a lead form may well be the remarks section, an area where the sales person can explain nuances or why the lead was taken," notes Edward Chapman, Jr. "And if an order is written for a new customer, try to obtain some credit information for follow-up."

Then, most importantly, *do* follow-up with a price quote, sales call, literature, whatever. Too many companies fail to follow up on sales-call requests after the show. Yet trade show visitors are ready and able to buy. In a survey of exposition leads taken from twelve different shows, the Trade Show Bureau found that 40 percent of respondents reported they had purchased one or more products of the type exhibited within four to twelve weeks after the show. Although 54 percent of the orders placed by companies that exhibited at the twelve shows were closed without follow-up calls, another 36 percent of sales occurred following one or more calls. (The number of calls required to close the remaining 10 percent of sales was not known.)

In measuring response to your trade show, be aware that "two-thirds of all sales aren't achieved until 11 to 24 months after a show," states Dr. Allen Konopacki, president of INCOMM International. So if increasing sales was your primary objective in a show, don't cross off the show as a failure if you don't see an immediate jump in orders. Make sure that your sales staff gets a full report on leads following the show and then stays in touch with those prospects.

The most important single measure of booth performance may be how well your display is remembered. In the *Journal of Small Business Management,* Browning and Adams note, "In 1986, about 75 percent of visitors to a sponsor's exhibit were able to recall the visit and the sponsor eight to ten weeks after the show closed. Cases of low memory impact were generally attributed to lack of interpersonal contact during the show and to insufficient follow-up activity at the show's conclusion."

While you should measure how well each particular show you participate in achieves the quantifiable objectives you set, don't forget to compare show results with each other as well. That will provide a track record of performance and help you decide which future shows to enter.

Resources

Two sources of trade show information are the *Trade Shows Worldwide,* published by Gale Research Inc., Detroit, MI, which lists dates, locations, number of exhibitors, attendees, and other descriptive information for more than 4,500 trade shows and exhibits held in 60 countries each year. The cost is $195. Call (313) 961-3707 for details. Another source is the *Trade Show & Exhibits Schedule,* published by Bill Communications, P.O. Box 3078, Southeastern, PA 19398. This annual directory lists all trade shows held in the United States and is available by calling 1-800-253-6708.

One way to locate exhibit design professionals in your area is to contact their trade association, the Exhibit Designers & Producers Association, 611 E. Wells Street, Milwaukee, WI 53202; Telephone: 414-276-3372. You can also find exhibit designers and suppliers by checking the yellow pages under "Exhibits" or "Expositions."

For a complete listing of up-to-date costs contact the International Exhibitors Association, 5501 Backlick Road, Suite 200, Springfield, VA 22151, phone (703) 941-3725 to order *The Budget Guide.*

CHAPTER 27

Seminars

Why Seminars Can Be Used As A Marketing Tool

Seminars, once thought of as strictly a means of training, educating, or informing an audience, have become effective marketing tools for both business and consumer marketers. On the high-tech end, mainframe software vendors hold half-day product demonstrations/education sessions to educate MIS Directors and systems analysts on how the software can fit into the corporate data center. On the consumer side, a producer of baby toys and products conducts seminars on child care.

"Seminars can be effective marketing promotions," writes Herman Holtz. "The Evelyn Wood speed reading school advertised weekly free seminars for a number of years, offering a demonstration lesson along with a sales presentation. Albert Lowry, the butcher turned real estate tycoon, has used many free seminars to promote his $500 weekend seminar on how to make money in real estate."

Why are seminars so effective? Because they fit in nicely with the transition sellers and consumers have undergone over the past two decades. Twenty years ago, consumers were more open to traditional advertising messages. Salesmen were perceived as peddlers whose job it was to "move merchandise"—regardless of whether that merchandise was right for the customer. "Pressure selling" was the predominant technique. We tended to feel an adversarial relationship with salespeople while believing much of what was force-fed us through TV commercials and magazine ads.

Today, the consumer is more educated, more savvy, and more skeptical of advertising in all its forms. Consumers know what they want and are not afraid to question authority. Nowhere is this more evident in the aggressive manner today's consumers are taking with health-care providers, especially physicians. The family doctor, who once held a status second-in-command to God, is now routinely questioned, and many patients find themselves more well-read and aware of the latest developments than their doctors.

The peddler/salesperson finds he/she can no longer push unwanted goods on unwary buyers. Today's consumer questions, doubts, and actively seeks the best in all things. Selling has shifted from an adversarial to a *consultative* role, with the salesperson acting as an advocate for the consumer, helping him or her fill needs, wants, and desires with appropriate products and services. Indeed, books have been written on "consultative selling" and the master of sales training, Tom Hopkins, frequently refers to salespeople as "consultants" and buyers as "clients" in his books, tapes, and seminars.

As the consumerism movement grows, consumers shift from being passive buyers to informed buyers. And to be informed buyers, they need information. Information on products. Information on trends. Information on the very problems and applications the products address. This is where seminars come in.

The Role Of The Product Seminar

A "promotional" or "product" seminar—a seminar designed to ultimately sell a product or service rather than be a profit-center in itself—helps move the consumer one step closer to a purchase decision. It does so by providing the knowledge the consumer feels he needs to intelligently make that decision.

There is some common ground between seminar-giver/product-seller and consumer—and some difference. The goal they share is to exchange information and make the consumer more knowledgeable, thus helping him solve his problems and meet his needs. The point of difference is that while the consumer doesn't care which manufacturer gets his business, you do. You naturally don't want to spend time and money educating consumers to buy your competitor's product. You want them to buy *yours*.

How do seminars help promote products and services? In two ways: By (1) establishing the seminar giver as the authority and (2) "setting the specs" for a product purchase.

1. *Establishing the seminar giver as the authority.* Even if your seminar does not promote your product directly, just the mere fact that *you* and not your competitor are giving the seminar establishes you as the authority in your field, putting you in a superior position to make the sale to your attendee/prospect. Those who write books, publish articles, make speeches, or give seminars are perceived as experts, as authorities, as leaders in their field. And who do you want to buy from? An expert, of course. The seminar giver is perceived as more knowledgeable and better able to solve problems, and therefore is more likely to get the order.

2. *Setting the specs.* A common technique in a seminar is "setting the specs." In plain English, this means using the seminar to educate prospects on what they should be looking for in your type of product—the specifications to include in their request for proposal (RFP), the features they should want, the questions they should ask. Of course, you set these specs in such a way that *your* product satisfies them best. Your seminar tells the prospect, "This is how you should shop for [name of product or service.]" Of course, when he follows your shopping guidelines, your product or service clearly emerges as the logical choice.

Determining Whether You Can Use A Seminar To Promote Your Product Or Service

It depends on your marketing situation. Product seminars work well when introducing new products or technologies. They are also ideal for products which require an in-person demonstration, such as software or computer systems.

Seminars are also effective for introducing new *concepts,* new approaches to business, and professional and consulting services. For service firms, the seminar is the first opportunity to allow the prospect to "sample" the service before he makes a commitment to buy a larger chunk of it. Also, if your product or service solves or addresses a major business problem or issue (e.g., plant safety, computer security, employee benefits planning, life insurance), a seminar is a good place to educate your prospects on the subject.

Price is another factor. In most cases, seminars are appropriate only for expensive items, since it doesn't pay to rent a hotel room, mail invitations, and spend staff time presenting a seminar to people in the hopes of selling them a single product that only costs $10. However, there are exceptions. "Tupperware" parties are, in a sense, "mini-seminars" on how to store food in the home, and the unit of sale at such events is typically small.

Seminar Or Sales Pitch?

At this point, you might ask, "Aren't most product seminars thinly disguised sales pitches for a specific product and not really seminars?"

Yes, and that's why they fail. Obviously, your purpose in presenting the seminar is to convince people to buy your product. But if the seminar is a blatant promotional pitch, people become annoyed—even disgusted.

On the other hand, if you present information of genuine value, attendees will think well of your firm and be more inclined to do business with you. Attendees know they will be sold but want to learn something, too. They realize they cannot master a complex subject in a two or three-hour seminar, but if you can present them with one or two new ideas, or a few practical how-to tips or techniques, you'll dazzle them. They'll walk away delighted with the seminar and will become "fans" of your firm—a desirable result.

Setting The Seminar Fee

One early consideration is: Should you charge for your seminars or give them for free?

As a rule, seminars designed primarily to sell a product or service should be free. Every activity in business—promotional or otherwise—should have one primary goal and be wholly directed toward achieving that goal. Therefore, if your goal is to sell product and not generate revenue, the seminar should be free so that you (1) maximize attendance to get the largest number of prospects in the room to hear your message and (2) you feel free to do at least some product selling.

Attendees at free seminars expect to get *some* sell and find it acceptable if not overdone. But if someone has paid $295 to attend a one-day session on "Relational Databases," he wants to learn how to manage, choose, or design relational databases. He doesn't want to hear what amounts to a reading of your sales brochure—and if he does get that, he will feel cheated.

Some companies break this rule successfully, charge large fees for their seminars, and manage to generate both sales and immediate revenue at the same time. But they are the exception. If your goal is to sell, give free seminars and treat them as promotion, not profit-centers.

Some companies seek a happy compromise by charging a nominal fee; say, $10 or $25. The idea is to qualify attendees. The reasoning is: "Someone who pays $10 or $25 must really be interested, and someone not willing to pay it is not a good prospect."

This sounds sensible, but it may not be a sensible strategy. Free offers should be free. You are not likely to impress prospects or make the seminar seem more valuable by charging $25 or some other nominal fee.

What's more, if you charge the same fee as *regular* paid seminars ($50 to $125 for the general public and $100 to $300 per day for business seminars), then it would be inappropriate to do *any* selling, and the presentation would have to be 100 percent educational—which isn't your goal. If your purpose is to sell a product, make the seminar free.

Typical Response Rates To Seminar Promotions

The mere fact that the seminar is free is not going to get people to come running to your door. Executives, managers, and professionals in business are flooded with invitations to attend free seminars and don't have time to go to even a small fraction of them.

Worse, many people don't think that anything free is valuable. So they have an aversion to attending.

Most companies invite attendees to free seminars using direct mail. Response rates for free seminars in fields where the free seminar offer is common (e.g., software, computers, telecommunications) are generally not much higher than for paid seminars. Your response rate will probably be anywhere from 1/2 to 3 percent. If you assume a 1 percent response rate, and want 25 people in your seminar, you will need to mail 2,500 invitations and probably should mail 5,000 to be safe.

You might get a higher response when giving free seminars on a topic not usually presented in such forums. Gary Blake, a management consultant specializing in writing seminars, recently gave a free three-hour seminar on "Effective Business Writing" and got a 10 percent response.

Another way to increase response is to have a celebrity as your featured speaker. This need not be a show-business celebrity but preferably someone well-known in your industry.

Example: One software distributor recently sponsored a free lunch seminar at which Bill Gates, chairman of Microsoft, was the speaker. The seminar invitation consisted of a card listing only the location, date, and the fact that it was a lunch with Bill Gates. The banquet room was packed to overflowing with busy MIS vice presidents and DP managers—and the invitation hadn't even mentioned the topic or content.

The Best Length And Date For Your Seminar

Most free seminars run half a day in length, typically two or three hours, either in the morning or the afternoon.

What about food? If you hold the seminar in the morning, you have two choices:

1. Serve a hot breakfast as your main meal; invite people to stay around for questions after the presentation but do not serve lunch. Keep coffee and tea available throughout the morning.
2. Serve coffee and tea only in the morning (perhaps having a few Danish available), then give a lunch after the presentation.

If you have it in the afternoon, you can serve lunch first, then give the seminar. Or you can invite them to come after lunch, serve coffee and soft drinks only, then have a happy hour with open bar and hors d'oeuvres after the presentation. Dinner is usually not a good idea since people want to get home at the end of the day.

What day is best? Howard Shenson says that for seminars aimed at business, Wednesday or Thursday are the best days, followed by Tuesday, Friday, and Saturday. Monday and Sunday are the worst days.

For seminars aimed at consumers and the general public, Thursday and Saturday are best, followed by Wednesday, Sunday, Tuesday, and Friday. Monday is again not a good day.

Are some months better than others? The best seminar seasons seem to be March through May and September through mid-November. Summer interferes with vacations. Winter brings the danger of cancellation due to bad weather in most regions of the U.S. And from mid-November to January 1st, people are concentrating on their holiday fun.

Naming Your Program

Does it matter whether you call the event a 'product demonstration,' 'seminar,' or 'workshop'?" Yes. The title is very important as it connotes value.

"Product demonstration" is least desirable and should be used only when the event is indeed a pure and straightforward demonstration of a system. "Seminar" implies that the attendee will gain useful knowledge. "Workshop" implies hands-on participation and should not be used for most free seminars.

Copywriter David Yale suggests calling the seminar a "forum" and has gotten good results doing so. "Briefing" can be used for a session aimed at executives and managerial types. Programs aimed at consumers can also be "luncheons" if a light meal is served around noon or "parties" if given in a leisure atmosphere.

Obtaining The Mailing List

Mail your seminar invitations to the people who are likely prospects for your product.

You will get the best results by mailing to your *house list* or *database* of current and past customers, clients, and prospects. People who know you, have had dealings with you in the past, or have in the past asked for information about your product or service, are much more likely to attend than people who don't know you. A seminar is an ideal forum for reawakening interest in prospects who have not taken action as well as reactivating inactive accounts.

When renting mailing lists, select people who are the most likely prospects for the product being featured in the seminar, and be sure they live within a 100-mile radius of the seminar site—ideally, within 50 miles.

Timing

Mail your seminar invitations third-class about eight to nine weeks in advance of the seminar date if you are targeting a business audience. If you study the seminar mailings that cross your desk, you will probably see that most arrive four to eight weeks in advance of the seminar date.

You can probably mail on shorter notice for consumer seminars. Print ads can be placed a week or two, or even a few days, before the event to attract last-minute attendees.

Because the attendees do not pay, you don't collect money, but you still want them to register. Copy in ads and mail should read: "There is no fee to attend this seminar, but you must register in advance because attendance is limited. To reserve your seat, call [phone number] today."

And what about the mailing piece itself? There are a wide variety of formats. Some companies use self-mailers; others send personalized letters of invitation that include a circular or flier outlining the key points or benefits of attendance.

Must the copy be lengthy, complete, persuasive, and hard-hitting as it is in direct response mailings selling costly paid seminars? You don't have to sell your free seminar as hard as a paid seminar—but you probably have to sell it 75 percent to 80 percent as hard. The copy might not be as long or detailed as for a paid seminar promotion, but it should still tell the prospect what he will learn at the session and the benefits of attending.

If you offer a gift, stress this in your letter and on the cover of your brochure or self-mailer. Gifts have tremendous pulling power. If the gift has a retail value, say, "FREE GIFT—guaranteed to be worth $35." Many people will come just to get the gift. And if it's a sample of your product or related to your product line, that's fine.

The design of your mailing should be consistent with the event and audience. If you are inviting executives to a briefing on "Competing with the Japanese," the piece should be serious, somber, even urgent. If you are holding a party for expectant mothers to sell them on your diaper service, the mailing should be colorfully illustrated with pictures of babies, families, cribs, nurseries, and the like.

Copywriting Tips

In your mailing, make it clear that the seminar is free—but don't make this fact your central theme or trumpet it in your headline.

You should write copy that makes the reader say, "This sounds wonderful. I would really love to go. How much does it cost?" Then, tell him or her it's free.

You should *not* take the approach that all you have to do is say the seminar is free and people will want to attend. "Despite being free, [free seminars] must be *sold,* just as anything else is sold," warns Herman Holtz. "The word free is one strong inducement to attend, of course, but few, if any, would attend if they were not promised a benefit they find attractive enough to merit the expenditure of their time."

Expenditures

Free seminars are not a terribly expensive promotion, at least as far as incurring outside costs. If you know your product, there's no reason why your people can't develop the presentation in-house and present it themselves.

The main expense is in the mailing. Sending out 5,000 invitations will run approximately $2,000 to $3,000, depending on the format. Self-mailers generally cost much less than packages with outer envelopes, personalized letters, insert brochures, reply forms, and reply envelopes. If you use a full-scale package, you should split test a self-mailer; often, you get the same response at far less cost.

You can hold the seminar at your company facilities, although a nice room in a good hotel is more pleasant and easier for attendees to find. In the suburbs, a seminar room can be rented for $100 to $300 a day; in a major city, it might run $300 to $500. The smaller your audience, the smaller the room and the lower the cost.

Food is the big expense. Coffee and tea run $1 to $2 per person per serving; soft drinks run $2 to $2.50 per can or bottle. Meals involve significantly greater expense but may be necessary if attendees expect to be fed.

Other expenses include development and reproduction of overheads, slides, hand-outs, and invitations. These development costs can be amortized over the lifetime of the seminar. Because of the time, expense, and effort required to create an effective seminar, one-shot events do not pay off as well as repeats. So to maximize the benefit of the seminar, you should plan on giving it at least three or four times during the year in several different locations.

To develop a product seminar and give it once, a budget of $5,000 should be sufficient assuming you do the work yourself and do not hire outside consultants.

How To Sell At The Seminar

The key to making your seminar an effective promotional event is to give a good seminar—one that lives up to the promise of its brochure or mailing and delivers an interesting, useful, helpful, informative presentation prospects will appreciate. If they walk away happy and pleased, you've achieved your primary goal: to make them "fans" of your company.

To further enhance selling effectiveness, you can sell your product before, during, and after the seminar. This is acceptable (because your seminar is free, and they expect it), but only if done in a gentle, reasonable, unpressured way. Don't push your product onto people or mention it every minute. When people ask questions, don't answer every one by saying, "Buying our product solves it!" Instead, give them an answer that helps them regardless of whether they become customers.

More Tips On Maximizing The Sales Effectiveness Of Product Seminars

In advance of the seminar:

- Mail a questionnaire asking them what topics they want addressed during the seminar. Ask them to return the questionnaire. Answer those topics at the seminar.
- If appropriate, send a sample of your product so they are familiar with it and can begin to become users even before your presentation.
- Put them on your mailing list so they get at least one promotional mailing from your company before the seminar.
- Put them on the subscription list to receive your free company promotional newsletter.
- Send a confirmation letter acknowledging registration. Include easy-to-follow directions to the seminar site—both by mass transit and car.
- Call them to confirm that they are coming.

Before the seminar starts:

- Serve coffee and tea.
- Meet and shake hands with attendees. Welcome them to the seminar. Engage them in conversation to learn more about them.
- Leave product literature on a table at the back of the room and put one copy of your catalog or brochure on each chair in the room.
- Distribute an article reprint or other interesting piece for them to read before the seminar starts. Some people come early; others come late; and you want to give the early people something to do.
- Have an unannounced door prize to create additional interest and excitement. Hold the drawing at the first break. (This prevents people from walking out.)

- Give them a simple survey or questionnaire to complete while they wait for the session to start. These will be useful tools in planning your sales approach to these people. If possible, address some of the concerns expressed on the questionnaire during your talk. (Don't identify the person asking the question unless they volunteer their identity.)
- Use name tags so attendees feel comfortable mingling. The session will be more meaningful and enjoyable if attendees can network with their peers.

During the seminar:

- Work your product into your presentation and mention it briefly two or three times each hour. But only for a sentence or two. And don't overdo it. Let common sense be your guide.
- At the end, it's okay to give a five-minute pitch from the podium. After all, the audience expects it. A good lead-in is, "Okay, some of you have been sitting here for 3 hours and wondering, 'Where's the product pitch?' Well, I don't want to disappoint you, so here it is . . ."
- At the end of the pitch say, "You've been a great audience. Thanks for your attention." Then name the company salespeople in the room and ask them to identify themselves by standing or raising their hands. Then say, "Rick, Sue, and I (or whoever the salespeople are) will stay around awhile to talk to you if you have more questions about (topic of seminar) or want more information on (name of product). We welcome your questions and comments."
- Let people come to you. Don't have salespeople descend like hawks to "capture" prospects or put on the hard-sell. If people want to leave, let them. But be sure they have your catalog or brochure and business card before they go.

After the seminar:

- Send a follow-up note thanking them for coming along with a form they can use to place an order or request more information.
- Follow-up on any specific inquiries or concerns expressed to salespeople or on questionnaires.
- Place all prospects on your in-house database list to receive future mailings.
- Do not forget to deliver any gifts you promised to distribute if they were not handed out at the seminar.

- When giving out a free product or sample or literature, include price-off coupons the attendees can use to purchase your products at a discount at retail outlets.
- Did the mailing piece generate the desired attendance? If not, why not? Are you using the wrong lists, or is the piece itself ineffective? Maybe your topic does not appeal to your intended audience.
- Did the right people attend for the right reasons? Did you get a room full of eager prospects who showed interest and enthusiasm in your proposition? Or were you talking to the wrong people, or prospects who just wanted the free doughnuts and couldn't care less about your widgets?
- Did the seminar itself generate the desired sales results? That is, did prospects show interest, becoming involved, approach salespeople, and take the next step in the buying process?
- What percentage of attendees were genuine prospects? What percentage demonstrated real interest in your product? What percentage eventually become customers or clients?
- If the results were not satisfactory, is there anything you can do to improve attendance or the quality of the presentation? Or is it possible that free seminars simply don't work for your type of offer?

CHAPTER 28

Speeches, Slide Shows, and Presentations

Public speaking—giving speeches, lectures, talks, papers, and presentations at public events, industry meetings, conventions, and conferences—is a marketing technique that is widely used by individual entrepreneurs and small business. But many larger companies don't take full advantage of such opportunities.

Why? Because we advertising managers and professionals tend to concentrate on big projects. There's a lot of excitement and glamour in producing a national ad campaign or prize-winning annual report. But most advertising managers don't get excited helping a company engineer or manager prepare a speech for a local chamber of commerce or business club. Yet, for many firms, that speech can have more impact and generate more immediate business than the ad campaign or annual report.

Why is public speaking so effective as a promotional tool? For many of the same reasons seminars and articles are. When you speak, you are perceived as the expert. If your talk is good, you immediately establish your credibility with the audience so that they want *you* and your company to work with them and solve their problems.

But unlike an article, which is somewhat impersonal, a speech or talk puts you within hand-shaking distance of your audience. And, since in today's fast-paced world more and more activities are taking place remotely via FAX, computer modem, and videoconferencing, meeting prospects face-to-face firmly implants an image of you in their minds. If that meeting takes place in an environment where you are singled out as an expert—as is the case when you speak—the impression is that much more effective and powerful.

When To Use Speaking

Speaking is not ideal for every product or marketing situation. If you are trying to mass-market a new brand of floppy disk on a nationwide basis to all computer users, television and print advertising is likely to be more effective than speaking, which limits the number of people you reach per contact. On the other hand, a wedding consultant whose market is Manhattan would probably profit immensely from a talk on wedding preparation given to engaged couples at a local church.

In *Effective Communication of Ideas* George Vardman says speaking should generally be used in the following situations:

1. When confidential matters are to be discussed.
2. When warmth and personal qualities are called for.
3. When an atmosphere of openness is desired.
4. When strengthening of feelings, attitudes, and beliefs is needed.
5. When exactitude and precision are *not* required.
6. When decisions must be communicated quickly or when important deadlines must be met rapidly.
7. When crucial situations dictate maximum understanding.
8. When added impact is needed to sustain the audience's attention and interest or get them to focus on a topic or issue.
9. When personal authentication of a claim or concept is needed.
10. When social or gregarious needs must be met.

Finding Speaking Opportunities

Unless you are self-sponsoring your own seminar, as is discussed in Chapter 27, you will need to find appropriate forums at which your company personnel can be invited to speak. How do you go about it?

First, check your mail and the trade publications you read for announcements of industry meetings and conventions. For instance, if you sell furnaces for steel mills and want to promote a new process, you might want to give a paper on your technique at the annual *Iron and Steel Exposition.*

Trade journals generally run preview articles and announcements of major shows, expos, and meetings months before the event. Many trade publications also have columns which announce such meetings on both a national and a local level. Make sure you scan these columns in publications aimed at your target market industries.

You should also receive preview announcements in the mail. If you are an advertising manager, professional societies and trade associations will send you direct mail packages inviting your firm to exhibit at their shows. That's fine, but you have another purpose: To find out whether papers, talks, or seminars are being given at the show, and, if so, to get your people on the panels or signed up as speakers. If the show mailing promotion doesn't discuss papers or seminars, call up and ask.

Propose some topics with your company personnel as the speakers. Most conference managers welcome such proposals, because they need speakers to fill time slots. The conference manager or another association executive in charge of the "technical sessions" (the usual name for the presentation of papers or talks) will request an abstract, or short 100 to 200-word outline of your talk. Work with your speakers to come up with an outline that is both enticing—so as to generate maximum attendance—but also reflects accurately what the speaker wants to talk about. After all, it is his/her talk, and he/she must be comfortable with it.

Because many advertisers will be pitching speakers and presentations at the conference manager, the earlier you do it, the better. Generally, annual meetings and conventions of major associations begin planning 8 to 12 months in advance; local groups or local chapters of national organizations generally book speakers 3 to 4 months in advance. The earlier you approach them, the more receptive they'll be to your proposal.

If you are not on the mailing list to receive advance notification of meetings and conventions of your industry associations, write to them and request that they place you on such a list. You will find their names and addresses in *The Encyclopedia of Associations,* published by Gale Research and available in your local library.

Screening Speaking Opportunities

On occasion, you may find meeting planners and conference executives calling you up and asking you (or a representative from your firm) to speak at their event, rather than you having to seek them out and ask them.

This is flattering. But beware. Not every opportunity to speak is really worthwhile. Meeting planners and committee executives are primarily concerned with getting someone to stand at the podium, and do not care whether your speaker or your firm will benefit in any way from the exposure. So, before you say "yes" to an opportunity to speak, ask the meeting planner the following questions:

- What is the nature of the group?
- Who are the members? What are their job titles and responsibilities? What companies do they work for?
- What is the average attendance of such meetings? How many people does the meeting planner expect will attend your session?
- Do they pay an honorarium or at least cover expenses?
- What other speakers have they had recently and what firms do these speakers represent?

If the answers indicate that the meeting is not right or worthwhile for your company, or if the meeting chairman seems unable or unwilling to provide answers, thank him politely and decline the invitation.

Plan Your Objective

Of course, your objective is to sell. But be careful. People attending a luncheon or dinner meeting aren't there to be sold. They want to be entertained. Informed. Educated. Made to laugh or smile. Selling your product, service, or company may be your goal, but in public speaking, it has to be secondary to giving a good presentation, and a "soft-sell" approach works best.

Terry C. Smith, author of *Making Successful Presentations,* lists the following as possible objectives for business presentations:

- Inform or instruct.
- Persuade or sell.
- Make recommendations and gain acceptance.

- Arouse interest.
- Inspire or initiate action.
- Evaluate, interpret, clarify.
- Set the stage for further action.
- Gather ideas and explore them.
- Entertain.

You could also add "establish credibility" to this list; a good talk can go a long way toward building the image of the speaker and her firm as authorities in the field.

"Perhaps you are aiming for a combination of these," says Smith. "For example, there is nothing wrong with being both informative *and* entertaining—the two are not mutually exclusive. In fact, the two may complement one another."

Let's say your talk is primarily informational. You could organize it along the following lines: First, an introduction that presents an overview of the topic. Next, the body of the talk, which presents the facts in detail. Finally, a conclusion that sums up for the audience what they have heard.

This repetition is beneficial because, in a spoken presentation, unlike an article, the reader cannot flip back to a preceding page or paragraph to refresh his memory or study your material in more detail. For this reason, you must repeat your main point at least three times to make sure it is understood and remembered.

And what if your talk is primarily persuasive or sales oriented? In their book *How to Make Speeches for All Occasions,* Harold and Marjorie Zelko present the following outline for a persuasive talk:

1. Draw attention to the subject.
2. Indicate the problem, need, or situation.
3. Analyze the problem's origin, history, causes, manifestations.
4. Lead toward possible solutions, or mention them.
5. Lead toward most desired solution or action.
6. Offer proof and values of solution proposed.
7. Prove it as better than other solutions. Prove it will eliminate causes of problems, will work, and has value.
8. Lead toward desired response from audience.
9. Show how desired response can be realized.
10. Conclude by summary and appeal as appropriate.

Janet Stone and Jane Bachner present a similar outline for persuasive organization in their book, *Speaking Up:*

1. Secure attention of audience.
2. State the problem.
3. Prove the existence of the problem.
4. Describe the unfortunate consequences of the problem.
5. State your solution.
6. Show how your solution will benefit the audience.
7. Anticipate and answer objections you know are coming.
8. Invite action.

Many other organizational schemes are available to speakers. For instance, if you're describing a *process,* your talk can be organized along the natural flow of the process or the sequence of steps involved in completing the process. This would be ideal for a talk on "How to Start Your Own Collection Agency" or "How to Design Mixers for Viscous Fluids."

If you're talking about expanding a communications network worldwide, you might start with the United States, then move on to Asia, then cover Europe. If your topic is vitamins, covering them in alphabetical order—from vitamin A to zinc—seems a sensible approach.

Lyle Surles and W.A. Stanbury, authors of *The Art of Persuasive Talking,* provide the following advice to speakers who want to persuade or sell as well as inform.

- Be sincere.
- Be honest.
- Show conviction.
- Be empathetic.
- Show respect for your audience.

And finally, Albert J. Beveridge, in *The Art of Public Speaking,* advises speakers to follow these rules:

- Speak only when you have something to say.
- Speak only what you believe to be true.
- Prepare thoroughly.
- Be clear.
- Stick to your subject.

- Be fair.
- Be brief.

The Most Important Part Of Your Talk

A talk has three parts: beginning, middle, and end. All are important. But the beginning and ending are more important than the body. Most people can manage to discuss a topic for 15 minutes, give a list of facts, or read from a prepared statement. And that's what it takes to deliver the middle part.

The beginning and ending are more difficult. In the beginning, you must immediately engage the audience's attention *and* establish rapport. Not only must they be made to feel that your topic will be interesting, but they must be drawn to you, or at least not find fault with your personality.

To test this theory, a well-known speaker put aside his usual opening and instead spoke for five minutes about himself—how successful he was, how much money he made, how in demand he was as a speaker, why he was the right choice to address the group. After his talk, he casually asked a member, "What were you thinking when I said that?" The man politely replied, "I was thinking what a blowhard you are."

How do you begin a talk? One easy and proven technique is to get the audience involved by asking them questions. For example, if addressing telecommunications engineers, ask: "How many of you manage a T1 network? How many of you are using 56 K DDS but are thinking about T1? And how many of you use fractional T1?"

If you are speaking on a health topic, you might ask, "How many of you exercised today before coming here? How many of you plan to exercise after the meeting tonight? How many of you exercise three or more times a week?"

Asking questions like these has two benefits. First, it provides a quick survey of audience concerns, interests, and level of involvement, allowing you to tailor your talk to their needs on the spot. Second, it forces the audience to become immediately involved.

After all, when you are in the audience, and the speaker asks a question, you do one of two things—you either raise your hand or don't raise it, don't you? Either way you are responding, thinking, and getting involved.

While the beginning is important, don't neglect a strong closing, especially if you are there not just for the pleasure of speaking but to help promote your company or its products. As Dorothy Leeds observes in her book *PowerSpeak:*

> Speakers, as you now know, are also in the selling business, and the conclusion is the time to ask for the order. Nothing will happen if you don't ask. And you ask by telling the audience what you want it to do with the information you've presented and *how* they can take that action. An effective speaker presenting a central idea ends by pointing out to those in his audience exactly what is needed from them to put that idea to work. For example . . . if you've been persuading them to give blood, tell them where. And make it sound easy to get there.
>
> Action doesn't always have to be literal. If you simply want the people in your audience to mull over your ideas, tell them this is what you want them to do.

Although you want a great opening that builds rapport and gets people to listen, and an ending that helps "close the sale," don't neglect the body or middle of your talk. It's the "meat"; it's what your audience came to hear. If your talk is primarily informational, be sure to give inside information on the latest trends, techniques, and product developments. If it's motivational, be enthusiastic and convince your listeners that they *can* lose weight, make money investing in real estate, or stop smoking.

If your talk is a how-to presentation, make sure you've written it so your audience walks away with lots of practical ideas and suggestions. As actor and toastmaster Georgie Jessel observed, "Above all, the successful speaker is sincerely interested in telling his audience something they want to know."

When speaking to technical audiences, tailor the content to the technical expertise of the listeners. Being too complex can bore a lot of people. But being too simplistic or basic can be even more offensive to an audience of knowledgeable industry experts.

Matters Of Length And Timing

Talks can vary from a 10-minute workplace presentation to a two-day intensive seminar. How long should yours be? The event and meeting planner often dictate length. Luncheon and after-dinner talks to local groups and local chapters of professional societies and business clubs usually last 20 to 30 minutes, with an additional 5 to 10 minutes allotted for questions and answers.

For technical sessions at major conferences and national expositions, speakers generally get 45 to 75 minutes. For a one-hour talk, prepare a 45-minute talk. You'll probably start five minutes late to allow for late arrivals, and the last 10 minutes can be a more informal question and answer session.

The luckiest speakers are those who get invited to participate in panels. If you are on a panel consisting of three or four experts plus a moderator, it's likely that you'll simply be asked to respond to questions from the moderator or the audience, eliminating the need to prepare a talk.

Richard Armstrong, a freelance corporate speech writer, says most of the speeches he writes are 20 minutes in length. James Welch, author of *The Speech Writing Guide,* says that a typed double-spaced page of manuscript should take the speaker 2½ minutes to deliver. This means an 8-page double-spaced manuscript, which is about 2,000 words, will take 20 minutes to deliver as a speech.

That's about a hundred words a minute. Some speakers are faster, talking at 120 to 150 words a minute or more. So the 20-minute talk can really be anywhere from 8 to 10 typed pages.

Preparing the Talk

What is the advertising department's role in arranging and preparing speeches for company executives, managers, and technical professionals? It varies widely. In some cases, you may be totally unaware that the speech is being given, and you find out only by accident. Some advertising managers are upset by what they consider "unauthorized" speaking, and insist that every talk funnel its way through the communication department. Some adopt a more liberal policy. Why inhibit speakers or make the process more bureaucratic than it need be?

In other situations, you may be called upon to coordinate the details of the presentation and help with its preparation. This can range from writing the entire talk, to simply coaching the speaker or assisting with production of slides or other visual aids.

Individuals vary on how much assistance they want or require. As a rule, top executives with severe time constraints will have their speeches written, or at least work from an initial draft prepared by the communications department, while most engineers, scientists, and technical managers prefer to prepare their own papers and presentations.

Don't be too quick to volunteer to write everyone's speech for them. While such activity can get you into the good graces of your "clients" at your company, it can easily become an overwhelming commitment as you underestimate the amount of work involved. According to *Best Sermons,* a religious magazine, it takes clergymen about seven hours to prepare a 20-minute sermon. You will find that this figure also holds true for business, sales, and technical presentations.

Allow at least one full day for preparation and rehearsal of any new short (20 to 30-minute) talk. Terry Smith says that for every brand new presentation, his ratio is one hour of preparation for every minute he plans to speak. "This is the preparation level at which I feel comfortable that I'm giving my very best," says Smith.

Tip: The trick to reducing preparation time is to have two or three "canned" (standard) talks which you can offer to various audiences. Even with a "canned" presentation, you'll need at least several hours to analyze the audience, do some customizing of your talk to better address that particular group, and rehearse once or twice.

Once the presentation is written, check it against the following list, provided by Dorothy Sarnoff in her book *Speech Can Change Your Life:*

1. Have I honored all the requirements of the talk? (For example, if you submitted an outline or abstract, were all points covered?)
2. Have I researched the topic enough?
3. Have I taken into account the nature of the audience?
4. Have I rechecked to make sure the talk fits the allotted time? (This is done by rehearsing *aloud* and timing yourself with a stopwatch.)
5. Have I constructed the talk so it has a clear purpose and makes a point at the end?
6. Have I enough strong ideas in the body—and have I developed them sufficiently and arranged them in good order?
7. Have I asked enough questions and used "you" enough?
8. Have I an appropriate introduction and a strong conclusion?
9. Does the talk include enough specifics?
10. Have I used *too many* statistics?

One Expert's Advice On How To Give A Speech

Professional speaker Rob Gilbert charges $3,000 to $7,000 to give a speech or presentation. Here are 41 of Gilbert's most effective techniques:

1. Write your own introduction and mail it to the sponsoring organization in advance of your appearance. (Also bring a copy with you for the master of ceremonies in case he lost your original.)
2. Establish rapport with the audience early.

3. What you say is not as important as how you say it.
4. Self-effacing humor works best.
5. Ask the audience questions.
6. Don't give a talk—have a conversation.
7. Thirty percent of the people in the audience will never ask the speaker a question.
8. A little bit of nervous tension is probably good for you.
9. Extremely nervous? Use rapport-building, not stress reduction, techniques.
10. The presentation does not have to be great. Tell your audience that if they get one good idea out of your talk, it will have been worthwhile for them.
11. People want stories, not information.
12. Get the audience involved.
13. People pay more for entertainment than education. (Proof: The average college professor would have to work 10 centuries to earn what Oprah Winfrey makes in a year.)
14. You have to love what you are doing. (Dr. Gilbert has 8,000 cassette tapes of speeches and listens to these tapes three to four hours a day.)
15. The first time you give a particular talk it will not be great.
16. The three hardest audiences to address: engineers, accountants, and high school students.
17. If heckled, you can turn any situation around ("verbal aikido").
18. Communicate from the Heart + Have an Important Message = Speaking Success.
19. You can't please everybody, so don't even try. Some will like you and your presentation—and some won't.
20. Ask your audience how you are doing and what they need to hear from you to rate you higher.
21. Be flexible. Play off your audience.
22. Be totally authentic.
23. To announce a break say: "We'll take a five-minute break now, so I'll expect you back in 10 minutes." It always gets a laugh.
24. To get them back in the room (if you are the speaker), go out into the hall and shout, "He's starting; he's starting."

25. Courage is to feel the fear and do it anyway. The only way to overcome what you fear is to do it.
26. If panic strikes: Just give the talk and keep your mouth moving. The fear will subside in a minute or two.
27. In speaking, writing, teaching, and marketing, everything you see, read, hear, or do is grist for the mill.
28. Tell touching stories.
29. If the stories are about you, be the goat, not the hero. People like speakers who are humble; audiences hate bragging and braggarts.
30. Join Toastmasters. Take a Dale Carnegie course in public speaking. Join the National Speakers Association.
31. Go hear the great speakers and learn from them.
32. If you borrow stories or techniques from other speakers, adapt this material and use it in your own unique way.
33. Use audiovisual aids, if you wish, but not as a crutch.
34. When presenting a daylong workshop, make the afternoon shorter than the morning.
35. Asking people to perform a simple exercise (stretching, Simon Says, etc.) as an activity during a break can increase their energy level and overcome lethargy.
36. People love storytellers.
37. Today's most popular speaking topic: Change (in business, society, lifestyles, etc.) and how to cope with it.
38. There is no failure—just feedback.
39. At the conclusion of your talk, tell your audience that they were a great audience—even if they were not.
40. Ask for applause using this closing: "You've been a wonderful audience. (Pause) Thank you very much."
41. If you want to become a good speaker, give as many talks as you can to as many groups as you can. Dr. Gilbert has some speeches he has given more than 1,000 times.

Slide Shows

What's the difference between a talk, a speech, and a presentation? A talk is a lecture given for free, while the term "speech" implies that the speaker receives a fee or honorarium. A presentation is a talk accompanied by slides, overheads, or other audiovisual aids.

When I was a marketing trainee at Westinghouse in the late 1970s, slides were all the rage in the corporate world. Nearly every presentation was an audiovisual presentation. Two managers could literally not get together for an informal chat without one pulling out a slide projector and dimming the lights.

Slides are still popular today, as are overhead projectors, but audiovisual aids are not necessary for most presentations. Most corporate presentations are dependent on slides or overheads and they are boring. Most professional speakers—people who earn thousands for a brief talk—do *not* use audiovisual aids. Today, businesspeople, especially in the corporate world, have become dependent on the visuals and have lost the spontaneity and relaxed manner that come with "having a conversation" rather than "making a presentation."

The problem with the corporate approach to visuals is that the audiovisual aid is seen as something that must run continuously and concurrently with the talk. So, although only 10 percent of the presentation requires visuals, the slide projector runs for 100 percent of the time, and the speaker fills in with stupid "word slides" that are wasteful and silly.

For instance, if the speaker is going to talk for 3 or 4 minutes on quality, he hits a button, and the word "QUALITY" appears on the screen in white against a black background. Such a visual adds nothing to the talk and is in fact ridiculous.

A better approach is to have visuals you can use when appropriate, then deliver the rest of your talk unaided. You can use flip charts and magic markers, but don't prepare them in advance. Rather, draw as you speak, which adds excitement and motion. It also creates anticipation: The audience becomes curious about what is being created before their eyes.

Slide projectors and overhead projectors are prone to mechanical failure. Errors in presentations, such as difficulty sorting through a pile of overhead transparencies, or slides that are upside down or out of order, confuse and embarrass the speaker; they also cause the audience to snicker or lose interest.

Some speakers, interrupted by a jammed slide tray, lose their train of thought and never fully recover. Errors or mishaps with audiovisual support can be extremely disconcerting, especially when making a good impression is important or the presenter is not comfortable with public speaking in the first place.

At times, high quality visuals are needed. You may need a visual to demonstrate how a product works, explain a process, show the components or parts of a system, or graphically depict performance. For instance, if you are trying to promote your landscape design practice by giving a talk on "How to Design a Beautiful Front Yard," you want to show pictures of attractive front yards you have designed. In this case you can prepare overhead transparencies, a videotape, flip charts, or similar displays which can be shown for a brief period and then put away. If you use slides, turn the projector off and the lights up when visuals are not in use.

According to a research study from 3M, it's estimated that we retain only 10 percent of what we hear, but by adding visual aids, the retention rate increases to 50 percent. And a report from Matrix Computer Graphics notes that 85 percent of all information stored in the brain is received visually.

22 Tips For Improving Slide And Other Audiovisual Presentations

1. Simple is better. Use slide presentations that can be shown using a single projector. Multi-projector presentations, while dazzling, require special equipment and trained personnel to present.

2. The best length for a slide show: 5 to 10 minutes if prerecorded; 10 to 20 minutes if live.

3. The proper pace for a slide show: one slide for each new thought.

4. To test the readability of a slide: Hold the slide at arm's length. If you can't read the text, your audience won't be able to either.

5. Pick a narrow topic. In 20 minutes, you can't cover much ground. If there's more detail, put it in a printed hand-out your audience can take with them.

6. Slides and overheads are used to show, demonstrate, create excitement. They are not a good medium for transmitting complex detail. Too much detail in a slide or overhead makes it unclear.

7. Use pictures. Keep use of "word slides" to a minimum.

8. Make the visuals clear, bold, and simple. For example, a graph should only have one curve and three or four data points. If there's more data to show, break it up into several slides.

9. Write narration for the ear, not the eye. Your talk will be heard—not read. This means shorter sentences, use of sentence fragments, pauses, and conversational tone.

10. To test your talk: Read it aloud. Rewrite portions that sound awkward or that you stumble over.

11. Slides today are an inexpensive medium. Cost per slide ranges from $7.50 to $50 for word slides, simple special effects, charts, graphs, and pictures taken from existing negatives or photos.

12. Resist the temptation to use silly or humorous slides. What one person finds funny and witty strikes another as offensive or juvenile.

13. "Tell them what you're going to tell them. Tell them. Then tell them what you told them." Your presentation should have an introduction, body, and recap or summary. According to Matrix Computer Graphics, a manufacturer of presentation and imaging equipment, you should spend approximately 20 percent of your speaking time on the introduction, 70 percent on the body, and 10 percent on the conclusion.

14. Slides with the most visual appeal include people (especially shots of people in the audience), familiar settings (e.g., their workplace), familiar problems.

15. Before you start, say: "There's no need to take notes. We have hard copies of this presentation for you to take home." This relieves the listener of the burden of note-taking, freeing him to concentrate on your talk.

16. The leave-behind can take one of several formats: hard copy of the slides or overheads, brochures, article reprints, or reprints of the narration (with visuals incorporated, if possible).

17. If the slide tray jams, insert a dime into the screw in its center and turn counter-clockwise. This will usually release and allow you to remove the jammed slide. Put it aside and go on to the next slide. Do not try to show it—the slide may be damaged.

18. Try to have someone else handle the audiovisual equipment, so you won't be bothered by such problems. If the problem cannot be fixed within 30 seconds, continue talking without your visual aids.

19. When travelling, always carry your slides, lecture notes, and other audiovisual materials with you. Do not pack them with luggage. Luggage gets lost.

20. Arrive early, set up early, and do a dry run in the room. Get there in plenty of time to make sure all equipment, electrical outlets, markers, and other material you requested is there—also to rearrange the room to your liking. The speaker should always check out the lecture room at least one hour before the talk is scheduled to start.

21. The big advantage of slides: They are modular. You can quickly change, rearrange, update, or revise the presentation at virtually no cost.

22. Keep originals or "masters" under lock and key. Make several duplicate sets available in trays for others in your firm. Also keep copies of individual slides in a light cabinet (illuminated storage rack system) so people can have access to individual visuals as needed.

CHAPTER 29

Films and Videos

Video and film, with their mesmerizing effect, have a potentially greater sales impact than print media. Reading takes effort and requires concentration. But few people can resist the impulse to stop and stare at a TV or film screen, which always seems a relaxing pastime.

Computer Video Productions, based in Minneapolis, specializes in "video sales brochures." Craig R. Evans, CVP's marketing director, points out that video (and, for our purposes, film) "is a very intimate medium. It appeals to both the audio and the visual sense. A paper brochure just sits there. With video you can see the product and also hear it. And you have a captive audience. People tend to watch your video brochure from start to finish, in the order you want the information presented."

Granted, a video or film is less convenient to watch than sales literature is to read. And it will surely be more expensive to produce. But it is also less likely to be thrown away or easily misplaced. Pallace, Inc., a Maryland-based advertising agency, puts it thus: "In today's junk-mail jungle, a videotape stands out from the pack."

Audio-visual media are also cost-competitive compared to the salary of a full-time salesperson. "And unlike the salesman," says Craig Evans, "your video never has a bad day."

Applications

Videos and Films as Sales Tools

A film or video may be the ideal sales solution for services or high-tech products which are too big to lug around from client to client, or for reaching potential consumers at point-of-sale locations. Non-broadcast commercial films can run in department store windows, airport terminals, hotel lobbies, and at trade shows. If you are selling a system of some kind, the audio-visual approach can demonstrate an entire step-by-step process.

New products can be introduced or explained. If a pharmaceutical company is marketing a new drug, a videotape can be distributed to doctors to make them aware of the availability and benefits of the new drug.

Sales videos can be mailed directly to customers, or left at their offices during sales calls, for viewing at the prospect's convenience. Most executives welcome the opportunity to turn out the lights and watch a little TV during the course of a day's work.

Using Audio-Visuals to Produce Employee Motivation

Audio-visuals can be presented to the sales force at conventions, conferences, seminars, or smaller meetings. These productions can be used to launch new products or kick-off promotion campaigns, or to instill team spirit by chronicling company successes. Presentations geared to top management can showcase accomplishments, introduce new concepts, or offer projections for the future.

Video and Film as Training Devices

Audio-visuals can be used to orient new employees or update the skills of your current staff. Big-screen presentations are useful with large groups, and could be used in conjunction with live instruction. Audio-visuals can also be used for recruitment.

Using a Video as a Public Relations Tool

A video could show community service projects, or document a pioneering research program behind new product development. It can be sent to civics groups, such as the Rotary Club, Elks or B'nai B'rith, libraries, or schools. These films often have educational overtones, but always reflect well on the company. A utility company could distribute audio-visuals on how to clean a furnace, how to conserve energy, or the importance of recycling.

Videos as Tie-ins

Films or videos can be used as part of a larger presentation, which can include live speakers, multi-media displays, product demonstrations, or supplemental print literature to take home after viewing the film.

Interactive Videos

In this format, instead of sitting passively, the viewer participates directly by responding to choices presented.

Kings Supermarkets provides culinary tips to shoppers via interactive videos. A shopper presses a button to select a choice of video offering helpful kitchen advice, such as how to cook a salmon or carve a turkey.

Interactive videos linked to computers are also used in training such technicians as auto mechanics or hospital personnel. In the latter case, the video simulates an emergency situation, and an on-screen menu gives the trainee a choice of response A, B, or C. If the wrong answer is selected, the video explains why and demonstrates the proper procedure.

Film or Video: Which is Best for You?

Video is the predominant format of industrial audio-visual presentations nowadays. It is an instantaneous technology. On a set, you can see results immediately, and mistakes are easier to rectify on the spot. If you didn't get what you wanted on the first take, you can re-shoot. With film, you have to wait to see the *rushes* (unrefined, developed prints), usually the next day; if the results are unsatisfactory, you may have to re-setup the entire shoot, which may be impractical, cost prohibitive, or impossible.

Production time for film and video is about equal, but in terms of overall efficiency (especially from the producer or director's standpoint), video clearly has the edge. It is, overall, a more convenient technology.

For viewing, it also has the edge over film. A client is likelier to be equipped with a VCR and TV monitor than a projector and screening room, and this trend will accelerate in the coming years.

Image clarity differs between the two formats. Video tends to look more "live," hence, more immediate. But it also looks flat, not fully dimensional. Video lighting often lends a harshness to the image. Film, on the other hand, is richer, softer, and has more depth of field. Film looks permanent, almost timeless. (Music videos, in fact, are often shot on film and then transferred to video.)

Steve Dovas, a Brooklyn-based filmmaker specializing in animation, admits: "I'd be hard-pressed to advocate film production over video for corporate and industrial purposes. Costs for video are getting a lot lower. In terms of aesthetics, film is more intimate, warmer. It requires a lot less glaring, directional light. But video equipment is smaller, and you've got a lot more mobility. And with film, costs are always escalating. If your bottom line matters, you can do better with video on the cheap than with film. But I'd have to say as bad as a low-budget film looks, cheap video in inexperienced hands looks even worse."

Regardless of which medium you use, it's possible to convert at a later stage. A film can be transferred to video (and vice-versa, though there are fewer instances where this would be desirable). There will be some loss of image quality in the process, but if you need to distribute quick copies of a film to clients who only have VCRs, the option is available.

The Key Qualities Of Audio-Visuals

Visual Impact

It's important that pictures tell as much of the story as possible. The client may have distractions while viewing—phone calls, conversations with colleagues, or surrounding noise. But while their ears or mouths may be otherwise engaged, the eyes are likely to remain fixed on the screen to catch what the ears miss.

Motion

The advantage of a film over print literature or a slide show is movement (although *multi-imaging* slide shows—using as many as 20 screens at once—almost resemble animation). The medium should be used to this advantage. Keep the action paced for comfortable viewing. Stills may be inserted where motion pictures aren't available, but these images shouldn't linger.

However, the kind of rapid-fire, quick-cut action editing so stylish in rock videos should be avoided, or you may succeed only in confusing the viewer. Quick cuts may be good for an opening or closing, but for product depiction, the viewer should be given time to assimilate the visual.

Length

This will always vary, depending on the purpose of the production. Gloria Piliero, of A.D. Venture Video, Fairfield, NJ, gives some indication: "If you have a captive audience that has to watch, it can be as long as it takes to get the information across. An orientation video for banks to train new tellers can run 10 to 30 minutes. But if it's going to run longer than 30 minutes, it should be segmented. If you're targeting people you want to sell services or products to, they're not going to spend a lot of time with a prolonged commercial. So, as short and sweet as you can make it while still getting the necessary information across—may be between four and seven minutes. Ten minutes is probably too long, unless the visuals are interesting, or it's funny. But just because it's longer doesn't mean it'll prove the point better. As soon as you get the message across—stop!"

Pacing is the key, and when the audience's patience is tested, attention begins to flag. As a general rule, shorter is always better than longer.

Plot

The most engaging productions involve storytelling. A conflict, struggle, or problem is presented, that must be resolved. Introduce characters with whom the viewer can identify, either by age, economic status, gender, or profession. Use real people, rather than glamorous dreamboats or starlets. Show how the character's problem is resolved, either by using your product, or by following the correct procedure.

If the subject is an institution, such as a hospital, corporation, bank, or international agency, never forget that such organizations consist of *people*. Emphasize these folks doing their jobs. No one can relate to a large bureaucracy, except as individuals working as part of a team.

Language

Your script language will depend on the projected audience and their familiarity with the subject. Unless they are highly trained technicians, it's best to keep the tone conversational. Use familiar, but descriptive language, and avoid "bureaucratese." Freelance scriptwriter John Baldoni recommends using "words for the ear, not for the eye . . . active verbs, colorful words and phrases." Never lose sight of the "human interest" element.

Let the visuals do most of the talking. It isn't necessary to point out everything that's happening on-screen. Keep it tight, don't meander or throw in gratuitous digressions. In a film or video, narrative should be used for reinforcement or continuity, but rarely for primary information.

Dynamics

Use different elements: voiceover narrative; musical interlude; various on-camera spokespeople; anecdotal material; on-screen text (captions, titles); illustrations (charts, graphs, diagrams); animation; special effects. Keep the production moving, using as much variety as your budget permits.

Estimating The Cost Of Your Audio-Visual

The breakeven point between video and film seems to be about 30 seconds in length; cost for either will probably be equal. For longer productions, video is usually cheaper. And most non-broadcast audiovisual productions are longer than 30 seconds.

However, there is no rule of thumb for film or video costs. Fees will vary depending on the following factors:

—sophistication of production;

—editing time;

—scriptwriting;

—music (and whether score is original or "canned");

—director;

—actors;

—voiceover announcers;

—technical assistance;

—props;

—special effects;

—animation (computer or hand-art);

—travel (and lodging for extended shoots).

A low estimate for a professionally made industrial video runs about $4,000. For that price, you can get what looks like a fancy home video. The image will be decent, but not top-notch, scripting will be minimal, and there will probably be no voiceover announcer or special effects. Such a budget could cover one day of on-location shooting, relatively little editing, and more than likely no director. It could be just a technician with a videopack and tripod aiming his camera and shooting from a stationary position. Such an approach might be suitable for in-house productions, or for short-term usage with restricted distribution. However, to create an image or market to a broad consumer base, it will cost much, much more.

One video studio quoted a figure of $13,000 to produce a seven-minute short spotlighting an industrial hire-the-handicapped program. Price included minimal special effects, two days' on-location shooting, a "canned" (pre-recorded, generic) music bed, no voiceover, some direction, and three days of reviewing and editing footage. This was for a non-profit organization with a limited budget.

On the high end, a corporate video could run between $50,000 and $250,000. Not exactly Spielberg, but the result would be an excellent, high-quality production, full of glamour and glitz.

To give an indication of how costly special effects are: one second of computer graphics for a slick video opening costs about $1,000. And that opening could run four to seven seconds.

Some of the reasons film costs more than video are explained by Steve Dovas: "A lot of the cost of film is more than just setting up the camera and shooting. You have an entire run of laboratory costs. Titling (adding captions and credits) gets very difficult. With any additions to the raw image, costs multiply geometrically. Video production editing can cost as high as $200 to $300 an hour. But with video, even on the low end, you get a fully assembled tape, with titles and any other weirdness you need for presentation purposes."

Regardless of which medium you choose, copies are relatively inexpensive. The major investment is in producing the master.

Cost of duplication varies, based on transfer format, number of copies, packaging, and vendor. One copy of a 20-minute ¾″ master to ½″ VHS costs between $15 to $25. Per copy cost for quantities over 25 are between $8 and $15; 100 copies, $7 to $10 each; 500, $6 to $9 each; 1,000, $3-5 each. These are basic duplication costs, including a cardboard sleeve, with no fancy labeling or packaging. The field is competitive, however, and comparison shopping is worthwhile.

The Stages Of Production

Video Production

Original footage is recorded on ½″ Betacam (a trademarked name used, incorrectly, to generically refer to portable, on-location video equipment).

Original footage can also be recorded on ¾″ videotape, but ½″ is more practical and convenient. In the studio, the raw footage is stepped up to 1″ tape for the final mix (or if you're budget-conscious, onto ¾″ tape, which is slightly cheaper). This process is called *interformat editing.* The original footage is referred to as *source* tape, and the final version is the *master.* (Jargon varies, however. Some technicians refer to original footage as the master, and the final version as the *edited master.*)

All copies (called *dubs* or *dupes*) are made from this final version. Copies can be made on either ¾″, VHS, or Beta. Beta and VHS are both ½″ tape, but the cartridge sizes differ, and they cannot be played on each other's machines. VHS is the more popular for in-house corporate screening; an advantage to VHS is that a client can take your video home for viewing on the family VCR.

Film Production

Following ideas developed in a *storyboard* (hand-rendered, panel-by-panel approximation of major sequences of the film) or in a shooting script, raw footage is shot in either 16mm or 35mm film. 35mm captures a superior image, but is more expensive. The raw footage is then developed into a *work print* and a negative. The work print can be *scratched* (rough cut) to conform to the director's conception of the film. A *slop print* is a black-and-white composite of the film, also a work print, which contains the basic soundtrack elements, including dialogue, ambient effects, or off-camera noises. The negative is then conformed to the rough-cut work print, creating a *fine cut.* The negative at this stage is "married" to the soundtrack mix.

The lab will then send back an *answer print,* based on all work so far. The director will diagnose the film for necessary color changes, flaws in synchronization, damage to the negative, or other imperfections. After corrections to the answer print, the *release print* is made. This is the copy which is distributed to the public.

Tips On Getting What You Want

Pre-Planning

Know what you want and what you hope to achieve. This applies to the conceptual framework, script, storyboard, mood, and the target audience. Plan. The unexpected will always arise, and though you can't avoid every hindrance or delay, you can thwart Murphy's Law as much as possible with purposeful planning.

Editing

Always sit in on editing sessions. This is standard procedure. Editing time is expensive and revisions can be costly. You should be present to steer the edit. If you have a specific direction or cut in mind, the time to talk about it is during the editing process, not later.

Copying

Copies should be made from the edited master. Each step of duplication from the master is called a *generation,* and there is loss of clarity with each subsequent generation. It may not be noticeable from a second to third generation, but from the third on, the image will lose sharpness, colors will look flat, and the soundtrack will build up hiss or distortion. For optimum quality, avoid making copies of copies.

Where To Find Film Or Videomakers

There are many elements to video or film production, such as lighting, camerawork, scripting, set design, acting and voice talent, editing, special effects, and duplicating. When contacting video technicians, filmmakers, or studios, inquire whether they offer full production capabilities, or merely one specialized aspect of production. If you hire all the separate vendors yourself, you become the producer. The alternative is to hire an independent producer or large production house, who will take care of the myriad details. It could save you a lot of headaches later by having an experienced professional handle the entire package.

If you see an industrial video or film you like, watch the credits at the end for a contact name or studio.

Referrals

Ask your colleagues or other advertising managers who have worked with videomakers for referrals. As with any creative vendor, artistic vision and experience are never the whole story. When seeking recommendations, inquire about temperament and cooperativeness.

Vendors in related disciplines (e.g., scriptwriting, set design, makeup, music) might be good sources for recommending film or videomakers with whom they've worked.

Many large corporations use independent video and filmmakers. Ask their advertising departments for recommendations. Some, such as Prudential Insurance, have their own in-house video department which can be hired for outside work.

Service Organizations

Any film or video service organization or union will publish member directories, or offer referrals of qualified members. The ITVA (International Television Association), headquartered in Irving, Texas, is one of the largest such associations, with regional chapters around the country. Their phone number is (214) 869-1112.

Yellow Pages

Under "Film," "Video," "Audio-Visual," and sometimes under "Photography." There are a few companies which do both film and video, but most do one or the other.

Publications

Magazines (regional and national) that deal with video and film feature advertisements for freelance technicians or production houses. *Video Systems,* an excellent professional journal, is available from Intertec Publishing, P.O. Box 12901, Overland Park, KS 66282-2901 phone (913) 341-1300. *Backstage,* a tipsheet geared heavily towards the entertainment industry and available at many newsstands, also has listings for commercial and industrial production talent. *Audiovisual Communications Monthly* (Horizons Media, 475 Park Avenue, NY 10016 phone 212-682-7010) is aimed at corporate in-house media production. *In Motion* (1203 West Street, Annapolis, MD 21401 phone 410-269-0605) is helpful for "professionals working in film/video production and related imaging media."

Knowledge Industry Publications, Inc. (KIPI), offers authoritative books on video graphic design, computer animation, and scriptwriting for corporate productions. Their catalog can be acquired by calling 1-800-800-5474. They also publish the magazine *AV Video.*

Trade Shows

Keep abreast of creative trade shows and expos in your area. They are sure to include exhibition booths hosted by local producers seeking your business.

CHAPTER 30

Billboards and Signs*

Billboards

If you want to expand your advertising reach, consider venturing into the great outdoors. Depending on your company's market and message, you may not have to go too far—just to your local highways or town streets to find the right billboards to advertise your company's services.

Billboard advertising can be effective for small, local firms as well as big consumer companies. It can help you reach prospects, impress customers, build your image as a successful company, attract future employees, even strengthen your position as a creditworthy client at your local lending institution.

Despite the public outcry in recent years over the proliferation of billboards, and the subsequent restrictions by local governments in the number and location of signs—or perhaps because of it—billboard advertising is an effective way to get your company's name before prospects and "open doors" when the sales staff calls.

*Material in this chapter is reprinted courtesy of the National Association of Printers and Lithographers (*Printing Manager*, January/February 1989) and the U.S. Small Business Administration (Aid No. 4.016).

According to the Institute of Outdoor Advertising, "Outdoor advertising is ideal for product introductions, store openings, or promotional events where timing is critical. Outdoor advertising bridges the gap between the in-home message from other media and the out-of-home purchase."

All-Day Selling

The big advantage billboard advertising has over radio, TV, direct mail, and newspaper advertising is that once your message is up, it's there 24 hours a day. John Selix, the owner of an 11-store graphic arts chain in Milwaukee, WI, points out, "Prospects can't shut their eyes when they're driving."

Billboards come in two forms: bulletins, which are most often 14′ by 48′ and can be painted on or posted with preprinted paper; and poster panels, which are smaller structures that measure 12-¼′ by 24-½′ and contain either bleed posters or 30-sheet posters.

Bulletins have relatively high circulation compared to poster panels because they are located only on major thoroughfares. However, poster panels are more widely distributed and achieve a broader and faster market reach. While bulletins are bought on an individual unit basis, posters are bought by "showing," which means the intensity with which a various number of poster panels cover a market. Common showing sizes are #100, 75, 50, and 25.

For example, a #50 showing delivers 500,000 daily exposures in a market with one million people. A #25 showing would deliver 250,000 people in that same market. An average #50 showing will reach over 80 percent of all adults in one month, and more than half are reached the first week.

In addition, retailers benefit when manufacturers place outdoor advertising close to their stores. In return, they may give the manufacturer prime shelf space and carry higher inventory for the advertiser.

Location Is Critical

As with buying real estate, location is the essential factor to consider when purchasing billboard advertising. Will more prospects see your billboard in town or on a nearby highway? Do you want to target an upscale neighborhood or a commercial district? A distinct advantage of outdoor advertising is that it can offer a more highly targeted placement than other media, since poster panels can be placed in communities of different ethnic backgrounds and levels of income.

After a year and a half of using a rotating bulletin system, Gilbert Thompson, President of Thompson Printing in Belleville, NJ, signed an 18-month contract for a billboard on a busy highway that leads into New York City. "I wanted that location because most of our clients, who are advertising and businesspeople, at one time or another go into New York," explains Thompson. "In fact, about half the population of New Jersey takes that road into New York at one time or another, so it's worth the $2,000 a month price tag."

But for Bob Fellman, President of five consumer service stores located in four Wisconsin cities, the only good locations are city locations. "Our customers are mostly individuals who live or work close to our shops," he explains. "So I would never use a highway billboard." For the past five years, Fellman has personally selected every board, and he changes their locations every month to get the broadest exposure possible.

Other important factors to consider include reach (how many people drive by the sign) and frequency (the average number of times an individual has the opportunity to be exposed to an advertising message during a defined period of time), speed and volume of traffic at the site, height and dimensions of the sign (displays that "break above the skyline" are better, as are larger signs), the number of other signs in the area (too much clutter could cut down on the readership your sign receives), and whether the sign is illuminated so it's visible late at night in high-traffic locations. Also, proximity to a stoplight or intersection will increase readership.

While outdoor advertising companies will provide demographics and traffic circulation statistics on various locations, common sense and personal experience are good guidelines. The president of a Connecticut company chose his bulletin location as a result of his own experience as a commuter on a major highway close to company headquarters. "The billboard was rather sizeable—about 24′ square—and positioned right before the toll booths, where everyone was slowing down," he says. "You couldn't help but read that sign." Although he had to wait a year before the billboard was available, the results were worth the wait. "I've probably gotten more attention from that billboard and from advertising placards on commuter trains into New York City than from any other promotion I've done in the last 10 years," the president of the $12 million company comments. Moreover, the placards, a cousin of billboard advertising, produced more than 30 leads during the two years the company used the promotion.

Impact On Sales

The Institute of Outdoor Advertising claims that "dollar for dollar, outdoor advertising delivers a greater audience than any of the major media." Table 30.1 from *Adweek's Marketer's Guide to Media* gives cost per thousand comparisons:

Outdoor advertising has a unique target ability, in that the outdoor message is the last one potential buyers see on the way to the store. "It's the most local medium, but it can be as national or regional as you want it to be," says Andrea MacDonald, marketing manager for the Institute of Outdoor Advertising. "A lot of advertisers use outdoor as the design basis for their other ads to enforce a one-idea, one-benefit message. But it's also a very flexible creative medium—one advertiser we know of lit up the headlights on a car featured on his bulletin, which had a dramatic effect at night. Another advertiser uses fiberoptics to create simulated lightning on his board."

Currently, there are 260,000 billboard and poster structures in the United States available for leasing. Ten thousand of that number are poster panels, the rest are billboards. In 1988, total revenues generated by the leasing of billboards came to $1.42 billion.

Tracking sales results from billboard advertising is difficult. Im most cases, determining effectiveness relies largely on feedback from customers, salespeople, and business associates. As part of a media campaign, outdoor advertising can strengthen sales results through improved audience delivery, higher frequency, and more gross rating points (the total number of impressions delivered by a media schedule as expressed by a percentage of the population) per dollar. While billboards reach every population strata, Simmons Market Research Bureau (SMRB) shows an above average performance in the younger, affluent, and working market.

TABLE 30.1. COST PER THOUSAND OF OUTDOOR ADVERTISING

Cost Per Thousand	*Men*	*Women*
Outdoor (50 showing)	$ 1.70	$ 2.15
TV (30 seconds) (Prime Time)	12.90	10.25
Radio (30 seconds)	4.10	3.30
Newspapers (600 lines Black & White)	7.00	6.75
Magazines	7.30	4.60

Thompson notes that "a billboard gives extra punch to our sales force so when they go out, prospects have seen the name and our logo. It opens doors more easily."

Another indication of the bulletin's effectiveness, says Thompson, "is that we're getting many more requests for quotations from people we haven't contacted. More importantly, the quality of the responses has gone up. We're not interested in doing one-time projects, we want high-quality leads that translate into steady business. That's what we're getting from billboards."

To obtain a more accurate analysis of sales impact, Fellman has recently begun tabulating the results of his stores' various advertising efforts through customer reply cards that customers pick up with their orders. Although the cards only ask whether customers have seen the boards, not whether they responded to them, 70 to 75 percent of customers indicate they've seen the poster panels. That places the medium above newspapers—and about even with radio—in terms of effectiveness for the company.

Not only do billboards reach prospects, but they seem to convince customers that the advertiser is a sizeable and stable company that's good to do business with.

Says one company president, "Here's my 125-employee company out there on the billboards side by side with Coca Cola and Dewar's Scotch. That gives our buyers a sense of security. And it reinforces the message that we're a pretty big company in this area."

Thompson echoes those sentiments, noting, "We started using billboards when we moved to our present location in 1984, because we thought they would give us great exposure and help build our image. The strategy has surpassed our expectations. Our customers have told us they're impressed with the sign. They know putting up a billboard isn't something you do if you don't have money and aren't interested in growing, and they feel good about doing business with a company that's on the upswing."

Short On Copy, Big On Design

Billboards must state their message clearly and quickly, since the reader is usually in a car going 50 or 60 miles per hour and will only glance at your billboard for a few seconds. All outdoor messages are viewed at distances ranging from 100 to 400 feet. Copy must be kept to a minimum, and the design has to grab attention.

In fact, the Institute of Outdoor Advertising tells advertisers "The fewer the words, the larger the illustration, the bolder the colors, the simpler the background, and the clearer the product identification, the better the outdoor advertisement."

Thomas Lavey, President of Lakeland Outdoor in Manitowoc, WI, offers this advice on design: "Try to come up with a graphic or visual that tells the story. If you have to add copy, use a play on words—it will result in a more memorable message."

The vivid colors that can be used on outdoor displays are a distinct advantage of the medium. Outdoor advertising professionals recommend using colors that are dissimilar in both hue and value—such as yellow and purple. White will work with any dark-value color, and black is ideal for colors of light value.

"Hire a top designer," advises one company president, whose company billboard won an award from the Printing Institute of America. "It will pay off."

Outdoor advertising companies will give you the specifications to contract out the design work, or in some cases, they have art departments that will help you design your billboard. Bulletins are either hand-painted in an artist's studio, and then put up in sections on location, or painted directly on-site.

Ninety percent of bulletins today are hand-painted on poster board, but messages can also be applied by posting pre-printed paper or using computer-generated painting. Poster panels are lithographed or silk-screened and then shipped to the outdoor company. "The industry is moving towards high-technology, computer-aided design systems," says Lavey. "They speed up the design process and make it easier."

Gannett Outdoor, the nation's largest outdoor advertising company, hopes advertisers will switch to a new material it has developed called "Superflex," a combination of canvas and plastic stretched over a billboard frame. A computerized painting system sprays the design directly on the material, eliminating individual variations in execution. The new material costs about 25 percent more than paper, but provides brilliant color and a consistent, high-quality reproduction for advertisers who want to use the same design on more than one billboard.

Purchasing Outdoor Advertising

There are hundreds of outdoor advertising companies in the United States. Once you have selected the markets for outdoor advertising, you can look up those markets in the *Buyer's Guide to Outdoor Advertising.* It will identify the outdoor company in each market and the cost of poster panels and bulletins in those markets. For more information on the *Buyer's Guide,* contact: Leading National Advertisers, 136 Madison Avenue, New York, NY 10016; telephone 212-696-4533. Or, if you're interested in using a particular board, you can usually find the outdoor advertising company's name posted at the bottom. Another option is to look in the yellow pages under "Advertising: Outdoor."

Contracts generally run on either a 12-, 24- or 36-month period for bulletins, or on a monthly basis for poster panels. You should contact the outdoor advertising company at least 90 days before you would like your ad to appear. While poster production takes from 21 to 45 days, artwork for painted bulletins must be sent to the outdoor company 60 days in advance.

Costs vary tremendously, according to region of the country, specific billboard location, number of billboards leased, designer, complexity of the design, whether the sign is illuminated, whether the billboard is a bulletin or a poster panel, and whether the billboard is hand-painted or computer-printed.

Average costs for poster panels are $200 to $400 per month, plus about $80 each to produce. But the average cost of a bulletin is typically $1,000 to $3,000 per month, plus about $1,000 each to produce.

You can keep down production costs by agreeing to let the outdoor advertising company rotate the location of your billboard every 60 or 90 days. For the outdoor company, this kind of agreement can take advantage of unrented space. The plus side for the advertiser is that balanced coverage of the market can be achieved with just one billboard. Some companies also give discounts based on volume and length of contract, so that if you rent four or five billboards for a two, three, or even one-year period, 10 to 30 percent may be knocked off the price.

Even without such discounts, cost efficiency can be high. As promotional literature published by the Institute of Outdoor Advertising notes, "Outdoor is seen all day, every day. It cannot be turned off like television, tuned out like radio, or discarded like newspapers and magazines. And the mere size of your ad makes it difficult to ignore."

For more information on outdoor advertising, or to request the "File Cabinet" information kit that charts cost comparisons between billboards and other media and explains how to buy and design outdoor advertising, contact the Institute of Outdoor Advertising, 12 E. 49th Street, New York, New York 10017. Telephone: 212-688-3667.

Signage As A Promotional Tool

Signs are one of the most efficient and effective communication media. Most businesses depend heavily on signs to help people find them, advertise their business, and present an image of their business. In short, signs tell people who you are and what you are selling.

Signs are such a powerful communication medium that it is difficult to estimate the extent of their influence. Other media require the directed attention of the person receiving the message. Signs, however, can convey a message while creating a mood or feeling of atmosphere. It is not necessary for people to give full attention to your sign in order to derive meaning from its presence.

What is a Sign?

A sign is the most direct form of visual communication available. In fact, so many people use signs without a second thought that it is easy to overlook their importance. When we cannot talk to other people directly in a given location, we put up signs: wet paint, beware of dog, enter here, garage sale, et cetra. Signs are the only form of mass communication directly available to everyone—they are the people's street communication system.

What Signs Can Do For Your Business

Signs perform three major communication functions for your business:

1. *Signs give information about your business and direct people to your business location.* Signs index the environment so people can find you. This is especially true for travelers, new members of your community, and impulse shoppers who may be on a journey to purchase the particular goods or services that you sell. Americans are mobile. Each year 40 million of us travel over 1.7 trillion miles by automobile and approximately 19 percent of us change our place of residence. A primary source of customers for your business is the large number of people who are new to your community or who may be just passing through. Your sign is the most effective way of reaching this mobile or transient group of potential customers.

Signs can help correct a poor location by substituting effective communication for poor site characteristics. If your business is located on a site which is not visible or in a building which does not correspond with the goods or services offered, your sign can overcome this disability. For example, most buildings are not built to conform to the design needs of any particular type of tenant. Without an effective sign it is often impossible to determine what type of business is being conducted in a given building. In addition, when your site is located off a busy traffic artery or in an area which is not easily accessible, your sign can communicate to people who are passing on a busy street several blocks away. If you are located off a busy freeway but far from an exit, your sign becomes your main device for directing people to your business. High-rise signs are used when a business is located away from potential customers' normal pathways of travel.

2. *Signs are street advertising.* Your sign provides an easily recognizable format for the goods or services you are selling. For most businesses, the street is where potential customers are. The message displayed on the street reaches people who are close enough to make a purchase. Street advertising also helps people develop a memory of your business name and the products and services you sell. People tend to buy from businesses they know.

3. *Signs build image.* Signs can build an image for your business and help you identify with the market segment you are trying to reach. Through materials and design, a sign can appeal to a given group of potential customers. For example, some firms attempt to capture the youth market, other senior citizens, other unmarried single people and so forth. If you have a particular market segment that you wish to attract to your business, your sign can be an important means of bringing these people in.

The Advantages of Signs

On-premise signs are your most effective and efficient means of commercial communication because they are inexpensive, available, practical, easy to use, always on the job, and directly oriented to the trade area of your business.

Your sign is an integral part of your advertising program along with the other forms of commercial communication such as television, radio, newspapers, magazines, and billboards. There are four basic criteria used to judge the effectiveness of these advertising media: (1) coverage of the trade area; (2) repetition of a message; (3) readership of a message; (4) cost per thousand exposures of a message. Two other criteria important for the small business owner are (5) availability and (6) ease of use. Here's how signs measure up to these criteria:

1. *Signs are oriented to your trade area.* Signs do not waste your resources by requiring you to pay for wasted advertising coverage. The people who see your sign are the people who live in your trade area.

2. *Signs are always on the job repeating your message to potential customers.* Your on-premise sign communicates to potential customers twenty-four hours a day, seven days a week, week after week, month after month, year after year. Every time people pass your business establishment they see your sign. The mere repetition of the message will help them remember your business.

3. *Nearly everyone reads signs.* Signs are practical to use, for nearly everyone is used to looking at signs and using signs, even small children. Studies have shown that people do read and remember what is on signs. When special items are displayed, sales increase for these particular items within the store.

4. *Signs are inexpensive.* When compared to the cost of advertising in some other media, the on-premise sign is very inexpensive. Unless your trade area encompasses an entire city or region, where you must rely upon broad-based media coverage, there is no better advertising dollar value than your on-premise sign.

5. *Signs are available to each and every shopowner.* There is no need to schedule the use of your sign. Your sign is available to you whenever you need it and to be used however you please.

6. *Signs are easy to use.* No special skills or resources are needed to operate a sign once it has been installed. If it is an illuminated sign, all you need to do is flip the switches and that may not be necessary with timing equipment. Once the initial expenditures are made, no special resources or professional services are needed. You need only operate and maintain your sign.

Checklist for Ordering a Business Sign

Before you select a sign for your business, there are several things you need to consider. A competent sign company in your area can help you with the answers to some of these questions.

1. *Who are your customers?* Potential customers for your business are people who reside in your trade area. Most of your customers come from the immediate area within a half mile to a mile of your business location. Trade areas come in assorted shapes and sizes depending upon the business. Trade areas may also vary seasonally.

2. *How do you get information on potential customers?* Plot a dot map of your customers as soon as you begin business. This is easily done by plotting the addresses of people who shop in your store as a dot on a

street map of your city. Within a few months time you will have a fairly clear idea of the trade area from which you are drawing your customers. You will then be able to decide what type of sign would best meet the needs of the people in that trade area. For example, if your customers can only reach you by automobile or if you are located on a very busy street, the type of sign that you use will be very different than if you have a shopping center location and people must walk to your store from parking lots.

Obtain your street profile from a city traffic engineer. Since your sign communicates to people who pass your business establishment, you can direct your message to potential customers if you know what type of traffic passes your door. Your city traffic engineer can provide information which will tell you: where people begin and end their trips, how people travel, when people travel by time of day, why people travel, and where they park when they reach a destination. Even small cities and towns have traffic volume maps available to tell you how many people pass by your business every day.

Know how many new people move to your area each year. This is a potential market for your business. This type of information can be obtained from any board of realtors, chamber of commerce, or police department.

3. *How are you going to communicate with customers?* In order to communicate effectively, a sign must be noticeable and readable. After a while a sign becomes part of the landscape. It loses some of its ability to attract attention. By periodically changing some small design element or by using changeable copy, a sign can continue to attract interest. Time and temperature devices or rotating and moving parts can be used to maintain interest in a commercial message. Time and temperature displays also provide a much-needed public service.

A sign needs to be large enough to read. How far will someone be from your store when he first sees your sign and what is the real speed of traffic on your street? With this information, a competent sign company can use a formula to calculate the necessary size for your design and build you an effective sign.

4. *What are you trying to say?* Decide on a message that is clear and simple. First, focus on key words. Choose one or two words which describe your business. Clever or strange names may attract only certain customers.

Second, be brief. The cleaner and clearer the message, the more impact is has. Listings of names or unclear symbols confuse rather than communicate.

5. *What image are you trying to portray?* Design of your sign is important. Your sign tells people a lot about your business. Stark, simple design and materials may suggest discount prices and no frills. Elegant and expensive sign materials may suggest luxury goods and services. Two basic design considerations are important when ordering a sign—physical elements and graphic elements.

Physical elements include considerations such as size, placement, materials, and structure. The size of the sign is an important consideration for your business. The biggest sign that you can afford may not necessarily be the best one for your needs. A sign should go with its surroundings. A sign which is either too big or too small will not communicate your message effectively.

The number of signs is also important. Too many signs compete with one another and reduce the effectiveness of your message by presenting an image of confusion to potential customers. The materials used by your sign determine its appearance and performance. For example, differences in cost, appearance, color, durability, flexibility, and reaction to extreme weather conditions can be found in the many types of plastics available. The structure of a sign also contributes to its effectiveness. Pole covers and cantilevered construction (signs displayed at right angles to a vertical surface) help portray an attractive message.

Graphic elements include layout of the message, colors, lettering, shape, symbolism, harmony, and daytime versus nighttime lighting conditions. If your sign is well designed, it will be easy to read. Legibility means that the letters or characters on the sign are distinct from one another. Certain color combinations of background and letters are much more legible than others. To test your sign's legibility, drive past your business and see if you can read it from a distance. Look at it both day and night. Some signs are difficult to read because of illumination problems such as glare from street lights, signs on nearby business establishments, or shadows caused by buildings. A well-designed sign blends with the environment, has a message impact, and overcomes viewing problems.

6. *How much should your sign cost?* You should consider several factors when determining the cost of your on-premise sign.

A sign is an investment. Your sign is one of the most permanent parts of your business and is exposed to weather and constant use. The average life of signs varies from five to eleven years, depending on type of materials used, construction, and other factors. Find out how many years of service to expect from your sign. It pays to purchase good materials if you intend to use the sign over a period of years.

Don't forget maintenance costs. No business can afford to have its sign fall into disrepair. A dilapidated sign tells the public that you are not concerned with your business image or their visual environment. Some types of signs are virtually maintenance-free while others require more attention. Find out how to replace burnt-out bulbs or tubes in your sign. Determine who is responsible if the wind blows your sign down and someone is injured.

Consider all energy consumption costs. New technological developments now enable some types of signs to achieve energy savings without sacrificing effects. Inquire about new energy-saving bulbs and internal materials.

Decide between owning and leasing. Many sign companies have programs whereby you can lease a sign for a given period of time and they will maintain it for you. This may be more economical for a new business, especially if there is any chance that logos or names may change in the first few years of operation. Statistics show that if a small business fails, it will happen somewhere between the first and second years of operation. Leasing a sign during this period of time might help save some of the initial capital needed for operating expenses.

Should your sign be custom or standardized? Some large companies offer standardized types of signs which are cheaper than signs which are custom designed and constructed. Many of these standardized units can use ingenious design techniques to enhance creativity and individuality. Often the standardized units can be arranged in different configurations depending on your needs. Some standardized sign units use the highest quality materials and are designed to be relatively maintenance free. Mass production enables these units to be sold much cheaper than if designed and produced from scratch.

7. *Signs communicate in a shared environment.* A sign's ability to send its message beyond its location requires that you be sensitive to the effects of your message on others. Since you share your space with others, consider their rights and responsibilities, too. They are potential customers.

Consider city or town planning goals and regulations when ordering a sign. Some types of signs are not permitted. Determine what the regulations are in your community before you discuss design with a sign designer. Most sign companies are well aware of the regulations in any given community and can guide you in selecting a sign which is not in violation of the law.

CHAPTER 31

Miscellaneous Sales and Business Promotion

Business promotion is a combination of advertising and public relations. It is distinguished from advertising in that it doesn't necessarily sell products *directly* (though it can); but it is more than PR because, in the long run, it is intended to increase profits *indirectly.*

Besides generating sales, sharp business promotion can foster goodwill, increase brand name recognition, shape an image, change buying habits, or elicit responses for compiling a prospect mailing list.

Some of the best business promotion is *interactive.* It involves the consumer in a participatory way: clipping coupons, sending in postcards, wearing fashionable attire bearing company logos, or phoning for information. Offering discounts or rebates, sponsoring a grand-prize sweepstakes, or giving away free premiums are all tried-and-tested methods for attracting attention and gaining a competitive edge.

Of course, as in advertising, the imaginative entrepreneur knows the best approaches are often the *un*tried and *un*tested.

Seven Rules Of Effective Promotion

Set Goals

Know what you're striving to achieve. Regardless of the method employed, promotion must have an objective. It could be to:

- Introduce new products or increase consumer awareness of ageless standbys that span generations.
- Expand customer base, or romance the sustaining market.
- Move merchandise off the shelves at point-of-sale.
- Test consumer response to a new product, or improvements in an existing one.
- Improve overall company image and visibility.
- Increase recognition factor of company name or logo.
- Foster a cooperative working relationship with retailers.
- Any of the above, with either short- or long-term impact.

You must give careful consideration to what a specific promotion can accomplish, and what it cannot.

Keep It Simple

You have a limited time to make your pitch. A four-step promotion is more complicated than three; three more complicated than two; and two more so than one. Any extra effort on the part of the consumer that can be avoided is *always* preferable. Whether it's a contest, coupon, giveaway, or free consultation, anything that requires extra work or concentration on the part of the prospect will discourage a good percentage of responses. A certain amount of effort is expected, but if the process can be streamlined at all, do it.

This includes graphic design. Lots of "fine print" and excessively busy layouts may be necessary to convey a lot of information, but care should be taken to edit and cut what isn't essential. Key phrases must stand out to intrigue upon first glance.

Promotion campaigns should also attempt only ONE objective at a time. A price-off coupon combined with a sweepstakes, or promotion of two unrelated products in one campaign could contradict or confuse.

Be Consistent

All promotion should complement and enhance your product or service. For a product with a macho image (cigarettes, Canadian beer, Jeeps), a promotion should reflect the rugged adventurousness associated with the merchandise. William A. Robinson, in his "Ten Commandments of Creative Promotion," asks: "What would you think about Kraft offering a recipe book of potent drinks or Marlboro offering pantyhose free in the mail? Especially for image-sensitive brands and categories . . . it's important to get creative about supporting positioning and image."

For years, the Tower Records chain has been publishing a glossy, fashionably written music magazine called *Pulse,* which is given away free at all Tower locations. Each issue contains profiles of new artists and old mainstays, all of whom "coincidentally" happen to have new releases. By keeping on top of industry trends and new faces, *Pulse* enhances Tower's image as a retailer that keeps current with the music market. And though no direct sales pitch is conveyed in the articles, it's easy to see how such "journalism" can stimulate sales.

Coordinate

Promotion should be carefully scheduled to dovetail with other marketing strategies, including product improvements and line extensions, trade allowances, and national ad campaigns. Don't launch a major promotion the same week your sales force is attending a convention in Cincinatti. Parallel scheduling requires inter-departmental communication within your company, so you don't undercut each other's efforts.

An effective promotional campaign should be supportive of the company's sales force, making their job easier. Broadly applied, the advice of advertising whiz Gene Mahany is for "promotion people (to) take the initiative and ask sales management what materials they can provide to make sales calls more effective." He feels the job of promotion is to "provide additional top spin to the brand-sell media advertising." He amplifies this by referring to promotion as "a bridge in the marketing mix."

Know Your Medium

In fact, know the *media.* Point-of-sale display has certain advantages over magazine ad support, and certain limitations. Direct mail, free door-to-door samples, or T-shirts with your company's logo are different approaches with differing effects. Economy, efficiency, and maximizing coverage are important considerations in selection of a medium.

If selecting print, there are thousands of publications to choose from, both general-interest and specialty. How broad is your target audience? What are their demographics? Choosing the appropriate forum is both a creative and a scientific judgment. This is usually not a decision you should make by yourself. Account executives, product managers, researchers and sales directors should all have input in selecting the best medium.

Tailor Your Appeal

You have to reach your audience on a level that excites, intrigues, or flatters. To do this, you have to know what it is about your promotion that appeals to their hopes or needs. Are they looking to save money? Do they like participating in contests that require creative thinking (such as taking photos, completing limericks, or answering personal questions in 25 words or less)? Are they seeking state-of-the-art updates on technology they're already using?

Despite overwhelming odds, lottery tickets continue to sell because a million-dollar windfall is the stuff of dreams. A coupon offering 50 cents off a quart of low-cholesterol salad dressing may not send consumers into a swoon, but a chance at a Caribbean vacation for two probably will. Small stakes may be good for small-ticket items, such as supermarket shelf goods, but bigger fish require bigger bait. A promotional discount on an office copier (or automotive rebate) could go into hundreds of dollars. You have to know what your typical consumer normally spends, and how much of a discount they'll go out of their way for.

Know the Rules Before You Break Them

Effective sales promotion is not a matter of luck. For every example of accidental astronomical payback (such as Reese's Pieces being used in the movie *E.T.* instead of M&Ms), there are thousands of unprofessional shots-in-the-dark that backfire.

This shouldn't discourage a company from experimenting with sales promotion, or trying something off-beat. But since promotion can be an expensive proposition (with a potentially lucrative payoff), approaches should be scrutinized carefully before being put into action.

Though excessive complexity can be detrimental, it can work if the intricacy of a promotion incorporates an element of fun, or if the consumer stands to gain considerably. There may be legal restrictions, and ways around them. Smirnoff Vodka once sponsored a "Break a Silly Rule and Win a Year's Vacation!" contest. Among the rules for entry was included this suggestion: "If contests are null and void in your state, move to another state."

A Few Common Types Of Promotion

These are far from the only ones that work. The important element in any campaign is *imagination,* which means a new twist on traditional methods, or an innovative combination of existing technologies. Computers, in particular, have radically altered promotional methodology, but the overall intent is still to attract attention. As author Kurt Vonnegut, Jr., is fond of saying: "Technology changes, but sociology remains the same."

Giveaways

Someday, an ancient merchant's equivalent of the Dead Sea Scrolls will be unearthed, and etched in parchment, scrawled in a long-forgotten language requiring scholarly translation, it will say: "Everybody Wants Something for Nothing." This is one of the oldest pieces of marketing wisdom in the world.

It's a gimmick used everywhere in the business community, from banks giving away dishware and toasters for new accounts, to Sunday supplement coupons redeemable for *FREE!* (it's always in caps) laundry detergent. The purpose is to get customers in the door and have them spend money on your business, rather than your competitor down the block.

The best way to broaden your market is to give away free samples of your product, usually in small "trial-size" quantities. With household or kitchen items, this may be feasible. But with larger items (e.g., appliances, cars, or backyard sundecks) the more practical approach may be to give away a small premium, which may or may not have anything to do with the product or service you sell.

The graphics revolution of the past twenty years, by making it easy to imprint a brand name on just about anything, has changed the giveway emphasis from practical items to recreation-oriented freebies. Instead of a useful appliance, businesses have found a willing acceptance on the part of consumers to provide a lot of "free" promotion through display of bumper stickers, T-shirts, posters, and athletic caps bearing product logos. Radio station WFMU, which doesn't have a tangible "product" to sell, pioneered some interesting concepts, including custom-designed night lights and snazzy refrigerator magnets sporting the station call letters.

You can popularize your company's name (and, as space permits, address and phone number) by emblazoning it on calendars, coffee mugs, umbrellas, notepads, pens, key chains, clocks, frisbees, beach gear, stuffed animals, tote bags, salt and pepper shakers, jigsaw puzzles. The possibilities are unlimited and, sometimes, outrageous. At the 1989 New Music Seminar in New York, at least three different recording equipment manufacturers at the Exhibitors' Showroom gave away free condoms with suggestive (and, in one case, unrepeatable) slogans on the package. No doubt, each of the three thought they had an original idea.

Though not, strictly speaking, a "giveaway," many manufacturers offer *salable samples,* which are small, trial size packages at irresistible prices, perhaps 29 or 59 cents. Retailers prefer these over in-home sampling because they bring in customers while generating a small profit.

Coupons

Manufacturer's coupons, which appear in newspapers, magazines, circulars, or direct-mail packets, offer discounts on specific products, redeemable at local retailers. They involve an extra step for the merchants who accept them from customers—these coupons must ultimately be redeemed by the merchant back through the manufacturer. But, besides bringing customers through the door, there is usually a small per-coupon handling fee paid to the retailer, which compensates for the inconvenience of playing middleman.

Gene Mahany wrote in *Advertising Age,* in 1977: "I predict the growth of on-label refund offers, since they provide a hard-working package flag at the critical in-store moment of truth." As usual, he was right. The trend has accelerated in recent years, as customers tear coupons off boxes of cat food, frozen waffles, and lightbulbs right at the front register.

Retailer coupons, generated by merchants in-house, and requiring a product to be bought in a specific retail outlet, cut out the middleman. Retail coupons are likelier to build store loyalty, rather than brand loyalty.

Many regional business associations offer coupon booklets to local residents, featuring dozens of tear-off coupons for car washes, restaurants, movie theatres, florists, and family recreation centers. Restaurants and theatres, in particular, benefit from offering two-for-the-price-of-one coupons. To find out how your business can be included in one of these bonanza packs, ask any merchant whose coupon appears in one.

Point-of-Purchase Displays

This approach reaches the consumer where the decision to buy (often on impulse) is triggered: in the aisles of shopping centers. P-O-P (also known as "point-of-sale") can feature life-size cardboard models, ingenious product stacking set-ups, or colorful display bins with risers touting new or on-sale merchandise. The idea is to grab the shopper's attention. Many new foods are introduced in supermarkets by a "chef" with a hot-plate offering free samples of burritos, deep-dish pizza, or imported cheeses.

Any P-O-P will, of course, require the authorization and cooperation of store management, who may be more interested in increasing store traffic than promoting brand loyalty. P-O-P displays may also have to conform to certain aesthetic standards of each retailer. As George Donahue, president of GTD Marketing, points out, "The retailer stands between you and your customer. He can either sell your product or your competitor's. Treat him as an equal partner and he'll push your products."

AMD Industries, of Chicago, distributed a free "P-O-P Analyzer" to marketing executives, consisting of a 20-point questionnaire designed to help with initial display planning. It inquired about such matters as, "What is the anticipated life expectancy of the display?" and "By whom will the display be installed?" A review of the answers suggested the best course for P-O-P promotion. (And, of course, it made AMD a knowledgeable choice to help develop the campaign, which is a good example of the following category.) AMD's "P-O-P Analyzer" is reproduced as Figure 31.1.

Free Advice

Giving helpful advice to consumers is a good way to foster a trusting relationship with business prospects, and at the same time, inform them (implicitly or explicitly) of the services you offer. When such courtesies are extended on a "no-strings-attached" basis, potential customers sense they have something to gain or learn, without spending money. It is a gesture of goodwill. But by providing professional counsel, your position as an expert is solidified; when services are needed, you become the logical place to turn. This corresponds to one of my favorite sales techniques: "Don't sell. *Solve.*" In this way, the emphasis is not on your need to sell, but on the customer's need for a solution.

Good media for disseminating helpful advice are:

—Printed literature: brochures, booklets, article reprints, newsletters, press releases

—Personal visits by appointment

(*list continues on page 586*)

Figure 31.1 P-O-P Analyzer

As a marketing executive, you are interested in developing a point-of-purchase program that will deliver the greatest possible return on your merchandising investment. In achieving this goal, nothing is more important than your initial planning activity. The effort you spend now in preliminary thinking and planning will be repaid many times over in attaining top merchandising performance at the point of sale.

This "P-O-P ANALYZER" has been developed to assist you during the preliminary planning stages of your P-O-P program. It is not meant to be all-inclusive. It *does*, however, outline the basic objectives to be considered before pencil is ever put to paper in the initial design of your merchandising display.

Company Name: ____________________ Telephone: ____________________

Address: ____________________ Contact: ____________________

City, State, Zip: ____________________ Title: ____________________

Project Title: ______________________________

1. **What is the purpose of the proposed display?**

   _____ Introduce a new product _____ Replace a current display

   _____ Introduce a new package _____ Increase sales on an existing product

   _____ Other ______________________________

2. **What type of display are you currently using?**

   _____ Permanent (over one year) _____ Semi-Permanent (6 to 12 months) _____ Promotional (3 to 6 months) _____ None

3. **What type of displays have you used in the past?**

   _____ Permanent (over one year) _____ Semi-Permanent (6 to 12 months) _____ Promotional (3 to 6 months) _____ None

   To what features do you attribute the ☐ success of ☐ failure of these displays?

   ____

   ____

   ____

   ____

4. **Do your competitors use displays?**

   _____ Yes _____ No

   If yes, who are they; what type do they use: ______________________________

   ____

Figure 31.1. (continued)

5. Have you seen features on any other display that you would like incorporated?

_____ Yes _____ No If yes, which ones _____

6. Should your display tie-in with your total advertising program?

_____ Yes _____ No

If yes, should there be similarity in: _____ Copy _____ Color _____ Style

Comments: _____

_____

7. In what type of outlets will you place these displays?

_____ Drug _____ Variety _____ Food _____ Hardware

_____ Discount _____ Service Stn _____ Other _____

8. What merchandise will be displayed?

Product _____

Number of packages _____

Size of packages _____

Weight of packages _____

9. Are there design limitations to be considered on the proposed display?

_____ Yes _____ No

If yes, check and describe:

_____ Height _____

_____ Width _____

_____ In-Store Location _____

_____ Trade Practice _____

_____ Pilferage Protection _____

_____ Other Comments _____

10. Do you have a preference for the material to be used?

_____ Yes _____ No

If yes, (please circle) steel, wire, tubing, wood, plastic, other _____

11. What is the anticipated life expectancy of the:

Display _____

Total Program _____

Figure 31.1. (continued)

12. How many displays will be needed?

_____ Initially _____ Reorders _____ Total Potential

13. By whom will the display be installed?

_____ Company Salesman

_____ Retailer

_____ Other

14. Would simple on-site assembly be acceptable in order to achieve shipping and storage savings?

_____ Yes _____ No

15. How will display be provided to dealer?

_____ Offered with product assortment ordered

_____ Placed at no cost

_____ Other _______________

16. Will merchandise be packed with the display?

_____ Yes _____ No _____ Not Determined

17. What is your estimated budget?

_____ Per Unit _____ For the entire program

18. When will delivery of the finished displays be required? _______________

19. How will the display be shipped to dealer?

_____ Truck-LTL

_____ United Parcel (UPS) (50 lbs. maximum with length and girth not to exceed 108″)

_____ Parcel Post (40 lbs. maximum with length and girth not to exceed 80″)

_____ Other _______________

20. Are there any other special factors to consider? _______________

____

____

____

Review these points, and you will note that you have begun to develop the concept of a display. You have the reasons for its use; the product or products to be merchandised; and how, where, and by whom it will be used. You have considered a tie-in with other media programs, thus making *all* your media advertising more effective. You have considered costs and budgets. You have an idea of the life expectancy of a unit and of the entire program. You have decided on the method, time and place for shipment which answers other questions concerning carton development, delivery dates, warehousing and transportation.

Now that you have considered these questions, let AMD help you analyze, design and produce your display. We want your business and want your company's name listed among AMD's satisfied customers.

—Sponsoring seminars

—Cassette tapes (especially geared for decision makers on the go)

—Telephone services (see below)

—Computer software programs (including fun, business-oriented games)

Consultant Don Hauptman hit upon the "computer-generated" memo. He had prepared a marketing strategy report for a client on his word processor. But, said Hauptman, "as every consultant quickly learns, clients' problems are usually more alike than different." Taking a boilerplate of the report, he used his "search-and-replace function to plug-in client-specific references (like company and product names)," and sent out a "personalized" 10- to 14-page "Marketing Opportunities" memo to clients and prospects. "Electronic technology," he pointed out, "made it a snap to produce."

Telephone Services

Getting people to call (either toll or toll-free) to hear a pre-recorded message is a good way to get across a pitch while providing helpful information. If your phone system is set up to receive messages as well as dispense them, you can compile a prospect database by having callers leave their address and phone number for follow-up information.

Such services are infinitely more considerate than telemarketing, which, dispatched at the seller's convenience, often arrives at the buyer's *inconvenience.* If you've ever had your dinner or privacy interrupted by a solicitation for basement waterproofing (especially if you live in an apartment complex), you already know that telemarketing is one of our nation's fastest-growing public nuisances. Unfortunately, it is often an effective promotional sales vehicle, due to the small percentage of affirmative responses required to make it pay. Such "success" is unlikely to hasten its demise as a promotional sales tool. But for generating consumer goodwill (and, hopefully, sales), it's better to let them call you, rather than you calling them. This also ensures that those who actually call are already somewhat intrigued by your product or service.

One consultant created the Advertising Hotline, a nationwide service providing marketing tips on advertising, direct mail, and publicity. By dialing 201-XXX-XXXX, callers could hear a taped 3 to 5 minute "mini-seminar" on such topics as "10 Ways to Stretch Your Advertising Budget," or "How to Write and Publish a Trade Journal Article." The tape is changed each week, addressing a fresh topic. At the end of the tape, a message, encouraged calls about specific problems and questions. The consultant mailed out press releases and Rolodex cards announcing the Hotline. Response was excellent.

The cost of setting up the Hotline was about $500. The benefits:

—Editors find the service unique and newsworthy. The consultant was called and interviewed for the trade press. This provided immeasurable free publicity.

—Follow-up calls to his office put the consultant directly in touch with prospects, who may be in a position to use his services.

—A brief message at the end of the tape advertises helpful mail-order merchandise: books; transcripts of the seminars; article reprints. This generates additional income, which over time, will pay for the cost of the Hotline.

TIAA-CREF (Teachers Insurance Annuity Association—College Retirement Equities Fund) provides a service to members, who call toll-free for the closing value from the previous business day's stock and money market funds, and interest rates. Though not directly intended to "sell" a product, it provides a helpful, 24-hour service and keeps clients informed and up-to-date.

Scott, the lawn-and-garden people, set up a toll-free number for harassed suburbanites to call and address crabgrass problems to a lawn-care expert. At the end of the call, an offer was made to mail free literature on gardening hints and the Scott product line.

Hold a "Party"

Hosting a "coming out" party for a new product is a good way to generate publicity among trend setters and opinion makers who network in the trade. An author who makes appearances at bookstores autographing copies of a new work can increase sales and stir up publicity from event-hungry newsmedia. Record labels often stage "listening parties," at which invited journalists and industry hipsters sip Chablis, nibble Jarlsburg, and glad-hand each other while a new album blares at deafening volume from boxcar-sized Marshall amps. No sales appeal is necessary; the point is to get insiders talking and writing about the new release.

Housewives have long known the value of Tupperware parties, using the pretext of an afternoon coffee klatsch to demonstrate plastic food storage containers. Princess House Crystal of Massachusetts uses the same approach: field reps (often, but not necessarily, women) invite friends and neighbors over, serve refreshments, and show off samples. Orders are placed, and shipped UPS the following week to the representative, who distributes the merchandise. In this way, contact is made with the client twice—once during the "party," and again upon delivery. The personal service is conducive to follow-up purchases.

Reader Info Cards

Most slick trade magazines offer *reader information services.* You've probably noticed at the bottom of display ads the wording: "Check No. 87 on Reader Service Card," or something to that effect. Near the back of the magazine will be a tear-off, pre-addressed, business reply card. Readers can circle designated numbers, fill out their name and address, mail in the postage-paid card and receive promotional literature from advertisers. This service is offered in specialized trade periodicals, such as *Personal Computing* and *Marketing Communications,* as well as popular general interest magazines, such as *Rolling Stone* and American Airlines' in-flight magazine, *American Way.*

These cards may also feature survey-type questions for compiling demographic profiles of the magazine's readership. Reader information service participation is usually offered to advertisers at an additional charge above the cost of the display ad, but often at a tie-in discount.

Resources

The above is a mere sampling of promotional vehicles. There are countless books on the subject, available from libraries and bookstores. Many trade periodicals, from the large (*Adweek, Business Week,* and, of course, *The Wall Street Journal*), to the less well-known (*Business Ideas Newsletter* and *New Ventures*), publish promotion-related features. Keep in mind, the more widely circulated the publication, the more widely applied the ideas they suggest. Small, independent entrepreneur-oriented publications are often good sources of original ideas not yet tapped-out in the marketplace.

If you are contemplating setting up a promotional telephone service, Hello Direct, Inc., of San Jose, sells a full array of state-of-the-art, business-oriented phone accessories for setting up your own system. Their catalog can be acquired by calling 1-800-HI-HELLO.

If you want to tie in a special event promotion to a particular calendar day (e.g., an Evlis look-alike contest on Elvis Presley's birthday), consult *The Promotional Sourcebook*, published by Caddylak Systems (Brentwood, NY).

CHAPTER 32

Graphic Design

A graphic designer can be likened to an orchestra conductor. The job of a conductor is to take individual elements (in this case, musical instruments), and with a particular direction in mind (symphonic score), coordinate them faithfully and imaginatively. The result is a brilliant work of art.

The graphic designer, too, must take individual elements (text, photographs, illustrations, headlines) and coordinate them in a layout to create a stunning work of art. The object, in this case, is to attract attention and sell the goods.

Products can sell on their own inherent quality. But the marketplace is logjammed with meritorious merchandise, and some not-so-meritorious. Your sales edge comes from advertising and promotion campaigns. And what makes these campaigns effective is great design.

As with text and visual elements, design must complement and enhance your product or service. It must also intrigue, excite or flatter the reader. A direct-mail pitch for Rockliff & Bundy Studios expressed its importance thus:

"Your sales media should work as hard as you do. Effective graphic design doesn't punch out at 5 o'clock. It doesn't take three-day weekends or bank holidays. Sick days? Good heavens! It works all the time, or not at all. . . .

"You work hard. Good design media may not make your work easier. But it should create more of a demand for it."

Graphic designers (also called "graphic artists") may or may not be visual artists themselves, but their job is to work with artists and art. They are the intermediary stage between creation and print production. A B/PAA White Paper defines the role as "problem solving. Developing a solution to a particular problem within a given time frame, budget, materials availability and client objectives. If the graphic designer is to be effective, he must be knowledgeable enough to function in many areas."

Imaginative design is an expert mix of art and science that, capably executed, is the invisible partner in a campaign. Everyone praises the copy, admires the illustration, and raves about the product. But it was the graphic designer who brought all these elements together to create the whole package.

Where To Find Graphic Services

Directories

There are a number of national and regional directories which list vendors in the graphic design field, such as *The Creative Black Book* (New York, NY), *RSVP* (Brooklyn, New York), and *Adweek Portfolio* (New York, NY). In these annual publications, artists (arranged by category) pay a fee and are usually alloted one page to display a sample of their work. Because of the space limitations, displays tend to be highly specialized, rather than indicative of any broad range of design skill. These publications are sold in art stores and distributed to advertising agencies and art directors.

The Graphic Artists' Guild (212-463-7730) and the American Institute of Graphic Artists (212-246-7060) publish member directories. Both organizations have regional chapters around the country.

The Yellow Pages

Check under "Graphic Design," "Graphic Art," "Design," or "Art." You may find either freelancers, design studios, or "creative boutiques."

Freelancers

Many independent designers compile mailing lists of former and prospective clients. Read and keep on file any direct mailers that cross your desk.

Printers

Printers work with graphic designers in the normal course of their business. If a particular printer does not have a graphic artist on staff, they can easily recommend local talent.

Referrals

Ad agencies, photographers, illustrators, magazines, and newspapers can all recommend freelancers with whom they've worked.

Awards Annuals

A number of expensively produced awards annuals are published by graphic arts organizations. These high-visibility volumes exhibit prize-winning designs by the best studios. They are a prestigious showcase and, as one envious designer (who wasn't included) said, "You can't buy your way into those books." These include *Typography,* published by the Type Director's Club (New York, phone 212-983-6042); *Design Annual,* put out by Communications Arts (Palo Alto, California, phone 415-326-6040); and, perhaps the most coveted of all, *The Graphis Design Annual,* published in Switzerland, which features international award-winners. These books are the source for locating cutting-edge talent, and probably the most expensive talent as well.

The Stages Of Graphic Design

Planning

In the initial phase, you (and your art director, if you have one) sit down with the graphic designer and explain your needs, which can be artistic (creative input) or technical (executing production). You may have a specific concept in mind, or just broad parameters. Lacking a total overview, you can confer a certain degree of creative freedom to the designer.

What makes a graphic designer's job easier? Clients who know the business, know what they want, and what to expect. Conversely, a client who is stubborn about ideas but has no concept of the technical aspects was described by one graphic designer as a "living nightmare." If you know what you want, but don't know how to achieve it, rely on the graphic designer's advice, and don't tell them how to do their job.

Bill Graef, an Applied Artist based in New York, also has misgivings about design-by-committee. "Unfortunately, things are getting more that way. Advertising works like that, and publishing is becoming more that way. Everyone wants to get their fingers in the pie so they can say they had something to do with it. As a result, design either gets very bland and watered down, or the look becomes overly ambitious. It's depressing, but it's a consequence of big business."

Background

In the early design stages, the graphic artist may be required to do some research, to see what's been done on the subject, or to find supportive material or appropriate visuals. The designer may look through a *swipe file* (a collection of pictures clipped from magazines or miscellaneous illustrations for conceptualizing). These visuals are used for reference, to give an idea of atmosphere, model positioning, or prop placement.

Execution

The graphic artist uses tracing paper and pencil or marker to draw a *thumbnail* sketch. (A thumbnail isn't as tiny as the name implies; it can be full-size, or smaller, perhaps 25 percent of actual size.) Also referred to as a *layout,* or *rough comp* (short for *comprehensive*), the point is to visualize the direction of the design. Samples from the swipe file may be xeroxed or copied on tracing paper and inserted into the rough comp. The artist may do three to ten thumbnails for the client's inspection. The client may pick one, or suggest a combination of two or three, or send the designer back to the drawing board.

The graphic artist will select type styles and typefaces. Bill Frederick, a graphic designer for Frederick and Froberg Design Offices in Montville, New Jersey, estimates that "an ad manager spends a good 25 percent to 50 percent of his time dealing with the 'word' element—having text approved by the product manager, making sure it's proofread. Then he'll have the designer experiment with typefaces to suit the flavor and finally make the type fit the format. Every time an ad manager sees text, he'll probably want to change something. Or have to." (In the final phases, however, type*faces* are rarely changed, except for size.)

During this stage, the designer will also select colors, borders, and special effects to be achieved during print production. Unless you have expressly relinquished control over these decisions to the designer, you reserve the right to have each element approved before final inclusion. In any case, the final product will be your responsibility, so every element should require your approval.

Next, the graphic artist will produce a *finished sketch,* or *comp.* (Be advised, these terms are used somewhat loosely, depending on who you're talking to. In discussions with a designer, you could be using different jargon while talking about the same thing. A rough can also be called a *pencil sketch,* and a finished comp a *tight comp.*) In the finishing stages, you will know exactly what typeface, colors, visuals, and text will be used, and their relative placement.

When the comp is approved, a *mechanical* can be prepared, which involves affixing all the elements to stiff art board, in position, and *camera ready* (ready to be photographed for printing). This process is discussed in greater detail in Chapter 34.

What To Look For In Good Design

The newsletter *Communication Briefings* suggests the following method for judging the stength of a layout: "Hold (it) at arm's length and squint at it. The weak elements will disappear, and you'll be able to see the powerful ones that attract and direct the eye." This will also give an overall impression of the layout's balance, contrast, unity, and proportion.

Bill Graef believes "the most important aspect of good design is refinement. There is no excess. Every detail in a design either serves a purpose, or it's removed." You should also judge your design by the following characteristics.

Originality

Once described by some anonymous wag as "the art of concealing your source." There are standard cliches in any field, and traditional approaches. The most imaginative, adventurous applications are often the product of the more glamorous (and expensive) design studios. But even within a limited budget, it's possible to find talented vendors who aren't satisfied churning out assembly-line design. Even cliches can be played with and twisted.

One designer referred to "business paranoia, (where) everybody wants to look like everybody else." Just because a design worked for them is no reason to assume it will work for you. It will most likely succeed in making you look like a copycat. If you want your appeal to stand out from the competition, resist the impulse to make it look like everyone else's.

Readability

Having devoted considerable attention to text and headlines, does the typography enhance your message, or obscure it? Do the typefaces complement the overall visual impact of the design? Are type sizes sufficiently large enough to be read easily and understandably? All text elements should be "friendly" to the eyes. Unusual type could attract attention but hinder readability. Large blocks of copy set in italics, upper case, or gimmicky typefaces are a must to avoid.

Judging a design's readability goes beyond mere words; it should also apply to visuals. Are your illustrations "readable?" Is your product recognizable? Do essential details stand out? Were any details lost in the design process? Does the overall atmosphere convey a favorable impression? Every one of these questions deserves an affirmative answer in judging the effectiveness of design. A single untoward element could handicap an otherwise worthy production.

When superimposing type over a tint or visual, the reader may get the picture, but lose your words. High contrast between these elements is essential.

Color

Do the colors flatter your design, or cheapen the impact? Do they create interplay with the text, or distract the reader? How "pure" are the tints? Are they muddy, or so bright they almost blind?

Are they appropriate for the context? If your product is food, some colors stimulate the appetite, while others, such as brownish-green khakis, are downright unappetizing. Certain colors excite, others soothe. They should be selected and arranged to maximize the intended effect.

White Space

Mark Twain once referred to "the eloquence of silence." Because white space represents "nothing," it is often overlooked as an effective attention-getter. But when competing with "busy" adjacent layouts (in a magazine, for instance), a block of white space may be a startling eye-catcher.

A balance is best, neither too much nor too little, evenly distributed throughout the design. But again, there are no firm rules. Uneven layout can be used to good effect if the intention is to throw the reader off-balance.

Consistency

Keeping your design consistent shapes an image. Related elements, used in your campaign over an extended period, lend an air of continuity that the audience comes to identify with your company, product, or service.

You've no doubt seen the long-running ad campaign touting *Forbes* magazine as a "Capitalist Tool," illustrated by noted designer Seymour Chwast. *Forbes* is one of the most respected and widely read publications among businesspeople, a community noted for dignified behavior. Yet the Chwast campaign features coloring-book style cartoons and playful, pun-filled captions. As a result of this offbeat approach, *Forbes* stands distinctively apart from other business publications, appearing bold, unafraid, almost devilish. What years ago must have seemed a daring tactic, has evolved into a familiar image on the American publishing scene.

The series of ads for Pallace, Inc. (Figures 32.1, 32.2, and 32.3) demonstrate how several relatively simple elements, slightly reconfigured and re-worded, can be used effectively in an ongoing campaign. Each successive ad builds upon the previous, reinforcing Pallace's image as a knowledgeable and common-sense advertising agency.

Desktop Publishing

Computers have brought about a "D.I.Y." Revolution, which means "Do It Yourself." Jobs which formerly would have been farmed out to studios, agencies, or independent vendors, can now be completed in-house at a tremendous savings in cost and time.

The applications of design software are far-reaching, and can facilitate every aspect of production, from conceptualization to printing. In Chapters 33 and 34, you will see how computers aid photographers, illustrators, and print production houses. They perform miracles no less for graphic designers. Bill Frederick paints the inevitable scenario: "If you don't have a computer within five years, you won't be able to compete (in the design field)."

The name *desktop publishing* has become generically associated with design software that allows the user to produce any sort of document elec-

Figure 32.1. Pallace, Inc. ad.

High-Tech Marketing Executives

If you want to increase your sales, you must stand above the competition.

Positioning: Determine how your company and its products will be perceived by the marketplace.

Setting yourself apart from and superior to the competition. Building preference for your products and services.

A complex and never-ending job. It involves how you answer the phone, the reliability of your products, the integrity of your people, the quality of your advertising and sales literature, and much more.

At Pallace inc., we can do the research to determine your current position in the market. We can help formulate the strategy to enhance or alter your position.

We can develop the advertising, the literature and the publicity that will help you implement the strategy. And set you above the competition.

To learn more about our services, call Joy McIlwain or Bob Pallace at (301) 622-5100.

Pallace inc.

A High Technology Advertising Agency

11961 Tech Road, Silver Spring, MD 20904
(301) 622-5100

Figure 32.2. Pallace, Inc. ad.

High-Tech Marketing Executives

If you want to increase your sales, you must increase your visibility.

Awareness: The first step toward making a sale.

Create, in the mind of a potential buyer, an awareness of your company and its products.

Each time you increase this level of awareness, you effectively increase the size of **your** market.

And the most effective means of creating awareness are advertising and publicity.

At Pallace inc., we specialize in the advertising and publicity requirements of high-technology firms, particularly those that market electronic hardware, computer software, and technical service. We have a proven track record and twenty years of solid experience.

We can develop common-sense, cost-effective programs that will increase your visibility in your marketplace. And will lead to increased selling opportunities for your salesforce.

For a no obligation analysis of your advertising and PR needs, call Bob Pallace or Joy McIlwain at (301) 622-5100.

Pallace inc.

A High Technology Advertising Agency

11961 Tech Road, Silver Spring, MD 20904
(301) 622-5100

Figure 32.3. Pallace, Inc. ad.

High-Tech Marketing Executives

If you want to increase your sales, you must bring the customers to you.

Response: It has been demonstrated over and over again that advertising actually lowers selling costs.

But this shouldn't surprise anyone. Interview one salesperson who has spent the day cold calling and one salesperson who has spent the day following up qualified leads. Who was more productive?

Making your sales force more productive can begin with a call to Pallace inc.

We can develop direct response programs that will put qualified leads into the hands of your sales force. We have been doing this for over 20 years.

For one client, we generated 17,000 sales leads in one year on a relatively modest budget.

If your sales force needs qualified leads, call Joy McIlwain or Bob Pallace at (301) 622-5100.

Pallace inc.

A High Technology Advertising Agency

11961 Tech Road, Silver Spring, MD 20904
(301) 622-5100

tronically. (The CRT screen, or monitor, is the "desktop.") You can compose and incorporate all elements, including text, visuals, color, typography, positioning, borders, and special effects. Instead of leaning over a drafting table, the artist punches keys and slides around a *mouse* (a little box linked to the computer by a thin cable, that affects the on-screen movement of a pointer; instead of typing keys to move a cursor, you slide the mouse, which moves the pointer to the work area, then click a button which executes the application). The on-screen layout is sometimes referred to as an *electronic pasteboard.*

Like the traditional graphic artist's workshop, design software features a "tool box," consisting of on-screen methods for creating, modifying, and positioning the various elements in a design. Depending on the program, tools are usually represented by symbolic images, such as knife-blades (for cutting), pencils (for sketching), paint brushes (for coloring), or boxes (for squaring or enclosing). In addition, many programs include ready-made *templates* (a standard pattern to form an accurate copy of a shape or sectional arrangement).

Any number of desktop publishing programs are available. The two leading programs for IBM users are Ventura and Aldus PageMaker. IBM systems also use GEM (short for Graphics Environmental Manager) and First Publisher. These programs are updated on a regular basis (usually every six months), as improvements are developed. Each subsequent update is called a *release.*

For Macintosh users, there's Quark and Ready Set Go! In addition, Aldus PageMaker and Ventura are available to run on Macintosh.

A complete desktop publishing system is linked by component programs, commonly consisting of:

- A personal computer (e.g., a Macintosh, IBM or IBM-clone);
- A graphics or "paint" program, such as McDraw or Adobe Illustrator, for creating visuals;
- A word processing program, such as MicroSoft Word or MacWrite for creating text;
- A page-making program, such as Aldus PageMaker or Harvard Publishing's version;
- A laser printer, which reproduces the entire work on paper.

These systems are infinitely flexible. Whatever can be designed by hand can probably be done just as effectively (and more efficiently) on computer. And it takes no less artistic skill to execute fine design. A desktop publishing system is ultimately just a toolkit. What's done with it depends on the person facing the screen.

Some of the materials which can be produced on desktop publishing systems include:

- Newsletters;
- Press releases;
- Business cards;
- Proposals;
- Announcements;
- Menus and price lists;
- Reports;
- User manuals;
- Small directories and catalogs;
- Mailers, including postcards; and
- Sales literature.

As you can see, practically any printed material that serves your business needs can be produced on computers. The few (generally larger) jobs they cannot do at present, they will probably be capable of doing with subsequent generations of technology.

These systems, however, are not foolproof. In terms of artistic application, they are capable of anything—including human error. A computerized design system will not turn a careless, unimaginative designer into a genius. Hugh P. Curley, of Direct Marketing Consultants, Inc., refers to the final product as "WYSIWYG," which stands for "What You See Is What You Get." In a mini-report on the state-of-the-art, he notes: "We've seen many examples of newsletters produced by companies using desktop publishing where it was patently obvious that the fine touch of a good graphics artist was sorely lacking . . . (M)any of these in-house productions all have that same 'boxy' appearance that doesn't lend itself to leading readers quickly and easily through the copy. Even the best newsletter we've seen produced via desktop . . . was set up by an outside design team working closely with its editors."

Computer systems are extensions of the human mind, and as such, are only as good as the people who use them. But a top-notch designer accustomed to using traditional means can adapt his or her talents to the electronic pasteboard and create designs that will astonish, delight, turn heads and sell.

CHAPTER 33

Photography and Illustration

If the purpose of an ad is to introduce a product to a prospective consumer, think of a visual as a "handshake." Blocks of copy, on casual glance, look pretty much alike; photographs and illustrations catch immediate attention, welcoming the reader into an ad. Without an attention-getting visual, your target reader may never make it to the first sentence.

Unbroken blocks of text also intimidate readers. Graphic art (and white space) allow a page to breathe, and ultimately they give an ad (and your company) style.

Consequently, much thought should be given to a number of concerns:

—Which is more appropriate: photo or illustration? Color or black and white?

—How do you judge the impact of a visual?

—Should you create a new visual image, or use existing stock?

—Can you do it yourself, or should you hire a pro?

—How and where do you find the *right* technician for the job? What's a fair price?

—What's the step-by-step process in getting your concept accurately materialized in the final image?

—What's your design budget? Often this last factor determines the other variables in the equation. Without exception, color will cost more than black and white.

Photos Or Illustrations

Having decided that visual art is a key part of your campaign, the next decision is: photograph or illustration? Cost is always a factor, but there is no rule-of-thumb. An illustration can be rendered at a drafting table less expensively than airlifting a photographer to the polar icecaps. On the other hand, a LeRoy Niemann color painting of a racehorse will probably cost more than a color photograph of same. Budgeting aside, the following factors will determine your choice:

The Advantages of Photographs

Some of the advantages of photos are:

—They are real, hence, more believable. Terry C. Smith, communications manager at Westinghouse attests: "Nothing beats an actual photograph for adding authenticity."

—Certain products demand it, especially if stylishness is part of their appeal (e.g., cars, sportswear, fine china, jewelry), or if the package is particularly eye-catching.

—If the product is new and unfamiliar to consumers, a photo proves that it exists.

—"Before-and-after" comparisons are possible.

—Photos depict tangible benefits of a product, such as compactness (laptop PC shown carried by consumer), or design innovations.

—Product use can be demonstrated, especially through a step-by-step photo sequence.

The Advantages of Illustrations

Some advantages to using illustrations are:

—Generally speaking (with many exceptions, however) art costs less than photography.

—It's easier to make changes to an illustration. It's usually too impractical (and expensive) to reschedule and re-create an elaborate photo shoot.

—With repeated use, artwork, especially a logo, becomes emblematic of your company's product. You can save money, and reinforce an image, by recycling illustrations.

—For instructive, or data-supportive purposes, you can use flow charts, diagrams, maps, and scales. Nowadays, these can be done inventively and precisely with computer graphics.

—Simple illustrations are good for symbolic shorthand. Think of highway signs, which convey important information (steep grade, deer crossing, two-way traffic) via simple drawings that are universally recognizable.

—If your product is unattractive, a drawing can give an "impressionistic" artist's rendering, softening harsh features.

—If the product doesn't exist yet, a building under construction, design samples, or next-year's model can be depicted to create anticipation with the reader.

—Cross-sections or exploded views detail the inner workings of appliances, or complex technology.

—Because photographs must reflect reality (even if surrealistically staged), the medium has inherent limitations. The wilder the effect, the higher the cost. The more your desired visual is inclined towards the land-of-make-believe, the likelier it can be created by an artist, whose only limitation is, after all, the imagination. Cartoons and caricatures, in particular, give ads a fun, mischievous appearance.

Photography

An effective photograph has to accomplish many things:

- It must be eye-catching; it should hook a viewer with something familiar, or something strikingly different.
- It should stand out distinctively from its surroundings, including other photographs.
- It should avoid cliches.
- By conveying tone and mood, it must reflect on the product (and your company) in a complimentary fashion. An ad does more than direct sell; it provides public relations.

- A photo should look professional, rather than like a high-school internship project. It should be crisp, with true colors and appropriate special effects.

Perhaps the "ideal" negative role-model for the above is the proverbial bikini-clad vixen posed alongside, say, a high-pressure containment vessel. Scantily clad females are eye-catching, especially advertising a sauna, wine coolers, or Carribean resorts; badly used, they can distract from the product, add gratuitous salaciousness to ads that don't require it, and convey a mood ranging from frivolous to absurd. So used, they require and demonstrate no imagination on the part of ad designers. Another reason bikini-bait can backfire is that a growing number of business prospects are female, and they resent this sexist approach to advertising.

Know the Field

Having decided to go with a photograph, the first step is to study the competition. What do others in your field use in their ads? Are they effective or ineffective by the above standards? Scrutinizing other ads can give you ideas on what to do, what not to do, and how to avoid the obvious and overdone. Positioning yourself distinctively vis-á-vis the competition demands that you be familiar with their approaches.

Get the Picture

There are three ways to acquire photographs:

1. hire a photographer;
2. take them yourself; or
3. buy existing prints.

1. Hiring Pro's

This is the most expensive way, but the best assurance of quality. Photographer fees vary widely, from a hundred dollars per day, to several thousand. As with most independently contracted creative services, there are many patterns, but few standards.

Price will depend on the level of sophistication you desire, as well as the particular level of workmanship and fee schedule of the professional you hire. Rates may be negotiable. Day rates are often determined by the target medium, such as the number of different magazines in which an ad will run, or the circulation of a specific periodical in which the ad will appear.

Know what you're getting for your money: does the fee include expenses (film, props, processing, special effects), or will these be extra? Is travel included? Avoid the shock of last-minute surcharges by asking up front.

Where to locate a photographer: Yellow pages; studios; camera shops may recommend local pro's. Newspapers either have staff photographers who moonlight, or editors can recommend reliable freelancers. Regional magazines are also good sources of freelance talent; check photo credits of shots you find appealing and call the editor. The fine arts department of nearby colleges or universities can recommend faculty or qualified students (the latter a good source of inexpensive, promising talent).

During an interview, examine their portfolio for craftsmanship. Technical skills are important, as is personal style. Since you'll be paying for both, you should have a good idea what to expect. If your ad photo will be in color, make sure they present color samples. Pay attention to details such as purity of colors, range of tones, whether the prints are clean and the composition attractive. Note special effects (and overuse of such). If your requirements call for shooting in an industrial setting, is the person behind the lens suited to the task? All photographers have specialties, from glamour and fashion to meticulously sculpted stills of inanimate objects. Others focus best on nature panoramas, or machinery. Some can handle any challenge. Your product, standing alone under the harsh glare of studio lights, may lack dynamic. But, as New York lensman and *LIFE* magazine contributor Jan Staller explains, "A professional can make a boring subject interesting with good photography."

Ask for references, and don't be afraid to call them. One question you might ask is: does this photographer follow instructions and deliver as promised? Is he or she cooperative and easy to work with?

You can describe your ideas to photographers and have them shoot to your specs; or you can allow them a free hand to work their creative magic within certain guidelines. Often, the result is a combination of the two. But you should know what you want, and be able to explain it so the assignment is understood.

Generally, a layout is provided, sketching your (or an art director's) conception of the ad, including size, placement of copy and visuals, color (if any), and graphic parameters. It may help for the artist to talk with the graphic designer about type specs and the particular reproduction process being used. The more a photographer knows about the final application, the chances improve that the final prints will be what you asked for, and that no loss of quality will occur in reproduction.

A written agreement or purchase order should be drawn up, specifying fees, obligations, deadlines and definitions of "satisfactory" completion of assignment. This will hopefully avoid misunderstandings, hidden charges, or your having to pay for substandard work (not to mention inconvenient court appearances).

2. Taking Your Own

This can be an exciting adventure, a risky proposition, or both simultaneously. By clicking the shutter yourself, you have greater control over the final product. And, consequently, no one to blame but yourself if you don't achieve it.

If you're fairly proficient with a camera and darkroom techniques (or work closely with someone in a developing lab), you can save a lot of preliminary headhunting and interviewing by getting behind the lens yourself.

But if your forte is vacation snapshots with an Instamatic, creating your own ad photo could be iffy. Although modern cameras boast ever-simpler operation while eliminating a lot of guesswork, achieving an ad-ready shot isn't as easy as it sounds. Such variables as color, lighting, depth of field, and tonal range require a trained eye. You could waste a lot of time (and money) trying to do it yourself, only to end up having to hire a professional to get it done right.

Legal note: Shots of people add life to an ad. However, courts have ruled a person's privacy can be violated if their recognizable image—not just their face—appears in an ad without permission. When shooting candids (e.g., at the beach, office, or supermarket) or using old pictures, if you intend to use anyone other than a hired model in your ad, get them to sign a release. And get their signature *before* you shoot, to avoid having to retake the shots if they refuse permission.

3. Buying Stock Shots

Stock photo houses keep files of photographs by category, which they supply for a price. This method is obviously impractical if you intend to depict your own product. But for illustrative effect—such as a sunset, a traffic jam, or a clock striking midnight—stock photos might be the easiest and least expensive route.

You can also acquire photos free or at reasonable cost from libraries, newspapers, PR agents, museums, and government agencies.

Software companies (such as Comstock) publish photos in computer format, including vacation, business, household, and technology images.

When using any of the above sources, be aware of possible copyright infringement. Inquire if a particular photo is licensed for commercial use.

Plan your Shots

Draw up a *shoot list.* This is an agenda of photos that must be taken, and it should be organized in such a way as to maximize convenience. This will save time, and since many photographers charge by the day, it also saves money.

The shoot list should specify location (including travel), sets, models, costumes, props and special effects. Make sure each element is ready (or will be delivered) in time for the shoot, hopefully beforehand to avoid last-minute anxiety when something (or someone) is missing. Shooting at the photographer's own fully equipped studio will always save travel expenses, and probably time, because of the home-turf advantage.

If traveling, arrange to complete all shots on one location before moving on to the next. Schedule locations in a geographically logical sequence to minimize travel and backtracking.

Think ahead: if you envision a long campaign for the same product, have extra shots taken to stockpile for future use. If you're planning a slide presentation of your product line, have the shots taken with slide film, from which prints can easily be made for ads. As long as you've contracted the cameraman's services and all the elements are in place, everything may as well be done at once. Get the maximum number of shots possible out of your agreement with the photographer. The greater the volume of material generated (provided quality is not spared), the wider your selection and the greater its possible application.

Preparing the Set

If you watch a professional arrange a set for a shoot, you will notice great attention paid to minute, cosmetic detail. Since many details aren't detectable until viewing a finished print, the advantage of hiring a seasoned pro instead of doing it yourself is obvious.

Cameras do not see what the human eye sees. They magnify certain characteristics, and completely miss others. But in the final analysis, your ad photo shouldn't imply: "You had to be there." It either captures the essence, or it doesn't. If the shoot is prepped by a knowledgeable professional, the wrinkles, shadows and stray lint will be instinctively taken care of.

If, however, you're doing it yourself, the following is a (necessarily partial) checklist of details to note. And even with a competent professional behind the lens, remember that you are the client, and the finished product should reflect your needs, not the photographer's. When you (or your art director) are supervising a session, if something seems amiss or not quite what you wanted, point it out before the shutter clicks.

Framing

This is the actual composition of the photo as seen through the camera's viewfinder. Composition can, of course, be corrected in the darkroom via "cropping" (editing) and retouching. But while you can take away during processing, it's more difficult to add something left out of the original shot. You must guide the photographer, especially regarding use of props, arrangement of models, color, and lighting. By working closely with the technicians, you can orchestrate an entire tableau to tell a story.

Background

Your background should be harmonious with the objects being photographed. Backgrounds can also clash for dramatic or humorous effect, but they should not distract to the point of upstaging the photo's focal point. Excessive clutter makes a photograph "busy," reducing its impact.

"Shmutz" (pronounced "shmoots," Yiddish word for dirt)

Shmutz (everything from stray threads, dust and fingerprints on windows, to bits of tape and exposed clips, perhaps even the odd insect wandering across the set) should be removed.

Unwanted Lettering

Avoid anything that can be "read" on props. Wall signs, brand names (other than your own), book titles, and newspaper headlines are examples, unless these are conspicuous for deliberate effect.

Sweat

Unless you're advertising athletic shoes or air conditioners, watch for it. Sweat can create glare from a flash, or just look plain grungy. Adjust the temperature in the studio, mop the model's brow, or apply pancake powder to avoiding unnecessary shine.

Shooting Time

Shooting models early in the day guarantees a fresher look, and avoids "clothing fatigue" (wrinkles and wilted collars).

Colors

Sharp, solid colors, often contrasting with the product or model, have an immediate impact, and grab attention. Even shooting black and white, sharp visual juxtapositions prevent muddiness and highlight important features.

Dates

Unless intended for one-time immediate or seasonal use, don't "date" your shots. Wall calendars, holiday trappings, and soon-to-be-out-of-fashion attire can make photos obsolete by the time they reach print.

Keep in mind at all times that even though there are tried-and-true formulas for successful photos, the most imaginative often break the rules and create the most visual excitement. If you can afford to experiment, don't be afraid to try something different.

Processing

Developing and printing are as important as shooting in the photographic arts. Such techniques as burning in (darkening), dodging (lightening), toning, airbrushing, and screening are available to the darkroom technician. Different grades of paper, lens filters, enlargements or reductions can all improve the impact of photos. Special effects, such as multiple exposures or silhouetting, can create stunning dreamscapes. Conversely, if done carelessly or artlessly, they can ruin an otherwise effective shot.

Discuss your ideas with the photographer, and hear any suggestions. He or she knows from experience what's possible. When skillfully applied by adept veterans, corrective touch-up is undetectable and can improve a print's impact by as much as 50 percent.

For photo selection, the photographer will supply *contact sheets.* These are pages of actual-size (meaning, small—20 to 35 per page) positives of all negatives from a session. They should be examined with a magnifying glass.

As a photo is enlarged, the sharpness of the image is reduced, with increasing graininess. However, if its final destination is a highway billboard, the graininess won't matter, since from a distance, the eye automatically reduces the larger-than-life image to a smaller, less-detailed size. Reductions of 8″ × 10″ prints lose incidental detail and subtle textures. These inevitable consequences should be taken into account during the shooting stage.

Except in rare instances, you will not be accompanying the photographer into the darkroom, so your processing instructions should be carefully explained.

Storage

Negatives, contact sheets, and prints should be stored in protective folders, away from light and high temperatures. When handling negatives, do not touch either surface with your fingers. If jotting down notes on the back of photos, do not use a sharp ball-point pen (which will make an impression) or certain indelible markers (which may bleed through). You should avoid scratching negatives and prints, so don't attach paper clips or store with stapled literature.

Illustrations

With illustrations, more so than with photos, the sky's the limit. A photograph, even one employing spectacular darkroom wizardry, ultimately must capture the "real." An illustration can more easily explore the "unreal." You can't photograph a unicorn, but you can draw one. The following are 10 categories of illustrations.

Drawings

A free-hand sketch, using any writing utensil: pen and ink, pencil, crayon, felt-tip marker, or chalk. Any of these media can be used to different effect. For a new line of kid's jumpsuits, a playfully rendered crayon scribble could catch the attention of parent-readers. Drawing tools, skillfully applied, can convey elegance, economy, or stylishness. Cartoons, once considered juvenile, are excellent visual accompaniment for youth-oriented products, or for creating a mischievous, "pants-down" image. Caricatures can also add flair in the right context.

Painting

Easy enough to visualize, ranging from a few abstract splashes of acrylic to Hieronymous Bosch's nightmarish "Garden of Earthly Delights." Hiring painters can be an expensive but classy way to make your ad stand out.

From watercolors and pastels to airbrushed designs, paintings are distinctive and add a touch of sophistication. The only thing they lack is realism; hence, paintings are better suited to creating moods, rather than depicting products. Many corporations have made effective use of timeless masterpieces from da Vinci to van Gogh; discretion should be used, however, to avoid pretentiousness.

Map

Maps express location with greater visual impact than words. The phrase "30 outlets nationwide" says less than 30 red pinpoints on a map of the United States. Depending on the scope of your sales network, maps can depict towns, states, countries, continents, worlds, or galaxies. They can be rendered by hand or by computer graphics.

Diagram

Diagrams can visually express how your product, system, or process works. They can consist of a few basic lines and arrows, or a complex *schematic* diagram which may be understood only by technical specialists. *Block* diagrams show a series of boxes representing related elements in a network or system, with each box separately labeled and connected by arrows. Each box could represent steps on an assembly line, or a mainframe linked to user-terminals, or the manufacture-to-marketing process of garden supplies. *Flow charts* are also used to depict sequential steps.

Cross-Section or Cutaway

Details the internal assembly of appliances and machinery, or in-wall or underground installations. Some devices, such as security systems, motors, or hi-tech audio circuitry, are best illustrated "in use." But they can be difficult to photograph or express in a surface drawing. Cutaways provide a glimpse of what goes on inside. Similar to the cutaway is the *exploded view,* which depicts a product's component elements pulled apart (exploded) to show how it's put together. Assembly instructions for the home craftsman best typify this type of drawing.

Graph

A graph depicts a trend or patterns plotted against a web of horizontal (x) and vertical (y) axes. A wavy line, parabola or series of zig-zags illustrate the linear progress or cumulative rating of the x variable charted against the *y*. Such data as fuel efficiency, cost-effectiveness, and sales trends can be easily conveyed via graphs. A number of computer software programs are available to plot graphs. *Bar charts* convey similar information, but use a series of solid bars (often color-contrasted) to show comparisons in quantities or time frames, with longer bars representing higher values.

Pie Chart

A circle, cut in slices to represent proportions and percentages. With the entire circle representing 100 percent, pie charts can reflect population breakdowns, budgetary allocations, or market shares. Often, each pie slice is shaded in a different color. These, too, can be easily—and accurately—created on computer.

Table

Often rows of numbers, or characteristics, arranged in columns for logical organization and comparison. Otherwise dull tables can be dressed up by imaginative use of color, or the inclusion of *icons,* which are tiny, symbolic drawings (usually silhouettes) to represent units (e.g., cars, chickens, homes).

Symbol

Symbols are a good way to express broad concepts by simple, familiar visuals. Some can be devised especially for your ad, others are universally recognized. A skull-and-crossbones on a label says one thing: Poison! And anyone who sees an image of Smokey the Bear knows not to play with matches. If you've ever seen the old "Alfred Hitchcock Hour," you remember the opening credits superimposed over a few very basic contours, instantly recognizable as the Master's profile. Granted, your product may not be as familiar to the public, so symbols should be intelligently designed to evoke the broadest recognition from readers.

Clip Art

As the name implies, these are small, often thumbnail-size images which can be clipped and pasted onto a layout. Art stores carry inexpensive clip-art catalogs, which feature thousands of illustrations in color and black and white. Many are cute and campy, some outrageously looney, others generic or broadly symbolic. Sometimes you can find just the right clip for your purposes. But bear in mind that because others have equal access to the catalogue, your "artwork" may turn up in someone else's ad.

Computer Graphics

The computer graphic state-of-the-art is such that almost any form of visual can be created on a computer. An entire generation of illustrators has grown up concurrent with the computer graphics revolution, and they are no less artists simply because they accomplish with a scanner and mouse what previous generations did with a sketchpad and T-square. There's a burgeoning industry of desktop publishers and computerized design studios serving every corner of the business and advertising community.

These highly skilled specialists can save time and money by executing in 15 minutes what previously took a whole day. Another time-saving advantage is pointed out by Norman Cahn, who trains artists on computer-aided design systems. "Neither clients nor artists ever have to settle for anything they are not completely satisfied with because changes take only minutes," says Cahn. "There is less temptation to 'go with what we've got,' and more incentive to 'go for the best we can do.'"

Graphs, pie charts, and perspective grids can be created with microscopic accuracy. As technology advances, possibilities astonish. Kevin O'Rourke, vice-president of Whitman Studios (Clifton, NJ), explains: "An illustration job will come in that the client is not necessarily requesting to be done on computer. But we look at it and realize it's a natural for this high-tech approach."

Computers will not put traditional artists out of business. A canvas, a sketchpad, and a CRT all serve the same purpose: They are media on which an artist visualizes an idea. Smart illustrators, accustomed to grease-pencils and Exacto-knives, are learning new tools to materialize their creative concepts.

In addition, computer clip-art libraries are available on disk from a number of software publishers. *CD ROMs*, which look and are packaged like musical Compact Discs, feature high-resolution illustrations in a variety of styles, from a palm tree to a chimpanzee, from cat's paws to Santa Claus. One CD ROM can hold as much as 500MB of storage space (almost 700 times that of a disk). The advantages are obvious. Larry Orchier, of Lawrence Computer Systems (New York), attests: "A clip-art library that would have taken up a foot's worth of disks, I now have on one CD ROM, indexed and easily accessed. There's no deterioration or loss of image. It's always there."

Some clip-art sources may limit commercial use without permission, others are licensed for unlimited use.

What to Look For in an Illustration

Judging an illustration, you should use many of the same criteria as for photography: clean design; the periphery shouldn't distract from the focal point; all elements should complement each other and the ad as a whole (unless shock or humor is intended).

Illustrations create moods, and they should reinforce the image you wish to project for your company and products. Every aspect of an illustration has an effect on the viewer, often subconsciously. Hanks and Belliston, in their book *Rapid Viz* (William Kaufmann Inc., 1980), which teaches techniques for making rapid sketches of ideas, point out:

> "People naturally tend to see visual things in common patterns. They have a tendency to read from left to right, . . . (and) things are usually viewed from top to bottom. If a circular pattern is used, people feel more comfortable seeing it in a clockwise direction . . . Horizontal lines suggest a quiet, stable movement . . . The vertical line becomes very active, suggesting movement from top to bottom. A diagonal line is dynamic. It feels like it's falling down, and suggests danger and temporariness."

Colors can create tension, or alleviate it. Reds are exciting, dark colors foreboding; icy blues are cool, and rainbow patterns look festive. Give careful consideration to every nuance of an illustration before it is used in your campaign. If subject to misinterpretation, it could cause reader confusion. If offensive, it could lead to consumer backlash. Once it's out there in the world, you can't recall it. All you can do is expend a lot of effort at damage control. Study an illustration's impact from every conceivable angle, and get second opinions.

Finding and Working with Illustrators

Qualities

The person you want is an *illustrator,* as opposed to a *graphic artist.* The latter designs and prepares printed literature for publication (supervising typography, color, layout and paper selection). There is some overlap between fields, but many graphic artists don't illustrate, and many illustrators know nothing about graphic design. All illustrators have specialties, and you must hire the person with the right qualifications. If you want line art, don't hire a portrait artist. If a caricature is required, look for these skills in an artist's portfolio. If you need graphs and charts, make sure the artist has experience with these formats.

Note quality and style of previous work, and suitability to the assignment. You should be comfortable with an artist's approach, because it will reflect on your company. What you see is what you're going to get. Personality should also be a factor. Some artists refuse to relinquish creative control, failing to accept the realities of the business/advertising world. Such unprofessional attitudes will ultimately drive them from the field or force them to adjust. Make sure the artist you're considering is accustomed to servicing the needs of clients. This will usually be obvious from a brief conversation and a glance at their portfolio, so it isn't necessary to ask.

Where to Locate Illustrators

Many illustrators work freelance. The thing to keep in mind is that artists are looking for clients, and that requires visibility. They are trying to attract your attention; you have to know where to look.

Publications: Artwork that impresses you in periodicals—either illustrating articles or ads. Contact the editor, advertiser, agency, or (if signed) the artist directly. Publications that serve the interests of creative professionals may contain display or classified ads for studios or freelancers.

Referrals: Ad agencies, creative consultants, book publishers, and art studios can all recommend available talent. Unions and creative service organizations serve as resource clearinghouses, linking talent with prospective clients. Neighborhood print shops, if they don't have illustrators on staff, may farm out work to reliable independents. Ask your colleagues. Explain your needs, and follow leads. Art schools can also recommend faculty or gifted students.

Directories: National, state, and regional directories are available in a variety of fields. The Yellow Pages are a good place to start. Creative service organizations usually publish member directories, which can be purchased or acquired free. Additionally, books such as *The Creative Black Book* (phone 212-254-1330) or the *Adweek/Art Directors' Index* (phone 212-529-5500) will be helpful.

Working With Illustrators

Know what you want. In discussing concepts, be as specific as possible: color or black and white; painting, line art, or cartoon? How many drawings do you require? If you saw samples in the artist's portfolio that approximate your needs, say so. Point out similar ads that have features you like or don't like.

Without clear instructions, an artist can neither give a reliable cost estimate, nor guarantee meeting your needs. They may be good at visualizing what's in their mind, but they can't read yours. Either your art director or the hired illustrator should produce a "thumbnail" sketch (so named for its small scale) to indicate positioning of all the ad's elements.

Indicate the final size of the illustration, as well as the target medium (e.g., magazine, billboard, retail display), accompanying text, and type specs. It may be necessary for the artist to consult with the graphic designer about the particular reproduction process, to ensure the finished work can be compatibly reproduced with as little distortion as possible.

The illustrator should be provided with as much background material as available: product samples, photographs, blueprints, instruction manuals, and examples of the effect you want achieved.

An agreement or purchase order should be drawn up, stating nature of the work-for-hire, fees, deadlines, revisions, payment provisions, and a definition of "satisfactory" completion of assignment.

Stages of Development.

Work should proceed in stages, with incremental review of progress. The initial thumbnail (or larger) sketch will determine the direction. Once this is agreed upon, work proceeds. Stage two is your review of the half-completed illustration; stage three, the artist submits the work for final approval. By reviewing in stages, if changes are required, they can be done before the job is finished.

Bear in mind that artwork prepared for publication rarely looks *exactly* as it will after printing. Reduction, enlargement, screening, and paper stock will all affect the final image. Hopefully, care taken during pre-production will avoid unforeseen complications.

Upon completion, you are the judge of whether the work is "satisfactory." Reviewing artwork pasted to a piece of board is a less than flattering context, so you'll have to imagine the art as it will appear in the ad. Is it what the artist was hired for? Is it what you paid for? Even if the answer to either of these questions is "no," a more important consideration should be: "Will it do the job?" Does it convey the essence of your product or service? Is it helpful, instructive, eye-appealing? If you came across this image in a publication, would it grab your attention?

If not, it's either back to the drawing board for modifications, or start over again, with the attendant unpleasantness of a dissatisfied client and (probably) a dejected or defensive artist. At that point, there's the matter of your agreement/purchase order, final settlement of which may or may not be in dispute.

CHAPTER 34

Print Production

Having created text and illustrations for your campaign, the next step is turning these raw materials into a finished, printed product.

As in photography, where darkroom technique is 50 percent of the artistic process, so it is with print production. These are the last crucial steps before your ad, brochure, or flier is submitted for final approval *to your prospective customer.* The impression your presentation makes depends on the care and professional expertise of whoever attends to print production. Your photograph may be as dynamic as Avedon's; the text could be clever, or rich in metaphor and subtlety; the illustration outright gallery-worthy. Yet sloppy, careless, or substandard print production could defuse an otherwise explosive sales pitch.

There are three possible elements of any printed product: text, photography, and illustration.

The first stage after creating the elements is putting together a *layout* (or *mock-up*), which in its early form is known as a *rough layout,* or simply a *rough.* The final layout is called either a *finished* or a *comprehensive* layout (*comp,* for short). It indicates positioning of text and visuals, and should leave no doubt as to the appearance of the final product.

A *mechanical,* also known as a *paste-up,* is the actual assembly of all art and text elements. A mechanical consists of copy and visuals pasted on stiff art board, ready for reproduction. The actual process of reproduction involves a special camera photographing the mechanical. Printing plates are made from the resulting negatives. Finally, the plates are duplicated on the press, and your job is run, hopefully resulting in the final product you envisioned.

With computers playing an increasingly pivotal role in graphic design, layout and mechanical stages can be tremendously streamlined. Razor blades and rubber cement, once the tools of layout specialists, collect cobwebs in many studios, as design-oriented software captures a larger share of the graphics market. And just because computers are used is no reason to assume your printed material will look "sterile" or "untouched by human hands." It will, however, turn out closer to your specifications: alignments are scientifically-precise, and there will be virtually no loss-of-quality between *generations* (each time material is duplicated).

Regardless of the process used, care should be exercised in selecting production services, and progress should be monitored at each stage to ensure a quality final product.

Text

Blocks of text are also known as *copy.* They are the "word" component of your presentation. The printed letters themselves are called *type,* and they must be processed via *typography,* which is the art of arranging type for printing. Type must also be set (transcribed into reproducible form) by a *typesetter.* This is usually done by manual entry from a keyboard.

Typewriters and word processing printers are, in a sense, basic typesetting machines. Many executives still use typewritten documents for presentation purposes. But according to a Boston University study, noted in *Communications Briefings,* "300 professionals . . . considered typeset documents to be more credible, persuasive and professional than those turned out on a typewriter or dot-matrix printer." It will invariably be worth the extra time and money to have your text typeset.

Any words you read in published material contain the following characteristics, which must be considered during (or preferably *before*) the typographic stage:

Size

The height and width of the lettering, usually measured in *points* (72 per inch) or *picas* (12 points or $^{1}/_{6}''$), For comparison, most newspaper columns are set in 8- or 9-point type; headlines are generally 18- to 54-point. Extremely small type is difficult to read, causing eyestrain. Any type smaller than 8-point is likely to be ignored by readers (hence the phrase "fine print," referring to legal details of secondary concern set in tiny type). Type size may depend on the *copyfitting* requirements—that is, the amount of space alloted for text in the final design.

Font

This is the style of type. Fonts run in families, with upper- and lower-case variants, which evolved from ancient styles of calligraphy (hand-lettering), such as *roman* and *gothic.* There are hundreds of styles to choose from, each conveying a different effect. Some look modern; others have an 18th-century charm. Through careful selection of fonts, it is possible to convey such qualities as urgency, politeness, or even aristocracy. The tone of your text will, on a subconscious level, be affected by your choice of font. Printers provide catalogs displaying font samples.

Typeface

Particular variations within a font, including *boldface* (thicker lettering), *italics* (slanted type), or such special effects as *shadowing* (ghost letters behind the type) or *outlining* (the basic configuration of the letter with no internal fill).

Kerning

The space between letters. Most fonts are computer based so the kearning is controlled by the computer.

Leading

Pronounced "ledding," the space between lines of type. Space between paragraphs can be different from line spacing, depending on desired readability.

Justification

Type which is justified has a square look with both column edges being perfectly straight. Unjustified type has a ragged edge, either on the right (*left justified*) or on the left (*right justified*). Lines which are justified have corrective spacing between words, either uneven or even (*microjustification*), depending on the typesetting system. This makes the column edges optically straight.

Column Width

Measured in inches, picas, or characters. Avoid making columns too wide, since a reader's eyes may lose their place shifting from one line to the next.

All the above choices comprise the *type specifications* (*specs,* for short). Specs are provided to the typesetter, to set text per your instructions.

Copy Preparation

Copy should be sent to the typesetter on standard 8-½″ × 11″ bond. It should be typed neatly, double-spaced, on one side only. Any corrections should be absolutely clear. Typesetters are not paid to decipher sloppily altered copy, and if they can't make sense of your corrections, time and money will be wasted (probably yours). Before you send copy to the typesetter, have it proofread. Any corrections should be made in ink, not pencil, and indicated directly on the copy, rather than on little scraps of paper stapled or taped to the margins, which can be lost or misunderstood. Any mistakes in spelling or punctuation will not be corrected by the typesetter; they will be set as submitted.

Make certain that the pages are numbered consecutively, and that each page is identified at the top by any helpful title: company name, assignment, or project heading, to avoid possible mixup if the pages get separated.

After the copy has been typeset, you will receive *galleys,* which are long sheets of copy to be cut and pasted onto the mechanical (either by the printer or a graphic artist). Galleys must be proofread, preferably against the original text. Typesetters make mistakes: words get misspelled, lines are left out, paragraphs become transposed. If mistakes are the fault of the typesetter, indicate corrections on the galleys (usually in blue, non-reproducible pencil, or in the margins). However, if errors appeared in your original document, you could have difficulty amending the galleys. Major editing may be prohibitive without having the entire job (paragraphs or pages) re-done—at extra charge. That's why you should double check all text before sending it to be typeset.

Typesetting Via Computer

The entire process explained above can be done on computer, particularly on *desktop publishing* systems with all text entry, editing, type specs, and proofreading done on screen. Many programs (such as *PageMaker* and Aldus *FreeHand*) are available which allow the user to incorporate visuals for constructing an entire layout on-screen.

You can save a lot of time and money by doing your own typesetting. Any of various Macintosh programs, or an IBM Composer, allow more immediate control over the typesetting process—including editing, corrections, last-minute revisions, and paste-up. The Composer features over 100 fonts, but ultimately offers a limited flexibility. If you plan to generate a lot of printed material, you should consider shopping around for your own in-house typesetting system.

If your text was generated on a word processor, you may be able to submit your documents to the printer on disk, or over the phone via modem. Check with your printer on the compatibility between your respective software. Though there are industry standards (such as *ASCII,* a common encoding system for binary data), not all computers can communicate with each other directly. However, it is possible to have data converted from one format to another via *conversion programs.* The advantage to using disk or modem is that it eliminates having a typesetter re-*key* (enter on a keyboard) the text. The disk (properly converted to compatible format) is loaded, and the text pops up on the screen. This saves time, reduces production costs, and avoids errors during retyping.

Optical character scanners are also available, which work like a fax machine hooked up to a computer instead of to a telephone. A document is fed into the unit, which reads a page of text, recognizes characters (in hundreds of fonts and dozens of languages), and converts to any of several standard formats on screen, at which point the text can be edited.

Photography

Graphics arts photography (preparing photos for print) uses much the same technology as creative art photography: cameras, film, negatives, and light-sensitive paper.

The actual processing of the photo will be done by the printer. But an understanding of the process is important so you know what to expect, and what can and cannot be done.

Black-and-White Photos

Before a black-and-white photo can be printed (for most purposes), it must be *screened.* This involves converting *continuous tones* to *halftones.*

Continuous tones are the broad range of solid and graded images the eye sees when looking at a camera-produced creative photograph. Inks cannot produce graded tones, only solids. In order to print a photograph, a halftone screen breaks a continuous-tone photograph into millions of tiny, but clearly defined dots (which can be seen under a magnifying glass). The dots represent solid points having equal spacing and ink density, but different area. This creates the optical illusion of a screened photo appearing to consist of continuous textures, while actually made up of a broken pattern. The human eye is "fooled" into seeing solid patterns.

Screening is done by a printer. The actual halftone-processed picture is called a *velox,* which can be pasted directly onto a mechanical.

There are different kinds of halftones, such as square, highlight, vignette and outline, which can be used for impact. *Duotones,* which are two-color halftones, can make a black and white photo appear colored. Ask your printer for samples of each technique.

Color Photos

Color photos must undergo *color separation* before printing. These can be done by the printer or by a graphic artist. It involves breaking down full-color images into primary color (red, blue, and green) negatives using a camera and filters. A fourth color—black—is added as a *color corrector* to compensate for imperfections in the process. What appears to the viewer as a full-color reproduction of the original image is actually a collage of microscopic, single-colored dots either next to or overlapping one another.

Thanks to the introduction of laser-scanners—which use electronic technology—the quality of color reproduction has risen, while the cost has dropped. Camera color tends to be more expensive, and though many professionals still swear by camera-quality, each new generation of scanner improves laser possibilities. Ask your printer about the respective advantages of each, depending on their own in-house state-of-the-art.

Regardless of the process used, contrast is important in a photo to be reproduced. Calvin York, of Danbury Printing, laments: "You'd be amazed at the number of people who bring in art work that has a white product against a white background, or dark against dark. Using monotone colors like pinks and reds doesn't work either." There are also certain combinations which create hallucinatory effects, such as red on green, and fluorescents. York adds, "What you spend on good photography, you will save at the printer. Sharp, well-lit, good contrast pictures, in which you don't have to hunt for the product, are the key to good color printing."

The color of the paper upon which the photo is printed will also affect the final image. For the purest color reproduction, a neutral shade of white works best.

Basic Checklist For Preparing Photos

There are a few things to keep in mind when preparing your photos for printing:

—*Protect photographs.* Store and ship all photos in plastic protective sleeves or attach a tissue overlay.

—*Don't write on the front or back of photos.* If you need to label a photograph for owner identification, placement, or captions, use adhesive labels—and write the information on the label before applying it to the back of the photo. Writing on the back of a photograph with a pen or pencil will leave a welt across the photo surface, and certain inks will bleed through to the front.

—*Submit original photos to the printer, rather than reproductions.* Each generation loses sharpness in color and tone.

—*Specify the degree of reduction or enlargement of photo.* This is expressed in percentages: 50 percent is half-size; 75 percent is three-quarter size, and so on. A 20 percent reduction means the final image will be one-fifth the size of the original. Art Service Technical Promotions (Loveland, Colorado) recommends that you avoid enlarging color prints more than 150 percent, to minimize loss of quality.

—*Indicate cropping instructions.* Cropping is how photos are edited; any portion of the image you don't want to appear in the final reproduction can be cut. There are three ways to indicate cropping: 1) make a xerox and draw crop lines; 2) indicate crop instructions on a tissue overlay; or 3) have the picture mounted on a sheet of paper with horizontal and vertical axes (*drop marks*) indicating the desired cuts.

—*Do not paste photos directly on mechanicals.* Though a velox can be inserted into a mechanical, original photos are handled differently. Boxes on the mechanical are labeled by the artist and *keyed* to visuals, indicating their respective position, such as Photo A in Box A, and so on. To assure correct keying, apply an adhesive label to the back of photos and write key references with a soft felt-tip pen; or, attach the photo to a sheet of paper or art board, and note key match-ups in the margin.

—*Mount photos (and illustrations) on stiff art board,* leaving a wide enough margin to accommodate key references or special instructions. However, *if laser scanning is to be used, do not mount prints on art board.* They will not be flexible enough to wrap around the scanning cylinder.

Illustrations

There are two types of illustrations: *line art* and *continuous tone* images. Line art includes simple sketches, diagrams, maps, charts, and most hand-drawings. Line art does not have to be screened and can be pasted directly onto a mechanical.

Complex artistic renderings can be continuous tone images. Like photographs, they must be converted to dot-pattern halftones before they can be reproduced. Continuous tone color illustrations must also undergo color separation to create overlay transparencies.

Here, again, traditional "hands-on" methods are giving way to modern means. Through computerized graphic arts systems, images—including continuous tones—can be fed onto magnetic tape, for instance, going directly to separation and other pre-press stages without the need to create color transparencies. This eliminates an entire generation in the production process, with virtually no loss of quality. In addition, it's possible to do retouching, repositioning, color control, image enhancement, and layering, all on screen. Special effects, such as *warping* (distorting) or *reflecting* (creating a mirror image) are simple and quick. Nancy Faherty, art director at Graphics One Fifty, a New Jersey-based design studio, attests: "By going directly from the magnetic tape format and eliminating the intervening transparency stage . . . I am experiencing a new stage of design freedom."

Checking your Mechanical

Before the mechanical goes to the printer, refer to the following checklist:

- *It should be clean.* Not just dirt-free, but free of pencil marks, glue smudges, white-out, and paperclips. The less touch-up the printer has to do, the better.
- *Everything should be pasted into final position,* including headlines, text, veloxes, line art, captions, and boxes keyed to photos or other visuals to be "picked-up" by the printer and inserted.
- *Check spelling,* one last time. An error in copy could cause acute embarrassment if caught by a reader. Triple-check all text, including capitalization. Headlines, in particular, the most obvious attention-getters, are sometimes overlooked while concentrating on small details.
- *Alignment—is everything cut and positioned squarely?*
- *Make sure all elements are pasted securely,* so they don't slip off on the way to the printer.
- *Double-check all key cross-references,* so their placement is clearly indicated.
- *Place a tissue overlay atop the mechanical,* for protection.
- *Include samples of the paper stock* to be used, to avoid mistakes.
- *Make sure your company name is on every piece of artwork that is sent to the printer.* Your phone number, too, and the name of the job or purchase order number.

Paper

Selecting the right paper for your printed material is a major decision, and because of the wide variety available, it's rarely simple. Paper thickness, weight, weave or texture, color, and ink sensitivity are factors. The importance of good paper is emphasized in "How to Buy Printing and Related Services," which states: "The cost of taking color pictures and having separations made is so high that these projects should be protected with . . . good paper to give the color work the best support possible."

Just to give a brief idea of the multitude of factors affecting choice, consider the following examples:

—Color photos always look better on glossy (coated) stock. However, because glossy finishes reflect light, they can affect readability.

—The lifespan of a piece of paper varies: is your printed material expected to last for years, or a few days? Permanent documents require a higher grade of paper.

—Will your literature be folded, stapled, or bound? Certain grades of paper are better suited for such use.

—Are illustrations featured? Are they two color, four color, or black and white? Tinted stock will affect visuals, regardless of format.

—If you plan to mail your literature, postal costs must be considered in selecting the weight of the paper.

The choices that go into paper selection are limitless, and could (and probably do) fill entire books. Zona Meravi, of Printer's Place, says they routinely offer advice on paper to clients. "Colors, weights, card stock—there's so much. Certain tints make illustrations stand out better. Different colored inks reproduce better on certain stocks," she says. "We always recommend flyers on brightly colored paper to make them more noticeable."

Your printer will, of course, be familiar with the pros and cons of various papers and can steer you towards the right paper for the job. You should also consult your art director for ideas.

Finding a Printer

If you intend to do a lot of printing, it would be in your best interest to develop a solid working rapport with a reputable shop. Allen Glazer, founder of Berkeley House Publishing, recommends: "Of all your business relationships, the relationship with your printer is among the most important . . . You should plan on devoting some time to locating a good one—maybe even a perfect one."

Good places to find the perfect printer:

—Those your company has used in the past with success.

—Printers who actively solicit your business, either by phone or mail. Read and file any sales literature that comes across your desk.

—The Yellow pages. Look under "Printing," "Copying," "Duplication Services," "Invitations and Announcements," "Artists—Commercial," "Advertising Art," "Layout and Production Service," or "Graphic Designers." Some of these may not offer printing services, but they all must work with printers and can probably give you references.

—Industry trade associations. The Printing Industries of America has over 9,000 members (which is less than 20 percent of all printers). The PIA has regional offices in many metropolitan areas, and they can recommend printers in your region to meet your exact requirements. The PIA's phone number is (703) 519-8100.

Another printing industry trade group to contact is the National Association of Printers and Lithographers, phone (201) 342-0700.

By shopping around, you will discover quite a range of available technology, some more advanced than others. Depending on your needs and your budget, inquire about the particular services each offers and get several cost estimates before selecting the right one for you. Glazer points out that, "in most cases, 25 to 75 percent of a direct mail budget will go to the printer. And . . . you'll discover that prices can vary greatly—often by as much as 30 percent or more."

Besides saving money, a trusted, reliable printer is an adjunct to your business. He or she can offer advice and helpful shortcuts. Printers, like any entrepreneurs, appreciate repeat customers; a shop to which you bring a steady flow of work will go out of its way to deliver exactly to your specifications.

CHAPTER 35

Market Research*

According to *Business Marketing's* 1986 Starmark Report, nine out of 10 business marketers say that research is important in their communications programs. Market research helps businesses learn more about their customers and prospects, including their needs, wants, likes and dislikes. As defined by the American Marketing Association, market research is "the systematic gathering, recording, and analyzing of data about problems relating to the marketing of goods and services."

"Anyone who thinks he doesn't need to understand marketing because he has enough business is courting disaster," warns Dr. Richard Lancioni, Professor of Marketing at Temple University. "You need to have a longer view of maintaining profitability. Don't assume you know what your customers' needs are. Conduct surveys and audits at least once a year to develop a pro-active approach of anticipating those needs."

*Some of the information in this chapter is reprinted with permission from the following sources: *Researching Your Market,* Management Aid Number 4.019 of the Small Business Administration, written by J. Ford Laumer, Jr., James R. Harris, Hugh J. Guffey, Jr., and Robert C. Erffmeyer, Ph.D.; *Reality Based Market Research: Factors to Consider,* White Paper Series Number 19 of the Business/Professional Advertising Association; "Mail, Telephone, or Focus," published in the *Research Reporter,* CMP Publications, Inc.; Vol. I, No. 3, July 1988.

While long-time experience and continuing contact with customers will give you an edge in understanding the market, they are not infallible. Information about markets gained from long experience may no longer be timely enough to base selling decisions on. And customers don't always tell you how they really feel or what they really want, even if they are unsatisfied with some aspect of your service or product. That's why market research is a valuable tool to maintaining and increasing your company's market share.

Uses Of Market Research

Market research covers a broad range of topics, including product research, market performance research, copy testing, ad testing, pricing research, distribution channel research, new market research, competitor research, even finding out why a salesperson in one area of the country isn't doing as well as a salesperson in another part of the country. It can be applied specifically to a product problem, sales problem, or corporate situation. Without market research, your ad campaign, TV commercial, direct mail program, or other promotions may "miss the mark" and waste a lot of money.

The goal of market research is to gather facts that will help your business solve problems, avoid problems, allocate funds better, and continue to grow. It provides what you need to:

- Reduce business risks;
- Spot problems and potential problems in your current market;
- Identify and profit from sales opportunities; and
- Get basic facts about your markets to help you make better decisions and set up plans of action

Obviously, it's much easier to sell people what they do want than what they don't want. Market research is useful in uncovering what's important to your prospects and customers, what products or services are in demand, and what problems your company can help your prospects solve. It can also open doors to new opportunities, whether it's a previously untapped segment of the marketplace, a new application of a product, or the creation of additional products or services to meet a need in your current market.

Even if you think you know your customers and how they perceive your products or services, research may surprise you. One large manufacturer, for example, was surprised to discover that customers highly valued the cleanliness of its plant. A commercial printing shop polled its customers and discovered that they wanted a variety of graphic arts services, so it invested in developing those additional services. And a corporate book supplier found that many of its prospects wanted to receive a single detailed invoice instead of many separate invoices addressed to each department that bought books, so that the companies could then issue a single check in payment. So the book supplier switched to a new computer program that enabled it to provide the necessary information—and convert more prospects to customers.

What You Need To Know

Judy Bjorling, Managing Director of Bjorling & Associates, a Glenview, Illinois-based marketing consulting firm, says you can increase useful marketing information inexpensively by asking yourself the following questions at least every six months:

- Who are our customers?
- What do I know about them?
- What do they think they're buying?
- What are we selling?
- What do customers think our strengths and weaknesses are?
- What *are* our strengths and weaknesses?
- Who are our competitors?
- What do our customers think about them?
- How long has it been since I talked to a salesman about our customers?
- How long has it been since I talked face-to-face with one of our customers?

Marketing research should also answer such questions as:

- Am I offering the kinds of goods or services customers want, at the best place, best time, and in the right amounts?
- Why have old customers left us?
- What attracts new customers to buy from us?
- Are my prices consistent with what buyers view as the products' values?
- Are my promotional programs working?

- How does my business compare with my competitors'? What are my competitors' strengths and weaknesses, and how can we capitalize on them?

Marketing research must be timely, since customers' likes and dislikes shift constantly. It's better to get a little information rapidly than to get too much late. If you take too long to gather information, it may be out-of-date by the time you've collected it all.

Researching Your Market, a publication of the Small Business Administration, lists the steps involved in conducting market research as:

1. Define the problem.
2. Assess available information.
3. Assess additional information, if required.
   a) Review internal records and files.
   b) Interview employees.
   c) Consult secondary sources of information.
   d) Interview customers and suppliers.
   e) Collect primary data.
4. Organize and interpret data.
5. Make decision.
6. Watch the results of the decision.

Defining The Marketing Problem Or Opportunity

Before you begin to collect marketing information, know your goal (i.e., what you hope to accomplish with that information). Market research may be exploratory, predictive, or diagnostic.

An example of an *exploratory* problem is trying to decide what a new market is looking for, or whether you can find a new market for an existing product. Or trying to decide which acquisition you should make or which of five new product designs you should implement.

A *predictive* problem occurs once you have chosen an option and you want to know what it is likely to achieve. How profitable is the option likely to be? Can you sell enough of these widgets to make it a viable product? What progress are you making generally, and how does your progress compare to what your competitors are doing?

Some market research is *diagnostic*—for example, what particular problem are you trying to solve? The fact that a product is selling in one area but not in another, or that you are losing current customers, is a symptom of a problem, not the cause. You need to come up with a list of possible causes (i.e., a hypothesis) before you begin your marketing research efforts. For starters, you might consider if there has been:

- A change in the areas your customers traditionally come from.
- A change in customers' tastes.
- Price-cutting by a competitor.
- Increasing competition.
- Turnover or reduction in your customer service department that has adversely affected customer relations.
- Decline in product quality.
- A decrease in product distribution efficiency.
- A change in direction or media placement of advertising or promotional materials.
- A change in fulfillment of requests for company literature.

Only when you've formally defined the problem can you assess your ability to solve it. You may realize you have all the information you need to determine if your hypothesis is correct, or solutions to the problem may have become obvious in the process of defining it. Or you may realize you can get the necessary information through secondary research—published or readily available information from various sources outside your company—or that you need more data. Realize that there is a big difference between information you would like to know and information that helps solve the problem.

Then, you can set a specific objective for your market research. What are you going to use the information for? What will it help you accomplish? If your objective is very important, the information is worth much more than information for a smaller objective. "Reality Based Market Research," a B/PAA White Paper, notes that "Some companies have spent a hundred thousand dollars for research on a product whose most optimistic sales would net a profit of no more than ten thousand dollars."

By categorizing the information you need and deciding on your research objective, you can determine the research methodology best suited to your task. If the objectives cannot be met through available secondary research, or if it's too hard for your company to be objective about the information it needs, a market research consultant or firm should be called in.

Market research is also valuable in assessing marketing opportunities. Perhaps you want to find a new application for your product in either the same market you currently sell to or a different one. Based on your product's features and capabilities, you may be able to brainstorm a list of possible new uses for it. But will those uses fill a need in the marketplace? Before you spend thousands or hundreds of thousands of dollars touting that new use, it makes far more sense to spend several thousand dollars—or more—on market research to find out if the idea has any validity in the marketplace.

Your goal in conducting market research will determine who should be polled and what questions should be included. For example, if you manufacture lawn mowers and your current customers are mostly men, but you are interested in finding out whether weight and color adaptations in your product would increase sales to women, polling your current customer base would be a waste of time and money. Instead, your ideal group of respondents would be women homeowners—especially heads of households—who live in suburban or rural areas.

Assess Available Information

Often, the information you need to solve a marketing problem is available within your company. All you may need to do is go through your files, check with sales staff or marketing staff, or use your company library.

Available information typically includes credit information about your customers you have on file; sales staff or customer service reports on customers; any recent surveys or studies you have conducted regarding your market, product, or service; recent articles about your industry, competitors, the economy in your selling area, changing demographics in your marketplace, and so on; competitors' literature; customer complaint letters; and records of product sales and returns.

If you have the information you need to solve the identified problem, stop there. Further market research will only be a waste of time and money. If, however, you're not sure if you need more information, you must make a subjective judgment to weigh the cost of more information against its usefulness.

Assess Additional Information

If you feel you need additional information, there are several inexpensive routes to consider before undertaking expensive surveys, field experiments, or hiring an outside consultant. For example, addresses on cash receipts can tell you where your customers live so that you can cross-reference their geographic area with the products they purchase. This, in turn, may tell you the effectiveness of your advertising placements.

Another valuable source of customer information is your employees. You can either talk to them informally or ask them to fill out a survey revealing their perceptions of customers' likes and dislikes. A good source of information about your competitors is *their* employees—you can even call anonymously and speak to the receptionist or sales staff about the company's products, new developments, sales, or *their* competition. The B/PAA report *Reality Based Market Research: Factors to Consider* states ". . . most confidential information leaks do not come from the hiring of outside consultants that work in your industry. They come from within, from the receptionist or salesman who is trying to make a sale or a variety of other internal sources."

Another excellent and relatively inexpensive source of information is secondary research. It involves using already-published surveys, books, and magazine articles—especially trade journal articles and their authors—to find information relevant to your industry and customers. Writers are often happy to direct you to their secondary sources of information, which can save you considerable time. Libraries, universities, trade associations, government agencies, newspapers, chambers of commerce, local TV and radio stations, computer database services, even economic development offices, are other sources of secondary research information. If your business is concerned only with a local market area, look for local statistics and newspaper articles that report on market potential in your geographic area.

Primary Research Activities

If your internal files and secondary sources of information don't provide the data you need, the next step is to conduct primary research. This can be as simple as asking your customers or suppliers how they feel about your store or service firm or as complex as the surveys done by the sophisticated professional marketing research giants.

What kinds of research will help you achieve specific goals? *Business Marketing*'s 1986 Starmark Report identifies the most successful market research projects and the goals they help reach:

- Focus groups provide an in-depth view of sales prospect attitudes.
- Key market surveys identify potential markets and clarify the needs of individual accounts.
- Market position studies identify perceptions of a company's product lines.
- Product feasibility studies point out market needs and allow the company to capitalize on them.

The most popular market research studies are listed in Figure 35.1. These primary research activities may be accomplished through direct mail questionnaires, telephone or "on the street" surveys, experiments, panel studies, test marketing, or behavior observation. Primary research can be classified as *reactive* or *nonreactive.* Reactive research tends to be the most expensive, consisting of surveys, interviews, and questionnaires. It's best left to marketing research experts, who know what kinds of questions to ask and how to elicit unbiased responses. There's also the danger that either people won't want to hurt your feelings when you ask them their opinions about your business or they'll answer questions the way they think they are "expected" to answer, rather than the way they really feel.

Nonreactive research involves observing your customers, specifically how they are dressed, how old they are, how educated they appear to be, and how and when they purchase your products. It may also involve noting:

1. which products and prices appeal to them the most, as determined through comparing sales results, split testing of direct mail and ads,

Figure 35.1. The Top Ten Marketing/Advertising Research Studies Used by Today's Marketers (Percent Responding)

Study	Percent
Market Position Studies	56%
Readership Studies	46%
Customer Attitude Studies	42%
Focus Groups	37%
New Product Feasibility Studies	37%
Competitive Environment Analyses	35%
Brand Preference Studies	33%
Market Potential Studies	31%
Company Image Studies	27%
Prospect Feedback Studies	20%

(Response adds to more than 100% due to multiple mentions)

coded business reply cards or observation of in-store traffic patterns; and

2. where your customers live, through license plate analysis, checking phone numbers on checks and credit slips, or using coded coupons or "tell them Joe sent you" radio and TV advertising.

One unusual example of nonreactive research was conducted by a discount merchandiser who gave away "all the roasted peanuts you can eat" during a three-day promotion. At the end of the third day, he could see which product displays and store aisles attracted the most attention from customers just by looking at the peanut shell trails and heaps that had been left behind.

Purchasing Market Research Services

At most companies, the marketing manager is responsible for conducting or arranging market research. Other company staff who may be responsible for this activity are the product manager, marketing director, vice president of marketing, sales manager, or advertising manager.

Marketing information can be gathered by an in-house staff or by an outside marketing agency. *Business Marketing's* Starmark Report shows that 61 percent of top marketers use an in-house department for market research activities; 28 percent hire a marketing research firm; 16 percent use magazine publishers; 15 percent rely on an ad agency; and another 15 percent hire a consultant.

Reasons to hire an outside firm include time limitations on your in-house staff; lack of market research expertise within your organization; a sensitive political situation—such as having to tell your company president his pet product may bomb if you suspect lack of marketplace interest; the need for international market information, which outside consultants are often able to get more easily; or the need to collect information anonymously, such as when contemplating the acquisition of another firm.

In hiring an outside firm, you should consider industry expertise and experience, reputation, price, how capable the firm is at defining measurable and meaningful research objectives, and how quickly the market information can be delivered to you.

Good market research consultants don't have a bias. They are able to look at a situation, help you address what your information needs are, what your goals are, and what's necessary on an objective basis. They can also put concentrated time against a marketing problem when you need information fast and they know where to go to get the best information. Custom research can also reduce your overhead. You don't have to have a market research professional or information source on staff 52 weeks a year for the two or three times during the year that you need market information.

Organizing And Interpreting Data

Once you have assembled all your information, how do you analyze it? This step requires both keeping an open mind so as not to jump to early conclusions and checking out inconsistencies. You must also be careful to look at all the data, not just selected segments of it.

Writing in the *B/PAA Intelligencer,* Dr. Arnold Diamond, Vice President at Harry Heller Research Corp., explains: "Correlation does not mean causation. The classic example is in stating that there is a high correlation between the number of fire engines at a fire and the extent of damage at the fire, suggesting that fire damage can be lessened by limiting the number of fire engines at a fire. Obviously, it is the third variable 'size of fire' which is highly correlated with the number of engines present at a fire and the extent of damage that is 'causing' things to happen."

Likewise, if the demographics of your respondent groups are not similar, you may draw incorrect conclusions. Demographic differences in age, income level, education, sex, marital status, and other variables between two groups of respondents can throw off results. For instance, if one ad for a high-priced product appears to generate a great deal more interest than another, it may be simply that those who saw the first ad are in a higher-income group. To make a valid assessment of the effectiveness of the two ads, your two groups of respondents must be balanced demographically.

Proper analysis requires looking beyond basic data to a variety of possible correlations which may affect the final conclusions. For example, the fact that Brand A is bought and used by more people may not be related to superior attributes, but rather to the fact that Brand B is not advertised enough—or that the advertising is ineffective.

For a study to be successful, you must discriminate between executions, products, ad concepts, etc. And your market research should not only point to revelations about product performance and customer preferences, but to the reasons behind them.

Consistencies in responses, and especially consistencies in the *reasons* behind those responses, increase the confidence you can place in your findings. But, according to Dr. Diamond, "sometimes it is the inconsistencies in the data which produce the most meaningful results in a study. Inconsistencies may reveal errors in the data. So they must be verified as true before proceeding with an analysis. Then, the inconsistency in the data must be resolved by looking at other measures to try to determine, for instance, why buyers apparently prefer a product but won't purchase it." Possible reasons might include that the preferred product is too expensive, too large, or the wrong color. Armed with that information, you can then make product modifications that will lead to improved sales.

Choosing The Right Research Methodology

The type of research methodology you use to gather information depends on several factors, including the purpose of the research, the type of data desired, the nature of the individuals being researched, and timing and cost considerations. In general, research methods fall into either subjective or objective categories.

Subjective research is best suited for the preliminary or early phases of researching a new market: to investigate why products are purchased, how the purchase process occurs, what potential market segments exist, etc. Subjective techniques are appropriate when qualitative information is desired, that is, information related to the "hows" and "whys" of product selection. They are used for generating ideas for new products or promotional strategies, for understanding complex issues or decision processes, and for identifying areas for further research. They are not appropriate for gathering quantitative information (e.g., size of the market, proportion of subscribers in certain job functions). A subjective technique would involve an unstructured interview in which questions are phrased in a conversational context and topics explored in a flexible fashion.

The *objective* approach is best suited for the later phases of research, when quantitative information directly tied to decision making must be gathered. Size of the potential market, relative importance of various product features, and extent of interest in various industry segments are all types of information that should be gathered through objective techniques. An objective technique might be a mail survey or questionnaire that permits the interviewer little or no latitude in what is asked or how it is recorded. Telephone surveys as well are often objective, with the interviewer essentially reading from a pre-arranged script and recording responses in a standard fashion. Personal interviews may also be objective, as in an exit poll in which voters are briefly questioned as they leave the polling place.

Telephone Vs. Mail Surveys

Mail surveys are often selected over telephone surveys because they are less expensive. The most common reason for choosing telephone surveys is speed. However, the nature of the study, the questionnaire, and the characteristics of the respondents should also be considered.

Longer questionnaires are usually better done by mail since respondents may tire before a long telephone interview is completed. Sensitive or controversial topics are also better covered in a mail format, since a live interviewer may limit respondents' candor or bias their responses. Technical subjects that are difficult to discuss over the phone are also easier to cover by mail. It is difficult to reach people in certain positions or in certain types of companies on the telephone, so a mail survey may be more productive.

Telephone surveying, on the other hand, affords the researcher a great deal more flexibility, which can be essential if not enough is known about the market to cover all bases in an objective format. A well-designed telephone survey can combine both subjective and objective elements.

Inexpensive Market Research Techniques

Owners and managers of small business often have an advantage in conducting market research more efficiently, since they are closer to their customers. They can go out and learn much more quickly and react faster to what their customers like and don't like. For the large firm, market research usually involves hiring experts to sift through their mass markets for clues as to what makes customers buy or not buy. But even large companies can conduct market research inexpensively by following these tips from Judy Bjorling:

1. Make a list of assumptions you, your boss, and others make about your business for which there is little supporting data. The longer the list, the more likely it is that you need a better system for gathering useful information.

2. Provide incentives to your sales force for accurate and insightful information. Make the sales force aware of the importance you place on up-to-date information and insights about loyal customers, those customers who have recently switched to another firm, new customers, and potential customers who have thus far eluded them.

3. Listen to customers yourself on a regular basis. There is no substitute for direct exposure to customers. Asking their opinions (and actually modifying your products based on their input) makes them increasingly loyal.

4. Form a good customer panel which meets periodically to volunteer information. Be sure that R&D, Engineering, and Production Managers have the opportunity to interact directly with this panel.

5. Make it easy for customers to complain about your product. Resolution of complaints leads to increased loyalty. Complaints provide a legitimate source for product-improvement ideas.

6. Attend meetings. Your competitors suffer many of the same problems you do and often will share information and solutions on the trickiest problems.

7. Whenever you realize that an executive from a competitive firm is speaking at a meeting, be sure someone in your company attends the meeting. Executives often reveal future directions for their company, as well as insights about the industry.

8. Make yourself, or designate someone in your company, to be the *industry expert.* Read and subscribe to trade publications, but don't keep the information to yourself. Plan regular meetings to update your associates on trends and new developments.

Tips For Conducting Successful Surveys

Surveys are one popular way to gather market research information. They can be used to assess customers' opinions of your product or company, establish a "customer profile" that tells what common characteristics your customers share, find out what customers want or need from your industry, or solicit their reactions to a new service you are thinking of offering. Richard P. Gorman of Association Management, Inc., Washington, D.C. offers these tips for designing a survey that will increase response rates:

1. Set your goals. Define what you want your survey to accomplish.
2. Identify your sample group and define your boundaries, such as size, type of industry, or whatever.
3. Recognize any particular limitations or problems associated with your survey topic or sample group. For example, do you need the results in

a very short time? Were previous surveys on this subject too difficult to answer?

4. Keep your survey as short as possible.
5. Keep your questions unbiased and unambiguous. Make them easy to answer.
6. Discard questions with obvious answers or those with illegal implications.
7. If you are seeking an answer that is long or complicated, break it up into several simple questions rather than one long question that is difficult to understand.
8. Make as many responses as possible simple check-offs or multiple choice. This makes it easier for respondents to reply and for you to tabulate the final results.
9. Make your survey stand out; dare to be different, but keep it professional looking.
10. Set a deadline for returns.
11. Prepare a cover letter that encourages people to respond.
12. Pretest your survey on a small portion of your sample in order to debug any problem questions.
13. Offer an incentive for reply. For example, explain that respondents will be entered in a drawing for a $100 savings bond.

CHAPTER 36

Copyrights and Trademarks

Copyrights and trademarks are used to protect your creative work (i.e., ads, brochures, campaigns, slogans, logos, tag lines, and product names) from being copied. Generally, you copyright a manuscript, advertisement, commercial, or other work of visual art, and you trademark a product name, company logo, or package.

Getting Your Work Copyrighted

Under a law passed by Congress in 1976, which took effect January 1, 1978, a work is automatically copyrighted at the moment it is created in a fixed form, such as a manuscript or audio recording. Copyright protection endures for the life of the author plus 50 years and is available for both published and unpublished works.

This is a major change from the old 1909 law, which stated copyright originated only upon publication. If you write advertising copy or articles as a freelancer, your work is automatically copyrighted at the time it is created. You, not the publisher or purchaser of your work, are considered the owner of your visual creation. A copyright gives you the right to sell, lease, license, give away, or donate ownership of your material. It also gives you the right to terminate a sale or transfer of rights.

Copyright is provided by the laws of the United States for "original works of authorship," including advertising copy, literature, drama, music, art, even computer software programs. The copyright protects such creations from being copied, reproduced, distributed, performed, or displayed without authorization from the author. This means that mere possession of a material work does not automatically give the possessor the copyright to that work.

To let the public know that a visual work is copyrighted—especially if the work is published—you should type the word "copyright," the letter "c" in a circle, or the abbreviation "Copr.", the date the work was first published, and your name in a prominent place in your manuscript, such as the top of the first page. If the work is a sound recording, such as a record, the notice on the recording should consist of the symbol "P" in a circle, the year the sound recording was originally published, and the name of the owner of the copyright.

Although it is not necessary to register a work with the Copyright Office (as it was before the 1976 law went into effect), it is a good idea to do so, since registration establishes a public record of the copyright claim and gives you more ammunition in court. The copyright fee is $10. For more information, write to Register of Copyrights, Library of Congress, Washington, D.C. 20559. (For telephone numbers, see the *Resources* section at end of chapter.)

The Berne Convention

In March of 1988, the United States officially subscribed to the Berne Convention, an international copyright agreement. This gives additional protection to writers who register their work in the United States. If the work is published in another member country, it automatically earns copyright protection under the law of that country.

Work Made For Hire

The exception to the rule that the person who creates a work is considered the author concerns "work made for hire" arrangements. As an advertising manager employed by someone else, the work you create for your company is termed "work made for hire." Under these circumstances, the employer—not you, the creator—is considered the author and owns all rights to the work. These works are copyrighted for 75 years after publication or 100 years from the date of creation, whichever is less.

In addition to the definition of "work made for hire" as "a work prepared by an employee within the scope of his or her employment," there is another kind of "work made for hire," which must meet three conditions. First, the copyright law states the work must be "specially ordered or commissioned" by the person who requests it; second, both parties must agree in a written contract that the work shall be considered a work made for hire; and third, the work must fall within certain categories specified by law. Those categories are as follows: contributions to a collective work, including a movie or other audiovisual work, a translation, a supplementary work to another author's work (such as a foreword, index, charts, maps, or illustrations), a compilation, an instructional text, a test or answer material for a test, or an atlas. Since advertising material is not included in these categories, ads, direct mail, broadcast scripts, capabilities brochures, and other advertising copy can only be considered "work made for hire" if it is created by an employee within the scope of his or her employment. So employees of an advertiser or ad agency or direct mail agency who produce copy or art as part of their jobs are doing "work made for hire" and their work does not belong to them.

To ensure that the work you commission through your ad agency is owned by you and copyrighted in your company's name, you may want to talk with your agency and have their principals sign a contract stating that the work they produce for your company is on a "made for hire" basis. For legal advice, consult your attorney.

Protecting Your Copyright

As with trademarks, much of the job of watching out for copycats is up to you. If someone reprints your work without permission, you may not ever hear about it. But if you do, you should notify the infringer in writing and warn him or her against future use of your material without permission, ask for a published correction attributing the work to you, or, if all else fails, seek compensation for damages.

Sometimes, however, work can be copied and distributed without violating its copyright. This is covered by the "fair use" doctrine of the Copyright Act, which states that fair use constitutes "purposes such as criticism, comment, news reporting, teaching, scholarship, or research." Granted, this is not very specific and leaves "fair use" open to different interpretations. In the end, the courts must decide each case of copyright infringement based on its own merits.

The Trademark Symbol

According to the Patent and Trademark Office of the U.S. Department of Commerce, "*Trademarks* may be a word, symbol, design, or combination word and design, slogan, or even a distinctive sound which identifies and distinguishes the goods or services of one party from those of another." When a trademark identifies a service—such as the emblems of Blue Cross and Blue Shield—it may be called a *service mark.* A trademark for products is usually the word or design on the product or its package, while a service mark is typically the word or design used in advertising to identify the owner's services.

Your trademark establishes your product's name or package as belonging to you, so that others cannot use the same or a similar mark to identify their products. It also can serve as a guarantee of quality and help advertisers sell their product. Unfortunately, sometimes trademarks become so well identified with a particular type of product that the trademarked name slips into common use as the name for that product. Cellophane and aspirin used to be trademarked names, but were lost over time as people used them as synonyms for the products they identified. Kleenex tissues and Xerox copies are other trademarked names that are often used generically and incorrectly. It is up to the trademark owner to regulate the use of a trademark and prevent it from being incorrectly used by the public and media or infringed on by competitors.

A trademark does not have to be federally registered in order for it to have protection. In fact, before you can apply for a trademark, you must use the word, design, or symbol on goods which are shipped or sold, or on services provided, in federally regulated commerce. Registering a trademark is a good idea, however, because it provides the following advantages:

- The right to sue in Federal court for trademark infringement.
- Recovery of profits, damages, and costs in a Federal court infringement action and the possibility of treble damages and attorneys' fees.
- Notice of a claim of ownership.

- The right to deposit the registration with the Customs Department in order to stop the importation of goods bearing an infringing mark.
- *Prima facie* evidence of the validity of the registration, registrant's ownership of the mark and of registrant's exclusive right to use the mark in commerce.
- The possibility of incontestability, in which case the registration constitutes conclusive evidence that the registrant has exclusive right, with certain limited exceptions, to use the registered mark in commerce.
- Limited grounds for attacking a registration once it is five years old.
- Availability of criminal penalties in an action for counterfeiting a registered trademark.
- A basis for filing trademark applications in foreign countries.

Trademark registration is given for 20 years and costs $175. (See trademark application information in *Resources* section at end of chapter.) Registration can be renewed for 20 additional years for another $300. But between the fifth and sixth years following registration, the trademark owner must file an affidavit stating the mark is currently in use in commerce. If this is not done, the registration will be cancelled.

The trademark symbol is a capital R in a circle raised slightly above the line of type following the trademarked name. The phrase "Registered in U.S. Patent and Trademark Office" may also be used. If registration has not been applied for, you can use a TM (trademark) or SM (service mark) symbol to designate ownership of the product, logo, or phrase.

How To Use Trademarks Correctly

Advertising managers have the responsibility of safeguarding their company's trademarks by knowing how to use them correctly in advertising. The following tips are reprinted with permission from "Rights Rules," *Business Marketing:*

1. A trademark must be distinguished from other words in print, even if only by capitalizing it. For example, Herculon olefin fiber or HERCULON olefin fiber is correct. But herculon olefin fiber or Herculon Olefin Fiber are incorrect uses of a trademark.

2. Whenever possible, a trademark notice should follow the mark. If that is impossible, it should be used at least once in copy and preferably,

the first time the mark appears. If the trademark is registered in the U.S. Patent and Trademark Office, the registration notice ® or "*Reg. U.S. Pat. & Tm. Off." should be used. If the trademark isn't registered, ™ or Trademark of Widget International can be used.

3. The trademark should always be used with the generic name. Therefore, "Vaseline petroleum jelly is good for burns" would be correct, but "Vaseline is good for burns" would be wrong. The simple way to remember this is to think of the trademark as an adjective.

4. Trademarks should never be used in the possessive form. "Karastan's fine quality" is wrong, but "Karastan carpets' fine quality" is correct.

5. Trademarks should always be used in the singular. They aren't nouns so they can't be made plural. So "Band-Aid brand adhesive bandages are good for cuts," is correct but "Band-Aids are good for cuts" would be wrong.

6. Thinking of the trademark as a proper adjective is perhaps the best way to avoid two common pitfalls. Never use a trademark as a verb or common adjective. "Simoniz your car" is wrong but "Polish your car with Simoniz paste wax" is correct. "Buy a Dacron shirt" is an example of using the mark as a common adjective but "Buy a shirt made of Dacron polyester fibers" is correct.

7. Companies should identify their ownership of a trademark. For instance, "Plexiglas is a registered trademark of Rohm & Haas."

Resources

For more general copyright information, call 202-479-0700 to speak to a Public Information Specialist at the Copyright Office, Office of Information and Publications, Library of Congress, Washington, D.C. 20559. The Copyright Office provides assistance and how-to information on copyright and how to register claims to copyright. Or you can call 202-707-9100 to leave a recorded message requesting specific copyright forms. If you want to copyright advertising and promotional material that is mostly text, request form TX. If the material consists mostly of art work, request form VA.

Another information resource is the Copyright Clearance Center, Inc., located at 2 North Street, Salem, MA 01970. Or telephone 508-745-

7837 and ask for the Publisher Coordinator. This center gives permission to photocopy copyrighted material for personal or internal use to corporations, academic and research libraries, information brokers, government agencies, and others. It provides information on copying from journals, books, proceedings, newspapers, newsletters, and consumer and trade magazines. The Copyright Clearance Center also collects photocopying royalties on behalf of 6,400 member publishers from nearly 1,000,000 titles.

To apply for a trademark, you must fill out an application form, which is included in *Basic Facts About Trademarks.* To receive the form and brochure, send $1.75 to the Superintendent of Documents, Washington, D.C. 20402. Or call 703-557-INFO for general trademark or patent information. The brochure spells out the exact filing requirements as well as the registration process, waiting times, and trademark search procedures.

CHAPTER 37

Newsletters

One proven promotional tool is the company newsletter. In today's age of specialized information, newsletters are popular. There are more than 10,000 newsletters published in the United States. Most of these are paid subscription newsletters, sold for profit by entrepreneurs for whom the newsletter is their primary source of income.

In this chapter, we will deal with another kind of newsletter—the *promotional newsletter.* It is also called the *company newsletter* or *house organ.* This is a newsletter, magazine, tabloid, or other publication regular published primarily as a promotional tool. They range from simple sheets published in-house to elaborate, four-color company magazines with photography and professional writing rivaling newstand magazines.

The Function Of Promotional Newsletters

The main purpose of such a newsletter is to establish your image and build your credibility with a select audience (the people who receive the newsletter) over an extended period of time.

Instinctively, most marketers recognize that they should be in touch with their customers and prospects far more often than they actually are. You know, for instance, that there are many people in your life—business and social—who you don't think about, see, or talk to for long periods of time simply because you are busy and not thinking of them.

Well, your customers and prospects are busy, too. And while you may be agonizing over why Joe hasn't placed an order from you recently or called your firm to handle a project, Joe isn't even thinking about you . . . because he has so much else on his mind.

You know you should be doing something to keep your name in front of Joe and remind him of your existence. But how? You may want to call or send a letter, but you think this is too pushy . . . and besides, there's no real *reason* to call, and you don't want to seem begging for business.

The newsletter solves this problem. It regularly places your name and activities in front of your customers and prospects, reminding them of your existence, products, and services on a regular basis. And, you need no "excuse" to make this contact, because the prospect *expects* to receive a newsletter on a regular basis. The newsletter increases the frequency of message repetition and supplements other forms of communication such as catalogs, print ads, and sales letters.

Frequency And Size

How long should your newsletter be? How often should it be published?

Four pages seems to be the ideal length for a promotional newsletter. Eight pages is too much reading, and two pages seems insubstantial—more like a flier or circular (which is perceived as *junk mail*) than a newsletter (which is perceived as a useful publication). If you need to go longer than four pages, use six, not eight.

As for frequency, four times a year—once every three months—is ideal. Publish fewer issues, and people aren't aware you are sending them a newsletter *per se;* they perceive that they're just getting a piece of mail from time to time. Four times per year is enough to establish credibility and awareness. Publishing six times or more per year is unnecessary, because some months you may prefer to make contact with your prospects using other media, such as the telephone or direct mail or catalogs.

What's more, experience indicates that most companies don't have enough news to fill six or more issues each year, and if your schedule is too frequent, you may find yourself putting unnecessary fluff and filler in the newsletter just to get something in the mail. Your readers will be turned off by the lack of quality and poor content, so this would hurt you rather than help.

Building Your Subscriber List

Who should get your newsletter? Basically, it should go to anyone with whom you want to establish a regular relationship. These people can include:

- Current customers.
- Past customers.
- Current prospects.
- Past prospects.
- Expired accounts (e.g., past subscribers, "expires," etc.).
- Employees.
- Vendors.
- Colleagues.
- Consultants, gurus, and other prominent members of your industry.
- Trade publication editors, business columnists, and other members of the press who might possibly use material in your newsletter in their own writings.

Here is how you build the subscriber list:

1. First, put all current and past prospects and customers on the list. But don't use names that are too old. For past prospects and customers, for example, you might go back two or three years—but no more than that.

2. Next, get your salespeople to give you all the names of the people they call on regularly. Salespeople have their own favorite prospects, and these people may not be in the advertising inquiry files. So get salespeople to give you names of people who should get the newsletter. You essentially want to convert the dozens of individual rolodex™ files kept by various salespeople and sales reps into a single, integrated subscriber list for your newsletter.

3. Go to your PR department or agency and add their media list. Get the names of all editors who should receive the newsletter.

4. Make sure all new inquiries and new customers are automatically added to the subscription list.

5. At trade show booths, create a subscription application form and offer a free one-year subscription to anyone who stops by your booth and completes the form.

6. Make sure the subscriber lists contains the names of your immediate supervisors, your product and brand managers, your sales and marketing managers, your CEO, and any other key personnel whose support you need to run an effective advertising department. Company managers enjoy getting the newsletter and often will offer ideas for articles and stories you can use. You might also approach your most important colleague and ask her to contribute a regular column.

Promoting The Newsletter

In addition to compiling the list in this manner, there are a number of things you can do to promote the newsletter (and to use the newsletter offer as a promotion):

1. You can offer the newsletter as an extra incentive to people who respond to your direct mail. This can be as simple as adding a line to your reply cards with a box that says, "☐ Check here if you would like a free one-year subscription to our quarterly newsletter, [title of newsletter]." You could also stress the newsletter offer in the P.S. of your sales letter.

2. You can offer the newsletter as an extra incentive for responding to your space ads. Again, add an option to the response coupon that says, "☐ Check here for a free one-year subscription to our newsletter, [title of newsletter]."

3. At speeches, seminars, and presentations, your company representatives can use the newsletter offer to get listeners involved in conversations with them. At the end of the talk, the presenter says, "Our quarterly newsletter, [title of newsletter], will give you more information on this topic. Just give me your business card and I'll see to it you get a free one-year subscription to it]." This way, the presenter will collect many business cards for follow-up—far more than he or she would get if there was no newsletter offer.

4. You could rent a list of names and send them the newsletter for free two or three times. The third or fourth time, you send it with a cover

letter that says, "We hope you find [title of newsletter] informative and helpful, and we would be happy to continue sending it at no cost. To continue your free subscription, just complete and mail the reply card enclosed." Then you continue sending the newsletter only to those who return the reply card, which eliminates the cost of continually renting names.

5. Send out a press release offering a free sample copy of the newsletter to people in your industry.

6. Run small space ads with a picture of the newsletter. Offer a free sample copy to anyone who responds.

Designing Your Newsletter

Newsletters do not have to be elaborate. But the design should be consistent from issue to issue, in order to build recognition and awareness. After a time, many recipients will come to welcome your newsletter, even seek it out from among the pile of mail in their basket. But this can only happen if the newsletter has a distinctive, recognizable design that is consistent from issue to issue.

Although many paid subscription newsletters are typewritten, you probably want a design that is a little slicker, so as to enhance your image. Text is generally typeset in two or three column format. Paper stock may be white or colored, and the newsletter is usually printed in one or two color inks. The key to the design is a distinctive masthead highlighting the name of the publication.

The look, content, and "feel" of the newsletter are usually arrived at after a couple of issues. By the third issue, you know the approximate length of copy, the type of visuals needed, the technical depth of the content, and the types of articles to be featured.

For instance, you might decide that each issue will contain two feature articles, one biographical profile, a regular question-and-answer column on technical issues, one product-related story, three or four short news tidbits, and a box with short previews of the next issue. Your newsletter may be different, of course, but the point is, you'll eventually find a formula that works and stick with it from issue to issue.

Readers like this consistency of format because they know what to look for in each issue. For instance, some people opening the Sunday paper turn to sports first; some go to the comics; others read Dear Abby first. In the same way, some readers might check your "technical tips" column first, while others will read the profile. Make these features look and read the same in each issue (even position them in the same spot) so readers gain a comfortable familiarity with your publication.

Charging A Fee For Your Newsletter

One common question is, "Since so many newsletters charge hefty subscription fees, what about charging a fee for my newsletter?" Don't do it. A promotional newsletter is *not* the same as a paid-subscription newsletter.

The paid subscription newsletter must deliver unique and valuable editorial material to the readers—otherwise, they will not continue to pay a hefty price for it month after month. This material must be useful, informative, new, and special. In short, it must be material the reader cannot easily get elsewhere. The newsletter's purpose is to be the reader's source of critical information in the area covered by the publication.

The promotional newsletter is quite different. Although it should contain helpful and interesting information, the reader expects less from a promotional newsletter than from one he pays to receive. As a result, he will accept a blend of how-to and technical information mixed with production information, company news, and sales talk. And this is the mix you want to give him. Remember, the ultimate goal of the newsletter is not to educate the reader (you are not in the business of educating people for free) but to get him to do business with your firm and buy your products.

Because your newsletter is free, you're entitled to make some subtle (and not-so-subtle) sales pitches. But if you were charging, the reader would not accept this. So your newsletter should be free. Another reason not to charge is that paid newsletters typically capture only a small percentage of any market as subscribers. So if you want to reach a broader base of prospects, you must offer your newsletter free.

Putting Your Newsletter Together

Putting your newsletter together is not terribly difficult. The first step is to make a list of possible story ideas. (Later in this chapter, I provide a checklist of 29 such ideas).

Key Point

The material in your promotional newsletter does not have to be original, nor must it be created solely for the newsletter. In fact, a company newsletter is an ideal medium for recycling material from other sources—speeches, articles, press releases, annual reports, presentations, and so on.

This helps you get maximum use out of material you've already created while minimizing the time and expense of writing and producing the newsletter.

The second step is to review your story ideas and select the ones to be featured in the next issue. If you are unsure as to how much room you have, it's better to select one or two extra ideas than one or two too few. You can always use the extra material in a future edition.

The third step is to create a file folder for each article and collect the material which will serve as background material for the person who writes the story. This background material typically includes sales brochures (for product stories), press releases (which are edited into short news stories), and reprints of published trade journal articles on a particular topic (which are often combined and compiled into a new article on a similar topic).

The fourth step is to write each story based on this material. Many advertising managers hire freelance writers to write and edit their company newsletters. A few hire their ad agency to do it. Using freelancers is usually more cost effective. Besides, while most freelancers relish such assignments, most ad agencies don't like doing company newsletters, because they find them unprofitable.

Some articles may require more information than is contained in the background material. In this case, supply the writer with the names and phone numbers of people within your company who he or she can interview to gather the additional necessary information. You should call these people ahead of time to let them know a freelance writer will be calling them to do an interview for the newsletter. If they object, find someone else to take their place.

Once you get the copy, the fifth step is to edit it, send it through for review, and make any final changes. The sixth step is to give the final copy to your graphic artist or printer, who will create a mechanical for the newsletter. This should be carefully proofread and reviewed before it is printed. Many companies nowadays use desktop publishing systems in-house or hire outside desktop publishing services for newsletter layout and creation.

Once the mechanical is completed and approved, you print the newsletter. You may want to order a small run above what you need to mail to the subscribers. These extras can be kept on file for people who request a back-issue. If your newsletter is truly perceived as valuable by the subscribers, as is Niagara Lockport's *Tissue Issues,* you can periodically offer back issues as a "bait piece" in your ads and mailings.

If your subscriber list is small—say, only a few hundred names—you can have your computer generate gummed mailing labels and affix them in-house. Once you have a thousand or more subscribers, you might want to use a letter shop, fulfillment house, or similar mailing service to handle the mailing and distribution of your newsletter on a regular basis. This will not be terribly expensive.

A Checklist Of 29 Newsletter Story Ideas

1. *Product stories:* New products; improvements to existing products; new models; new accessories; new options; and new applications.
2. *News:* Joint ventures; mergers and acquisitions; new divisions formed; new departments; other company news. Also, industry news and analyses of events and trends.
3. *Tips:* Tips on product selection, installation, maintenance, repair, and troubleshooting.
4. *How-to articles:* Similar to tips, but with more detailed instructions. Examples: How to use the product; how to design a system; how to select the right type or model.
5. *Previews and reports:* Write-ups of special events such as trade shows, conferences, sales meetings, seminars, presentations, and press conferences.
6. *Case histories:* Either in-depth or brief, reporting product applications, customer success stories, or examples of outstanding service or support.
7. *People:* Company promotions, new hires, transfers, awards, anniversaries, employee profiles, customer profiles, human interest stories (unusual jobs, hobbies, etc.).
8. *Milestones:* Use of such phrases as "1,000th unit shipped," "sales reach $1 million mark," "division celebrates 10th anniversary," etc.
9. *Sales news:* New customers; bids accepted; contracts renewed; satisfied customer reports.
10. *Research and development:* New products; new technologies; new patents; technology awards; inventions; innovations; and breakthroughs.

11. *Publications:* New brochures available; new ad campaigns; technical papers presented; reprints available; new or updated manuals; announcements of other recently published literature or audiovisual materials.
12. *Explanatory articles:* How a product works; industry overviews' background information on applications and technologies.
13. *Customer stories:* Interviews with customers; photos; customer news and profiles; guest articles by customers about their industries, applications, and positive experiences with the vendor's product or service.
14. *Financial news:* Quarterly and annual report highlights; presentations to financial analysts; earnings and dividend news; reported sales and profits; etc.
15. *Photos with captions:* People; facilities; products; events.
16. *Columns:* President's letter; letters to the editor; guest columns; regular features such as "Q&A" or "Tech Talk."
17. *Excerpts, reprints, or condensed versions of:* Press releases; executive speeches; journal articles; technical papers; company seminars; etc.
18. *Quality control stories:* Quality circles; employee suggestion programs; new quality assurance methods; success rates; case histories.
19. *Productivity stories:* New programs; methods and systems to cut waste and boost efficiency.
20. *Manufacturing stories:* SPC/SQC (statistical process control/statistical quality control) stories; CIM (computer-integrated manufacturing) stories; new techniques; new equipment; raw materials; production line successes; detailed explanations of manufacturing processes; etc.
21. *Community affairs:* Fund raisers; special events; support for the arts; scholarship programs; social responsibility programs; environmental programs; employee and corporate participation in local/regional/national events.
22. *Data processing stories:* New computer hardware and software systems; improved data processing and its benefits to customers; new data procession applications; explanations of how systems serve customers.
23. *Overseas activities:* Reports on the company's international activities; profiles of facilities, subsidiaries, branches, people, markets, etc.

24. *Service:* Background on company service facilities; case histories of outstanding service activities; new services for customers; customer support hotlines; etc.
25. *History:* Articles of company, industry, product, community history.
26. *Human resources:* Company benefit programs; announcement of new benefits and training and how they improve service to customers; explanations of company policies.
27. *Interviews:* With company key employees, engineers, service personnel, etc.; with customers; with suppliers (to illustrate the quality of materials going into your company's products).
28. *Forums:* Top managers answer customer complaints and concerns; service managers discuss customer needs; customers share their favorable experiences with company products and services.
29. *Gimmicks:* Contents; quizzes; trivia; puzzles; games; cartoons; recipes; computer programs; etc.

*Company Magazines**

The company magazine, or *house organ,* is a larger, more ambitious effort than the company newsletter. The term newsletter implies a slimmer publication, with simple graphic and short, concise, to-the-point write-ups. The term magazine implies a larger, slicker, more visually oriented publication, with photos, illustrations, more pages, more text, and lengthier, feature-type articles.

There's nothing mysterious about custom-published magazines. Companies, associations and other organizations have been using them for years to promote products and services, bolster sales efforts and strengthen relationships with customers and members. They come in a variety of shapes and sizes. They may contain outside advertising or only ads for the sponsoring firm. Most rival the publications available on the newsstand.

The best custom-published magazines present a positive image of their sponsors while providing helpful and useful information to readers. They may cover several subjects or focus on a single item such as travel, food, health, or finances, much as newsstand magazines do.

*The information in this section is reprinted with permission from "An Inside Look at Producing Company-Sponsored Magazines: A Special Report by KL Publications, formerly Webb Custom Publishing.)

But custom-published magazines are not aimed at general audiences. They're carefully constructed for the customers and prospects their sponsors want to reach. Their content is designed to support the sponsor's products and services by targeting values and lifestyles.

The first custom-published magazine was developed by DeWitt Wallace at The Webb Company before the turn of the century. Wallace took articles about farming practices and farm life from the pages of other magazines and reproduced them in digest form. Banks purchased them and gave them to customers. He eventually left Webb and founded one of the most successful magazines in the long history of American publishing—Reader's Digest.

The most familiar contemporary custom-published magazines are probably the airline "in-flights"—magazines tucked into the seat pockets of commercial jets. They combine information a traveler can use (whether it's feature material about vacations or practical tips about business travel) with promotional and advertising information for the airline. There are several custom-published magazines for farm audiences providing information about farm management, progressive farming practices and other topics focused on today's farm audience—their value systems and lifestyles. Other magazines appeal to insurance purchasers, car owners, brides-to-be and dozens of other consumer groups.

What Magazines Can Do That Other Media Can't

Custom-published magazines combine the trustworthiness of print, the visual appeal of consumer magazines and the targetability of direct mail. They cost much less per customer contact than a sales call while providing audience involvement no television or radio station can hope to match. The pages in these magazines can be read, re-read, underlined, torn out and even mailed back.

With marketing costs increasing, companies are becoming more and more concerned with the effectiveness of their advertising campaigns. And no other vehicle provides the same capability for accurate media and marketing research as does a magazine. Company-sponsored magazines can include mail-back questionnaires designed for a known audience.

Magazines also build company and product loyalty as nothing else can. They build positive corporate and organization images in addition to selling products and services. More than 3,000 sponsored magazines are published in the United States, a good indication of how popular they are with companies and groups that have made them part of their marketing strategies.

Several strengths of custom-published magazines were outlined in "Marketing & Media Decisions"—

- Ability to target an audience of prospects identified by dealers or company management.
- Total control of the message, free of competitive advertising clutter.
- Elimination of placement problems in general circulation media.
- Ability to stimulate floor traffic at dealerships with coupons and special offers.
- Seasonal timing—which puts the message into customers' hands when they are planning purchases.
- Space to present specific and detailed product information with charts, graphs, etc.
- Penetration of hard-to-reach markets.

Other strengths:

- Service to readers through education and updates on product lines.
- Image building in a positive, controlled environment with each issue creating its own environment.
- Direct sales support as part of an overall sales strategy.
- Semi-confidential distribution of the marketing plan.
- Reinforcement after the sale.

Getting Started

The first step in developing a magazine program is to set goals and objectives. How important is it for you to establish regular contact with your customers and top prospects and to encourage customer involvement with your sales/distribution network? Is your first priority to enhance the image of the company, or should direct sales support be the primary objective? Is the company most interested in cross-selling its goods and services, getting feedback from customers, reducing sales costs, lobbying decision-makers, customer retention or consumer education?

All are worthy goals. However, it's important to establish one or more objectives so the magazine can have a clear focus.

The next step in planning your magazine is the last step of the publishing process: distribution.

Companies and associations have different problems getting their magazines to the right people at the right time. An association can simply use its membership roll to develop a circulation list. A business usually doesn't have members (co-ops and buyers' clubs are exceptions), so it has to develop its own list. This takes time and money, but a good list is invaluable as a sales-lead developer, a market survey tool and the start of a direct-mail program. And a confidential customer-prospect list is a recognized business asset.

Here are some good places to start building a circulation list:

- Current customers.
- Respondents to mass-media advertising.
- Existing lists, assembled by professional list brokers and rentable.
- Professional association lists, also rentable.
- Dealer-supplied names, available two ways. (The term "dealer" represents the closest-to-consumer level in your distribution network, whether it's dealer, agent, sales person or franchisee.) Dealers can supply names to you for computer storage, either in your computer or in your publisher's. Computer printout labels can then be mechanically affixed to magazines after they are printed. Magazines also can be bulk-shipped to dealers, who will distribute them. While this is less satisfactory, it is sometimes necessary because independent dealers often have a stake in keeping their customer lists confidential.
- Dealer imprints. When dealers pay part of the magazine cost, it is often extremely important to them to have their name, address and phone number on each issue. This imprint can be as simple as a double computer label with "from" and "to" printed on each part of the label. A more uniform look can be achieved by typesetting the information and imprinting it during the printing process. Finally, you can provide dealers a full-page ad or their own newsletter bound into the magazine.

Ink-jet printing will permit matching of dealers' names on insert cards with the correct labels imprinted on the outside. Sophisticated dealer imprint systems use a specialized computer program that does far more than just produce labels. A well-designed program can provide a treasure of demographic information. It can provide printouts on participation by dealers, districts, regions, ZIP codes, etc. This is particularly important if dealers are billed for their participation in the program.

In any case, if you are selling the program to dealers on a cost-sharing or cost-liquidation basis, you must educate and sell them on the program to ensure participation.

There are other ways to distribute the magazine.

- Point-of-service: distribute the magazine when customers purchase products or services.
- Focal-point distribution: place magazines where potential customers gather. Farmers, for example, might receive it at a county fair, stockyard, or grain elevator; teachers might receive it at school in the teachers' lounge.
- Piggyback distribution: the magazine is physically attached to a product, such as a packing crate or included with a company's annual report so it acts as an incentive as well as a marketing device.

  The next step is to decide what kind of magazine to publish, taking into account your marketing objectives, the kind of image you want to project and how these can best be supported by a publication.

There are three elements to consider: graphic design, publication size and format.

Size and Shape

Among the basic formats are magazine, tabloid, newsletter, bulletin, booklet and specialty piece. Magazine format is a clear choice when you aim for a top-quality marketing publication with four-color photos and illustrations. Usually the page is a press-efficient size about 8 × 10-¾″. Digest-size magazines (5-⅜ × 8″) offer a smaller alternative. Booklet form can be effective for one-time use, partly because it is unusual and easy for a reader to keep. Newspaper formats—tabloid and broadsheet—offer low cost, but can be messy to handle and have shorter retention than magazines.

Specialty pieces are the most expensive pieces to produce, but often are the most impressive custom-published products. Some examples: a fold-out poster that resembles an 8 × 11-¾″ magazine when folded; a circular book; square or other odd-shape pages (this wastes paper in longer press runs but might make sense in shorter ones); calendar/magazines with articles on page-backs; or die-cut publications with special ink combinations or unusual paper.

The Editorial and Graphic Approach

The corporate image a publication conveys can be enhanced by the heft, feel and appearance of the publication as well as by its editorial approach. There are two very basic editorial questions to ask:

- What message should be conveyed?
- What does the selected audience want to read?

The first question really isn't difficult to determine because most companies have been trying to communicate effectively with people for a long time. The second isn't difficult, either. Most companies probably have demographic and psychographic data on their audiences and can list topics that will attract readership. They can select subjects that best support the goals they want to achieve.

For example, a financial institution with a strong community reputation for supporting the arts and a clientele with an upper-income socioeconomic base might start a magazine covering the regional arts scene. An airline whose audience consists mostly of business people might produce a magazine that emphasizes business topics and stories featuring destinations on its flight routes.

Success isn't guaranteed by the best editorial approach and a sophisticated corporate message. A custom-published magazine has to be well-written and well-designed with a specific readership in mind.

Magazines that make it are not overloaded with corporate promotion material. If readers get the idea that a magazine is little more than a montly sales brochure, they'll throw it out. At the same time, properly presented articles about a company's services and products can be perceived by readers as interesting, useful and helpful

Once a planned approach is chosen, it's time to bring in a topflight editor and art director to establish the editorial focus, graphic design and budget.

It is their job to clearly understand marketing objectives and then plan the proper mix of stories, photographs and illustrations to ensure both good readership and effective reception of the sponsor's message.

Control is a primary concern for any sponsor of a custom-published magazine. If an editor and art director can't or won't take direction and produce what's expected, the sponsor will be unhappy with the final product. How much the sponsor wants to be directly involved with the creative staff depends on time, expertise and inclination. At the very least, the sponsor will review all copy and layouts before magazine production is so far down the road that changes become expensive.

The keys to properly producing the magazine are communication and control. The sponsor and the creative staff must be on the same wavelength before and throughout production.

Be sure to establish checkpoints before production starts. In a typical publishing situation, the sponsor should review work on the magazine at four steps:

1. Editorial planning
2. Manuscripts
3. Rough layouts (including photos)
4. Blueprints or color-keys

This four-point checklist lets the sponsor direct every step from initial planning through final check. If properly used, this system will not cause costly delays, whether the editor and art director are across the hall or half a continent away.

Superior graphic design ensures magazine readability and creates a distinctive personality for the publication. A conservative financial firm may want a more formal look, for example, than a company selling records and laser discs. The effects of appearance may be subliminal, but if they clash with the desired image and editorial content, the discord will jar readers even though they may not be able to recognize what's wrong.

Good production planning and control are essential, too. In almost any magazine with a circulation of several hundred thousand, the cost of physically producing it exceeds creative costs. Therefore, you can save more money by making excellent production decisions than by cutting creative costs. Because there are many cost-saving options in producing any publication, experienced production managers are invaluable.

A production manager can help answer questions about the most economical way to produce a magazine. For example, does it need to be published with full-color photos throughout or will black-and-white do? That decision could mean a significant savings. Should inserts be slid into the magazine, glued in or stapled in with the rest of the pages? What are the paper stock alternatives? Which other production options are available? Each decision contributes to the final cost of the magazine.

At the same time, graphic skill can frequently make a one-or two-color publication look as sophisticated as a full-color magazine, and production can be organized so some pages are printed one-color and others four-colors.

If the production manager is on your staff, that person can help decide which printer should be employed. Is the lowest bid the best bid, or is the added experience and capability of a higher-priced printer worth the difference? Are reliability, longevity and proven ability to meet schedules more important than price? Does a bid cover everything, or are there additional hidden costs? A production manager can help answer these and other questions about the publishing process, review costs, and establish an accurate, workable budget.

Costs

Magazines can be expensive or inexpensive depending on the number of copies distributed and the quality of the publication. Because the work that goes into producing a magazine is a substantial part of the cost, the price per copy drops rapidly as the size of the press run grows. Here is a breakdown of the costs involved in publishing a magazine:

Production

Except when dealing with short press runs—less than 30,000 for example—production dollars will dominate all costs. In press runs of several hundred thousand, cost of paper is the biggest item, as much as 60 percent or more of the total budget. As a result, most long-run magazines are printed on standard-size pages to save money.

The cost of large printing jobs varies little among most large, reputable printers. Quoted figures may vary because some printers price items such as stripping and platemaking as options, while others include them as basic costs. Production costs also are influenced by the kind of paper used, the number of pages, size of pages, number of copies and the number of color separations needed for art work. Service and quality will also affect cost.

As in most industrial production, the cost-per-unit for magazines goes down as press runs get longer. At about 500,000 copies, the cost curve becomes almost horizontal. Variable costs versus fixed costs is another way to express volume efficiency. Fixed costs get the first copy of the magazine off the end of the press: creative, administrative, list development, separations, film, stripping, plates, etc. Variable costs are the additional costs of continued press run, including stitching and mailing.

This fixed cost/variable cost concept is important in certain types of cost sharing. For example, a sponsoring company can pay fixed costs, then charge dealers only variable costs. This helps dealers pay for promotional material while the company controls content and its part of the budget.

Postage and Handling

The second largest cost is usually postage (depending on method of distribution), but it is often overlooked in initial plans. Third-class bulk mail, used by the majority of sponsored publications, will cost a minimum of 12.5 cents per magazine at current rates. In addition, it costs another penny to label, tie, sort and bag for the post office.

Creative

In both editorial and art, there are two costs: outside purchases and staff production. A large number of custom-published magazines buy some articles, photographs and artwork from outside suppliers, partly because it is more efficient than producing everything in-house and partly to take advantage of a variety of talents. A typical magazine may pay between $200 and $1,000 for an article.

How much creative time does it take to put out a magazine? Again, it's going to depend on the size and quality of the magazine. A 32-page monthly magazine that uses about eight stories with some photos for each, but doesn't get into in-depth, investigative editorial material and whose literary standards are positioned somewhere between the *New Yorker* and your basic club bulletin probably will require a full-time editor and a half-time artist. There are magazines with heavy emphasis on graphics where the ratio would be reversed. Magazines need research, secretarial and clerical support, too.

Administrative

This is another cost often overlooked. With a custom-published magazine there is invariably administrative time spent by the sponsor. Someone must set marketing direction, monitor editorial material, approve copy through channels and monitor production.

Miscellaneous Costs

There are always costs to be planned for, such as libel insurance in case someone whose name or photo appears decides to sue. Correspondence generated by the magazine will require substantial administrative and secretarial time even if it's viewed as a plus for the magazine's image.

Total Cost Guidelines

The way to estimate magazine costs more precisely is to sit down with people whose business it is to do just that. Talk with someone who has extensive publishing experience, especially with custom-published magazines, to find out what all the options and costs are before you begin to figure out the bottom line.

Are custom-published magazines for everybody? Probably not. Here are some questions to answer before deciding if they're right for your company or organization:

- How important is repeat business to maintain a profitable volume or keep membership levels high?
- How important is it to maintain contact between sales?
- Can your staff locate sources of probable future business or membership for building a mailing list as well as for follow-up calls?
- Can you expect higher sales volume from more frequent calls on potential customers or members?
- Is your company's sales force already overloaded with more customers and prospects than can be served satisfactorily?
- Does your company line include several distinctively different major products as opposed to several similar products? (Special alloys are similar products; sheets, plates and beams are different products for a steel company.)
- Are your products sold in more markets than you can effectively reach with purchased advertising within your budget?
- Do you have potentially profitable fringe markets whose chief buyers could be contacted for less than it costs to run a standard advertising campaign?
- Does your product line include more minor products than you can afford to advertise adequately in existing publications?
- Could an educational emphasis stimulate your sales volume, using articles on "How to Install," "How to Apply," "How to Service," and so on?
- Do your employees, salespeople, dealers, or jobbers need to be better informed about products and sales methods?
- Does your company sell through exclusive representatives—the kind of people who would appreciate having their names or advertisements appear in a publication going to customers and prospects?

Finding the Money to Launch the Program

New company-sponsored publications, often financed by newly created budgets, sometimes have difficulty getting started because it's hard to justify additional expenditures when corporate belts are being tightened.

A creative manager, however, may discover money is already available in existing budgets. For example, a review of advertising budgets may indicate a magazine should be included as the most efficient, on-target medium for reaching prime customers and prospects without waste.

Public relations budget dollars may be reallocated to sponsor a magazine that functions as the ideal vehicle for "corporate image" articles, new product and service news, and major personnel changes.

A solid case can be made for using the sales promotion budget for a custom-published magazine, especially when the publication promotes local purchases by identifying local retail outlets with imprints or special promotion inserts at less cost than separate mailings. A high-circulation magazine mailed bulk rate may cost only a few cents per copy more than a letter mailed first class.

If research is important, the research budget may be tapped for part of the magazine cost. Surveys can be very effectively and economically conducted, either inserted into the magazine or bound with the rest of its pages.

Corporate communications budgets can reasonably be applied to a magazine. An all-important letter from the chief executive officer is especially significant in the company's own magazine.

In other words, your magazine may require no new dollars, but simply a readjustment of existing budgets. There are two other options for financing the magazine: advertising and cost sharing.

When a magazine can help generate floor traffic for a retailer who sells your product or when it is used as a value-added extra to help sales, the cost of publishing the magazine can be shared with dealers. This report has already discussed the hypothetical mechanics of cost sharing in the sections on distribution and costs.

In addition there are many compelling reasons to consider selling advertising in a custom-published magazine, but some equally compelling ones that may mitigate against it. Theoretically, non-competitive advertising should be beneficial to the sponsored magazine through the revenue generated.

Making a company-sponsored magazine self-liquidating through advertising is a considerable challenge. Consider the high failure rate for ordinary consumer magazines that are designed solely to make money for their publishers, with no mandate to carry a company message. How difficult would it be to sell enough advertising in a magazine designed for something other than pure readership?

It is even more difficult for a custom-published magazine to be competitive because consumer magazines will have additional revenue streams including newsstands sales, paid subscriptions, list rental and book sales to help support the publication.

Remember that sponsored magazines are driven by specific marketing objectives for the sponsoring company. Whether or not some of the costs can be reduced by outside advertising should be a detail in evaluating the overall need for a publication, but not the final decision factor. Even if everything is done right to launch a magazine advertising sales program, most advertisers take a wait-and-see attitude on any new publication.

Does this mean advertising in a custom-published magazine should be discouraged? Yes and no. There are some magazines that sell ads successfully. A great deal depends on the circulation and editorial justification. In-flight magazines are just one example of successful, company-sponsored magazines carrying paid advertising.

However, Webb's experience selling advertising in a wide variety of such publications leads us to recommend a very cautious and realistic appraisal of advertising revenue and cost projections before investing dollars in an ad sales program.

Starting an ad sales program is expensive. In the best situation, only about 50 percent of revenue is returned to finance the cost of the magazine. In addition to the cost of retaining an advertising representative firm, sales commissions generally run about 20 percent, ad agencies get 15 percent of the sale, rate cards and promotions claim another 5 percent and bad debts take another 5 percent.

These considerations will help you decide how to use advertising in your publication:

- Start a company-or association-sponsored magazine only when a clear marketing justification exists.
- In the initial stages, sell paid advertising to your own company's other divisions.
- Establish the publication as a solid marketing tool, obtaining feedback from customers about their interests, level of readership, demographics, etc. Make certain the publication works well for the company before figuring in the costs of selling advertising. Convincing evidence that the publication is proving effective for you is strong sales medicine for outside advertisers.

- Ask potential outside advertisers if they would advertise when the publication is established. Their reactions to page count, frequency, distribution method and content will help you determine the economic feasibility of outside advertising. Be careful, though. "What-if" commitments are a long, long way from signatures on contracts. It may take 10 "what-ifs" to equal one sale.
- Make careful economic projections of cost-versus-income before deciding to sell outside advertising.

  Suppose, after all this, you find your magazine is attractive to advertisers and you are willing to underwrite the costs. How do you capitalize on the potential?
- Hire an experienced advertising sales manager to lead an internal staff; or contract with one or more reputable advertising rep firms with proven results in your field; or work with an established contract publisher who can supply solid advertising sales experience and results along with the complete professional package of creative and print production.

Doing It In-House

In general, establishing a magazine division within your company or association can cost more in time, money and headaches.

Unless a sponsor already has a need for publishing experts on staff, taking the work to a professional contract publisher is a better choice. There are many capable suppliers that can produce travel publications, health, sports and general interest magazines. Outside editors are likely to produce a magazine more efficiently and smoothly than in-house editors because of their experience with the subject matter and relationship with free-lance writers and photographers.

Still, most decisions are not clear-cut. Internal company politics and policies also enter the picture, but here are some things to consider when making a decision:

- Is the magazine viewed as a long-term commitment? If it's not, you'll have to fire or absorb staff members with skills foreign to the company's other operations when you shut it down. It might be better to contract with an outside supplier until the company is ready to make a firm commitment.
- Do current staffers have magazine experience? Public relations specialists have different skills than magazine editors and publication design-

ers. Producing a magazine will probably require hiring full-time publication specialists or contracting for the services.

- Do you have a realistic estimate of the time necessary to prepare the publication for printing? It always seems to involve a great deal more than most people think. Editors, for example, assign stories, write them, do research, gather background information, handle editorial correspondence and coordinate work with art directors and photographers. They also coordinate material with someone responsible for company policy and work with production specialists, printers and sometimes an advertising manager. Let an experienced magazine professional assess the total requirements before someone is assigned to handle the job in spare time.
- Is it cheaper to buy expertise from outside than develop it within? Hiring one or two people to produce a company magazine misses the opportunity to tap a reservoir of expertise provided by a full-time publisher.
- Do the company's politics indicate that an internal editor would be under pressure in the selection or slanting of editorial content from within the company? An outside supplier, dealing with only one highly placed contact at a company, is free of those pressures.
- Will publishing, if handled internally, coordinate well with regular responsibilities? Starting a new division from scratch to produce a magazine takes an astounding amount of administrative time.
- Is there enough management time to oversee an internal staff? This is a cost not usually considered when you begin to total the financial commitments to an internally produced company-sponsored magazine.
- Do you, or someone you might assign, have experience and time to keep the many facets of a publishing operation moving on schedule? Printers' time is tightly scheduled and missing deadlines can be costly. If magazine material is tied to an advertising or promotional campaign, missed deadlines could ruin the entire effort.

PART III

ADVERTISING MANAGEMENT

CHAPTER 38

Choosing and Working with Ad Agencies, PR Firms, and Freelancers

Getting Help

If you are like most advertising managers, you will need to use many outside vendors to get your ad campaign created and implemented. Although some companies have complete in-house advertising departments or even in-house ad agencies, the trend today is to "downsize" or reduce internal staff and buy most of what is needed on the outside. Even those firms with large internal resources buy a lot of services on the outside.

Why do companies go outside? For a number of reasons. First, most of the services required are used only on an occasional basis, for example, photography or illustration. It doesn't make sense to have a full-time person on staff.

Second, as freelancer Eugene A. Hosansky observes, advertising and public relations have a "crisis-lull-crisis rhythm." Things can be slow, then suddenly get busy. During the peak periods, the internal staff becomes overloaded, and freelancers are needed to handle the extra work.

Third, outsiders offer the benefit of a fresh point of view. While staff members gain a superior knowledge of the product and familiarity with the company and its procedures, these can in fact become disadvantages in doing good work. Anyone doing the same thing repeatedly for years tends to repeat himself or herself eventually. Outsiders are not so jaded and bring fresh thinking to marketing problems.

Fourth, there are certain skills which are rewarded so handsomely that a corporation cannot afford to keep such people on staff. A top direct mail copywriter, for example, can earn upwards of $200,000 a year as a freelancer; few copywriting staff jobs pay nearly that amount. Thus, the best talent is sometimes available only at an agency or from freelance resources.

This chapter is written to help you select and work with ad agencies, PR firms, and freelancers.

Is An Ad Agency Right For You?

You probably need an ad agency if:

- You place a lot of newspaper and magazine ads or run a lot of TV and radio commercials.
- Your firm is marketing-driven and needs strategic direction as well as creative implementation of marketing communications ideas.
- You market to several different niche industries or to a broad consumer marketplace.
- You advertise and market aggressively, on a continuous basis, and spend at least $50,000 to $100,000 a year on marketing communications.
- You have a small or nonexistent internal advertising staff and need an outside firm to manage and coordinate advertising activities for you.

You probably don't need an ad agency if:

- You run few or no ads or commercials.
- Most of what you do in marketing consists of producing brochures, data sheets, price lists, and other collateral materials.
- Your management is not marketing-oriented, does not view marketing as an activity that needs to be planned strategically, and prefers a straightforward rather than a creative approach to marketing communications.
- You market to only one or two narrow vertical markets that are small, easy-to-reach, and which you approach mainly through a single vertical publication or a group or association.

- You spend less than $50,000 a year on marketing communications.
- You have a well-staffed advertising department or an in-house advertising agency—with both professional and administrative/clerical staff—capable of handling the planning as well as the day-to-day paperwork of implementing and managing an advertising program.

Some Observations About Ad Agencies

These random observations may be helpful to you in selecting, working with, and understanding the mentality of advertising agencies.

- Agencies come in all shapes and sizes, but most are small, ranging from one or two employees to 40 or 50. Most agencies in suburban locations near local industry probably have between five and 15 employees.

- Many people who work for ad agencies do so because they perceive the business as both creative and glamorous. While the owners and upper managers often understand and appreciate the marketing objectives behind your ad campaign, some of the writers and artists may have as their primary objective the creation of work which is creative, clever, aesthetically pleasing, "stylish," and which wins awards. They are not likely to enjoy working for a client who wants pedestrian advertising or otherwise puts limits on their creative expression.

- Agencies, unlike freelancers and other vendors, provide a single-source service, handling each project from concept to finish. This is a big advantage. It ensures single-source responsibility for getting the project done on time and within budget. The agency, not you, acts as project manager and coordinator. This greatly reduces the administrative and paperwork associated with advertising management, freeing you to concentrate more on creative aspects. With an agency, you're more of a quality control supervisor. When you use freelancers, you take on heavy administrative, coordination, and project management burdens.

- Agencies are not oriented toward project work. Most want to handle all of the advertising for your company, division, product line, or product—not just a brochure here or an ad there. Their reasoning is that it takes so long for them to familiarize themselves with the product and the market that they cannot make a profit handling just one job. Many agencies today, in fact, *will* do a single project for you—but usually to allow a potential client to "sample" their service before assigning an entire account to them. If you tend to have project work rather than ongoing ad campaigns, freelancers might be better for you.

• Agencies are set up primarily to do major ad campaigns—both print and broadcast. For the agency to be enthusiastic about handling your account, at least half of the work you give them should involve preparing and running print ads for magazines and newspapers or commercials for radio and television. Agencies know this work well and are skilled at it. They will probably do a good job for you, giving you a fresh, original approach more different and arresting than you would have thought of on your own. And, because they make money placing the ads or buying air time on your behalf, their fees for the actual production work—copy, design, photography—will be reasonable (though not inexpensive).

• Agencies are *not* oriented toward other marketing communications. Their writers and artists are unenthusiastic about producing your brochure, catalog, manual, or data sheet. And the accounting and billing procedures used by agencies make having such materials produced by them an expensive proposition. Many clients routinely have their collateral materials produced by agencies when it would be more cost-effective and better for all parties concerned to use internal resources or freelancers.

• As with most professional service providers, advertising agencies are paid on the basis of materials produced, not results achieved. This system encourages advertising agencies to advise their clients to do more advertising, regardless of whether this is in fact the most profitable course of action for the client. An independent marketing consultant, on the other hand, gets paid to render objective advice, not run or create ads. Such a consultant may, at times, give you a more realistic appraisal of the efficiency of your marketing communications, actually advising you to do *less* space advertising rather than more. That's a recommendation you'll rarely get from your agency.

• Agencies would rather do big jobs than little jobs. They would rather run ads in *Newsweek* than *Sludge Journal;* and they prefer to create four-color one and two-page ads rather than tiny black-and-white fractional ads. When an agency gets a 15 percent commission every time an ad or commercial runs, the tendency is to tell the client to run lots of ads and commercials—and to run full-page ad that costs $10,000 ($1,500 commission) rather than a quarter-page ad that costs $3,000 ($450 commission).

• What about getting help with strategy and planning? Agencies are more oriented to handling this type of work than they were a decade or so ago. In years past, the agency was simply a place where ads were made, type was set, and insertion orders were typed up. Today, many agencies seek—and can offer—a more active role in helping clients plan marketing and advertising strategy. Yet too few clients take advantage of these services or see their agencies in the role of advisor. If you need strategic guidance and not just implementation, it's probably better to retain an agency or consultant than to rely solely on freelancers and other vendors.

A Seven-Point Checklist for Ad Agency Selection

Stan Merritt, president of Stan Merritt Advertising, New York, provides the following advice on selecting an ad agency.

1. First and foremost, look at your needs and budget. What do you want an agency to accomplish? How much do you have to spend? When you've determined the services you really need—after eliminating the obvious fluff and ego-building departments you'll probably never use—get a firm grip on your actual promotion dollars (not the funds you hope you'll get but probably won't). Look at your company through the eyes of the potential agency.

With what you have to spend, will your account be significant to the agency? For example, if you choose an agency with $300 million in billings, and you have $3 million to spend, you'll get 3/300th or 1 percent of the agency's creativity, effort, and concentration. That $3 million may look big to you. But how will it be viewed by a potential agency? And, what happens if you only have a million dollars to spend—or even half a million or less?

It's not just in the cards for a small account in a large agency to expect mroe than a sliver of the time of the expensive management of that agency. What a small accounts receives is a wafer-thin slice of a creative person, a few minutes from a marketing person, a quick hello from the $125,000 creative director, and a quicker, but firmer, handshake from the $200,000-a-year president. In sum, a million-dollar account doesn't belong in a $50 million agency, no matter what the agency promises in any presentation. It just doesn't make dollars and sense.

2. Look carefully at the agencies whose billings would get a significant boost from your business. See how much compatibility really exists between the people you'd be working with on a day-to-day basis and yourself.

After an initial meeting, seriously analyze the personalities involved and, above all, trust your gut reaction. Remember, you met them on their best behavior—they won't get any better as time goes on. Unless you can honestly say, "I can live with those people," keep looking elsewhere.

3. Ask yourself, "Will I be paying for services I don't need?" Branch offices are terrific, but if they don't help you, you shouldn't be paying for services that benefit another account. It's difficult enough to justify the services you do require.

4. If you decide that a smaller agency meets your needs and budget, is the agency small because the principals like the intimacy of a smaller group and the chance to work closely with clients? Or, is it an agency that is small because it's staffed by small people with small aspirations?

5. Analyze the agency's clients. Is the quality of their business and service comparable to yours? When your product is quality and the agency's clients are shlock, do you want to be in their company?

6. Check for conflicts, accounts that would directly compete with yours. And check the agency's financial stability, duration of business, and likelihood of staying in business for at least the next five years.

7. Once having winnowed the choice of agency to a possible one, pay for a look at the kind of work they do.

Ask for and pay for a campaign that will show how the agency copes with your company's situation. The work they did for others may give a vague feeling of reassurance, but they'll probably never show you the ads that failed, only those that worked or at least look good even if they didn't work.

If you think the agency might be right for you, spend a little money and have your assumptions confirmed before you make a major commitment.

There are also some *don'ts* to keep in mind in agency selection. Avoid these reasons for choosing an agency:

- Don't pick an agency as a crutch or to boost you or your superior's ego. The potted palms, gorgeous secretaries, and innovative decor have nothing to do with the effectiveness that the advertising produces.
- Don't forget that the buck stops with you. The agency will perform only as well as you let it.

The best thing for any businessperson's ego is to see his company's profits soar. The right agency can make a real contribution to the cause. The wrong one will provide an incredible financial and emotional drain, benefitting you little if at all.

As a marketing person, you should look at every decision analytically, not emotionally. Don't select an advertising agency any differently.

More Tips on Ad Agency Selection

In addition to Stan Merritt's comments, here are a few more thoughts on selecting an ad agency.

- Examine their portfolio carefully. Take a close look at the work. Most agencies quickly flip through portfolio cases showing samples at their presentation. Ask them to send you copies (photocopies are fine) of some of the more interesting pieces so you can read them at your leisure and get a feel for their copy style and creative approach. The work should be studied carefully, not casually, as is usually done.

- Select an agency whose style and creative approach is "in sync" with yours. That is, you should like their work and feel it's the type of work you'd like to get. Don't pick an agency whose style doesn't fit yours, or whose approach you don't like, thinking that they can simply create work in any style you specify. Agencies all have styles and cannot easily switch on command. For instance, an agency that does hard-sell mail order copy is not the right agency to handle your high-class, image-oriented corporate ad campaign. When you see an agency's work, realize that the work they do for *you* will have a similar quality and flavor to the materials already in their portfolio.

- If you need strategic assistance, marketing planning, or want an agency that is more of an advisor than just an "ad maker," select an agency with experience and expertise in your industry. There's much debate whether it's better to hire a general agency or an agency that specializes in direct response, financial services, industrial advertising, hi-tech, fashion, or whatever. Both the general and the specialized agency probably can turn out first-rate work on your account. But the specialized agency can get "up to speed" faster, because they work in your industry on a daily basis. Which means they know the market, the competition, and the media. Also, the specialized agency is more likely to be able to provide marketing advice and guidance based on a thorough knowledge of your business. A general agency will have to learn from you, rather than be able to teach you. On the flip side, general agencies may offer a fresh approach, while specialized agencies may be giving you versions of campaigns done for past clients (not necessarily a negative if the campaign works).

- Many agencies today push desktop publishing, computer graphics, and other in-house computer capabilities as a competitive advantage. Are they? It depends. If your primary need is for print ad campaigns and TV commercials, having computers in-house is a nice plus but hardly a major reason to choose the agency. On the other hand, if you produce a lot of printed materials—data sheets, price lists, manuals—then it may be important that your agency have a desktop publishing system or at least a computer system compatible with your own computers.

• As Stan Merritt observed, personal chemistry is important. You should meet not only with agency president and account executive but all the people who you (and your staff) will deal with on a daily basis. If the copywriter is a snob who hates talking to clients, and your advertising is copy-driven, you're going to have problems.

• Make a list of services you require from your agency and check to see whether the agency currently provides these services to its clients. The agency you choose should *already* offer these services as standard; beware of the agency who says "We don't do it but if you give us the account, we'll get someone who can." You want to hire an agency with all the services, equipment, staff, and procedures you need already in place.

• Small agencies can be good, but that does not always mean that a large agency always treats small accounts with minimal service. Some large agencies have divisions or subsidiaries created specifically for smaller accounts. Others are set up to handle such accounts profitably and welcome the smaller advertiser.

• On the flip side, a small agency may not have the resources to handle a large account. They may lack computer resources, media buying clout, specialized departments, staff, office space, secretarial support, and even the cash flow required to lay out money for art, printing, production, and media. Don't pick an agency that would be overwhelmed by the size and complexity of your account.

• Do not ask agencies to do speculative campaigns. Typically, an advertiser picks a number of agencies and says, "It's between you and three other agencies. Do a campaign for us and show us how you work, and"—and this part sometimes goes unspoken—"we don't expect to pay you for this effort." Because advertising is such a competitive business, and many agencies are desperate for work, you can probably get them to do these spec campaigns for you. But don't. Instead, do as Stan Merritt advises—pick *one* agency you like, have them do a campaign (or initial test project), and *pay their full fee* for the work. This is the only fair test. Spec campaigns usually produce work that is colorful, wildly creative, and—because the agencies have no access to the proper information and are not being compensated to do the careful planning and research that normally precedes ad preparation—totally off base. A reputable agency may meet with you and prepare a cost estimate or proposal at no charge, but it will not engage in spec work.

• Contrary to conventional industry practices, there's no reason why you have to "give your account" to any agency you feel you'd like to work with. Instead give them a few projects or put them to work on a special assignment or portion of your account. Or retain them, but for a six or 12-month trial period. Test them out. Sample their work—and the working relationship. This is the best way to see if things will work out.

How To Locate Advertising Agencies

Finding advertising agencies is not at all difficult. If you are the advertising manager of a sizable firm, you undoubtedly get many phone calls, mailing pieces, and other solicitations from local ad agencies seeking your business. If not, you can ask colleagues, competitors, and space representatives from the media to recommend some agencies. Or, consult the local Yellow Pages or *The Standard Directory of Advertising Agencies* (see *Resource* section at end of chapter). This book lists 4,400 advertising agencies in alphabetical order and is indexed by city and state. Each listing gives the agency's name, address, phone number, specialties (if any), number of employees, year founded, billings (gross income), breakdown of billings by media, key personnel, and major accounts.

Working with Your Agency

Who's responsible for the up-front planning of the marketing campaign? According to a special report published by Starmark, Inc. and *Business Marketing,* only 20 percent of companies rely on their advertising agencies to assist with the internal planning function. Yet many of these marketers say they would like the agency to be *more* involved with planning.

Why aren't agencies more involved in planning? According to the survey, some 40 percent of top marketers regard their agencies's planning expertise to be only fair to poor. Other areas ranked "fair to poor" include account service, cost control, and the match of the size of the agency to the size of the client.

Most of these answers agree with common-sense observation. As stated earlier, while there is an ongoing debate between whether to select a general or specialized ad agency, one-fifth of the clients surveyed clearly feel their agencies do *not* have enough experience in their specialized industries.

Table 38.1. Clients' complaints about ad agency performance.

According to the Starmark report, the most common complaints marketers had about ad agencies:

Lack of industry experience	20 percent
High costs/lack of structure	15 percent
Inability to listen	8 percent
Tendency to overact	6 percent
Slow response	4 percent
Unqualified employees	2 percent
Undefined objectives	1 percent

Also not surprising is that *cost* is the second-biggest complaint. Unfortunately, professional advertising services are expensive, yet many clients are not sophisticated enough, knowledgeable enough, or operationally able to track advertising results and link them to sales and profits. As a result, many business executives feel they are spending a huge amount of money with their ad agency, and getting no tangible result in return.

Slow response is a not a big problem, cited by only 4 percent of the client surveyed. This too is not surprising. Whatever their faults, agencies are known for their willingness to "jump through hoops" and meet impossible client deadlines. However, agencies may be mistaken in their willingness to do so. Good work takes time to conceive and create. Rushing the agency usually produces a mediocroe result, puts a strain on their employees, and results in substantial overtime charges for the client from printers and other vendors. The shame of this is that it's unnecessary: most client deadlines are artificial, and there's no reason why due dates can't be set to allow the agency the time it needs to do the job right.

The survey also revealed the clients wanted to see the following from their agencies:

- Stronger creative, adapted to specific selling strategies.
- More in-depth media review and more integration of media strategies with planning objectives.
- More market research services tailored to specific client needs.
- Increased telemarketing and direct mail services.
- Stronger inquiry qualification methods and more creative solutions to inquiry follow-up.
- More in-house capabilities such as photography and typesetting as a means of improved cost control.

- More cost flexibility, such as more modestly priced services for smaller projects.

Some Additional Tips on Working with Your Agency

Account Executives

Your agency will assign an account executive to handle your account and serve as liaison between you and the rest of the agency's staff. Matters of planning, scheduling, coordination, and administration should always be dealt with through your account executive; the creative director or media buyer is not authorized to give cost estimates or agree to delivery dates. However, make clear that you welcome direct contact from agency staff on matters pertaining to the work at hand (for example, the copywriter can call you directly if he needs more information about the product).

The account executive function was created to prevent chaos and to provide a smooth, efficient mechanism for a client to communicate with its agency. And for the most part, it works. But don't be ruled by it. In situations where direct contact between you and people within the agency would be more efficient, encourage that direct contact. Let the copywriter, media planner, traffic manager, and art director know they can contact you directly.

Make Experts Accessible

Others within your company will have to function as "sources of information" for your agency. Product managers, engineers, quality control managers, designers, research scientists, and others have first-hand knowledge of facts that may be vital to the success of the ad campaign.

Whenever possible, encourage these people to have direct communication with the agency. The briefing will be more accurate and take less time. If the information is passed on from the engineer to you, from you to the account executive, from the account executive to the creative director, and from the creative director to the copywriter, much will be lost in the translation. Far better to have your engineer and copywriter speak directly.

Responsiveness

You and the account executive must establish how rapidly you expect the agency to respond to requests and problems. Some veteran account executive feel the account executive should always get back to the client within *one hour,* regardless of whether he was in the office, traveling on business, or on vacation. It is reasonable to expect someone from the agency to return and acknowledge your call within a few hours. This is part of the extra service you're paying agency rates for.

Conference Reports

Conference reports are reports written by the account executive and distributed to the client and agency staff after each client/agency meeting. The report summarizes what was said in the meeting and what actions, plans, and projects were initiated, if any.

Most agencies generate such reports not for the benefit of the client but to create a written record and protect themselves if a misunderstanding or disagreement about what was said arises later on. If you're an agency, and you have reason to need such protection, conference reports are probably a good idea. If you're a client, unless you really read and like getting call reports, they're a waste of paper and money (even if you aren't billed directly for them, the account executive's time is valuable, and believe me, you're paying for it in your overall monthly bill). If you don't read the call reports, save time and money by instructing your agency that you don't want them.

Meetings

Meetings can take place in the agency's offices or the client's. Account executives typically travel to the client's office to meet with the advertising manager and his or her staff to discuss ongoing business once a week or less frequently. New campaigns can be presented either at the agency or client offices, depending on the preferences of the parties.

Although many agencies don't give you a bill for the account executive's time spent in meetings and travel with you, this cost is factored into the overall fees you pay. You can do business more efficiently by reducing the number of meetings and doing more by phone and fax. The agency will likely pass some of the savings on to you and keep some as profit. Even the latter is beneficial, since the more profit the agency is making on your account, the better the treatment you'll get.

Cost Estimates

Let your agency know that small, incidental items, such as getting prints of a photograph or reprinting 500 copies of a price list, can be done without the need for you to approve the fee or review a cost estimate. Making the agency do a written cost estimate or proposal and get approval for mundane tasks which they'd rather not handle, make little or no profit on, and do for you only as a service, is counter-productive to the relationship. If you're uncomfortable giving your agency a blank check, establish a minimum expenditure above which they must get your approval. This could be $1,000 or $3,000 or any figure you're comfortable with.

For projects that are still routine but more expensive—say, producing a new ad or mailer—tell the agency you want to approve the cost estimate before they proceed. This will prevent unpleasant surprises. The estimate can be oral or in writing.

For major projects that require management approval—a new brochure, catalog, or trade show booth—get a detailed estimate in writing which you can circulate to the appropriate executives for their okay.

Establish with the agency how precise you expect estimates to be. Keep in mind that in the early stages, before the project has been conceptualized and formulated, it's difficult for the agency to provide a firm, to-the-penny projection of what the job will cost. For instance, how can the agency tell you a brochure will cost $35,890 when you don't know what size, how many colors, how many pages, or how many photographs it will contain?

One common solution is to get estimates with a "contingency," typically 10 percent. This means that the estimate is accurate, plus or minus 10 percent. Thus, a $20,000 job with a 10 percent contingency can cost anywhere from $18,000 to $22,000. Keep in mind that jobs estimated on a contingency usually end up costing the top fee and sometimes the middle fee, but almost never come in at *below* the original estimate. Agencies tend to estimate on the low side because they're afraid a high estimate will prevent them from getting the job (which is often true).

Haggling

A common tendency of smaller clients or clients with limited budgets is to haggle. That is, when the agency presents an estimate for a job, the client protests it's too expensive and they can't afford it—in the hopes the agency will lower the price.

Occasionally, you will feel a fee is more than you can or should be asked to pay; by all means, raise the issue with your account executive. But don't become a chronic haggler. Agencies dislike such clients and cannot make a profit on them. They may keep you as a client, but a minimum of time will be spent on your account.

Many clients think they're smart because they consistently get ad agencies, printers, electricians, and service providers of all types to lower their prices. But that's not smart. A smart client knows that his ad agency (or any other service firm) will only serve him enthusiastically and happily if they are making a profit. Smart clients go out of their way to make sure agencies, vendors, freelancers, and others are making a decent profit. They know that the vendor who is getting paid well gives the best effort.

If the price is too high, don't try to get your agency to do the same work for a lower fee. Instead, redesign the project so it costs less. For instance, instead of a four-color, 12-page brochure, do a two-color, eight-page brochure. Instead of five new ads do three ads. And so on.

Compensation

Most agencies today charge a 15 percent commission for placing ads and get an additional fee for the preparation of TV commercials, print ads, brochures, and other materials. Many agencies have hourly rates established for each function at each level (e.g., different hourly rates for account supervisors versus account managers, media planners versus media buyers, copy supervisors, versus copywriters, etc.) and can supply you with a copy.

Other agencies maintain detailed job cost records on computer, which yield averages of what clients can expect to pay for color ads, black-and-white ads, direct mail pieces, and other common assignments. Make a list of typical projects and ask your agency to give you a rough range (not an exact cost estimate) for each category.

Payment

Prompt payment of agency invoices can rapidly put you at the top of their "favorite client" list. Slow payments from clients cause severe cash flow problems, especially in smaller agencies, and have even put some agencies out of business. Agencies are expert in finding creative solutions to marketing problems, yet their corporate clients—who, for the most part, are far wealthier, with far greater cash reserves—expect the poor agencies to act as their bankers. When your agency lays out $100,000 to the media, and you take six months to pay their invoices, you're asking them to give you an interest-free loan for six months. Once they pay overhead and salaries, the commissions they get hardly justify the effort.

The agency business is such that most agencies shell out a tremendous amount of money up front—or incur large indebtedness on behalf of their clients—to printers, typesetters, media, and other vendors. Pay your bills promptly, or consider paying the media and other vendors directly. Do not use ad agency "cash floats" to your advantage. It's wrong and unethical.

Conflicts of Opinion

Because the creation and approval of advertising campaigns hinge on subjective judgment, there are bound to be conflicts of opinion between clients and agencies. This is natural. As Brian Cohen, CEO of Technology Solutions notes, "When clients and agencies meet, it's to discuss important things, and so there are going to be strong opinions and differences." How you handle these differences sets the tone for the client/agency relationship.

In an ideal world, agencies are the total experts on advertising and clients always defer to agency judgement because the agency is always right. Sadly, in the real world, such is not the case. This will be discussed more fully in Chapter 39, "Managing Creativity."

Nonadvertising Tasks

Use your advertising agency when you need advertising. Don't have them print business cards, design letterhead, get folders produced, or typeset price lists. Printers, freelance graphic artists, and other vendors should be used to handle more routine tasks that do not require great creativity or ingenuity and would therefore be inappropriate as an agency assignment. As one advertising executive puts it, "Don't use a machine gun when the jobs calls for a water pistol." Agencies are geared toward handling major advertising projects and should not be assigned routine work that's more efficiently and less expensively done elsewhere.

Rights

When you pay an agency for an ad or photograph, do you own the rights to the work for all time? You'd think so. But there's some debate here. Photographers, for example, will tell you that when you hire them to take a photograph for your new ad or catalog, you're buying rights to use that picture in a specific medium aimed at a particular market for a specified period of time. You're not getting all rights or the photo itself. So when you want to put that picture in next year's catalog, you may find yourself facing a photographer who wants to bill you (or your agency) a hefty fee for the additional usage.

In the same way, there has been a recent debate in the copywriting field about whether clients or freelance writers own the copyright to the work. You would think that if a client pays a freelancer $5,000 to write a direct mail package, the client owns the rights. But articles in *Who's Mailing What?* and other industry publications say the copyright may very well belong to the writer.

As a client, you want to make sure you're buying all rights. You might have the agency sign a blanket agreement to this effect or put this wording in all your purchase orders; consult your attorney for details. The key point is to make clear that you are buying all rights to the work. This is what most clients *think* they are getting when they hire an agency or a freelancer, and so this is what they should get. Make sure you do.

Improving the Client/Agency Relationship

Why is it important to have a good working relationship with your ad agency? Because advertising, unlike, say, dentistry, medicine, or home repair, is a *team* effort. Your dentist doesn't need your help in filling your cavity: He can do it on his own quite nicely. But your ad agency *does* require your cooperation to create good advertising for you. Not only do they depend on you for all the background information needed to write and design the ad, but they cannot proceed without your approval at every step.

How do you improve the agency/client relationship? Here are four suggestions: First, determine what you're looking for in an agency. This refers to quality of work and service, prices, philosophy, and attitude. For instance, do you want an agency that will simply comply with your orders, meekly accepting all your dictates? Or do you want fighters who will stand up for what is right, even if it means risking your wrath? (You may legitimately want the former or the latter. The important thing is to choose one or the other.)

Next, choose the right ad agency—one whose work is in sync with what you're looking for, and whose employees are people you can get along with. Most problems occur because the relationship should not have been established in the first place.

Third, provide leadership which encourages excellence and allows for intelligent risk-taking. Don't impose unnecessary restrictions, unworkable budgets, unrealistic deadlines, or rules that prevent effective work from being created. Give your agency the freedom to do good work; but be clear enough about what you want so they don't waste your money creating unrealistic materials that won't be approved or run.

Finally, use the most potent phrase in the motivational manager's vocabulary: thank you. Make sure everyone on the agency team receives your personal thanks from time to time for jobs exceptionally well done. Creative people thrive on praise, but seldom receive it. Most client communications are to request revisions or voice complaints—things which *de*-motivate rather than motivate. A simple thank-you is a profitable investment in a good agency/client relationship.

The Myth of Full Service

The term "full service" is used to designate an advertising agency that provides a broad gamut of advertising services, as opposed to design studios, freelancers, "creative boutiques," and other vendors offering a limited or specialized service. Typically, a full-service advertising agency provides all of the services you need—marketing, planning, copy, art, photography, illustration, production, media buying, account management, market research—under one roof. The advantage to the advertiser is that the agency manages the project, eliminating the need for the advertising manager to hire multiple vendors and manage their various activities.

If you want a full-service ad agency, by all means hire one. But don't get too caught up with "full service." Many agencies that promote themselves as full service don't do all the activities in-house; they hire freelancers and other vendors to do things like write copy, take pictures, or set type. Some agencies make it clear to clients this is what they're doing; others attempt to conceal the use of subcontractors, or keep it low key.

But with the trend toward "downsizing" and the proliferation of independent contractors in all business service areas, few full service agencies really are. For instance, even the biggest agencies buy much of their printing in-house, and virtually all hire freelance directors to direct national TV commercials for their major clients. Full-service doesn't really mean that the agency has all the capability in-house anymore; it means the agency will provide a total package to the client, encompassing all of the services required.

As the years go by, your needs may change. For instance, when you first hired your agency, you didn't think desktop publishing was important; now, you do. Should you fire the agency and get a new one, simply because your current agency does not use desktop publishing? Probably not. Keep in mind that the services your agency does not provide in-house can easily be purchased by them or by you from independent contractors. Don't insist they have a capability, piece of equipment, or specialized employee in-house unless it's clearly in your and their best interest to do so. (And let them be the judge of this.)

Agency Reviews

Some advertisers periodically hold "agency reviews." This consists of asking their current agency plus four or five potential new agencies to make a pitch for their business based on a new campaign, often prepared on a speculative or low-pay basis. The message to the current agency is that they must produce better work or lose the account. The lure to the new agencies is that if they do a superior job, they will replace the current agency.

Do not conduct agency reviews. If your current agency is not performing to your satisfaction and you wish to continue the relationship, explain precisely what is wrong. Tell them the changes you want (be specific) and give them an opportunity to make those corrections. If the relationship is beyond saving, fire the agency and get a new one according to the procedures described earlier.

But do not hold agency reviews. They're unfair to the new agencies, because the new agencies rarely have a fair chance to win the business and are thus being exploited. Agency reviews are also insulting to the existing agency—if they have your business, they have your business, and they don't want to compete for an account that's already theirs. Even if they win, the agency review is likely to leave a bitter taste that sours the relationship.

Handling Public Relations

The first question to answer is, "Should public relations (PR) and advertising be handled by separate agencies?" The answer depends on several factors:

1. Do you handle both advertising and PR, or is PR handled by another manager within your firm? If you are responsible for both, you may want to buy both services from a single source. If PR is a separate function, it's likely that your PR manager will choose the agency he feels will best serve him, which may or may not be your ad agency.

2. Does your ad agency also do PR? Some do, and some don't. If yours offers PR services, you can certainly put them on your list of potential PR firms. If they don't, go elsewhere. Don't ask them to do something they're not set up to do.

3. How important is it to you to get advertising and PR from a single source? The advantage of getting both from one vendor is that it eliminates the need to brief and deal with multiple suppliers. If you use separate firms, you have to spend a lot of time educating both your PR and your advertising account executives about your business, strategies, products, technology, and so forth.

On the other hand, many ad agencies offer PR services but are not as expert and are not comparable to firms that specialize in PR. It may be worth the extra effort having a separate PR firm if they get better results.

Finding a PR Firm

As with advertising agencies, finding a PR firm is not at all difficult. If you're an advertising manager with a sizable firm, many PR firms will approach you each month seeking your business. You can also consult colleagues and the yellow pages, or look up local PR firms in directories such as *O'Dwyer's Directory of Public Relations Firms* (see the *Resources* section at end of chapter). This book lists approximately 1,700 PR firms including their addresses, phone numbers, key executives, number of employees, and areas of specialization.

Selecting a PR Firm

Here are 10 questions to consider when selecting a PR firm. (Reprinted with permission from "The Ten Most Commonly Asked Questions About Public Relations," Smith & Shows, Menlo Park, CA).

1. *What can public relations do for me and my company?* Professional and well-programmed public relations creates market awareness, establishes a position, builds and reinforces credibility for a company, its management, and products over an agreed upon and pre-determined period of time.

The public relations professional accomplishes these objectives by talking to your intended marektplace through the media—newspapers, business and trade publications, and various broadcast avenues. The PR firm sets strategic goals and controlled, consistent program objectives.

2. *How much will a good PR program cost?* Typically, a public relations budget for a manufacturing company will run about 20 percent of the established advertising budget—but that rule may vary depending on the tasks to be accomplished.

One rule of thumb is that the broader the company marketing objectives (the broader the product lines or types of messages—recruitment, investor, original equipment manufacturers, dealers, consumers), the more costly the program.

Using a PR firm simply to introduce a product, for example, will cost between $8,000 and $40,000 depending on the size of the press community to be addressed and the nature of the product to be introduced.

3. *What am I paying for?* Time, contacts, and results are all any PR agency has to sell. The more important the project or marketing problem you have to solve, the more time and contacts are required to produce results. An agency's time will be used to create a plan of action, consult with you about each step of the process, write materials, contact the many reporters and editors of newspapers, magazines, trade publications, broadcast outlets and your own target audiences directly as well. Time is required to gather approvals from your management, groom your spokespeople, take descriptive photographs, analyze editorial opportunities, and so on.

Because the business of public relations is a fairly technical process, your PR firm should be experienced and comfortable with all the many segments of that process.

4. *How can I measure results?* While there are very formal procedures for measuring communication program results—awareness studies, publication studies, secondary research data, and so on—the results of PR programs can be evident without such expense.

You must be prepared to track and monitor leads that come into the company. Many of them are inspired by an article or news announcement. Beyond that, read the publications pertaining to your market to see if you're included in them. Listen to your market, your employees, your investors, your prospective employees and customers. What are they saying about you? If a trend is developing, your PR program is working. If the message is negative, your PR program needs to be strengthened or more strategically directed.

5. *How can I tell if I'm getting my money's worth?* If you've set clear objectives with your PR firm, you will know approximately in four months whether your program is giving you value.

If the objective was to determine a position for your company and a positioning study and consultation has taken place and an appropriate, acceptable position has been agreed upon, your objective has been met.

If the objective was to be visible in three key publications which speak to your prospective customers, and your message was carried in those publications in a given time period, that objective has been met.

And if your objective was to educate an audience about a particular feature of your product through a sales seminar, and that seminar took place with good attendance and feedback, that objective was met.

Objectives must be targeted realistically. *Business Week,* for example, is one of the most difficult publications to penetrate and has very specific information criteria that interests the editors. Achieving such an objective depends on both strong news and plenty of time to develop a relationship between your company, its story and growth, and the publication editors.

After six months or a year, you can review your PR plan and determine how many of the objectives set out in the plan have been met.

6. *Should I use an outside agency or an in-house PR person?* The broader and more complex your program objectives, the better chance you'll have of accomplishing them if you use an agency with extensive contacts and the system in place to produce your press materials.

Many companies will use an in-house PR person to write or handle the voluminous details and coordination work required in a good PR program, leaving the press contact up to an outside PR firm. Because the PR firm has multiple clients, and multiple reasons to talk with members of the press every day, that relationship can be leveraged for each client, providing many more opportunities for press exposure.

Whether you determine to use an in-house professional, or an outside agency, or a combination of both, it is important to realize that creating and following a strong strategic PR plan as your company emerges and grows is essential. A good PR plan begins the day your company opens its doors and drives the visibility campaign on a consistent basis ever afterward.

7. *If I use an outside agency, will I have the attention of top agency management?* You should make certain your relationship with the agency gives you access to the principals or top management when necessary. Typically, an account is managed by an account manager or account executive. Upper management will be called in during the strategic planning phases of the program, and for the extensive personal press contacts that may not be available to less experienced PR professionals. Conversely, the more mechanical day-to-day functions such as production or event coordination may be assigned to an agency support person such as an assistant.

8. *How will I know what kind of a program is best for me?* A general session with your agency will help you focus on the market challenges and opportunities to be addressed in your PR program. A plan will be designed with specific objectives based on those realities.

9. *How should I select an agency?* Do some homework first in order to cut down on the number of agencies you want to see. Talk with your peers, your competitors, and most importantly, the press. If you think a particular company of your size has a good PR program, find out what PR firm they are using.

Prospective agencies should have experience in reaching your markets, understanding your types of products, and have a good solid reputation with the press.

Select up to five agencies to meet with. Any more than that will prove confusing to you. Look for strategic planning, strong press contacts, and a sense of a well-managed company in this first meeting.

Select two finalists and meet with them at their offices. Meet the people who will be working on your account, particularly the account manager in charge of it. Look for creativity, leadership ability, and chemistry between yourself and the account team. If you haven't a sense of confidence in your account team, you'll never be comfortable that the agency is doing the best job for you, no matter how good its reputation or results may be.

10. *How can I, as a client, make sure the PR program is successful?* One critical concept to understand is that PR is a deadline-driven business—daily and hourly deadlines as well as weekly and monthly. Respecting that reality is a key to making your PR program work.

Here are some very simple rules:

- Trust your agency's advice and recommendations.
- Give your account team all the information it requires and the time to develop a solid program and press materials for you.
- Keep the agency informed about all new or changing situations. It should know as quickly as you do about production schedule changes, new management additions, etc.
- Be realistic. *Business Week* really isn't for everyone. Don't insist that your PR firm "get you in" *The Wall Street Journal* when (a) there's nothing about your company that would interest *The Wall Street Journal,* (b) getting in *The Wall Street Journal* really wouldn't benefit your company all that much, and (c) you want to reach chemical engineers and so the right publications for you are *Chemical Engineering* and *Chemical Engineering Progress.*
- Be accessible. Many valuable opportunities are lost because an executive doesn't bother to return a phone call and a publication deadline passes by.
- If you have a concern, call your account supervisor as quickly as you recognize your concern. Allowing the situation to wait may mean it never gets resolved.

- Pay your bills promptly. Few agencies are large enough to exist on 60-to 90-day pay cycles. Work might be halted just as a big break is developing because your accounts payable department has assumed the PR agency's bill isn't that important.

Don Levin, president of Levin Public Relations, offers the following additional tips.

Chances are the first thing you'll do in your search for a firm is ask a few friends for recommendations. Ninety percent of Levin PR's new business approaches them based on the word of others. But don't rule out the firm that contacts you. Instead, learn from them. Review their materials; save the information that might help you make a decision about their firm. Take them up on a free consultation meeting if you have something to gain from their knowledge. Three excellent client relationships of Levin PR's developed out of one phone call Don made over four years ago.

Paying for PR

The most effective method of paying for PR is with incentives. Motivate the PR firm to give their all. The worst arrangement is a flat monthly fee without accountable staff charges or time statements. This invites the PR firm to spend as little time as possible on the account and to generate minimal acceptable results.

The best method of payment is a minimum monthly fee against time/action statements plus the incentive for additional productive work through additional payments. The PR firm will then be driven to pursue more useful work. Be sure to indicate a ceiling beyond which written consent is required for additional work and payment. This will protect you against excessive charges and ensure that the ongoing work is well under control before your firm creates new projects.

Managing PR Services

Expect a flow of exciting ideas. Ensure continual access to top management and feedback from them. Make sure your PR firm is operating according to your own agenda, not their own. Pat them on the back when they deserve it.

Test them. Make a little mistake on purpose and see if they pick it up. Be sure they offer constructive advice and criticism, not just serve as "yes men."

Choosing Between Big and Small

Use a big firm when you need instant national and international service or a wide variety of highly experienced specialists (e.g., in SEC regulation or environmental law). Large firms have the most diverse resources.

But when you want a general public relations program on a limited budget, a smaller firm may be better suited to your needs. Remember that regardless of size, you are actually hiring only one account manager and some helpers.

Levin reports that one small PR firm is getting frequent projects (some elementary, some sophisticated) from a company that already has a big PR firm. Why? The big firm has a junior account manager coordinating client work. He doesn't really know or use his own firm's resources, but enormous overhead forces the large firm to be costly.

Freelancers, Consultants, Independent Vendors, and Self-Employed Professionals

From time to time, you may want to hire a variety of self-employed professionals and small service firms providing services to advertising managers and their companies. These include:

- Copywriters
- Graphic artists
- Photographers
- Illustrators
- Desktop publishers
- Computer service bureaus
- Copy editors
- Proofreaders
- Typesetters
- On-line information researchers
- Market researchers
- Telemarketers
- Printers
- Letter shops (direct mail production houses)
- Slide houses

- Audio-visual production studios
- Marketing consultants
- Advertising and "creative" consultants
- PR consultants

Why should you, as an advertising manager, turn to outside freelancers and vendors, especially if you already have an ad agency or PR firm? Freelance copywriter Richard Armstrong says there are seven basic reasons:

1. *The advertising department is overloaded.* The staff is busy with other work, and they don't have time to do the project. Or, they could do it, but not by the deadline. The outside vendor is called in to help when your own staff is overloaded.

2. *The advertising department is understaffed or there is no staff.* There are busy times and slow times. Rather than overstaff and have people sitting around doing nothing in the off-season, most companies prefer to understaff and hire freelancers during busy periods. Some companies may not have any advertising staff aside from the ad manager and must depend on outside sources for all their work.

3. *Quality.* In some situations, a freelancer may be able to do a better job on specific assignments. One of the advantages of using outside specialists is that you can pay for top talent on an "as-needed" basis, choosing the freelancer who is exactly right for that particular job. Joan Lipton, president of Martin & Lipton Advertising Agency observes: "Freelancers are apt to be even more talented than the permanent staff."

4. *Fresh perspective.* In-house and agency personnel can get bored dealing with the same products and accounts year after year. For this reason, companies turn to independents for renewed enthusiasm, new concepts, a new point of view, and fresh ideas. Freelancers can appraoch a project with the sense of excitement and vigor staff and agency personnel may have lost.

5. *The company or ad agency can't do the job themselves.* This happens when an assignment comes up that is outside the company's or agency's regular area of expertise. A corporation that has never used direct mail before would benefit by hiring a graphic artist who knows how to design pieces to comply with postal regulations. An ad agency that specializes in fashion and then acquires an account in telecommunications will

probably look for a freelance copywriter specializing in hi-tech. A fashion writer just doesn't understand the ins and outs of the telecommunications field as thoroughly as a writer who specializes in that field.

6. *The company is dissatisfied with its current suppliers.* For a variety of reasons, you may become unhappy with the work you are getting from your ad agency or other resources. If this displeasure continues, you may decide to farm out more and more projects to independents until you decide what to do about hiring a new agency.

7. *The independent can do the job cheaper.* Most advertising agencies and PR firms shy away from handling one-shot projects, such as a single ad, brochure, or press release. PR firms work on monthly retainers, which usually start at $1,000. Ad agencies expect clients to have an established annual advertising budget, with $50,000 a common minimum figure. For the company with the occasional rather than steady need for advertising and PR services, freelancers are a cost-effective solution. Most freelancers are available to handle single projects on a fixed-fee or hourly basis, and with their lower overhead, they can charge less than your agency.

Overall, corporate executives are satisfied with outside advertising and creative services, according to a survey conducted by Jenkins & Jenkins Market Research and reported in *Adweek.*

Of those surveyed, 62 percent said they use freelance writers and photographers and 67 percent said they would consider using freelance help if the freelancers could provide a service not already provided in-house. Of those who used freelancers, 78 percent said they were satisfied with the work that was produced.

Today the trend is clearly toward doing less in-house and with agencies, and more through freelancers. Alfred Brown notes that the main advantage to using freelancers over in-house or agencies is access to a broad range of specialized talent on an as-needed basis.

"The main idea is to utilize the talents and skills of individuals who are uniquely suited to a particular project," writes Brown. Using freelancers "provides broader, more flexible access to the best creative talent [and] a broader range of ideas than you can get either in-house or through an agency," he maintains. The major advantage of freelancers is:

- Getting access to the best talent;
- Getting access to a broader range of talent;

- Getting access to highly specialized talent tailored to the project at hand; and
- Paying for this talent only when you use it.

The main disadvantage of using freelancers and independents is that the advertising manager must coordinate the activities of many different suppliers who, although they are working on the same project, rarely communicate with one another, and certainly are not working as a team. "The danger is lack of control," says Brown. "It's like shopping at 10 specialty stores rather than writing one check to Sears." No one vendor on the team takes single-source responsibility for getting the job done right and meeting the deadline, and if there's a slippage, independents can easily blame it on others, citing their own lack of control over the total project.

Elaine Tyson suggests these 12 steps for getting the best work from your freelancers:

1. Avoid prima donnas.
2. Hire the right people.
3. Know how much you're paying (and what you're paying for).
4. Provide enough information.
5. Be prompt with feedback.
6. Critique copy constructively.
7. Streamline the approval process.
8. Build and maintain good relationships.
9. Pay fairly and promptly.
10. Be cooperative. Get freelancers the information they ask for promptly, and answer all questions as soon as possible.
11. Don't waste their time.
12. Give everyone several printed samples of the finished job. Discuss results.

Finding Freelancers and Other Vendors

As with ad agencies and PR firms, finding a freelancer, consultant, or other specialist is usually not difficult. Most likely, they will contact you by phone or mail, asking for work. Save the mailings and request the resumes, then save them in a file for future reference.

If you need a specialist and don't know one in that field, call friends, colleagues, and competitors for a recommendation. Your ad agency or PR firm account executive is also a good source for names. Many freelancers and independents also advertise in the classifieds sections of magazines such as *Adweek* and *Advertising Age*. You can also find them listed in *The Creative Black Book* (see the *Resources* section at the end of chapter) which lists audio-visual producers, typographers, retouchers, graphic designers, photographers, printers, engravers, and many other specialties.

Unlike advertising agencies and PR firms, which tend to be generalists, freelancers and self-employed professionals today are specialists. You can find someone to handle whatever you need, whether it's setting up a telemarketing operation and writing telephone scripts, or creating a computer system to track leads and sales, or building a three-dimensional model for your trade show exhibit. Do not settle for a generalist; look for a vendor with expertise in what you need, whether it's PR or direct mail or brochure-writing.

Hiring Freelancers and Independent Vendors

Here are 10 steps to finding and hiring independent service providers:

1. *Ask around.* Need to find a writer, artist, or photographer? The best way is through referrals. As discussed, ask friends, colleagues, and acquaintances to recommend names to you. The people most likely to know the names of independent advertising professionals include:

- Local advertising and PR firms
- Magazine space reps and editors
- Printers, typesetters, design studios
- Advertising managers of local companies
- Other independent advertising professionals

2. *Choose someone with experience in your industry.* When you use someone who is already knowledgeable about your business, you spend less time briefing him/her and bringing him/her up to speed in your technology and your markets.

Because this person speaks your industry lingo, he/she'll have an easier time communicating with engineers, product managers, and others within your firm.

Third, his/her superior knowledge of your markets and industry will enable him/her to critique your ads, make suggestions on strategies, and come up with new ideas based on his/her experience working with clients whose products are similar to yours.

3. *Hire someone at the right level.* In every business, there are beginners and old pros. Those with average skills and those with superior talent. The best costs more, but you may not need the top pro for every job.

Matching the right freelancer or vendor to the right assignment ensures a competent job at reasonable cost. For instance, don't hire a $2,500-a-day fashion photographer to shoot routine black-and-white photos of the company picnic. Not every project justifies top-dollar talent. Know which do, and pick freelance talent accordingly.

4. *Use service providers whose style is in sync with your own.* Freelancers and independents are mercanaries. The term freelance comes from "free lance," where knights and warriors would serve as lances for hire to the highest bidder.

So, while freelancers can do a good job and provide talent and expertise you can't get elsewhere, they're not going to change your corporate culture for you. The relationship is too brief, too tenuous, too temporary. Management is not going to change the style of your advertising dramatically because some freelance guru says so. More likely, they'll reject the work and ask for something similar to "what we did in the last ad."

You will be most successful if you choose freelancers and independents whose styles are in sync with your own. The work done by freelancers should complement, not revolutionize, what was done previously. Only a large ad agency with a multi-million dollar budget can create a brand-new image or campaign with any hope of getting it approved and implemented. Freelancers can't.

5. *Get their information.* Most freelancers and independents have brochures, checklists, article reprints, samples, resumes, bios, and a variety of other information they'll happily send you. Ask for it, get it, read it, and keep it. You'll get a good idea of who's available, what they charge, and what jobs you can use them for. You may also get some good free marketing advice by studying their articles, booklets, and samples.

Start a file labelled "FREELANCERS" and save all this material. From experience, I've learned that the best time to evaluate a freelancer is at your leisure, not when a project deadline comes crashing around the corner. That way, when you need someone with a specialized expertise, you know who to call and have their phone number handy.

6. *Don't try to get something for nothing.* It's human nature to want to get something for nothing; few people *volunteer* to pay for something if they feel they can get it for free.

Many prospective clients take this attitude with freelancers. They call up the freelancer and promise all sorts of lucrative work, but say they just want to ask a few questions and then proceed to pump the freelancer for all the free advertising advice he or she is giving out that day.

Even if you can get away with this, don't do it. Your interviewing of the freelancer should be solely to ascertain whether the freelancer is the right person for the job and what it will cost—not to get free advice, service, or consultation which you should be paying for.

One of the biggest gray areas in rendering freelance service is when to stop talking for free and when to start charging the client. If you are a client, points out consultant Howard Shenson, it's really in your best interest for you to disclose to the freelancer whether you intend to pay for an initial meeting or conversation. Why? Simple.

If the freelancer and you both expect money to change hands, the freelancer will be a lot more forthcoming with ideas, strategies, and useful suggestions. In short, he or she will be working with you to solve your problem.

On the other hand, if you expect to pay for the initial consultation but the freelancer doesn't know this—and thinks it's a free, sales-type meeting—he or she won't be forthcoming with ideas, suggestions, and strategies. The freelancer will be holding back the "good stuff" for when you sign on the dotted line. And you'll be disappointed unless you've agreed that this initial meeting is really just a sales call during which you're looking the freelancer over and making a decision about whether to hire him or her.

So don't try to get free advice, and communicate to the vendor when you expect to begin paying for advice and service.

7. *Discuss fees up front.* Get an exact estimate for the project, and get it in writing. To make this estimate, the freelancer needs as much information from you as possible about the job. For example, if it's a brochure, what's the topic? How many pages? How many words? What size? How many colors? How many drawings? How many photos? What research is required? Will there be original photography or illustration or will you use existing materials? What background information can you provide? Will travel be required? Where and to how many locations?

If you can't provide detailed job specifications, then ask the freelancer to give you a fee schedule or an explanation of how jobs are billed and what the charges are. Does the service provider charge by the project, by the hour, or by the day? How much per hour? How much per day? If by the project, ask for typical fees or a range of fees for projects similar to what you need. Most independent firms have a written fee schedule explaining rates, charges, terms, and conditions in detail.

Terms and conditions are also important. Does the freelancer require a purchase order, or will you be asked to sign a standard agreement or contract? Can you review a copy of the form agreement or contract in advance? What are the terms and conditions? Is payment due upon completion? Or is an advance retainer required? If so, how much? What happens if you want changes—how are revisions handled? What happens if you are not satisfied?

8. *Provide complete background information.* The more background information and more complete job specifications you provide, the more accurately the freelancer can estimate the cost of the job. If you are vague or uncertain about the parameters of the job, the freelancer will be "flying blind" because he/she doesn't know how much work is really involved—and his/her high estimate will reflect this degree of uncertainty.

You'll get the best price by giving the freelancer whatever information is required to make an informed, accurate estimate of what the job will cost.

9. *Get it in writing.* Put the fee, terms, deadlines, and a description of the assignment in a purchase order or letter and send it to the vendor.

A written agreement eliminates confusion and spells out what you are buying and what the vendor is selling. Too many buyers and sellers in all fields of business have gone to court because they made their deals orally. Don't you make that same mistake.

When you write the job description as you see it and send it out as a purchase order or letter, that becomes the understanding and agreement unless the vendor notifies you otherwise, in writing. A written agreement protects you, so don't just shake on it. Put it in writing.

10. *Stand back.* Once you've hired the vendor, stand back and let them do their job. Don't interfere, don't ask to "take a look at the first few pages," don't badger them with constant "how's it going?" calls. You've hired a professional. Now let the professional do his job. You'll get your work by the deadline date, or sooner. And if you've hired the right person, you'll get quality work.

Resources

An aid in locating an advertising agency: *The Standard Directory of Advertising Agencies,* published by Reed Reference Publishing Company, 121 Chanlon Rd., New Providence, NJ 07974, phone 800-521-8110.

A directory to help you find a PR firm: *O'Dwyer's Directory of Public Relations Firms,* published by J.R. O'Dwyer and Company, Inc., 271 Madison Avenue, New York, NY 10016, phone 212-679-2471.

A resource to help you find freelancers, consultants, or other specialists: *The Creative Black Book,* published by Friendly Press, 401 Park Avenue South, New York, NY 10016, phone 212-870-2586.

CHAPTER 39

Managing Creativity

One of the most difficult aspects of advertising management is supervising, reviewing, commenting on, and handling the work of "creative" people—copywriters, graphic artists, illustrators, photographers, consultants, TV directors, and others who conceive, plan, write, design, and produce advertising campaigns and materials.

The difficulty comes mainly in managing the relationship between these people—who are usually employed by the ad agency but sometimes work on-staff in an advertising department—and the client employees, who are usually business executives and managers rather than creative types.

The specific trouble comes when the business types want to make changes to the work submitted by the creative types, who feel they are the experts and the client's request for changes is unwarranted. Is the client right? Are the creatives prima donnas who judge work solely on artistic merit, with no regard to the marketing, business, or budgetary aspects which is so important to making a campaign profitable?

Or are the creatives right? Are all clients boobs who meddle in things they know nothing about, thus destroying any chance of getting work that is clear, original, forceful, and effective?

And can anything be done to improve the situation? Or will the relationship between client and its vendors always be, to a degree, adversarial? Let's take a look at these issues and see what we can do to make things better.

A Look At The Problem

Recently, the head of a large public relations agency said to me, "I don't envy you being a freelance copywriter. That's got to be a tough job, writing copy and then having clients make all those changes and revisions."

To a degree, he's right. Someone once observed that there is no greater human urge than the desire to rewrite someone else's copy. Or redo their layout. Or redraw their sketch. Or retake their photograph. And certainly, if you've been in this business any length of time, you know that the most tedious portion of any promotional campaign is routing the copy and layouts around, making changes, generating revisions, and getting approvals.

And that raises a question: Namely, if the standards of professionalism in our industry have risen dramatically over the last several decades, as many experts claim, then why is there still so much revising of copy and layouts by clients?

Aside from the possibility that the copy and graphics being submitted are simply lousy, I think there are two major reasons why so much ad copy is revised and rewritten to the point of absurdity.

The first reason is that copywriting and design are one of the few activities in the business world where there is no RFP or *request for proposal*—no predefined and agreed-upon specification to which the work must conform.

For example, if you order a computer system to be installed in your office, part of the vendor's selling process is to precisely define your needs and requirements. In their proposal, the vendor will spell out exactly what is to be delivered—down to the height of the computer console, the functions of the software programs, even the temperature and power requirements. As a result, it's rather simple to determine whether the vendor has accurately fulfilled the requirements.

But in the creation of advertising, it's different. It would be absurd for you, as the client, to request in advance a brochure with so many headlines, so many subheads, so many commas, so many charts, so many sentences beginning with the words *and* or *the,* so many paragraphs of such and such length. In fact, one could argue that even specifying the *type* of marketing communication required (e.g., an ad versus a booklet versus a telemarketing script versus a mailer) is usually done prematurely, without the proper thought, planning, and analysis.

And here's the root of the problem: If you cannot define a specification or requirement for the work before you order it from your ad agency, how can copy be written to clearly fulfill your desires or expectations? It can't, of course; hence, the tendency to edit and rewrite any piece of copy submitted.

For this reason, the advertising business is a business where an inherent degree of client dissatisfaction and discontent is literally built into the process of creation of the ads and rendering of the service!

The second reason why copy is rewritten is best summed up by an account executive from the television show *thirtysomething* who, when asked to defend a campaign idea conceived by Michael Steadman, replied, "Nobody knows anything." To some degree, he is right: There is no formula that guarantees a successful ad or winning campaign. All creative efforts are at best educated guesses; all campaigns are tests which determine the validity of our approach to the market.

Because advertising is more of an art or craft rather than an exact science, the professional advertising person's opinion is always subject to question and debate—in part, because he cannot with certainty say he is right.

Few people constantly and boldly challenge the opinions of their neurosurgeons, accountants, attorneys, or electricians, because these professions are viewed as scientific, and the practitioners are seen as technical experts with arcane knowledge beyond the understanding of an ordinary mortal.

But in fields where decisions are more subjective—copywriting, graphic design, interior decorating, landscape architecture—clients frequently question the practitioner, because the client believes his opinion to be equally valid. Even if the client gives the professional *carte blanche* at the beginning of the project, the instant he sees something that is not exactly the way he would have done it, a revision or change is demanded.

Can anything be done to correct this situation and enable clients and vendors to work more harmoniously with one another? Before exploring various methods in detail, here are three quick suggestions:

First, your ad agency or consultant needs to be involved much earlier in the marketing process. Too often, clients come to the agency and say "do an ad," when in fact print advertising may be the *least* effective means of promoting the product. Agencies are treated as order-takers or ad-makers, but to succeed, they need to be more involved as strategists, planners, and problemsolvers. As a client, you should view your agency as a source of ideas and marketing knowledge, not a place where mechanicals are made or insertion orders typed.

Second, in some instances, clients and their agencies may want to establish a set of specifications or guidelines for certain projects. For instance, if all your brochures are written in terse, technical terms, let your agency know if you are open to a different approach or just want another brochure written in the same style. Understand why they may want to pass on the project if you insist on having it done in a manner which they feel would be ineffective or inappropriate.

Third, a reply mechanism and tangible, measurable direct-response offer should be built into all marketing communications—not only ads and direct mail but brochures, video, and PR too. While your product managers and CEO may all think they have a way with words, they are always impressed by numbers—and if you can quantitatively show that your agency's approach outpulled their old version, they will be less inclined to argue with you.

The "Creative" Worker Versus The "Business" Worker

Creative worker or *creative types* are the copywriters, artists, and others who write and design ad campaigns. (The trade press generally refers to such people using the more concise term *creatives.*)

To deal successfully with agencies or freelancers who are creatives, you must understand how they think and what motivates them and how this is different than the client mind-set. Basically, there are three personality types in advertising: creatives, corporate managers, and entrepreneurs.

Creatives write and design ad campaigns, and they love writing and design work for its own sake. This is a trait that clients do not share. There are pros and cons to dealing with a group of people who love writing and design. The advantage is that they're good at it: They can usually write better than you and design better than you. You use them because they can communicate with a freshness, originality, and clarity that the typical corporate executive lacks. Also, they have the technical skills and knowledge to put together communications materials from start to finish.

The disadvantage is that creatives are sometimes too much "in love" with their craft. Writers love writing so much they cannot imagine anyone not loving to read; yet many people targeted by their copy are not readers and do not appreciate the craft behind the written word. Designers love design so much they cannot conceive of anyone who doesn't appreciate the beauty and technique that goes into their creations; yet many buyers are unaware of the fine points of design and unmoved by graphic innovation.

Corporate Executives

Corporate executives involved in advertising consist of managers operating on three levels: top executives (CEOs, presidents, etc.), product management (product managers, brand managers, sales and marketing executives), and communications (advertising managers, marketing communications staff, corporate communications).

Top executives are usually overconcerned with corporate image and getting a "company message" across. They do not understand that most buyers are unconcerned or minimally concerned with the company and are much more interested in the benefits and features of the product or service. Top executives are also overly concerned with communicating in what they believe to be an "appropriate manner" (i.e., using dignified, important-sounding, stuffy language) rather than motivating the readers, getting their attention, and speaking to them in *their* language.

Problems arise when presidents, CEOs, and other top executives get too involved in the nitty-gritty of reviewing layouts or editing copy. Their changes tend to overemphasize the corporate viewpoint and company information, which detracts from the power of the ad. They also have a tendency to delete strong language and substitute flabby, bland corporate prose which turns off readers and makes the whole effort a waste of time and money. This bores prospects, loses sales, and demoralizes the ad agency staff.

Product Managers

Product management includes product managers, marketing managers, and brand managers who usually have the same goal as advertising managers and ad agencies: to produce powerful ads and commercials that *sell the product.*

Unfortunately, their review of materials often turns into a rewriting session which, like the CEO's commentary, can destroy the ad, but in a different way. Because they work so closely with all aspects of the product on a daily basis, product managers are *too close* to the product. They want to make sure the copy mentions every last fact or feature lest some specification go unmentioned. They don't understand that prospective buyers don't care about every fact and feature; they only care about the benefits or the features that can specifically help them.

Some product managers will hand the ad manager or ad agency a sheet listing features and specifications and insist, "This has all got to go into the ad (or the brochure or the video). By making such a demand, they sabatoge the agency, not realizing that effective copywriting involves selectivity. The agency, unable to find an effective way to present all the information in a short ad or commercial (because there is none), complies with the request, turning in work that is dull and ineffective.

You will often hear product managers say, "It's important to say [this or that] about the product." Their viewpoint starts with and focuses on the product. Unfortunately, to be an effective salesperson, you must start with and focus on the *prospect,* not the product. Remind your product people of this fact. Maybe it will sink in.

Communication Managers

Good *communications managers* are hard to find. There are some communications managers working in corporate America today who are excellent, but many are not. It's not a lack of skill holding them back; rather, with all the downsizing and staff reduction going on today, there are too few of them doing too much work. Also, much of the work tends to be of a routine or administrative nature (e.g., routing materials for approval or overseeing the mechanical aspects of print or audio-visual production), which requires diligence but can get boring.

As a result, communications managers become overburdened and overtired, and they lose their positive attitude. Instead of seeing each ad or brochure as an exciting marketing challenge or problem-solving assignment, they see it as another piece of paper to get produced. Thus, when the top executives and product managers make changes that are not healthy for the project, they accept them too easily and don't defend good work. Many are heard to say, "We can't argue over every copy change; we have too much going on and too many deadlines, and we just have to get it approved and through the system."

This attitude is understandable but not acceptable. When your ad fails to motivate anyone to buy your product, will you tell your boss, "I didn't think it was good, but I didn't want to make waves or create extra work"? When your customers complain that your brochure lacks information and is unclear, will you say, "I know it's a mess but that's the way management approved it"?

Part of your responsibility is to stand up for good work, defend it, and get it through. If your reviewers make changes that you or your agency feel are no good, say why and fight to get the best work produced. Naturally, you can't make an issue every time someone says to use blue paper instead of yellow, or wants to airbrush the lips red instead of pink, or changes "the" to "a." But don't accept every harmful change just because that's the easiest thing to do. If you do, the work will be mediocre, the ads won't sell, your agency will become demoralized, and the same executives and managers who made those changes will complain to you that "no one's responding to the ad."

Entrepreneurs

Entrepreneurs, unlike corporate communications managers, for whom getting things approved is a big task, are more concerned with getting sales and generating profits than with making sure everything's corporately "acceptable."

As with any group, there are pros and cons to working for or with entrepreneurs. On the plus side, they make decisions quickly, without routing copy and layout through endless layers of management. Therefore, the work is likely to emerge from the approval process with a minimum of changes (the creatives love this). Another plus is that entrepreneurs want advertising that produces immediate, tangible results in the form of leads, orders, and money. So copywriters, agencies, and artists who do that type of hard-sell work will enjoy working with entrepreneurs.

On the negative side, many entrepreneurs don't really understand advertising and marketing (they're more likely to come from a sales background). They often insist on having a certain look for their materials without regard to what the designer feels will work best for the market they are trying to reach. And they can be insensitive when critiquing materials or requesting changes—which offends some of the more "delicate" creatives. Also, while creatives want to do highly original work, entrepreneurs often instruct their ad manager or agency to copy or "knock off" a particular brochure, mailing, ad, or promotion they saw, liked, and saved in their swipe files.

Another problem with entrepreneurs is that, unlike their corporate counterparts, they are doers, not planners. While most sophisticated ad agencies today are planning oriented, many entrepreneurs find the planning process slow and do not think it necessary; they tend to dream up promotional ideas on the spot and want to implement them right away.

Clashes Between Creatives and Clients

You can readily see why there are problems when creatives have to work with corporate or entrepreneurial types; each comes from a different background, with different interests and perspectives. The corporate executive wants to hype the company; the product manager wants to talk about the product; the entrepreneur wants to make money as fast as possible; and the agency or freelancer wants to create fresh, original work he or she can be proud of. While all may claim a unified goal (a good ad or campaign) they may privately disagree on what defines a good ad or campaign and may each have their own agendas.

Here are some specific reasons or situations which cause conflict between clients and ad agencies (or other creative vendors):

1. The client goes too far in dictating the content, style, and approach of the work. The agency feels overly constrained, complaining that they are being prevented from doing good creative work before they even get started. The client believes the agency is being a prima donna, unwilling to take direction.

2. The client insists on putting too much corporate or product information in the copy. The agency protests that all this detail will overload the ad and be a barrier to effective communication. The client feels the agency is too lazy to read the material or not creative enough to "solve the problem." The agency is forced to include the information and becomes unenthusiastic about the project.

3. The client instructs the agency to make the new ad or brochure conform to the look and style of previous ads or brochures. The agency feels the existing design is lousy and proposed a new look. The client wants consistency and feels the agency is changing the design just to create more work.

4. The client requests revisions which the agency feels are unwarranted and would harm the work. The agency resists making the changes, explaining why they are not sensible. The client becomes annoyed at the agency's seeming inflexibility and regrets hiring "that bunch of prima donnas."

5. The client reviews work or requests changes in a way that offends the artists and writers who did the work. The artists and writers begin to hate the account and stop giving it their best effort. Although nothing is

said, the client can tell that the agency resents him/her and, in turn, becomes miffed.

6. The client makes major changes in content, direction, and strategy and expects to get the work for the fee specified by the original estimate. The agency points out that the assignment is different and will cost more. A dispute arises over this. The client feels the agency is trying to take advantage of what was simply a misunderstanding. The agency feels undercompensated and resents the extra work.

7. The ad manager and account executive get along famously, but people within the client and agency staff do not work well together. For instance, a product manager on the client's staff dislikes the agency and is not cooperative with the account manager or creative director.

8. The advertising manager lacks real authority within his corporation and tries to hide this fact from the agency. Thus the agency spends a lot of time working on projects approved by the advertising manager, only to have managers above him say, "No, this is totally off-base."

9. The client does not pay on time or argues over previously agreed-to invoice amounts.

10. The client kills a lot of projects in mid-stream and the agency never recovers its real costs in kill-fees it receives. Also, doing work that is not produced is demoralizing to agency staff.

Just recognizing these situations can help prevent them and make the working relationships better. Below are some additional suggestions and ideas for getting the best work from your creatives.

The Three Types Of Client Revisions

Client revisions fall into one of three categories:

1. One-quarter of all client revisions are sensible and actually will improve the copy.
2. One-quarter don't make sense and will make the copy worse.
3. Half of the comments won't make a difference one way or the other.

Naturally, all changes that improve the copy can be made; both the client and the writer want the best copy possible.

All the revisions that don't make a difference one way or the other can be made, too. After all, if it doesn't make a difference, why not let the clients have their way?

The revisions that will make the copy worse are the ones your agency or freelancer will object to, and here is where conflict arises. If you're a client, and you want to make a change that's going to hurt your ad or mailing, the writer should let you know it. It's his/her professional obligation to do so, since you're paying him/her to create advertising to sell your product or service. (If you don't care about sales, and simply want "pleasing" copy, you probably shouldn't be working together in the first place.)

What Clients Don't Know About The Vendor's Objections

Many clients feel that agencies and freelancers who "give them a hard time" over revisions and changes are being prima donnas and enjoy arguing with clients. Nothing could be further from the truth.

Creative-types *hate* arguing with clients. In fact, when a client requests a revision that the vendor feels is wrong, the easiest thing for the agency or freelancer to do would be to *say nothing.* After all, making an issue of it only delays the job and makes the vendor wait longer before he/she can finish the project, bill the client, and get paid. Getting involved in a discussion over the content or design also means the vendor is spending more time on the work, probably without an extra compensation. So his profit on the job is lower.

The reason a vendor questions the client's revisions and changes, then, is not for his benefit, but for the client's. As professionals, vendors have the obligation to give the client the best advice possible and to produce advertising and marketing communications that get read, remembered, and responded to. If vendors think the client's change will interfere with one of those functions, they have a duty to report it—even though many clients will be aggravated and annoyed.

So when your agency or freelancer says, "I don't think we should make that change," keep in mind this is for *your* benefit. Not theirs.

How Clients React To Vendor Objections

When the agency or freelancer says a revision or direction given by the client is wrong, the client will react in one of four ways:

1. The client will ask for an explanation, listen to the reasoning, agree with it, and tell the agency or freelancer, "You're right. Leave it as it is."
2. The client will ask for an explanation, listen to the reasoning, think about it, but decide against it and tell the agency or freelancer, "I understand what you're saying, but I disagree. Please change it as discussed."
3. The client will ask for an explanation, listen to the reasoning, agree with it, but tell the agency or freelancer, "You're right—but this is what management wants. Please change it as discussed."
4. As the agency or freelancer begins to protest the change, the client interrupts and says, "Just do it the way I want."

Responses #1 and #2 are the most reasonable and will be respected by all creatives. Response #3 may not make your agency or freelancer happy, but it is within your right and certainly reasonable. After all, you are the client—you are paying for the ad, and you have a right to get it produced the way you want. Many creatives do not have enough healthy respect for the tremendous risk clients take by spending thousands of dollars running and placing ads in the hopes they'll pay off. Many creatives who insist their way is best would not gamble their own money on their copy or design if requested to do so.

Response #4 is the least desirable reply. If you give it consistently, you must realize that as far as the agency or freelancer is concerned, you are not a good client to work with and you are certainly not taking advantage of the marketing expertise vendors make available to you.

However, response #4 is reasonable if used occasionally—for instance, when the deadline is a rush and there is no time to come to a consensus. In these situations, you as the ad manager may need to be more dictatorial than you'd like in order to get the work through on time. But you should at least explain to your vendors *why* you have to pass on their advice this time.

How To Present An Objection

When I get into a disagreement with a client concerning the way a promotion should be done, here's how I handle it. I explain to the client *once*, calmly and directly, why I feel their idea won't work and why their change would be harmful. Then, if they don't agree, I go ahead and do it the way they want. I don't continue to argue, or get angry, or refuse to make the change.

However, if I feel that the change is doing major damage to the work, I point this out. I may even send a short letter explaining my disagreement and saying I don't think the ad or mailing will be effective because of what they've done.

This is for protection. If the client later claims, "Your ad didn't work," I pull the letter out of the file and remind them it wasn't my ad that failed, it was theirs. All of this is done politely, not argumentatively.

While it is important to get a quality job produced, you are not going to convince the client (or, if you're an ad manager, your product managers and president) every time. You must know when to press a point and when to let it go and move on. Clients may value vendors for their knowledge, but they also like working with people who are cooperative, not those who are argumentative.

Freelancer Cam Foote has this advice for agencies and freelancers:

> Once you have presented what you like and why [to the client], ask for approval to proceed . . . or discuss the changes the client suggests. If the client wants a totally different conceptual approach, or extensive changes to your concept, acquiesce pleasantly. Don't fight. Go back to the drawing board or word processor. Just as your first obligation to the client was to recommend, your obligation now is to follow direction. After all, it is the client's money you are spending.

Important Versus Routine Issues

The process of creating advertising will invariably involve conflict between creator and client; it's almost impossible to imagine an agency doing work for a client who loves everything and never requests a single change. It's equally difficult to imagine a situation where every change the client makes is for the better. So clients and agencies are going to argue, as will ad managers and their management. The key here is to let the unimportant matters pass and to only stand up and make a fuss over important issues.

If your president wants to add a short section about how the company was founded to the back page of a 12-page product brochure, don't fight him. It probably won't make any difference (the back page of most brochures is usually blank anyway).

On the other hand, if he wants to rewrite your direct mail letter and make it all about how he founded the company, instead of how your product can provide many wonderful benefits, fight him. Explain that his approach will reduce response to the letter to zero and effectively waste the money he is spending on the mailing.

Some people liken the client/agency debates over such issues to a chess game: don't fight over the pawns and bishops, but protect your king and queen.

Don't battle over every comma. Let minor changes pass. If you argue vehemently over every simple change, you will gain a reputation for being "difficult." Instead, choose your battles wisely. Fight only when you know it's important and when the success of the program is at stake.

Reducing Subjective Judgment

Although there are many so-called "rules" and "principles" in advertising, in the final analysis all creative work is reviewed by the client on a subjective basis. People look at it, and either they like the copy and design or they don't.

One way to reduce dependence on subjective judgment is to create guidelines or criteria by which the work is to be judged before the piece is created. Freelancer Jon Toigo creates a detailed outline for every piece he writes, submits the outline to the client, and writes the actual copy only once the outline is approved. If Toigo's copy addresses all the points in the outline, then (according to his contract), he has performed the job satisfactorily and the client must pay him. If people in the client organization, in reviewing the copy, discover additional points they want to add that were not in the original outline, Toigo is happy to do so for an additional fee.

You can create a set of guidelines or criteria against which the copy and design will be judged, either generically or for each specific assignment. Many professionals, like Jon Toigo, find an outline written and approved for each specific project provides a reasonable assurance that the final result will get a satisfactory rating from the client. Or, you might create checklists of specific points or information to be covered in each of your various promotions—ads, brochures, data sheets, and so forth.

An outline or checklist doesn't guarantee that the client will find the work acceptable, but it does provide a rational basis for reviewing work. Arguments resulting from subjective critiques won't be eliminated, but there will be fewer of them when you establish guidelines or specifications for each job at the start, then review the work in progress against these agreed-upon objectives and points.

Dealing With Creative People Who Take Things Personally

An important point to understand about creative people is that they take your comments *personally.* When you tell a copywriter you don't like the copy, doesn't he or she seem to immediately get rigid and defensive? Doesn't his or her manner become cold and annoyed?

You might consider this behavior inappropriate or unprofessional, but it's an unavoidable fact of life. Writers don't like having their writing criticized, and artists don't like having businesspeople tell them how to do design.

The solution is to be *tactful* in your criticisms. When sitting down with your artist, don't say, "I don't like this layout." Instead, say, "I like this layout and feel it's a really great start; there are just a few things we might need to add to it." Then proceed with your changes. The artist will be so flattered by the compliment you gave at the beginning, he or she will accept your critique and happily make the changes you ask for.

Dealing With Changes In Direction

If you change direction in the middle of a campaign and your agency has to redo a substantial portion of the work because of this change, tell them you expect to pay them an additional fee for the extra work. As a client, you have every right to change your mind. But you cannot expect your suppliers to foot the bill for your (or your management's) indecision.

If you want your agency to change or redo something because you don't like it, fine. That's part of the service, and you won't be billed extra for it (unless they bill you by the hour).

But if you change things on a whim, or for no good reason, or because of a management decision made *after* the work has been submitted, you should expect to see an additional bill for it.

When such situations arise, bring up the subject of money with your vendor. If you expect to pay extra for changes, let them know it. They'll be more willing to put extra effort into the revision when they know they're not paying out of their own pockets. You would expect the agency to keep you informed about when you're incurring extra charges, but many don't—probably because they're afraid of losing the account.

Many agencies operate in fear of the client, of the company president, of losing the account. If you can remove this atmosphere of fear, you'll get better work and service from them, because they'll be happier and more enthusiastic about your account.

Avoiding Ignorance And Arrogance

An ad agency owner once remarked, "I can work with a client who is either ignorant or arrogant—but not one who is both." This is an ideal description of what constitutes being a bad client to your agency.

If you are ignorant—that is, if you don't know how to create effective advertising or if your management does not understand basic marketing principles—you can still be a good client if you listen to your agency and rely on their advice and suggestions. Even though you or your management may be "marketing illiterates," you can still succeed if you have the smartness to select a good agency and the humility to take your lead from them.

If you are arrogant—that is, if you think you know everything there is to know about advertising and you dictate to your vendors exactly what you want done and how they should do it—that's probably okay if you're as expert as you think.

The one type of client no agency or freelancer can serve effectively, however, is the client who is both ignorant and arrogant. This is the client who doesn't know anything about advertising, but thinks he's an expert. He's too arrogant to listen to his agency's advice, and too ignorant to realize the mistake he's making. If your management fits this description, you have a big problem. You could try to educate them about advertising (for starters, have them read this book). You could suggest that they try listening to you and your ad team, and maybe test out a few of your ideas. Or, you could get another job.

Dealing With Artificial Deadlines

Another thing that drives creatives crazy is rush deadlines. Yet at times it seems as if every project is a rush. Agencies, being too timid to object and too eager to please, accept the most ridiculous, unrealistic rush deadlines imaginable. And so clients have become conditioned to making every job a rush job.

The problem with most deadlines is that they are artificial—that is, there's no event, milestone, or other driving force necessitating the deadline. The deadline exists because you or someone else in your company is impatient and wants to get the ad, brochure, or catalog done right away. Or because you are unaware of how much time the agency really needs to do the job right. Or because, as one communications manager put it, "rush jobs are part of the game."

Unfortunately, rush deadlines are a bad idea for the agency and the client alike. Creative work takes a certain length of time to produce, and this time period is not directly related to actual hours spent on the work. Writers and designers often speak fondly of their favorite part of creative assignments: the time spent thinking, reading, doodling, sketching, and "brainstorming" for ideas.

While this sounds like an excuse to avoid sitting down and writting the final copy or doing the layout, it's not. Good ideas need time to "ferment," to come to the surface. James Webb Young outlines five steps in the creative process:

1. Gathering raw material.
2. Digesting the information.
3. "Sleeping" on it (unconscious thought).
4. Coming up with the idea.
5. Analyzing and testing the practicality of the idea.

Creatives need separation between steps to allow the unconscious creative mind to do its work. Creatives are most comfortable when they have one or two days to rest between reading background material and writing a first draft, or between writing the first draft and reading and editing it. When they can literally put the project in a drawer, sleep on it overnight, and return to it refreshed the next morning, they can refine their work far more effectively than when forced to work on a job continuously until it's done.

Because most deadlines are artificial, you should always question deadlines if they do not allow your creative team enough time to do good work. When a product manager says, "We need this in two weeks," ask why. Nine out of ten times there's no reason other than a whim, and the job can be scheduled for completion in four, six, 10, or even 12 weeks instead of two.

Give your agency or freelancers all the time they ask for. They know best how much time is required to do this work. As a rough guideline, figure two to three months to complete a brochure or mailing from start to finish, including approvals, revisions, and printing. When jobs are rushed, the work is often second-rate and substantial overtime charges from printers, color separators, and other subcontractors is incurred by the agency, which is *always* passed along to you, the client, as an extra charge.

Vendor Management And Motivation

An argument in favor of using outside vendors has always been that, unlike employees, who need to be properly treated, managed, and motivated, vendors require no such motivation. You don't have to worry about whether the vendor is sick, tired, bored, angry, unhappy, underpaid, or unenthusiastic. You just assign the work and it gets done.

This is true, but only to a degree. As a manager, responsibility flows two ways. True, your employees work for you; but you also work for your employees. They give their labor, effort, and time in exchange for pay, but they expect a lot from you, too. Managers, many of whom are not comfortable being responsible for people's lives, find that employees demand to be taken care of. They want their supervisor to provide interesting work, a pleasant workplace environment, adequate compensation, motivation, career guidance, and assistance in completing tasks, when required.

Obviously vendors are much more independent. Yet it's not entirely true that you can take them for granted and not have to worry about human motivation. Vendors, like employees, want to be admired, appreciated, well-paid, praised, valued, and challenged. The advertising manager must work to nurture the client/vendor relationship just as he or she nurtures the employer/employee relationship with in-house staff.

For instance, many freelancers complain how difficult it is to get samples of their work from the client. Why should this be so? Most clients print far more copies than they can use, so why not give the artist or writer a dozen or two dozen copies or more, if he or she wants them? If you are thoughtful and provide plenty of portfolio copies for your vendors, you'll be doing something that 99.9 percent of their other clients don't do. For a simple effort that costs virtually nothing, you'll quickly climb to the top of their "favorite client" list.

And don't kid yourself: Not all clients are equal. Agency personnel and freelancers give their best effort to the best clients. So it pays to become a client they like rather than one they can't stand.

Thank-Yous, Business Gifts, And Bonuses

The two most powerful motivational words when dealing with vendors is "thank you." Most phone calls from clients are to request more service, discuss an ongoing project, or call in changes to copy or layout. Rarely does the vendor receive a call or letter that simply says "Thank you for all your fine work." If the work was good, send such a letter. Include a statement in your letter saying the vendor may use your letter as a testimonial. They'll be grateful and will work even harder next time to assure that they continue to please you.

Many larger corporations, especially those in the defense and aerospace industries, have strict policies against advertising managers accepting gifts from vendors. But this doesn't mean you can't give your vendors a small gift, bonus, or other token of your appreciation once in a while.

Don't make a habit of giving gifts and bonuses. It's unnecessary and costly, and if you do it all the time, it loses its motivational value. Rather, a small, unexpected but thoughtful gift, or a small performance bonus, will get your vendors motivated and working for you. Try it!

Briefings

Chapter 38 discussed how to work with and brief your agency. This also applies to creatives, who do their best work when given complete information in the initial briefing, direct access to experts within the company for follow-up, and immediate and complete additional background material upon request.

The initial briefing should be as thorough and complete as possible, though it should take no more than two hours. Beyond the two-hour limit, people's eyes begin to glaze over as they reach the limit of the amount of material they can absorb in one meeting. The solution is to provide an overview of the basics, then give the agency team back-up in the form of brochures, manuals, and other printed materials they can take back to the office.

Creatives should be briefed directly. Don't invite only your account executive and have him relay the information back to the creative team. Major briefings should be attended by the writer, artist, and creative director.

For follow-up, assign individual managers, executives, engineers, technicians, and others in your company as official "expert sources" the agency creative team can call on to get additional information or answers to questions. Permit direct contact between creatives and expert sources. For instance, have the copywriter call the quality engineer directly, if a question about quality control procedures arises. Translating questions and answers through several layers is wasteful, inefficient, and often results in inaccurate information.

If your agency team or freelancer is having trouble getting the information or reaching the right people, let them know they can call you anytime and that you will personally get them what they need right away. At times, lack of a key fact or resource (such as a prototype or drawing of a new product) can delay the entire creative effort. When the information stops flowing, step in and get things moving again. It's easier and more acceptable for you to badger others within your firm than for the agency or freelancer to do it. And that's not really their job, anyway.

Presentations

Most agencies and many vendors make a big deal of presenting concepts, layouts, and copy to clients. Opt for making such presentations informal rather than formal. In fact, the best way to review concepts or drafts is to have them sent, rather than personally presented, and to review them in the privacy of your own office, without the agency or vendor present. One exception might be in the review of color proofs, where it's desirable for you to be present at the printing plant so any desired color adjustments can be made on the spot. Another exception is photography: You may want to be in the studio to review Polariod test shots to make sure the shot is right before the photographer takes 35mm stills.

But copy, layouts, illustrations, and comps should be reviewed in private, without the agency or freelancer present. If the agency team is hanging around as your management reviews material, reviewers will feel pressured to render an immediate opinion rather than give it thoughtful consideration. Also, the agency is liable to become defensive if this review is done with them present; if changes are needed, you can present criticism more tactfully after the comments have been thought out, reviewed, and a consensus is reached.

Therefore, do away with "presentations." When the job is ready, just have it sent or mailed, read it, react to it, and send it for review and approval internally. The traditional method of having concepts and campaigns presented and critiqued on the spot sets up an undesirable tension between client and agency. Avoid it.

Trial Projects

If you have a significant amount of work that needs to be done, and you're thinking of farming it out to an agency, freelancer, or combination of the two, you might want to assign one small portion of the total campaign to a particular agency or vendor and see how they handle it before giving them more work.

Will the vendor find this offensive? They shouldn't. After all, you're not asking them to work "on spec." You're offering them a real project, at their usual rates. Some agencies may turn you down, saying they want the entire campaign or none of it. That's their perogative. But it's perfectly acceptable to want to do a "pilot program" on one or two assignments before handing over a big chunk of your business. You'll find plenty of creative vendors happy to take you up on this offer.

Do not try to get this initial project for a reduced rate by saying things like "If we like it and it works, we'll pay more" or "Do this cheap now and we'll give you a lot of work later." When dealing with vendors, always offer a fair day's pay for a fair day's work. If you want a professional quality ad, expect to pay the going rate, and don't haggle or try to get a discount. The vendor who is working on the cheap will resent it and rarely give you his best effort.

Get Involved

Advertising is a peculiar business in that success requires active participation of a knowledgeable, professional, sensible client. This isn't true in other fields. Your accountant can do your taxes without your input and assistance (aside from providing the basic financial papers and information). Your doctor doesn't require you to understand a surgical procedure in order to successfully perform the operation on you. And your dentist doesn't require your ongoing cooperation (except for having you sit still in his chair) to fill your cavities and give you check-ups.

But advertising is different. Rather than the vendor rendering service to the client unaided, advertising is a partnership, a unique collaboration between agencies and their clients. The agency provides project management capability, planning assistance, and talent in advertising creation. The client contributes his superior knowledge of the product, industry, buyers, and markets along with a thoughtful review and critique of the agency's work at every step.

For this reason, a good client is actively involved in his advertising and marketing. You cannot hand the agency a few brochures and say "go make me some ads." You need to provide ongoing guidance and feedback to ensure that the creative effort forcefully and accurately speaks to the needs, hopes, and wants of your target markets. Your agency may know *how* to communicate (creative execution and implementation), but you know *what* to communicate (product features and benefits of interest to various key markets and audiences).

A good client is not removed and aloof; a good client is involved in his advertising at every step. Advertising and marketing management is not just something the advertising agency or manager does; it should be a primary concern of top executives, including the president and CEO.

Respect Your Own Expertise

While you should listen to your agency, realize there are some things about which you have superior knowledge, some areas where they would do well to defer to your judgment. Clients often have superior knowledge of their product and markets. They have a more thorough understanding, based on years of experience in a given industry, of who the buyers are, what their main concerns are, and what they look for in the client's type of product.

Do not let your agency tell you all your feelings and thoughts concerning these things are invalid, and to relax and let them worry about persuading your market. An agency that does not listen to its client, claiming to be an expert in all things, is not an agency you want to deal with.

As Jo Coudert observed, "No amount of expertise substitutes for an intimate knowledge of a person or situation." The agency may indeed have much more general expertise in advertising than you do. But you and your colleagues have an intimate knowledge of your company's marketing situation and history that they do not. The agency should eagerly seek and absorb, rather than reject, any insights you can provide. This means not that they except everything you say at face value, but that they listen and consider each observation carefully.

Usually the client knows the key marketing problem or challenge but has not been able to articulate it. The agency, consultant, or freelancer, by questioning and probing, helps bring what is already known to the surface so it can be recognized, acknowledged, and then addressed by the advertising.

Avoid Using A Team Approach

The trend in advertising today is to get a lot of people involved in the planning, creation, review, and approval of campaigns. Unfortunately, this is often not an effective method of producing good advertising. Having too many people involved drives up the cost and inhibits, rather than generates, creative thinking. As political advertising consultant David Garth has observed, “When you have 15 of the greatest minds working, you come up with zero.”

Do not create advertising campaigns through group efforts, surveys, or company opinion polls. Old cliches like “too many cooks spoil the broth” and “a moose is a cow designed by committee” became accepted into the vocabulary because they are true. Yes, group efforts can be productive. But many great things have come from the efforts of individuals: The Mona Lisa, penicillin, Federal Express, *War and Peace,* and the personal computer.

Most ad agency people say the best combination is a writer and artist sitting in a room working together. But personally, I believe that most good advertising is created by one person locking himself or herself up in a room with a typewriter, word processor, desktop publishing system, or pad and pencil to think and write. I empathize with author Fran Leibowitz, who says, “I do not work well with people—nor do I wish to learn how to do so.” This viewpoint is perhaps too extreme but does acknowledge the fact that creativity is primarily an individual rather than a group activity, and should be treated as such.

The Fallacy Of Testing

Claude Hopkins believed subjective judgment had no place in advertising management. “Almost any question can be answered, cheaply, quickly, and finally, by a test campaign,” he wrote. “And that’s the way to answer them—not by arguments around a table.”

Unfortunately, while in theory his attitude is sensible, in reality things are not quite as Hopkins describes. Many large corporations that sell to mass consumer markets are unable to determine the effectiveness (or lack of effectiveness) of their advertising, because so many other factors—price, distribution, packaging, the economy, sales promotion—are involved in the marketing mix. By comparison, many small and medium-size companies are not sophisticated enough to track and measure advertising results. They don’t key code ads or mailings, don’t know where leads and sales originate, and cannot compare ads or mailings on a scientific basis to determine which is best. Many firms selling to specialized vertical markets use mailing lists so small and publications with such limited circulation that the returns are not large enough to provide statistically valid test results.

So, while a test may seem to be the best way to answer questions, we must recognize that most companies are not set up to conduct pure direct marketing tests as Hopkins talked about.

What to do? First, if you're not as scientific as Claude Hopkins wants you to be, at least try to be more scientific than you are now. Code your ad coupons, reply cards, questionnaires, and order forms—even if it means doing it by hand. Use some of the lead sheets, tracking charts, and other measurement tools provided in Chapter 41.

And, even if your results are not 100 percent complete or accurate or statistically valid, some information is better than no information. If your old ad pulled 100 replies a month, and your new ad is getting 500 replies a month, it doesn't take a scientist to figure out that the new one is better than the old. Try to do as much testing, tracking, and measurement as you can, even if it's not "scientific." In the same way a scientist needs to record the results of his experiments to know what works and what doesn't, you need to record, monitor, and analyze ad response to know which ads are most profitable and which are duds.

A Few Additional Tips On Working With Ad Agencies, Freelancers, And Other Creatives

1. *Pay fairly.* Pay fair rates for services rendered. An underpaid vendor is an unhappy and unproductive vendor. Everything is negotiable, but only so far. By all means, get the best price, but pay enough so your agency is making a decent profit on your account.

2. *Pay on time.* Pay on time (in 30 days or less) and your vendor will get a warm glow whenever you call. Better still, get a check out in 10 days or less, and the vendor will treat you with extra-special care. Few things are as annoying or unpleasant to the vendor as having to call or write you repeatedly to collect an unpaid invoice for work done, approved, and used by you.

3. *Cooperate.* Be available to answer questions, review rough layouts and outlines, or give direction. Review all materials submitted in a timely fashion, especially if the deadline is tight.

4. *Respect their time.* Avoid unnecessary meetings. Do as much as you can by mail, fax, and phone. When you ask vendors to see you, do not keep them waiting for their appointment with you. To the agency or freelancer, time is money. If you waste their time, your account will be less profitable and hence, less desirable.

5. *Let them hear from you.* Don't force the vendor to call you to get feedback. If you have something to say—positive or negative—get back to them right away. If things are delayed internally, call to let them know what the situation is. Don't let them sit there guessing and worrying that something's gone amiss when it hasn't.

6. *Critique work rationally.* "I don't like it" or "It doesn't send me" is a meaningless critique and a frustrating response for the agency to deal with. The key in reviewing advertising is to give specific, objective criticisms. Subjective and vague comments don't give the agency any guidelines for revision and often lead to hurt feelings, defensiveness, and a gradual collapse of the client/vendor relationship.

7. *Be specific.* How specific should your review of the material be? Instead of "I don't like the headline," tell your account executive, "The most important feature of our service is that we deliver on the same day rather than overnight, as our competitors do—and this same-day versus overnight delivery should be stressed in the headline versus the quality/customer service aspects the headline now talks about."

Remember: the ad agency people are not mind readers. It is not enough to say you want changes; you must specify, as much as possible, what those changes are.

Does this mean you rewrite the copy or redo the layout? No. That's the agency's job. But since you both have a mutual goal of producing an ad that makes you happy and meets your deadline, don't make their job unnecessarily difficult, either. Tell them what you like, and what you don't like. And be as specific as possible.

How to present your comments? If they are minor, and can be gone over in 10 minutes or less, a telephone call is appropriate. If they're extensive, or require a lot of additional information, give your instructions in writing, not orally. The very act of writing out your comments forces you to be more specific.

8. *The fewer levels of approval, the better.* Minimize the number of people to whom an approval copy of the ad must be routed; the fewer the better. If you require too many signatures for approval, you will have too many cooks spoiling the broth. You will end up with an ad that pleases no one and says nothing.

9. *Attach an approval form.* When routing any material for approval, attach an approval form that lists the reviewers in order in which the copy and layout should be routed (you start with the lowest-ranking reviewer and end with the person in highest authority, who as final say). People who want to see a copy for information purposes but do not have official authority to make changes are on a "cc" (courtesy copy) list; they get a chance to give their comments, but you are free to incorporate or ignore them as you see fit.

Once all comments are received, it is the advertising manager's responsibility to consolidate all reviewer's comments into a single corrected manuscript (and, if required) cover letter for transmittal to the agency.

Do not ask your agency to go through each reviewer's copy and consolidate the comments. First, it's not their job, and they'll have to bill you for the extra work. Second, they do not have the authority to make a decision regarding conflicting comments from different managers—that's something you must do from your end. The agency can only work efficiently with one person of authority at the client company (you), and it is your job to act as liaison between the agency and your management.

10. *Proofread everything.* Do not rely on your agency, printer, freelancer, or other vendor for proofreading. Have everything proofread by at least three people in your office.

This advice is not meant to save agencies and freelancers from extra work. They should and do proofread. But, once you've written and rewritten and read a piece of copy a dozen or so times, you can no longer proof it as effectively as someone who has not seen it before.

As a client, you—not your vendor—are responsible for the final proofreading of your job. Many printers and other vendors are asking clients to sign statements to that effect so as to remove liability in case an error appears in the printed piece. I think this is reasonable, especially if you produce technical materials or other literature containing jargon, acronyms, and specialized terms the agency proofreader will not be able to find in standard dictionaries. By all means, ask your agency to proof everything carefully. But you must do the same. And the final responsibility is yours.

CHAPTER 40

Working with Management

Just as your ad agency works for a client (you), you too serve clients within your company. As the advertising manager, or head of the advertising department, you provide advertising services to groups, divisions, or product lines requiring such services.

Generally, the advertising manager deals with managers in three areas. First, you provide advertising services to *product management;* these people may be called product managers, brand managers, or marketing managers, and are responsible for the overall marketing of specific products or product lines.

Second, you have a relationship with sales management, since in most cases advertising and sales work together to generate new business. Typically, advertising creates awareness, initial interest, and inquiries which are turned over to salespeople. Salespeople call on leads and prospects and get the actual purchase order or contract for goods or services.

Third, you must deal with top management. The company president, CEO, or division manager may all get involved with advertising, and often have the final authority to approve or veto advertising budgets, plans, and programs as well as specific ads and campaigns.

Perhaps you'd prefer to be able to do as you please without the cooperation or approval of others. Realistically, however, that's not likely to happen in the corporate environment. For this reason, it's important to get along well with others and to deal with your colleagues and bosses effectively. This chapter gives some advice on doing so.

Product And Brand Managers

At industrial firms, the person in charge of marketing a product or product line is called a *product manager* or a *marketing manager;* at a packaged goods or other consumer firm, this person is called a *brand manager,* because he or she is responsible for marketing a particular brand (e.g., Cheerios, Tide, Dove, Pepsi).

Under the product/brand management system, a manager is assigned the total marketing responsibility for one of the company's brands, products, product lines, or services. For instance, at Procter & Gamble, there is a different brand manager for each of the many brands. The brand or product manager may have assistant brand or product managers working under him or her.

The product or brand manager (and from now on, *product manager* will signify both) is responsible for such diverse responsibilities as planning, strategy, market research, product development, packaging, pricing, distribution, sales promotion, and advertising.

Does this mean the product manager designs the package, conducts the phone surveys, or writes the ads and commercials? No. These tasks are performed by other manager/departments within the corporation. For instance, a graphics manager might produce the logo and package design, while the advertising manager would get the ads and commercials produced. Proposals would be prepared by the manager of technical publications.

Product managers are *line* managers, meaning they have direct bottom-line profit-and-loss responsibility. They are rewarded if sales go up and held responsible if sales go down.

Advertising, on the other hand, is a *staff* or *support* function, meaning it is a service utilized by product managers as needed. The advertising department does the actual work of supervising, creating, and implementing advertising campaigns. However, this is done for each individual product manager under his or her direction and approval.

In most corporations, the product manager makes the final decisions, which the advertising manager carries out. A smart product manager will listen to the advice and suggestions of a knowledgeable, competent advertising manager. But usually, the product manager—not the advertising manager—has final say as to the content of an ad or the theme of a campaign.

The Product-Orientation Versus Advertising-Orientation

To get along with your product managers and serve them effectively, it's important to know the difference between how they think about their job and how you think about the job at hand.

Most advertising managers are, naturally, advertising-oriented, perhaps overly so. They tend to place too much emphasis on advertising, have the myopic view that advertising is the main or most important component of marketing a product, and focus on the *advertising itself* as the product of their own labors rather than as a tool to sell the product or communicate with the customer. It's a fact that most advertising managers I know get far more excited about looking at a new ad, brochure, or commercial than seeing a new design, prototype, or finished product.

This is a weakness advertising managers must work hard to overcome. Advertising is important, but in most industries, there are many other factors that play an equal role in making the sale. These include product design, technological advances, packaging, distribution, pricing, and salesmanship. In some industries, advertising may even be less important than sales representatives or price or channels of distribution. While your work is important, you must be realistic and understand what you can contribute to the company's success—and what advertising cannot do.

Advertising managers must also realize that most of their fellow managers are not advertising-oriented. Many product managers, for example, come from a sales, not an advertising, background. Sales-oriented marketing managers are more oriented toward short-term, immediate results, not long-term planning and business-building. In industrial firms, most product managers were engineers; engineers are enthralled with numbers and physical products (technology), not communications or selling. Many product managers with engineering backgrounds do not believe advertising is effective and think that technical buyers are not influenced by it.

Product managers have a different perspective than advertising managers in two important respects. First, product managers deal with the "big picture," while advertising managers are concerned with an important but narrow function. Product managers, in effect, are running mini-enterprises within the larger overall business of the corporation, and are responsible for all aspects of business marketing management. Advertising managers have the luxury of being specialists.

Second, product managers, as discussed in a previous chapter, are product-oriented. They are excited by the product, not the brochure, the ad, or the mailing. They view their product as a fascinating, unique invention composed of special features, and their urge is to want to tell everyone in the world about each of these wonderful innovations and features in great detail.

Advertising managers, on the other hand, are usually more excited by the idea or concept of the product, rather than the physical product itself. Advertising managers want to communicate specific benefits of the product and get excited when their ad or promotion influences a great number of potential buyers to take action. Advertising managers are happiest when writing copy, planning campaigns, or working with the ad agency on the creative aspects of advertising. Product managers are often happiest sitting over the shoulder of the design engineer as he adds a new feature to a prototype drawing of a widget.

Proof of this is that product managers are usually enthusiasts about the product they sell; for instance, it's not surprising to find that the product manager of sail boats at a boating company owns a boat and sails frequently. Advertising managers are often not enthusiasts; their interest is *communication* about the topic, not the topic itself. If they have an interest in the product, they tend to be *armchair* enthusiasts (i.e., they'd rather read about sailing than actually go out and learn to sail or they'd rather read a book on astronomy than go outside and look through a telescope).

These portraits border on being stereotypes and certainly don't apply in all cases. It's quite possible they don't apply at all to you or those you know. But you should have an idea of the attitude and approach your product managers may bring to the job.

Working Effectively With Your Product Managers

Here are some suggestions on how to have a productive, conflict-free relationship with your product managers:

1. Treat all product managers as equal. In reality, they are not equals; those managers who handle the big brands with highest sales re-

ceive the lion's share of the advertising department's budget and attention, while those who have been pushed off in a corner with a minor product line or unimportant brand receive a smaller allocation and minimal use of the ad department's resources.

Yet, you should handle the lesser product lines with the same courtesy, positive attitude, and good service you give to the superstars. It's a basic principle of business that the smallest client or account wants (and feels he deserves) just as much care and attention as the biggest client. This should be applied to the "clients" (product managers) you as the advertising manager provide service to.

Do not tell lower-ranked product managers that you don't have time for them or that you can't get to their work because you're doing a big project for Brand X. They will resent being treated as inferiors and will do everything in their power to retaliate (possibly by saying negative things about you to others).

Instead, be enthusiastic about working on smaller projects and campaigns for minor brands. What you can't give them in terms of budget, you can make up for with enthusiasm and creativity. Suggest alternative media and creative promotions (direct mail, sales promotion, publicity, product endorsements, new channels of distribution, etc.) that will give them the selling power of a big TV or print ad campaign within their limited budget.

The benefits? Successes in these small campaigns will give you a reputation as a smart, economic-minded marketer. And good treatment of other people can only bring good will for you in return.

2. Learn to allocate your resources—including time, budget, and agency personnel—fairly and sensibly between different product managers.

All will want a disproportionate share of advertising resources. Even those who don't understand advertising or say they don't believe it will want to see ads for their products in all the magazines their customers or prospects read. If they're missing from an issue of the industry trade, especially a special issue, expect them to come to your office with the magazine demanding to know, "Why don't we have an ad in here?"

Distribute your advertising plan and budget to all product managers. This shows them what things cost (many have no idea of the high cost of ad space, mailings, or print production) and helps them realize that your resources are not infinite. Also, when they see the master plan, they realize that you are serving many, many product lines with your limited resources—and will be less likely to push for more attention.

If a product manager wants additional services or promotions that are not in the annual budget, offer to help or provide the total program if they supply the funds out of their budget. Often in large corporations that complain "We don't have the budget," money previously deemed unavailable can be found somewhere, in someone's budget, if the project is wanted badly enough.

3. Learn how to say "no" politely. Before you say "no" to your product managers, ask yourself these questions:

- *"Is this project really so minor that we shouldn't handle it?"* Don't be a snob who only gets involved if it's a major ad campaign or TV commercial. Often seemingly small or minor promotions can produce more impressive results.

- *"Am I so important that this task is beneath me?"* Don't get overly obsessed with raising the image and prestige of the advertising department within the corporation by taking on only "important" jobs. Yes, prestige and image are important; you don't want to be doing every two-bit editing or printing job that comes along. But don't get too big an ego. It is not beneath your status to do a routine task for someone if they ask it as a favor. If you truly feel the job is beneath you, delegate it to a staff member or secretary, but still have it handled by your department. Your product managers will appreciate the extra help.

- *"If I don't do it, who else will?"* A routine task like having business cards made up or ordering golf balls with the company logo may seem beneath you. But if you don't do it for your client, is there someone else in your company that will?

If there's another person or department that can handle it, by all means direct your product manager to that department. On the other hand, if the product manager truly doesn't know how to get the job done, and you do, and there's no one else to turn to, why not be a nice guy and help them out?

4. Be as helpful as you can. As an advertising manager, your philosophy should be to do as much as you can to help your product managers—even if that means occasionally doing things you do not want to do or that you feel are beneath you. Whether it involves editing an article or technical paper, helping someone write their speech, or getting some slides produced, your product managers will appreciate the extra help. Product managers want to work with advertising managers who are helpful and cooperative, not those who are difficult and aloof. Which are you?

5. Connect your product managers with other resources that can help them. The advertising manager often serves as the unofficial "clearinghouse" of information on local printers, photographers, illustrators, technical writers, and others whose services product managers may require. If the job can be done with the product manager hiring the service firm directly without your intervention, by all means encourage direct contact between the vendor and the product manager. It will eliminate the middle-man and save you time and money. Insist on being involved only when your expertise will enhance the final result or when the vendor or product manager would prefer it.

6. Become a product enthusiast. If you work for a company that makes golf balls and you don't play golf, learn. Your product managers will respect you more—and relate to you better—when you become an enthusiastic user of their product. If you don't use the product, they'll question whether you're really enthusiastic and knowledgeable enough to do the job. Their argument is: "If he doesn't use the product, how can he understand why our prospects and customers buy it?" There is more than a little validity in this argument, although it is not an absolute that you must use a product or service in order to promote it effectively.

7. Teach them to be advertising enthusiasts. Just as you must learn to become a product enthusiast, your product managers must become enthusiastic about advertising if it is really to work for them. They must understand what it is, how it works, what it can do, what it cannot do, and what is required of them to make it work.

The best way to get a product manager who doesn't believe in advertising to become enthusiastic about it is with small pilot programs—for instance, a limited market ad campaign or mailing which generates immediate, measurable, tangible results proofing the effectiveness of the advertising. Remember, product managers are results-oriented. They won't like a campaign because you say it's good. They won't believe in advertising because you say it works. But if you can get them some results, they'll believe.

8. Be in on the planning. Don't be the type of advertising manager who just "gets it produced" or "makes brochures." You should be a part of the planning process from the early stages. The more input you have in the planning of marketing activities, the more effective the advertising will be.

Often, a marketing campaign does not generate the desired results because of some fundamental defect in the product, such as design, pricing, construction, features, benefits, distribution, or target audience. Your job is to work with the product manager to make sure what you're offering is what the customers really want. If that's the case, you'll both be more successful. Remember, while advertising can make a good product more desirable, it usually cannot make a bad product a best-seller in its field.

9. Establish realistic goals. Most advertising managers over-promise in terms of what they will deliver or the results it will achieve. At the same time, they also under-estimate the costs of producing campaigns and promotions. No wonder so many product managers complain, "I spent a lot of money and it didn't work!"

Do not over-promise. Be honest about what you can and cannot achieve. Don't tell the product manager you'll get him publicity on the front page of *Business Week* when you know you can make no such guarantee. Instead, explain what's involved in sending out a press release—the cost, how and why it works, and typical results he can expect.

10. Build measurement and accountability into every marketing communication. Instead of just getting a message out, generate an immediate, tangible response. Include reply cards with every sales letter you send out. Put a coupon in every ad. Insert questionnaires in your sales literature packages. Always ask for a response from the prospect. Product managers like to see immediate results and are less thrilled with things like readership, preference, and awareness studies.

11. Make them look good. The more successful you make the product manager, the better he'll like you. You need to give him an advertising campaign he can "sell" to management, but one that will also sell the product to the consumer. That's not an easy task. But anything you can do to make his life easier or more successful will be appreciated.

Working With The Sales Force

The second department advertising managers work with on a fairly frequent basis is sales—specifically, sales managers and salespeople.

To deal effectively with sales management, you must understand their mindset and how it differs from the advertising manager's mentality.

Here are some observations about salespeople and their view of advertising:

1. Most salespeople are present-oriented, not future-oriented. They are doers, not planners. They want to make a sale today, not build a mar-

ket for tomorrow or next year. This is the opposite of marketing, which seeks not only immediate results but also to build a business that will be successful and profitable over the long haul.

2. Many salespeople believe that advertising doesn't work, that it doesn't sell or help sell products, and that advertising people don't know anything about selling. And they're partially correct—in some cases, advertising people *don't* know anything about selling, and the ads they create don't help sell the product.

3. Advertising and selling are closely linked, so salespeople resent it when advertising is created without their input and the advertising department shows no interest in speaking with salespeople about markets, products, or selling strategies.

4. Many salespeople believe that leads generated by advertising are of little value. This can also be partially true, especially when the advertising and marketing program does nothing to qualify the lead in advance of turning the leads over to salespeople. The salespeople call a few leads generated by bingo-card (reader service card) response, and when the prospects brush them off, they complain that they are getting worthless leads.

5. Many salespeople are uncomfortable with prospecting for new business. They would rather talk to existing customers than make calls to new prospects or leads. They would rather work existing markets than pursue unfamiliar territory. This is directly opposite from advertising, which has uncovering new leads as one of its goals.

6. Salespeople are generally paid a commission based on gross sales; thus, they have a vested interest in selling those products that generate the highest commissions. Advertising people, on the other hand, generally like to work with products that are new, interesting, or innovative, or that have unusual or special features that can be dramatically promoted in advertising.

7. Salespeople believe they are on the "front line" of selling and view most advertising professionals as theoreticians. Most salespeople believe that advertising professionals would be inept in selling, and they have greater respect for advertising people who have done some selling or come from a sales background: They feel such sales-oriented advertising managers can better understand the needs and concerns of salespeople.

8. The greatest cause of salespeople's animosity towards the advertising department is a perceived indifference to their opinions and needs.

How To Work Effectively With Salespeople

Should the opinions of salespeople be given more weight by advertising managers when it comes to getting their input in the planning and creation of ad campaigns? The answer is yes and no.

Certainly, there are some advertising managers who do operate too remotely. They tend to like the theory and creativity of advertising; they rarely face prospects, speak to customers, or get input from those within the company who deal with the product and its end-users on a daily basis. While theory is fine, it is possible to get *too* wrapped up in reading John Caples and Claude Hopkins while ignoring the realities of today's marketplace.

Salespeople can be a valuable source of information concerning the market: their likes, dislikes, preferences, and buying habits. Make it a habit to talk with salespeople to get a "pulse" of how your products are performing in the marketplace and how prospects and customers react to them.

Here are some of the things an advertising manager can learn from speaking with his sales manager, field salespeople, and sales representatives:

- Which products are selling best? Which are slow movers?
- Who are our customers?
- What are their interests, concerns, likes, and dislikes?
- What is the biggest problem the customer has that our product helps solve?
- What feature or aspect of our product do customers like best?
- What feature or aspect is *most* important to them and should be stressed in advertising?
- What feature or aspect of our product do customers like *least?*
- How should this weakness be addressed in our advertising—if at all?
- How are prospects *using* our product? What are the most common applications?
- What *markets* does our product have success in? And in which markets does it not do so well? Why?
- What about competition? Which products/brands are taking sales away from us? When our prospects are considering a purchase, which products/brands do they look at in addition to ours?

- How do we compare to the competition? What are our advantages? weaknesses?
- What do the customers say about our product? Do you have customers who would be willing to give us a testimonial or endorse our product in an ad or commercial?
- How does the market view our price? Are we high-priced? low-priced? Is price a major factor for the prospect? Or are other factors—quality, reliability, delivery, speed, efficiency, operating costs, size—more important to the buyers?

What Salespeople Cannot Tell You

Salespeople can provide valuable insight into how your product is perceived in the marketplace. They know, better than we advertising people do, what the customers are looking for, what they're buying, what they're rejecting, and what they want. It makes sense to tap into this wealth of knowledge.

However, you should turn to salespeople for market, product, prospect, and customer information only. Do *not* rely on their comments concerning what they think of the advertising, what their customers say about it, or how to improve it.

You can certainly ask for their input, if you wish; it won't do any harm. Just be certain not to put too much weight on their judgments. Remember, they are experts in sales, not advertising. Just because they don't like an ad or think it should be rewritten a certain way doesn't mean that will work. Just because they heard a customer say he didn't like or understand your last ad doesn't mean it's a bad ad and you should immediately create a new ad based on that person's comments.

The problem with asking salespeople, customers, and other laypeople what they think of your ad is that they will then proceed to critique the ad *as an ad.* When they give their comments, they don't do so as a potential customer deciding whether to buy a product; your asking them to give an opinion automatically puts them in the role of ad critic, and their comments reflect their opinion of the ad based on what *they* think constitutes good advertising. So if the ad has a lot of copy, the salesperson will tell you it's lousy because people won't read "all that copy"—despite the fact that such ads have proven enormously profitable. If he doesn't like green, and your ad uses green, he/she'll say the ad looks terrible.

You are interested in the perceptions of salespeople as they concern the product, its features and benefits, and how customers react to those features and benefits. But you are the advertising expert—not the salesperson. It is your job to take the knowledge of which features and benefits have greatest appeal and translate them, using proven principles of persuasive communication, into an ad, brochure, or mailing that gets the desired result. The fact that a salesperson doesn't like long copy, or hates the photo, or thinks the color of the brochure should be green because he doesn't like the blue, is unimportant or irrelevant.

You should not, however, communicate to the salesperson that his opinion is unimportant or irrelevant. People love to give their opinions and are hurt when you dismiss them, don't listen, or tell them they're wrong.

So the best approach when speaking with salespeople and other "ad critics" about your advertising is to listen and be genuinely open to suggestions, criticisms, and comments. If you hear something that makes sense, by all means explore it further. In particular, if there is a consensus—that is, *every* salesperson tells you that his customers say they don't understand your latest ad—that's a sign that the criticism carries more weight and should be given further consideration.

Or, you may hear a comment from *one person* that is not repeated by others yet somehow rings true. The idea for the famous TV commercials showing how fried chicken absorbed far less of one brand of cooking oil than another came from *one* reply to thousands of market surveys completed; on the form a woman had written in the margin, "Although you didn't ask, I have noted that your cooking oil doesn't go into the food as much, so less oil is needed and the food tastes lighter and less greasy."

Many of the suggestions made by well-meaning salespeople, however, simply are not workable or applicable. In these cases, thank them politely for their time, but do not feel compelled to act on the suggestions. You are the authority in your company as to how to construct an ad campaign; remember, the salesperson didn't feel the need to ask *you* for tips on selling!

How to Win the Cooperation of Salespeople

If a salesperson gives you a critique of an ad, try to incorporate one or two of the suggested changes in the next ad if you think they will do some good or, if they don't improve it, if you don't think they'll do any harm.

When the ad is produced, send a copy to the salesperson with a note thanking him for his helpful suggestions and noting that the suggestions have been incorporated into the new ad.

Do this a few times and you will rapidly gain a reputation with the sales department as someone who listens to them and values the experience and knowledge of salespeople as it relates to promoting the company's products.

As time goes on, this technique will help you develop a friendly rather than adversarial relationship with the sales department. They will become less critical of advertising, more open to your ideas, and more eager to use and succeed with the leads you provide them.

This is the simple result you get whenever you treat people as if they matter rather than dismiss them out of hand, and can work with all your relationships in all facets of business and personal life.

How to Create Sales Support Materials Salespeople Like and Use

As much as possible, sales support materials should be flexible, modular, and easily tailored by the individual salespeople to the style and manner of presentation they make. When expensive sales kits are created without the input of salespeople, and then mass distributed to these salespeople, who are told "Use it," the results are seldom favorable.

One pharmaceutical salesperson told me, "The company regularly issues sales kits and presentation materials, which are created by the ad agency with no input from the salespeople. So when I get the material, I take it out and try it on a few sales calls. It invariably fails because the material has no relevance to what the doctor wants to know about the disease or the product. So after those three or four sales calls, I throw it away and develop my own presentation based on what I know will work."

Making elaborate presentation aids, charts, folders, and the like is generally a wrong strategy for several reasons. First, it forces a standardized presentation upon each salesperson, when in fact a sales professional can greatly increase sales results using his own skills and abilities to customize according to both his own personality as well as the needs of each different prospect.

Second, expensive flip-charts, color panels, and other such printed materials are fixed and cannot be altered. Yet the initial use by salespeople in the field should be considered "test drive" of these materials, and many useful refinements can be made based upon this feedback. It's better to have materials that are modular and easily updated so that they can be improved based on the reactions of the prospects. Telemarketing scripts, for instance, can be fine-tuned a dozen or more times during the first hundred or so test calls.

Third, and most important, salespeople are likely to reject "canned" presentations without your ever knowing it. Instead of telling their management, and risk being commanded to use the material, they accept the costly presentation folder or kit gratefully, toss it in the trunk under the spare tire, and use the presentation they had been planning to use all along. It is virtually impossible to force field salespeople to use materials or follow procedures they feel are not relevant or productive.

It's far better to provide modular, easily updated materials the salespeople can use and tailor to their needs. For example, instead of making a slide show presenting a new product, with script and all, that the salespeople will change, rearrange, and rewrite, until it suits them, you may find it more productive to produce the basic slides they needed (for example, photos of the product, charts, graphs, and so on) and store a quantity of each in a slide cabinet. Salespeople will appreciate this resource and take from it what they need, as they will always do.

The same is true with printed material. If the salesperson is to have a kit or book, make it a three-ring binder with three-hole-punched plastic sheets that hold the various sales inserts—price sheets, product photos, and so on. This allows the salesperson to add, delete, change, and rearrange pages in the presentation to suit his needs. If salespeople cannot tailor the presentation to their needs, they won't use it.

If you find salespeople are creating their own inserts, presentations, or visual aids, do not complain that they're encroaching on your territory. They are the ones who must give the presentation, and so they must feel comfortable with the materials they use. However, if the materials look amateurish and present an inappropriate image of the company, you can offer to redo them to improve the appearance.

Selling The Advertising Program To Top Management

In addition to product managers and sales, the third group advertising must deal with on a regular basis is top management. By this we mean the president, chief executive officer, general manager, owner, or any other executives who rank above the advertising manager and are the final decision-making authorities concerning how much money should be allocated to advertising and how it should be spent as well as what should be said in advertising, how it should be stated, and how it should look.

Few, if any, advertising managers have final say in these things. The advertising manager is the one responsible for the planning and implementation. The advertising manager recommends a plan and budget and presents specific campaigns and promotions for approval. But one or more higher-level executives has the final say. You do not.

For this reason, your success depends, in large part, on your ability to "sell" management both on the value of advertising in general and on the specific ads, campaigns, or promotions you want to run in specific.

Often this is a task which advertising managers find distasteful and for which they are ill-suited. There are several reasons for this.

First, many advertising managers are introverts by nature. Many come from an art or writing background and have liberal arts or English rather than business training. They would rather be writing or designing or thinking than selling or making management presentations, and this lack of comfort giving presentations comes across in the boardroom. According to a *Business Marketing* survey,[1] 24 percent of successful advertising managers communicate the results of their programs to management in presentations given at sales meetings. If you are uncomfortable doing so, you might document your plans and programs in a written report; 22 percent of those surveyed chose that route.

Second, many advertising managers come from an ad agency background, which has taught them to view management in a somewhat adversarial light. Just as some ad agency staff see the client as "the enemy," some advertising managers have a similar attitude toward top management. The most common complaints I hear from advertising managers are "My management doesn't understand advertising" and "When budgets are cut, advertising is the first thing to go."

Third, many advertising managers lack "political" skills. In their heart of hearts, they have not bought into the corporate culture the way many of their peers and colleagues in other departments have; many would rather be oil painting or sitting at home writing the Great American Novel or running their own small advertising firm. They are not good at "playing the game" and have not developed the skills necessary for "selling" management on their ideas and programs.

Fourth, advertising managers and corporate executives tend to speak different languages. When the advertising manager talks about things like *awareness, recall, brand preference,* and *readership studies,* it often falls on deaf ears. Top executives are very big-picture and bottom-line oriented. When you see an ad, you think of it as a communication tool. When a corporate executive (or, for that matter, an entrepreneur) looks at an ad, he or she is likely to ask, "How much money did we spend on this, and how much money did it make?"

Fifth, while product managers are product-oriented and sales managers are sales-oriented, top executives are *company*-oriented. When reviewing advertising campaigns, they are likely to ask such questions or make such comments as:

"The logo should be bigger."
"Our slogan should be featured more prominently."
"Put more about the company in the copy up front."
"Does this ad tell our company story?"
"Is this ad consistent with our corporate image?"
"Stress our quality and dedication to excellence more."
"Tell the reader what a good company we are."

Unfortunately, all of these things are of little interest to the prospect and can severely lessen the effectiveness of the ad. Through books, articles, memos, clippings, seminars, training, or whatever means available, top executives must be made to understand these fundamental truths of advertising:

- Prospects don't care about your company or your image or this year's corporate "theme." All the prospect wants to know is, "What's in it for me?"
- You cannot insert this type of "corporate-drive" copy into an ad, brochure, or mailing on the theory that it is simply an addition. Company-centered copy, wherever it appears, bores and turns off readers, destroying the ability of the ad or mailing to generate the results you want.
- "Quality" as a copy motivator is ineffective. The word is so overused that it has lost all meaning. To say in an ad "We care about quality" is like saying "We make products"—it is not a sales point in any sense.
- Other words executives like that are awful in copy (this list courtesy of freelance annual report writer Bob Otterbourg: challenge, opportunity, fundamental achievements, pioneering efforts, state of the art.
- The size, reputation, and financial stability of your corporation may be relevant to some prospects in some situations. But it is *always* secondary to the benefits that your product or service provides.
- The reason many ad writers and designers make the corporate slogan small and unnoticeable is that most corporate slogans are meaningless fluff phrases that say nothing and should not therefore be the center of attention when used in an ad or brochure. Does this apply to yours?
- Do not allow corporate advertising requirements (e.g., the need to conform to some graphic standard or incorporate certain boilerplate language) interfere with the creation of advertising. These requirements,

designed to ensure a consistent graphic design and copy style, are secondary in importance compared to the main goal of *selling products.*

- If you insist on getting a "corporate message" across do so in separate corporate advertising and communications pieces. Do not mix corporate and product messages in the same ad. (Most corporate advertising is a waste of time and money, but if the CEO insists, remember its his company.)

Here are some additional guidelines for dealing productively with your top management:

1. *Understand who is in charge.* Who is the real decision maker? It's not always the vice president of advertising or marketing or corporate communications. You may have to sell someone else—the president, the chairman of the board, the owner, the owner's son—to get your program through.

2. *Know the background of your executive decision makers.* Is the president a former engineer? Then he is likely to hold the viewpoint that the function of advertising is to transmit technical information. Does he have a financial background? Many financial people place little value on advertising because it cannot be measured as precisely as, say, a monthly profit-and-loss statement. Know the background and prejudices those above you bring to their responsibilities as it relates to your function.

3. *Find out whether they believe in advertising.* Some will lie and say yes to protect your feelings or avoid confrontation. But many others will be candid about where they see advertising in the hierarchy of "important things to worry about." If they're believers, great! If not, you have a selling job to do.

4. *How to sell top management on the concept of advertising.* Rather than guess what will convince them, ask, "What would I have to do to show you, and have you believe it, that advertising works?" Some (the MBAs, perhaps) will want to see case studies and articles from the *Harvard Business Review* proving the effectiveness of advertising. Others will say, "Set up a program where you can measure the responses generated by ads and which of those leads converts to sales and the total dollar sales generated per dollar spent on advertising."

Although it may be overly simplistic for me to say, "Just do it," that's essentially the best advice. You can talk about all the advertising theory you want, but you'll only convince your management by showing them the proof *they* need, not what you *think* is proof.

5. *Trace all major orders to their source.* One sneaky, but fairly effective way, to sell management on advertising is to prove that large contracts and substantial new business originated from a lead generated by an ad, article, mailer, or press release. A short note or memo with the original ad attached might read: "Bill: Congratulations on winning the Boeing Contract. I searched through the records and found they originally came to us through our ad in ELECTRONIC NEWS—so the campaign has already paid for itself many times over from this one sale alone."

Although this is overstating the case (obviously in industrial selling large contracts are secured through many sales and marketing contacts, not a single exposure to one ad), it's an argument that most executives find compelling and convincing: namely, that advertising must be worthwhile if it brings in big customers and sales revenues that exceed its cost.

6. *Document your successes and demonstrate results.* Whenever your advertising program produces a tangible, measurable result, communicate this to management. For instance, don't just send them a color reprint of the new ad, as many advertising managers routinely do. Instead, send it with a cover memo that says, "FYI: Our new ad was the second-best read ad in the last three issues of HYDROCARBONS TODAY and the number-three lead producer, generating 1,250 inquiries—more than any other ad we have run in that publication to date." Management is interested in results, not ads.

7. *Don't make promises you can't keep.* When pressured by skeptical management to defend advertising expenditures, nervous advertising managers tend to make claims that are overstated and promises they cannot keep. Avoid this syndrome.

For example, you know that it is scientifically impossible to predict the response to any ad or mailing, so don't tell management, "If you let me run this ad it will make us a lot of money"—because you don't know for certain this is so. Instead, explain the type of response such an ad typically generates (or has generated in the past) and then show why you think this ad is likely to do as well or better. But don't make promises you can't keep. Doing so destroys your credibility.

Selling Specific Campaigns And Promotions To Management

In large consumer goods companies, the presentation of major campaigns by the ad agency involves major hoopla and a carnival-like atmosphere that is both stupid and detrimental.

Typically, a huge contingent from the agency and every executive from your company who has nothing better to do that day gather in the boardroom to watch "the show." These executives generally have no idea of the objectives of the campaign and have reviewed no copy, outlines, or other materials prior to the presentation.

The agency nervously presents the print ads or TV story boards, lamely explaining why they think their approach is great and creative and should be loved by client and consumers alike, while the audience sits in stoney-faced silence.

After the presentation the uncomfortable silence continues either until the highest-ranking executive opens her mouth to give her opinion, or someone (either the agency president or the ad manager) turns to the group and asks, "What do you think?"

The problem with this scenario is that it forces ad reviewers to be clever and opinionated instead of thoughtful and contemplative. If they were reviewing the advertising in the privacy and leisure of their own offices, their comments would be well thought out and most likely constructive. Instead, the executives at the meeting feel pressured to have an immediate opinion, even if they haven't formed one yet. And further, they want to make sure it's the *right* opinion (i.e., an opinion that won't be laughed at or make them look stupid, or an opinion that mirrors the opinion of others at the meeting—(especially their boss, the CEO, and others who outrank them).

I am wholly opposed to the idea of having the agency, freelancer, or whoever creates your advertising "make a presentation."

Those who are in favor of the presentation method for selling new campaigns argue, "But isn't it important to have the agency there to explain why things were done the way they were, in case people have questions or don't understand it?"

My reply is simple. The ad or commercial has to communicate to the consumer without the agency being there. When the buyer picks up a magazine and sees the ad, the creative director won't be standing at his side, saying, "Do you have any questions? Do you get the concept?" Advertising must communicate everything—the concept, the selling point, the main theme or proposition, the offer, the product description and features—wholly on its own. If you can't understand the ad or commercial as written without explanation from your agency, then your agency has not done a good enough job writing the ad.

How then, should advertising be submitted to management for approval? In most small and medium-size companies, no presentations are made. The text, layouts, story boards, or other materials are sent via mail or messenger to the client, who reviews them at leisure in the privacy of his office, makes any comments on the manuscript or a separate memo, and sends the material back to the agency for revision and correction.

What if many people must review the material? Simply make copies and route them to the individuals with a cover sheet instructing them to review it and return it to you by a specific date. If there is an approval hierarchy—that is, the review material must pass through the hands of several managers in a predetermined, specific order—then simply attach a "route to" sheet to one copy of the material, indicating the order of review and instructing each reviewer to make changes and then pass the material on to the next reviewer. The final reviewer is instructed to return the material to you.

If some of the comments are conflicting, it is your job, not the ad agency's, to resolve them. The agency should receive one clear, unambiguous set of comments and instructions for revision. They should be completely removed from the politics of resolving internal differences of opinion concerning the content and execution of advertising materials. Handling those situations is the responsibility of the advertising manager.

CHAPTER 41

Monitoring Results and Handling Inquiries

For many advertisers, a prime objective of advertising and promotion is to generate inquiries and sales. Indeed, American business spends billions of dollars each year to generate, track, and follow-up on sales leads.

For some companies, the sales lead program represents a tremendous investment in time and money. For instance, a marketing communications manager at Digital Equipment once reported that his company processed 120,000 inquiries per year. A survey conducted by *Business Marketing* magazine[1] found that nine out of ten marketers believe that proper handling of inquiries is important. (Tables 41.1 through 41.4 are from this survey.) The responses are summarized in Table 41.1.

The survey also found that counting leads generated was one of the two methods of advertising measurement most favored by successful marketers—the other being measures that relate advertising to sales or profits. The results are shown in Table 41.2.

Interestingly, these concrete measures—leads, sales, and profits—were the only ones advertising managers really valued. They do not apparently put much faith in ad benchmark studies, readership studies, company awareness research, and other "soft" methods of measuring

Table 41.1. How top marketers rate the importance of inquiry handling.

Extremely important	59 percent
Very important	21 percent
Relatively important	11 percent
Not important	4 percent
No answer	5 percent

Table 41.2. Preferred methods of measuring advertising progress.

Relating communications activities to sales and profits	39 percent
Number of leads generated	28 percent
Ad benchmark/readership studies	13 percent
Company awareness research	12 percent
Sales force feedback	12 percent

communications effectiveness. Nor do they value feedback from the sales force, although this may result from an unfortunate animosity toward salespeople rather than logic.

Yet, despite the importance placed on inquiry handling, only three out of ten of these marketers use a computerized system for inquiry fulfillment, and nearly as many (27 percent) have no inquiry handling system at all.

What's Important In Inquiry Handling

The key to successful inquiry handling is speed. Experience proves that the value of a sales lead decreases almost exponentially in proportion to the delay in responding to it. You should try to fulfill all inquiries within 48 hours of receipt of the lead. Prospects will not wait to receive your material before seeking proposals from vendors or making purchases. Instead, they will consider only those vendors who respond promptly.

Some marketers mistakenly believe there's some benefit to being the last to respond to an inquiry. They reason that the prospect is more likely to remember the *last* brochure he received and will have already forgotten the first ones by that time.

Unfortunately, this isn't true. The best strategy is to respond quickly, then follow up several times to keep your name at the top of the prospect's awareness. But delaying response is inappropriate. Many prospects reason, "If they're this slow in sending a brochure, I can imagine how unresponsive they'll be when we order from them!" First impressions are important, and a slow response to the initial inquiry is a poor first impression indeed.

Aside from speed in responding to inquiries, qualifying the sales leads—that is, making sure you turn over only quality leads to the salespeople—is the second key function of inquiry handling.

What is a qualified lead? It's a response from someone who has the money, authority, and desire to buy your product or service and is interested in what you are offering. It is *not* the person who says, "I just want a brochure for my files; don't call me—leave me alone!"

Either the initial marketing communication (ad, letter, mailer) or the follow-up material must qualify the prospect so that leads turned over to salespeople are of good quality and serious intent. Qualification of leads may also be done over the phone by support staff or telemarketing representatives. Some of the typical qualifying questions include:

"What is your specific application?"

"When do you think you will be making a buying decision? within three months? Six months? One year?"

"What size/capacity/volume/power unit do you require?"

"Who else in your company will be involved in making this purchasing decision?"

"What is your budget for solving this problem or handling this application? Under $1,000? Under $10,000? Under $50,000? Under $100,000? Under $1 million?"

"Do you currently use this type of service or product? If so, who is your supplier?"

Table 41.3 lists the elements marketers consider most important in an inquiry follow-up and handling program:

Business Marketing also asked these marketers what improvements they were likely to make to their inquiry handling systems. Half said they were thinking about computerizing their inquiry handling systems (remember, only three out of ten currently use a computer to handle inquiries). Table 41.4 shows the other potential upgrades and improvements these marketers said they would consider making to their inquiry handling systems.

Designing The Inquiry Handling System

Whether computerized or manual, an effective inquiry handling system must perform the following functions:

Table 41.3. The elements marketers consider part of a successful inquiry program (responses add up to more than 100 percent due to multiple mentions).

Fast turn-around	80 percent
Qualification process	53 percent
Relation to sales process	47 percent
Use with telemarketing and research	23 percent
Reporting methods	18 percent
Economy	15 percent
Flexibility	15 percent
Customization	15 percent

Table 41.4. Inquiry handling improvements marketers would consider (response adds up to more than 100 percent due to multiple mentions).

Computerized handling	52 percent
Telemarketing	49 percent
Dial-in reader service	27 percent
Multiple prospect mailings	27 percent
Electronic mail	17 percent
Dial-in computer service	16 percent
Other	3 percent

- Record all necessary information about each lead.
- Respond to the inquiry in the appropriate fashion.
- Pass the lead information on to salespeople and others who require it.
- Provide a mechanism for future follow-up and promotion.
- Track the buying decisions of each lead.
- Report on inquiry and sales results.

Let's look at these functions one at a time.

Record All Necessary Information About Each Lead

You should design your system so that a computer operator, secretary, or other member of your support staff records into the inquiry handling system all necessary information about the prospect. This can include (but is not limited to):

- Name of prospect
- Title
- Company

- Address
- City
- State
- Zip code
- Daytime phone number
- Evening phone number
- Fax number
- Date of inquiry
- Source of inquiry
- Method of response (reader service card, letter, phone call)
- Nature of prospect's business
- Type of application
- Timeframe of need (immediate, three months, six months, one year, no immediate need, etc.)
- Quality and urgency of lead (i.e., whether the prospect has an urgent need, a less urgent need, or is just collecting brochures for future reference)
- Date literature was sent
- Dates and summary of follow-up contacts
- Salesperson's opinion as to the probability of closing the sale (can be ranked from one to 10)
- Comments

When designing your inquiry handling system, make a complete list of the information you think you need, then show it to salespeople, product managers, and others. They may want to add additional information to the inquiry records.

It's important to do this analysis carefully. Especially with computer databases, it's much easier to take time at the beginning to design it right; and much more difficult to go back and *change* the database once you've been using it.

Think about any specific information not on the above list that would be important to your sales and marketing efforts. For example, if in ad coupons and direct mail reply cards you ask prospects to indicate whether they have life insurance, it would make sense to add this information to your prospect database.

Respond To The Inquiry In The Appropriate Fashion

As discussed, you should respond to inquiries promptly and by sending the appropriate materials. These materials include the specific catalog, brochure, or other information the prospect asked for along with any other materials you think would help sell the prospect on using your product or service. An effective inquiry fulfillment package typically consists of the following elements:

Outer Envelope

This should be imprinted or rubber stamped with a teaser which, in large bold letters, proclaims, "HERE IS THE INFORMATION YOU REQUESTED." Without such a teaser, the prospects or their secretaries might not remember asking for the material, will think it's unsolicited direct mail, and are more likely to throw it away. When you remind them that they asked for it, they're likely to at least open and look at it.

Brochure or Other Information the Prospect Requested

The most important element in the package is the brochure or other sales literature the prospect asked you to send. Ideally, the brochure should be about the specific topic featured in the ad or mailing to which the prospect responded.

For instance, if you did an ad offering information on "Circular Widgets," the most effective response is a brochure specifically about circular widgets, not a general all-line widget brochure. If you must send a general all-line piece, clip the appropriate pages with a paper clip and attach a note to the cover that says, "The information you asked for on circular widgets appears on pages XX-YY."

Additional Brochures and Sales Literature

Without overwhelming the prospect by sending too much literature, selectively include additional materials you feel would be effective in selling the prospect on your product or service. These pieces can include user stories, case histories, testimonial sheets, article reprints, technical papers, applications bulletins, and corporate capabilities brochures.

You can often "cross-sell" a prospect interested in one product or service on other products or services by including a statement of your full capabilities, either as a page in a larger brochure or as a separate piece. For instance, if you are responding to an inquiry about floppy disks, that prospect would also be likely to buy computer paper, printer ribbons, and other PC supplies. Sending a catalog or full-line brochure could quite possibly stimulate additional sales.

Sales Letter

Your inquiry fulfillment package should be accompanied by a persuasive sales letter that thanks the prospect for their interest, explains a little more about your products or services, tells them what you've sent in the package, and encourages them to take the next step in the buying process.

The letter can be personalized or nonpersonalized. A form letter works well and eliminates the need to run off a personalized letter on the computer for each prospect. But it's up to you.

The letter can be long or short. In some situations, it's better to be brief, and let your brochure do the selling. But if your literature doesn't do the whole selling job, you can turn the letter itself into your main selling tool.

Dealer List

If inquiries are fulfilled from a central location rather than by the local rep or regional office responsible for sales in the prospect's territory, you need a mechanism in your inquiry fulfillment package that gives the prospect the name, address, and phone number of a contact or salesperson he can call to get more information or arrange an appointment.

This can be done in the sales letter; the computer can pull the appropriate salesperson or dealer's name and insert text that says, "The salesperson handling your account is (name, address, phone)." If you use a form letter, you can staple or clip the appropriate sales representative's card to the letter and put in a line that says, "For more information, contact the dealer (or sales rep, or whatever) whose card is attached to this letter. Or call us directly at the corporate office at (phone number)." The latter is in case the card becomes detached or lost.

An alternate method is to enclose a typeset list of your dealers, agents, or sales offices nationwide and check or circle the appropriate name for the prospect to contact. Copy in the form letter would say, "The name and phone number of the dealer (or agent or sales rep) assigned to your account is indicated on the attached Dealer List (or agent or sales rep list)."

The important thing is to give the prospect access to the name and number of a local contact. All else being equal, prospects would rather by from someone local than from someone far away. If you have a branch office, dealer, outlet, rep, or field salesperson in the prospect's territory, it's a competitive advantage and should be made clear in the inquiry fulfillment package.

Reply Form

It's important not only to tell the prospect what the next step is, but also to make it easy for him or her to take it. For this reason, you should always include some sort of reply element in every inquiry fulfillment package you send.

The reply element can be a survey form, questionnaire, specification sheet, or order form. Encourage prospects to fill it in and return it to you by mail or fax as the next step in getting more information on how you can help them solve their problems.

One strategy is to print the reply element on a brightly colored piece of paper, usually gold, yellow, blue, pink, or green. Then in your inquiry fulfillment letter say, "To order (or to get more information), just complete and mail the pink (or blue, or whatever) form today." The prospect's eyes immediately seek out the response form and find it, because it's a different color than the rest of the package.

Business Card

Always include your business card or the business card of the salesperson or representative handling the prospect's territory. This personalizes the package. Also, many people routinely keep and file business cards.

Tip: If you sell a product or service which the prospect is likely to need later instead of now, and if it's the type of product or service which is bought on an as-needed basis (e.g., printing, office suppliers, mailing lists, etc.), you can increase the likelihood of your prospect contacting you when in need by enclosing a Rolodex™ card with your company name, phone number, and a description of what you offer. Business cards printed to fit in Rolodex card files have become increasingly popular in recent years; and many, many prospects automatically remove such cards from mailings and put them in their Rolodex, even if they have no pressing need for the product or service advertised.

Keep in mind that the dual goals of the inquiry fulfillment package are (a) to promptly provide the prospect with the information he requested—that is, the data he *thinks* he wants and needs to make a decision about buying your product or service, and (b) to actually *sell* him the product or service by including additional material which, although he didn't specifically ask for it, will gain his attention, get read, and persuade him to take action favorable to you.

Pass The Lead Information On To Salespeople And Others Who Require It

The next function of the inquiry handling system is to distribute information about the lead to salespeople. This is typically done by geographic region (territory) or by product line, depending on how your sales force is organized.

With a manual inquiry handling system, you can use a carbon form so that as mailing labels are typed or leads are recorded, duplicates are created; the copies are routed to the appropriate salespeople. Or, you can simply photocopy the sheet or ledger in which you record leads and distribute them to salespeople.

A computerized system can generate, for each salesperson, a listing of the leads (with complete information on each) he or she is assigned to follow up on. These leads should be passed on to salespeople for follow-up.

How quickly should salespeople or telemarketing staff make the first follow-up call? For consumers at home addresses, allow one week after you mail the inquiry fulfillment material. For business prospects at corporations, one and one-half to two weeks seems about right (this allows enough time for delivery by the post office and corporate mailrooms and assumes the material will sit in the prospect's in-basket a few days before he or she gets around to reading it).

Provide A Mechanism For Future Follow-Up And Promotion

If you mail out a brochure to your prospect and don't follow up, you won't get a lot of response. Marketers who want to convert more leads to sales realize they must follow up, again and again, to overcome intertia and get the prospects to take action toward acquiring the product or service they offer.

How much should you follow up? Keep making follow up phone calls and mailings until the latest mailing or call in the series doesn't at least pay for itself. How much is this in practice? Author Jeffrey Lant says seven follow ups in 18 months is needed to get prospects to take action. Consultant Robert Sieghardt says that if you send an inquiry fulfillment package, then follow up with a series of three mailings, approximately 55 percent of prospects will respond.

The inquiry handling system should make prospect names easily accessible for follow-up and should be organized so you can determine which prospects should be followed up this week, next week, next month, and so on.

A computerized inquiry handling system can be designed to generate reports listing leads according to original date of inquiry as well as date of last contact, so you can easily get a list of those who are due for a friendly follow-up phone call or letter.

A manual inquiry handling system can be organized in a notebook with 12 sections, each for a different month. The prospects in section one all get called in January, the prospects in section two get called in February, and so on. This is cumbersome but can work.

Track The Buying Decisions Of Each Lead

Another desirable feature of the inquiry handling system is the ability to track the status of each lead. For instance, one service firm uses direct mail to generate leads. All leads are mailed a brochure, then followed up by telephone. Those who are interested get a more in-depth discussion of their specific need, then receive a price quotation and proposal to do the work discussed. Some of them sign the proposal and buy the service; others who receive proposals do nothing.

The firm's in-house inquiry handling system identifies each lead according to these categories:

- *Inquiry*—the person has requested a brochure but has not talked with a salesperson.
- *Open quote*—the person has talked with a salesperson and has been sent a proposal and cost estimate for work to be performed.
- *Sale*—the person has accepted the price quotation and bought the service.

- *Dead lead*—after six months, those who received a proposal and do not buy are no longer considered potential customers and go in a "dead" file.

The inquiry handling system can print a report showing the status of each lead. For this level of sophistication, you need to computerize your inquiry handling; it's nearly impossible to keep track of this information accurately using a manual system.

When should a lead be considered "dead?" Your own experience will determine it. Selling cycles vary by the industry and by the product. In general, the more costly the product, the longer it takes the prospect to make a buying decision.

In my copywriting and consulting business, I find that many prospects who request my information do so for future reference; only a minority who call have an immediate project they are ready to assign me on the spot.

Of those who say they have a future need, the ones who end up hiring me generally do so within 12 months after making the initial inquiry (and most do so within two to six months). If they don't contact me after 12 months, then they are not sufficiently motivated or genuinely interested in my service, and I move them from the "active lead" to the "dead lead" file.

You must observe your own prospects' buying patterns and make a similar decision as to when leads should be moved from active to inactive status.

Report On Inquiry And Sales Results

In addition to tracking individual leads, you also want to get a picture of the success of your advertising and sales programs. For instance, how many leads did your last ad produce? Of those, how many just wanted a brochure and how many were really interested and requested a proposal? This tells you whether your ad is generating leads of good quality or poor quality. Of those who requested a proposal, how many actually became customers? This tells you how effective your sales program is in converting leads to sales. Of those who bought, what were the total sales and average sale per order? This tells you how profitable your ad was.

Here is some (but not necessarily all) of the information you may want your lead handling system to be able to produce for you:

- Name and source of promotion (e.g., January mailing to *Forbes* list).

- Total cost of promotion (in dollars).
- Total number of leads generated.
- Cost per lead (divide total cost of promotion by total number of leads generated).
- Number of leads who requested a proposal, sales presentation, or took some other action step.
- Percentage of leads that took the above step (divide number of leads taking action by total number of leads, then multiply by 100).
- Cost per "qualified" lead (defining a qualified lead as someone who took the above step; to calculate, divided total cost of promotion by number of leads who took the action step).
- Number of orders generated.
- Cost per order (divide total cost of promotion by number of orders generated).
- Percentage of leads converted to orders (divide number of orders by number of leads, then multiply by 100).
- Total sales generated
- Ratio of total sales to cost of promotion (this tells if the promotion is profitable or not; to calculate, divide total sales in dollars by cost of promotion).

Without such information, you have no way to tell if your advertising is making money for you, hence no way to rationally judge the effectiveness of any promotional effort you produce.

This level of sophistication is generally available only in computerized inquiry handling systems. You can track it manually only if you receive a small quantity of leads (say a few hundred per month).

Manual Inquiry Handling Systems

First, we will look at how one small marketer uses a manual inquiry handling system to track leads. Then we will examine the computerized handling systems required by larger firms with more leads.

A simple form (Figure 41.1) to record and track leads is all that's needed to manually track leads. Leads come from several sources, including directory listings, small space ads in trade journals, referrals, articles, publicity, and occasionally, from direct mail.

Figure 41.1. Lead sheet for manual inquiry handling system.

Date____________ Source of inquiry____________ Response via____________

NAME________________________ TITLE____________________

COMPANY____

PHONE________________________ FAX____________________

ADDRESS____________________________ ROOM____________

CITY____________________ STATE____________ ZIP____________

Type of business:

Type of projects: ☐ marketing assistance ☐ marketing plan ☐ ad

☐ direct mail package ☐ sales letter ☐ brochure ☐ feature article

☐ press release ☐ newsletter ☐ other:

FOR: ☐ immediate project ☐ project within________weeks/months ☐ future reference

STATUS:

☐ Sent package on (date):________________________________

☐ Enclosed these samples:________________________________

☐ Next step is to:____

☐ Probability of assignment:______________________________

☐ Comments:____

CONTACT RECORD:

Date: Summary:

Let's take a look at how to use this form. The date at the top is the date the prospect contacted you. Source of inquiry tells whether it's a referral, ad, mailing, and the exact source. "Response via" means did they write or call (those who call are usually better leads for me because they have taken a more aggressive role and have actually spoken to me).

Underneath, fill in the usual information: their name, title, company, phone, fax, and mailing information. Knowing the type of business they're in and the type of project they need will help you tailor your inquiry fulfillment package. Ask if they have an immediate project, a project coming up soon, or if they're calling just to get my material for file reference.

Under "STATUS," list the date you sent the package, what you sent, what you think the next step is (did they ask you to call on a specific date or keep them on my mailing list?), the probability you will get work from them (rated on a scale of 1 to 10), and any miscellaneous comments the prospect made you feel are important (for example, "We need this in a hurry" or "We're a small company and we don't have much money"). Under "CONTACT RECORD" record the date of each follow-up call and brief notes on what was said.

Keep leads for the past 12 months in a three-ring binder in chronological order, with the most recent lead first. When a lead gets older than 12 months without buying from you, put it in an "inactive leads" file organized alphabetically by company name. When a prospect buys from you, their sheet goes into a "CLIENTS" notebook which is again organized alphabetically by company name. Thus you have three notebooks: one for leads which I hope to sell to, one for your clients (current, ongoing, and past), and one for old leads—people who asked for my information but never hired you.

Computerized Inquiry Handling Systems

The following eight criteria are the building blocks on which an effective computerized inquiry handling system is built:

1. The system should be easily understood and accepted by staff and sales force. It should also be planned and sponsored by top management to assure cooperation and compliance.
2. It should be relevant and timely, providing requested materials while inquirer interest is still high and forwarding qualified leads to the sales force without delay.
3. It should be qualification-oriented with the facility to determine the best candidates for sales force follow-up.
4. It should be follow-up oriented with the ability to determine the level of sales force participation as well as inquirer action.
5. It should be measurable and accountable.
6. It should provide information with which management can properly evaluate both the advertising program and the system communication.

7. The system should be accurate, efficient, and disciplined, recording all data correctly and consistently. It should not become a self-defeating ocean of paper.
8. Finally, it should be flexible and accessible. It should be able to handle hundreds or thousands of inquiries per month and provide needed information in a reasonable time frame.

In most cases, experience indicates an inability within a company to achieve these goals because of prioritization within the company. Lack of top management concern and priority can lead to using an outside service in spite of very good reasons to process sales inquiries internally.

What are the pros and cons of handling inquiries in-house? Advantages of processing leads internally include shorter lines of communication and the potential to develop reports with greater detail. Disadvantages include the high cost of initial software development (or purchase), lack of access to company computer because of low priority (solvable if the advertising department has a dedicated micro or minicomputer), and the extra cost of inquiry handling personnel and supervisors.

Some advantages of using an outside computerized sales inquiry service are:

- Guaranteed turnaround time for literature fulfillment and reports.
- Fixed cost per inquiry—often lower than what a company would incur internally.
- More sophisticated system reporting, such as field sales tracking and prospect follow-up.

Disadvantages of using outside services include problems in communications, the high cost of customization of special programs for your company (if required), and the hesitancy of management to release information to an outside service for what is traditionally an inside operation.

The greatest cost internally for a *manual* inquiry handling system is labor. The cost to stuff envelopes and type labels, including fringe benefits, runs somewhere between $13,000 and $16,000 or more annually per clerk. Assuming an individual worker can do 10,000 fulfillments a year (that's 40 per day or five per hour), the per inquiry cost is $1.30 to $1.60 or more in labor alone. In your area of the country, cost for labor may be greater, so adjust these figures accordingly.

In addition, there are postage and literature costs. Inquiry packages can range from $1 to $4 per piece for literature and postage costs. More elaborate packages can run $5 apiece or more! Space is also a consideration. Some companies that are dealing with 30,000 to 35,000 leads a year use considerable cubic foot area. In an organization where three to four or more people are employed to handle leads, there is also the cost of employing a supervisor, which could easily be an additional $20,000 to $25,000 a year.

Case Study: How IBM Created Its Lead Processing System

Here is how IBM handled its need to computerize inquiry handling, as explained by a sales program administrator of the IBM National Marketing Division:

> "About two years ago, IBM found that the need for mass marketing was rapidly growing. McGraw-Hill says that it costs about $137 (1980 figure) just to have a salesperson make a call. And with that, we actively moved into the area of mass marketing. What we found is we could identify our prospects very easily using direct mail, advertising, and business shows, but what made sales was the lead processing, getting those leads out to the salespeople in the most timely situation we could. We were faced with the problem of not being able to turn those leads around quickly enough, which resulted in the loss of the money we'd invested to find the prospects. So we tried to establish a system that would meet several objectives.
>
> "The first one was to reduce the number of lost leads. Since we support over 200 locations across the country, those leads also had to have a very quick turnaround to our branch offices. We also needed to track the progress and the results of each of our different campaigns. So we had to have the result from each of these leads. Did they close? If so, what did they buy? If they did not close, why not?
>
> "We also wanted to build a database for future mailings to those who indicated that they are interested. They may not buy at the present time, but many buy later when we have a new product.
>
> "We looked at developing our own lead tracking system. First, we considered using outside services and saw both the pros and the cons. We were given 90 days to put a system in place, and with that facing us, we also looked at developing our own system since we had in-house expertise. The key question, however, was do we use one of our own large systems or a small commercial business computer? We found in view of the short time frame lack of access to a large system that the answer to our problem was a small business computer. We've installed our own, with several key functions.
>
> "The first thing we looked at is lead capture: the name, the address, and any key qualifying data to transmit to the salesman. That obviously

leads us to having to do lead distribution—taking it from when it comes into our headquarters in Atlanta and distributing it to the appropriate location, one of 200, so that it reaches the right marketing rep in the field.

"We also wanted to offload the burden of the field having to do any fulfillment of literature. So we then moved into a system of automating the fulfillment. And of course, the key was tracking those leads once the lead was fulfilled and the salesman had received it, as to what was the final result and how much business we actually generated.

"The last function was lead management. If a prospect doesn't buy, could we bring him back into our system and put him in a different series of mailings or a different means of contact, possibly telephone prospecting or salesman follow-up, based on what the request was from the actual prospect?

"What were some of the results of our new system? We've developed several ways of getting reports, so that we can actually sit down and analyze the time that it takes to get a decision made as well as what the decision is. Then we can analyze what is the best offer. We can also analyze what the cost of closing that order is, which is a key factor considering how much money is spent.

"We found that we get good field participation, and that was probably the most difficult thing we had to face. How do we get nearly 1,800 salespeople across the country participating in this program? We found that we had to devise our own internal direct mail and advertising campaign. We sent each rep a simple pre-addressed check-off form to be put into our internal mail system and sent back to us. We explained that they would be able to get better prospects in the future because we would know what mailings were better campaigns and resulted in better ways of qualifying prospects. So far our response rates have increased, our sales force is getting higher and higher closing rates. Now, with the total mass marketing program, they're beginning to rely more and more on us doing lead generation.

"I think we took the right route, and that the in-house system fit us best, with the expertise and assistance we had on hand, and the number of people we had to handle."

To Computerize Or Not To Computerize?

There is a distinct dividing line between when a company should computerize—whether they do it in-house or with an outside service—and when they should handle lead processing manually.

Most of the companies involved in lead generation either via direct mail specifically or via space ads and other direct response promotions are not large *Fortune* 500 companies. There are many more companies nowadays that have gotten into direct mail and direct response as the primary vehicle for the sales of their particular products. It takes a lot of in-house analysis for them to determine whether to computerize, because automating any type of system depends on the quantity that you're trying to process.

If you're a firm trying to process 100 or 200 leads a month, it's probably not worth the expense to automate that system. You can follow the same guidelines and routines that you would if you automated a system by doing it manually.

There are three basic requirements or objectives for automating an inquiry handling system:

The first is to decrease the response time to the respondent. If someone is taking the time to respond, there is some type of interest. The company should make every effort to minimize turnaround time to that respondent—whether it's via computer transmission or whether using the mail or a telephone response. Even prior to when the sales rep actually gets the lead, some means of acknowledging the response is effective.

The second step is to try to qualify that respondent as well as you possibly can with what information and material you have in-house before the lead gets out to the sales rep. Nothing turns a sales force off quicker than ten leads where eight of them are coupon clippers.

There are a number of ways to analyze response. You can refer to printed source material. You can use automated systems that firms such as Dun & Bradstreet offer, where you can have on-line access to their data files, so that when a response comes in, you key in the name of that company and the computer will sort through four or five million names and print out for you all the data Dun & Bradstreet has on that company—size, number of years in business, type of business, location, and so on.

That might get fairly expensive, but suppose you were a very large firm generating thousands of leads a month, such as an IBM, or a Lanier Business Products, or any firm that uses the mail heavily. A sophisticated qualifying system may not be all that expensive, considering the cost of a sales call. Figure the cost of a sales rep making five out of ten sales calls on unqualified prospects and you've spent $700 or $800 fruitlessly. There are trade-offs involved that need to be analyzed.

The third requirement is analyzing the response received from whatever kind of system you're using. You have to capture data to be able to analyze, then compare it to a base you've set up before.

You can analyze by type of business, size of business, other demographics, or geography. You can analyze by census information, income information, or zip code.

Analyze where you get your best results from any type of a direct mail program, then start on that program, continuing to test before you roll-out with a full-scale direct mail campaign. You can do that only if you spend time analyzing the responses you've received, continuing to mail to them, or making sales calls or sending your information. But also take a look at your marketplace. If you received a 4 percent response, say, from the southern half of Atlanta to a particular program sent out, look at everybody that's in the southern half of Atlanta, so you can go back to them because that seems to be where you're getting the best response.

In summation, the keys are to respond quickly, to respond personally, to analyze what a company is doing, whether it's an automated or manual system.

Qualified Leads Versus Coupon Clippers And Brochure Collectors

It's one thing to generate responses. You may be able to go out with some type of promotion that has either some giveaways or special little triggers and generate a 4 percent response. But if your field sales force can only sell a small percentage of the leads you've generated, you really have not generated a 4 percent response of *sales.*

You have to look at it from this standpoint: "We received responses of *X*, we made presentations of *Y*, and that resulted in a sales factor of *Z*." Of course sales made is really the bottom line. Just to generate responses doesn't do a whole lot for you or for the company unless you've been able to close on those responses you did receive.

Consider the coupon clipper—the person who responds to get a free brochure but is not a genuine prospect. If eight out of 10 of your leads are of low quality, you'll have a sales force problem. That's significant and you want to consider what is a "lead" that you're going to send to your salespeople. How does the salesperson tell which are the leads he should spend his first few moments on, and which are the ones he goes to when he has no one else to talk to? The coupon clipper is probably your biggest problem; the person who reads a magazine and circles everything he sees or just likes to send for brochures to have a full mailbox. The inquiry handling system should rank leads, distinguishing between hot leads and the coupon clippers.

Many companies believe that the sales force should get a lead form on every lead that comes in. They feel it's the responsibility of the individual salesperson to qualify either by telephone or by personal visit. But others feel the sales force would be deluged with a sea of paper. Although every request for literature is fulfilled, it's up to the individual salesperson whether to follow-up or not.

In some cases, salespeople may be getting 50 to 100 leads a week. If the salesperson is ill one week or out one week, he has 200 pieces of paper in his hands to qualify.

Leads can be separated into four preselected categories of qualified leads. The first category is any prospect who comes to a trade show and says he wants to see a sales representative. That is a prequalified lead. The second category would be any direct mail campaign prospect who checks off a box and says, "Yes, I would like to see a sales representative."

The third category is phone inquiries; any telephone call that comes in from a prospect is considered a qualified lead. Letters are also considered a qualified lead. These are the primary categories for sending a sales lead notice on to the salesperson. The salesperson gets a reduction in paper, but the leads that he does get are fairly qualified. A fifth category would be people who clip a coupon from an ad and mail it in and check the box indicating they would like a salesperson to call.

To fill that salesperson in on all the activity in his territory, a monthly report listing all prospects who inquired or requested literature supplements his leads. Now the salesperson has the opportunity at his discretion to go over a master register and decide whether any individual secondary lead warrants a telephone call. There are no gaps in the information. The salespeople get their hot leads on a weekly basis, but also get a monthly report outlining in detail all the prospects in their areas.

Computerizing The Priority Of Leads: A Case History

One industrial advertising manager reported:

> "We have evolved from assigning the priority of lead processing by any secretary who had the time availabile to using a computerized service and assigning a high level of priority to specific sales leads. We identified the needs that were required in a lead processing system and went through several stages of development.
>
> "First, we formalized a manual system and operated this for about one year. It was satisfactory, even though it was not allowing us to get all of the information we could get from all the names that we were spending hard marketing dollars to generate. It was sufficient to fulfill a prospect's request and it was sufficient to gauge quantities and to assign a priority to a source

of the lead. As far as getting other additional marketing information out, it was insufficient.

"We then looked at the computer as a solution to all of our problems and found somebody with a computer who thought it could do what we wanted it to. We thought it could do that. But the service was not completely debugged. It was a mail list maintenance program designed to do one thing where we were trying to make it do another. This proved fatal. Retrieving information from the system was almost as difficult as a manual system. Again, throughout the manual and the first computer lesson stage, we were fulfilling all requests on a timely basis and notifying the field on a timely basis. It's primarily in the area of getting additional information, or getting the names back out to do other promotions, where we had difficulties.

"We decided that the major features we wanted in a new computerized system would be timely fulfillment of the inquirer's request, timely reporting to field sales, and timely reporting to management, with the addition of being able to draw data from that system for other promotions, direct mail and so forth, in support of other promotional areas, trade shows as well as special campaigns.

"We identified the type of service that we wanted now and the future service, based on a given lead quantity that we would be generating many years hence. We wanted a versatile system that would give us the information we wanted now, with the options of several different types of reporting that would be valuable to marketing as the company as a whole became used to a more sophisticated database and to using the information that was available from a database.

"We now fulfill inquiries within 48 hours after they are received. We send notifications of every lead to our field salespeople at the time of fulfillment. On a monthly basis, we send a status report of all leads in a given territory to the field sales offices as well as to the regional managers' offices. We also have a quarterly system which is a status report of all the leads broken down by sales territory, by the lead type source (whether it be direct mail, advertising, trade shows) and specific medium, and it also identifies the numbers that have been generated and the cost per inquiry.

"Other types of reports are also available to us. We've used this computerized inquiry system for one year and are at a level where we think we can use additional reporting and additional data to make our promotions and our field sales follow-up still more efficient.

"Follow-up mailings to a prospect can be extremely valuable. If a manufacturer is paying anywhere from $10 to, in some cases, $200 for an industrial sales lead, plus from $3 to $7 for the package of literature plus the postage and the labor required to get that material out, and the prospect does not respond, why drop that prospect right then and there? Reinvest another 30 or 40 cents and contact him a month later. Ask him basically the same set of questions. There may be some very good reason why he didn't respond the first time, and if you don't hear from him that time, try it again a month later. Try two more comparatively inexpensive mailings to him over a two-month period to see if you can get a response that says, 'Yes, I'm ready to see a sales representative now.'

"In some cases two follow-up mailings have generated a 125 percent increase in qualified leads over the original bounce-back card (reply card) and the four categories of prequalified leads mentioned earlier.

"With an inquiry database, you own a ready-made list of people who were interested in you earlier, and that's another opportunity of using those names once again. For example, re-awaking interest when you have new products, a change in terms and conditions, or new prices. That's a major announcement to someone who had a stumbling block in making a decision to buy it from you before.

"Each new contact will increase your response rate by some percentage. There's a trade-off as to when it becomes non-cost-effective. Names you get from any type of a direct mail program are precious to you. It's so much more valuable than going to a compiled field and buying 200,000 raw names that previous analysis has indicated *should* be prime prospects. Responses you receive are people that you know definitely *are* prime prospects. The overwhelming majority of them will be qualified prospects for you, so you should continue to work that list just as frequently as you can allocate the money or as response continues to justify.

"The file of names can be used for other promotions, such as product newsletters and special offer direct mailings that are broken out by the individual product of interest category. Those names are also a valuable source of market information for market research surveys.

"The list can also be a source of revenue for a firm because there is an increasing amount of rental and usage of response names to noncompeting lines. A firm may have a file of 50,000 or 100,000 companies or individuals who have responded to a certain type of offer. Someone else may be looking for a list that would closely coincide with the type of an offer they have. By getting up with a list broker or a list management firm, renting the list can be a profitable source of revenue."

Note: The revenue from list rentals can be from 50 cents to $3 per name per year. If you have 100,000 names and earn $1 a year from renting them, that's an additional $100,000 per year in revenue.

This is significant when you realize that the list rental costs can help finance (or in some cases totally pay for) the inquiry handling system.

Seven Steps To Computerizing Your Inquiry Handling

The first step is analysis of what your problem is. Is it volume? Is it lack of information? Determine your key problem, because that's the area that should be your priority in addressing the use of the computer.

The second step is to pursue the proper solution. How can you handle that? Is it ability to do more processing of leads, or is it reports that you need? Investigate the financial benefits. Often they're quite easy to justify, whether it's in-house or a service, because you're talking about handling of an asset, something of real value.

The third step is to select the right system. It has to fit into your business. Consider ease of use and ability to solve your problems.

The fourth step is to develop a plan of how you're going to go about installing this computer system into your company.

The fifth step is a training program for your people, including your salespeople, your administrative people, and your management team.

The sixth step is preparing accurate data, taking what you currently have and putting it into the system.

The seventh step is looking at what you have to do in the future and having that growth capability by designing the system (or asking your service bureau to design a system) that's going to address your future needs as well as your current ones without going through a complete redesign.

The Literature Fulfillment Center

If you decide to handle inquiry processing in-house, then in addition to the computer system you will also need a "literature center"—a separate work area dedicated to the physical storage, assembly, and mailing of inquiry fulfillment materials.

This literature center can be a separate room or the corner of an office. It can require the services of a single worker or (depending in the number of inquiries you receive) a staff of several employees stuffing envelopes, entering leads into the computer, and distributing lead reports.

The important thing is to make the distribution and management of literature a separate function, not something your secretary does when he or she has some extra time. If lead handling is given a priority below other routine tasks, these routine tasks will fill the secretary's day and the inquiries will not get fulfilled on time.

Here are ten additional points to keep in mind when setting up your literature center:

1. The best set-up is to have a completely separate room or area set aside for literature storage and distribution. Don't ask secretaries to do

the job in their normal work space. They will quickly run out of room and become overwhelmed. Handling and mailing multiple pieces of literature, and storing the leads, takes space.

2. Equip the literature center with shelves for stocking an ample supply of brochures. The best shelves are the metal type found in warehouses; shelf height can be easily adjusted. Shelving allows workers to quickly find and pull the material they need. Do not store your working supply of brochures in boxes; this makes the material hard to get at.

3. Shelving, of course, holds a limited supply and must be restocked at intervals. The rest of the brochures are best stored in the original cardboard boxes in which they arrived from the printer. Be sure the literature center has enough room to stock these boxes. Stacking boxes in a large, open room is best because it allows easy access. Piling boxes atop one another in a cramped closet discourages people from looking for the materials they need.

4. When estimating space requirements for your literature center, consider all the things you'll need. These include workstations for each secretary or clerk; room for the computer system; shelves to hold the literature; space for one or more postage meters; file cabinets to hold lead reports, forms, and other materials; and a place to keep outgoing mail (which may be substantial in volume) until the mailroom pick-up person or mail carrier arrives.

5. The literature center should be dry, well-lit, and kept at normal room temperature. Excess humidity and extreme temperature changes can cause printed material to wrinkle and fade, creating a poor impression.

6. Put in a few extra work areas in the literature room to accommodate temporary help you may need to hire if the volume of leads suddenly increases. It's better to hire extra help and keep current rather than save money on labor and fall behind on fulfillment (which can cost you orders).

7. Set up the literature center as a pleasant, efficient workplace. Workers should have everything they need within easy reach. If, for example, literature is to be bound into spiral or hard-spine covers, keep the binding machine on a table in the literature room with ample area for people to spread out and work. Make sure the people can do the steps involved (collecting materials, assembling packages, typing labels, keying computer data, putting materials in envelopes, affixing postage) with minimal movement and travel.

8. Stock the literature center with an ample supply of all essential items. In addition to an inventory of sales literature, this can include: envelopes, stamps, postage meters, cardboard backings, paper clips, rubber bands, mail bags, address labels, rubber stamps, ink pads, form letters, notebooks, forms, pencils, pens, and computer supplies.

9. Since there will be a steady flow of mail into and out of your literature center, try to locate it near your mail room or or near where the mail-room clerk comes by with his cart to pick up your mail each day. Don't force literature center employees to drag or cart heavy bundles of outgoing literature to a distant location for sorting and mailing.

10. Ideally, one or more employees should work in the literature center full time. If workers complain that this is boring, you could rotate assignment to the literature center among available clerical personnel.

The main idea behind all this is to process leads and get the literature into the mail quickly and efficiently. Hot leads can cool off fast, and the longer you sit on your inquiries, the more business you lose. As discussed earlier, speed is of the essence when it comes to turning leads into sales.

Computerized Inquiry Handling Vendors

The following companies offer either software or complete computer systems for handling of inquiries, leads, and prospect and customer databases.

Applied Information Group
720 King Georges Road
Fords, NJ 08863
Phone 908-738-8444
Product: Advertiser Response System

Brock Control Systems
2859 Paces Ferry Road
Suite 1000

Atlanta, GA 30339
Phone 404-431-1200
Product: Brock Activity Manager

Claritas Corporation
201 N. Union Street
Suite 200
Alexandria, VA 22314-2645
Phone 703-683-8300
Product: COMPASS

CoLinear Systems, Inc.
2814 New Spring Road
Suite 217
Atlanta, GA 30339
Phone 404-578-0000
Product: Response

Compusearch Market and Social Research Ltd.
16 Madison Avenue
Toronto, Ontario M5R 2S1
Phone 416-348-9180
Product: Compusearch

Data Absolute
PO Box 784
Nevada City, CA 95959
Phone 916-265-4779
Product: TeleMOM

Donnelley Marketing Information Services
70 Seaview Avenue
PO Box 10250
Stamford, CT 06904
Phone 203-353-7261
Product: CONQUEST

Richard L. Fleischer & Associates
135 Village Road
Roslyn Heights, NY 11577-1522
Phone 516-621-2826
Product: Zip + 4 Coding and Mailing System

Geographic Data Technology, Inc.
13 Dartmouth College Highway
Lyme, NH 03768
Phone 603-795-2183
Product: GeoSpreadSheet ZIP Code

Group I Software
Washington Capital Office Park
6404 Ivy Lane
Suite 500
Greenbelt, MD 20770-1400
Phone 301-982-2000
Products: List Conversion Management System, Accu-mail, ArcList

Inquiry Plus
814 Eagle Drive
Bensenville, IL 60106
Phone 708-595-5059
Product: Inquiry Management Software

Inter Active Micro, Inc.
PO Box 478
Bradford, NH 03221
Phone 603-938-2127
Product: The Front Office

Key Systems, Inc.
512 Executive Park
Louisville, KY 40207
Phone 502-897-3332
Product: Prospecting, Accountability

LEADtrack Services
595 Colonial Park Drive
Suite 302
Roswell, GA 30075
Phone 404-587-0412
Product: LEADtrack

Market Power Computer Innovations
101 Providence Mine Road #104
Nevada City, CA 95959
Phone 916-265-5000
Product: The Sales Manager

Nashbar Associates, Inc.
4141 Simon Road
Boardman, OH 44512
Phone 216-788-9000
Product: Quick Order Processor

PER Software, Inc.
38109 87th Street
Burlington, WI 53105
Phone 414-537-4131
Product: Direct Marketing/400

Inquiry Handling Services

If you prefer not to handle inquiries in-house, here are some outside inquiry handling service bureaus that can help you:

Epsilon Data Management, Inc.
24 New England Executive Park
Burlington, MA 01803
Phone 617-273-0250

Fala Direct Marketing Inc.
70 Marcus Drive
Melville, NY 11747-4278
Phone 516-694-1919

LCS Industries, Inc.
120 Brighton Road
Clifton, NJ 07012
Phone 201-778-5588

McGraw-Hill
The Qualified Lead System
1221 Avenue of the Americas
New York, NY 10020
Phone 212-512-2000

Fulfillment Houses

If you don't want the hassle of setting up a literature center, or don't have room in your office to store all your brochures, fulfillment centers can help. They'll fulfill inquiries, sending the literature you specify, and some can even maintain your customer database for you on computer. There are hundreds of fulfillment houses nationwide; here is just a sampling:

Controlled Distribution
1100 Boston Avenue
Bridgeport, CT 06610
Phone 203-334-4060

Fala Direct Marketing, Inc.
70 Marcus Drive
Melville, NY 11747-4278
Phone 516-694-1919

Four Star Associates, Inc.
1560 Fifth Avenue
Bay Shore, NY 11706
Phone 516-968-4100

Fulfillco Fulfillment Center
90 Dayton Avenue
Passaic, NJ 07055
Phone 201-471-5980

Mailco, Inc.
150 S. Main St.
Wood-Ridge, NJ 07075
Phone 201-777-9500

Progress Distribution Services, Inc.
5505 36th St. S.E.
Grand Rapids, MI 49512
Phone 616-957-5900

White Mountain Fulfillment Services
2625 S. Roosevelt Ave.
Tempe, AZ 85282
Phone 602-894-9618

Figure 41.2.

Bob Bly's
Business-to-Business
Marketing Communications Audit

In today's economy, it pays to make every marketing communication count.

This simple audit is designed to help you identify your most pressing marketing communications challenges—and to find ways to solve problems, communicate with your target markets more effectively, and get better results from every dollar spent on advertising and promotion.

Step One: Identify Your Areas of Need

Check all items that are of concern to you right now:

- ❑ Creating a marketing or advertising plan
- ❑ Generating more inquiries from our print advertising
- ❑ Improving overall effectiveness and persuasiveness of print ads
- ❑ Determining which vertical industries or narrow target markets to pursue
- ❑ How to effectively market and promote our product or service on a limited advertising budget to these target audiences
- ❑ Producing effective sales brochures, catalogs, and other marketing literature
- ❑ How to get good case histories and user stories written and published
- ❑ Getting articles by company personnel written and published in industry trade journals
- ❑ Getting editors to write about our company, product, or activities
- ❑ Getting more editors to run our press releases
- ❑ Planning and implementing a direct mail campaign or program
- ❑ Increasing direct mail response rates
- ❑ Generating low-cost but qualified leads using postcard decks
- ❑ How to make all our marketing communications more responsive and accountable
- ❑ Designing, writing, and producing a company newsletter
- ❑ Creating an effective company or capabilities brochure
- ❑ Developing strategies for responding to and following up on inquiries
- ❑ Creating effective inquiry fulfillment packages
- ❑ Producing and using a video or audio tape to promote our product or service
- ❑ Writing and publishing a book, booklet, or special report that can be used to promote our company or product
- ❑ Choosing an appropriate premium or advertising specialty as a customer giveaway
- ❑ Getting reviews and critiques of existing or in-progress copy for ads, mailings, brochures, and other promotions
- ❑ How to promote our product or service using free or paid seminars
- ❑ How to market our product or organization by having our people speak or present papers at conventions, trade shows, meetings, and other industry events
- ❑ Training our staff with an in-house seminar in:

  ____
  (indicate topic)
- ❑ Learning proven strategies for marketing our product or service in a recession or soft economy
- ❑ Other (describe): ______________________________

  ____

  ____

– over –

Figure 41.2. (continued)

Marketing Communications Audit

Step Two: Provide a Rough Indication of Your Budget

Amount of money you are prepared to commit to the solution of the problems checked off on page one of this form:

❑ under $500 ❑ under $1,000 ❑ under $2,500 ❑ under $5,000

❑ under $10,000 ❑ other: ______________________

Step Three: Fill in Your Name, Address, and Phone Number Below

Name ______________________________ Title ______________________

Company ______________________________ Phone ______________________

Address ____

City ______________________ State ______________________ Zip ______________

Step Four: Mail or Fax Your Completed Form Today

Mail: Bob Bly, 22 E. Quackenbush Avenue, 3rd floor, Dumont, NJ 07628
FAX: (201) 385-1138
Phone: (201) 385-1220

If you wish, send me your current ads, brochures, mailing pieces, press releases, and any other material that will give me a good idea of the products or services you are responsible for promoting. I will review your audit and materials and provide a free 20-minute consultation by telephone with specific recommendations on how to solve your marketing problems, implement programs, and effectively address your key areas of concern. To schedule a specific date and time for your free, no-obligation phone consultation, indicate your preferred date and time below:

Preferred date and time______________________________

Alternate date and time______________________________

Mail or fax your audit form today. There's no cost. And no obligation.

Bob Bly • Copywriter/Consultant • 22 E. Quackenbush Ave, 3rd floor • Dumont, NJ 07628
Phone (201) 385-1220 • Fax (201) 385-1138

CHAPTER 42

Legal Aspects of Advertising Management

This chapter is provided for general information only. Keep in mind that (a) the law may have changed since I wrote it, (b) the laws in your state may be different, (c) I'm not an attorney and therefore I may not have interpreted the law in correct legal context, or (d) all of the above. In any event, don't use this chapter as the final authority. Instead, ask your lawyer.

False Advertising

There are laws preventing advertisers from running ads that are unfair, deceptive, or that contain false information or mislead consumers. Since virtually every ad is at least intended to *lead* consumers—to cause them to take some action or convince them to accept some proposition—it's difficult to know when you've gone too far.

How do you determine how far you can go in your advertising copy? The best method is to try not to get away with anything. Err on the side of being too honest rather than too full of hype. This is the surest way to prevent abuse of Federal Trade Commission (FTC) regulations.

Section 5 of the FTC Act and various amendments added to the act over the years, as well as decisions in a number of court cases, have helped define what the FTC considers unfair or deceptive advertising. Basically, the FTC does not permit advertising that is (1) false, deceptive, or unfair and that (2) injures either the consumer or your competitors or (3) violates the accepted standards of public policy.

What does this mean?

- False advertising is advertising that contains untrue statements.
- Deceptive advertising is advertising that contains misleading statements, whether deliberate or otherwise.
- Unfair advertising is advertising that is immoral, unethical, oppressive, unscrupulous, or that violates some other accepted standard of "fairness."
- Injury to consumers means consumers are harmed either financially, physically, or otherwise through purchase of products induced by your advertising.
- Injury to competition means your competitors lost business because your ads unfairly, deceptively, or unethically got consumers to buy your products instead of those of your competitors.
- Violation of public policy means the advertising violates commonly accepted, established concepts of fairness as defined by statutes, the common law, or other means.

The burden of making sure your advertising does not violate these admittedly nebulous FTC regulations is on you, the advertiser, not on the general public or the government. That is, it's not okay to run an ad you think may be in violation of the rules and wait for the FTC to catch you. You have to weigh each ad against the established standards of fairness, ethics, and honesty and—to the best of your ability—make sure the ad satisfies these standards before you run it.

How does the FTC judge whether an ad is in violation of current regulations? There are three criteria. First, the ad must be written and designed so that it is likely to mislead the consumer. This is determined not only by what you say but also by what you *don't* say; for example, if you sell bug spray by mail and fail to mention that it is likely to cause cancer in household pets and infants, that's deceptive.

Second, the consumer's interpretation of or reaction to your ad message must be considered reasonable. For example, if I order your bug spray, it's reasonable for me to think it's safe to use unless you warn me otherwise.

On the other hand, if I order a meat thermometer and then complain to the FTC that I put my eye out on the sharp end of it, it's not reasonable for me to be sticking a sharp object in my eye because the ad copy didn't warn me against doing so. Specifically, the FTC does not want to make you, the advertiser, responsible for misinterpretation of your ad copy by stupid people or idiots. However, you are responsible for writing ads that can be understood and are not subject to misinterpretation by the *average* reader.

Third, if your ad is found to be misleading to the average intelligent consumer, the false or misleading information must be substantial enough that it affected the consumer in some way—that is, it caused him harm or financial loss, or at least affected his choice of product purchase. Yes, even if the only result of your unethical or deceptive copy was to get the consumer to buy your product instead of another, that's cause for action.

And what's the action? If the FTC says your ad is false or misleading, they'll issue a cease-and-desist order telling you to immediately stop running the ad, airing the commercial, or mailing the literature. You have to be especially careful about direct mail, because *each piece* mailed might be held a separate violation! This can be dangerous when mailing thousands or millions of pieces. Also, each day you fail to withdraw the deceptive or misleading ad is considered a separate violation. As of this writing, the penalty for violation of the FTC's deceptive advertising regulations is a whopping $10,000 a day.

Is there any way to combat the FTC if they deem your advertisement unfair or deceptive? Yes. The easiest way is to simply rewrite the ad to eliminate the offensive portion and create an ad that in no possible way could be considered unfair or deceptive.

On the other hand, perhaps you feel the FTC is wrong and that everything they say is false in your advertising is actually true. In that case, the FTC will allow you to submit evidence that product claims made in the ad copy can be verified through lab testing, research, and other documented results.

Retail Advertising

One deceptive practice you should particularly avoid if you are a retail advertiser is "bait and switch" advertising. In a bait and switch, the store's ads stress discount merchandise at big discounts. The consumer, upon arriving at the store, finds that the advertised discount items are "sold out," or else the salesperson says that the advertised sales items, while inexpensive, are inferior, and tries to sell the consumer a more expensive alternative brand.

According to the FTC, bait and switch is illegal. If you feature special sale items in your ads, these items must be available in your store during the sale period at the discount advertised. If you do legitimately run out, you are not allowed to try to sell the consumer an alternate, more costly brand; instead, you should offer a "rain check" on the advertised sale item—that is, allow the consumer to come back at a later date to purchase the sale item at the advertised discount price.

Another deceptive retail advertising practice to avoid is to advertise a sale for a chain of stores and then not have the sale items available at certain locations. If advertised discount items are not going to be available at certain locations, you must name these locations prominently in your ad copy. Saying "available at most of our stores" is considered deceptive and not good enough to satisfy FTC regulations.

Product Packaging

Product packaging is really just another form of advertising and promotion and, as such, is also regulated by the FTC. The FTC regulates the packaging of most consumer products. The Federal Food, Drug, and Cosmetic Act regulates the packaging of certain foods, drugs, cosmetics, and devices.

Basically, the FTC's Truth-in-Packaging Act requires that your package prominently display:

1. The name of the seller, advertiser, manufacturer, or distributor.
2. The quantity of product contained in the package (fluid ounces, grams, etc.)
3. The number of servings, if contents can be designated in servings
4. A complete list of the ingredients.

In addition, there are a wide number of regulations specific to various industries, too numerous to be listed here. In food and dairy, for example, the percentage of milk content determines whether your product can be labeled "cheese" vs. "cheese food." In the clothing industry, garment labels must identify the fiber content by percentage of material used (e.g.,

40 percent cotton, 60 percent wool). In the furniture industry, law prohibits removal of tags and labels on mattresses, sofas, and certain other items. Labels must also identify whether clothing or furniture is flammable.

Protecting A Company Name, Product, Name, Logo, Or Slogan

Do you have a name (for a company, service, product), slogan, phrase, or other marketing term you want to protect? The best protection is to register it as a trademark with the United States Patent and Trademark Office in Washington, D.C., phone 703-557-4636. Call them for the appropriate instructions and forms.

A trademark indicates the source and origin of the product, service, or slogan being trademarked and distinguishes these items from others. You may apply for a trademark if you use or intend to use the trade name in commerce. Filing fee is $200 as of this writing.

The first step is to put a "TM" as a superscript after the name you intend to trademark. This lets people know you are trademarking the name and that they cannot use it. Once the trademark is registered with the U.S. Trademark office, you can substitute a circle "R" ® for the TM in your superscript: Writer's Profit Catalog™ would be changed to Writer's Profit Catalog®.

Why would you want to make a phrase or name a trademark? To prevent others from using it. Sometimes, a phrase, slogan, or name becomes a unique marketing tool, a signature that identifies you and makes you stand apart from the crowd. If you invent a term like Vaseline and it becomes popular, you want to be the only maker of petroleum jelly allowed to call your product Vaseline. A trademark will give you that protection.

The main problem with trademark registration is that it is not permanent or all-protecting. As the trademarked word works its way into the popular vocabulary, it becomes almost generic. A good example is Vaseline used as a substitute for petroleum jelly. Many people say Vaseline when they mean petroleum jelly. Petroleum jelly is that greenish oily stuff you rub on your body to keep it moist and prevent dryness. Vaseline is simply one specific brand of petroleum jelly.

If a brand or trademark becomes so popular that it becomes, in essence, a part of the vocabulary, then the company holding the trademark *may actually lose trademark protection.* Trademark registration is not permanent; the FTC can rule at any time that a currently trademarked term has become so "generic" that the trademark no longer holds and other manufacturers may start using the word to describe their product.

What can you do to prevent this? Here are some suggestions:

1. Trade names, when written in your copy, should be capitalized and followed by the appropriate symbol—™ or ®.
2. Some advertisers take occasional ads in magazines explaining to the general public that their product name is a trademark and should not be used generically.
3. Some advertisers monitor violations of their registered trademark and take appropriate action. One story says that a major soft drink manufacturer planted "agents" in various restaurants around the country. When patrons ordered their beverage by the brand name (which was becoming used more and more as a generic term for a particular flavor of soft drink), and the server served a generic equivalent, the manufacturer's agent intervened and told the server that if patrons asked for the brand by name, they should either be served that brand or be told that the restaurant was serving a different brand.

Here are some commonly encountered trade names, along with the generic equivalent on the right. Use the term on the left only when referring to that particular brand or product; when referring generically to the *type* or *category* of product, use the term at right.

Trade Name	*Generic Equivalent*
Astro Turf	artificial grass
Band-Aid	adhesive strip, bandage
Coke, Coca-Cola	cola
Escalator	moving staircase
Formica	laminated plastic
Jacuzzi	whirlpool bath
Jello	gelatin, gelatin dessert
Kitty Litter	cat litter, cat box filler
Kleenex	facial tissue
Liquid Paper	correction fluid
Mace	chemical repellant
Magic Marker	marker, marking pen
Nautilus	exercise/weight machine
Novacain	anesthetic, pain killer
Pampers	disposable diapers
PC (IBM)	personal computer
Ping Pong	table tennis
Q-tip	cotton swab

Rolodex	rotating card file
Sanka	decaffeinated coffee
Scotch Tape	clear tape, plastic tape
Sweet 'N Low	artificial sweetner
Tabasco Sauce	red pepper sauce
Valium	tranquilizer
Vaseline	petroleum jelly
Velcro	fabric fastener
Walkman	portable cassette player
White Out	correction fluid
Windbreaker	nylon jacket, waterproof jacket
Xerox	copy, photocopy

Contests And Sweepstakes

Many advertisers fasten on the idea of a contest or sweepstakes as a way to gain attention and boost sales. And they can work. Richard Benson, in his book *Secrets of Successful Direct Mail,* says a sweepstakes can increase response to direct mail by as much as 50 percent.

Sweepstakes, games, and contests are legal in many states. Lotteries, except for state lotteries, are not. Therefore, you must make sure your promotion can be considered a sweepstakes, contest, or game but cannot be considered a lottery.

According to the U.S. Postal Service, "A lottery is a scheme where a consideration is furnished for a prize that is dependent upon chance." This means that for your promotion to be illegal, all three elements—prize, consideration, and chance—must be present.

- *Prize* is money or merchandise given to the winner.
- *Consideration* means the participants have to buy something (your product) in order to be eligible to win the prize.
- *Chance* means that winning is not guaranteed by purchase of the product but depends on a random drawing or other random selection method.

The way to make your sweepstakes, contest, or game legal, then, is to remove one of these elements from the mix. You don't have to remove all three. You just have to remove one. In a sweepstakes, for example, sending in proof of purchase is the consideration, because it requires the consumer to buy your product to be eligible. Scratching off a game card, is the chance. Winning $25,000 or that dream vacation cabin is the prize.

In sweepstakes, the element of consideration is removed by allowing consumers to become eligible by mailing in *either* proof of purchase (such as a package label or receipt) or just their name and address printed on a plain postcard or piece of paper. As The Independent Judging Organization observes in their book *The Sweepstakes and Games Planning Guide,* "Consideration may be *requested* as long as it isn't *required.*"

In a contest, on the other hand, the lottery element removed is not prize or consideration but *chance.* That is, in a contest you may require entrants to write a 25-word essay on why they like Ookie Gookie cereal. This removes the element of chance, because the prize is awarded on merit rather than in a random drawing. For the contest to be legal, it must be valid (that is, require skill, not luck) and judgeable (able to be evaluated on the basis of the quality of the entries).

Cooperative Advertising

Cooperative advertising is also regulated by the Federal Trade Commission in its *Guides for Advertising Allowances and Other Merchandising Payments and Services.* The main thrust is to ensure fairness to retailers. That is, if you're a manufacturer, make sure you don't put one retailer at a competitive disadvantage by offering better coop discounts and terms to other retailers you deal with.

Here are some of the key points of FTC laws and regulations concerning coop advertising:*

1. All retailers who buy your product are considered customers of your company, whether the retailer buyers direct from you or through a distrubutor, agent, or other intermediary. Therefore, the rules of fair coop treatment apply to both direct and indirect buyers.
2. If you're a wholesaler or distributor, and you do a coop program with your retailers, you are held to the same standards and practices as the manufacturer.
3. The FTC prefers that coop plans be in writing.
4. All retailers participating in your coop plan should be offered the same terms with regards to cooperative advertising, product discounts, and all other elements of the program.

*Source: *Cooperative Advertising* by Edward C. Crimmins (New York: Gene Wolfe & Co., 1984).

5. It's unfair (and therefore illegal) to favor a retailer with better terms under your coop program because the retailer is large or favored by you.
6. All your retailers must be informed of your coop program.
7. You must make the plan available to all of your retailers.
8. You are not required to make *sure* all your retailers participate.
9. You can't dictate to participating retailers what prices they can feature in their ads, and you can't refuse to reimburse retailers for advertising featuring pricing different than your suggested list prices.
10. You have to monitor your coop program to make sure participating retailers are getting the reimbursements and other services they paid for and are not overpaying you.
11. As a manufacturer, you can limit your coop program to a specific market area; however, you can't discriminate and must offer the program to all retailers trading within that geographic marketplace.
12. Retailers whom you reimburse for coop advertising must in turn pass on to you any discounts or rebates they receive from local media.

Mail Order Advertising

If you advertise products for sale by mail, you must ship the product within 30 days of the receipt of the order. If you can't fulfill the order that quickly, you must send the customer a card or letter telling the customer that his order is delayed, when he may expect to receive it, and giving him the option of either agreeing to this delay or else requesting a full refund.

The response device included in this notice must be a postage-paid or business-reply envelope or postcard or possibly a toll-free 800 telephone number; the consumer should not have to spend his own money to reply to such a notice. Refunds, if requested, must be mailed within seven days.

On occasion, through a clerical error, computer error, or some other mishap, you might accidently ship a consumer something he or she did not ordered. Under the law, consumers are not required to return unordered merchandise sent by mail. You can request that the consumer return the material, but you cannot order or tell her to do so. I recommend sending a postage-paid business reply envelope to make the return of materials easier. However, the consumer has the right to keep any unordered merchandise you sent without payment to you.

References

In writing this chapter, I drew upon information presented in a number of books. The most valuable are:

The Complete Guide to Marketing and the Law by Robert J. Posch, Jr. (Englewood Cliffs, NJ: Prentice Hall, 1988), hardcover, 817 pp.

Personal Law: A Practical Legal Guide by Robert D. Rothenberg and Steven J. Blumenkratz (New York: John Wiley & Sons, 1986), trade paperback, 475 pp.

Legal and Economic Regulation in Marketing: A Practitioner's Guide by Ray O. Werner (Westport, CT: Quorom Books, 1989), hardcover, 193 pp.

I suggest you consult these books and your attorney for advice on the legal aspects of advertising. In this brief chapter I'll just touch on a few key points.

Index

A

B

C

K

L

M

R

S